California's topography is characterized by great variety. Its coastline varies from the low, sandy beaches of Southern California to the rocky headlands of Cape Mendocino and other northward protrusions. The Coast Ranges, one of the state's two great mountain systems, runs generally parallel to the coast.

Within the spurs of the Coast Ranges lie many of the state's most fertile and agricultural valleys. Eastward is the Central Valley, California's richest agricultural region, which has a width of up to fifty miles. The Central Valley is walled in to the east by the Sierra Nevada rampart, which at Mount Whitney, the highest mountain in the continental United States outside Alaska, reaches an altitude of 14,496 feet.

From the summit of Mount Whitney one can see the weird sink known as Death Valley, 282 feet below sea level, the lowest spot in the United States. Stretching southward are the nation's two largest deserts, the Mojave and the Colorado. By contrast, the topography of northern California contains such large bodies of water as Lake Tahoe and Clear Lake.

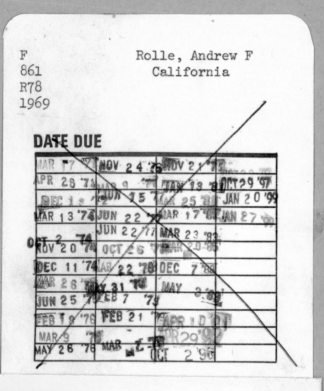

LENDING POLICY

IF YOU DAMAGE OR LOSE LIBRARY
MATERIALS, THEN YOU WILL BE
CHARGED FOR REPLACEMENT. FAIL-
URE TO PAY AFFECTS LIBRARY
PRIVILEGES, GRADES, TRANSCRIPTS,
DIPLOMAS, AND REGISTRATION
PRIVILEGES OR ANY COMBINATION
THEREOF.

California

A History

ALSO BY ANDREW F. ROLLE

Riviera Path, 1946

An American in California:
The Biography of William Heath Davis, 1956

The Road to Virginia City:
The Diary of James Knox Polk Miller, 1960

Lincoln: A Contemporary Portrait, 1961
(with Allan Nevins, Irving Stone, and others)

Occidental: The First Seventy-Five Years, 1962

California: A Student's Guide to
Localized History, 1965

Helen Hunt Jackson, ed., *A Century of Dishonor:*
The Early Crusade for Indian Reform, 1965

The Golden State: A History of California
(with John Gaines), 1965

The Lost Cause: Confederate Exiles in Mexico, 1965

Los Angeles, A Student's Guide to
Localized History, 1965

The Immigrant Upraised: Italian Adventurers
and Colonists in an Expanding America, 1968

California

A History

Second Edition

ANDREW F. ROLLE

ROBERT GLASS CLELAND PROFESSOR OF HISTORY
OCCIDENTAL COLLEGE

Thomas Y. Crowell Company · New York · Established 1834

Designed by Barbara Kohn Isaac

Manufactured in the United States of America

First Printing, January, 1969
Second Printing, November, 1969

We aim at a life beautiful without extravagance and contemplative without unmanliness; wealth in our eyes is a thing not for ostentation but for reasonable use, and it is not the acknowledgment of poverty that we think disgraceful, but the want of endeavor to avoid it.

PERICLES, FROM HIS FUNERAL ORATION
FOR ATHENIAN SOLDIERS WHO FELL IN
THE PELOPONNESIAN WARS

Preface

There is a largeness about the very name California that transcends its open style of life, unpredictability, and expansive tone. First, the name brings to mind extremes and paradoxes in both geography and climate. California's mountains are the highest in the continental United States outside Alaska, her rains, floods, and fires often the most catastrophic, her droughts among the driest, her fogs the densest, her earthquakes the most damaging; her redwoods are the oldest and tallest, and her deserts among the most naked and forbidding in the western hemisphere.

Just as California's geography is grand and diverse, so is her history. The record of man in California offers the historian a subject matter of dimension and significance equal to that of a sovereign nation. As the nineteenth-century English observer James Bryce once wrote of California, no other American state would, if isolated, be so truly a nation in itself. A 1906 article in *Munsey's Magazine* put it this way: "It will never be easy for an Easterner to believe that this one state is larger than the six kingdoms of Belgium, Holland, Greece, Denmark, Portugal, and Rumania; that it is as long as from New York to Indianapolis."

California's development has been influenced by all manner of people—explorers, Indians, *padres*, trappers, traders, whalers, miners, cattlemen, and farmers of every nationality. A history of California must first do justice to her Indian beginnings and then to the long years of Spanish colonialism which contributed so much to the shaping of her past and present. It must consider her enrichment by later immigrants too—the Chinese, French, Germans, Italians, and Japanese, It must describe and analyze the many changes brought by California's American era, changes that become increasingly dramatic in the twentieth century. Such a study must give special attention to minority unrest and the population explosion, as well as to industrial and cultural expansion, particularly since the close of World War II.

The aim of this book is to recount the state's history from its origins to the present. It seeks to interpret every phase of the story, for both students and general readers, without recourse to burdensome detail. After six printings and the passage of over five years, it is now time to offer a revision of the book, originally published in 1963. A half-decade has brought many changes to California.

The selected bibliographies of periodical and book references which follow each chapter have been brought up to date. A new Index of Authors Cited recapitulates these bibliographies in the book's closing pages. New maps and illustrations are also provided.

Numerous specialists have directly or indirectly aided the improvement of this work. In addition to those persons mentioned in the first edition, the following colleagues offered advice: the late Professors Alfred L. Kroeber and Robert Glass Cleland, as did Professors Ray A. Billington, Oscar O. Winther, Allan Nevins, Richard G. Lillard, John A. Hawgood, Doyce B. Nunis, Jr., Max L. Heyman, Leon Litwack, John H. Kemble, Abraham P. Nasatir, Joseph A. McGowan, James Jensen, Ward M. McAfee, David Williams, Richard D. Batman, Dudley Gordon, Marjorie Phillips, Iris H. Wilson, Roger Daniels, Clement Meighan, John B. McGloin, John E. Baur, Don E. Fehrenbacher, Theodore Grivas, D. E. Livingston-Little, Jackson K. Putnam, Imre Sutton, and W. H. Hutchinson. I am grateful also to Frances and Alec Rolle, Albert Shumate, W. W. Robinson, Fred B. Rogers, and Governor Edmund G. Brown. Dr. John Barr Tompkins at the University of California's Bancroft Library was helpful in the selection of illustrations, as were Carey Bliss and Mary Isabel Fry at the Henry E. Huntington Library, as well as the Redwood Empire Association, the Standard Oil Company of California, the California Division of Mines, and all other organizations that furnished photographs.

A.R.

Contents

Maps and Photographs

Maps

Photographs

California

A History

1

The Distinctiveness of California

Regional variety has given tremendous richness to American life. Local differences encourage the interplay of conflicting points of view and thus develop national flexibility. The crisp quietness of New England, the leisurely comfort and courtesy associated with the Old South, the agrarian solidity and sobriety of the Middle West, and the scenic grandeur and sense of newness of the Far West have richly flavored our cultural life. In the case of California literature, for example, the expression of a distinctive regionality underlies the "local color" of Bret Harte, the wit of Mark Twain's tales, the humor and tragedy of William Saroyan and John Steinbeck, as well as the celebration of nature and scorn for mankind in the poetry of Robinson Jeffers. In architecture the fusion of the New England and Spanish heritages has produced the appealing Monterey-style house, with its wide balconies, adobe walls, and white woodwork. Like the southwestern states of New Mexico and Arizona, California represents a picturesque mingling of a Spanish colonial influence with the mainstream of an increasingly mechanized, industrial way of life.

California's Population Growth

California has become in many ways one of the most prominent states in the Union. With its 158,693 square miles, California is third in size among the states in area (after Alaska and Texas).

1

In population alone, its growth has been phenomenal. When admitted to statehood in 1850, it numbered only 92,597 official residents, but since then, each succeeding decade has seen the state's population grow by about 50 per cent. In other words, the state has doubled its residents about every twenty years for more than a century. Population growth in the decade 1940–1950 was 53.3 per cent—greater than in any other state. From 1950 to 1960 California's expansion accounted for nearly 20 per cent of the total United States gain. California now has more people than the combined population of twenty other states and is the most populous in the nation.

The state grew from 10.6 million persons in 1950 to more than 18.5 million by 1965, a jump of 74 per cent. From 1955 to 1960 alone, 1,938,130 new residents arrived in California. At times in its recent history, California's population grew at a rate of 5 per cent a year—more than five times the rate of the nation. The average annual growth rate is 3.8 per cent. California viewed the 1960 census results with great satisfaction: In the previous decade its population increased by 48.5 per cent, thereby earning eight additional congressional seats in the national legislature.

By the 1960's, the growth rate had slowed down somewhat, but the state attracted up to 600,000 new residents annually, or 1,000 to 1,500 per day. In the fiscal year 1967–1968, California grew by 447,000 persons, or more than 1,200 per day. At this rate of growth it would bypass the current population of such nations as Poland and Spain before the end of this century.

In 1969 one American in ten lived in California. If the state were once more to grow by 600,000 per year—or 6 million in ten years—in the year 2000 it would have as many people as there are in Great Britain or France today. By 1969 California's overall population approached 21 million. Demographers predict that there will be more than 25 million persons in California by 1975, up to 30 million by 1985, and from 36 to 42 million by 2000. The latter projection is more than double its 1967 population.

During the 1950's and 1960's most newcomers settled in southern California. One five-county area—Los Angeles, Orange, Ventura, Riverside, and San Bernardino—contained 10 million persons in 1967. Between 1950 and 1960, Los Angeles County alone gained more people than any state in the nation except Florida, New York, and the whole of California itself. In the early 1960's Los Angeles became the most populous of the 3,103 counties in America. By 1968 the city proper approached 3 million inhabitants while Los Angeles County then numbered close to 7 million. The city disputed with Chicago the title of second most populous metropolis in the nation. After Oklahoma City it is the second largest

POPULATION OF CALIFORNIA BY 1975

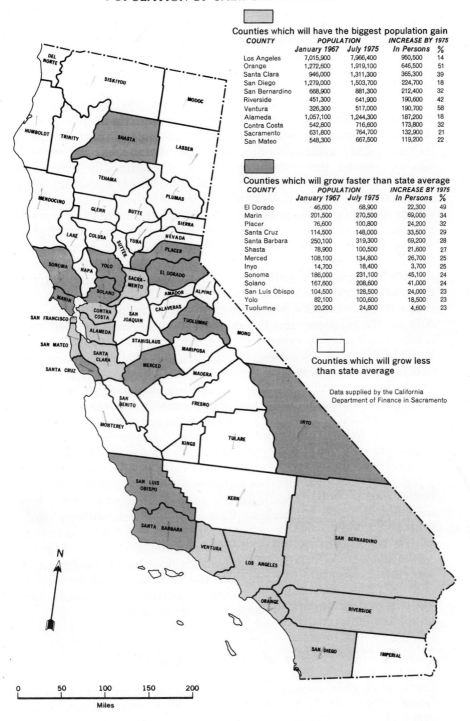

Counties which will have the biggest population gain

COUNTY	POPULATION		INCREASE BY 1975	
	January 1967	July 1975	In Persons	%
Los Angeles	7,015,900	7,966,400	950,500	14
Orange	1,272,600	1,919,100	646,500	51
Santa Clara	946,000	1,311,300	365,300	39
San Diego	1,279,000	1,503,700	224,700	18
San Bernardino	668,900	881,300	212,400	32
Riverside	451,300	641,900	190,600	42
Ventura	326,300	517,000	190,700	58
Alameda	1,057,100	1,244,300	187,200	18
Contra Costa	542,800	716,600	173,800	32
Sacramento	631,800	764,700	132,900	21
San Mateo	548,300	667,500	119,200	22

Counties which will grow faster than state average

COUNTY	POPULATION		INCREASE BY 1975	
	January 1967	July 1975	In Persons	%
El Dorado	46,600	68,900	22,300	49
Marin	201,500	270,500	69,000	34
Placer	76,600	100,800	24,200	32
Santa Cruz	114,500	148,000	33,500	29
Santa Barbara	250,100	319,300	69,200	28
Shasta	78,900	100,500	21,600	27
Merced	108,100	134,800	26,700	25
Inyo	14,700	18,400	3,700	25
Sonoma	186,000	231,100	45,100	24
Solano	167,600	208,600	41,000	24
San Luis Obispo	104,500	128,500	24,000	23
Yolo	82,100	100,600	18,500	23
Tuolumne	20,200	24,800	4,600	23

Counties which will grow less
than state average

Data supplied by the California
Department of Finance in Sacramento

N

0	50	100	150	200

Miles

3

in the world as to area. In 1968 some 37 out of every 100 Californians resided in Los Angeles County and over 9 million (almost half the state's population) lived within a sixty-mile radius of the city's old plaza. Orange County, the second most populous in the state, had 1.3 million inhabitants in 1968.

Net annual migration into California had, by 1968, leveled off, however, to about 300,000 persons per year. The state's growth has been a prime stimulant to the local economy, but population increases have aroused controversy too. Although some authorities minimized the wrenching effects of continually expanding urban centers, others maintained that intolerable crowding, civic decay, suffocating air pollution, and the sacrifice of basic human values would be inescapable. Whatever the arguments for growth, pro and con, it seemed unlikely that the growth rate would slow appreciably. State and municipal officials, therefore, prepared for the task of governing more and more millions of persons.

With 90 per cent of California's inhabitants now in urban areas, the state's early pastoral economy has undergone great change. As its frontier rurality has developed into an industrial and urban culture, the missions and the ranchos of the Spanish period have made way for such expressions of modernity as Hollywood, oil derricks, aircraft factories, steel mills, residential subdivisions, and television studios. The grape vineyards and orange groves of the early twentieth century have surrendered space to tourist attractions, housing projects, and jet-propulsion laboratories. These recent material changes have not all benefited the state. Crowded highways, the noxious fumes of "smog," and serious state and municipal problems have damaged the charm California once held for health seekers, tourists, and lovers of the out-of-doors.

Yet the allure of California remains. In the twentieth century it has drawn to it both some of the nation's richest citizens, who wintered at Santa Barbara or Pasadena, especially before World War II, and some of its poorest. The latter group included the Middle Western "Dust Bowl" refugees of the 1930's, disparagingly called "Okies" and "Arkies." California's present population represents, in its size and composition, the culmination of an intense process of westward migration, rapid social acculturation, high social mobility, and continuous material growth.

The Effects of Geographical Diversity

California's vivid contrasts in climate, in topography, in flora and fauna, all contribute to the state's appeal. It offers man virtually every physical, climatic, geologic, and vegetational combination:

the wettest weather and the driest; poor sandy soil in the south-eastern desert regions and rich loam in the great Central Valley; some of the hottest recorded temperatures on earth and also the coldest; the highest mountain in the United States outside Alaska (Mount Whitney, 14,496 feet) and the lowest point in the country, only sixty miles distant in the grim wastes of Death Valley (at Bad Water, 282 feet below sea level); scrub brush in southern California and the world's largest trees in the rugged High Sierra. In the summertime, it is actually possible to leave a temperature of well over a hundred degrees in the Central Valley and in half an hour travel by auto to the shores of San Francisco Bay, often fogbound at less than fifty degrees. Similarly, the orange groves of southern California are in the wintertime frequently to be seen against a backdrop of snowy peaks in the distance. One can travel from snow- and ice-clogged Idyllwild, a resort atop the San Jacinto mountains, to the burning sands of Palm Springs in less than an hour. (In fact, a direct funicular line connects these spots.)

California's physical characteristics have been closely related to its development. Three-fourths of the surface of the state consists of rolling hills and mountains; the remaining fourth of fertile valleys and deserts. California has more land area and more diversity of natural resources than many foreign nations. Partly as a result of this diversity, the people of the state have created a variegated economy: more than half the people and industry are in southern California, while much of the raw materials and 90 per cent of the water are located in northern California. Each section, of course, is highly dependent upon the other. The increasing importance of southern California as a center of manufacturing and industry has helped make California the nation's sixth-ranking manufacturing state. However, industrial areas—north and south —occupy only a small percentage of the state's surface. California has over 7 per cent of all the forest land in the United States, much of it concentrated in northern reserves, and the state is a major producer of the nation's lumber.

California is also the top agricultural state in the nation. For decades it has ranked first in the production of lemons, apricots, avocados, figs, grapes, olives, peaches, pears, plums, and many other fruits. Because it is possible to raise crops during three growing seasons—instead of the usual one—agriculture continues to flourish. Yet today only 5 per cent of California's people live on farms. Many of the state's orange groves, once the major producers of citrus fruit in the United States, have toppled before the axes of subdividers; nevertheless, more oranges are grown in California today than ever before. Moving out of zones of high population density, growers have opened up new agricultural areas in the

San Joaquin and Imperial valleys and on the western slopes of the southern Sierra foothills. The same sort of decentralization has occurred with other crops, including grapes. Despite urban encroachment upon land devoted to vineyards, California produces most of the nation's wine. Los Angeles ranks sixth among the counties of the United States in total income from farm products but is number one in dairy production. Similarly, the El Monte, Petaluma, and San Fernando regions continue to be important in the production of poultry and eggs. Sebastopol remains a major apple-growing center, and the warm Santa Clara Valley a region full of apricot and prune orchards. The temperate Sierra foothills are renowned not only because of earlier gold-mining activities, but also because of the heavily-laden peach and pear trees their slopes sustain. In California's rich river-delta zone, rice, asparagus, and sugar beets grow in profusion. And the Salinas area is the nation's major producer of lettuce.

Today, it seems surprising that Gaspar de Portolá, the Spaniard who, in 1769, led the first overland party of whites into California, was discouraged by the appearance of the land, and remarked that the Russians should be made welcome to such a desert. California's natural resources were virtually unexploited by either the Indians or the Spaniards. Magnificent, dense timber stands remained untouched. The melting snows of the Sierra ran wasted in rivers rushing to the sea; the power of California's waterfalls was unharnessed. Subterranean reservoirs of petroleum were untapped. Gold remained locked deep in the rocky Sierra awaiting the picks and shovels of ambitious men. The Spaniards, who lived primarily off their flocks and herds, were—almost unknowingly—the wardens of California's wealth. Under the Americans, after the Gold Rush of 1848–1849, mining techniques were developed in California that were later used throughout the world. American mining law, too, was largely evolved in California. Early in the twentieth century oil and gas gradually displaced gold as a cornerstone of the state's mineral wealth. Today California ranks third among the states in the production of crude oil, exceeded only by Texas and Louisiana. Until recently, California produced about a million barrels of petroleum daily, which amounted to some 6 per cent of the world's annual crude oil production. For a long time after 1900, the state was second, and is now third, among the other states in total mineral output. California leads the nation in the production of chromite, diatomite, quicksilver, metals of the platinum group, sand and gravel, sodium carbonate and sodium sulphate, as well as tungsten, mercury, iodine, and various borate minerals. Over fifty new minerals have been found in California, of which thirty-nine have not been found in other parts of the world.

Topography and Climate

California spans the Pacific seaboard for 1,200 miles, counting all coastal indentations, between the thirty-second and forty-second parallels. The maximum length of the state is 824 miles; the maximum width 252 miles. The chief surface features, apart from its coastline, are the two mountain chains that traverse almost the entire length of the state, and the great Central Valley lying between them. The mountains of the Coast Range are generally below 4,000 feet in height, but a few peaks—San Antonio, San Bernardino, San Gorgonio, and San Jacinto—range from 10,000 to 11,600 feet. Inland, more than forty peaks of the Sierra Nevada mountain chain rise to 10,000 feet in height. A dozen Sierra peaks exceed 14,000 feet. The western slope of the High Sierra country is seamed by many watercourses, turbulent in their youth, calm and serene in maturity. However, the Sacramento and San Joaquin are the state's only navigable rivers.

A glance at the map gives one the impression that, except for its dividing plain, California is mostly mountainous. But closer inspection discloses numerous mountain passes, including the Tehachapi, the Cajon, and the San Marcos, as well as long, narrow valleys that nestle between the summits of the Coast Range. In these valleys, some large, some small, each producing its distinctive products, lies much of the agricultural wealth of California. In the Napa, the Salinas, and the Santa Inez valleys, as well as in the Los Angeles Basin, people live and work in a generally pleasant environment conducive to economic productivity. Easily the most important of California's agricultural areas is its enormous San Joaquin–Sacramento Valley. When John Charles Frémont first saw this valley it was a natural bed of wild flowers four hundred miles long and fifty wide, where large heads of antelope grazed. This valley is today one of the best granaries of the world, as well as an area of increasing industrialization.

It is more accurate to speak of California's "climates" than to refer to one single climate. Richard Lillard, in describing "the varied factors which help keep weather prediction in a prescientific stage," speaks of "scores of microclimates," that give California "more little specialized climates per square mile and more square miles of specialized climate than perhaps any other equal area on earth." No traveler in the Sierra in midwinter would recognize the generally arid, almost subtropical, climate that tourist advertisements often ascribe to California. What is usually thought of as "California climate" prevails in the area lying south of San Francisco to the Mexican border, and between the coastal mountains and the Pacific Ocean. In this region the seasons seem to drift mildly from one to another, almost unperceived. Frost occurs, but normally it is not heavy enough to stop the greening of the hills under the winter rains. Light breezes and cooling fogs generally keep the temperature at a comfortable level. The heat of the day is fanned by prevailing westerly winds. In summer, near the coast, climatic equability is also maintained by low clouds, known as *veloes*. The climate is, therefore, rarely humid or soporific. Less than 1 per cent of the earth's surface enjoys such ideal weather.

Rainfall varies markedly throughout the state. Annual rainfall in the extreme northwest corner of the state, above Eureka, reaches 110 inches, making the area a virtual rain forest. Precipitation in the central valley is heavier at Sacramento and Stockton than at other cities farther south, including Fresno and Bakersfield. At San Francisco, the average annual rainfall is nearly 23 inches; at San Luis Obispo it falls to 19 inches, and then to less than 15 inches at Los Angeles. At San Diego, near the Mexican border, rainfall generally amounts to only 10 inches per year. Seasonal precipitation averages only 6 inches at Bakersfield and as little as 1 or 2 inches in desert areas. Drought conditions sometimes exist from Monterey southward to San Diego. Furthermore, practically all of California's precipitation—both rain and snow—falls between November and April. Thus, although the state as a whole receives sufficient water for its needs, water must be stored carefully and transported over long distances for the steady distribution not provided by nature.

The coastal mountain ranges partly control California's weather. In winter, heavy North Pacific storms, moving counterclockwise, and sometimes cyclonic in their fury, crash down on the northern California Coast Range. The rain clouds, carried by heavy winds, push through the canyon gaps in these mountains into the central valley. Because many eastward-moving storms are broken up on the Sierra's crest, there is much less rain east of the Sierra, and therefore on their western slopes numerous dams impound water for urban use. Indeed the transportation and distribution of water in California has become a major preoccupation of its citizens.

Water remains a major determinant of California's future growth. Below the eastern side of the Sierran cordillera the temperature rises as high as 134 degrees, and so little water falls upon areas like Death Valley that there exists hardly any substantial vegetation. Along the volcanic plain which covers much of north-eastern California, agriculture and animal grazing are also limited by climate and a rocky topography.

DESERT FLORA. (From the author's collection.)

The uneven distribution of water has given rise to the tongue-in-cheek observation that California's unusually "high fogs" sometimes cause drowning among the unwary. In the north the danger of floods is no joking matter. Since the Gold Rush days the northern communities of Sacramento, Stockton, Oroville, and Marysville have been plagued by massive winter inundations which sometimes burst through artificial dikes raised along the sides of the American, Sacramento, and San Joaquin rivers. Paradoxically, one of the most serious flood threats also exists in semi-arid southern California. There, although the rainfall is the lightest in the state, the scarce, partly burned-out natural chaparral provides but a poor cover for the watershed. Many inexperienced people build their homes on low flats, alluvial fans, or in canyon mouths, thereby making themselves vulnerable to such disasters as the southern California flood of 1934, the La Crescenta holocaust of 1936, and the serious flood in 1938. In the north almost annual inundations occur throughout the upper Sacramento Valley.

From this brief review one can see that perhaps the key word to describe California's climate—as well as most of her other natural characteristics—is variety, indeed grandiose variety. Newcomers, more frequently in recent years, sometimes express disappointment over California's prolonged spells of dryness, heat, and, quite rarely, cold. Some critics even persuade themselves that the one normal characteristic of California's weather pattern is summed up in the word "unusual." There are Californians who blame climatic changeability upon atomic bomb explosions, or upon man's pollution of the atmosphere. There is, however, little objective evidence for these speculations.

Flora and Fauna

The wide range of climate in California makes possible a corresponding variety, as we have seen, in vegetable and floral products. Almost every plant, tree, or shrub that grows in temperate zones, and many indigenous to the tropics, can be grown somewhere in California. The state also is known for certain unique forms of vegetation, especially for its giant Sequoias, which have their roots deep in the past. Along with the ancient Bristle Cone Pines of the state's White Mountains, these lords of the forest are probably the oldest living things on earth. Some Sequoias now standing were in their prime at the time of Christ. In fact, their age may be five thousand or more years. Most "Big Trees" that have perished have been the victims of man's ravages, or of burning, lightning, or fierce storms. Sequoias are virtually immune to diseases that afflict other trees, and their tannic bark is generally resistant to fire.

The gnarled Monterey cypress, a weirdly picturesque denizen of the seacoast, likewise commands attention. It is found only along a small and rugged section of the Monterey County shoreline. These trees, often clinging precariously to unsheltered promontories like Cypress Point, are totally exposed to the Pacific storms. Heavy winds have twisted them into fantastic forms, and yet they survive. Similar in their tenacity are the Torrey Pines of the coastline above San Diego.

California's skies were once darkened by flocks of geese, ducks, and other migrating birds who wintered there. In recent years the wildlife has been greatly depleted by the ravages of man. Nevertheless, 400 species of mammals and 600 varieties of birds make the state their home. From the horned toad and desert tortoise to the bobcat, weasel, and black-tailed deer, California's fauna is as diversified as numerous other features of the state. In the wilderness, coyotes, mountain lions, wolverines, and cougars still roam. Big-horn mountain sheep and wapiti, or elk, once rather common, are now rare and the distinctive California grizzly bear is virtually extinct. The condor and California sea otter have also barely escaped extinction. Perched on the brink of extinction, the condor—largest land bird in North America—reminds us of the way in which California is paradoxically old and new. Despite the diminished wild life, outdoorsmen still hunt and fish in California annually. Fresh-water streams are stocked with striped bass, rainbow trout, and steelhead, and in diminishing numbers one can still find king and silver salmon and even, rarely, in northern waters, sturgeon.

Geology and Scenic Grandeur

Geologically, California is young. The great 400-mile-long Sierran scarp, caused by uplifting and faulting, and the volcanic Cascades and the nonvolcanic Klamaths in the north are in youthful stages of development. The California coastline, pushed up out of the Pacific's depths at Points Pinos and Lobos, as well as at Cape Mendocino, is a rocky one, with headlands jutting out to sea. California's coastline, unlike our eastern shore, is at the present time one of emergence, rather than submergence; in fact, the entire Pacific shoreline, down to Cape Horn in South America, is sharply uplifted. This geologic pattern has produced few good meandering, navigable rivers or inland estuaries and harbors comparable to Boston, New York, Philadelphia, or Baltimore. With the exception of San Diego in the south, San Francisco in the middle, and Humboldt Bay in the far northern corner of the state, significant natural harbors are virtually nonexistent in California (Los Angeles is not a natural harbor).

Stupendous changes, frequently abrupt, sometimes gradual, have shaped the face of California in past geologic ages. The two principal mountain chains, the Sierra Nevada and the Coast Range, were created by titanic upheavals from beneath the earth's crust. The fiery origin of California's Cascade mountains to the northeast is revealed by their many lava formations and extinct cinder cones. One supposedly dead volcano, Lassen Peak, came alive in 1914 and spouted out a holocaust of hot mud and ash which poured down its sides and devastated everything in its path. At intervals, Lassen floats a pennant of smoke from its summit to warn careless hikers that its inner fires still smolder. Mount Lassen is the only active volcano in the United States outside Alaska, but Indian traditions still exist of former eruptions in California's northern mountains. John Muir once wrote of these:

They tell of a fearful time of darkness, when the sky was black with ashes and smoke that threatened every living thing with death, and that when at length the sun appeared once more it was red like blood.

Seething geysers and innumerable hot sulphur springs—safety-valves of subterranean heat and pressure—testify that underlying fires are far from extinguished.

Many physical forces have combined to change the configuration of California's mountain chains. The movements of glaciers, the changes of weather and temperature, the volcanic and chemical action, the eroding effect of running water, the successive earthquakes—all have had a part in sculpturing the mountains of California into some of the most impressive in the world. The Yosemite chasm, in particular, is noted for its incomparable domes, its peaks, and its glacier-formed perpendicular walls nearly a mile high, with their matchless waterfalls—all within a radius of half a dozen miles. In 1850, when California became a state, the east coast was already well-settled. The Yosemite Valley was not officially seen by white men until a year later. For decades California's remote interior remained a frontier. The scarred Sierra, created and shaped by avalanche, by earthquake, by rasping glaciers, by gale-force winds, and by rain and frost, stands aloof with the ice and snow on its peaks, far above the verdure of its valleys.

FLOOR OF YOSEMITE VALLEY BEFORE SILTING OF MIRROR LAKE OCCURRED. (From the author's collection.)

Serious earth tremors, which still startle Californians, as in 1812, 1870, 1906, 1933, 1952, and 1957, indicate that these forces are still strong, and that shocks similar to those of the past may be expected to occur again. The sheer precipice which forms the eastern walls of the Sierra, facing Owens Valley and the state of Nevada, drops 10,000 feet in the Mount Whitney region. This area provides a striking example of a series of vertical faults caused by successive earthquake shocks.

Although the California coastline is currently in an emergent stage, its geologic story has been one of repeated rising and sinking. Sea shells, whale bones, and beach boulders are to be found on mountain tops far above the present level of the sea. Ages ago ocean waves washed the base of the Sierra Nevada, but as geological forces heaved up the floor of what is now the great Central Valley, the ocean waters were forced to recede. The most recent phase of the geologic development of the coastline was the flooding of the mouths of several streams that helped form San Francisco and San Diego bays. Relatively little geological change of California's shoreline has occurred in the past few thousand years. Estimates of the age of shell mounds along the shore indicate that Indians in the area between three and four thousand years ago literally picked up their living along California's coastline. Had the English navigator Francis Drake been fortunate enough to see the bay of San Francisco when he landed in California in 1579, he would have found the bay almost exactly as it is now.

Prehistoric California went through numerous transitions of climate, including both arctic cold and tropic heat. A few small glaciers still exist in the Sierra, as mementos of the ice age. Similarly, the tropical past is locked into the asphalt beds at Rancho La Brea, now a municipal park in Los Angeles. During the tertiary age, the quaking, sticky surface of this prehistoric swamp became a death trap for animals and birds long since extinct. The blackened skeletons of creatures caught in the mire of these tar pits furnish evidence of the tropic life that once existed. The re-creations of museum dioramas can only partly portray the oversize mammoths, camels, horses, saber-toothed tigers, and ground sloths that once roamed through California's primeval forests of vines and palmetto fronds. Carbon-dating techniques have established the age of certain animal and mineral objects taken from La Brea as more than 28,000 years.

Isolation

California's discovery came late in history. Its remoteness from the civilizations both of the East and of the West, as well as the tremendous physical difficulties of approaching the area, kept it an isolated locale on the globe. To the eastward was a vast, unexplored continent with rugged, often snow-covered mountain ranges, almost unfordable rivers, and waterless deserts. Added to these obstacles were widely dispersed, fierce Indian tribes. Even after the eastern half of North America had been settled, travelers faced numerous barriers in attempting to cross the great western stretches of country. When Frémont entered California early in 1844, he and his troop of men narrowly escaped death from exposure and starvation amid the snows of the Sierra. The tragic story of the Donner Party, demoralized, lost and starving in these mountains two years later, is even better known. Death Valley acquired its lugubrious name from parties of travelers whose horses and cattle perished in its arid wastes. California did not invite exploration or settlement.

The seemingly endless waste of water to the west of California kept earlier explorers away from its shores. When Ferdinand Magellan sailed out of the Atlantic through the straits that bear his name and came upon an unknown ocean on the other side of Latin America, he called it the "Peaceful Sea" (Pacific). Later navigators who experienced its frequent tempests resented this name and thought it should have been called the "Restless" ocean. As European mariners crawled along the Pacific coastline from the south, their approach was impeded by head winds which drove their ships hundreds of miles backward and off their course, sometimes far out to sea. Only by the patient tacking of sails and beating to windward, at times for weeks at a stretch, could tiny sailing vessels make a northing. In 1539, Francisco de Ulloa, the first white man to round the point of Lower California, complained bitterly of the northwest wind, which so hindered him from making progress that he angrily called it the "king of all that coast." Added to the wind and weather was scurvy, for which no remedy existed. On the earliest Spanish expeditions so many sailors died or were incapacitated from this disease that not enough were left to man the vessels, which were obliged to drift at the mercy of wind and wave.

Though Spain's mariners died by the hundreds, and ship after ship of hers sank, nothing could halt the indomitable spirit of her navigators. League by league, each expedition reaching a slightly higher latitude, these men made their way up the coast, from the early sixteenth century onward. In time they won the distinctive and still unexplored "terrestrial paradise at the left hand of the Indies" named California.

SELECTED READINGS

For the regional flavor and for descriptions of the physical, geologic, and natural wonders of California see: John Muir, *The Mountains of California* (New York, 1894); Mary Austin, *The Land of Little Rain* (Boston, 1903), and, with Sutton Palmer, her *California: The Land of the Sun* (New York, 1914); Roderick Peattie, ed., *The Pacific Coast Ranges*

(New York, 1946), and his *The Sierra Nevada* (New York, 1947); Carey McWilliams, *Southern California Country* (New York, 1946).

R. W. Durrenberger, W. G. Byron, and J. C. Kimura, *Patterns on the Land* (Los Angeles, 1957), is a handbook of maps of California. Consult also Clifford M. Zierer, ed., *California and the Southwest* (New York, 1956), for physical and economic geography, as well as David W. Lantis, Rodney Steiner, and Arthur E. Karinen, *California: Land of Contrast* (Belmont, California, 1963). Titus Fey Cronise, *The Natural Wealth of California* (San Francisco, 1868); Gilbert E. Bailey, *California: A Geologic Wonderland* (Los Angeles, 1924); and several earlier works cover the same field. Discussion of California's earth tremors is in Robert Iacopi, *Earthquake Country* (Menlo Park, 1964). A modern guidebook was produced by the Federal Writers Project of the W.P.A. as *California: A Guide to the Golden State* (New York, 1939, revised, 1954).

Early multi-volume histories of the state include Hubert Howe Bancroft, *History of California* (7 vols., San Francisco, 1884–1890); Theodore H. Hittell, *History of California* (4 vols., San Francisco, 1885–1897); and Zoeth S. Eldredge, ed., *History of California* (5 vols., New York, 1915). These were followed by Charles E. Chapman, *A History of California: The Spanish Period* (New York, 1921), and its companion volume, Robert G. Cleland, *A History of California: The American Period* (New York, 1922). Rockwell D. Hunt and Nellie Van de Grift Sanchez, *A Short History of California* (New York, 1929), for its time a distinct contribution, preceded Cleland's later books, *The March of Industry*, with Osgood Hardy (Los Angeles, 1929), *From Wilderness to Empire* (New York, 1944), and *California in Our Time* (New York, 1947). See the compact revision, also entitled *From Wilderness to Empire*, edited by Glenn S. Dumke (New York, 1959). A general history is John W. Caughey's *California* (New York, 1953). A useful paperback is Don E. Fehrenbacher, *A Basic History of California* (New York, 1964). Consult two brochures by Andrew F. Rolle, *California, A Students' Guide to Localized History* (New York, 1965) and *Los Angeles, A Students' Guide to Localized History* (New York, 1965).

Valuable as bibliography is Robert E. Cowan's *A Bibliography of the History of California and the Pacific West, 1510–1906* (San Francisco, 1914), a second edition of which appeared, in three volumes, in 1933. One should also consult the extensive files of the California Historical Society *Quarterly* and the *Quarterly* of the Historical Society of Southern California, as well as the *Pacific Historical Review*, for a wealth of monographic articles concerning California's past.

John Crow, *California as a Place to Live* (New York, 1953), is useful for prospective residents and newly-arrived citizens. The same purpose characterizes Philip H. Ault, *How to Live in California* (New York, 1961). Remi Nadeau, *California: The New Society* (New York, 1963), is a recent popularization. N. Ray Gilmore and Gladys Gilmore, *Readings in California History* (New York, 1966), is a book of valuable selected readings.

2

The Indian

The California Indians, like other minority groups, have sometimes been portrayed in an unfortunate manner. It was once believed that these Indians could not be measured favorably against other tribal groups in North America. As compared to the land they inhabited, rich in natural products and attractive in physical beauty, this first inhabitant did represent something of a contrast. Despite the mild climate and the abundance of wild plant and animal foods, the first Californians did not advance very far toward developing a "civilized" way of life. But they should not be measured only against Caucasian standards. From ancient times, these Indians arrived at an adjustment to their environment which they considered adequate. Though their general culture was simple, the California Indians acknowledged no peers in certain specialized activities. Among these were their well-developed, even complex, cult religions, their intricate basket designs, their clever acorn-leaching operations, and their skill in flint chipping. Their dependence upon acorns as a basic food possibly discouraged interest in organized agriculture. Similarly, their excellent and serviceable basketry work may have accounted for their neglect of pottery, an art form brought to a high state of achievement by tribes living to the south and east. Like other North American Indians, these first Californians did not understand the principle of the wheel, had no real system of writing, and in general led a Stone Age level of existence.

Living close to the soil, these natives achieved stability in a generally comfortable environment. Usually happy and peaceful in outlook, they possessed an uncomplicated, yet successful, culture, in tune with their environment. A few tribes, among them the Hupa and the Yurok, showed some highly-developed culture traits. These Indians preferred their simple way of life to a more complex one, featuring systematic agriculture or handicrafts. It is difficult to generalize about so many different tribal groupings, but the basic fact about the California Indians is that, relatively isolated from other North American Indian cultures by mountain barriers and deserts, they developed a society suited to their own geographic needs. Theirs was a style of living built around food gathering and fishing, rather than sowing, planting, or harvesting. Instead of describing that way of life in terms of a culture lag, it is more accurate and contemporary to speak of the California Indian's culture as uncomplicated but effective in providing them with a livelihood. Their social system remained essentially intact for thousands of years, until historic times.

Physical and Ethnic Characteristics

Short, and with small skulls, most California Indians did not possess the copper complexion, the aquiline features, or the proud bearing usually associated with the American Indian. Instead, according to anthropologist Alfred Louis Kroeber, they "were flat-nosed and broad-faced, with an apathetic carriage." Yet they were strong, sturdy, and long-lived, and there were some handsome individuals among them. Chief Solano of the Suisunes, for whom Solano County is named, was six feet, seven inches in height and broad in proportion. Such a chieftain would have done honor to any tribal society. The Colorado River tribes were among the tallest groups of California.

That these Indians were not dull-witted is shown by the facility with which they acquired use of the Spanish language. They soon learned to speak it clearly and correctly. The Spaniards also taught them to read music and to sing church chorals, and they learned to intone Latin with astonishing accuracy. In view of the fact that California's aborigines were without education in any modern sense, such accomplishments as they acquired in a very few years of mission instruction seem remarkable. Their ability to learn mechanical arts finds a silent but impressive witness in the remains of California's missions, erected almost entirely by Indian workmen under the direction of friars. In the industrial schools of the missions Indians became fairly skillful carpenters, weavers, and farmers. There were no better cattle herders, although the Indians had never seen domesticated animals, including horses, before the coming of the Spaniards. There is reason to feel some amazement at their capacity, rather than shock at their lack of it.

Native Arts and Dwellings

Native Indian crafts or arts were relatively few in California. Basket making was the chief industry, and it was largely in the hands of the women, who were also expert in dressing skins and in making rush mats for beds. California's coastal Indians built dugout canoes with no better tools than wedges of elk horn and adzes with mussel-shell blades. Household utensils included basket pots into which hot stones were dropped, stone mortars and pestles for grinding seeds and acorns, horn and shell knives, and flat spoons or paddles for stirring acorn gruel. The Indians also used looped sticks for cooking with red-hot stones, nets of vegetable fiber for fishing and carrying small objects, and wooden trays and bowls.

Indian dwellings were of the simplest construction, varying usually in accordance with the climate. In the northwest, and also in central California, they were sometimes partly excavated, with sides and roof of heavy wood slabs laboriously split or hewn from trees; center posts held up the roofs of larger structures. These "houses," half above and half below ground, kept the Indians warm in cold weather, but the damp fetid atmosphere of their interiors would have been unendurable to modern whites. The dwellings of the Klamath River tribes were built above the surface; they were rectangular, with walls and roof constructed of redwood planks. The Yurok and Hupa built frame houses. Mountain Indians usually preferred bark or wood-slab buildings. Among the Chumash, along the Santa Barbara coast, houses of "half-orange" shape were built of poles drawn together and tied at the top. Thatched grass, foliage, or wet earth covered these dwellings, whose light construction was suited to the mild climate of the area. Cave habitation was also practiced to a limited extent by various Sierran Indians, but in the warmest parts of California the natives were satisfied with a thatch or brush shelter, piled up heavily on its windy side.

As a result of these latter habitations, the Indians' interest in housing has been described as deficient — a basically incorrect indictment in view of the many different types of dwellings they actually constructed. Whatever the style, however, in one respect these structures were alike: the state in which they were generally kept was one of filth. When the collection of bones and other refuse strewn on the floor became too offensive, and the fleas and vermin too numerous, an Indian family sometimes set fire to their "house" and built a new one elsewhere.

Food and Clothing

The food of the primitive Californians was more often vegetable than animal, but roots formed only a part of it. Thus these Indians do not deserve to be called by the once popular epithet "diggers" —a term first applied to them, in contempt, by Americans who were arriving from the Great Basin, where there was more reason for its use.

The first sound to be heard on approaching an Indian village was the pounding of pestles in mortars. The major food staple of the California Indians, corresponding to the maize consumed elsewhere, was the acorn. Carefully gathered in season and stored in raised cylindrical cribs, acorns constituted, with dried salmon and nuts, the basic provisions stored by most natives for winter. Before acorns could be eaten they had to be hulled, parched, and pulverized, and the tannic acid had to be leached out. This last operation was done in a basket, or in a sand basin. Next, the Indians boiled the sweetened ground acorn meal. The Shastas roasted moistened meal, while the Pomo and other groups mixed red earth with their meal, sometimes baking it; the resultant mixture was eaten or stored. The Indians also ate, after boiling them, the green leaves of many plants. Certain roots, otherwise poisonous, were made fit for food by long roasting underground. The natives possessed no intoxicating drinks, but a mild form of inebriation was sometimes produced by prolonged smoking of wild tobacco and jimson weed.

California's Indians ate the flesh of animals whenever they could obtain it. Weapons were few in number and relatively poor in quality—usually small bows and arrows, and flint-tipped lances. When hunting large game, the Indians made up for lack of efficient weapons by strategy. Wonderfully deft and skilled in stalking game, they contrived disguises with the head and upper part of the skins of animals. They also set out decoys to attract birds within arrowshot. Game drives were organized, with the animals being directed past hidden hunters. Less common was the technique of running down a deer by human relays, until he fell from exhaustion. Pits and traps were used to catch larger game, except the grizzly bear. The Indians held this animal in such fear and respect that they let him alone, believing him possessed of a demon. Wood rats, squirrels, coyotes, crows, rabbits, lizards, field mice, and snakes were all, however, fair game. Cactus apples and berries were a special treat. The Indians were not fastidious in their tastes, and they did not disdain to eat snails, caterpillars, minnows, crickets, grubs found in decayed trees, slugs, fly larvae gathered from the tops of bushes in swamps (these had a texture rather like tapioca pudding), horned toads, earthworms (used in soup), grasshoppers (roasted and powdered), and skunks (killed and dressed with due caution). Fish, especially salmon and shell-fish, formed an important part of the diet of coastal Indians, often excellent fishermen who jealously guarded their "salmon waters," as the northern rivers where these fish spawned were called. Incursions upon salmon fishing areas by intruders caused bloody conflicts.

Food, whether animal or vegetable, was provided almost wholly by nature. Although the Colorado River Indians were settled agricultural tribes, most of the other natives of California followed no form of agriculture, except the occasional scattering of seeds of wild tobacco. Indeed, after the coming of the padres, male Indians frequently opposed such radical notions as organized crop cultivation, involving backbreaking labor in the fields.

Nature, in addition to furnishing the Indians with food, also gave them the basic ingredients for their clothing. Originally most of the men went entirely naked, wearing not even a breechclout, although rude moccasins, sandals, and (in the north) snowshoes, were usually worn. The Indians' complexions were dried, hardened, and cracked by exposure to wind, sun, and water. Only in the coldest weather did they utilize rabbit or deerskin cloaks and skin blankets. Some natives were known to roll in the mud on cold mornings and to wash off the surface of their bodies when the sun came out. Women either wore a pretense of a skirt made of tule grass, reaching from the waist to the knees, or narrow skin aprons, front and back. In cold weather they wore a cape of deerskin or rabbit fur and sometimes they covered their breasts with furs, including those of the otter and the wildcat. They were fond of ornamentation, and painted both faces and bodies in grotesque patterns. They decorated their hair with small shells, bones, and even stones. For ceremonial occasions they used elaborate headdresses of feathers and beads. Some Indians wore basketry hats, while those of the central region bound their heads with hair nets.

Social Customs and Organization

The women and children did much of the drudgery among the California Indians, while the men, when not engaged in hunting and fishing, sometimes roamed from house to house and from village to village. The women hunted small animals, gathered acorns, caught fish, scraped animal skins, fashioned robes, hauled water and firewood, wove baskets, barbecued meat, and constructed some dwellings. Creation of a male paradise on earth seems almost to have been the Indians' objective. Yet it is incorrect to label the males as lazy. They specialized in certain occupations. Among the Hupa Indians, for example, these included making bows, arrows, nets, and pipes, dressing hides, and preparing ceremonial fire-sticks from cottonwood roots.

California's natives were considerably different in their typical behavior from the taciturn Eastern Indians of James Fenimore Cooper's Leather-stocking tradition. The California Indians impressed visitors as a joyous race, evidently among the happiest and most gregarious of all American aborigines. Far from resenting the coming of most white men, they gave them a friendly welcome. Indeed, a major complaint of numerous Spaniards was that the singing and dancing was so continuous, day and night, that they had little opportunity for sleep. The Indians, of course, were not always so joy-ridden or garrulous. A day might pass in some villages with nothing more than a few grunts being exchanged.

The Indians were extremely fond of dancing, in which they engaged not only for amusement, but also in connection with the numerous ceremonials with which they celebrated every important event, public or private. The northwest Indians, for example, had the salmon dance; special dances for the newborn child, for the black bear, for the new clover, for the white deer, and for the elk; the dance of welcome to visiting Indians; the dance of peace; and of course war dances, for which the braves were painted and dressed in finery of plumes and beads. Dancing also took place at the separate puberty rites for boys and for girls. The Yurok held a first-salmon dance at the mouth of the Klamath River. The Hupa, in addition to a first-eel ceremony, also held an autumnal first-acorn feast. Some of these first-fruit ceremonies bore a resemblance to the Thanksgiving feast of the Puritans of New England.

Along with dancing, singing and chanting formed a significant part of the lives of the Indians, who possessed both a greater power of tonal imagery and a lyric sense than is generally credited to them. Musical activities became especially spirited whenever the Indians indulged in the chewing or smoking of jimson weed,

MEMBERS OF THE DIEGUEÑO TRIBE, MESA GRANDE, 1906. (Museum of the American Indian.)

whose narcotic effect is similar to that of mescaline or marijuana. Some of the religious rituals, such as that of the Toloache cult, made particular use of music as an adjunct to narcotics in apprehending the extrasensory aspects of life. On such occasions, accompanied by the hum of bull roarers (these consisted of a slat of wood swung at the end of a thong), chanting and singing would go on late into the night.

Among other types of celebrations were those at which the Indians boasted about their successes—the huts they had built, the victories they had won; defeats were sometimes duly glossed over. All these achievements were recounted by wizened elders in long orations, to which their people listened in solemn silence. Afterwards they did not proceed to gorge themselves with a great feast, in our fashion, but often ate abstemiously. The California Indians had good reason to be proud of their achievements, however meager we may consider them. A special source of pride was their watercraft, which they handled with dexterity and skill. One of the most common types was the tule balsa, a sort of raft made out of river rushes; this craft, used for fishing, was usually poled or paddled on inland waters. The Indians also made much use of wooden plank canoes, which were burned or chopped out of large trees.

A special ceremony was that which took place late each summer when the southern California and Sierra Nevada tribes held a memorial dance for the dead in the village cemetery. There they built a large fire into which clothing, baskets, and other possessions were thrown as offerings to the departed. Indian braves then danced in a circle around the fire, accompanied by the hoarse rattle of the mourning chant, terrible to a civilized ear. Organized mourning for the dead by close relatives was practiced by nearly all tribes. This took the form of smearing the face with a wet paste mixed from the ashes of the deceased. The Indians kept this facial covering on until it wore off, sometimes for as long as a year. A few tribes buried their dead; others practiced cremation.

The morals of the California Indians were unrestrained by our standards — but no more so than among the other Indians of North America—and many of their customs might seem strange to us. In northwestern California a wife could be purchased for strings of shell money or deerskins. A man was disgraced if he secured his wife for nothing. Polygamy was practiced by some who could afford the purchase price of more than one wife, and rich men sometimes had many wives. Some Indians were inveterate gamblers, who would risk their last possession, even their wives, in games of chance. A "strip poker" guessing game was popular, as were other gambling games involving the use of stone pebbles under sea shells. The Indians were also fond of athletics, in which they displayed considerable proficiency. In various ball games, and in leaping, jumping, and similar contests, they generally accepted defeat with the same sportsmanship as they did victory; but there was, nevertheless, a certain amount of familial and local pride in achievement.

Each family was a law unto itself, and there was no fully systematic punishment for crime. Yet atonement for injury was not unknown. Sometimes serious offenses could be excused for "money." A murderer could even buy himself off by paying the family of the deceased in skins or shells, after which friendship might be restored between him and the aggrieved.

In these days of super-nationalism we best understand social organization as practiced by the nation-state. In Indian California, however, where approximately 135 different dialects were spoken, a strict political or tribal system cannot easily be discerned. Kroeber cautions that it is wise to avoid the term "tribe." Except for a minority of well-defined tribes or tribelets, including the Yumas and some of the Indians of California's northwest coast, the basic political unit was the village community settlement. The Spanish called these separate village units *rancherías*. They were loosely knit groupings of several hundred aborigines; within each there were clans, identified by their individual totems. A *ranchería* typically had a patrilinear leader, who was paid ceremonial deference, but whose authority was generally limited to giving advice. One can apply the term "chief" to him only with considerable qualification. Sons of clan chieftains inherited the father's power only if they were potentially of similar capacity. Wealth played a part in chieftainship, but personal ability to inspire confidence had to be demonstrated anew by each generation.

California's Indians were not generally nomadic. Boundaries were defined, and to pass beyond a local boundary sometimes meant death to the trespasser. This led mothers to teach children the landmarks of their own family or tribal limits. These lessons were imparted in a singsong enumeration of the stones, boulders, mountains, high trees, and other objects on the landscape beyond which it was dangerous to wander. Women and children, of course, depended upon husbands and fathers for protection against enemies. Controversies between occupants of different villages sometimes led to "wars," at times over the abduction of women or quarrels about food sources. Rock and arrow fights took place round acorn groves or salmon streams. The name of one of California's northern counties, Calaveras ("skulls"), was earlier given to one of its streams by the Spanish Lieutenant Gabriel Moraga; he found a large number of skulls scattered along the banks of the stream, probably evidence of a bloody Indian struggle.

Because the California Indians seemed less warlike than many Eastern tribes, their comparative mildness of character led early writers to speak of them as cowardly. Actually the Spaniards had many sharp encounters with them before they were finally subjugated. General Mariano Guadalupe Vallejo called them a brave people. Moraga led as many as forty-six campaigns against them. Americans, later finding them already subdued by the Spaniards, failed to realize how much "frontier work" had been accomplished before their arrival. On those relatively rare occasions when the California Indians fought systematically, it is to their credit that they never tortured prisoners of war, though some of them took the scalps of dead opponents. Cannibalism was, however, occasionally practiced to the extent of eating parts of the body of a dead enemy—particularly the heart—with the idea of acquiring his valor.

An institution which the Californians had in common with most other American Indians was that of the sorcerer, or "medicine man," and they had profound faith in his ability to cure illness. His shamanistic treatment consisted mainly of reciting incantations, after which he placed one end of a hollow tube, a basic tool of the trade, against the body of the patient. He then pretended to suck out the cause of the disease, which might be a sliver of bone, a sharp-edged flint flake, or a dead lizard or other small animal, which he had previously secreted in his mouth. His success, in fact, depended partly upon his ability to fabricate incredible stories. Notwithstanding the pretenses of these practitioners, they had some knowledge of the medicinal properties of herbs and roots and other natural remedies, and often used it to benefit their patients. Even the Spanish sometimes consulted Indian medicine men when all other means failed to cure them of afflictions such as dysentery. Until the coming of the Spaniards the Indian seems not to have suffered from such white man's diseases as smallpox, influenza, and measles. Tuberculosis was unknown to them, the common cold was rare, and venereal disease did not exist. Constant scratching from lice and fleas, however, bloodied their bodies, and they were kept awake nights by the vermin from the filthy animal skins they used as bed clothes.

Though not universally used, one of the favorite treatments of Indian illnesses was the *temescal*, or sweathouse; this was a mound-like structure, usually made of timbers hermetically covered with earth, with only one small opening. A large fire was built inside the sweathouse, the patient entered, the door was closed, and there, clustered around steaming hot stones, a sick Indian remained until dripping with perspiration. Then he rushed out and leaped into the nearest lake or stream, sometimes into ice-cold water. This was a sort of "kill or cure" remedy. The Spaniards attributed to its use large numbers of deaths among the Indians from smallpox and similar diseases. The cold-water plunge was, however, most effective in eliminating vermin. Personal odors also must have been thereby diminished. Because the *temescal* was restricted to men, one early chronicler wrote that the women smelled like long-dead fish. (Among some tribes, however, both sexes were accustomed to take a daily plunge in the nearest stream.) Some men preferred to sleep at such a clubhouse or lodge rather than at home.

Religion

The Indians' religion, as moderns prefer to understand it, was primitive. Yet they had a well-defined system of shamanism, designed not only to cure disease, but also to serve a definitely formulated religious purpose. There were various cults based on distinct ideas about the creation of the world and about the primeval flood. Each family unit believed that the creation took place at a spot within their local territory. A general tradition held that at a remote time in the past a billowing sea rolled up onto the plains to fill the valleys until it covered the mountains. Nearly all living beings were destroyed in this deluge, except a few who had gone to the high peaks. There was some vague notion among the Indians of a supreme being, known by various names among the different groups. They also held to a concept of immortality: in eternity good Indians would go to a happy land beyond the water, where food would be plentiful without effort, and there would be nothing to do but eat, sleep, and dance. When the coming of the new moon was celebrated, an old man would dance in a circle, saying, "As the moon dieth and cometh to life again, so we also, having to die, will live again." California Indian mythology was extensive and complex. About it Kroeber wrote: "Their legends evince a higher power of primitive speculation than might be anticipated in view of their being largely animal tales, with [a] coyote as the chief figure." The most unusual of the Indian folk tales and village traditions were preserved and passed on eventually to invading whites, doubtless garbled at times.

In the practice of their religion, the Indians sometimes conversed with a supernatural being while in a trance. Dreams too were a source of communion with heavenly deities, as in a vision. Individuals sought to cure themselves of disease, actual and imagined, by rituals involving singing, dancing, and smoking. A guardian spirit oversaw one's quest for freedom from pain, aided, of course, by local medicine men, who sometimes engaged in a "doctors' dance"; there were rain, rattlesnake, and bear doctors, each possessing special clairvoyant and curative powers.

The Toloache and Kuksu cults were among those that figured most significantly in the religious life of California's Indians. The

Toloache ritual featured the smoking of jimson weed, an ancient rite that induced supernatural visions, perhaps even hallucinations. The Kuksu cult was originally a male secret society with an esoteric set of initiation rites. So complex were these that young boys were schooled at length in the use of masks, disguises, and ritualistic dancing. Ritualistic chambers, usually earth-roofed, were designed for use by the Kuksu faithful. Other "closed cults" also existed in California, perhaps the most prominent of which was the "World Renewal" religious system of northwest California. It too had an esoteric ritual and a relatively small membership.

The Indians had few or no traditions relating to their origin in some other land. They must have lived in California from a very distant age. So many generations had passed that their beginnings had literally been forgotten. Although anthropologists and historians generally agree that the Indians of America originated in Asia and came eastward via the Bering Straits, no primary evidence exists to connect the Californians directly with Asia. Their origin and migration across the North Pacific remains speculative. There is a possible physical resemblance to Asiatics, but no significant traditions pointing to an Oriental cultural inheritance exist.

The Indian Languages

The Indians possessed a veritable babel of languages. No less than twenty-two linguistic families are identifiable. All but one of these (Yukian) extended beyond the borders of California. Within the present boundaries of California there were, as already noted, 135 regional dialects. This confusion of tongues was one of the principal difficulties with which the missionaries had to contend. Because it was laborious to learn so many dialects, native interpreters were not easily found. Many Indian groups could not understand each other's speech, though separated in distance sometimes by only the width of a stream. It is a feat of memory merely to list the dozens of different Indian groups in California. Among the better known linguistic classifications are the Hupa or Hoopa, Pomo, Modoc, Maidu, Mono, Yurok, and Yuma (see map on facing page). Many smaller groups have become extinct.

The Indians of California have left behind little of greater permanence than the place names taken from their various dialects. The meaning and origin of most of these place names remains cloaked in mystery; linguistic scholarly investigation was not in-

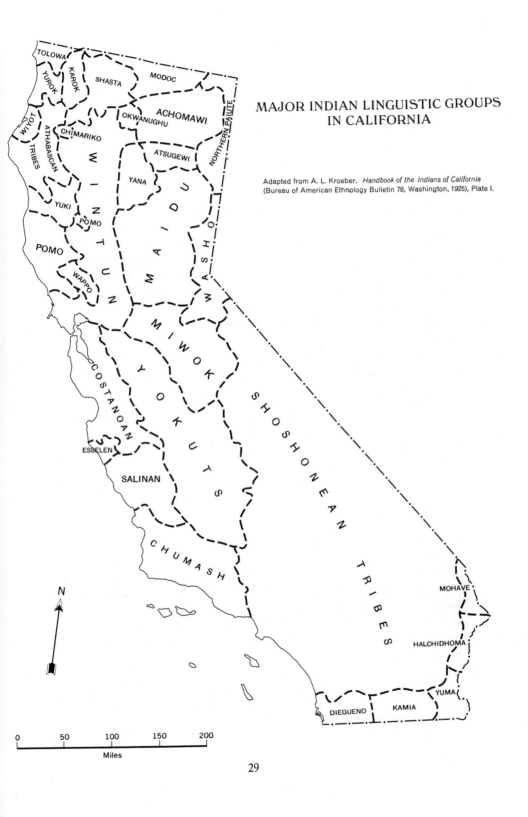

MAJOR INDIAN LINGUISTIC GROUPS
IN CALIFORNIA

Adapted from A. L. Kroeber, *Handbook of the Indians of California*
(Bureau of American Ethnology Bulletin 78, Washington, 1925), Plate I.

TOLOWA
YUROK
KAROK
SHASTA
MODOC
WIYOT
ATHABASCAN
CHIMARIKO
OKWANUGHU
ACHOMAWI
NORTHERN PAIUTE
ATSUGEWI
W
I
N
T
U
N
YANA
M
A
I
D
U
YUKI
POMO
POMO
WASHO
WAPPO
M
I
W
O
K
COSTANOAN
Y
O
K
U
T
S
SHOSHONEAN TRIBES
ESSELEN
SALINAN
CHUMASH
MOHAVE
HALCHIDHOMA
YUMA
DIEGUENO
KAMIA

N

0   50   100   150   200
Miles

29

stituted until most of the aborigines were dead. Those who remained had forgotten almost everything connected with their
tribal past. Thus an "unanalyzed residuum of meaningless names,"
to quote Kroeber, was lost forever. Not until the Indians had almost vanished did the white man realize the loss which he had
caused to the ethnological record.

Considering the prevailing disregard in which the Indian was
held by the whites, it is remarkable that the names of nine California counties—Colusa, Modoc, Mono, Napa, Shasta, Tehama,
Tuolumne, Yolo, and Yuba—have been taken from the language
of the Indian. Two more county names—Inyo and Siskiyou—are
of possible native origin. In general, the significance of the native
names borne by towns, rivers, mountains, and counties has been
hopelessly lost. Modern man must be content with the historic interest that the sound of these names, sometimes pleasing, sometimes harsh, gives to California. They remain the only enduring
monument to the first lords of its soil.

Indian Population

As compared with most regions of North America, California had
a dense native population, doubtless as a result of the mild climate
and relatively ample food supply. An early estimate placed the
number of Indians when California was discovered at from 100,000
to 150,000,* or one-eighth the entire Indian population in the area
now covered by the United States, although the territory these
Indians occupied was only one-twentieth of that total land area.
After disastrous diseases were introduced among the Indians by
the Spaniards, their numbers were drastically reduced. Despite a
tradition for cruelty given the Spanish by their enemies (the
"Black Legend," or *leyenda negra*), they were not generally hard
taskmasters. When the Indians entered the confinement of the
missions, however, they gave up the habit of burning down their
"houses" occasionally, as well as their use of the sweathouse. The
abandonment of these practices removed the only methods of
sanitation the Indians had known, and thereby increased the in-
cidence of disease.

* Professors Alfred L. Kroeber, C. Hart Merriam, and S. F. Cook have all
given different figures concerning the California Indian population prior to
the arrival of the first Spaniards. Kroeber's figure, arrived at in 1925, was
133,000. In a letter of January 22, 1960, to the author, Kroeber stated: "The
population has been estimated, after detailed analysis, at around 133,000,
and again at about a quarter of a million." Kroeber referred to population
studies by other anthropologists.

Following secularization of the missions in California's Mexican period (1834), the condition of the Indians deteriorated further. Their numbers diminished even more severely after the discovery of gold in the American period, which brought more disease, as well as mining operations that destroyed the Indians' food sources. Northern "salmon waters" were so roiled up that fish no longer swam up some of California's streams to spawn. Miners cut down acorn groves for firewood. The whites also seized valuable Indian campsites, to such an extent that the loss of their lands became a prime cause of the Indians' destruction. Induced to sign treaties they did not understand, the natives were, still later, moved off fertile lands into rocky deserts. Starvation and malnutrition brought down their numbers to a remnant estimated at only 16,000 by the year 1900. Western history has seldom if ever seen such destruction of human life—through famine, disease, and killing, but above all by confiscation of land—as that practiced upon the Indians of California. The full story of the decimation of the Indian is told in a later chapter. Though less picturesque than other American Indians, and less addicted to appearing in plumed headdress and beaded buckskins for the entertainment of tourists, the California Indian has made great progress, despite great difficulties, in becoming a member of the new order in which he lives.

SELECTED READINGS

Basic to an understanding of the California aborigines are Stephen Powers, *Tribes of California* (Washington, D.C., 1877); Alfred L. Kroeber, *Handbook of the Indians of California* (Bureau of American Ethnology Bulletin 78, Washington, D.C., 1925); and Frederick W. Hodge, *Handbook of the American Indians North of Mexico* (2 vols., Washington, D.C., 1907–1910; repr. New York, 1959). Kroeber published numerous monographs in the University of California's *Publications in Archaeology and Ethnology*. Especially useful is his "California Culture Provinces," in Volume XVII of this series (Berkeley, 1920). One of Kroeber's last efforts, written with S. A. Barrett, is entitled *Fishing Among the Indians of Northwestern California* (Berkeley, 1960). Most useful also is *Aboriginal California: Three Studies in Culture History* (Berkeley, 1963), the combined work of A. L. Kroeber, James T. Davis, Robert F. Heizer, and Albert B. Elsasser. Consult the penetrating study by Sherburne F. Cook, *The Conflict Between the California Indian and White Civilization* (Berkeley, 1943), and C. Hart Merriam, *Studies of California Indians* (Berkeley, 1955). These studies attempt to gauge the effects of white contact upon the Indians, as does C. Alan Hutchinson, "The Mexican Government and the Mission Indians of Upper California, 1821–1835," *The Americas*, XXI (April, 1965), 335–362.

From earliest times to the present the Indian has attracted the attention of popularizers and scholars alike. Non-anthropological works include: Fray Gerónimo Boscana's "Chinigchinich" in the Appendix to the first edition of Alfred Robinson's *Life in California* (New York, 1846) and Helen Hunt Jackson, *Ramona* (Boston, 1844). There is a reprint of her 1887 volume, *A Century of Dishonor*, ed. by Andrew F. Rolle (New York, 1965). See also, in Zoeth Skinner Eldredge, ed., *A History of California* (5 vols., New York, 1915), V, the essay, "Types of Indian Culture in California," and Robert F. Heizer, "The California Indians, Archaeology, Varieties of Culture, Arts of Life," California Historical Society *Quarterly*, XLI (March, 1962), 1–28. John W. Caughey, ed., *The Indians of Southern California* (San Marino, 1952), contains the useful B. D. Wilson report.

General works on the Indian include Clark Wissler, *The American Indian* (New York, 1922), and Warren K. Moorehead, *The American Indian in the United States . . .* (Andover, Mass., 1914). See also J. R. Swanton, *The Indian Tribes of North America* (Bureau of American Ethnology Bulletin 145, Washington, D.C., 1952) and Harold E. Driver, *Indians of North America* (Chicago, 1961). Examples of more specialized interpretation are Nils Christian Nelson, *Shellmounds of the San Francisco Bay Region* (Berkeley, 1909); Galen Clark, *Indians of the Yosemite Valley and Vincinity* (Yosemite, 1904); R. F. Heizer and M. A. Whipple, *The California Indians: A Source Book* (Berkeley, 1951). See also R. F. Heizer and J. E. Mills, *The Four Ages of Tsurai* (Berkeley, 1952), as well as C. D. Forde, *Ethnography of the Yuma Indians* (University of California *Publications in Archaeology and Ethnology*, XXXI, Berkeley, 1928), and, in the same series (Volume I), P. E. Goddard, *Life and Culture of the Hupa* (Berkeley, 1903). A discussion of the Indian's traditional stories of the creation of the world, his vision of man, fire, sun, thunder, and the meaning of life appears in Edward W. Gifford and Gwendoline H. Block, *California Indian Nights Entertainment* (Glendale, 1959). In a similar but more literary folk vein is Theodora Kroeber's *The Inland Whale* (Bloomington, 1959) and her realistically exciting *Ishi in Two Worlds: A Biography of the Last Wild Indian in North America* (Berkeley, 1961). See also Edith B. Webb, *Indian Life at the Old Missions* (Los Angeles, 1952). Harry C. James, *The Cahuilla Indians* (Los Angeles, 1960), reviews the history of that group of Indians native to the deserts and hillsides of southern California east of the San Bernardino mountains.

The origin of Indian and other place names can be determined from the following: Erwin G. Gudde, *California Place Names* (Berkeley, 1960); Phil Townsend Hanna, *The Dictionary of California Land Names* (Los Angeles, 1951); Nellie Van de Grift Sanchez, *Spanish and Indian Place Names of California* (San Francisco, 1914); and A. L. Kroeber, *California Place Names of Indian Origin* (Berkeley, 1916).

3

Discovery

California's name was derived from a fifteenth-century Spanish book, *Las Sergas de Esplandían (The Exploits of Esplandían)*, written by Garcí Ordóñez de Montalvo. This volume was one of those impossible romances of chivalry, including those about King Arthur and his Round Table, which grew out of the Crusades of the eleventh century. Although these romances had Christian knights for their heroes, they also sometimes featured Amazons, giants, griffins, and other mysterious creatures living on land, on sea, and even in the air. During the sixteenth century a semi-pagan literary craze ran to such extremes in Spain that there was talk of prohibiting fiction that featured the supernatural. Had the Spanish Crown banished the chivalric romances entirely, California might not today be called by its present name. Such literature finally received its death blow from the ridicule heaped upon it by Cervantes in his *Don Quixote*.

Las Sergas de Esplandían centers around Esplandían, a perfect knight, the son of Amadís of Gaul, bound to vows of courage and chastity, and sworn to follow in his father's footsteps as *conquistador* of all his enemies. In this second-rate novel of chivalry, the word *California* appears as the name of a wonderful island of tall, bronze-colored Amazons, ruled by a pagan queen, Calafía, who goes to the assistance of the pagan forces besieging the city of Constantinople. The fact that these women repelled all male suitors excited the Spanish imagination. The description of the island in *Las Sergas de Esplandían* runs as follows:

33

Know ye that at the right hand of the Indies there is an island named California, very close to that part of the Terrestrial Paradise, which is inhabited by black women, without a single man among them, and they lived in the manner of Amazons. They were robust of body, with strong and passionate hearts and great virtues. The island itself is one of the wildest in the world on account of the bold and craggy rocks. Their weapons were all made of gold. The island everywhere abounds with gold and precious stones, and upon it no other metal was found. They lived in caves, well excavated. They had many ships with which they sailed to other coasts to make forays, and the men whom they took as prisoners they killed. In this island, named California, there are many griffins. In no other part of the world can they be found. And there ruled over that island of California a queen of majestic proportions, more beautiful than all others, and in the very vigor of her womanhood. She was desirous of accomplishing great deeds. She was valiant and courageous, and ardent, with a brave heart, and had ambitions to execute nobler actions than had been performed by any other ruler.

How did the name of this mythical island reach America and become attached to a region on its western shore? The novel was at its height of popularity when Hernando Cortés was carrying on his explorations in America, and the likelihood is great that he and his men were familiar with it. The fact that he asked for the prohibition of such romances of chivalry in the American colonies probably indicates that the craze had affected the discipline of his soldiers. Following the conquest of New Spain, or Mexico, in 1519–1521, Cortés himself wrote to the Spanish King about a rumored "island of Amazons or women only, abounding in pearls and gold, lying ten days' journey from Colima." The Spaniards then still believed the peninsula of Lower California to be an island, an impression possibly gained from the Colima Indians of Mexico, who told them of land lying across the Gulf of California.

It is not clear whether the name California was first applied to the bay where the discoverers of Lower California ultimately landed, or a small island off that bay, or a number of islands in the gulf, or the cape at the end of the peninsula, or the peninsula itself. The earliest maps bearing the name vary. Whatever it first designated, the term California came to mean all that territory on the western shore from Cape San Lucas as far as the mysterious Strait of Anián, as the Spaniards called the long-sought northwest passage through the Arctic.

The region was known by several names in the first years of its discovery, but the one which was ultimately retained is probably the most euphonious. Neither "New Albion," the name bestowed upon it by Drake (by which it appears on numerous early maps), nor "Islas Carolinas" (in honor of King Charles—Carlos II—of Spain), appeals so much to the ear or to romantic instincts as does "California." Most historians give credit for the first use of the name California to the explorer Francisco de Bolaños, who in 1541, a year before the celebrated Cabrillo expedition, explored the coast above the tip of Lower California. But before that time, in the mid-1530's, the mariners of Cortés had already landed in Lower California. Whoever first named the province, there is no reason to doubt that California was so called not in mockery, but in anticipation of finding there the pearls, gold, and other riches mentioned in Montalvo's romance about the mythical island of Queen Calafía.

California and the Orient

Some years ago, the historian Charles Edward Chapman advanced the notion that there might possibly have been Oriental contact with California prior to the arrival in 1542 of the Spanish naviga- tor Juan Rodríguez Cabrillo. He suggested that Oriental ships could have found their way to California by mistake. Professor Chapman based this speculation upon a number of factors. These included the falsity of Mercator-projection maps, which had led some historians to overestimate the actual distance to California by way of the northern Pacific Ocean (the largest distances be- tween the Commander and Aleutian Islands in actuality being approximately 100 to 200 miles); the influence of the Japanese Current, which could drive a sailing junk 75 to 100 miles per day; and Chapman's belief that about sixty such craft traversed the Pacific Ocean to North America during the eighteenth and nine- teenth centuries. Professor Chapman was also greatly impressed by the discovery along the Northwest Pacific coast of such arti- facts as a Chinese bronze fan and ancient Chinese coins. In addi- tion, numerous glass Japanese globes, used to hold up fishing nets, continue to wash ashore in California. Chapman also saw material "evidence" of cultural transfer from the Orient to America's Indian civilizations. This argument emphasized particularly the Mayan and Incan rope bridges, in Peru, which resembled those constructed of similar fibers in Asia; there was also a similarity between the Aztec priesthood and the monastic societies of the East; and certain Indian hieroglyphics were like those employed in China. Chapman's writings also cited anew an old tale about "a regular trade that existed between China and California in the first century of the Christian era." From the third to the fifteenth centuries A.D., Chinese oceanic adventuresomeness (including improved navigation, cartography, and mathematics) was highly active. The Chinese had a magnetic compass from the tenth century onward. Chapman referred to "definite literary evidence" indicating that as early as the fifth century the Chinese knew of a land called Fusang—discovered by one Hwui Shăn and a party of Buddhist monks—which "many writers have identified as the Pacific Coast of North America." As late as 1697, Doctor Francesco Giovanni Gemelli-Careri, who traveled in a Manila galleon along the California coastline, believed that North America "bordered upon Great Tartary," in the Far East.

Today—in an age when the Kensington Stone, the Cardiff Giant, and the Piltdown Man have been exposed as hoaxes by modern research—historians are highly skeptical. Fifty years ago such dramatic flights into the past as the "discovery" of California by the Chinese enjoyed more widespread appeal and were given greater credence than they have come to have since. Just as one may say that, despite the Vikings, the first *effective* discovery of America was made in 1492 by Columbus, so it can be said that California was first *effectively* discovered by the Spaniards fifty years after that date.

The modern historian must seek the roots of California's discovery and colonization in an examination of the ideals and purposes of Spain's colonial system in the New World. In Columbus' time, the chief motive of exploration was to discover a new and shorter route to the "Spice Islands," whose commodities were eagerly desired by all the nations of Europe; trade with these islands had previously been carried on only by means of long, laborious voyages around the Eastern Hemisphere. The vast mass of land in the Western Hemisphere, which unexpectedly blocked the path of Columbus, seemed to him at first an obstacle, rather than a stupendous discovery.

The Search for a Northern Passage to the Orient

Columbus' original purpose of finding a route to the Orient was not abandoned. In 1513, when another explorer, Vasco Nuñez de Balboa, sighted "the great mayne sea heretofore unknowen," lying west of the new continent, his discovery gave rise to an active search for a way to get from the Atlantic Ocean around the continent to the Pacific. Spain's explorers hoped then to continue the quest toward the islands of the East. At first Balboa called the ocean that washed the southern shore of the Isthmus of Panama the South Sea, in contrast to the North Sea, or the Atlantic—which bathed the northern shore of the Isthmus. In 1520 the passage of Ferdinand Magellan, also in the service of Spain, around the South American continent and into the South Sea throught the strait bearing his name, made it clear that this entrance was too stormy for the small European ships of that period. This encouraged a search for still other routes, north and south, into what then came to be known as the Pacific Ocean. As eagerly as Ponce de Leon looked for the fountain of youth in Florida, his countrymen ardently sought the mythical passageway to the Orient, the "Strait of Anián" (or "Northwest Passage," as it was called by other explorers).

Rich cities and other marvels were rumored to be located on the banks of the northern strait that led to Cathay. A number of other legends also led the Spaniards onward, similar to those which had spurred them on previously to make explorations farther south—including tales of the Seven Cities of Cíbola, the kingdom of La Gran Quivira, even the gold hoard called El Dorado. During the 1520's and 1530's highly colored reports led the Spaniards into a futile search for a group of fabulously wealthy interior villages of the Zuñi Indians, said to be called the Seven Cities. As for La Gran Quivira, it too was rumored to be a place where even common kitchen utensils were made of gold. The story of El Dorado (the Gilded Man) was based on the reputed existence of an Indian chief in the mountains of Bogotá, today located in Colombia, whose body was painted with gold dust every morning and washed off again in the evening, and whose followers allegedly threw objects made of gold into a nearby lake (Lake Guatavita); this fable too had its counterpart in a North American setting.

Such mythical tales as these, combined with the continuing Spanish urge to find the Strait of Anián in order to open a shorter route to the Spice Islands, made Spain's quest for riches the most powerful factor in the ultimate discovery of California. The historian Hubert Howe Bancroft once wrote, "But for this influence it may almost be doubted that Spanish occupation at the end of the sixteenth or even the seventeenth century would have extended above Colima on the Pacific or Pánuco on the Atlantic." The Spaniards realized that some enemy nation, particularly England or Russia, might conceivably find the Strait of Anián before they did and that such a power might fortify it; consequently, Spain's mariners were in particular haste to get there first. In time the fear of foreign colonial interference, along with the quest for profit, came to overshadow other considerations in the search for the supposed strait.

The Pacific Explorations of Cortés

Once Cortés had completed his conquest of Mexico (1519–1521) he turned toward the newly discovered western sea. He had been commissioned by the King of Spain, Charles V, to engage in the search for the legendary northern Strait of Anián, and it seemed to him that the best plan was to launch exploratory voyages from the western coast of Mexico. With no remaining continent to conquer, he proposed to equip a fleet at his own expense with which to subdue the Moluccas and Spice Islands. The most important of Cortés's reasons for sailing into the Pacific was his lingering hope to find the isle of the Amazon Queen, whose location was rumored as constantly farther and farther north. Cortés, in his orders to one of his lieutenants, wrote that on the coast near Colima "there is one province which is inhabited by women without any men; and it is said of them that they produce their progeny in the same manner as is related in the ancient histories of the Amazons; and in order to learn the truth of all this and of whatever there may be on that coast you shall follow it down, so that you may learn the secret of what is related above." In the years from 1527–1539 Cortés was to sponsor numerous discouraging expeditions into the Pacific.

Besides the search for the Strait of Anián, and the lure of mythical riches, Cortés had another potent reason for undertaking explorations in the Pacific. When Magellan, in 1520, had entered and named the "Peaceful Sea," he struck straight across it, and the next year discovered the Philippines, an archipelago consisting of thousands of islands. Spain became increasingly interested in establishing a maritime trade between America and these islands, named for the future king of Spain, Philip II. In the middle 1520's Cortés established for this trade (to be described later) a shipbuilding station at the heavily-timbered harbor of Zacátula on the western shore of Mexico. There he sent carpenters and shipwrights to build four stout vessels. The construction of these primitive ships in colonial Mexico was a remarkable feat. All their iron work and rigging had to be laboriously brought from the Atlantic port of Vera Cruz on the backs of Indians and animals.

In the spring of 1527, after supply difficulties had been overcome and the ships were ready, three of them sailed for the Moluccas. Cortés placed these vessels under the command of Alvaro de Saavedra, a cousin of his and an explorer now virtually forgotten. Saavedra's expedition reached the Moluccas, but the Portuguese were too strongly entrenched for him to carry on trade. He therefore started back on the return voyage with a cargo of cloves but died about midway. Near Papuas (New Guinea) Saavedra's leaderless ships were scattered by a tempest. Two of them were never heard of again. The crew of the third vessel turned about and went back toward the Moluccas. They were captured by the Portuguese,* then at war with Spain; Saavedra's voyage had done little to open up a Spanish route to the Far East.

In 1532, Cortés resolved anew to push his discoveries northward up the coast from what is now Mexico, and for this purpose sent out two ships under Diego Hurtado de Mendoza. This expedition ended in mutiny, and its fate is uncertain; in any event its commander was never heard of again. Still not disheartened, the indefatigable Cortés set to work to outfit two more ships; these he dispatched the next year under Captain Diego de Becerra. This voyage involved a mutiny, led by the pilot Fortún Jiménez, who slipped up on Becerra in the night, while he slept, and killed him. The mutineers then continued the voyage and finally landed, either late in 1533 or early in 1534, in the Bay of La Paz above the southern tip of the gulf shore of the peninsula. Rumor had it that pearls were located there. This place, generally believed to be identical with modern La Paz, in Lower California, was inhabited by savage Indians. When the Spaniards, twenty-one in number, went ashore to get water they were attacked and all were killed but two sailors, who had been left on the ship and who made their way back to Cortés on the mainland. Jiménez himself was killed. In spite of the disastrous outcome of the voyage, it had succeeded in touching for the first time the peninsula (believed to be an island) of Lower California; and thus it contributed to the discovery of what is now the State of California. Furthermore, the two survivors brought back rumors of pearl beds just off the Lower California cape, which stimulated later exploration.

* The Indian Archipelago was discovered by the Portuguese who came by way of the Eastern Hemisphere and landed at Sumatra in 1509. When Magellan, in the employ of Spain, came from the other direction in 1521 and discovered the Philippines, hostilities immediately ensued between the two countries. Dissension continued until 1529, when a treaty was made fixing the boundary between the Spanish and the Portuguese at 17 degrees east of the Moluccas, a line which remained a source of dispute thereafter.

Cortés and Ulloa on the Peninsula

After this third expedition, Cortés determined to send no more captains into the Pacific but to go himself. On the third of May, 1535, he entered the Lower California bay where the massacre had occurred and took formal possession in the name of the King of Spain, calling the place Santa Cruz. At this time, however, Cortés found himself surrounded by political enemies both in America and in Spain. To a degree his New World successes had aroused the jealousy even of the King, and he was thereafter harassed by the intrigues of various opponents, who envied his success. Angry, frustrated, and discouraged by this constant opposition, and desiring greatly to rejoin his wife and children in Spain, he decided to return there. He had not, however, yet abandoned his "hopes of mighty treasures to be found and the vast city of Cíbola," and in 1539, before his departure, he ordered Francisco de Ulloa to make a further voyage to the north.

Ulloa's little fleet consisted of three small vessels, of 120, 35, and 20 tons in weight. According to the quaint contemporary English translation of the expedition's diarist: "We imbarked ourselves in the haven of Acapulco on the eighth of July in the yeere of our Lord 1539, calling upon Almighty God to guide us with his holy hand into such places where he might be served and his holy faith advanced." Ulloa's men turned their prows towards the almost unknown Sea of Cortés, or Vermillion Sea, as the Gulf of California was then called.

Following the mainland shore, Ulloa made his way to the head of the gulf, expecting to find a passage around the "island" to the open sea. After vain efforts to find this passage, he returned southward, this time carefully hugging the eastern shore of the peninsula, until he reached the port previously discovered by Jiménez. The failure to find the passage at the head of the gulf weighed heavily upon the minds of the voyagers. The expedition's diary reads: "Whereat we were sorry, because we were always in good hope to find some outlet in some place of that land, and that we had committed a great error in not searching out the secret whether that were a strait or a river which we had left behind us unsearched at the bottom of this great sea or gulf." The "strait or river" mentioned was the Colorado River, into which the gulf then ebbed and flowed.

After resting in the harbor of Santa Cruz for eight days, taking on wood and water, Ulloa's men next determined to run along the outward western coast and examine it. In their attempt to round the point of the peninsula they met heavy contrary winds, finally

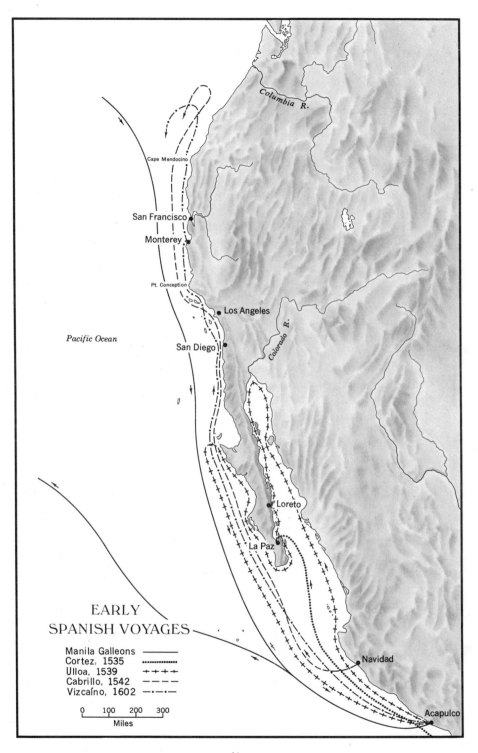

Columbia R.

Cape Mendocino

San Francisco
Monterey

Pt. Conception

Los Angeles

Pacific Ocean

Colorado R.

San Diego

Loreto

La Paz

Navidad

EARLY
SPANISH VOYAGES

Manila Galleons ————
Cortez, 1535 ••••••••••
Ulloa, 1539 ＋＋＋＋
Cabrillo, 1542 – – – –
Vizcaíno, 1602 —·—·—

Acapulco

0   100   200   300
Miles

running into a violent tempest which forced them to navigate on
the open sea. For eight days they beat up and down the coast in
a storm, riding before the wind during the day and returning upon
their course at night, while they prayed for a wind that would take
them forward on their journey. Finally they rounded the point of
Lower California and Ulloa turned northward. So started the first
lap of a series of voyages which would lead others to the discovery
of Alta (Upper) California.

Harassed by a strong northwest wind, observing the lights of
Indian fires on the land, and going ashore at one point for a sharp
encounter with hostile natives, the voyagers kept on up the coast
until January 5. On that date Ulloa's men came in sight of Cedros
Island, so called because of the tall cedars on its summit. Here
they landed and took possession in spite of the Indians, who attacked with sticks and stones. The Spaniards stayed at Cedros
only a short time. After battling opposing winds, they rounded the
island, and sent back the largest ship to its home port. Ulloa continued in one of the smaller vessels to about 29 degrees north latitude. There he was compelled by northern winds and lack of provisions to turn about, missing by a narrow margin the chance to
be the first white man to see the shores of Upper California. Some
historians have maintained that Ulloa himself never returned from
this expedition. Today, from time to time, treasure hunters assert
that they have found the remains of Ulloa's party in a variety of
places. There is, however, some evidence that Ulloa did return to
New Spain or Mexico. He is alleged to have been a court witness
in a trial there after the date of his 1539 expedition.

The chief results of Ulloa's voyage were the revelation that
Lower California might be a peninsula, the discovery of the island
of Cedros, and further exploration of both the inner and outer
coasts of Lower California. Ulloa received little credit for his
achievement, possibly because there was much disappointment
over his failure to bring back news of the Strait of Anián, the
fabulous Seven Cities of Cíbola, and other alleged terrestrial
paradises. The old geographical error, representing California as
an island, was again repeated, and appeared on maps as late as 1784.

Cabrillo and the Discovery of Alta California

When Cortés angrily departed from Mexico, he left behind his bit-
terest personal enemy, Viceroy Antonio de Mendoza. In full charge
of future explorations, Mendoza, who had been sent to apply
restraints on Cortés, did an effective job of eradicating the

memory of the Cortés exploits. Relieved of his principal rival, the Viceroy eagerly launched his own search for the Strait of Anián. Mendoza also sponsored new quests for the "Seven Cities" reported by Fray Marcos de Niza, a priest who in 1539 had penetrated northward on foot to the land of the Pueblo Indians, and whose reports had been wildly exaggerated in passing from mouth to mouth.

Numerous sea and land explorations of the early 1540's represented a continuation of the Cortés search for treasure. Expeditions in and around Lower California were led by such men as Melchior Díaz, Hernando de Alarcón, and Bolaños, already mentioned as the explorer who probably gave California its name. These attempted probes, however, extended but slightly Spain's knowledge of northern waters. And they hardly led to the discovery of new riches. Similarly, the military expedition of 1540, led by Francisco Vázquez de Coronado into the area today called Kansas, failed to find the riches it was seeking.

Viceroy Mendoza, in yet a further attempt to discover the Strait of Anián and the treasures to which it might lead, decided to send another exploratory party north by sea. This one would proceed with orders to explore the coast beyond the latitude reached by Ulloa. Mendoza gave orders to put two ships in readiness, the *San Salvador* and the *Victoria*. A leader was found in the person of Juan Rodríguez Cabrillo, described as a "navigator of great courage and honor and a thorough seaman." Little is known of the personal background of this sailor, the actual discoverer of California, except that he was Portuguese by birth and had participated in the expedition in which Cortés conquered Mexico. It was common practice for Spain, as well as for other maritime nations, to employ experienced navigators and seamen from other countries. In this tradition Columbus, a Genoese, had navigated under the protection of the King and Queen of Spain, and Giovanni Caboto, another Italian, who anglicized his name to John Cabot, sailed in the service of England.

The two small vessels to which Cabrillo entrusted the lives of his men along an unknown coast were poorly built and badly outfitted. Their anchors and ironwork had, like those of the ships built by Cortés, been carried across Mexico to the Pacific. They were manned by conscripts and were sparsely provisioned; the crews were subject to that deadly peril of the sea, scurvy. One can only admire the courage and perseverance of such men, who, with crude instruments and no accurate navigational maps, fought their way from the tropics to the remote north of the Pacific, regardless of the seasons.

The usual prayers having been offered to Almighty God for the success of the voyage, Cabrillo's sails were unfurled and the start made at midday on June 27, 1542, from the port of Navidad, on the western coast of New Spain. Seven and one-half months were spent in this voyage, during which the Pacific Coast, at least as far as 41 degrees and 30 minutes north latitude, was explored. It was folly to start the expedition so late in the season; violent winter storms battered the ships and protracted the voyage so that it had to be abandoned before its purpose was accomplished. Nevertheless the discovery of California makes this the most important voyage Spain had yet made on the western coast.

The crews of Cabrillo's two little ships, at times beaten back by the northwest wind, at other times becalmed and rocked idly on the waves for days, were unable to make a northing. Their captain, the documents say, paced the deck, peering anxiously into the mists ahead. He did not realize that he was about to make a great discovery and to lay down his life in doing so. The adventurers were on the threshold of an important event, yet the shoreline along which they sailed was unvaried to their eyes, with no visible dividing line anywhere to show where a new California began.

On Thursday, September 28, 1542, after three months at sea, Cabrillo's two ships entered a "very good closed port." This was the future harbor of San Diego. Their entrance into this bay formally marked the discovery of California—or Alta (Upper) California, as it was called in distinction to the peninsula of Baja (Lower) California. In later years English writers claimed the discovery of California for Drake; but Cabrillo's landing, almost thirty-eight years earlier than Drake's, on a legitimate voyage of exploration, clearly established Spain's prior rights to California.

When Cabrillo's party landed, they found Indians, who exhibited great fear. In fact, all the natives fled but three, from whom the Spaniards learned that people like themselves, bearded and wearing clothing, had apparently been seen eastward, toward the interior. The Indians made gestures to show how the white men threw their lances, and by galloping along the ground showed that the strangers had been on horseback. They also indicated that the white men had killed some natives. Writers have speculated that stories about the Ulloa expedition several years before, or perhaps even the Coronado land expedition of 1540, may have reached the Indians of the San Diego area. Cabrillo gave these Indians gifts of beads and other trifles, and endeavored by his kindness to win their confidence. In contrast to the early history of Mexico and Latin America, that of California was not marked by the widespread shedding of Indian blood.

At Santa Catalina Island the Spanish visitors encountered other astonished but passive natives. Cabrillo then cruised onward. Along the shoreline opposite Santa Monica, he noted an indentation on the mainland which he called "the Bay of Smokes": even in those days before smog, Indian campfires covered the bay near today's Los Angeles with spirals of smoke. Cabrillo's party found the Santa Barbara Channel above Ventura teeming with a dense Indian population, whose seaworthy boats presented a marked contrast to the primitive rafts the Spaniards had seen on the Lower California coast.

Upon rounding Point Conception, just above today's Santa Barbara, the voyagers encountered a heavy northwest wind which forced them out to sea. There they came in sight of the islands now known as San Miguel and Santa Rosa. Seeking refuge from the wind, they ran into a snug port on San Miguel Island, known later as Cuyler's Harbor. They took possession of this port, calling it La Isla de la Posesión; and the harbor became a sailors' refuge during many a future storm. This island too was populated by Indians, who lived by fishing and who traded beads, manufactured from fish bones, with the Indians on the mainland. In their long hair were intertwined cords into which were thrust daggers of flint, bone, and wood. They wore no clothing, and painted their faces in squares, like a checkerboard. Cabrillo spent a week on this island, in the course of which he suffered a fall, breaking his arm near the shoulder. Early accounts state that Cabrillo's accident reopened an old military wound.

Despite this painful accident, and the severe winter storms, the commander gave orders to continue the search for the Strait of Anián. The vague Spanish quest for a great river or strait kept luring them onward. Braving severe storms, the Spaniards beat their way to a cape, near Fort Ross, having skirted such landmarks as Monterey Bay and the Golden Gate without seeing them. They then drifted south again, and on November 16 discovered what is today known as Drake's Bay. Here they dropped anchor in forty-five fathoms of water, but, because of heavy seas, dared not land. After two days they set sail once more, again missing the Golden Gate, and ran southward.

On November 23, unable to make a landing on the rocky coast north of Point Conception, Cabrillo's crew were glad to sail southwestward and to re-enter their snug harbor at San Miguel Island. Almost continuous storms and high winds over the next two months compelled them to winter on the islands of the Santa Barbara Channel, chiefly at San Miguel. Here the expedition sustained a grave misfortune. On January 3, 1543, its commander

died, probably as a result of his earlier fall and the exposure of the
hard northern voyage. After his men laid Cabrillo to rest they re-
named the island La Isla de Juan Rodríguez. Drifting sand and
cliffs which have since fallen into the sea long ago obliterated his
last resting place; not even the name of the island has been retained to commemorate his achievement. That Cabrillo was beloved of his men is implicit in a statement found in the expedition's records: "They returned to Navidad sorrowful for having
lost their commander."

As he lay dying, Cabrillo had charged his men to resume their
quest and to explore the coast as far northward as possible. His
pilot, Bartolomé Ferrer (commonly misspelled Ferrelo), took
command after his death; and the expedition set sail again. Scud-
ding northward before a storm, on March 1 Ferrer reached the
northern limit of his voyage, possibly at the Rogue River in
Oregon, but at least as far north as the Eel River of California. At
this point the crews, in an almost crazed condition from scurvy,
forced Ferrer to turn back. He returned to the harbor of Navidad
in New Spain on April 14, 1543.

This first true voyage to California had failed to find the Strait
of Anián, or the gold sought by Mendoza for Spain. Cabrillo had
seen no cities with gold and silver walls—indeed no advanced
Indian civilization with treasure lying in its streets, no *Otro Mejico*
or *Otro Pirú*, no "other" lands so rich as the Aztec and Inca empires. Yet the expedition had proved a magnificent success in gaining new geographical knowledge; and Cabrillo and his men had
opened the sea route to a province now familiar to all the world.

SELECTED READINGS

Conjecture about the origin of the name California appears in Herbert D. Austin, "New Light on the Name California," Historical Society of Southern California, *Publications*, XII (Los Angeles, 1923);
Ruth Putnam, *California, the Name* (Berkeley, 1917); Irving Berdine
Richman, *California Under Spain and Mexico, 1535–1847* (Boston,
1911), pp. 362–366; and George Davidson, *The Origin and Meaning of
the Name California* (San Francisco, 1910). Richman's work is greatly
under-consulted. See also Donald C. Cutter, "Sources of the Name
'California,'" *Arizona and the West*, III (Autumn, 1961), 233–243.

Discussion of possible Oriental contact with California is in Charles
E. Chapman, *A History of California* (New York, 1921), pp. 21–42;
Edward Payson Vining, *An Inglorious Columbus; or Evidence that*

Hwui Shǎn and a Party of Buddhist Monks from Afghanistan Discovered America in the Fifth Century A.D. (New York, 1885); Naojiro Murakami, "Japan's Early Attempts to Establish Commercial Relations with Mexico," in *The Pacific Ocean and History* (New York, 1917), pp. 467–480; Zelia Nuttall, "The Earliest Historical Relations Between Mexico and Japan," University of California *Publications in Archaeology and Ethnology*, IV (Berkeley, 1904), 1–47. On this theme see also Douglas S. Watson, "Did the Chinese Discover America?" California Historical Society *Quarterly*, XIV (March, 1935), 47–57, and Charles G. Leland, *Fusang, or the Discovery of America by Chinese Buddhist Priests in the Fifth Century* (London, 1875). Further conjecture is stimulated by C. W. Brooks, "Report of Japanese Vessels Wrecked in the North Pacific Ocean From the Earliest Records to the Present Time," *Proceedings, California Academy of Sciences*, VI (San Francisco, 1876), 50–66.

Basic works on the discovery and coastal exploration of California are Francisco Preciado, *Diary of the Voyage of Ulloa to Baja California in 1539–1540* in Hakluyt's *Principal Navigations* (Edinburgh, 1885–1890), Volume III; Miguel Venegas, *Noticia de la California y de su conquista temporal y espiritual hasta el tiempo presente* (Madrid, 1757); Henry R. Wagner, *Spanish Voyages to the Northwest Coast of America in the Sixteenth Century* (San Francisco, 1929), as well as his *Juan Rodríguez Cabrillo, Discoverer of the Coast of California* (San Francisco, 1941) and *Cartography of the Northwest Coast of America to the Year 1800* (2 vols.,Berkeley, 1937); Francisco López de Gómara, *Historia de la conquista de Mexico por Fernando Cortés* (Mexico, D.F., 1943); Martín Fernández de Navarrete, *Colección de viajes; documentos inéditos* (Madrid, 1825–1827); Juan Paez, *Relation of the Voyage of Juan Rodríguez Cabrillo*, translated and edited by Herbert E. Bolton in *Spanish Exploration in the Southwest* (New York, 1916); Antonio Pigafetta, *The First Voyage Around the World 1519, '20, '21, '22* (London, 1874). Other useful references regarding exploration are: Maurice G. Holmes, *From New Spain by Sea to the Californias, 1519–1668* (Glendale, 1963); Jack D. Forbes, "Melchior Díaz and the Discovery of Alta California," *Pacific Historical Review*, XXVII (November, 1958), 351–357; and two volumes of basic documents concerning such mariners as Pedro de Unamuno, Vizcaíno, and Cermenho, *California: Documentos para la Historia de la Demarción Comercial de California, 1583–1632*, ed. by W. Michael Mathes (Madrid, 1965).

The concept of California as an island is discussed in R.V. Tooley, *California as an Island: A Geographical Misconception Illustrated by 100 Examples from 1625 to 1770* (London, 1964).

On the Spanish northward advance by land see Herbert E. Bolton, *The Spanish Borderlands* (New Haven, 1921), and Philip W. Powell, *Soldiers, Indians and Silver: The Northward Advance of New Spain, 1550–1600* (Berkeley, 1952). The flavor of the Spanish mining frontier comes to life in Bernard Moses, *Flush Times at Potosí* (Berkeley, 1910).

4

Continued Exploration

Though the dreams of finding great cities and other mythical marvels slowly faded, from the sixteenth through the eighteenth centuries Spain continued the search for a Northwest Passage to the Spice Islands. Her efforts were complicated by the fact that she was constantly obliged to protect her provinces, including California, against the expansionism of other nations. Her quest proved fruitless. That such a passage actually existed was not to be proved until the twentieth century, for only in 1906 did Roald Arnundsen, a Norwegian explorer, traverse thousands of miles of Arctic waters to reach the Bering Sea from the Atlantic Ocean.

After the discovery of the Philippine Islands by Magellan in 1521, the lure of fabulous profits from trade with the East Indies produced a new movement of Spanish ships across the Pacific from ports on the western coast of the New World. Though the outbound voyage was relatively easy, the return was extremely difficult. Favorable winds blew the ships toward the Orient, but on the return trip the same gusty winds beat them back. For this reason numerous early voyages to the Philippines ended in disaster.

The Philippine Trade

In 1564 King Philip II ordered a Spanish fleet sent from New Spain to find a practicable return route from Asia to America. This task could be entrusted only to the most skilled navigator in

New Spain, Andrés Urdaneta, who had taken holy orders. He consented to leave his cloister to serve the King, ostensibly as chaplain of the fleet, but in reality as a chief cartographer and sailing master. In effect, he was in command. On November 24, 1564, the expedition left the port of Acapulco on the west coast of New Spain under its titular commander, Miguel López de Legazpi. It reached the Philippines and succeeded in making its way back to Acapulco after a voyage of 129 days.

Urdaneta's feat showed that the most feasible way for ships to make the return trip was to sail northeastward. After leaving the Philippines the Spanish vessels took advantage of heavy westerly winds, at from 30 to 40 degrees latitude, and ran before them to the North American coastline. Establishment of this route, with its first landfall on the coast of Upper California, at about the latitude of Cape Mendocino, was to help speed the occupation and settlement of California, whose earliest history was thus bound up with that of the Philippines. Trading ships ran between the continents for two and a half centuries after 1564, carrying silver bullion from Acapulco to be exchanged for Oriental goods at Manila. This Philippine city was the collecting point for two great staples—silks from further north in the Orient and spices from the south. The silks in particular, together with other manufactured rarities from China, formed the foundation of Spain's Pacific commerce. The slow and lumbering galleons returning from the Islands were also filled with the riches of the Indies—precious stones, musk, aromatic resin, wax, amber, porcelain, metals, carved and inlaid chests, knickknacks of all kinds, and exotic birds that "talked and played tricks." Bales and chests were piled so high in cabins, and on the decks up to the gunwales, that one traveler wrote: "We had hardly room to stand. Nobody could live under deck, it was so full of provisions and commodities. All men lay exposed to the sun and air."

The commodities brought to America by the galleons found a ready sale among the Spaniards in Mexico and Peru who had enriched themselves from mining silver. Some of the Oriental luxuries were also reshipped to Spain by way of Mexico. The Philippine trade was originally a government enterprise, both maintained and officered at royal expense; in time however, it came under the control of private merchants. Even today the name "Manila galleon" conjures up thoughts of adventure by men who risked their lives on small and insecure craft. Although never more than tenuous, the almost ethereal connection of these galleons with California nevertheless persists. Eventually, the Spanish Crown placed restrictions upon this traffic, including its limitation to one galleon a year—standard mercantile practice for Spain. The mother country did not welcome competition from her colonies. Finally, in 1815, after lending peripheral color to California's history for 250 years, the galleons ceased to sail altogether.

The voyages of these luxury-laden ships involved intense misery for their sailors. Although the outward trip from Acapulco required only two or three months of fair sailing, the return took from seven to nine months. The food became rancid or filled with maggots and the water supply failed altogether, compelling reliance upon rainwater, caught in sails, barrels, or any other handy receptacle. Scurvy then set in; as some galleons approached the coast of America, body after body was thrown into the sea. Crews were so decimated that by the time they sighted California there were often not enough able-bodied men left to go ashore for fresh water, or to raise an anchor if it were dropped—even though they were tantalized by the sight of the land. So the ships limped on, without stopping, down the coast, with their battered, leaky hulls, spoiled provisions, putrid water, and sick and dying crews, until they reached Acapulco. The loss of one of these vessels cast a deep gloom over both Manila and Acapulco, for nearly every citizen had a stake in its cargo, or relatives among its crew. Moreover, the failure of one of these ships to arrive caused a great scarcity of the exotic commodities to which the Spaniards had become accustomed.

After 1564, the government in Mexico was increasingly troubled at the loss of so many men on the return voyage from the Orient, and the miserable condition in which they arrived at the home port. Obviously the best means of relieving this state of affairs was by discovering and occupying a safe harbor on the coast of Upper California, and establishing a way station where ships could stop for sorely needed repairs and fresh food and water. Although this objective was never accomplished, the quest for such a port made the Manila galleon important in the subsequent settlement of California.

Drake and Cavendish

The need for wood, water, meat, and repairs was not the only reason for Spanish determination to seek a haven for the galleons on the coast of the Californias. The intrusion in those waters of the English privateers, Drake and Cavendish, rudely shocked the Spaniards. By the late sixteenth century, when the English achieved access into the "Spanish lake" known as the Pacific, news of Spain's rich galleons in the Pacific had spread around the world. English privateers, little more than licensed pirates, then began to brave passage through the Strait of Magellan in order to reach the western coast of the Americas. There they could lie in wait for galleons returning from Manila. Henceforth the Spanish ships were armed with small cannon, muskets, and catapults for hurling stones, ineffective though these weapons were against fast corsairs.

In 1577 the magnificent sea dog, Francis Drake, bearing a secret commission from Queen Elizabeth to "annoy the King of Spain in his Indies," set sail from Plymouth in England on a voyage that would last several years. In his famous vessel the *Golden Hind*, he made his way through the Magellan passage, and swooped down upon unsuspecting Spanish outposts on the Pacific like a hawk among barnyard fowl. Boldly attacking both coastal settlements and Spanish vessels, Drake captured ship after ship, sending them to run before the wind with all sails flying after taking off their treasure and crews. He stopped in the ports of Lima—in present-day Peru—and Guatulco—today in the Mexican province of Oaxaca—long enough to sack these towns before the terror-stricken populace of either could collect their wits sufficiently to make any defense. He was a courtly robber, and in his operations on the western coast of the New World never killed a man; instead, he treated his prisoners like honored guests, even giving them money and clothing after he set them free.

The *Golden Hind* was loaded almost to the sinking point with treasure—some say to the amount of 800,000 English pounds. In constant danger of capture, Drake finally set sail for England, by way of California and the northern Pacific. Fearing that Spanish ships would be lying in wait back at the Strait of Magellan, Drake sought a passage through the Arctic. According to some accounts, this was a major purpose of his voyage. In any case, Drake sailed north along a route that took him to the Upper California coast. On June 17, 1579, his lookout sighted a "convenient and fit harborough," at 38 degrees and 30 minutes latitude on the California shoreline. Into this sandy bay he entered for the purpose of repairing his ship. Drake remained there until July 23, during which time his men tipped the vessel onto her side, caulked and careened her, and mended a bad leak. The exact location of Drake's anchorage in California has long been a matter of controversy. Strong arguments have been advanced for the bight under Point Reyes, today called Drake's Bay, a white-cliffed harbor then held by the Miwok Indians. Some believe that Drake anchored at Bodega Bay, a few miles farther north.

As to San Francisco's spacious bay, no convincing evidence has been produced that Drake or his men laid eyes upon it, even though his landing parties several times went ashore north of the location of the present city. The Englishmen probably did not anchor in a spot where they, or their shore parties, could see San Francisco Bay. Books and articles on the subject of Drake's anchorage still debate its whereabouts. Hopefully one day new documentary evidence will be unearthed. A basic contemporary source (not listed in the bibliography of this chapter) is *The World Encompassed by Sir Francis Drake* (London, 1628), written by persons closely connected with that expedition. By studying this basic document and other sources, anthropologists, among them Professor Robert F. Heizer, generally conclude that Drake landed at Drake's Bay. In 1775 the Spanish *San Carlos*, the first ship to enter San Francisco Bay, was seriously damaged by battering against rocks and tides, a clear indication that Drake's earlier expedition entered a bay distinctly different in character. As a result of still other evidence, most historians also believe that Drake could not have entered San Francisco Bay.

During his stay on the California coast Drake kept up friendly relations with the Indians, exchanged gifts with them, and went through ceremonials that the English later chose to regard as acceptance by the natives of England's sovereignty. These symbolic acts probably corresponded to the smoking of a "peace pipe." After completing repairs on their ship, Drake's party held religious services, during which—the documents of the expedition solemnly assert—the natives made loud responses, possibly incantations similar to those of their own medicine men.

Before he departed from California, Drake claimed title to the country for his Queen by leaving behind

a plate of brasse, fast nailed to a great and firm poste, whereon is engraven her grace's name and the day and year of our arrivall there, and of the free giving up of the province and kingdome, both by the king and people, into her Majestie's hands; together with her highnesse picture and armes in a piese of sixpence currant English monie shewing itself by a hole made of purpose through the plate; underneath was likewise engraven the name of our General.

In 1934 such a plate of brass was allegedly found near the Laguna Ranch on Drake's Bay; after being thrown away it was supposedly "rediscovered" in 1936 under circumstances that led skeptics to question its authenticity. Following an internal and external analysis (including a metallurgical study of the plate), historians still disagree as to whether this artifact is genuine.

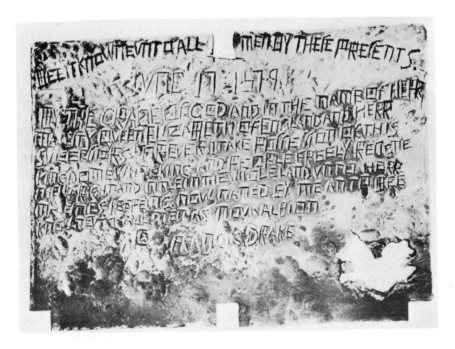

THE "DRAKE PLATE." (By courtesy of The Bancroft Library, University of California, Berkeley.)

There can, however, be little question concerning the vivid imagination possessed by the first English chroniclers who described Drake's relations with the California Indians. Their accounts made a princely personage out of an Indian chieftain, who would actually have been attired poorly in rabbit skins; his rude basketwork hat was transformed into a royal crown, and every gesture into a courtly mannerism. The three main accounts of the Drake voyage were set down by writers who did not hesitate to embroider the original reports, so that their highly embellished descriptions of California's geography and primitive people conformed to seventeenth-century European standards of etiquette. Drake's own full account was never printed; in all probability it was suppressed lest it should cause further complications with Spain.

Abandoning hope of finding a passage through northern waters, Drake turned his back upon the shores of California, to which he gave the name "New Albion," and continued his voyage westward around the world via the Moluccas. His explorations on the western coast of North America were of little importance, the chief result of his stay in California being to hasten the occupation of that region by the Spaniards. Neither did Drake add much to the general knowledge of the Pacific, for in all his voyaging he used Spanish navigational charts taken from captured ships.

In 1586 another English corsair ravaged the Pacific coastline. This was Thomas Cavendish, very different in character from the suave and courtly Drake. Cavendish, a rascal of reduced fortunes from the county of Suffolk, was seeking to recoup past gambling losses by a voyage to the "South Sea." He sailed up and down that ocean robbing and burning Spanish ships, torturing and killing prisoners, and conducting himself in general like a pirate flying the black flag. After considerable destructive poaching, Cavendish returned to England. His sails were lined in silk, his banners fashioned of cloth-of-gold, and his sailors dressed in fine damask, each with a golden chain around his neck. On his return Cavendish, like Drake, became a hero of Elizabethan England. His exploits in the Pacific were rivaled by those of his countryman Richard Hawkins and the Hollander Van Noort, the latter as merciless a pirate as ever made his victims walk the plank. The activities of such marauding buccaneers, lurking off the Lower California coast, made it clear that Spain must move to protect not only the Californias but also the returning Manila galleons.

The Voyages of Gali and Cermenho

The viceregal government at Mexico City, aroused by the continued threat of foreign interlopers, in 1584 ordered Francisco de Gali, the seasoned commander of the Manila galleon, to sail along the Upper California coast on his return from the Philippines. Gali was instructed to make careful nautical observations to be used as a basis for formulating future plans. As has been noted, a new port in California waters would offer at least temporary protection for the galleons. On his return from the voyage, Gali reported observing a "very fair land, wholly without snow, and with many rivers, bays, and havens," although he had not debarked from his galleon. His report stimulated a number of further explorations; among these, perhaps the most significant occurred ten years later, when Viceroy Luís de Velasco appointed a Portuguese navigator, Sebastián Rodríguez Cermenho, to explore and mark out Gali's entire course, beginning where the galleon bound from the Philippines reached a point below the islands off the California coast. These are today called the Channel Islands.

On July 5, 1595, Cermenho's ship, the *San Agustín*, sailed out of the port of Cavite in the Philippines, its decks crowded, as usual, with boxes of merchandise, chicken coops, and barrels of ship's stores. On November 4 the first North American landfall of the *San Agustín* occurred, probably a little north of Eureka, above 41 degrees latitude. Next, Cermenho entered the same bay in which Drake is supposed to have anchored sixteen years before, went ashore with a party, and took possession of the land and port in the name of the King of Spain.

At this shallow roadstead, Cermenho met with disaster. On November 30 the *San Agustín* was driven ashore by a squall and completely wrecked, scattering the fine silks and porcelains in her cargo along the beach for the Indians to pick up—as a chronicler says, "like pearls before swine." Fortunately the crew had completed the building of a launch for shore use. Into this craft they crowded themselves, seventy in all, with such provisions of acorns as they could obtain from the Indians, and proceeded to make their precarious way down the coast. The meager accounts of this voyage in the launch *San Buenaventura* reveal it to have been one of the most remarkable for endurance and courage in the annals of the Pacific. The commander, Cermenho, notwithstanding uncomfortable conditions, continued to make careful observations. He noted, for one thing, the entrance to Monterey Bay, thus qualifying as its real discoverer rather than the later explorer Vizcaíno, to whom the credit is usually given. On January 7, 1596, Cermenho's launch arrived at its home port of Navidad with the crew almost dead.

This voyage was regarded by Cermenho's contemporaries as a failure, and he was threatened with a lawsuit by the owners of the lost cargo of the *San Agustín*. His great effort, however, was not wasted; he not only brought back a quite accurate description of the California coast, but his disastrous voyage awakened the government to the folly of trying to make such explorations with heavy, unwieldy galleons, risking the loss of their precious cargoes. It became clear that future expeditions to California should make use of smaller ships, of light draught, to facilitate shore observations. Such vessels would sail directly from New Spain, loaded only with provisions. This plan was tried with complete success seven years later when Viceroy Monterey sent out another California expedition under the command of Sebastián Viscaíno, a Basque merchant-navigator with much experience on the galleon route, having been involved in expeditions to the Philippines in 1586–1589 and to Lower California in 1596–1597.

Vizcaíno at Monterey

Sailing under the protection of Our Lady of Carmel, Vizcaíno's "fleet" of three tiny vessels passed out of the harbor of Acapulco on May 5, 1602. The party proceeded up the coast, stopping at many of the points visited by Cabrillo and renaming them. To the Vizcaíno expedition we owe many familiar place names—San Diego, Santa Catalina Island, Santa Barbara, Point Conception, Monterey, and Carmel. At 36 degrees latitude Vizcaíno, on December 16, 1602, sailed into Monterey Bay. This became the principal event of Vizcaíno's voyage and he named the place after the viceroy who sponsored his expedition. Under an oak tree which stood so close to the shore that its branches were wet by the incoming tides, the explorers took part in a religious ceremony:

The mass of the Holy Ghost was held so that God might give light to the general and those of his council, in order that they might decide what would be most conducive to the service of the Lord and of his Majesty.

As Vizcaíno looked about him at the ring of hills, dark with the growth of pines covering them from base to summit, he became so enamored of the place that he wrote a fulsome description of it to the viceroy. His praise of a harbor defended from all winds was so misleading that the Spaniards who next saw Monterey, in 1769, failed to recognize it. Vizcaíno, continuing the voyage to the north, passed Cape Mendocino; then he decided, due to the miserable condition of his crews, to turn about and make for Acapulco.

On the way down the coast Vizcaíno's men were unable to land. The number of able-bodied men was so reduced that they dared not let go of their anchors lest they not be able to raise them again. Crew members died like flies from scurvy and starvation. Because of their sore mouths and loss of teeth, Vizcaíno's crew could not eat the coarse food they had on board. At Cedros Island most of them were able only to crawl ashore on their hands and knees; by a supreme effort, they somehow managed to take on wood and water. Forty-five men, probably half the crew members, died on the voyage, which lasted eleven months. Yet they had made a detailed exploration of the coast as far north as Monterey. They had also reached and sketchily mapped the northern limit (to about the latitude of Drake's Bay) desired by the viceroy, and they had visited as well the fine harbor of San Diego.

In 1612–1613 Vizcaíno made one further—but obscure—voyage, apparently to establish commercial relations between New Spain and Japan. He took along some Franciscan missionaries and appears to have also been in search of some mythical islands named Rica de Oro (Rich in Gold) and Rica de Plata (Rich in Silver). Viscaíno probably died on the coast of New Spain in 1629 after combat with Dutch invaders; little else is known about him.

A change of viceroys, and a lessening of Anglo-Spanish tensions, had occurred after Vizcaíno returned to New Spain from his California voyage. The new viceroy, the Marqués de Montesclaros, proved lukewarm toward the prospects of colonizing California. In the years from 1602 to 1769 no ship is known to have entered California waters from the south, while the Manila galleons left few records of what they saw as they sailed past the shores of the area. Their crews generally refused to risk valuable cargoes by venturing too near Alta California's unfamiliar coastline. As a result, the miles slipped by with only slight incident, as these ships usually turned southward as soon as they sighted the floating seaweed that signaled the presence of rocky shoals. For more than a century and a half, there was little addition to the knowledge produced by Vizcaíno's voyage.

SELECTED READINGS

A basic source on the Manila galleon trade is the account by Dr. Giovanni Francesco Gemelli Careri, an Italian passenger who published the gruesome details of his voyage in *Narrative of a Voyage on a Spanish Galleon from Manila to Acapulco in 1687–1688;* a translation is in *Churchill's Collection of Voyages and Travels,* IV (London, 1752). See also William L. Schurz, *The Manila Galleon* (New York, 1939).

Useful to an understanding of Drake are Henry R. Wagner, *Sir Francis Drake's Voyage Round the World: Its Aims and Achievements* (San Francisco, 1926); C. G. Fink and E. P. Polushkin, *Drake's Plate of Brass Authenticated . . .* (California Historical Society, Publication No. 14, San Francisco, 1937); R. B. Haselden, "Is the Drake Plate of Brass Genuine?" California Historical Society *Quarterly,* XVI (September, 1937), 271–274; Robert F. Heizer, *Francis Drake and the California Indians* (Berkeley, 1947). Richard Hakluyt's *Principal Navigations . . .* (London, 1903–1905) contains the three eye-witness narratives of Drake's voyage to California. Over the years numerous articles on Drake have been scattered throughout the California Historical Society *Quarterly.* The most recent of these is Francis P. Farquhar and

Walter A. Starr, "Drake in California: A Review of the Evidence and the Testimony of the Plate of Brass." This appears in Volume XXXVI (March, 1957), 21–34. Robert H. Powers, "Portus Novæ Albionis Re-Discovered?" *Pacific Discovery,* VII (May–June, 1954), 10–12, puts forth the view that Drake anchored in northern San Francisco Bay. Walter A. Starr, "Drake Landed in San Francisco Bay in 1579, the Testimony of the Plate of Brass," California Historical Society *Quarterly,* XLI (September, 1962), 1–29, re-opens the controversy unconvincingly. The most well-reasoned summary article on Drake is Adolph S. Oko, "Francis Drake and Nova Albion," California Historical Society *Quarterly* XLIII (June, 1964), 135–158.

On Cermenho see Sebastián Rodríguez Cermenho, *Diario* (1595), in manuscript form at the Bancroft Library, University of California, Berkeley. This and other documents at the Bancroft Library are transcripts from the Archivo General de Indias, Seville, Spain. Consult also Henry R. Wagner, "The Voyage to California of Sebastián Rodríguez Cermenho in 1595," California Historical Society *Quarterly,* III (April, 1924), 3–24. In the same journal Robert F. Heizer's "Archeological Evidence of Sebastián Rodríguez Cermenho's California Visit," XX (December, 1941), 315–328, offers a fascinating identification of artifacts, including Chinese pottery shards left after the wrecking of Cermenho's *San Agustín* at Drake's Bay. On Vizcaíno, see William Michael Mathes, "Sebastián Vizcaíno and Spanish Expansion in the Pacific, 1580–1630," Ph.D. dissertation, University of New Mexico (1966).

A general, but imperfect, account of buccaneering in Pacific waters is Peter Gerhard, *Pirates on the West Coast of New Spain, 1575–1742* (Glendale, 1960). Michael E. Thurman, *The Naval Department of San Blas, New Spain's Bastion for Alta California and Nootka . . .* (Glendale, 1967), is a useful study of a key supply base.

5

The First Colonizers of the Frontier

Nearly a century before the first English colonists landed at Jamestown, on the eastern shores of North America, Spanish soldiers and priests went to New Spain to spread their civilization northward from Mexico City. In small bands—and sometimes individually — these representatives of King and Church sought treasure for Spain and converts for the Church, while bringing order to the frontier. For the padres the principal object was the wealth of men's souls; but Spain's government was astute enough to realize the value of missionaries also in subduing wild peoples with a minimum of expense and bloodshed, and hence in securing the riches that would hopefully flow from colonization. In the Spanish colonial system the cross marched side by side with the sword.

During the period between the Vizcaíno expedition of 1602 and the permanent settlement of California in 1769, New Spain's northern border extended in a sort of arc, from a series of garrisons located along the Red River in present-day Louisiana to a remote chain of Jesuit missions spread throughout northern Mexico and Lower California. Along this colonial frontier were established increasing numbers of missions, mining camps, cattle ranches, and crude adobe *presidios*, or forts. Most of the colonization took place below the present border of California, but it laid the groundwork for later advances toward the north and thus was important to the history of that province.

Three Jesuit clerics contributed notably to the colonization of the approaches to California. Foremost of these was Eusebio Francesco Kino (sometimes spelled Chino or Chini), a native of Trento, Italy, who had been highly educated in German universities. As explorer, cartographer, and mission builder, Kino was responsible, in the years 1678–1712, for the founding of numerous missions on New Spain's northern frontiers. It was also Kino who, by his explorations and maps, proved in 1702 that California was not an island. Aiding Father Kino was another Italian Jesuit, the square-jawed, flinty Juan María de Salvatierra, who in 1697 founded the first of a chain of missions in Lower California. Salvatierra went on to become Provincial of the entire Jesuit order in New Spain. The third major blackrobe was Father Juan de Ugarte, a gigantic cleric, so strong that he could lift two men simultaneously and bump their heads together. Ugarte labored for many years among the Indians. These priests, educated and yet hardened by years of missionary work, gave a solid foundation to the frontier establishments from which later military and clerical officials would move toward Upper California.

By the middle of the eighteenth century, representatives of the King of Spain had pushed the frontier up to the Gila and Colorado rivers. Kino's early surveys and those of other explorers and navigators had revealed much about Lower California, the tip of which had been occupied steadily since the first mission was built. It would only be a matter of time before the coastline of Upper California, past which Spain's galleons had so long been sailing, would be fully explored and settled by Europeans.

In spite of the success achieved by her colonizers, Spain was still beset by fears of competition from other nations. At the end of the Seven Years' War between France and England, in 1763, the British took over most of North America from the French. As a result, Spain came to share a common frontier with England in the Mississippi Valley. Might this advance of the British encourage them to attempt colonization further west, perhaps from ports in California? Or might the Russians, probing across the northern Pacific in search of furs, decide to enter California waters?

Gálvez and the Proposed Occupation of California

In 1765, Charles III, a vigorous Spanish monarch (as compared to other Bourbon kings), appointed José de Gálvez *visitador-general*, or inspector general, of New Spain. Gálvez' chief mission was to increase the royal revenues. As an enthusiastic expansionist, he was also deeply interested in fortifying New Spain's northern frontier. Gálvez sailed to Lower California from the port of San Blas, on the west coast of New Spain; his personal inspection of the peninsula lasted almost a year. During this tour he reorganized missions and repaired the royal revenues. He also developed preliminary plans for a future land expedition to Upper California.

While Gálvez was in Lower California in the spring of 1768, there came an order from King Charles expelling the Jesuits from the Spanish colonies—in part because of fear and distrust of their political power on the part of various European monarchs. They were replaced in Lower California by a determined knot of fourteen gray-robed Franciscan friars under the fifty-five-year-old Junípero Serra, who arrived at La Paz to continue the work begun earlier by Kino. As mission builders and instructors of the Indians, these men would serve a useful colonizing purpose for Gálvez, a leader of colossal ego who became absorbed with plans to mount an assault upon Upper California. The Russians provided him with his best excuse for this projected expansion.

Russian encroachments from the north upon Spain's Pacific preserves—particularly the voyages to the American Northwest led by Vitus Bering and Alexei Chirikof in 1741, disturbed the Spanish lethargy that had prevailed since Vizcaíno's voyage to Monterey in 1602. As Russian otter-hunting ships extended their cruises farther southward each year, these threats added decisively to those of the increasing English entrenchment in the lower Ohio Valley and of the Dutch and English corsairs lurking off the coast of Lower California. Gálvez became convinced that he must safeguard Spain's future on her northern frontiers, and that he must occupy Upper California to achieve this purpose. Gálvez was fortunate in his close association with an energetic viceroy of New Spain, the Marqués Teodoro de Croix. Together they cut the red tape that kept Spain's colonial bureaucracy from countering the attacks of enemy powers.

Without personally setting foot on the soil of Upper California, Inspector General Gálvez planned a four-pronged expedition to occupy and settle the ports of San Diego and Monterey. Two divisions were to go by sea and two by land; if one party should fail, another might succeed. The four groups would meet at San Diego and then press onward to Monterey. Religious supervision of the expedition was entrusted to the Franciscan order, which had recently yielded control of Lower California to the Dominicans. This trust was almost joyfully accepted by the Franciscans; in fact, when these missionaries heard they were to turn over the peninsula to the Dominicans and move on to Upper California, they celebrated the news by ringing bells and holding a thanksgiving mass. Ever since Cabrillo and Vizcaíno had reported the existence of a large population of docile and friendly natives in California, an ardent desire to convert them had possessed the Franciscan friars.

Serra and Portolá, Torchbearers

Officials in New Spain took great care to select the right man to lead the Franciscans into the new land; never was better judgment used than when they chose Fray Junípero Serra for the purpose. The selection of Don Gaspar de Portolá to lead the military branch of the expedition was equally wise. Instead of a Cortés or a Pizarro, Serra the idealist and Portolá the dutiful soldier were the first colonizers to have a hand in shaping the development of California.

Serra was a native of the Mediterranean island of Majorca, who had first come to America with a party of missionaries in 1749; he gave up prestige and a brilliant future to labor among the sav-

FATHER JUNÍPERO SERRA AT HIS LAST COMMUNION, A PAINTING IN THE COLEGIO DE SAN FERNANDO IN MEXICO 1785, CERTIFIED BY WILLIAM RICH IN 1853. (By courtesy of The Huntington Library, San Marino, California.)

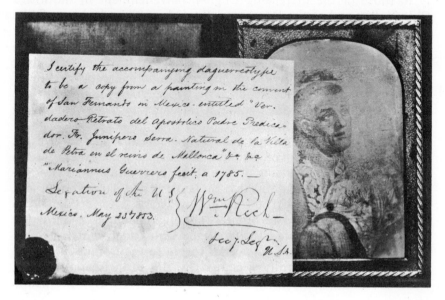

ages of the New World. Before he was called to take up the presidency of the missions of the peninsula, and afterwards those in Upper California, he served for nine years among the Pamé Indians in the Sierra Gorda mountains of eastern Mexico. His fame was, however, won in the missions of the north. In the inception and carrying out of a plan for the occupation of California, Serra was figuratively the right hand of Gálvez; his zeal brushed aside obstacles that would have stopped lesser men. One of the worst of these was his own frail health, aggravated by a lame leg, from which he suffered nearly all his life. When he set out on the 1769 expedition to Upper California, he was so weak that it was necessary for two men to lift him into the saddle of his mule; but when his friend, Fray Francisco Palóu, discouraged by the sight, bade him an eternal farewell, Serra gently rebuked him, and insisted that with the aid of God he would reach Upper California and there raise the cross.

Serra's military companion, Portolá, was a member of a noble family of Catalonia, Spain, and had served in various European campaigns as a captain of dragoons. A steadfast soldier, he was sent to Lower California as its first governor at the time of the expulsion of the Jesuits. On hearing of Gálvez' plan, he volunteered to lead the expedition to occupy and colonize the unknown north.

Embarkation of the First Colonizing Expedition

In addition to occupying the ports of San Diego and Monterey, Portolá and Serra hoped in 1769 to establish five missions in Upper California. Church ornaments and sacred vessels did not constitute all of Serra's cargo, however; the seeds of flowers and vegetables from both Old World and New, carefully packed by the priest, were transported to California to become the basis of future mission gardens. It also was arranged for the two land expeditions to take a herd of two hundred cattle from the northernmost mission of the peninsula. From these few animals were descended the herds which in time roamed the hills and valleys of Upper California—the chief source of her wealth for several generations during the pastoral era of the province. The peninsular missions were called upon to contribute—besides the cattle, and church vestments and furniture—all the horses, mules, dried meat, grain, flour, cornmeal, and dry biscuits they could spare. Lower California is thus entitled to the sobriquet, "The Mother of

California"; it provided the first material nourishment for Upper California.

Two small vessels, the packets *San Carlos* and *San Antonio*, were made available for the two prongs of the sea expedition. On January 9, 1769, the *San Carlos* was ready to start at La Paz in Lower California, under the command of Captain Vicente Vila. Added to her crew were twenty-five Catalan volunteers from that province in Spain, under Lieutenant Pedro Fages, primarily in order to have a military party that could overcome any native resistance in landing. (Fages later became one of the Spanish governors of Upper California.) After a solemn mass and an address by Gálvez, in which he exhorted all to do their duty in the sacred and historic mission on which they were embarking, the little ship, with a total of sixty-two men aboard, unfurled its sails, doubled the Lower California cape, and was off. The *San Antonio* was not ready until February 15, when, after another exhortation from Gálvez and a last shout of *buen viaje* from those who remained ashore, she also shook out her sails for California. The first stop for both vessels was to be San Diego, far to the north.

Meanwhile preparations for the two land expeditions were actively under way in Lower California. By the latter part of March, Captain Fernando Rivera y Moncada, in command of the first division—his force strengthened by twenty-five leather-jacketed soldiers from Loreto in Lower California and forty-two Christian Indians—was ready to start from the northern frontier. This division was accompanied by Fray Juan Crespi, an intimate associate of Serra. Crespi was a missionary pathfinder and provincial record keeper whose name was also to become prominent in the later story of California. He eventually accompanied Portolá all the way to San Francisco, and left a journal of the entire march. Crespi's careful account, which records much of the early history of California, is valued as a major source concerning the expeditions of 1769. On March 22, 1769, Rivera's small army, made up of veterans seasoned in frontier life, set off northward into the desert; it became the first overland party to reach California. The other land contingent, under Portolá, accompanied by the father-president of the missions, Serra, started last of the four groups bound for California. This second overland party, with Portolá, bronzed and bearded, riding at its head, set out on its march to San Diego on May 15, 1769.

San Diego was, of course, also the objective of the two sea expeditions which had gone in advance. Contrary to expectations, the *San Antonio*, which started a month later than the *San Carlos*, was the first to arrive, on April 11. When the *San Antonio* sailed into port, the terror-stricken Indians at first mistook it for a great whale. On April 29, to the joy of those on the *San Antonio*, the long-delayed sister ship sailed alongside and dropped anchor. When no boat was lowered from the *San Carlos*, however, Captain Juan Pérez became apprehensive. A visit, in one of the *San Antonio's* boats, revealed a frightful state of affairs. The long voyage— one hundred and ten days from the cape—had caused such ravages from scurvy on the *San Carlos* that there were no men aboard able to lower a shore boat. Twenty-four crew members were dead.

The survivors were removed to land by the *San Antonio's* crew, who made tents of sails to shelter the sick. Pedro Prat, who came on the *San Carlos* as surgeon, scoured the shore in search of green herbs with which to heal them. To add to their trouble, Pérez's men were attacked by dysentery, and many of them died along with members of the other party; finally, less than a third of the soldiers and sailors from the *San Carlos* were left alive. All thought of continuing the voyage to Monterey was temporarily abandoned. Every moment and every man were occupied in caring for the sick and burying the dead. Those who died were buried at a point which has ever since borne the name La Punta de los Muertos, or Dead Men's Point. The expedition's two vessels remained anchored offshore, near what later became New Town, in San Diego. A third ship, the *San José*, apparently a supply vessel, had also been dispatched by Gálvez; she failed to appear at San Diego, apparently having been lost at sea.

The Settlement of San Diego

On May 14, 1769, the gloom was greatly lightened by the appearance of Captain Rivera, with his band of leather-jackets, muleteers, and native bearers from Lower California. To get a better water supply, Rivera quickly moved the camp nearer the river, at the foot of today's Presidio Hill in Old Town. There the party built a stockade, Upper California's first military fortification. The sick were moved into a handful of rude huts and for six weeks the officers and priests cared for them, completely unloading the *San Antonio* while they awaited the arrival of Governor Portolá and Father Serra with the last overland party. At the end of June the camp was thrown into confusion by the sound of musket shots, announcing the approach of Portolá, the military commander and governor. Not burdened by so many animals as Rivera's division, Portolá's men had experienced an easier land trip, and arrived in good condition. As previously noted, they had not left Lower California until May 15, a day after the arrival of the first land party at San Diego.

More than a third of the three hundred men who had set out for Upper California, both by land and by sea, had failed to survive the trip. Half of those still alive were physically incapacitated. Portolá and his sea and land commanders now held a consultation, during which they decided that the loss of so many men, mostly sailors, made a change in plans absolutely necessary. They also decided to send the *San Antonio* back to the peninsula for supplies; then they would leave the friars with a guard of soldiers in care of the sick at San Diego, while Portolá pressed on to Monterey with the main force.

The outlook was bleak for the new colonists. Deaths were still occurring; most of the men were seriously weakened by hunger, dysentery, and scurvy, and no relief was in sight. But Portolá, a dedicated soldier, set to work at once to prepare for the advance to Monterey. Serra, equally determined, and remembering the thousands of natives living in heathenism, declared that if necessary he would remain in Upper California alone to carry on his labors among them. Portolá wrote a friend about his preparations for the journey to Monterey:

Leaving the sick under a hut of poles which I had erected, I gathered the small portion of food which had not been spoiled in the ships and went on by land with that small company of persons, or rather skeletons, who had been spared by scurvy, hunger, and thirst.

After singing a final *Te Deum*, Portolá's party left San Diego on July 14, 1769. The sixty-four members of the expedition included men whose family names later become well known in California's history—such names as Ortega, Amador, Alvarado, Carillo, Yorba, and Soberanes. These troops, wearing protective leather jackets of seven thicknesses of deer skin, carried bull-hide shields on their left arms. Lances and broadswords were among their weapons, as well as short muskets. At their head rode Portolá, while Rivera brought up the rear with extra mules and horses. Short marches were the rule, with frequent stops to rest the men and animals. The route they followed may still be traced by the place names left by this expedition—Santa Margarita, Santa Ana, Carpintería, Gaviota, Cañada de los Osos, Pajaro, and San Lorenzo.

The Failure to Recognize Monterey

The Indians were friendly, and they furnished the party with food. Portolá pressed on until he reached the shallow Salinas River. He then marched along its banks to the sea, near Monterey Bay. There he stood upon a hill and saw an open *ensenada*, or gulf, spread out before him. Although it was in the latitude of Monterey, it did not fit the descriptions of Monterey Bay given by early navigators, including Vizcaíno, as "a fine harbor sheltered from all winds." The bay of Monterey, though beautiful, cannot be called a well-protected port. Mystified, the little company gazed over the expanse of dark blue water which lay before them. The sand of the long curving beach glistened in the sun. But where was the grand landlocked harbor Vizcaíno had described? Great swells from the ocean rolled in without obstruction, and there was no safety from the wind except in the small hook of the horseshoe where the town of Monterey now stands. The party, in effect, had failed to recognize the bay of Monterey.

After holding a solemn mass at the mouth of the Salinas River, Portolá's group concluded that their only hope of finding Monterey was by continuing the journey to the north. The party pushed on up the coast, with eleven of the men now so ill that they had to be carried in litters swung between mules. Near Soquel they had their first sight of the "Big Trees," which Portolá named *palo colorado*, or redwood, because of the color of their wood. At one stopping place they saw a giant tree of this species which they called *Palo Alto* (high tree), and the town located there still bears that name.

The Discovery of San Francisco Bay

Weak and confused, Portolá's men passed northward over land never before trodden upon except by Indians. Their path was hindered by numerous *arroyos*, or gulches, over which bridges had to be built to permit the animals to pass. After exploring in the direction of Point Reyes, an advance party excitedly reported to Portolá their discovery of a "great arm of the sea, extending to the southeast farther than the eye could reach." This, of course, was San Francisco Bay, whose magnificent panorama the whole party viewed for the first time on November 2, 1769. Astonished by the sight of so vast a body of water, the explorers concluded correctly that Monterey Bay must now be behind them and that this was yet another large estuary. For decades ships had passed by the opening of the bay of San Francisco. Yet it remained for a land expedition to discover the greatest harbor on the Pacific Coast. (Not until 1846 did this landmark receive, from John Charles Frémont, its name the Golden Gate.)

After a feast of mussels, wild ducks, and geese, which abounded in the region, the group decided to return southward to Point Pinos, near Monterey, taking nearly the same route by which they

had come. When Portolá and his men reached Carmel Bay they
set up a large cross near the shore, with a letter buried at its base;
if future ships should come into the vicinity they would thus be
informed that Portolá's expedition had been there. His men then
crossed Cypress Point, and very near the bay which they still did
not recognize as that of Monterey they erected another wooden
cross. On its arms they carved these words with a knife: "The
land expedition is returning to San Diego for lack of provisions,
today, December 9, 1769."

The Return to San Diego

Retracing their route, Portolá's men found themselves in dire
need of food. Winter was coming on and snow already covered the
Santa Lucia Mountains, which they had to cross. In their plight
the party welcomed any sort of food. For posterity Portolá wrote:
"We shut our eyes and fell to on a scaly mule (what misery) like
hungry lions. We ate twelve in as many days, obtaining from them
perforce all our sustenance, all our appetite, all our delectation."
As their mules disappeared, the party, upon approaching San Luís
Obispo, obtained fish from the Indians. "Smelling frightfully of
mules," they finally returned, on January 24, 1770, to the makeshift wood and adobe walls of their San Diego palisade. With
foreboding they approached the camp, not knowing whether any
of the company they had left behind were still alive, or whether
they would find the place a mortuary. Their fears were exaggerated, however; and when they fired their muskets as a salute,
those who were still alive rushed out to exchange greetings.

The accomplishments of this expedition, sent out by Gálvez a
year before, were already significant. The first mission in Upper
California had been founded, July 16, 1769, and named San Diego
de Alcala. A good part of the coast to the north had been explored.
On the other hand, trouble clearly lay ahead. The Indians had
quickly lost their awe of white men and they began to steal even
the bed sheets from under the sick. One sharp encounter had
taken place in which a boy belonging to the garrison had been
killed and several men wounded by arrows. Death continued its
ravages, and provisions grew alarmingly short. Now Portolá became disheartened. Earlier he had sent the ship *San Antonio* back
to San Blas on the Mexican west coast for supplies. It had not yet
returned. On February 10, 1770, Portolá sent Captain Rivera and
a small party of the strongest men back to Lower California by
land to seek supplies. Rather than expose his men to starvation he
reluctantly decided to abandon the enterprise and return to the

peninsula himself if no relief ship should arrive by March 20.

It may seem odd that men should starve in a country like California; but little could be obtained from the Indians, who lived precariously off the countryside, raising nothing. As for wild game, ammunition was too precious for defense against possible attack to be spared for such purposes. Around San Francisco Bay wild geese were so abundant and tame that they could be knocked down with a stick, but this was untrue elsewhere.

The decision to depart was a deep disappointment to Serra and his friars, for they knew that if the party withdrew it would probably be years before another attempt would be made at exploration and colonization. The rest of the company clamored for departure, and the whole camp waited tensely to see if new supplies would arrive by the appointed time. Each day the missionaries knelt in supplication for the coming of a supply ship and began a nine-day prayer, or novena, to San José, patron saint of the expedition. On the afternoon of the last day of grace, the nineteenth of March, 1770, as twilight began to obscure the horizon, a loud cry of "The ship! The ship!" rang through the camp. For a moment a sail was dimly seen, then it disappeared. The *San Antonio* had run on northward, probably through a mistake in reckoning. In four days, it mercifully sailed back into the harbor and dropped anchor.

The Rediscovery of Monterey

Their hunger and despair relieved by a large feast, the Spaniards again started preparations for a new expedition to find Monterey. Sending the *San Antonio* ahead by sea, Portolá led a land party over the same route as before, and finally reached the spot where they had set up the second cross, near Monterey Bay, the previous winter. They found the cross still standing, but now surrounded with a circle of feathered arrows thrust in the ground, as well as some sticks on which were hung sardines. This they accepted as an offering of friendship on the part of local Indians.

This time Portolá recognized the bay of Monterey; and he, Crespi, and Fages, as they walked along the beach, observed that the bay resembled a round lake. The *San Antonio* arrived a week later. On June 3, 1770, beneath the very oak tree under which the Vizcaíno expedition had held services in 1602, Father Serra conducted a solemn mass amid the ringing of bells and salvos of artillery. Here was founded the second mission in Upper California, dedicated to San Carlos Borroméo. For convenience in obtaining wood and water, the mission was later removed to the little bay of Carmel, about four miles from Monterey. From Carmel, which became Serra's headquarters, he wrote his friend Father Palóu, "If you will come I shall be content to live and die in this spot." A second presidio was established overlooking Monterey Bay. This site, later occupied by United States Army forces, is still called the Presidio of Monterey.

On July 9, 1770, Portolá turned the military command over to Pedro Fages, and sailed away on the *San Antonio;* California heard no more of him. In its history he must always be a prominent figure, as the first of its governors, the leader of the first expedition over the thousand-mile trail from the peninsula, and the discoverer of San Francisco Bay.

SELECTED READINGS

The best portrayal of Kino is Herbert Eugene Bolton's *Rim of Christendom* (New York, 1936). Another biography is Rufus Kay Wyllys, *Pioneer Padre: The Life and Times of Eusebio Kino* (Dallas, 1935). See also Eugenia Ricci, *Il Padre Eusebio Chini, Esploratore Missionario della California e dell' Arizona* (Milan, 1930), and Kino's own *Favores Celestiales*, translated and edited by Bolton as *Kino's Historical Memoir of Pimeria Alta* (2 vols., Cleveland, 1919). See also Bolton's *The Padre on Horseback* (San Francisco, 1932) and Frank C. Lockwood, *With Padre Kino on the Trail* (Tucson, 1934). Kino's astronomical activities are discussed in Ellen Shaffer, "The Comet of 1680–1681," Historical Society of Southern California *Quarterly*, XXXIV (March, 1952), 57–70, and in Kino's own *Esposición astronomica de el cometa* (Mexico, D.F., 1681). Finally, on Kino, consult Ernest J. Burrus, trans. and ed., *Kino Reports to Headquarters* (Rome, 1954). On Salvatierra see Miguel Venegas, *Juan María de Salvatierra*, translated and edited by Margaret Eyer Wilbur (Cleveland, 1929). For other early Jesuit activity in the Southwest see J. J. Baegert, *Observations in Lower California*, translated and edited by M. M. Brandenburg and Carl L. Baumann (Berkeley, 1952); see also the following volumes by Peter M. Dunne: *Pioneer Black Robes on the West Coast* (Berkeley, 1940), *Pioneer Jesuits in Northern Mexico* (Berkeley, 1944), *Early Jesuit Missions of the Tarahumara* (Berkeley, 1948), and *Black Robes in Lower California* (Berkeley, 1952). See also Theodore E. Treutlein, ed., *Pfefferkorn's Description of Sonora* (Albuquerque, 1949).

On Gálvez see Herbert I. Priestley, *José de Gálvez, Visitador-General of New Spain* (Berkeley, 1916). See also the translation of Father Javier Clavigero's *Storia della California* (1789) in Sara E. Lake and A. A. Gray, *The History of Lower California* (Stanford, 1937).

Regarding the Russian threat to California see Frank A. Golder, *Russian Expansion on the Pacific, 1641–1858* (Cleveland, 1914), and the same author's *Bering's Voyages* (2 vols., New York, 1922–1925).

Good general accounts of the first colonization of California are Charles E. Chapman, *The Founding of Spanish California* (New York, 1916), and Irving Berdine Richman, *California Under Spain and Mexico, 1535–1847* (Boston, 1911). See also Douglas S. Watson, *The Spanish Occupation of California* (San Francisco, 1934).

Missionary activity has been widely chronicled. The *diario* of Fray Francisco Palóu appears, in translation, in Herbert E. Bolton, ed., *Historical Memoirs of New California* (5 vols., Berkeley, 1926). Crespi's *diario* (or journal) is also in these volumes. The relationship of Governor Fages with the padres is treated in Herbert I. Priestley, ed., *A Historical, Political and Natural Description of California by Pedro Fages* (Berkeley, 1937). See also Donald Nuttall, "Pedro Fages and the Advance of the Northern Frontier of New Spain," Ph.D. dissertation, University of Southern California (1964). Lives of Serra include Abigail H. Fitch, *Junípero Serra* (Chicago, 1914), and the less satisfactory but more recent *Junípero Serra: Pioneer Colonist of California* (New York, 1933) by Agnes Repplier. A serious adulatory treatment of Serra and his fellow Franciscans has been written by a member of the order, Father Zephyrin Engelhardt, *The Missions and Missionaries of California* (4 vols., San Francisco, 1908–1915). See also Charles J. G. Piette, *Evocation de Junípero Serra, fondateur de la Californie* (Washington, D.C., 1946). The best modern work on Serra is Father Maynard J. Geiger's *The Life and Times of Fray Junípero Serra* (2 vols., Washington, D.C., 1959); the same author has translated and edited Palóu's *Life of Fray Junípero Serra* (Washington, D.C., 1955). See also Geiger's "Fray Junípero Serra: Organizer and Administrator of the Upper California Missions, 1769–1784," California Historical Society *Quarterly*, XLII (September, 1963) 195–220.

Regrettably, no life of Portolá exists. See, however, Robert Selden Rose, ed., *The Portolá Expedition of 1769–1770; Diary of Vicente Vila* (Berkeley, 1911); and the *diario* (1770) of Miguel Costansó in its English version, *The Spanish Occupation of California*, ed. by Douglas S. Watson (San Francisco, 1934), as well as Costansó's *The Narrative of the Portolá Expedition of 1769–1770*, edited by Frederick J. Teggart (Berkeley, 1910). Also useful is Zoeth S. Eldredge, ed., *The March of Portolá and Discovery of the Bay of San Francisco, Log of the San Carlos, and Original Documents* (San Francisco, 1909).

The Spanish techniques of claiming their California discoveries by specific acts of sovereignty are discussed in three excellent articles: Henry Raup Wagner, "Creation of Rights of Sovereignty Through Symbolic Acts," *Pacific Historical Review*, VII (December. 1938) 297–326; Manuel P. Servín, "Symbolic Acts of Sovereignty in Spanish California," *Southern California Quarterly*, XLV (June, 1963), 109–121; and Servín's "The Instructions of Viceroy Bucareli to Ensign Juan Pérez," California Historical Society *Quarterly*, XL (September, 1961), 243–246.

6

Missions, Presidios, and Pueblos

Among the three institutions used by Spain to colonize Upper California—the mission, the presidio, and the pueblo—the mission must take first place. The other two served mainly to support and defend this primary establishment. Spain's ostensible purpose in the operation of its missions was the saving of the souls of aborigines, but actually it sought to win them to Spanish allegiance. Long experience had shown that well-trained missionaries could be highly successful in carrying out both objectives. By working with the Crown in giving the Indians practical as well as religious training, California's Jesuit and Franciscan priests hoped to keep both the souls and bodies of these natives safe from paganism and savagery.

By 1776, the central and dual role of the church was evident in the recommendations made by Father Serra to the governor of California. For example, he suggested that a survey be authorized for a new overland route to California from Sonora, itself a frontier province in the north of New Spain. In making this recommendation, Serra hoped for an increase in the population of California, expansion of its agricultural and pastoral possibilities, and further vital exploration along its northwest coast. Without these developments, California would not grow and prosper as a frontier community. The claims of Serra as "Founder of California" rest upon such secular contributions to its success, as well as on his missionary labors.

The Establishment of the Missions

California was one of Spain's last colonies. Its missions were among the youngest of all those scattered throughout the Western Hemisphere from Buenos Aires to Sonoma and from Tallahassee to San Diego. Though the mission system operated practically the same as elsewhere in the Spanish empire, the circumstances of its founding in California were somewhat different. From the time of Kino, it was considered foolhardy for individual missionaries to face the dangers of the frontier alone. Those priests who went to the Upper California mission stations were accompanied by guards, and supplied with provisions until the missions could gather Indian colonies around them and become self-supporting. A total of twenty-one missions were established in California, forming a chain from San Diego to Sonoma. They were separated by about a day's travel on horseback—some thirty miles apart. The King's Highway, or *El Camino Real* of the tourist literature, was then scarcely more than a dusty path, the only road from mission to mission and from presidio to presidio. Serra founded nine missions, either in person or through his helpers. The succeeding nine were established by Fray Fermín de Lasuén, a name as important in the history of California's development as that of Serra.

MISSION SAN LUÍS REY, FROM ROBINSON'S "LIFE IN CALIFORNIA BEFORE THE CONQUEST" (1846). (C. C. Pierce Collection; by courtesy of the Huntington Library, San Marino, California.)

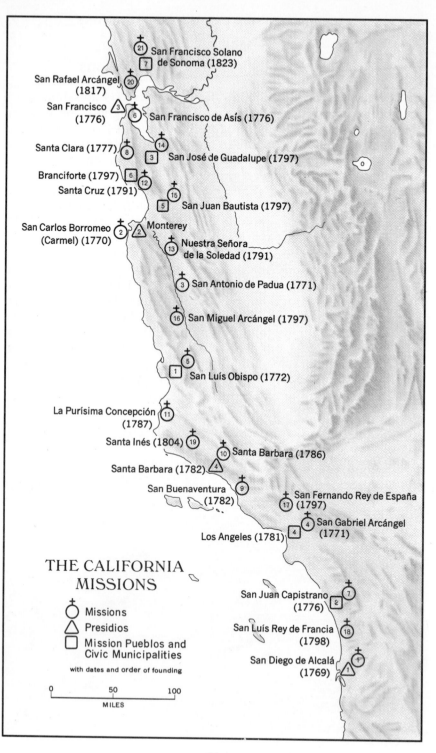

San Francisco Solano
de Sonoma (1823)

San Rafael Arcángel
(1817)

San Francisco
(1776)

San Francisco de Asís (1776)

Santa Clara (1777)

San José de Guadalupe (1797)

Branciforte (1797)

Santa Cruz (1791)

San Juan Bautista (1797)

San Carlos Borromeo
(Carmel) (1770)

Monterey

Nuestra Señora
de la Soledad (1791)

San Antonio de Padua (1771)

San Miguel Arcángel (1797)

San Luís Obispo (1772)

La Purísima Concepción
(1787)

Santa Inés (1804)

Santa Barbara (1786)

Santa Barbara (1782)

San Buenaventura
(1782)

San Fernando Rey de España
(1797)

San Gabriel Arcángel
(1771)

Los Angeles (1781)

THE CALIFORNIA
MISSIONS

✝ ◯ Missions
△ Presidios
☐ Mission Pueblos and
Civic Municipalities

with dates and order of founding

San Juan Capistrano
(1776)

San Luís Rey de Francia
(1798)

San Diego de Alcalá
(1769)

0   50   100

MILES

74

Three prime requisites determined the choice of a mission site
—arable soil for crops, a convenient water supply, and a large
local Indian population. Observation of their sites even today indicates the good judgment of the missionaries. By the time the
twenty-one missions were established, the friars had in their possession much of the choicest land in the province, a fact that led
to later resentment.

The first mission buildings were of the rudest thatch construction, mere huts of sticks, plastered with mud or clay, and roofed
with tule. Mission chapels too were made of these materials, and
were distinguished only by an altar and other crude wooden
church furniture. The permanent adobe-brick or cut-stone buildings, with which tourists are familiar, still appear dignified
though they are in partial ruin. These missions were slowly built
with Indian labor, for the most part after the era of the pioneer
missionaries. Today's stone walls at Mission San Carlos Borroméo

COLONNADES IN QUADRANGLE, MISSION SAN JUAN CAPISTRANO, FOUNDED 1776;
PHOTOGRAPH TAKEN 1885. (C. C. Pierce Collection; by courtesy of The Huntington Library, San Marino, California.)

were never seen by Father Serra, even though he died there.

Architecturally the missions of Upper California are distinctive, differing in many particulars from those in other parts of America. The California padres, in their isolation, evolved a plan of their own; the result was a combination of Moorish and Roman influences, with certain modifications appropriate to the environment. California's primitive isolation probably prevented the overdecoration rampant on the Iberian peninsula, inherited by Spain from the Moors. "California mission architecture" is characterized by open courts, long colonnades, and numerous arches and corridors. The typical red-tiled roofs were adopted as one solution to bitter experiences with fire. Similarly, the destruction of many of the earlier buildings by earthquakes led to the use of thick walls, sometimes reinforced with heavy buttresses. These give mission buildings their massive, imposing appearance.

California's First System of Government and Instruction

The missionaries instituted a form of patriarchal government, assuming a paternal attitude toward the Indians and treating them as wards. There were usually two friars at an establishment, the elder of whom had charge of interior matters and religious instruction, while the younger attended to agricultural and other outside work. Each of the mission administrators was subject to the authority of a father-president for all of California. He in turn bowed to the orders of the College of San Fernando, the headquarters of the Franciscans in Mexico. Except in the punishment of capital crimes, the friars had full control of the destinies of their Indian charges; and these padres became virtual rulers of their mission domains. Floggings and other corporal punishments were occasionally administered to the Indians for various offenses. The Comte de la Pérouse, an early French traveler, as well as other enlightened foreign visitors, regarded such punishments as a violation of the natural rights of man. The missionaries defended their discipline on the ground that it was the only effective means of controlling the childlike natives.

The missions were not devoted entirely to religious instruction. Each was also a sort of industrial school, in which the natives learned the formal meaning of work for the first time and where they were taught various trades. Native strength was harnessed with missionary inventive genius and mechanical skill to produce remarkable results—for example, irrigation works. The Franciscans, indeed, were the pioneers of California's future water system; and some of the mission dams and canals whose construction they directed are still in a good state of preservation.

The friars, by the nature of the task confronting them, served as teachers, musicians, weavers, carpenters, masons, architects, and physicians of both soul and body. In addition, sometimes putting their own hands to the plow, they raised enough food for mission use, and occasionally a surplus of meal, wine, oil, hemp, hides, or tallow. This was shipped down the coast to New Spain; at Acapulco principally these products were exchanged for articles needed in the new Alta California colony—clothing, furniture, implements, and tools. At mission farms and orchards the missionaries tried to adapt various crops to the climate and soil. Semitropical fruits, such as oranges, lemons, figs, dates, and olives, flourished in the mission gardens, and their cultivation preceded the development of California horticulture. Even cotton was grown at some missions, in quantities sufficient to prove the feasibility of raising it in that environment.

After 1771 a leading factor in the success of the early efforts to colonize California was the presence in Mexico City of a strong and able new viceroy, Antonio María Bucareli. Spain's interest in California waxed and waned, depending in part upon her viceroys; and Bucareli's determined support helped the struggling mission establishments greatly. As already noted, California was also fortunate in the personal character of its first missionaries. To serve in this capacity Spain sent numerous university men, high in spiritual and intellectual attainments. Early visitors to California all mentioned the talents of the men who had come to live among the neophytes, as the Indian savages were called. Father Serra's reputation naturally stands especially high, but he had several remarkable companions, among them Francisco Palóu, founder of Mission San Francisco, and Lasuén. Palóu had been among the last of the Franciscans to turn over their Lower California missions to incoming members of the Dominican order, and in 1773 he joined Serra in Upper Californa. Palóu was not merely a missionary, but also the author of the first book ever written in California, *Noticias de la Nueva California;* this and his *Vida de Junípero Serra,* are basic works about its early history. Lasuén, another cleric of notable talents and character, filled the post of president with distinction after Serra had died and Palóu had asked to be relieved of that responsibility.

At the time of Serra's death, in 1784, he and his followers had been in California sixteen years; out of a primitive culture they had fashioned the beginnings of civilization in the province. The nine flourishing missions they had founded claimed a total of 5,800 converts. The flocks and herds of these establishments ranged over thousands of acres, and in the busy workshops of each the Indians labored at spinning, weaving, carpentry, and masonry, besides raising crops for daily sustenance.

In addition to these accomplishments, the missionaries had been directly or indirectly associated with the establishment of the first towns in California. These were of three types: the military, which grew up around such presidios as those of San Diego and Monterey; the civic, founded under secular, civilian auspices; and those which developed around the missions themselves—the "mission pueblos." In this last category were San Luís Obispo, founded September 1, 1772; San Juan Capistrano, November 1, 1776; San Juan Bautista, June 24, 1797; and Sonoma, July 4, 1823. These towns were eventually transformed into civic municipalities, which still bear their original names.

Presidios and Military Towns

California's presidios, or frontier fortresses, were originally built to protect the missions from hostile Indians and to guard Spanish claims to the area against foreign aggression. These presidios were located at strategic positions, generally at the entrances of the best ports. Small groups of houses, inhabited principally by settlers, traders, and the families of soldiers, grew up around the presidios, and such "military towns" developed into colonial centers. These presidial pueblos included San Diego, founded July 16, 1769; Monterey, June 3, 1770; San Francisco, September 17, 1776; and Santa Barbara, April 21, 1782. At first they were under military rule, but each eventually acquired its own civil government. An early presidio typically consisted of a square enclosure surrounded by a ditch and rampart of earth or brick, within which were located a small church, quarters for officers and soldiers, civilian houses, storehouses, workshops, wells, and cisterns. Outside were grouped a few dwellings, and at a little distance were fields for crops and pasturage for the horses and mules of the garrison.

In addition to strictly military pursuits, such as exploring, hunting, capturing run-away neophytes, and carrying the mails, the duties of the soldiers who manned the presidios included the erection of buildings, the care of herds and flocks, and cultivation of the soil. These occupations were not always to their liking, and they soon learned to employ Indians for many services. For their labor the neophytes received such pay as a string of beads, a dish of porridge, shoes, or a bit of cloth.

The soldiers of the early presidios were poorly outfitted, wearing a uniform that consisted of a long leather jacket over their leather armor, as in medieval times. From this costume they acquired the name *soldados de cuero*, or "leather soldiers." With a few bronze cannon mounted on ramparts, and often without powder to charge them, these men were equipped to resist attack only by still more poorly armed Indians. Not one of the presidios could have stood up against a well-equipped ship of war. Indeed, they were maintained more as a warning against possible enemies than with any expectation of making a fight. In time the cannon rusted and the presidios took on an air of dilapidation.

Even the officers, the aristocracy of the presidios, lived under primitive conditions that awakened the pity of foreign visitors. Like exiles in a strange land, they waited for the day when they might return to more comfortable homes. The Englishman George Vancouver, visiting in 1792, described the house of the *comandante* at San Francisco as consisting of two rooms with earth floors, not boarded or even leveled; the windows had no glass, and furniture was almost completely lacking. Yet such was the warmth of hospitality of the officer's family that the visitor admitted he forgot their lowly surroundings.

The story of the founding of the presidios, in the light of hindsight, seems somewhat more heroic than that of the conditions which prevailed in them. Portolá's settlement of San Diego in 1769 and of Monterey in 1770 has already been described. His discovery of San Francisco Bay was to lead to the establishment of a third military outpost, largely through the efforts of Juan Bautista de Anza.

Anza was, like Portolá, a military man—one of the significant trail breakers and tough Indian fighters of the West. He learned his vocation from his father and grandfather, also frontier captains. Anza had long planned to explore a route northwestward from Sonora to the ocean, believing that such a land passage would obviate the delay and perils of the sea voyage, on which California still relied for major contact with the outside world. Viceroy Bucareli, convinced of the importance of strengthening the California settlements, saw in Anza's proposal an opportunity not only to open a new land route, but also to send additional colonists under the protection of a thoroughly capable leader. Women settlers, provisions, and domestic animals were in particularly great demand in California. Bucareli therefore empowered Captain Anza to reconnoiter the proposed route. In January, 1774, with the trails-priest Father Francisco Garcés as his guide, and a band of thirty-four men, Anza set out westward from Tubac in northern Mexico. Theirs was the first sizable crossing by white men into southern California from the Colorado basin through the San Jacinto Mountains. Another key to the success of this party was Garcés, a fearless missionary who three years before had penetrated into California well beyond the junction of the Colorado and Gila rivers, to the walls of the southern Sierra. (Later this trail would be followed by some of the United States gold seekers of 1849.) On March 22, 1774, Anza's party reached Mission San Gabriel in California, where they were received with enthusiasm by the padres. Anza and his men then moved on to Monterey, returning later that year to Tubac on the Sonora frontier. An overland route to California some 2,200 miles long had now been opened. Except for the dearth of water across the sand dunes of the Colorado, it was a fairly practical route.

In 1775, preparations were made to send Anza with another party of colonists, recruited throughout Sinaloa and Sonora, and so impoverished that they had to be given clothing and pay in advance. On October 23 Anza left Tubac at the head of this second company, consisting of 240 men, women, and children. Their commander led them and a herd of two hundred cattle beyond the Colorado River once more to Mission San Gabriel, and on to Monterey. A few colonists then accompanied him to the site of the future San Francisco. On June 27, 1776, the party arrived at the lagoon known as Dolores, built brush huts the next day, and celebrated mass on the twenty-ninth. Anza made this second trip from Sonora with the loss of only one life. Indeed, eight more persons had been added to his party by births along the way. Though Anza selected sites for a presidio and a mission, he did not remain long at the Golden Gate, returning instead to frontier service in Sonora and Sinaloa. He pursued a later career in New Mexico which resembled in adventurousness his activities in blazing the trail to California.

On September 17, 1776, the presidio of San Francisco de Asís was formally dedicated, and on October 9 the mission was founded by Father Palóu, acting for Serra. Palóu personally helped build its first little chapel, a wooden structure with a thatched roof. This building served the mission for eight years, until the present adobe structure was finished. Because it was located near Dolores Creek, it became known as Mission Dolores. It happens that the Franciscan missions in California were founded at about the time of the American Revolution; the year this mission at San Francisco was established also saw the signing of the Declaration of Independence.

Though a mission and presidio now existed at the future site of San Francisco, the community was not yet a real pueblo. Its potential, however, was well understood by the Spanish officials, who sponsored other expeditions into the area in addition to those led by Anza. In March, 1775, acting upon Serra's recommendation, the viceroy had also sent Captain Juan Manuel Ayala, in command of the vessel *San Carlos*, to explore further the vast bay which still had no name. No known ship had yet passed through the Golden Gate, and Ayala feared danger along its narrow, rocky shoreline. At nightfall on August 5, 1775, the *San Carlos* moved into the entrance of the bay, cautiously dropping her lead line every few moments. The wind blew strongly, and threatened for a time to tear out a mast; but the little vessel moved on until she reached a point one league within the mouth, near North Beach. Then the wind suddenly died down. Ayala remained in San Francisco Bay a total of forty-four days. He named two of its islands—*Nuestra Señora de los Angeles*, shortened later to Angel Island, and *Alcatraz*, or "Pelican," so called because of the large number of those birds flying over it.

Civil Pueblos

In addition to the mission and presidial pueblos, there was a third category of early California towns, those established under a definite civil government. The first of these were San José, founded in 1777; Los Angeles, 1781; and Branciforte (now extinct), 1797. The civil pueblos are usually considered the first real municipalities of California. They were established according to a plan administered by California's Governor Felipe de Neve in his code of laws, or *Reglamento*, issued in June, 1779. Neve's regulations, derived from the Laws of the Indies, theoretically granted each pueblo four square leagues of land, laid out according to the topography of the country. First a plaza was marked out—in inland towns a rectangular space in the center, but often on the waterfront in the case of a town on a river or bay. Facing upon the plaza were such public buildings as the council house, the church, storerooms, and the jail, the remaining frontage being occupied by settler's houses. The life of the community revolved around these central squares; even bullfights took place in them. Spanish plazas are still to be found in some California towns, notably in Los Angeles, Monterey, and Sonoma.

Valuable inducements were offered to settlers who would make their homes in these pueblos. Each was entitled to a house lot, stock and implements, an allowance in clothing and supplies amounting to $116.17½ for each of the first two years and $60 for each of the next three, the use of government land as common pasture, and, finally, exemption from taxes for five years. In return for this aid the settler was required to sell his surplus agricultural products to the presidios, and to hold himself, his horse, and his musket in readiness for military service in any emergency. He was also required to build houses, dig irrigating ditches, cultivate the land, keep his implements in repair, and maintain a specified number of animals. Each pueblo was expected to construct its own dams, canals, roads and streets, church and other town buildings, and to help till the public lands. From the town's agricultural production municipal expenses were theoretically to be paid.

These arrangements were provisional for the first five years, at the end of which settlers were to receive permanent title to their lands. As a safeguard against the carelessness of improvident persons, no one had the right to sell or mortgage his land. This measure was intended to protect people from their own folly, but it was sometimes evaded.

Municipal officers—consisting of an *alcalde* (similar to a powerful mayor), or two *alcaldes* in the larger towns, and a board of councilmen (*ayuntamiento*)—were at first appointed by the governor, but were afterwards elected by the people. The *alcalde* decided all cases of minor importance, which were punishable by fine or imprisonment, while cases of murder and other high crimes were brought before the governor at Monterey. His judicial decisions were final. Anyone could demand trial by "good men" (*hombres buenos*)—three or five jurors, as ordered by the magistrate. The powers of an *alcalde* were almost unlimited in his own domain, and generally these officials were honest in their administration of justice. The *alcalde* was in effect the "little father" of a town, to whom all carried their troubles, public and private.

The *ayuntamiento* performed numerous and onerous duties. It managed the public business not only of the town but also of a large contiguous territory. For instance, the Los Angeles *ayuntamiento* at one time had jurisdiction over territory as large as that of Massachusetts. It was a dignified body whose members were attired in black, to add solemnity to their meetings. The *ayuntamiento* received petitions and complaints from dissatisfied citizens, ranchers as well as townsmen, and it passed ordinances for the regulation of municipal matters, including amusements.

There was no pay attached to the office of *alcalde* or *regidor* (councilman). The honor of holding public office compensated the holders for their labors. As a symbol or badge of office the *alcaldes* carried a silver-headed cane. They and the *regidores* were entitled to considerable public respect. Functioning within the *ayuntamiento*, they were the arbiters of local town life, socially as well as governmentally. Later, under Mexican rule, *alcaldes* and *ayuntamientos* were suppressed, except in Monterey, and justices of the peace exercised the judicial functions originally performed by *alcaldes*.

Brief descriptions of California's first three civic pueblos will illustrate the pattern of their development. The earliest of these was San José de Guadalupe (now simply San José), founded November 29, 1777, when a few mud huts were erected on the banks of the Guadalupe River and occupied by soldiers and their families. Not until 1786 did the residents receive formal legal possession of their lands. The growth of the town was slow; for years it consisted of a few scattered houses of settlers who barely eked out a living.

Further south the second civic pueblo, Nuestra Señora la Reina de los Angeles de Porciúncula, abbreviated today to Los Angeles, was founded at sundown on September 4, 1781, by eleven settlers and their families. Recruited in Sinaloa, Mexico, they had trudged northward to San Gabriel Mission. From there, under the authorization of Governor de Neve, they had moved on a few more miles to settle "The Pueblo of Our Lady, the Queen of the Angels." Nothing could be more humble than the beginnings of this city. Its first citizens were mainly of Indian and African blood, with only a moderate admixture of Spanish. It was difficult to induce Spain's Mexican colonials of standing to accept a measure of exile to such a distant wilderness as California. Yet, by 1784 this motley band of colonists had replaced their first rude huts with adobe houses and laid the foundations for a church and other public buildings. Two years afterwards, when land titles were finally issued them, each Angeleño affixed his cross to these documents; apparently not one of Los Angeles' first citizens could write his name. Later the town assumed increased importance from its overland trade with New Mexico—over what came to be known as "The Old Spanish Trail."

California's third civic community, Branciforte, named after a viceroy of that name and designed for defense as well as for colonization, was founded in 1797 near the present city of Santa Cruz. It was a failure almost from the beginning, and soon passed out of existence. Its demise is usually connected to the type of colonists who founded it: these were partly composed of convicts sent by Spanish officials in Mexico to serve out sentences of banishment in California. Such colonization could only be degenerative in nature, weakening the colony.

SELECTED READINGS

Basic to an understanding of the mission, the most important institution of Spain's colonial frontier, is the article by Herbert E. Bolton, "The Mission as a Frontier Institution in the Spanish American Colonies," *American Historical Review,* XXIII (October, 1917), 42–61. See also Frank Wilson Blackmar, *Spanish Institutions of the Southwest* (Baltimore, 1891). Later works that treat the settlement of the California frontier include Theodore Maynard, *The Long Road of Father Serra* (New York, 1954), and Omer Englebert, *The Last of the Conquistadores: Junípero Serra, 1713–1784* (New York, 1956). One should consult also the *Publications* of the Academy of Franciscan History, including *The Writings of Junípero Serra* (4 vols., Washington, D.C., 1954), ed. by Antonine Tibesar, as well as Maynard Geiger's carefully edited translation of *Palóu's Life of Fray Junípero Serra* (Washington, D.C., 1955). A confusing subject, the background of the financing of the missions, is clarified in Francis J. Weber, "The Pious Fund of the Californias," *Hispanic American Historical Review,* XLIII (February, 1963), 78–94. Additional representative data concerning the missions is in *The Letters of José Señan, O.F.M., Mission San Buenaventura,* trans. by Paul D. Nathan and ed. by Lesley Byrd Simpson (San Francisco, 1962). Francis J. Weber, "The California Missions and Their Visitors," *The Americas,* XXIV (April, 1968), 319–336, pulls together a list of foreigners who visited the missions.

The founding of a pueblo at Los Angeles is discussed by W. W. Robinson in *Ranchos Become Cities* (Pasadena, 1939) and in *Los Angeles: From the Days of the Pueblo* (San Francisco, 1959), as well as tangentially in the same author's *Panorama: A Picture History of Southern California* (Los Angeles, 1953). A less successful example of pueblo founding is studied in Florian Guest, "The Establishment of the Villa of Branciforte," California Historical Society *Quarterly,* XLI (March, 1962), 29–50. The role of the most important Spanish official at the local level is portrayed in Theodore Grivas, "Alcalde Rule: The Nature of Local Government in Spanish and Mexican California," California Historical Society *Quarterly,* XL (March, 1961), 11–32. See also Francis F. Guest, "Municipal Government in Spanish California," California Historical Society *Quarterly,* XLVI (December, 1967), 307–335, and Edwin A. Beilharz, "Felipe de Neve," Ph.D. dissertation, University of California, Berkeley (1951). Bucareli's attitude toward the founding of municipal institutions in California is described in Bernard E. Bobb, *The Viceregency of Antonio María Bucareli . . .* (Berkeley, 1962).

On Anza see Herbert E. Bolton, ed., *Anza's California Expeditions* (5 vols., Berkeley, 1930). An entertaining diary of the last Anza expedition was written by its chaplain, Fray Pedro Font, and edited by Frederick J. Teggart as *The Anza Expedition of 1775–1776* (Berkeley, 1913). The story of the Anza trail and of the Yuma Massacre which followed is partly told by Douglas D. Martin, *Yuma Crossing* (Albuquerque, 1954).

7

California and Her Spanish Governors

The Spanish governors in California were almost uniformly men of intelligence and character who served their king faithfully. After the occupation of the province in 1769 by Portolá, Upper California was administered jointly with Lower California, the combined area being known as *Las Californias*. Until 1777 the official seat of government was at Loreto in Lower California, and rule over the northern territory was purely nominal. Then, as a result of increasing Spanish interest in Upper California, a decree of August 15, 1775, led to the moving of the capital in 1777 to Monterey during Governor Felipe de Neve's administration; a lieutenant governor in Loreto supervised Lower California affairs. These officials, of course, were themselves responsible to the Spanish viceroy at Mexico City.

Fages, Rivera, and Neve

In 1770 Pedro Fages followed Portolá as military commander of Upper California. Fages is remembered as a sturdy, faithful officer who labored hard to put the new colony on its feet. He was also an Indian fighter of repute and an explorer who, in 1770 and 1772, led two expeditions to San Francisco Bay and made a thorough reconnaissance of its shores. Fages kept the California colony alive for several precarious months, during a period when supply ships were delayed, by providing bear meat from the Cañada de los Osos (Bear Canyon), near San Luís Obispo. His brusque manners and hot temper involved him in many disagreements with the missionaries and with his young wife, Doña Eulalia, all of which the padres recorded in entertaining detail in the mission archives. Constant and sometimes petty wrangling also occurred between the religious and the military, an inevitable result of trying frontier conditions and divided local political authority. Friction between Fages and Serra became so acute that Serra asked for his removal. Fages' replacement as military *comandante* of Upper California was Captain Rivera y Moncada, leader of the second land party during the 1769 Portolá expedition. (Fages was to return to California in 1782.) These early administrative shifts involved relatively short tours of duty and, therefore, the period Rivera spent in office has not generally been considered that of a bona fide governor.

The change turned out to be a mistake; Rivera was not only nervous and erratic in disposition, but also procrastinating by nature. He even neglected to carry out specific orders of the viceroy, although in at least one case his obedience caused unfortunate results. In 1773 elaborate instructions were given him for the conduct of his office, including important regulations for the control of shipping. According to these, severe restrictions were to be imposed on the admittance of vessels into California ports, except those ships from San Blas and the Philippine Islands. This policy, which Rivera enforced, interfered with California's future trade with foreigners and aroused much discontent among her inhabitants.

In 1775 an uprising of the Indians at San Diego seriously frightened the Spaniards in California. A friar, Fray Luís Jaime, was killed in the fracas. Rivera, however, quelled the outbreak before it could spread and life resumed its peaceful tenor, the colonists thenceforth keeping a wary eye on their Indian neighbors.

In time the Spanish government recognized the increasing importance of the "New" California over the "Old" California. The royal decree of 1775 had reversed the relative dominance of Lower and Upper California. Put into effect in 1777, this decree established the governor's residence at Monterey, sent Rivera to Loreto in Lower California to rule that peninsula as lieutenant governor, and brought in a new and vigorous governor for Upper California. This active, enterprising administrator, Felipe de Neve, may well have been the best of the Spanish governors. Like his predecessors Neve was a soldier, but he had a statesman's mind. His fame is based chiefly upon the code of laws which he drew up during his term of office for the regulation of the civic and military affairs of California. His role in establishing principles for the founding of the early pueblos has already been mentioned.

The Yuma Massacre

Connected with the founding of these pueblos, notably San José and Los Angeles, is one of the most tragic occurrences in the entire history of the American West. Captain Rivera, after he became lieutenant governor of the peninsula, received orders in 1781 to conduct a party of settlers bound for the proposed pueblos from Sonora and Sinaloa. At the Colorado River, Rivera sent the colonists ahead, while he and his soldiers, accompanied by the trails-priest, Father Garcés, stopped at the river. On July 17, 1781, the Yuma Indians unexpectedly attacked two missions—Purísima Concepción and San Pedro y San Pablo—which had been established as way stations near the river crossing. All the friars at the mission, all the male settlers in the area, and all the men in Rivera's command, including himself and Father Garcés, were shot or clubbed to death before the Yumas had finished. Numerous women and children were herded off into slavery.

This incident, known as the Yuma Massacre, was largely due to the unfair treatment the Indians felt they had received. Earlier the Yumas had been promised supplies and good treatment by Anza. But when they saw Spanish forces marching through their corn-fields and pumpkin patches, their resentment was understandably aroused. After the massacre, when Fages, always a hardy frontier captain, arrived at the site with one hundred soldiers to bury the dead and to ransom the women and children, he learned that the bloody affair was probably caused also by personal injustices perpetrated upon the Indians by Spanish settlers and soldiers. For years neither pueblos nor missions were re-established on the Colorado River; the route opened with such great effort by Anza grew more dangerous than ever before. Governor Neve joined Fages in a later campaign against the Yumas, which was a complete failure. The Indians, who took refuge in rocky, inaccessible country, remained unpunished and hostile.

Felipe de Neve never returned to California after this campaign. He received an appointment as inspector general of the *Provincias Internas* of Mexico, while Fages went on to govern Upper California for a second term.

The Second Term of Fages;
Roméu and Arrillaga

During the second gubernatorial term of Fages, which began in 1782, California suffered a heavy loss in the death of Father Serra, on August 28, 1784. Of the seventy-one years he had lived, thirty-four had been spent in missionary work. His immediate successor, Palóu, occupied the presidency of the missions for only a year, which he spent chiefly in the preparation of the two volumes already mentioned. Perhaps more writer than missionary, Palóu ultimately asked to be relieved of the responsibilities of the office, and retired to Mexico. He was succeeded by Lasuén, who labored for eighteen years thereafter to carry out Serra's plan for the extension of the California missions.

Fages' second administration, commencing in 1782, covered approximately the second decade of Spanish occupation. It came to an end in 1790, when, worn out by anxieties connected with his office, and harassed by the constant urgings of his wife to leave this rough frontier post, he offered his resignation. He was succeeded by José Antonio Roméu, who took office on April 16, 1791. Roméu, although a man of ability, had slight opportunity to display it; he arrived in California already an invalid, and during the entire term of his office was physically unable to attend to most of his duties. He died at Monterey on April 9, 1792, and was buried in an unmarked grave. During his short term, however, two new missions had been founded—Santa Cruz, on September 25, 1791, and Soledad, on October 9, 1791.

José Joaquín de Arrillaga, who followed Roméu, served two non-consecutive terms, the first as governor *ad interim* between the death of Roméu and the appointment of a regular successor. A tall, blue-eyed, fair-haired, courteous native of Spain, Arrillaga was not only an efficient soldier, but a conscientious official as well. He labored diligently during his first term to straighten out the accounts of the presidios, which were in considerable disorder after the incumbency of the invalid Roméu.

Borica, Promoter of Reforms

The regular governor who relieved Arrillaga, a Basque named Diego de Borica, reached Monterey in November, 1794. One of the most progressive of the Spanish governors, Borica was also a good

soldier and administrator, who displayed much initiative in proposing new measures. He was, in addition, agreeable, fond of jest,
and so delighted with California that he never lost an opportunity
to sing its praises. "To live long and without care come to Monterey," he wrote his friends. "That is the most peaceful and quiet
country in the world; one lives better here than in the most cul-
tured court of Europe."

Among Borica's first acts was an attempt to inaugurate a system
of public education; but he received little encouragement from
either the government or the people. The Governor was especially
friendly to the friars, with whom, in spite of occasional disagreements, he established a harmonious working relationship. Borica
authorized Father Lasuén to have the regions not served by the
existing missions carefully explored for new mission sites; and
together they decided that five more establishments could be
founded. Borica believed that conversion of all the Indians west of
the Coast Range would make it possible to reduce the number of
provincial guards, thus saving about $15,000 yearly. Hitherto the
missions had been isolated units; Borica now proposed to link
them into one chain, with the links nearer together.

Under the supervision of Governor Borica and Father Lasuén,
the new missions were established in a relatively short time: San
José de Guadalupe, on June 11, 1797; San Juan Bautista, June 24,
1797; San Miguel Arcangel, July 25, 1797; San Fernando Rey de
España, September 8, 1797; and San Luís Rey de Francia, June 13,
1798. During the following years the California missions reached
a height of prosperity. Lasuén placed great emphasis on instruct-
ing the neophytes in artisan trades, as well as in agriculture and
stock raising. Carpenters, blacksmiths, and masons were sent from
Mexico to the province at royal expense, and this new talent
helped develop further the mission architecture and economic progress of California. The enterprising Governor Borica induced the
missionaries and the inhabitants of the pueblos to experiment
with sheep grazing and the planting of hemp and flax, which later
became moderately successful crops.

The years 1797 to 1799, however, also were a time of anxiety
over the increasing numbers of foreign ships arriving in California
ports. Although their ostensible purpose was trading or exploration, the Spaniards considered their real motivation to be espionage. The appearance in particular of vessels sailing under the flag
of the new American Union, to take on wood and water, caused
alarm among Spanish authorities who knew how poor their defensive potential was. Some attempts, however feeble, were made by
Governor Borica to repair fortifications at the presidios. He issued

instructions to those in command to resist any attacks as long as possible; then, if necessary, they were to retreat toward the interior, driving all livestock before them and taking all other supplies, so that these would not fall into the hands of the enemy.

Despite this threat, the accomplishments of Borica were considerable. In addition to helping sponsor new missions, the governor erected shore batteries at San Diego and Yerba Buena, instituted irrigation works, guarded the provincial revenues, and acted as censor of public morals. A steadfast friend of the Indians, he did what he could to see that they were not despoiled of their lands. He was a merciful magistrate who believed that, due to the ignorance of Indian offenders, no capital punishment should be inflicted upon them even for murder. Thus only imprisonment and labor were meted out as sentences for Indians. Borica also had a hand in the eventual separation of Upper from Lower California: at his recommendation, a dividing line was fixed some leagues below San Diego, and this afterwards helped determine the boundary between the United States and Mexico. Lastly, along with his busy official life Borica found time for society, and his genial personality helped make the period of his administration one of social distinction at Monterey.

Arrillaga's Second Term

Upon Borica's retirement in 1800, Pedro de Alberni filled the office temporarily until the arrival of the regular appointee—Arrillaga, who had already acted as governor *ad interim* before Borica's governorship. This second administration of Arrillaga was marked by continuing cordiality between the military and the religious officials in California, but it suffered from the fact that the Mexico City government had lost interest in the missions and consequently was sending no money to support them. The presidios and civil establishments too were allowed to fall into a deplorable state; buildings were half ruined by wind and rain; cannon rusted from exposure and disuse; the already spiritless troops remained badly equipped and idle, barely able to keep down miscreant Indians. These conditions are to be ascribed not to inefficiency on the part of any one Spanish governor, but to prolonged neglect by the central government. California's soldiers were left without pay for years. It is remarkable that they gave Spain so much loyalty and service.

On September 17, 1804, during Arrillaga's term, Santa Inés Mission was established. This, the nineteenth in California, was ultimately followed by the founding of two more missions, which completed the province's chain of twenty-one—San Rafael, on December 14, 1817, and San Francisco Solano, on July 4, 1823. In addition to their religious functions, San Rafael was designed to serve as a health retreat for padres and colonists, while the mission at Solano was to be an outpost against the Russian advance. In reality, the great period of mission expansion may be said to have come to an end with the death of Father Lasuén on June 26, 1803. The founding of Santa Inés filled the last gap between the older establishments. The missions then served the entire area from San Diego northward to San Francisco and between the Coast Range and the ocean. One could travel safely over a distance of five hundred miles and enjoy the hospitality of the missions each night without having to carry along provisions. Horses were plentiful en route, and, as communication became easier, visitors began to appear more frequently at the missions.

One of the principal worries of Arrillaga's administration was the founding of a Russian settlement in California in 1812. The Russians had come as early as 1806 to examine trading opportunities at San Francisco. Now they established Fort Ross, north of Bodega Bay, as a post to supply their Alaskan settlements with sea-otter furs, cattle hides, and foodstuffs. The Russian threat to California had, at last, become real. Such cares as these lay heavily upon Arrillaga, who took the duties of his office seriously. His burdens exhausted him, and on July 24, 1814, he died. He was buried under the floor of the church at Soledad.

Solá, Last of the Spanish Governors

California's next regular governor (after the *ad interim* appointment of José Argüello) was Pablo Vicente Solá. His arrival at Monterey in 1815 was marked by great rejoicing. There were days of feasting and dancing, exhibitions of expert horsemanship, gory bull and bear fights in the capital's muddy arena, and a grand finale in which the local Indians danced in their best feathers, beads, and war paint. The royalist governor considered this fiesta on his behalf to be an expression of California's loyalty to Spain, at a time when such allegiance was growing weaker throughout other parts of the Americas. Solá was a haughty official who actually expected the homage he was tendered.

The new governor found a multitude of troubles in California. His popularity diminished after his condescending attitude became publicly known. He was proud of his Spanish birth and inclined to look with contempt upon colonial Californians as incompetent and untrustworthy whelps. He was also angered by the smuggling that had grown up between the inhabitants and visiting foreigners. Yet, when he himself faced scarcities of clothing, furniture, tools, and other necessities—as a result of the shortage of supply ships during the colonial rebellions against Spain—he, like other local officials, grew more sympathetic to the plight of the Californians and began to wink at smuggling. Governor Solá's future eventually became entwined with California's change of political status. That confusing story, connected with revolutionary activities throughout Latin America, will be told when Mexico's independence movement is considered in terms of its effect upon California.

SELECTED READINGS

The Spanish governors of California have not been treated biographically in any systematic manner. One must therefore refer to such general works as the histories by Bancroft, Hittell, Eldredge, Richman, Chapman, and others. Palóu's *Serra* and his *Noticias* are, of course, basic. The latter work has been translated into English by Herbert E. Bolton, as *Historical Memoirs of New California* (3 vols., Berkeley, 1926). See also Pedro Fages, *A Historical, Political and Natural Description of California*, translated by Herbert I. Priestley (Berkeley, 1937), and *Letters of Captain Don Pedro Fages and the Reverend President Fr. Junipero Serra at San Diego, California, in October, 1772*, translated by Henry R. Wagner (San Francisco, 1936). Another valuable compilation is the *Writings of Fermín Francisco de Lasuén*, trans. and ed. by Finbar Kenneally (2 vols., Washington, D.C., 1965).

After the 150th anniversary of Los Angeles, the Historical Society of Southern California *Annual Publications*, XV (1937), published numerous articles concerning Governor Felipe de Neve, including Lindley Bynum's "Governor Don Felipe de Neve, a Chronological Note" and his "Four Reports by Neve, 1777–1779."

The Yuma Massacre is discussed in the previously mentioned volume by Douglas D. Martin, *Yuma Crossing* (Albuquerque, 1954). Father Garcés has been treated biographically in Elliot Coues, *On the Trail of a Spanish Pioneer* (2 vols., New York, 1900). Consult also John Galvin, ed., *A Record of Travels in Arizona and California, 1775–1776 by Fr. Francisco Garcés* (San Francisco, 1965). The punitive expedition undertaken by Fages after the Yuma Massacre is described in Pedro Fages, *The Colorado River Campaign 1781–1782*, translated and edited by Herbert I. Priestley (Berkeley, 1913).

The founding of San Francisco is the subject of Herbert E. Bolton's *Outpost of Empire* (New York, 1931).

The architecture of the California missions has been treated in a book of photographs by Kurt Baer, *Architecture of the California Missions* (Berkeley, 1958), and in his *Paintings and Sculpture at Mission Santa Barbara* (Washington, D.C., 1955), as well as Baer's "Spanish Colonial Art in the California Missions," *The Americas*, XVII (July, 1961), 33–54. Colored photos of Edwin Deakin's paintings are in *A Gallery of California Mission Paintings* ed. by Ruth Mahood (Los Angeles, 1966). Baer has also published other books on Missions Santa Barbara and Santa Inés. A revealing glimpse of the mission system appears in Herbert I. Priestley, *Franciscan Explorations in California* (Glendale, 1946). See also Henry R. Wagner, "Early Franciscan Activity on the West Coast," Historical Society of Southern California *Quarterly*, XXIII (September, 1941), 115–126. Useful also is John A. Berger, *The Franciscan Missions of California* (New York, 1948), and Maynard Geiger, *Mission Santa Barbara, 1782–1965* (Santa Barbara, 1965), as well as his "New Data on the Buildings of Mission San Francisco," California Historical Society *Quarterly*, XLVI (September, 1967), 195–205.

8

Exploration and Foreign Interference

The Spanish explorers along the California coast pursued their aims so energetically that much of the geography of that area had been mapped before other Europeans made a significant appearance there. The charting of the northwest coast in particular, the later opening of the interior valleys, and the pacification of many of the natives—each one an effect of Spanish occupation—proved to be major contributions to the opening up of California to further development.

Explorations along the Northwest Coast

After San Francisco Bay had been charted by the expeditions of Portolá, Fages, and Rivera, Serra had suggested to Viceroy Bucareli that other explorations be undertaken on the coast north of San Francisco. The Viceroy had also received reports from Madrid, long before the Russians settled at Fort Ross, of Russian designs upon California. He appointed Captain Juan Pérez leader of a new expedition to investigate both Russian and English activity above California, as well as to chart the northwest coastline. (Pérez was the commander of the relief ship which had sailed into San Diego in 1769 to save the Portolá expedition.)

Aboard the frigate *Santiago*, and accompanied by Father Crespi, Pérez set out from San Blas on January 24, 1774, carrying supplies for the California colonists as well as full equipment for a year's expedition. Above San Francisco the *Santiago* crept along a rocky, uncharted coastline; though opposed by almost constant winds, she succeeded in reaching the northern point of Queen Charlotte Island. There Pérez was compelled, by the suffering of his men from scurvy and exposure, to turn about and head for home. Although the fog, rain, and headwinds made it impossible for his expedition to land, Pérez made many observations. Coastal Indians came out to the *Santiago* in dugout canoes to barter dried fish, furs, carved wooden boxes, crude images, and hair mats for Spanish beads, iron, and sheets of thin copper. The Indians sang and scattered feathers on the water as a token of friendship. The *Santiago* was at one point encircled by as many as two hundred natives, whose concerted chanting and thumping of wooden drums stunned the whites.

When, late in August of 1774, Pérez' frigate dropped anchor in Monterey Bay, he had surveyed a large part of the coastlines of British Columbia, Washington, and Oregon, in addition to that of northern California. Pérez was deprived of his just renown because of Spain's policy of keeping such voyages secret. Thus even the names that Pérez gave to points on the northwest coast were eventually discarded in favor of place names left by other explorers.

A second Spanish exploratory voyage soon followed that of Pérez. Four government vessels sailed from San Blas in March, 1775—two bound for California with supplies, and the others for the far northern coast. Captain Bruno de Heceta, or Hezeta, commanded the expedition; under him were two young men, Juan Francisco de la Bodega y Cuadra and Francisco Antonio Maurelle, who were eager to dare danger and to win promotion in the King's service. To undertake a survey close to the shore Heceta took along a schooner, the *Sonora*, which he placed under the command of Bodega. This vessel was only thirty feet long, twelve feet wide, and eight feet deep, with its deck room so limited that there was no opportunity for exercise. Space below decks, invaluable as shelter during storms, was so low that the men had to remain sitting down while in it. Only four of the crew were experienced sailors.

Under such unpromising conditions these adventurers set out to reach 60 degrees north latitude, leaving the two supply ships behind in Monterey waters. At latitude 41 degrees the *Santiago* and *Sonora* headed into a fine bay. Its shores, covered with grass, wild roses, iris, manzanita, *yerba buena* (literally good grass), and tall pines, were most inviting, and the Spaniards landed and took possession in the name of the King. Since this event took place on the day of the Holy Trinity, they called the bay Trinidad, by which name it is still known. Friendly Indians, dressed in wreaths of flowers and feathers, trooped to the beach and assisted the strangers in taking on wood and water.

Farther north, the Spaniards encountered less friendly natives, and when a boatload of six Spaniards went ashore for water, they were set upon and cut to pieces before the eyes of their helpless companions on the ship, who had no other small boat in which to go to their aid. The natives next went out in canoes, and surrounded the schooner; they had to be driven off with musket fire.

To Heceta properly belongs the discovery of the Columbia River, on July 27, 1775, although the achievement is sometimes ascribed to the United States sea captain Robert Gray in 1792. Three days after Heceta first sighted the Columbia, the *Santiago* and the *Sonora* were separated in a driving rain and mist. They did not meet again until they returned to Monterey. Heceta and the *Santiago* eventually reached Nootka, a harbor on the west coast of Vancouver Island. At this point, because of the miserable condition of his crew, Heceta decided to turn about; he remained in sight of land on the way down, exploring the coast as he went.

The tiny *Sonora*, under Bodega, though short of food and water, and with a crew also crippled by scurvy, ran far to the north. When the cold autumn rains set in, however, the men suffered so severely from insufficient clothing and lack of shelter that Bodega, like Heceta, was compelled to return southward. The trip was a stormy one and great seas rolled over the ship, carrying away everything movable and filling the hold with water. On October 3, 1775, the *Sonora* found herself in a bay about four leagues north of Point Reyes, on whose banks bear and deer could be seen feeding. The local Indians welcomed the wary Spaniards, who named the bay Bodega.

On October 7 the *Sonora* sailed into Monterey Bay, where her crew found the *Santiago* calmly riding at anchor. In the years 1774–1775, the northwest coast, as far as 57 degrees 58 minutes, had thus been explored and formally taken into Spanish possession by Pérez, Heceta, and Bodega.

The Nootka Sound Controversy

To defend her rights on this coast, which she claimed up to 60 degrees latitude, Spain sent two more expeditions into the region in 1788–1789. Under the command of Estevan José Martínez, these parties had orders to establish a fort and mission on Nootka Sound as a clear symbol of Spanish sovereignty in the region. Ten years before, the English mariner Captain James Cook had first landed at Nootka. Martínez's instructions were to win over the Indians by friendly trading and then to have the missionaries in his party attempt their conversion.

At Nootka, Martínez found several English vessels already at anchor. The commander of one of these announced that he had orders from the King of England to take possession of the port and to fortify it. Martínez explained that Spain regarded the region as a northern outpost or extension of her firmly established California colony. Next, in fulfillment of his responsibility as the legal representative of Spain, Martínez seized the English vessels at Nootka and made prisoners of those on board. This act later nearly led to armed conflict between the two countries and created a major diplomatic incident with serious repercussions in Europe. Martínez eventually released the English vessels, having, meanwhile, taken possession of the port. A Spanish post was maintained at Nootka for five more years and was regularly provisioned by transport, as an extension of the California colony.

While Martínez was at Nootka in 1789 he encountered the American ships *Columbia* and *Lady Washington*. (The term *American* refers here and subsequently to the United States, not to the entire Western Hemisphere.) The captains of these ships, Robert Gray and John Kendrick, wisely did not involve themselves in the Nootka Sound controversy. Although relations between the Americans and Spaniards remained outwardly cordial, this appearance of the ships of the new republic caused great uneasiness among the Spanish. One more nation had entered the Pacific, thus posing further economic, political, and military threats to Spanish power. There was reason, of course, for the Spaniards' fear. America would one day occupy California itself. Long before her conquest of California, however, the United States would take over Spain's claims on the northwest coast. Eventually she was, in fact, to base her territorial sovereignty in the Far West partly upon the early voyages of Spanish navigators.

From 1790 to 1792 preliminary attempts were made to settle the controversy over Nootka between Spain and England. In the spring of 1792 Bodega, as Spanish commissioner, held a series of discussions at Nootka with George Vancouver, who had been sent out to oversee Britain's claims in the area. Arbitration proved too complicated, however, and the two officers left settlement of the Nootka controversy to their respective governments.

On January 11, 1794, a final Nootka Convention was signed at Madrid. England declined to accept any arbitration of Spanish claims and carried its point by superior strength; Spain yielded forever its early sovereignty on the northwest coast. By the terms of the treaty both Britain and Spain were free to occupy Nootka, and to erect temporary accommodations there. Neither was to make any permanent settlement or claim territorial dominion to the exclusion of the other. In 1795, however, both the Spanish and English posts at Nootka Sound were abandoned. This withdrawal was one of the most tangible steps in the progressive decline of Spanish power and influence.

The Visits of La Pérouse and Malaspina

For the first sixteen years of the history of Upper California as a Spanish province, its isolation was almost complete. Their geographic separation from Spain's other colonies, plus an unnaturally rigid mercantilist trade policy, forced the Californians to lead calm, even dull, lives. They knew the name of their king and that of the pope but very little more about events abroad. They did, however, realize that visiting ships flying the flags of other nations could bring them sorely needed goods which the decrepit Spanish supply system failed to provide.

Gradually, foreign vessels, as it happened, began to appear in California waters as a result of the activities of a man who never set foot in that province—Captain Cook. When he had landed in the Nootka area to obtain furs for sail in China, his voyage had attracted almost as much worldwide attention as his previous discovery of the Hawaiian Islands. A great fur trade began to develop on the Pacific northwest coast, and this led indirectly to the attraction of the European and American ships to ports further south, in California.

In particular, the publication of the details concerning Cook's exploit drew the attention of France and other European powers to economic possibilities in the Pacific. In August, 1785, the French scientist and navigator Jean François de Galaup de la Pérouse sailed from Brest, heading an expedition whose objects were geographic, scientific, and commercial. In addition to making a survey of the flora, fauna, native population, and geology of various Pacific regions, its commander was under orders to inquire about the new North American fur trade. On September 15, 1786, La Pérouse's two vessels anchored in Monterey Bay among a school of whales spouting vile-smelling water. News of the visit had already reached California. Since Spain and France were then on cordial terms, the California officials had received orders to accord the foreigners the same hospitable welcome as vessels of their own nation.

During La Pérouse's ten-day stay his French crews took on wood and water while his geologists and botanists collected specimens and made drawings. The Californians supplied the visiting ships with cattle, vegetables, milk, poultry, and grain; for none of this would they accept even a *peseta* in recompense. The visitors reciprocated with presents of cloth, blankets, beads, tools, and seed potatoes from Chile.

La Pérouse's report on his visit to California makes interesting reading. The country itself was enthusiastically commended for its agricultural fertility and mild climate, which were compared to those of southern France. La Pérouse found little to praise in the Indians, however, and rated the adults among them at the mental level of white children five years of age. Although he testified generously to the high purpose of the missionaries, he thought they erred in attempting to enforce a disciplined life upon a wild people, whose self-reliance, he felt, suffered from the mission system.

The Frenchmen, having finished their observations and charting of the coast, prepared to resume their cruise to undiscovered parts of the Pacific. *Comandante* Fages filled the hen-coops of the departing vessels from his own poultry yard, while the fathers at Carmel Mission supplied the La Pérouse expedition with vegetables and fruit. The expedition departed after a farewell which turned out to be final; except for a letter written by La Pérouse on February 8, 1788, at Botany Bay on the coast of Australia, giving the news of the murder of twelve of his men by natives of the Navigator Islands, nothing more was heard of the party until 1825, when the wreckage of two French ships was found on the reefs of Vanikoro, an island north of New Hebrides. Had it not been for the forethought of La Pérouse in forwarding installments of his journal to France at every port, the records of this important voyage would have been lost. This expedition is notable because it was the first official visit to Spanish California from the outside world, and because it resulted in the first scientific description of the province.

A few years later, in September of 1791, California received a two-week visit from another scientific expedition, this one a Spanish project led by an Italian, Alejandro (Alessandro) Malaspina. With the vessels *Descubierta* and *Atrevida*, Malaspina was on a round-the-world mission with special instructions to inspect the Pacific Coast more thoroughly than any Spanish explorer had yet done, and to find the long-sought Strait of Anián. Malaspina met Father Lasuén, then president of California's missions; the cartographic staff of the expedition made nautical observations, drew maps, described the avifauna of the region, and recorded the customs of both the Indians and the Spanish settlers. Malaspina wrote an account of his visit which, while valuable, is not as complete or as colorful as that of La Pérouse or the one composed subsequently by the Englishman Vancouver. His voyage is incidentally notable as having brought to California the first American to land on its shores. This was John Green, a sailor from Boston who had shipped as gunner's mate on the *Atrevida* at Cádiz; he died while in California, and his burial was duly recorded on a mission register.

Vancouver's Voyage

Although exaggerated by earlier historians, English interest in California was high during the eighteenth century. The poet John Dyer's book *The Fleece* (1757) forecast that there would come a day "when, through new channels failing, we shall clothe the California coast, and all the realms that stretch from Anian's streights to proud Japan."

Mention has already been made of the meeting at Nootka Sound between Bodega and George Vancouver. Vancouver had orders not merely to negotiate this controversy, but also to explore the entire coast, to examine the extent of Spanish possessions, and to seize unclaimed territory. Having crossed over from Hawaii, he made his first landfall on the California coast just below Cape Mendocino, and sailed northward from that point. After the fruitless meeting with Bodega, he ran back down the coast without anchoring, and on November 14, 1792, entered San Francisco Bay in the sloop-of-war *Discovery*. Despite strained relations between Spain and England, Vancouver was given a cordial reception by both the padres and the military officials, who wined and dined him and sent meat and vegetables aboard his ship.

Vancouver's party visited Mission Santa Clara—the first foreigners to penetrate so far into the interior—and were struck by the physical beauty of California's northern valleys. From Santa Clara they returned to San Francisco, where they gave the Spaniards presents of English culinary and table utensils, bar-iron, and a few ornaments for the church. Then they sailed out of the bay, which members of the party declared to be "as fine a port as the world affords."

Further south at the capital of Monterey, Vancouver was received as hospitably as he had been in San Francisco Bay. At Carmel Mission, only a few leagues from Monterey, the fathers constructed a ceremonial bower of green branches and entertained their foreign guests in the mission garden. This gesture was returned by a dinner which Vancouver tendered aboard the *Discovery;* next came a picnic in the garden of the Monterey presidio, and the festivities ended with a display of fireworks furnished by the visitors.

Despite this cordiality, Vancouver was in Pacific waters primarily to advance British interests, which were in conflict with those of Spain. Upon a return visit to California in 1793, he was greatly offended not to receive the same welcome as on the year before. Governor Arrillaga objected to allowing foreign officials like Vancouver to penetrate as far into the interior as the Englishman had gone on his first visit. Vancouver kept his eyes open, and remarked in his report on this trip to Califorina: "The only defenses against foreign attack are a few poor cannon, inconveniently placed, at San Francisco, Monterey, and San Diego."

Vancouver left Monterey in irritation at what he regarded as humiliating restrictions placed upon him, and moved down the coast, making observations and naming a number of points in honor of those Spanish officers and padres from whom he had received the best treatment.

United States Sea Traders and Whalers

In 1796 the first United States vessel actually to anchor in a California port, the *Otter* of Boston, with Captain Ebenezer Dorr in command, took on wood and water near Monterey. She secretly landed ten men and a woman on the Carmel beach at night, forcing them from a rowboat with a pistol. They were convicts from Botany Bay, an English penal colony in the South Pacific, who had used the *Otter* to escape. Governor Borica was much offended at what he regarded as a reprehensible and dishonorable trick on the part of the Yankee captain. Finding it, nevertheless, necessary to provide for the newcomers, Borica put them to work as carpenters and blacksmiths at nineteen cents per day; the ex-prisoners turned out to be so industrious and well-behaved that he would have kept them in California had not royal orders obliged him to send them to Spain the next year.

From that time, United States penetration of California waters was a frequent occurrence. Near the end of 1798 four sailors who had been left in Lower California by the American ship *Gallant* were brought to San Diego and set to work while awaiting a vessel to take them to San Blas. In May, 1799, James Rowan in the *Eliza,* also an American ship, anchored at San Francisco and obtained supplies on the condition that he would not touch at any other port in the province. In August, 1800, the *Betsey*, under Captain Charles Winship, obtained wood and water at San Diego. Four years later Captain Joseph O'Cain, a sea-otter hunter, went into San Quentin, on San Francisco Bay, for repairs and provisions in a vessel named after himself. He had sixty men, fifteen canoes, and sixteen guns, and left only when ordered off the coast. By 1806 Captain William Heath Davis, Sr., a colleague of O'Cain, was trading illicitly at Rancho Ortega, above Santa Barbara. A new world of contact with foreigners was coming alive for the Californians, and many of these outsiders were from the United States.

During the revolutionary years between 1808 and 1821, when Spain's New World colonies outside California were in rebellion, her supply ships bound for California were stopped by the revolutionists. Otto von Kotzebue, the Russian sailor-scientist, who made two visits to the coast during this period, described the people of California as almost without clothing and woefully neglected by their mother country. Their plight afforded rare commercial opportunities for American traders, who grew steadily bolder. Furthermore, the Spaniards were not, and never really became, a commercial people. Their background was, rather, pastoral and agricultural. Despite regulations against contact between foreign vessels and the Californians, a flourishing contraband business sprang up.

Local officials interposed only limited interference. They were powerless to prevent the trade with the "Boston ships"; and, besides, their own wants were nearly as dire as those of any other resident. In 1817 James Smith Wilcox, a Yankee trader, lean and lank, dressed in a beaver hat and swallow-tailed coat, excused his illegal smuggling operations on the ground that they "served to clothe the naked soldiers of the king of Spain, when for lack of raiment they could not attend mass, and when the most reverend fathers had neither vestments nor vessels fit for the church nor implements wherewith to till the soil." Other foreign poachers and traders, especially Americans, came to feel equally self-righteous about the role they played in smuggling goods to California.

The arrival in California of increasing numbers of foreign ships occasionally roused the viceroy at Mexico City to issue stricter orders against trading with them. Since, however, he had no means of carrying out such *pronunciamentos*, the Yankee poachers continued to operate—although at peril to themselves and their ships. On March 22, 1803, shots were exchanged between the American vessel *Lelia Byrd* and a shore battery at San Diego after a part of its Yankee crew had been captured while trading ashore. Although several shots struck the sails, rigging, and hull of the American ship, no one was hurt. The Yankee captain, William Shaler, got his men safely away to the Hawaiian Islands and China. The next year the *Lelia Byrd* was back doing a flourishing clandestine fur business with the missionaries and other Californians. But Captain Shaler and his leaky, worm-infested ship were careful this time to avoid the fortified ports of San Diego and Monterey. Shaler later published an account of his exploits in the *American Register,* and his vivid narrative greatly increased United States interest in California.

The stories of the contraband "Boston ships" form a fascinating record of the invasion of a culture by representatives of another society. The American traders became an important factor in breaking down the restrictions imposed upon California by the Spanish Crown, and accordingly they sometimes suffered severe consequences when caught. In 1806, Governor Arrillaga's guards seized members of the crew of the United States ship *Peacock* and sent them southward to San Blas as prisoners. In 1813, Captain George Washington Eayrs of the ship *Mercury* ran into a Spanish longboat in California waters. Unarmed, Eayrs and his men were captured and taken to Santa Barbara, where they were interned for two years. The captain wrote a series of pleading letters from his squalid California prison, but to no avail; he languished there at the pleasure of his captors—an example of how tough Spanish colonial officialdom could be. In 1822, also at Santa Barbara, the *Eagle,* a ship belonging to Captain William Heath Davis, Sr., was seized and its cargo confiscated.

The pattern repeated itself over and over again in the following years. Illegal coastal trafficking, by which New England wares or Chinese luxuries were exchanged for sea-otter furs, steer hides, tallow, and cow horns (to be made into buttons), continued to be most dangerous. Yet the rewards were great. In the first few decades of the nineteenth century the price of prime otter pelts at Canton, China, was from $50 to $100. As many as 18,000 skins were delivered to the China market from California in a single season. For visiting New England traders, therefore, this traffic became a significant branch of the great American China trade. Out of it grew also the fortunes of many prominent New England families.

One further economic link connected New England with California. In the later Mexican period of California's history a new approach to trade was forged by Yankee whalers. These seamen stayed away from their home ports as long as four years. Battered and bruised by the gales of the North Pacific, they were grateful to find in California protected ports of call in which they could repair their ships and spirits. Fresh meat, fruit, grains, and other provisions for the long homeward voyage around the Horn were readily obtained there. Richardson's Bay, near today's San Francisco, was an early rendezvous for whaling vessels, which made their presence known by their acrid, fishy odors. These ships carried small stocks of manufactured goods to exchange for gold and silver coins or for local products. Out of their sea chests came needles, stockings, jewelry, thread, bolts of cloth, and other comparatively luxurious commodities. On the eve of re-outfitting their vessels for New England, the whalers undercut the prices of other traders and thereby came to be especially popular among the native Californians. This trade conducted by the whalers served as the forerunner of the more systematic commerce that developed later during the hide- and tallow-trading era. At Monterey, one of their favorite retreats, these men of Nantucket and New Bedford left behind a permanent souvenir of their stay—a whalebone sidewalk—as a token of their appreciation for the shelter the town had afforded them. Whalers, furthermore, carried home glowing accounts of pastoral California, which helped popularize the province further.

Arrival of the Russians

The Russians came into California not with sword in hard, threatening violence, but, like their American competitors, as uninvited traders who gradually won governmental tolerance if not an official welcome. Since the 1740's, when Vitus Bering had prepared the groundwork upon which Alexander Baranov in 1799 established the monopolistic Russian-American Fur Company in Alaska, the Russians had slowly expanded their sphere of influence. They accumulated valuable caches of furs at their trading station in Sitka, but they were frequently on the verge of starvation in the midst of their riches; the harsh climate and barrenness of the country made agriculture virtually impossible. Cold, forlorn, and eager to purchase supplies from the Yankee sea captains, who were also seeking sea-otter and seal furs in the North Pacific, the Russians listened carefully to the Americans' reports about the abundance of wheat and other cereals to be found in California.

In 1803 the American captain Joseph O'Cain, after selling Baranov goods worth 10,000 rubles, suggested that the Russian send a company of Aleuts, natives of the Aleutian Islands, to California where they would, with their *bidarkas* (skin canoes) hunt otter "on shares." Baranov agreed to this proposal with reluctance, foreseeing danger as a result of Spain's aversion to foreigners in California waters; but he had heard of the abundance of otter to the south, and was anxious to secure information about Spanish California. The venture turned out to be profitable, and the Russians were eager to repeat it. This marked the beginning of the contract system by which, in partnership, Russians and Americans hunted land and sea otter on the southern coasts for a decade or more. The furs were secured partly by skilled Aleut hunters and partly by contraband trade with the Californians for goods. Notwithstanding the large number of skins they obtained in this manner, the Russians came to realize that it would have been wiser to keep the fur trade in their own hands and pay cash for such goods as they needed. The Russian American Fur Company later sent its own hunters south toward California, until they penetrated the bay of San Francisco; the Californians, who had not even a boat available to repel such operations, were suitably exasperated. Soon the Spaniards would complain that Russian hunters were infesting the coast.

Rezanov

In 1805 Nikolai Petrovich Rezanov, chamberlain of the Czar, was sent out to inspect the condition of the Russian colonies in the North Pacific. At Sitka he found the settlers reduced to eating crows and devilfish—almost anything that could be swallowed. Russian supply ships had faltered badly in caring for the needs of the colony. In this emergency, Rezanov decided to go to California in search of supplies. Accompanied by a German surgeon and naturalist, Dr. Georg Heinrich von Langsdorff, and by a crew already sick with scurvy, he sailed from Sitka aboard the former American ship *Juno*, on March 8, 1806.

Rezanov's party was courteously received at San Francisco, but Governor Arrillaga feared that furnishing such foreigners with supplies would be considered an act of disloyalty by his government. He thus balked at doing so, just as he had disapproved of Vancouver's visit. A novel element was, however, injected into the negotiations between the Russians and the Spaniards. The Russian envoy suddenly fell in love with the vivacious and beautiful fifteen-year-old daughter of the *comandante* of the port. Rezanov's private correspondence with his government suggests that in wooing this girl, Concepción Argüello, diplomacy as well as romance entered into his behavior; but there is no reason to suspect that his affections were not also genuinely involved. The betrothal of the couple required the permission of the girl's parents, Governor Arrillaga, and the friars; all of them consented, and thus Rezanov was placed in a new position. As a future member of the *comandante's* family, he had no trouble in persuading the governor to furnish supplies for the starving Russian colony at Sitka.

The *Juno* was laden with wheat, barley, peas, beans, tallow, and dried meat, and on May 8, 1806, Rezanov sailed away, while the Argüellos waved farewell from the fort. The understanding when Rezanov left was that immediately upon his return to St. Petersburg he would go to Madrid as an envoy from the Imperial Russian Court, in order to smooth over misunderstandings between the two powers in the Pacific. Thence he would return, via New Spain, to San Francisco to claim his bride and settle those matters relative to the commerce Russia wished to promote. Rezanov's farewell turned out to be forever. The departing Russian never returned to California; after years of waiting for news of him, Señorita Argüello, who had in 1850 taken the vows of the Dominican order at Monterey, learned of Rezanov's death in Siberia while on his way home from California. This romance has been used as a literary theme by Bret Harte and other writers.

Fort Ross

Although the immediate objective of Rezanov's voyage was to obtain supplies to relieve the Russian food scarcity at Sitka, he hoped in time also to extend Russian power southward. The Russians held that Spain's claim to the coast above San Francisco was slight, because of the Spanish abandonment of Nootka Sound after 1795.

In 1809 an officer of the Russian-American Fur Company, Ivan Kuskov, was sent to California from Alaska to select a favorable site for a southern outpost. He landed at Bodega Bay, which he reported to be a good harbor and a fine building site, possessing tillable lands, a mild climate, and an abundance of fish and fur-bearing animals. In 1812 Kuskov returned, this time with equipment for a trading station and with a number of Aleut Indians to fish for the community. Kuskov made no pretense of consulting Spanish officials, but simply chose a strategic shoreline site, eighteen miles north of Bodega on a plateau rising seventy-five to one hundred feet above high tide. A rectangular fort, surrounded by a strong palisade with bastions at the corners pierced for cannon, was built and mounted with ten pieces of artillery. Inside the stockade a wooden house of six or eight rooms, furnished with carpets and a piano, and boasting even glass windows, was built for the officers. In one corner of the enclosure was a chapel, which had a round dome and a belfry with chimes. Granaries, workshops, and redwood huts for the Aleuts were constructed outside the stockade, and on the beach the Russians erected a wharf, a tannery, a bath house, and a shed for *bidarkas*. Until a diary, only recently printed, told us that Fort Ross was, surprisingly, completely painted blue, most persons conceived of the establishment as an unpainted rough-hewn wood stockade and fort. These were practically impregnable to attacks by Indians or Spaniards.

This place was given the name "Ross," a derivation from the word "Russia"; because of its fortifications, it became generally known as Fort Ross. It lacked a good anchorage, and consequently the Russian ships wintered and made repairs at Bodega, where warehouses were built for the storage of goods. Attempts at raising vegetables were only moderately successful, and the Russians never did well with wheat cultivation; they were forced to rely upon the Spanish Californians for their grain.

While Kuskov was building Fort Ross, the Spanish officer Gabriel Moraga was sent to investigate Russian activity north of San Francisco. The Russians allowed the emissary to inspect the fort, and, after pointing out their deficiencies in wheat, indicated that they would like to improve trade relations with their California neighbors to the south. Moraga, on his return to San Francisco, reported to the officials of the province that the Russians seriously needed food. In January, 1813, he returned with three horses, twenty head of cattle, several *fanegas* (a Spanish unit of measure) of wheat, and limited permission from Governor Arrillaga to carry on trade with Fort Ross. The Spaniards thereby courteously allowed the Russians to evade their restrictions against foreign ships in California ports.

The trade established by Moraga was continued, though with growing reluctance on the part of the California government, throughout the Russian stay on the coast. Formal permission was never given the Russians to settle in the country or to trade directly with the people of California. In fact, as soon as the viceroy at Mexico City received word from Arrillaga of the Russians' arrival, he sent instructions to the governor to notify Kuskov that his occupation of California territory was in clear violation of a treaty between Russia and Spain. Through Arrillaga the viceroy requested Kuskov to remove his settlement immediately. But the Russians knew that Governor Arrillaga's weak garrisons were in no position to enforce the viceroy's order.

On October 2, 1816, another Russian trading party, aboard the two-masted schooner *Rurik*, sailed into San Francisco Bay, commanded by Otto von Kotzebue. Like the *Juno* ten years before, the *Rurik* had been sent to explore the coastline and to obtain more supplies. The Russians remained in port for a month; they were undoubtedly encouraged by the weakness of this Spanish outpost, less than fifty miles from the Russian settlement farther to the north. Outwardly, the Russians carried on polite relations with Spanish officials at the San Francisco presidio and the priests at the mission. The latter supplied them with fruit, vegetables, and other stores. Before the Russians left they entertained San Francisco's officialdom at a "parting dinner." The gaiety of that affair was recorded by Adelbert von Chamisso, naturalist of the *Rurik* expedition. After repeated toasts to the flags and monarchs of both the Spanish and the Russian nations, Von Chamisso noted that "a good missionary dipped his mantle too deep in the grape, and reeled visibly under the burden."

Later, Governor Solá, who viewed such fraternizing with disgust, and who was less friendly to the Russians than his predecessor, Arrillaga, again sent notice to them at Fort Ross to leave the country. The Russians paid no attention. Their colony continued to carry on a good business with the Californians, furnishing them articles of iron, wood, and leather in return for agricultural supplies. At Fort Ross the Russians tanned hides, fired brick and tiles, constructed barrels and kegs, and made rope from home-grown hemp. They also made a start at ship building by constructing four small vessels. The Russians even raised delicate plants in a glass hothouse, and the flowers they grew on their foggy peninsula gave the place a look of permanence.

Discipline at Ross was strict, and temptations few, but the Russian colonists surely preferred life there to the privations farther north. The population of the post was never large, ranging from about one hundred to four hundred persons, including the Aleuts and their Indian wives, with whom the Russians mixed socially. With the Aleuts as hunters, the Russians pursued the sea otters so assiduously that before long these animals were cleared out of the coast between Trinidad and San Francisco bays. From 1812 to 1840 the Russians also maintained an establishment at the Farallones Islands to secure fur seals and to kill gulls (as many as 50,000 per year) and sea lions—as food for the Aleuts.

Moraga and the Opening
of the Central Valley

The area of California occupied by the Spaniards was generally limited to the coastal region extending from San Francisco to San Diego. Soledad was the farthest inland settlement in the province, some thirty miles from the sea. The vast interior valley lying between the Coast Range and the Sierra Nevada, where herds of antelope grazed on wild oats, was termed *tierra incognita* (unknown land) in early documents. The southern part of the Central Valley was better known than the northern because of previous expeditions between the Colorado River and California. In 1774 Anza had crossed the desert diagonally from southeast to northwest, and the next year he had again traversed this region to bring the first colonists to California. Garcés had once gone across the mountains almost to Lake Tulare, exploring present-day Kern and San Bernardino counties.

By the beginning of the nineteenth century, a few of California's most exposed settlements were occasionally threatened by warlike tribes, bolder and more aggressive than the docile mission Indians. Gabriel Moraga, who was an outstanding organizer of military expeditions into the interior, took part in as many as forty-six campaigns against these Indians. He penetrated into the foothills of the Sierra Nevada during a number of these forays, which began in 1806. His *entradas* into the interior can still be traced by the names bestowed upon principal geographical features, especially rivers. The Kings River was explored and named by Moraga, as were the Merced River and Mariposa Creek. The Feather River was called *El Río de las Plumas* (the river of the feathers) in 1820 by Lieutenant Luís Antonio Argüello, Moraga's superior, because of the feathers of wild fowl which he saw floating on the surface of its waters. The county through which it flows has retained the original Spanish form of its name, Plumas, while that of the river has been translated into the English word, Feather.

Moraga, as a result of his pioneering leadership, is entitled to the credit for the opening of California's Central Valley. A robust explorer, he could be ruthless when occasion demanded; and he has been called the best soldier of his time. In 1811 he was made a lieutenant for his gallantry in an Indian battle the year before at the Carquinez Straits. After his death Moraga's forays into an unpromising interior of tule swamps and hot sands were continued by others. Later, during the Mexican period, similar parties went inland to recover stolen animals and to suppress Indian uprisings. Neither the Spanish nor the Mexican government, however, established towns or missions in the interior. The region remained of secondary importance until the arrival of the Anglo-Americans.

SELECTED READINGS

Both the land and the sea expeditions treated in this chapter are discussed in the Bancroft multi-volume *History of California*. The Spanish government's Dirección de Hidrografia published, in its *Anuario* for 1865 (Volume XVI), a monograph, "Viajes de Exploración, Primer Viaje de D. Juan Francisco de la Bodega y Quadra," a relatively technical account. Regarding Heceta, see Benito de la Sierra, "The Hezeta Expedition to the Northwest Coast in 1775," California Historical Society *Quarterly*, IX (September, 1930), 201–242. See also Francisco Antonio Maurelle, *Journal of a Voyage in 1775, to Explore the Coast of America, Northward of California* (London, 1781). An interesting account of another Spanish visitor to California is *Journal of José Longinos Martínez—Notes and Observations of the Naturalist of the Botanical Expedition in Old and New California and the South Coast, 1791–92*, trans. and ed. by Lesley Byrd Simpson (San Francisco, 1961).

Later expeditions are described in Henry R. Wagner, *The Last Spanish Exploration of the Northwest Coast and the Attempt to Colonize Bodega Bay* (San Francisco, 1931), and in Cecil Jane, ed., *A Spanish Voyage to Vancouver and the North-West Coast of America* (London, 1930). Vancouver's voyage and other English explorations are treated in George Godwin, *Vancouver: A Life, 1757–1798* (London, 1930), and in G. H. Anderson, *Vancouver and His Great Voyage* (London, 1923). See also V. L. Denton, *The Far West Coast* (Toronto, 1924).

A relatively recent reprinting, in French, of the La Pérouse expedition's report of 1786 is Gilbert Chinard, ed., *Le Voyage de Lapérouse sur les Côtes de L'Alaska et de la Californie* (Baltimore, 1937). An older version in English is *A Voyage Round the World, in the Years 1785, 1786, and 1788* . . . (3 vols., London, 1798).

George Vancouver's *A Voyage of Discovery to the North Pacific Ocean and Round the World* (3 vols., London, 1798) is the basic source on Vancouver. The California portions of this work have been edited and annotated by Marguerite Eyer Wilbur as *Vancouver in California, 1792–1794* (Los Angeles, 1953).

An account of the Malaspina expedition (containing translations from *Viaje politico-cientifico Alrededor del Mundo por las corbetas Descubierta y Atrevida* . . . , published in Madrid in 1885) is in an article by Edith C. Galbraith, California Historical Society *Quarterly*, III (October, 1924), 215–237. See also the work by E. Boni, *Malaspina*

(Rome, 1935), and Donald C. Cutter, *Malaspina in California* (San Francisco, 1960).

The *Lelia Byrd* episode is described in Lindley Bynum, ed., *Journal of a Voyage Between China and the North-western coast of America made in 1804 by William Shaler* (Claremont, 1935). Shaler's career is also treated in Roy F. Nichols, *Advance Agents of American Destiny* (Philadelphia, 1956). The experiences of Captain Eayrs are told in fuller detail in Cleland's *History of California: the American Period*, pp. 17–21. For Captain Davis's story see the vignette by Andrew F. Rolle, "The Eagle Is Seized," *Westways*, XLVI (December, 1954), 16–17. The California sea-otter commerce is admirably described in Adele Ogden, *The California Sea Otter Trade, 1784–1848* (Berkeley, 1941), and in the same author's "New England Traders in Spanish and Mexican California," *Greater America: Essays in Honor of Herbert Eugene Bolton* (Berkeley, 1945), pp. 395–415. Consult also William Henry Ellison, ed., *Life and Adventures of George Nidever* (Berkeley, 1937), and Magdalen Coughlin, "Boston Smugglers on the Coast (1797–1821): An Insight into the American Acquisition of California," California Historical Society *Quarterly*, XLVI (June, 1967), 99–120.

Regarding Russian contact with California, see T. C. Russell, ed., *The Rezanov Voyage to Nueva California in 1806* (San Francisco, 1926), and the same editor's *Langsdorff's Narrative of the Rezanov Voyage to Nueva California in 1806* (San Francisco, 1927). See also the biography by Hector Chevigny, *Lost Empire: The Life and Adventures of Nicolai Petrovich Rezanov* (New York, 1937), and that by Gertrude Atherton, *Rezanov* (New York, 1906). A bibliography relating to the Russians in California, as well as articles by E. O. Essig, Adele Ogden, and Clarence John Du Four, are printed in a special issue of the California Historical Society *Quarterly*, XII (September, 1933).

A contemporary Russian account by an expansionist author, who delivers some harsh judgments on California, is Otto von Kotzebue, *A Voyage of Discovery in the South Sea . . .* (3 vols., London, 1821). Another contemporary narrative is by Rezanov's associate, George Heinrich von Langsdorff, *Voyages and Travels in Various Parts of the World During the Years 1803, 1804, 1805, 1806, and 1807* (2 vols., London, 1813–1814). Recent Russian scholarship appears in S. B. Okun, *The Russian-American Company* (Cambridge, 1951), which builds upon P. Tikhmenev, *Historical Survey of the Formation of the Russian-American Fur Company . . .* (2 vols., St. Petersburg, 1861–1863).

Regarding Moraga, see *Diary of Ensign Gabriel Moraga's Expedition of Discovery in the Sacramento Valley, 1808*, edited by Donald C. Cutter (Los Angeles, 1957). On the same general subject see S. F. Cook, *Colonial Expeditions to the Interior of California's Central Valley, 1800–1820* (Berkeley, 1960), and his later *Expedition to the Interior of California's Central Valley, 1820–1840* (Berkeley, 1962). The observation concerning the color of Fort Ross is in Doyce B. Nunis, ed., *The California Diary of Faxon Dean Atherton, 1836–1839* (San Francisco, 1964).

9

Arcadia

In contrast to the settlers on North America's Anglo-American frontier, Spain's colonists were sustained by a relatively paternal government. The Crown tried, though sometimes without success, to send them supply ships periodically until they could become self-supporting. However useful such provisioning was, Spain's custodial attitude deprived its colonists of the self-reliance of the Anglo-American pioneers, who were ordinarily unsupported by any government. Once the Latin American independence movement broke out, the California settlers were abruptly on their own, obliged to govern themselves for the first time. Economically, too, as well as politically, the Californians had to learn how to care for one another. First under Spanish and then under Mexican rule, California faced a future that in large measure was to be determined by a combination of its heritage and its isolation. A glance at its picturesque colonial society and pastoral way of life may help clarify the events that both preceded and accompanied the revolt of the province from Spain.

Ranchos and Land Grants

Conditions in California during the colonial period seemed favorable to only one means of livelihood—the ancient one of the shepherd or rancher. The sparseness of the frontier population severely limited the markets available for both agricultural production and potential manufacturing. Ranching conditions, however, were almost perfect in California: abundant pastureland and water existed, in addition to a large supply of Indian labor. The climate was mild enough to permit animals to live throughout the year with little shelter, and there was no necessity to fence in stock. Ranching, moreover, was popular in the Spanish motherland and it suited the natural disposition of the Spanish Californians, who liked outdoor life on horseback. The small band of two hundred cattle brought to California by the Portolá expedition, and the few that survived the overland trip with Anza's party, provided the stock from which most of the California herds developed. These herds yielded hides and tallow for export in abundance.

In order to raise cattle, settlers had to have land. No phase of California history has produced more far-reaching consequences than the disposition of the large private land grants during the Spanish and Mexican eras. (The latter is generally considered as beginning in 1821 when Mexico declared its independence.) California land titles today are grounded upon these original grants, which the Californians regarded as the very origin of their wealth. Many California land grants are still known by their original names, including, for example, *El Toro* (the bull), *Los Laureles* (the laurels), and *La Sagrada Familia* (the Holy Family). The struggle over legal justification of such titles under United States rule will be discussed in a later chapter. In Spanish California, land was at first granted for pueblos, less than thirty grants being ceded to private persons during the Spanish period. The missionaries enjoyed only temporary rights to land, and they sought to preserve it intact from ownership by private persons because they feared that the Indians might be morally contaminated by settlers. On the other hand, the government was concerned at the impossibility of protecting outlying and scattered ranches from unpredictable native attacks. Consequently, settlers were generally required to live "in the pueblos, and not dispersed." In time, however, the private *rancho* became a needed institution. In 1775 Commander Rivera made such a grant to one Manuel Butrón, who thus became California's first rancher. In 1784 Governor Fages really began the land-grant system in earnest. Fages was empowered to make private grants, not to exceed three square leagues, each beyond the limits of the existing pueblos and not conflicting with the property of missions or Indian villages. The grantee had to agree to build a storehouse and to stock his holdings with at least 2,000 head of cattle.

It was during the Mexico regime, however, that most of the "Spanish land grants" were made; after the establishment of the Mexican Republic more liberal policies caused the number of land-grant applications to increase rapidly. A colonization law of 1824 promised security of both person and property to landholders, as well as freedom from taxes for five years. Any Mexican of good character, or any foreigner willing to become naturalized and to accept the Catholic faith, might petition for eleven square leagues of land. Nevertheless, Mexican citizens were preferred to foreign settlers, who could not ordinarily obtain grants within ten leagues of the sea coast.

The square leagues by which the grants were measured comprised a little more than 4,438 acres each (by modern standards this area alone would constitute a large ranch), and a *rancho* of four or five leagues was considered small. Boundaries were loosely defined by well-known landmarks, such as a chain of hills, a clump of cacti, or the center of a stream bed; in other cases the whitened skull of a steer might be placed so as to mark the limits of a grant. Beginning at a point marked by a pile of stones, called a *mojonera*, a horseman measured the tract by galloping at full speed with a fifty-foot-long *reata* trailing behind him. The quantity of land was roughly guessed at, the convenient phrase *poco mas ó menos* (a little more or less) being used to cover any deficiency or excess. This vagueness of description inevitably caused litigation when rancho properties later fell into the hands of American occupants.

Cattle and Horse Raising

Whereas in 1790 there were only nineteen private ranchos in California, by 1830 there were some fifty in existence, fourteen of them in the Monterey district. Many of the holdings were at first stocked with horses and cattle borrowed from the missions which the settlers returned whenever the increase permitted. As their endeavors proved profitable, some Californians came to own several ranchos, each with herds of cattle and horses. Many family fortunes were founded on the success of the ranchos, especially after the beginning of the extensive traffic with English and American vessels in search of hides and tallow.

William Heath Davis, Jr. (son of the American captain of the same name), a resident of California during its Mexican rancho era, once compiled a valuable list of the largest land and cattle owners of the times: Francisco Pacheco owned the San Felipe, San

Luís Gonzaga, and other ranchos, totaling 125,740 acres. The two ranchos alone contained 14,000 head of cattle, 500 horses and mares, and 15,000 sheep. David Spence, who married into the Estrada family, counted 25,000 acres in the Buena Esperanza rancho, with 4,000 head of cattle. Henry Delano Fitch, whose wife was Josefa Carrillo, held the Rancho Sotoyome; in its area of eleven leagues he had 14,000 head of cattle, 1,000 horses and mares, and 10,000 sheep. The Swiss Johann Augustus Sutter enjoyed the grant of a full eleven leagues of land, extending sixty miles in length, which was well stocked. Abel Stearns, an American, was the owner of a number of ranchos, comprising many thousands of acres on which grazed 30,000 cattle, 2,000 horses, mares, and mules, and 10,000 sheep. Mariano Guadalupe Vallejo of Sonoma had practically unlimited land, with stock in proportion. The sites now occupied by the cities of Oakland, Alameda, and Berkeley form only a part of what was once the Rancho San Antonio, the property of Don Luís Peralta; his lands furnished pasture for 8,000 head of cattle and 2,000 horses and mares. In totaling the figures for the California ranchos up to about 1840, Davis counted 1,045 holdings of all sizes. The number of private ranchos had, thus, greatly increased since 1830. About 800 of these were stocked, with an average of some 1,500 head for each rancho. That is, according to Davis' estimate, there were 1,220,000 head of cattle on the ranchos at this time, the height of California's pastoral period.

These cattle were the mainstay of the California economy. Beef was the principal item of food. Leather hides provided harnesses, saddles, soles for shoes, even door hinges; the long horns of cattle were used as added protection on top of adobe walls or fences in towns, as well as for shoe buttons. Tallow went into the molding of candles, in an age before kerosene lamps or electric lights.

Hides and tallow also became the main items of exchange. Trading accounts were kept in *pesos* and *reales*, but little cash was exchanged because of its scarcity. The Californians increasingly obtained their wearing apparel and other manufactured necessities by bartering with foreign trading vessels. The term "California bank note" came to be used widely for a dried steer hide, which had a value of approximately one dollar.

The term *rancho* was used primarily to indicate a farm devoted to stock raising, although sometimes crops were also planted on ranchos. (In Mexico, farms raising crops were called *haciendas*.) Some ranchos employed over a hundred Indian laborers, under a foreman or *mayordomo* who himself might be an Indian of exceptional intelligence. In fact, without Indians the ranchos could hardly have carried on. Despite their previous lack of experience with stock animals, Indians seemed to take almost naturally to handling both horses and cattle. They generally considered it an honor to work among the cattle or in a domestic capacity, and only Christianized Indians were so employed; the more lowly tasks of planting and plowing were left to other less adaptable natives.

Also indispensable in the care of cattle herds were the rancho's horses, usually mustangs. Far from being mongrels, as many believe, some were descendants of Arabian animals brought to the Americas by the Spanish *conquistadores*. During the rancho era they sold for a trifle: a passably good horse could be bought for three dollars—less than the cost of his saddle and bridle. Capable of great speed and endurance, the California horses acquired a skill in rounding up and handling cattle hardly less extraordinary than that of their riders.

These cowboys, or *vaqueros*, were required in large numbers because of the absence of fences in the territory over which the cattle ranged. Free-running stock became so wild and fierce that it was unsafe to go among such herds on foot or unarmed; any man who rode the range was as likely to need to defend himself against savage bulls as against ferocious grizzlies, then often encountered near the mountains.

The cattle continued to increase so that even a bountiful California could not furnish enough pasture in years of drought. It sometimes became necessary for ranch hands to "cut out" and kill the older animals. The horses too multiplied at such a rate that they often ran wild, so that similar measures were necessary to control them; some met their death by being driven over precipices into the sea and into rivers to drown.

The lack of fences also led to the institution known as the *rodéo* or round-up, devised to separate and brand stock belonging to different owners. Every rancher had his own distinctive brand, and each was registered. No one could adopt or change a brand without permission of the governor. The *rodéo* was conducted under a regularly appointed *juez de campo*, or field judge, who settled disputes over the ownership of animals. At intervals the rancheros also held bloody *matanzas*, or cattle slaughterings. Men rode at full speed through the herds and killed the animals with one cut of a knife directed at a vital part of the neck. Next skinners stripped off the hides, and butchers cut the meat into strips for drying. The tallow was melted and poured into bags made of hides, to be delivered to offshore trading ships, often by floating these bags out to the vessels. Most of the bloody carcasses, for which there was no market, were left on the field to be disposed of by the Indians and wild animals, or to rot. The artist Titian Ramsay Peale, who traveled to California with the Wilkes expedition in 1841, was only one of many observers to note that the hills and valleys of the province were dotted with carcasses in various stages of decomposition. So many bleached and brittle bones lay underfoot that when Peale once traveled at night, he was struck by the eerie effect of the continuous crushing of these bones under the hoofs of his horse.

Primitive Agriculture and Industry

A significant part of California's agricultural progress continued to be carried on at the missions, on whose lands oranges and grapevines were first planted successfully. It was from Mission San Gabriel that the wheat traded to the Russians came; and at Mission San Jose the padres planted a tract about a mile square in wheat. Their methods of sowing and reaping, however, were extremely primitive. Indian laborers usually scratched the ground with a rude wooden plow, fashioned from the crooked limb of a tree and shod with an iron point; they sometimes harrowed the soil by dragging large branches of other trees along the surface. Next the padres scattered grain in the furrows. Even with such methods the yield from the virgin earth was considerable.

The grain was cut with hand sickles and bound in sheaves, the missionaries being careful to cut the stalks so high that enough seed was left for the field to replant itself. For threshing, a flat, circular piece of ground was usually fenced in and its surface watered and pounded until, after drying, it became very hard. The wheat was then thrown into the enclosure and seventy-five or a hundred mares driven around and around until the grain was trampled out. Next came the winnowing, accomplished by tossing the wheat against the wind. At first the only means of grinding was by hand, with stone pestles and mortars. The padres later built water-driven grist mills at Missions Santa Cruz, San Luís Obispo, San José, and San Gabriel. The most common mechanical method of grinding was by the *arrastra*, which consisted of two crude circular millstones placed on top of each other. The lower stone remained stationary, while the upper was rotated when the cross beam attached to it was dragged around in a circle by a horse or mule. Thus the grain was crushed between the two stones, by a process that had been used in Spain for centuries.

California's colonials never held sheep in the same esteem as

they did cattle; nevertheless, each mission establishment and most
of the private ranchos raised small flocks of sheep for their mutton
and wool. The wool was coarse and wiry, but strong, and was
woven by the Indians on handmade looms into cloth called *serga*,
as well as into blankets. As for pork, neither Spaniard nor Indian
was fond of it. Hogs were raised mainly for their lard, which was
used in soap making, one of the few early California industries.
The padres also raised some flax and hemp in quantities sufficient
for the manufacturing of rope. In general, however, the combination of agriculture and manufacturing was of the rudest sort, in
both the Spanish and Mexican eras.

With the omniscience of hindsight, it seems remarkable today
that two of California's great natural sources of wealth were neglected by its earliest settlers—fur-bearing animals and gold. The
sea otter and the seal swarmed in the coastal waters of California,
but the inhabitants allowed this harvest to be reaped by American
and Russian hunters. And gold, of course, had yet to be discovered.

Pastoral Simplicity on the Ranchos

Life on the ranchos was carried on in accordance with a simple,
patriarchal system. The rancho family was a self-sustained economic and social unit, comparatively isolated from the outside
world. The *ranchero*, the family's major contact with life beyond
the rancho, was the unquestioned master of his estate. He was
implicitly obeyed by both his family and Indian retainers. Yet he
did not generally abuse his authority, for he was, ideally, a born
gentleman—kind-hearted and mild-tempered.

Probably no society ever existed in which a stronger bond linked
the members of a family, particularly parents and children. Families numbered from fifteen to twenty, or even more, to which
were added in-laws and orphans. To undertake the care of an or-
phaned child was considered a privilege rather than a burden. In
spite of its intensely affectionate ties, the family observed strict
discipline; fathers could administer corporal punishment to sons
even sixty years of age, and no son dared smoke in his father's
presence. Children even asked permission to sit down. Dances were
begun by elders, while young people stood by and awaited their
turn. Even where no family relationship existed, older persons
could inflict punishment upon young people when they saw fit.

Rancho life was a blend of abundance—principally in the things
each rancho could produce for itself—and barrenness. Ordinarily,
insufficient supplies of clothing, furniture, and other manufactured

articles existed in California. The mildness of the climate, however, made the scarcity of some of these things easier to bear than would have been the case in colder lands. The ranchero and his family, too, inherited a certain austerity from their Spanish ancestors; when they could not get the shoes, shirts, capes, black silk stockings, *rebozos*, or *mantillas* they wanted, they learned to do without or improvised substitutes. If anyone needed meat or corn he was encouraged to ask a richer neighbor for it and it was freely given, often without mention of price or indebtedness.

The ranchero, though not fond of hard labor, was usually a man of active and rather abstemious habits, arising long before dawn to partake of a slight breakfast of bread and chocolate, then to mount his horse and be off on the daily round of his lands. Evening saw the return of the master, who sometimes had not eaten during the day, and the gathering of this *patron's* large family around a well-laden table.

Food on the rancho was plain but nourishing and plentiful, beef forming the principal dish. Wine was used in moderation. This meat and drink, as well as grain, a little fruit, and certain of the more ordinary vegetables, were all produced by the rancho. Though sometimes beef, wheat, barley, and corn was supplemented by fish and wild game, it is accurate to say that each rancho supplied the basic needs of the people who lived and worked on it.

Housing and Clothing

The houses on the ranchos, as well as those in the towns, were generally square or oblong structures of *adobe* (sun-dried brick), as unadorned on the inside as on the outside. The fact that lumber was not used widely as a building material, in a country so rich in fine timber, is best explained by the absence of sawmills and woodworking tools. Adobe, however, offered advantages in addition to its availability: the dwellings made of it, with their thick walls and spacious rooms, were warm in winter and cool in summer. At first, homes were built on high spots, bare of surrounding trees or bushes, for defense against attacks by the Indians. As this fear receded, the rancheros planted gardens and fruit orchards around the rancho buildings. Interior furnishings, except among the richest persons, were usually confined to the most necessary articles. Those who could afford it, however, bought mahogany furniture made in South America or the Philippines and brought to California by trading ships. Almost every house had its altar for worship and a picture or two of Virgin and Child on the wall.

Even in the poorest homes beds were often covered with intricately designed spreads and pillow cases. The women were skilled seamstresses who took genuine pride in adorning their homes.

The well-to-do ranchero was sometimes quite a dandy. One of these, José Arnaz, describes a fashionable fiesta outfit as including these items:

Shoes of deerskin embroidered with gold or silver threads; breeches of cloth, velvet, or satin reaching to the knee, and open on both sides, bordered with gold braid and silver buttons; vest of velvet, silk, or cloth, and over it a short jacket of blue, black, or green cloth embroidered in gold and silver thread. Add to this outfit a gay sash of red satin bound around the wearer's slender waist, and a wide sombrero with a cord of silver or gold encircling the crown, worn jauntily tipped on one side.

The horse ridden by a ranchero dressed in this manner had to be equipped with almost equal ornateness. Embroidered trappings might nearly cover the animal, with a bridle heavily mounted in solid silver and long stirrups all but sweeping the ground.

In comparison to the dress of the men, that of the women was rather plain—although still colorful. Alfred Robinson, a trader, describes the costume of middle-class females in 1829 as consisting of

a chemise with short embroidered sleeves, richly trimmed with lace, a muslin petticoat flounced with scarlet and secured at the waist by a silk band of the same color, shoes of velvet or blue satin, a cotton *rebozo* or scarf, pearl necklace and earrings, with the hair falling in broad plaits down the back. Others of the higher class dress in English style, and instead of the *rebozo*, substitute a rich and costly shawl of silk or satin.

Such descriptions, of course, emphasize the extremes in rancho dress. Ordinarily, it was much less costly and elaborate. As a matter of fact, fancy attire was not often seen, and fashions varied but little in a culture where clothing remained scarce. It was literally true that a man might wear his grandfather's hat or coat.

Amusements

Of the various forms of entertainment, hunting grizzly bear, elk, and other game was one of the most popular. A grizzly sometimes took many bullets to kill, although he was not always pursued with a gun. Hunters met a grizzly on foot and in single combat, armed only with a long knife and an oxhide shield; as a rule, however, they had the assistance of their constant companions, the horses. The large California elk, extinct today, was also a dangerous animal, and when brought to bay required all the skill and alertness that a man possessed. The perils involved did not deter the women of the ranchos from taking part in hunting too. Some were almost as skillful as men in managing horses and throwing the lasso.

There were also entertainments of a milder sort, especially *meriendas*, or picnics, in which entire communities joined. Young people rode their best horses, while the older ladies and the children were satisfied to climb into clumsy, creaking two-wheeled carts, or *carretas*, to jog along to some grassy picnic place behind the slow oxen, with much chatter and laughter. These *meriendas* featured *carne asada* (roast meat), succulently barbecued on spits over a bed of glistening coals. After roast chickens, turkeys, *enchiladas*, or *tamales* were also disposed of, the rest of the afternoon might be spent in singing and dancing to the music of guitars.

Of all amusements, the dance was most in favor. Every event, public or private, from the birth of a child to the arrival of a new governor, was celebrated with this pastime. Sometimes as many as fifty guests would be accommodated at one rancho for an entertainment which might last for days. For such an occasion steers were killed, and the Indian women pounded corn in *metates* (stone mortars) to make *tortillas* (flat, thin corn cakes). Even in the absence of a special event, it was a rare evening when there were no guests at a ranch house to join the family, old and young, in the *jarabe*, the *fandango*, or any of the numerous other dances.

Pueblo Life

Town or pueblo life, though somewhat more elaborate than that on a remote rancho, consisted of the same round of simple family duties and pleasures, and included the same generous hospitality. A host sometimes carried his attention to a guest so far as to leave a few coins in a dish on a table in the spare room. This was done to save the visitor the embarrassment of asking for money. If the recipient neglected to return such a loan, most hosts politely forgot about it. A traveler who arrived with an exhausted horse found a fresh one ready in the morning, saddled and bridled for his use.

The number of persons who lived in pueblos and on ranchos grew slowly. The entire white population of the province as late as

1848 was an estimated 14,000, divided nearly equally between Californians and foreigners. By "Californian" is meant a person of Spanish birth or background who settled in the province as a resident during either the Spanish or Mexican era. In addition, a small percentage of the Indians, between 3,000 and 4,000, lived in or near the sleepy pueblos; so did perhaps 40 percent of the white population. Although mere hamlets, Los Angeles and Monterey were the social centers of the province.

Yerba Buena, as San Francisco continued to be called during its early years, was even smaller. It had grown up spontaneously on a spot known as *El Parage de Yerba Buena* (literally "the place of the good grass"), taking its name from a weed which grew locally in profusion. The importance of the pueblo, located about three miles from the presidio which defended the area, consisted in the anchorage for ships furnished by its little cove, an anchorage that later became the greatest harbor on the Pacific Coast. On June 25, 1835, William A. Richardson, an English seaman who, thirteen years before, was allowed by Governor Solá to stay on in California, had founded Yerba Buena.

Government of the California pueblos remained in the hands of *alcaldes,* usually under the supervision of a *comisionado* during the Spanish period. This official was a representative of the central government. There were laws against gambling, as well as regulations concerning the manufacture and sale of liquor and the keeping of late hours. A private citizen had to obtain a license before he could give a dance in a town house. The wealthier rancheros owned pueblo dwellings in addition to their ranchos, and divided their time between them.

In the towns bull-and-bear fights, a form of entertainment somewhat varied from that of old Spain, were popular. These blood-curdling events were generally conducted in an improvised arena of the public plaza, sometimes in front of the local church. A trapped bear was tied by one foot to a bull, after which the two beasts fought it out until one or the other was killed. The people gambled on the outcome. Cock fighting and horse racing afforded the Californians other ways to wager money or goods, including fine clothes. Most, including the Indians, were inveterate gamblers.

The dress in the pueblo tended to be somewhat more fashionable than on the rancho. Don Tomás Yorba, a gentleman ranchero who spent much time in town, wore a black silk handkerchief on his head, the corners of which hung down behind his neck. He also wore fine felt hats and sported an embroidered shirt, a cravat of white jaconet (a thin, cotton fabric), tastefully tied, a blue damask vest, short breeches of crimson velvet, and a bright green cloth jacket with large silver buttons. His shoes were made of embroidered deerskin. With his sword hanging by his side, he was every inch the Spanish *caballero*. On feast days, the cost of his personal regalia might exceed a thousand United States dollars.

Education, Health, and Public Morals

Despite the efforts of various governors to encourage education, provincial schools were limited in number and quality. School was sometimes held in empty granaries or in barracks. Among the teachers were superannuated soldiers, whose only qualification was some knowledge of reading, writing, and "figuring." Their chief instructional assistant was the *disciplina*, a sort of cat-o'-nine-tails, which was liberally applied to youngsters. Despite the discouraging conditions in public schools, ambitious young men managed to acquire some additional education through private instruction from priests, military officers, and especially foreigners. In the Mexican period the best-known foreign teacher was William E. P. Hartnell, a respected English trader who was also a scholar with a thorough knowledge of half a dozen languages. He settled near Salinas and regularly taught his own and his neighbors' children.

Working within the limits of a pastoral, decentralized society, the California governors could provide no better facilities for maintaining public health than they could for education. A surgeon, usually a graduate of a Spanish medical school, was in residence at the presidio of the capital, but California boasted few other doctors. Nevertheless, the health of the people was remarkably good, and astounding longevity was sometimes recorded. At a time when medicine was still in a relatively primitive state, even in Europe, California probably would not have benefited greatly from the arrival of more doctors. Its major health asset was a salubrious climate, combined with the moderate labor and open-air amusements in which most of the people participated.

Theft, murder, and other crimes were relatively rare in provincial California. Foreign sea captains would sometimes sell goods to rancheros along the coast on credit and return months later to receive their pay in hides and tallow. Banditry, except by Indians, was reputedly unknown until after the beginning of American occupation. The bandit Joaquín Murieta was said to have ascribed his criminal career to brutal treatment on the part of American miners, an alibi that seems plausible, if difficult to verify. "The era of crime in California," wrote J. M. Guinn, a local historian, "began with the discovery of gold." Though the statement is extreme, there is some evidence that crime was at a minimum during the Spanish and Mexican periods.

The missions, of course, played a part, at least initially, in the maintenance of law and order. With their extensive activities and control of society, the padres did much to stabilize California's provincial life. Baptisms, confirmations, marriages, and other vital ceremonies were, of course, performed at the missions. Even wedding dinners were held there. The missions also served as a sort of hospice for wayfarers, who could almost always count on a night's lodging. Mission accommodations were of the barest sort—usually consisting of a bed of rawhide, scratchy flaxen sheets, and the meals, cooked by Indian servants, were simple in the extreme. The warmth of greeting, however, often made up for the discomforts, and on a stormy night, as the wind whipped across mission tile roofs, travelers were thankful for the fragrant pine logs burning in their fireplace grates.

The Heritage of Spain

Modern California still retains many cultural reminders of its provincial, pastoral era. As in every part of the Western Hemisphere in which Spain planted its characteristic civilization, it left its imprint too in the institutions and language of California. Rivers, mountains, and towns often are known today by names that originated with the Spaniards; and a number of social, religious, economic, and architectural terms are of similar origin. Words growing out of the Spanish heritage include *adobe,* or sun-dried brick; *arroyo,* a creek or its dry bed; *cañada,* a deep valley; *cañón,* a narrow passage between high banks; *chaparral,* a thicket of low, brambly bushes; *corral,* an enclosure for livestock; *embarcadero,* a landing place; *fiesta,* a celebration; *placer,* a place where gold is found free in the loose earth; *plaza,* an open square in a town; *pueblo,* a chartered town; *rancho,* land used primarily for pasturage; *rodéo,* a round-up of cattle for branding; *sierra,* literally a saw, but frequently applied to a range of saw-toothed mountains; *tule,* water reed; *vaquero,* cowboy. This list might be greatly extended. (Some of these terms from Spanish have been anglicized: *cañón,* for example, usually takes the form *canyon.*)

Spanish place names are especially thickly clustered in the long, narrow strip of land between the Coast Range and the sea. They thin out markedly to the east, indicating clearly the limits of Spanish settlement. The frequent use of the prefix *San* and *Santa* (Saint) indicates the religious character of the first occupation, though in general, rather than piety, variety characterizes the names chosen by soldiers. Place names were first applied to the most striking natural features—the rivers, creeks, bays, mountains, and capes.

One of the earliest place names bestowed by the Spaniards was that of the bay of Monterey, so called in honor of Viceroy Gaspar de Zúñiga y Acevedo, Count of Monterey in Mexico. The Merced River was first called *El Río de Nuestra Señora de la Merced* (the river of Our Lady of Mercy) by Moraga's exploring party of 1806, as an expression of their gratitude at the sight of its waters after an exhausting march through dry country. The same expedition named Mariposa Creek after the butterflies found on its banks; and it was Moraga, too, who in 1808 named the Sacramento River (after the Holy Sacrament).

Among California's counties, Mendocino was named after Antonio de Mendoza, first viceroy of New Spain; the term was first applied to the cape, probably by the crews of ships coming from the Philippines. Several counties were given the names of missions —San Diego, San Luis Obispo, Santa Clara. Other counties, like Merced and Sacramento, took the names of their principal streams. Among these is also Kings County (from *El Río de los Santos Reyes*, or river of the Holy Kings). Fresno (ash) County was named after the abundance of those trees in the region, and Madera (timber) County after the forests which covered its valleys. The origin of the name of Plumas (feathers) County has already been noted. Many of these counties, of course, contain cities of the same name.

A few towns and cities bear the names of prominent early Californians. Martinez takes its name from the Martínez family. Suñol was christened for the owner of one of the most beautiful valleys in the state. The town of Vacaville commemorates the Vaca family. Alviso bears the name of one of the Anza colonists, and Benicia that of the wife of General Vallejo; the town of Vallejo honors the memory of Don Mariano himself.

Many California street names are of similar historical origin. There is an Alvarado Street, named after a prominent Mexican governor, in both Monterey and Los Angeles. One of the main streets of the latter city. Figueroa, honors another governor of the Mexican period, and dozens of other Los Angeles street names also commemorate the past—among them Pico, Los Angeles, San Pedro, Aliso, and Sepulveda. In San Francisco, there is a Junipero

Serra Boulevard, as well as streets named Noriega, Pacheco, Ortega, Rivera, Taraval, Ulloa, Guerrero, Valencia, and Palou. Oakland has two main avenues with Spanish names—Alcatraz
(pelican) and San Pablo (Saint Paul). Santa Barbara has rigorously restored its Spanish street names which had fallen into
disuse; no city in California, in fact, clings more strongly to its colonial past, including its many red-tiled and white-washed buildings.

Spanish place names and architecture, however, are only the
most conspicuous reminders of the past. Many other aspects of
California life also bear vestiges of earlier practices. The California
legal system retains a number of Spanish provisions, especially
concerning mining, water rights, trespass regulations, tribunals of
conciliation, and the property rights of women. In regard to water
rights, Spanish riparian law became the basis of municipal claims,
which Los Angeles pressed into the twentieth century, as did San
Diego.

Many social and religious customs also have become a part of
modern California life. The love of a fiesta still seems to come
naturally to Californians. Pageants and plays commemorating the
Spanish past include the Mission Play of San Gabriel, the Portolá
Festival of San Francisco, the "De Anza days" celebration at Riverside, and a yearly "Spanish" fiesta at Santa Barbara. In these
events colonial dress is worn by the participants, who are often
descendants of Spanish-Californians. In cookery too, Spanish colonial dishes, including *tamales, enchiladas,* and *tortillas,* are
widely consumed.

It is, of course, possible to exaggerate California's Hispanic inheritance. This cultural background has largely been submerged
by the advance of the Anglo-American frontier, yet one cannot
deny the heritage. For example, in this age of the television western one should not forget that the cowboy inherited his know-how,
horse, outfit (including reata, spurs, chaps and lasso), and lingo
largely from the Spanish era. Lingering aspects of the Hispanic
past are also to be found in the very faces of Californians of Spanish background, in their names, customs, and local ordinances.
With the best of intentions there is also considerable public genu-
flection to and exploitation of Spanish colonial history by sentimental antiquarians, genealogists, artists, architects, historical
societies, and tourist promoters.

At San Juan Bautista, the state has tastefully re-created a mission pueblo. With today's focus on refurbishing our "inner cities,"
communities like San Francisco, Los Angeles, and San Diego are
attempting to preserve the few authentic remnants of their Arcadian past.

SELECTED READINGS

Basic sources for the study of Spanish-Mexican society in California are William Heath Davis' books *Sixty Years in California* (San Francisco, 1889) and *Seventy-Five Years in California* (San Francisco, 1929). See also Andrew F. Rolle, *An American in California: The Biography of William Heath Davis, 1822–1909* (San Marino, 1956). Two Yankees who came to California wrote fascinating accounts of their stay: Richard Henry Dana, *Two Years Before the Mast* (New York, 1840), a minor American classic, and Richard J. Cleveland, *Narrative of Voyages and Commercial Enterprises* (2 vols., Cambridge, 1842). Perhaps the most perceptive analysis of Dana's *Two Years Before the Mast* is in D. H. Lawrence's *Studies in Classic American Literature* (New York, 1923). There is a somewhat unsympathetic biography of Dana by Samuel Shapiro entitled *Richard Henry Dana Jr., 1815–1882* (East Lansing, Mich., 1961).

See the useful reminiscences of José Arnaz, published as "Memoirs of a Merchant," in *Touring Topics*, XX (September–October, 1928), 14–19, 47–48, and those of Guadalupe Vallejo, "Ranch and Mission Days in Alta California," *Century* Magazine, XLI (1809–1891), 183–192. These are primary materials. One can also consult such romantic treatments as Nellie Van de Grift Sánchez, *Spanish Arcadia* (Los Angeles, 1929), Gertrude Atherton, *Before the Gringo Came* (New York, 1894), and the more popular revision of the latter, *The Splendid Idle Forties* (New York, 1902). See too Tirey L. Ford, *Dawn of the Dons* (San Francisco, 1926), as well as John Steven McGroarty's overly romanticized *California: Its History and Romance* (Los Angeles, 1911), in addition to Charles F. Lummis, *The Spanish Pioneers* (Chicago, 1893), and another of his hispanophile volumes, *Flowers of Our Lost Romance* (Boston, 1929).

Other appraisals include Hubert Howe Bancroft's *California Pastoral* (San Francisco, 1888), and Alberta J. Denis, *Spanish Alta California* (New York, 1927). Useful also are Susanna Bryant Dakin's *A Scotch Paisano: Hugo Reid's Life in California* (Berkeley, 1939) and *The Lives of William Hartnell* (Stanford, 1949). Medicine is described in George D. Lyman, *The Scalpel Under Three Flags in California* (San Francisco, 1925). An excellent reminiscence which unfortunately lacks an index is *The Blond Ranchero: Memories of Juan Francisco Dana*, as told to Rocky and Marie Harrington (Los Angeles, 1960). These books all overlap into the Mexican period, which is described more thoroughly in subsequent chapters; other bibliographical materials are suggested there.

10

Mexican California

After three centuries of dominance by the motherland, the Spanish colonies in the New World grew steadily more restive under what they considered to be an unjust system of economic, governmental, and social discrimination. Discontent kindled the flame of revolution, which spread from province to province in the years between 1808 and the middle 1820's. Almost to the last, Upper California, one of the most isolated of all Spain's provinces, remained loyal. This was partly because little news reached provincial California of revolutionary activities in Mexico and elsewhere in Latin America. Pablo Solá, last of California's Spanish governors, was an aristocrat who looked upon revolutionary activities farther south as the work of misguided fanatics. As late as 1822, he wrote emotionally to Luís Antonio Argüello: "The immortal Spanish nation has many and great resources with which to make herself respected." Possession of an effective armed garrison in California, with which to protect the province, was never one of these resources. Although intractably opposed to talk of independence, Solá was an apparently honest governor, interested in the welfare of California and skillful in managing its affairs.

The first significant manifestation of discontent in California occurred, as has been noted, when, after 1808, ships from San Blas failed to arrive in sufficient number to supply the populace. Increasing revolutionary attacks against Spanish ships aggravated the situation, so that fewer and fewer were able to visit the California ports. Along with the American and Russian trading ships which helped supply the gap, a number of privateers began to appear in the Pacific, some fitted out in the United States; these roamed the high seas, ravaging the ships and shoreline of Spain's colonies. News of the blockade of the South American Pacific colonial ports of Valparaíso, Callao, and Guayaquil by revolutionists and privateeers created considerable worry in California. Therefore Solá ordered a stricter watch along the shore for the approach of suspicious vessels. Although Californians made complaints against the viceroy in Mexico City for his failure to send supplies to the settlers and back pay to the soldiers, they had no initial thought of resisting his authority or that of Governor Solá. They were more concerned with their fear of restless pirates.

Bouchard's Visit to California

In November, 1818, two mysterious ships were sighted by a sentinel at Point Pinos on the coast near Monterey. The larger of the two vessels, the *Argentina*, was commanded by a Frenchman, Hippolyte de Bouchard, who had served in the patriot navy of the new "Republic of Buenos Aires." He was a big and brutal captain of fiery temper, who exercised an iron rule over his men. The other vessel, smaller in size, was the *Santa Rosa*. It was under the command of an English soldier of fortune named Peter Corney, whom Bouchard had picked up in Hawaii while Bouchard was trading gold chalices, silver crucifixes, and other valuables looted from churches throughout Latin America. Bouchard's crews were a motley lot of some 350 cutthroats, thieves, and revolutionists; among them were Malays, Portuguese, Spaniards, Englishmen, and Australians—all aiming to profit from the upset condition of the Spanish empire.

When the smaller of Bouchard's privateers, the *Santa Rosa*, dropped anchor in front of the Presidio of Monterey (with its eight dilapidated cannon), the "visitors" looked decidedly formidable. The *Santa Rosa* opened fire on the presidio. Corney and his crew, expecting little resistance, were surprised at the brisk return of cannon balls from the battery hastily established on the beach by the presidio's forty soldiers. Then Bouchard moved in with the *Argentina*, and sent ashore a flag of truce, along with a formal demand for the immediate surrender of Monterey expressed in the following peremptory terms:

To the *comandante* of the port of Monterey.

DEAR SIR: Since the King of Spain has declared "bloody war" on the Americans who do not wish to exist under his dominion, these same

Americans have to make defense by waging war on land and sea. They make war with all the seriousness of purpose and with all the rights of nations. Therefore, having crossed the Pacific Ocean to this coast, I now desire the surrender of your city with all the furniture and other belongings of the King. If you do not do so, the city will be reduced to cinders, and also the other surrounding villages. It is within my power to bring about this destruction. You may evade all the above spilling of blood by agreeing to my proposal. If so, I shall desist from what I say. Be good enough to reply to me as soon as possible. May God keep you many years.

Hippolyte de Bouchard.

Argentina, November 23, 1818.

Bouchard received a defiant reply to this message from Governor Solá, although the Californians had practically no means of resisting Bouchard. The pirate then landed several hundred men and a number of field pieces in the cove near Point Pinos, afterwards known as "the Beach of the Insurgents." Greatly outnumbered, Solá retreated, with a supply of munitions and the provincial archives, to the Rancho del Rey, near the present site of Salinas.

At Monterey wild excitement prevailed among the population, and many of the townspeople fled by night in haste and confusion. Some took refuge at Missions San Antonio and San Juan Bautista until conditions should permit their return to the capital. While the inhabitants were away the invaders sacked and burned both the presidio and town of Monterey. Few buildings escaped. Even orchards and gardens were destroyed.

Concerning the conduct of his crew during this pillage Peter Corney later wrote: "The Sandwich Islanders, who were quite naked when they landed, were soon dressed in the Spanish fashion; and all the sailors were employed in searching the houses for money and breaking and ruining everything." Something over a week was spent by the attackers in burying their dead, caring for their wounded, and repairing the *Santa Rosa*. They also made efforts to win over to their cause those of the inhabitants who had the courage to remain in the pueblo; but such propaganda, ostensibly promoting the cause of liberty, failed to impress a people whose homes had been despoiled.

After replenishing their larders, the *Argentina* and the *Santa Rosa* set sail on November 27, and Governor Solá returned to Monterey. The privateers next moved down the coast, stopping at various points on the way to burn and pillage. Rancho del Refugio was burned in revenge, so says Corney, for the loss of three pirates, who were lassoed and ignominiously dragged off by a party of *vaqueros*. San Juan Capistrano was one of the places sacked and robbed, especially of its store of wines and spirits, much of which immediately went down the throats of the pillagers. After taking two apparently willing Indian girls aboard to brighten their voyage, the pirates sailed south from that mission, and California was finally relieved of their presence.

This attack by Bouchard constitutes California's only active contact with outside revolutionists during the Spanish-American wars of independence. Once Bouchard left the province, life in California resumed its usual calmness; not long afterwards, events of great importance to the New World occurred in Mexico. In February, 1821, Agustín Iturbide, a colonel in the royal army in Mexico City, suddenly defected to the insurgent cause, raised a revolutionary flag, promulgated his later famous *Plan de Iguala*, and made New Spain independent. In September he took possession of the city, established an empire, and instituted a regency with himself in command.

The Beginning of Mexican Control

When news reached California of the astounding seizure of political control in Mexico, it was at first received with disbelief. In April, 1822, however, Governor Solá convened a *junta*, or caucus— consisting of officers from the presidios and padres from the missions—and swore allegiance to the new government. Former royal officials and some of the padres took an oath to Iturbide without undue hesitation, although the friars surely sensed that a non-royal government in Mexico would lead to an inevitable decline of the mission system. California's officialdom obviously acceded to Mexican control because they believed this act did not necessarily imperil future rule by the King of Spain if a truce were ever arranged between American colonials and the Crown. Also, the Californians had to face the fact that a new government was in actual control at Mexico City.

The California junta chose Solá as its delegate to the new Mexican *Cortés*, or congress. Before the governor could even leave for Mexico City, however, an official arrived at Monterey from that capital to preside over the transfer of authority from Spain to Mexico. Aware of California's royalist sympathies, this agent of the new regime, a worldly cleric named Agustín Fernández de San Vicente, canon of the Cathedral of Durango, arrived in a ship that flew a green, white, and red flag from its masthead. The eagle in the flag's center, the well-known symbol of Mexico, indicated to

the Californians who lined the Monterey docks to receive Fernández
that royalist rule was over. Solá's control over California had
clearly ended, although he, perforce, accepted the new government.

Soon thereafter the red and gold imperial banner of Spain had
to be lowered from atop the Presidio of Monterey. Cries of *Viva la
indepencia mexicana!* now dutifully rang out from the assembled
multitude. Almost before Commissioner Fernández could oversee
the establishment of a provincial legislative body, Iturbide (who
had quickly established his title as Emperor Agustín I) fell from
power. With that event began a succession of regimes under a new
and weak Mexican Republic, created on November 19, 1823. Almost like a mirror, California for decades to come would reflect
the basic vacillation of political power that gripped Mexico.

Succeeding Solá was California's first popularly chosen governor, Luís Antonio Argüello, a native Californian who was serving
as commander of the port of San Francisco. Argüello announced
that the decrees of the Mexican government would be accepted and
the title *nacional* would be substituted for *imperial* in all documents; public and private letters were thereafter to be signed with
the words "God and Liberty," and the old title *Don* was to give
way to *Ciudadano*, or citizen.

Such exterior signs of allegiance, and the various revolutions
that followed within Mexico, altered but little the political beliefs
of Californians. They remained more aloof than most other provincials within the former Spanish empire and continued to distrust foreigners, remembering with affection the Spanish pioneers
from Cabrillo to Serra who had first planted the flag of Castile on
California soil.

The change of the province's status was followed by the usual
aftermath of revolution—a long period of unrest. California was
fortunate in having been so far from the vortex of the struggle,
and lucky also to have received independence from Spain without
the fratricidal bloodletting which drenched Mexico's soil for many
years. Yet the province did not entirely escape the political turbulence and personal rivalries that afflicted the other Spanish colonies following their separation from the homeland. Scarcely a
California governor during the Mexican period served his term
unharassed by conspiratorial outbreaks against him. The bonds
that connected California with Mexico were even looser than those
with Spain had been, and no very violent jolts were required to
break them. The distance and the difficulty of communication,
feelings of resentment against Mexican power, and strong local
pride all encouraged the growth of sectionalism; Californians
identified themselves with California, not Mexico.

Argüello's Government

Luís Antonio Argüello served under three different Mexican authorities: Iturbide's regency, his "empire," and government by a constitutional congress. Argüello, who came from northern California, had been chosen governor over a prominent southerner, José de la Guerra. This circumstance began a rift between north and south, at first scarcely perceptible, which continued for decades. Working under the direction of Fernández de San Vicente, the cleric sent from Mexico to oversee California's new government, Argüello established a *diputación*, or legislative body, sometimes called a *junta* in California. This consisted of six representatives, one from each presidio and pueblo district.

Mexico's most distant new province now found itself without adequate funds to carry on its government. The demands for money seemed unending. The governor had to supervise the pueblos; he had to see to it that a *diputado* (deputy) was sent to Mexico City; he had to repair the roads, support schools, feed troops, and control the Indians. To help solve the money problem Governor Argüello in January, 1824, convened another assemblage at Monterey. This junta was composed of prominent citizens who were supposed to represent the military, civil, and clerical phases of California life. There were, however, no Franciscan friars, although the new taxes which California's government had to levy were bound to affect the missions. According to the provisions enacted by the body, local crops as well as all branded cattle were to be taxed as never before—at least officially, though these provisions were not always fully enforced. Fortunately the revolution in Mexico had removed some restrictions on trade with foreign vessels, thus opening a source of revenue for the collection of new customs duties on exports and imports.

One element remained lacking in the general approval of the new measures made necessary in California by a changed political situation. This was the cooperation of the missionaries. When the padres heard of the plans to tax the missions, they vigorously protested that these historic establishments, founded to care for the Indians, in fact belonged to the natives and were thus untaxable. Since the missions, however, held much of the best land in the province, to exempt them would have deprived the new government of a major means of support. Whether they liked it or not, the padres were destined to put up with increased surveillance over their operations. But compliance in full with regulations of the new California government violated, according to the friars, prior obligations of fidelity to the King of Spain. They feared that the new Mexican Republic would become a duplicate of postrevolutionary France, which had ruthlessly expelled its clerics from public life.

Despite the protests of the missionaries, their activities were not restricted in California. Some members of the new political *diputación* believed that the attitude of the friars merited rebuke, even that the management of the rich missions should be taken from them. While no direct steps toward secularization occurred during Argüello's administration, there were straws in the strong winds that blew out of Mexico which suggested that missionary rule might be nearing its end.

With or without the cooperation of the missionaries, Argüello's new government had a number of serious administrative problems to settle. The second junta that the governor convened also decided to maintain a professional military force of 290 men, as well as a militia to be composed of males between the ages of eighteen and fifty. *Alcaldes* were still to administer civil justice, with appeals to the governor being permitted. Criminal trials were to be by courts-martial, but sentences in these cases were to be executed as soon as pronounced—in order to avoid defeat of justice by legal delays. Almost as a matter of necessity the Californians were setting up their own new government. The Mexican Cortés, inefficient and inexperienced, was preoccupied with political and economic matters much closer to itself.

Increasing Foreign Activity

During Argüello's relatively stable governorship, there arrived in California increasingly large numbers of foreigners—both traders and settlers, and a number of people who were both. Although the new authorities of the province had inherited much of Spain's suspicion against strangers, the revolutionary atmosphere tended to modify their attitude and to bring about somewhat more liberal policies.

Argüello had been friendly with the Russians since the days when Rezanov had courted his beautiful sister, Concepción; and the Russians had long desired to enter into a partnership for fur hunting and trading with the Californians. As governor, Argüello signed a contract with the Russians which furnished his government with Aleut hunters, who were in return to be fed and supplied by the Californians. The Aleuts hunted in small skin canoes called *bidarkas*. The product of their hunt was equally divided; up to October, 1824, the share of the California government was 677 skins. This official hunting was done chiefly in San Francisco Bay, which still swarmed with sea otter, but it was also carried on as far south as San Pedro.

There was increasing acceptance, too, of English and American trading enterprises. In keeping with a former Spanish tradition of provisioning frontier outposts through foreign traders licensed by the government, California's padres now signed an agreement with the English partnership of McCulloch and Hartnell, a sub-sidiary of the firm of John Begg and Company, today purveyors of Scotch whiskey. Hugh McCulloch and William E. P. Hartnell came to California from Lima in 1822. Under their new contract they were allowed to bring at least one cargo a year to the prov-ince and take out all the hides the missions had to offer for $1.00 each, as well as suet, lard, tallow, wheat, wine, furs, and pickled beef. Known as "Macala y Arnel" to the Californians, the com-pany had entered into an agreement that legalized future Yankee trading in California and officially launched the prosperous hide and tallow traffic.

In the same year Henry Gyzelaar and William A. Gale, already well acquainted with the coast as smugglers, arrived in the ship *Sachem* from Boston and initiated the American side of the new hide and tallow trade. Gale, like his companion, was a trading supercargo, or roving merchant, representing a Boston trading syndicate; following the eventual secularization of the missions, however, ambitious Yankee middlemen—including Nathan Spear, William Heath Davis, Jr., John R. Cooper, Alfred Robinson, and Abel Stearns—replaced such supercargoes. The new group became mostly resident merchants, distributing their goods on land as well as from aboard ships. These trading arrangements especially pleased rancheros, for they were no longer dependent upon the uncertain arrival of government supply vessels. Ship captains also found the new system financially advantageous. They could now load and unload their vessels at central collecting points, rather than at numerous secret landfalls scattered up and down the coast.

One especially large Boston firm, Bryant, Sturgis and Company, maintained a chain of ship plying the sea lanes between that har-bor, California, Hawaii, and China. With Gale as its resident agent, this firm alone carried probably half a million hides from Cali-fornia to New England's shoe industry. Other sizable Boston firms included Marshall & Wildes and William Appleton & Company, both of which kept regular vessels trading on the coast. Stocked with hundreds of commodities, from silk stockings to tobacco, these were veritable floating commissaries.

For the purpose of trading with these vessels, rancheros brought great quantities of hides in a "green" state, or at best carelessly dried, from the interior. The smelly skins were soaked in sea water by hide "droghers," really working traders. Then the hides were stretched on the ground and pegged fast with wooden stakes. When they were dry the "droghers," local Indians, or Kanaka sailors from Hawaii would sprinkle them with salt, scrape them, and fold them lengthwise with the hair out. Next the skins were packed into the holds of the Yankee ships offshore, some of which held as many as 30,000 hides. Floated out to the ships beyond the surf went also the large cowhide bags filled with melted tallow.

During this period—from the middle 1820's to the outbreak of the Mexican War in 1846 — California added numerous Yankee traders to its population. Heretofore most of the foreigners landing on the shores of California had been visitors. After a short period of trading, their vessels had usually raised anchor and sailed away. Now a different type of outsider began to arrive largely as a result of the 1824 act passed by the Mexican Congress which promised security of person and property to foreigners settling in California and obeying its laws. Such traders took advantage of this virtual invitation to conduct business regularly in California; many settled in the province, married daughters of the country, and founded families. One of these men was John R. Cooper, who arrived in California in 1823 as captain of the American ship *Rover* and settled at Monterey. With Cooper came Daniel Hill and Thomas Robbins of Massachusetts, who decided to make their homes at Santa Barbara. David Spence, an Englishman, came to California from Lima to superintend the packing of hides, beef, and tallow for Begg and Company; like Cooper, he settled at Monterey, where he married into a leading California family. His countryman was William A. Richardson, who arrived in Yerba Buena on the English whaler *Orion*. Richardson was later baptized in the Catholic Church, married the daughter of the *comandante* of the port, and became a key figure in the settlement of that pueblo.

Among the many foreigners who came to play an increasing role in California affairs, however, the most prominent group was composed of the dozens of "warm-water Yankee" traders as distinguished from the "cold-water Yankees" of the eastern seabord. These California-bound traders reaped rich rewards from the marketing of their all-year stock of goods. Almost everyone, in fact, profited from their activities—except, occasionally, the Mexican customs collectors whose regulations the traders were expert at avoiding. Long before the Gold Rush a whole generation of pre-pioneer Americans in California enriched themselves and came to be, in part, the managers of California's destiny. They quickly acquired a thorough knowledge of the province, established the friendliest relations with its people, and made themselves indispensable in the exchange of the necessities and luxuries of life. These Yankees, who settled California long before the first overland parties crossed the plains, deserve more attention than they have received at the hands of historians. They came to represent in their own persons a blending of California's Spanish and Anglo-American cultures.

The Indian Revolt of 1824

Before he left office Argüello had to deal with an Indian disturbance of substantial proportions. Although there had been occasional uprisings in the past, the natives were so disunited that no general Indian revolt had ever occurred. Association with white men, however, gradually taught the Indians to appreciate the value of union, as well as to use firearms. In February, 1824, a revolt started simultaneously among the neophytes of Missions Purísima Concepción, Santa Inés, and Santa Barbara.

The cause is obscure, but it probably followed some outrage perpetrated upon the natives. Soldiers at Santa Inés, attacked by the Indians without warning, were surprised to find their assailants well armed. The Indians set fire to the mission buildings, partly destroying them; but when Sergeant Anastasio Carrillo arrived with reinforcements from Santa Barbara, the attackers yielded. At Purísima there was a more determined fight. After seven Indians and four whites had been killed, the mission guards were compelled to surrender. Later, following a parley, they were allowed to go to Santa Inés but the rebel Indians kept possession of the mission for nearly a month. At Purísima the rebels erected palisade fortifications, cutting loopholes in the church walls and mounting two rusty cannon hitherto used only during fiestas. But their inexperience in handling both guns and powder quickly brought about their defeat when they were attacked by Lieutenant José Mariano Estrada and a force of one hundred men. At Santa Barbara, Indians also entrenched themselves in the mission buildings, from which they fired both guns and arrows. *Comandante* de la Guerra attacked them there, and after a fight of several hours the Indians fled to the hills, taking with them all the property they could carry. Several succeeding expeditions were, however, required finally to quell the revolt. In mid-1825 Argüello reported to the Mexican government regarding the miserable state of the Indians, calling attention also to the injustice of keeping them any longer in virtual slavery.

Though considerable progress was made in California affairs during Argüello's term of office, his administration was never more than provisional, filling the time until Mexico appointed a regular governor. In October, 1825, Argüello retired to private life. Under him the change to Mexican rule had been quietly accepted by the people, a plan of local administration had been inaugurated, and a beginning had been made at representative government. Official commerce with foreign nations had also been initiated. But an era of revolution and unrest was about to open. California had exchanged the paternalistic, conservative regime of Spain for the unsettled sovereignty of Mexico. Governmental instability resulted in factional fights over such concepts as liberalism versus conservatism and federalism versus centralism—whose complications the citizenry scarcely understood. Continual disturbances followed, which were to terminate only with the stabilization of political control under United States rule.

Echeandía's Administration

José María Echeandía, Argüello's successor, was a lieutenant colonel of engineers, described as a "tall, thin, juiceless man, possessing but little enterprise or force of character, and much concerned about the effect of the California climate upon his not too robust health." At first Echeandía so feared the foggy weather at Monterey and northward that he came no farther into California than San Diego, where he summoned Argüello to meet him and surrender his authority. As commander of both Californias, Echeandía claimed that the southern town was more centrally located for transacting the business of the two provinces. Nothing in his instructions required this hypochondriac to live at Monterey, so he was acting within his rights in conducting California affairs from the city of his choice. Though no formal transfer of the capital was made, most southerners were delighted by Echeandía's residence at San Diego, while the natives of Monterey were correspondingly offended. Jealousy between north and south gained momentum from this affair, and the new governor started out handicapped by great unpopularity in northern California. A rivalry between Echeandía, who was a bachelor, and the young American sea captain Henry Delano Fitch for the hand of Señorita Josefa Carrillo of San Diego indicates that a romantic motive as well as reasons of health may have had something to do with Echeandía's stay there.

A more pressing question facing Echeandía on his arrival was that of supplies for the soldiers and their families, who had to be clothed and fed. The missions were the traditional source for these necessities, but the friars no longer gave willing support to local authorities. The padres were growing uncomfortable as they became aware of a rapidly increasing distrust of them and of other persons of Spanish birth in a revolutionary and secularist Mexico. Only with difficulty was Echeandía able to persuade the missionaries to furnish the needed food and clothing. Without such help the governor would have been at a loss; like most of California's governors during this period, he was plagued by lack of funds.

The financial state of the province, in fact, led to much resentment on the part of Californians toward the Mexican government that Echeandía represented, and to considerable ill feeling between California-born and Mexican residents — tensions that were to result eventually in a political break. For one thing, some of the California soldiers had not been paid for years. Once they saw that they were no better off than before Echeandía's arrival, they tended to blame him for their continuing misery. In 1828 part of the garrison at Monterey actually revolted. These troops were, however, persuaded by Romualdo Pacheco, a tactful young soldier-engineer who had gone north with the governor, to return to their duties. The more hostile of the mission padres likewise stirred up adverse sentiment against Governor Echeandía. Foreign residents seem to have joined in the controversy; some contributed occasional funds to encourage public ferment.

In 1829, this opposition to Echeandía was forcefully expressed by Joaquín Solís, a former convict, and José María Herrera, who had been sent to the province from Mexico as a governmental financial agent. Together they issued a *pronunciamento* accusing California's governor of tyrannical behavior toward the populace. Solís and Herrera led a "revolution," which symbolically began at Monterey; this movement was hardly more than a strike by the soldiers for their pay, but it extended as far south as Santa Barbara. After it subsided Solís and some of his fellow conspirators were arrested and sent to San Blas, where they were, however, set free. So ended the first of a series of minor uprisings against Mexican authority in the province, conflicts of *pronunciamientos* rather than of guns.

The Mexican government's practice of sending troublesome criminals to California was another circumstance that had much to do with the antagonistic feeling between Californians and Mexicans. Whenever government ships brought convicts, there was trouble in the northern districts. About the time of the collapse of the Solís rebellion eighty convicts arrived, and in spite of local protests, they were put ashore at Santa Cruz Island, giving them a few cattle and some fish hooks with which to maintain life. After experiencing a devastating fire, the convicts built rafts and made their way back to Carpinteria, below Santa Barbara.

In July, 1830, a vessel arrived from Mexico with fifty more criminals. No attempt was made to confine this batch, and they were distributed throughout the territory under the surveillance of local authorities. Echeandía was blamed for their arrival, although he had protested against it. At his suggestion California's *diputación* voted to request Mexico not to send any more such colonists to the territory. The practice of sending criminals by the shipload ceased, although many cor.tinued to enter the province as soldiers, an affront that outraged the Californians.

During Echeandía's administration another Indian outbreak also bedeviled the unlucky governor. The leader of this revolt of 1829, Chief Estanislao, put up an even more vigorous fight than had the rebellious Solís. Estanislao had at one time been *alcalde* of San José. Dissatisfied with conditions there, he ran away and joined a band of wild Indian renegades in the San Joaquín Valley. They fortified themselves in a dense wood and sent out defiant challenges. That summer, forty of Echeandía's soldiers, armed with muskets and a swivel gun, found the rebels. The Indians killed two of the soldiers and wounded eight others; the rest were forcd to abandon the siege when their ammunition ran out and the heat became insufferable. Estanislao's Indians were elated by the victory, and held a celebration with feasting and dancing to which neighboring Indian *rancherías*, or villages, were invited.

Because the uprising threatened to become widespread, Echeandía planned a counterattack. He sent against the Indians a force of one hundred men, a large army for the time and place—consisting of cavalry, infantry, and artillery—under Mariano Guadalupe Vallejo, commander in chief of the military forces of California. Vallejo's troops were met by a cloud of arrows. Since the woods in which the Indians hid were impenetrable, Vallejo set them on fire, forcing the Indians to the edge of the thicket. Although many were shot down by this strategy, Vallejo's reconnoitering revealed a series of Indian pits and ditches protected by barricades of trees. Entrenched behind these fortifications were more Indians. The Californians brought up cannon, but the Indians did not yield immediately. They were finally driven from the entrenchments, firing as they withdrew. In the darkness of the following night many escaped, including Estanislao. He took refuge with Father Narciso Durán, president of the missions, who concealed the Indian chieftain until a pardon was obtained from the governor.

Beechey and Du Haut-Cilly

Not the least important of the events of Echeandía's time were the visits of some notable foreigners. On November 6, 1826, the British ship *Blossom*, having just completed a year's cruise in the North Pacific and Arctic Oceans, sailed into San Francisco Bay under the command of Captain F. W. Beechey. A comparison of Beechey's description of the place with that of Vancouver shows that surprisingly few changes had occurred in the surroundings— and those in the direction of decay rather than improvement. Beechey commented, for example, on the ruinous condition of the fort on the bluff, seemingly ready to topple over the precipice into the sea. Like others before him, he was struck with the contrast between the natural advantages of the country and the lack of enterprise of its residents. Captain Beechey also observed real discontent among all classes, and he predicted that the Mexicans could not hold the land. Many of the friars, he noted, dreaded the worst, and would willingly have quit the country. "Some of them were ingenious and clever men," wrote Beechey, "but they had been so long excluded from the civilized world that their ideas and their politics, like the maps pinned against the wall, bore the date of 1772, as near as I could read for fly specks." Beechey's visit had no special significance in itself, but is important for the accurate and detailed description of the country and its inhabitants given in his narrative. Some remarkable water colors of California were painted by artists in his crew.

In January, 1827, another distinguished visitor arrived in California waters. This was Auguste Bernard du Haut-Cilly, commanding the French ship *Le Héros* on a trading voyage around the world. An educated, close observer, and an entertaining writer, this Frenchman was accompanied by Dr. Paolo Emilio Botta, an Italian archaeologist and scientist. More of the California mission and presidial establishments were visited by this party than by any of the foreigners preceding them. Thus the narrative of its commander is especially informative. As an interesting sidelight, the expedition spent much leisure time in hunting, and its members expressed astonishment at the multitude and variety of ducks and sea birds.

The Beginnings of Secularization

During Echeandía's administration no event was more important than his formulation in 1826 of a plan for the secularization of the missions. The governor, and the administration which appointed him, desired to place the missions under secular rule, and to convert mission towns into civic pueblos, but this action had to be approached cautiously. The friars, though in bad repute with the government, were recognized as the only ones who could keep the neophytes in subjection and induce them to work. Fear was great among the populace that if these priests should leave, California would be deprived of its major means of support and its people exposed to raids by hostile natives. The friars were in an anomalous position — unwanted and yet not permitted to leave. Some of them no doubt wished to depart, but most were old men, devoutly attached to their mission homes and their Indian wards. In general, these clerics wished to spend the rest of their days in the land where they had labored quite unselfishly.

On January 6, 1831, Governor Echeandía published a proclamation putting into effect his plan for the secularization of the missions. Under this plan—a reflection of then-current Mexican practice—the missions were to become pueblos, with each Indian family receiving an allotment of land and livestock, the friars remaining as curates of the missions. The immediate effect of this partial secularization was to make the Indians unruly and restive; some thereafter refused to work at all. The visiting Captain Beechey, a witness of this experiment, regarded secularization as discouraging. He reported that the neophytes quickly fell into excesses, gambled away their property, and were sometimes compelled to beg or steal.

Fulfillment of Echeandía's secularization plan was temporarily prevented by a change in the political administration in Mexico, and the appointment of a new governor for California, Manuel Victoria, "a friend of the padres and foe to secularization." Yet the forces working for secularization were strong and could not be stopped. The closing down of the missions would continue, greatly altering the Indian-white society that had grown up in California since its Spanish founding.

SELECTED READINGS

Peter Corney wrote a first-hand account of the Bouchard raid which is not entirely reliable. It is to be found in his *Voyages in the Northern Pacific* (Honolulu, 1896). The era during which Bouchard's raid occurred is the subject of an unpublished doctoral dissertation by Frances Carey Jones, "California in the Spanish-American Wars of Independence: The Bouchard Invasion" (University of California). See also the article by Lewis W. Bealer, "Bouchard in the Islands of the Pacific," *Pacific Historical Review*, IV (August, 1935), 328–342.

The actual transfer of government from Solá to Argüello has been scarcely plumbed by historical scholars; however, Bancroft, Chapman, and Richman all devote appropriate parts of their books to the transition from Spanish to Mexican control, as does Herbert Ingram Priestley in his *The Mexican Nation* (New York, 1924). The richest source of manuscript material in California for the study of this era, as well as the periods that precede and follow it, is again the Bancroft Library, University of California, Berkeley. Some of this material has been printed in the series edited by George P. Hammond, *The Larkin Papers* (10 vols., Berkeley, 1951–66).

Suggestive of further writing that needs to be done about Mexican California is George L. Harding's *Don Agustín V. Zamorano: Statesman, Soldier, Craftsman, and California's First Printer* (Los Angeles, 1934), a book about an important official who arrived in California shortly after the Mexican period began and who served there during the height of this era. Another biography that transmits the flavor of the Mexican period is Terry E. Stephenson's *Don Bernardo Yorba* (Los Angeles, 1941). Robert G. Cleland's *The Place Called Sespe* (Los Angeles, 1940, 1957) is a a local history with larger implications for the study of this period of California history. See also Myrtle M. McKittrick, *Vallejo: Son of California* (Portland, 1944).

There has been considerable research on the role of early Americans in California during the Mexican period. See Reuben L. Underhill's biography of Thomas Oliver Larkin, *From Cowhides to Golden Fleece* (Stanford, 1939, 1946), and Robert J. Parker's "Chapters in the Early Life of Thomas Oliver Larkin," California Historical Society *Quarterly*, XVI (March and June, 1937), 3–39, 144–171. Classic accounts of the hide and tallow trade are to be found in the previously mentioned volumes by Dana, Davis, and Robinson. One should also consult Adele

Ogden, "Alfred Robinson, New England Merchant in Mexican California," California Historical Society *Quarterly*, XXIII (September, 1944), 193–218, as well as her "Hides and Tallow: McCulloch, Hartnell and Company, 1822–1828," in the same periodical, VI (September, 1927), 254–264, and "Boston Hide Droghers Along the Califronia Shores," VIII (December, 1929), 289–305. See also Rolle, *An American in California*, and Raymond A. Rydell, *Cape Horn to the Pacific* . . . (Berkeley, 1952).

Regarding Indian disturbances, see Marion L. Lathrop, "The Indian Campaigns of General M. G. Vallejo," Society of California Pioneers *Quarterly*, IX (September, 1932), 161–205.

The visits of Beechey and Du Haut-Cilly fortunately produced literary by-products: Frederick W. Beechey, *Narrative of a Voyage to the Pacific and Beering's Strait* (2 vols., London, 1831), and Auguste Bernard du Haut-Cilly, *Voyage autour du Monde* . . . (2 vols., Paris, 1934). See the translation by Charles F. Carter, "Duhaut-Cilly's [sic] Account of California in the Years 1827–28," California Historical Society *Quarterly*, VIII (June–September, 1929), 131–166, 306–336. Edmond Le Netrel's *Voyage of the Héros Around the World with Duhaut-Cilly in the Years 1826, 1827, 1828, and 1829* has been translated by Blanche Collet Wagner (Los Angeles, 1951).

11

Infiltration and Revolt

The unrest that had led to revolution in many of Spain's former colonies was in part due to discontent caused by contact with foreigners. In California such contact came first by sea but also eventually by way of the seemingly impenetrable wilderness of desert and mountains that, for all practical purposes, had once sealed the remote province off from the east. California might have remained dormant and tranquil behind this barrier for perhaps another generation had it not been for a hardy band of American fur trappers. Since the founding of Jamestown and Plymouth, Yankees had been moving west. Englishmen, Frenchmen, and Indians had given way to their march; forests, deserts, wild animals, rugged mountains, and swollen streams had also failed to stop the tide. It was only a matter of time before Americans would establish overland contact with the settlements founded by Spain in the Southwest, a contact that would prove to be of profound significance to both sides.

Jedediah Smith, First Overland American

During Echeandía's governorship Jedediah Strong Smith, a young trapper of New England parentage, became the pioneer who blazed a trail from the newly formed United States to southern California. Smith, at the head of a small group of fur traders, was

145

in search of beaver and land-otter pelts. His southwestward trek, undertaken twenty-odd years after Lewis and Clark penetrated the American Northwest, has kindled the imagination of historians. Smith has become almost a legendary figure, a brave and adventurous "Knight in Buckskin." He earned this reputation through his indomitable personal courage and capacity for withstanding the perils of the wilderness. On one occasion a ferocious grizzly bear attacked him, taking his head between its jaws and leaving an ear and part of the of the scalp hanging from his bleeding skull. One of Smith's men stitched up the lacerated trapper with needle and thread and he was presently on his way again.

In the early 1820's Jed Smith found his first employment at St. Louis—then the center of the burgeoning fur trade—with General William Henry Ashley, the most successful fur-trading entrepreneur in the trans-Mississippi West. In the late summer of 1823, Smith undertook the first of many trips west for Ashley; his route made him one of the earliest white men to cross the continental watershed via South Pass, along what later became the Oregon Trail. In 1826, after an apprenticeship of several years with Ashley's trapping brigades, Smith and two other trappers, David E. Jackson and William L. Sublette, formed a partnership and bought Ashley's fur interests. Their new enterprise took the three men far beyond the known fringes of the Western frontier in search of pelts. On August 22, 1826, Smith led a trapping expedition of from fifteen to twenty men (there is uncertainty as to the number) and fifty horses out of Bear River Valley, in today's northern Utah. This departure signaled the beginning of an extensive penetration of the region between the Great Salt Lake and the Pacific shoreline, via the unexplored deserts of present-day Nevada and Arizona. Smith's party was composed of rough adventurers, capable of almost inconceivable endurance. His own tenacity, tempered with a sobriety unusual among "mountain men," had brought him the respect of these men. The party moved along the chalky banks of the Sevier River southwestward toward the Virgin River, continued to the Colorado, and then to the desolate Mohave villages. Venturing across sandy alkali wastes, over part of the route today traversed by transcontinental railroads, they finally headed in the direction of the California coast.

At the age of twenty-eight, Smith became the first white person to reach California overland, traveling through many hundred miles of wilderness, and undergoing Indian attack and severe shortages of food and water. Once he entered that remote area, Smith's adversaries were no longer the blistering white heat of the desert by day and the chilling winds that blew by night. With

these he knew how to cope. Quite another matter was the inquis-
itive Mexican bureaucracy he was about to face, a bureaucracy at
once polite and supremely suspicious.

Guided by two runaway Indians from San Gabriel Mission,
Smith's party moved across the desert area between the Colorado
River and the California pueblos. On November 27, 1826, he and
his remaining group of bedraggled men reached San Gabriel (the
Indians, of course, did not accompany them that far). The astonished priests at the mission received the uncouth-looking strangers warmly. In a singular exchange for the food, wine, and lodging
extended them, the trappers provided the friars with bear traps
to be used to catch Indians who poached oranges from mission
groves.

While his men relaxed for almost two months in the company
of the padres, Smith rode southward to see California's choleric
governor, Echeandía, about permission to trap in the province.
After several days he reached the muddy pueblo of San Diego,
only to have Echeandía demand an explanation of Smith's illegal
entry into California. When Smith failed to convince the suspicious governor that—lost and hungry—he had simply stumbled
into the province, Echeandía seized his weapons and placed him
under arrest. Smith protested angrily that he was "no Spy"; he
produced a passport and a diary listing all fifty-seven members
of the original Smith-Jackson-Sublette enterprise, in order to
prove that he and his companions were bona fide trappers. These
and other documents concerning Smith were confiscated and have
been lost; probably they are still hoarded in anonymity in some
remote Mexican archive.

The governor, unable to reach a decision about Smith, sent to
Mexico for instructions as to whether this Protestant alien should
be allowed to return overland to his own country. Languishing,
meanwhile, in a dirty San Diego *calabozo*, or jail cell, Smith
scrawled a letter in brown ink to the American minister at Mexico
City, Joel R. Poinsett, complaining: "I am destitute of almost
everything with the exception of my Traps (guns which I can
not now call mine), Ammunition, etc." There followed a strong
appeal also by visiting Boston shipmasters, to Echeandía and to
the American consul at Mazatlán. These sea captains maintained
that, lacking food and water, Smith's party would have perished
if he had not entered California. Smith was finally freed from his
humiliating imprisonment and allowed to return to San Gabriel;
there he was to pick up his men, upon condition that he leave
California posthaste, never to return. Echeandía considered Smith
and his men foreign interlopers, and doubtless anticipated that, if

this intrusion went unchecked, countless other trapping parties might eventually inundate the province which he was sworn, as governor, to defend.

Via the Cajón Pass, Smith recrossed the Sierra Madre range by which he had come, then slowly moved northward along the eastern foothills of those mountains into the San Joaquin Valley. In order to trap along the Stanislaus and Kings Rivers, as well as other streams, the party established a semipermanent camp in California's central valley. Early in the spring of 1827, Smith became most apprehensive over his prolonged stay in north-central California. While in the area under the jurisdiction of Mission San José, he addressed a letter of explanation to Father Narciso Durán, assuring the padre that he had made several efforts to cross the mountains, "but the snows being so deep I could not succeed in getting over." Smith had, in fact, attempted a crossing, but was blocked by both snow and sleet.

On May 20, Smith left most of his men in camp and, accompanied by two companions, set forth with seven horses and several mules to trudge through the High Sierra's "range of light" (a poetic term describing the effect which the Sierra has had on its conquerors), back toward the Great Basin of Utah. These were the first white men ever to cross the dangerous Sierra. Smith reached his destination beyond the Great Salt Lake on July 3, 1827, after about a month of travel. He and his one surviving companion were reduced, in Smith's words, to only a "horse and one mule remaining, which were so feeble and poor that they could scarce carry the little camp equipage which I had along. The balance of my horses," Smith wrote, "I was compelled to eat as they gave out." Smith was happy to arrive at Bear Lake in time for an Independence Day celebration with his partners.

California, however, had not seen the last of Jedediah Smith. On July 13, 1827, after spending only ten days at the rendezvous with his fellow trappers, he began the trek back to rejoin the men he had left west of the Sierra. Totally disregarding the warnings of Governor Echeandía, this time Smith headed a party of nineteen men, a party that was to meet even greater difficulties than had the former one. Near the Mohave villages, as Smith approached the Colorado River, his trail was blocked by Indians. Smith and his trappers rested for a few days in the vicinity; then, as they attempted to cross the river, the Mohaves attacked. The Indians killed ten of the Americans and wounded another, Thomas Virgin. Despite the loss of more than half his group, Smith finally succeeded in reaching Mission San Gabriel, where he obtained new horses and enough supplies to enable him to reach the encampment on the Stanislaus. He found the first party of trappers "in a very unpleasant situation; their supplies were almost exhausted and he without any to assist them." As their stay in California had been in violation of the governor's order, during Smith's absence the Americans had fallen under the displeasure of the Mexican authorities. In fact, Father Durán had warned the trappers to move on.

Smith himself, after making his way to Mission San José in search of needed supplies, was once more seized, this time by Father Durán. After being placed in the custody of Mexican officials at Monterey, Smith and his party were thrown into jail. Father Durán accused the Americans of enticing his Indian neophytes to desert from the mission. Stripped of his guns and under heavy guard, Smith again appeared before Governor Echeandía, who was then in the north. After much argument Smith was released for a second time. The fortunate presence at Monterey of the English trader William E. P. Hartnell and of four masters of American vessels made it possible for Smith to secure the supplies he needed. In December of 1827, he departed peacefully from California, under a heavy bond not to return.

Smith's route northward through today's Humboldt and Trinity Counties, and onward via Del Norte, proved extremely rough and difficult. He took more than six months to traverse northwestern California, paralleling the coastline in his march toward what is now the Oregon border. At one place it was necessary to spend a full six hours in order to get the horses of the party down a perpendicular slope fifty feet high; in spite of these precautions, one of the animals fell and broke its neck. Smith's men continued trapping as they journeyed northward in California, but had little success in hunting game.

On July 5, 1828, while in the Umpqua River country of southern Oregon, Smith's group suffered an Indian massacre from which only their leader and two other men were lucky enough to escape. The trio fled to the Hudson's Bay Company post at Fort Vancouver. Finally, after two years of separation, Smith found his way back to his partners, Jackson and Sublette, on the Snake River. Before long, he was off again, and on May 27, 1831, while marching across more of the burning stretches of the Southwest, met his death—probably at the hands of Comanche Indians while he was searching for a waterhole along a part of the Santa Fe Trail to New Mexico.

Jedediah Smith's influence upon the early history of western America overshadows even his dramatic, colorful adventures. He was a pathfinder whose descriptions of the terrain he crossed constituted a unique contribution to the development of overland communications. In the words of Robert Glass Cleland: "He had traversed the first of the great transcontinental routes to California, made known the valleys of the San Joaquin and Sacramento to the American trappers, and through them to American settlers; opened a line of communication from northern California to the Oregon country, a route the Hudson's Bay Company were quick to take advantage of; and traversed the Pacific Slope from the Mojave Desert to Puget Sound." The geographic barriers that once gave the Californians undisputed ownership of a choice land began to fall rapidly. Hunters, trappers, and traders crossed into the farthest West over at least half a dozen new trails. From Smith's first overland trek until the American military conquest of California, the movement toward that province of foreigners, most from the United States, was large enough to qualify as a "peaceful invasion."

Tension in California

There are various causes for the outbursts that continued to take place in California against Mexican authority. Resentment toward the central government was increasing, not only because of its indifference and neglect, but also because of the overbearing and mediocre governors sent out to rule over California. With some justification Californians felt contempt for these officials. They also nursed a half-conscious desire for complete freedom. Successive revolts following the Solís debacle were half-hearted, bloodless affairs; but they might have become precursors of a decisive movement for independence had not California's dissatisfaction been interrupted by American conquest.

Political changes in Mexico were naturally reflected in California, partially because it always experienced a change of governors at such times. On March 8, 1830, Echeandía was supplanted by Lieutenant Colonel Manuel Victoria, a militaristic conservative and an opponent of secularization. Echeandía, with the encouragement of the Mexican government, had made a number of moves towards secularization of the missions, as noted in the preceding chapter. In particular, on hearing the news of the change in administration, he had issued his decree of secularization of January 6, 1831, with the purpose of rushing the measure into effect before turning over the government to his successor.

When the new governor, Victoria, arrived in California, he found a particularly unfriendly reception awaiting him as a result of the fiery eloquence of José María Padrés. This enthusiast in the cause of liberty, who had recently come from Mexico, had a large and devoted following especially among the young Californians—members of such families as the Carrillos, Osios, Vallejos, Picos, Alvarados, and Bandinis. While Victoria impatiently waited at Santa Barbara for the retiring executive to come to meet him, he heard of Echeandía's decree of January 6, and took steps to annul it. Arbitrary by nature, and accustomed to the direct methods of the soldier, Victoria soon had increased the number of his enemies. He is described as a lean man of such dark complexion (he was half Indian) as to inspire the people to dub him "the black governor." Convinced that everybody opposed to him was in the wrong, Victoria made no attempt to conceal his contempt for the Californians, an attitude not calculated to help win them over.

During the rule of Echeandía justice had been carelessly administered, and such crime as existed had sometimes gone unpunished. Victoria had stricter ideas of discipline, and considered himself capable of fully enforcing the laws. He boasted that before long he would make it safe for any man to leave his handkerchief or watch lying in the Monterey plaza. The governor, however, set out to reform abuses without preparing the public for his changes, and with little concern for the constitution. In his haste to take a short cut to justice, he ordered the death penalty put into effect for the stealing of small sums and for other minor offenses. Californians were understandably shocked, and began to look upon their new governor as a bloodthirsty monster.

Victoria did not stop his undue severity with the punishment of ordinary criminals. He also rode roughshod over his political opponents, thereby provoking a revolution that was to prove his undoing. Several citizens—including the American Abel Stearns, who had become a naturalized Mexican, as well as José Antonio Carrillo, and Padrés—were arbitrarily exiled to Mexico, without trial or legal authorization. In refusing to convoke California's *diputación*, and in trying a local *alcalde* in a court-martial, Governor Victoria further overreached his constitutional authority. In effect, he took the government of the province into his own hands, and his acts engendered genuine hatred among the Californians. A movement to drive Victoria from office rapidly gained ground; even the friars restricted their approval to the governor's temporary abrogation of Echeandía's earlier decree of secularization. Victoria's punishment of Indian offenders was especially hard for the padres to endure, for they usually endeavored to stand between their wards and civil injustice. One missionary went so far as to throw himself at the feet of the governor to beg for the life of a young boy who had stolen a trivial sum. He was refused.

The foreign residents remained, for the most part, discreetly silent, although some of them were more favorable to the governor than they thought it advisable to admit. Increasing numbers of the foreigners were becoming naturalized citizens, but they were nevertheless primarily concerned with financial success rather than with politics. Revolution was destructive to their interests; thus some favored the "constitutional authorities" as most likely to preserve stable conditions—the kind most favorable to business. Victoria won their confidence by his firm stand against "evildoers" and his efforts to keep public order.

Nothing aroused the anger of the native Californians so much as Victoria's continued refusal to convoke the *diputación*. The governor was convinced that this body would interfere with his policies, and he ignored petition after petition sent to him in regard to the issue. He framed a manifesto stating that he was personally convinced of the illegal election of a large number of the members of the *diputación* and that he was determined it should not meet again until authorized by the Mexican government. On hearing this statement, the Californians sent complaints to Mexico about the governor's refusal to convoke the legislative body, calling upon the government to protect the people of the province against Victoria's arbitrary and oppressive measures.

The Revolt against Victoria

Active opposition to the governor was mounting. Among the most effective leaders of the movement were Stearns and Carrillo, in exile south of the border. Carrillo secretly returned to San Diego, and from there, in company with Juan Bandini and Pío Pico, he renounced allegiance to Victoria on November 29, 1831. The insurgents demanded the suspension of the governor, the vesting of the civil and military commands in the hands of two separate officials, and the return to power of Echeandía until such time as the *diputación* could meet. This *pronunciamento*, which was signed by Echeandía as well as by Stearns and Carrillo, gave the expatriation of the latter two men as one of the chief reasons for the rebellion. After taking possession of the presidio and garrison at San Diego, a force of about fifty rebels marched to Los Angeles, seizing control of that pueblo. There they found many prominent leaders in jail, by order of Victoria, and they prepared to fight the governor.

Victoria, having no doubt of his ability to cope with the Californians, set out southward from Monterey with a detachment of soldiers. A few miles from Los Angeles, near Cahuenga Pass, he experienced an unpleasant surprise when he encountered some of his own forces in battle array, accompanied by one hundred and fifty insurgent recruits from San Diego and Los Angeles. Victoria advanced alone and called upon these soldiers to come over to his side. They refused, and he then directed his men to fire a volley over the heads of the "enemy," probably to frighten rather than to harm them. The southerners replied with a few shots; then, their courage failing, they turned to run away, but Victoria was due for another surprise.

Among the Angeleños was a popular daredevil, José María Ávila, noted especially for his skillful horsemanship. Ávila suddenly rode out alone toward Victoria and his subaltern, Captain Romualdo Pacheco, and rushed at them with his lance leveled, as if in chivalric personal combat. When he came alongside Pacheco, Ávila drew an ancient pistol and shot Pacheco through the heart. The battle was then resumed and in the ensuing melee Ávila was unhorsed and killed, some say by Victoria himself, who received a deep lance wound in the face which prevented him from continuing to fight.

The continuing opposition to Victoria forced him to give up the governorship to the backers of Echeandía, but disagreements among the latter began almost at once. Echeandía took over the reins of government until the meeting of California's *diputación* at Los Angeles could choose another temporary governor. However, after Pío Pico was announced as its choice, on January 10, 1832, Echeandía refused to relinquish his office. Echeandía wanted no popular native son that he did not fully trust to take over the governorship. In effect, he temporarily succeeded in side-tracking Pío Pico from the office.

When Victoria had marched against the insurgents at Los Angeles, he had left in command at Monterey his secretary and friend, Captain Agustín Vicente Zamorano. Zamorano took no part in the rebellion of 1831, and made no effort to defend Victoria. After Victoria was driven out of the country, Zamorano realized that popular feeling in favor of Echeandía was lukewarm, especially in the north, and saw an opportunity to advance his own ambitions. He first won over to his side most of the foreign residents, who generally disliked Echeandía and distrusted Pio Pico, believing Zamorano's movement to be in defense of public order. Although Zamorano could, apparently, have relied upon a *compañia extranjera*, or body of foreigners, to fight for his cause, actual bloodletting proved unnecessary. Zamorano was wily enough to con-

clude a truce with Echeandía early in May, 1831. The two agreed
to divide California's military command between them: Echeandía's authority was generally to extend over all territory south of
San Gabriel, while Zamorano was to rule north of San Fernando
to Sonoma. This arrangement worked surprisingly well, enabling
California to enjoy a rare state of relative political quiet from
June to December, 1832; the Echeandía-Zamorano regime, however, came to an end with the arrival of a newly appointed Mexican governor.

Figueroa

Disturbed political conditions seemed to call for a strong but
understanding governor, and the choice fell upon the mestizo José
Figueroa, prominent in Mexican politics as *comandante-general* of
Sonora and Sinaloa. During a period of six years in that position,
Figueroa had learned something of California's disturbed affairs.
The new governor's talent for administration, his superior education, and his affable manners won for him personal popularity,
and helped overcome, temporarily, the prejudice against imported
Mexican governors. Figueroa was unostentatious and reasonably
democratic, making it a point to treat the poorest Indian with as
much consideration as the highest official. His first act was to
issue a proclamation granting amnesty to all who had taken part
in the disturbances of 1831-1832. Thus he met with no opposition
from the recent revolutionists; both they and the conservative
groups hastened to offer their allegiance to Figueroa.

Another important act of Figueroa's administration was his
move to take firmer possession of the territory to the north. By
a treaty of 1819 the Oregon region had been ceded by the Spanish
government to the United States, and the northern boundary of
Spain's holdings on the Pacific Coast was fixed at the forty-second
parallel. Mexico had fallen heir to these holdings, which gave it
undisputed claim to territory extending more than four degrees
latitude north of San Francisco; but the only establishments by
which it held its claim to this northern area were the missions of
San Rafael and San Francisco de Solano (commonly called Sonoma). Figueroa took steps to open this region by sending Mariano
Guadalupe Vallejo, afterwards known as "Comandante of the Line
of the North," to make explorations and look for a suitable site
for a presidio. Two colonies of settlers were established by Vallejo, one at Petaluma and the other at Santa Rosa, while he himself
built up a great private estate near Sonoma.

Further Secularization of the Missions

All other issues of the administration of Figueroa were overshadowed by the question of secularization. Figueroa has been attacked by some historians as the man who destroyed the missions. Yet he acted primarily as the agent of his government, attempted to mitigate evils that he saw could not be avoided, and urged that the loosening of mission control proceed gradually. Figueroa faced the fact that, originally, under the regulations of Spain, the Indians were eventually supposed to leave the missions and to be settled in pueblos, subject to the same laws as other citizens. He feared, however, that unconditional release of the Indians might lead to their destruction—a fear of a degree unfounded and exaggerated. Actually, considerable depletion of the Indian population occurred while they lived in the mission establishments. Also, there were many reasons why the missions, based on a paternal system, could no longer continue. Indian servitude was incompatible with Mexico's avowed republican principles. Conversely, the missionaries' contention that their Indian wards still required parental control, and that they were best qualified to exercise it, could not be wholly denied.

As the realities of secularization loomed large before him, Figueroa approached his task with a sense of dutiful reluctance. He made a tour of inspection of the missions, asking the padres for their opinions about his plans to secularize their establishments. His observations, and their protests, convinced the governor that the missions were not yet ready for secularization, and he warned the Mexican government that the Indians were still unfit for being placed suddenly on their own.

Figueroa's warning, however, came too late. Mounting sentiment in Mexico for emancipation of the Indians culminated in a sweeping decree of August, 1833. This provided for secularization of the missions of both Upper and Lower California. The missions were to become parish churches, in which the missionaries would remain to perform religious duties only because there were no substitutes available. An unfortunate loophole for corruption was left by the decree's omission of any rational plan for disposing of mission properties. Wide ranges of valuable land suddenly became available to the public, and some of the best soil in California haphazardly drifted under the control of private persons.

Governor Figueroa attempted to make the emancipation as smooth and gradual as possible. He allowed only a few missions at a time to be converted into parish churches. Half the land and livestock of these missions he ordered distributed among the Indian neophytes, while all remaining property was placed in the care of appointed secular administrators. The income from the latter property was to be used for the administrators' salaries and for the expenses of schools and other welfare requirements—especially those benefiting the Indians. To the surprise of Figueroa, the Indians did not accept their new freedom with joy. Instead, they hung about the missions, reluctant to leave the places which had been the only homes they had known, in some cases for as long as sixty years. As for the friars, they resigned themselves to the realization that their cause was lost and endeavored to adapt to the new conditions. It was impossible to obtain other clergy to take their places, and because outbreaks among the Indians were feared, without the traditional influence of the padres, Californians were not fully willing to let the missionaries go.

The Padrés-Hijar Colonization Venture

During the year 1834, in the midst of his difficulties over secularization, Governor Figueroa experienced further troubles as a result of the arrival of a particular party of colonists from Mexico. These settlers were under the leadership of José María Padrés, who had been banished from the territory by Victoria. Padrés, with money given him from the Pious Fund (a sum of money allocated earlier for missionary activity by the Mexican government), had paid the traveling expenses of more than two hundred persons desiring to settle in California. The government had no legal right to use missionary funds for this purpose. Nevertheless, with the prominent Mexican José María Hijar backing him, Padrés planned a new colony. The background of the settlers he had assembled was generally superior to that of any group yet sent to California. Among them were doctors, lawyers, teachers, goldsmiths, and artisans, but they were for the most part persons not especially fitted for the rigors of frontier life.

Padrés and Hijar did not meet as warm a welcome in California as they had expected. This was partly because they had brought with them twenty-one Mexicans to serve as administrators of the missions, whereas native Californians had planned to fill these places. Something had to be done with the settlers, however, and preparations were made to establish them on the northern frontier, as a bulwark against the Russians. The majority of the new colonists finally were sent to Mission San Francisco de Solano, from which most of them went into the Sonoma Valley. Failing to obtain employment in their various professions and trades, they spent a very uncomfortable winter, compelled to live upon the charity of Figueroa's government. In their disappointment some of them made violent threats to the governor, which caused Figueroa to take action against the most restless ones, especially after the Mexican central government withdrew its support of this hapless colonizing project. On May 8, 1834, the governor arrested both Padrés and Hijar as undesirables and sent them packing out of the port of San Pedro for San Blas, Mexico. Other colonists were, however, allowed to remain behind, and the descendants of some of them bear such well-known California family names as Coronel, Ábrego, Noé, Serrano, Prudón, and Covarrubias.

The Completion of Secularization

As the process of secularizing the missions continued, Governor Figueroa, harassed by many difficulties and worn out, had died on September 29, 1835. He left an honored name behind, and a reputation as probably the best of California's Mexican governors. Had more officials shared his concern for the welfare of the Indians, or had he lived to supervise the work, some of the ostensible purposes of secularization might have been accomplished. Figueroa is not to be blamed if few Indians got the land intended for them under the key secularization law of August, 1833. After his death, appointed mission administrators were allowed practically a free hand.

The government administrators and their friends, some of them members of the "first families," were enriched from the spoils of the missions. The natives consequently had little respect for these administrators. Frequent disturbances occurred, especially in the south, when Indians took former mission property they had been given and bartered it for liquor, so that they were left with no worldly goods. They failed to cultivate the land, and it passed to others. Buildings decayed from neglect, and the herds of cattle were depleted as some of the animals were carelessly killed by the Indians for food or sold to foreign traders often in exchange for gewgaws. For a brief period, from 1840 to 1845, secularization was virtually suspended, partly as a result of the pressure asserted by church authorities in both Mexico and California. On March 29, 1843, the proclerical Governor Micheltorena actually ordered restoration of the missions to the church fathers. But, with the approach of Mexico's war with the United States, the impoverished

Mexican government renewed the secularization process. Soon California's governors would rent and sell certain of the missions, also turning them into pueblos. In any case, deterioration of the missions never ceased once secularization began anew. Outright looting of mission properties went unchecked. Knaves stocked their ranchos with animals filched from dispersed mission herds. The mission Indians stood apathetically by as deeply confused, helpless witnesses. The dreams of Junípero Serra faded and California's missions began to crumble into dust. Within a very few years the mission era would be over forever.

SELECTED READINGS

The literature regarding Jedediah Smith has grown to sizable proportions. Consult Maurice S. Sullivan, *The Travels of Jedediah Smith* (Santa Ana, 1934), and the same author's *Jedediah Smith, Trader and Trail Breaker* (New York, 1936). A more recent biography is Dale L. Morgan, *Jedediah Smith and the Opening of the West* (New York, 1953). Robert Glass Cleland, whose *Pathfinders* (Los Angeles, 1929) represented some of the first scholarship on Smith, later included him in *This Reckless Breed of Men* (New York, 1950). Also basic to an understanding of Smith are Harrison C. Dale, *The Ashley-Smith Explorations and the Discovery of a Central Route to the Pacific, 1822–1829* (Glendale, 1918, 1941), and Donald McKay Frost, "Notes on General Ashley, the Overland Trail and South Pass," *Proceedings* of the American Antiquarian Society, LIV (October, 1944), 161–312.

Articles regarding Smith's route, the meaning of his explorations, and other aspects of the fur trade are scattered throughout numerous historical journals. One such treatment is A. M. Woodbury, "The Route of Jedediah S. Smith," *Utah Historical Quarterly*, IV (April, 1931), 35–46. Two articles that concern Smith's activities in southern California, both by Andrew F. Rolle, are "Jedediah Strong Smith: New Documentation," *Mississippi Valley Historical Review*, XL (September, 1953), 305–308, and "The Riddle of Jedediah Smith's First Visit to California," Historical Society of Southern California *Quarterly*, XXXVI (September, 1954), 179–184.

Mention has already been made of Harding's *Zamorano*, one of the few books that give us an insight into the fratricidal warfare involving Victoria and Echeandía. Useful also are *The Larkin Papers*, also previously cited.

Gerald J. Geary, *The Secularization of the California Missions* (Washington, D.C., 1934)), is the only book-length study of that sub-

SELECTED READINGS

ject. See also John B. McGloin, "The California Catholic Church in Transition," California Historical Society *Quarterly*, XLII (March, 1963), 39–48, as well as his life of Archbishop Joseph Alemany, entitled *California's First Archbishop* (New York, 1966).

Regarding the perimeter of Hispanic influence in northern California, a useful article is H. F. Raup and William B. Pounds, Jr., "Northernmost Spanish Frontier in California," California Historical Society *Quarterly*, XXXII (March, 1953), 43–48. Several articles by George Tays appeared consecutively in the *Quarterly* during 1937 (Volume XVI) under the general title "Mariano Guadalupe Vallejo and Sonoma—A Biography and a History."

12

On the Eve of American Rule

Governor Figueroa had managed to retain the allegiance of the people more by his personal charm than by the authority of his office. After his death Californians grew restless again, and this tendency was aggravated, as usual, by constant changes of governmental policies in Mexico. The old liberal (or federal) and conservative (centralist) struggle continued. Nicolás Gutiérrez, who succeeded Figueroa as governor *ad interim,* filled the office for four months until the next appointee arrived. This period was marked by only one significant governmental event—temporary recognition of Los Angeles as California's capital. As a result of the persistent pressure of such Southerners as José Antonio Carrillo and Pío Pico, an abrupt decree of May 23, 1835 announced the moving of the capital southward. While this news was jubilantly received by Angeleños, it hardly increased the popularity of Governor Gutiérrez in the north, especially at Monterey.

Chico and His Ouster

California's next regular governor, the Mexican-born Mariano Chico, was a reactionary in politics and therefore automatically unpopular with the majority of Californians; his unpleasant temper and disagreeable manners did nothing to ameliorate the situation. Public resentment quickly rose to the boiling point, and Chico was

expelled from California after only three months in office. The
ouster was adroitly and clandestinely accomplished, with the insurgent Californians managing to avoid open conflict with the
national government. Chico threatened to return with troops to
take vengeance, but it was an empty threat. The truth was that
Mexican governors were no longer welcome in California, and one
after another they found the place too hostile to hold them. Indeed, most provincials no longer called themselves *Mexicanos*, but
Californios.

Upon the expulsion of Chico the civil and military commands
again fell to Gutiérrez. This time he experienced a more stormy
tenure. Though easy-going and inoffensive, he was a Spaniard by
birth, and regarded as a foreigner. A petty quarrel between him
and Juan Bautista Alvarado, about the customs service, was seized
upon as an excuse for his overthrow. Although the Californians
had not yet reached the point of entertaining so radical an idea as
independence, they were determined to secure home rule for the
territory. Their attitude was not completely unreasonable. Why
should a Vallejo, an Alvarado, a Carrillo, or any other California
leader be in a position of permanent inferiority to an outsider
whom he considered his inferior? Contact with foreigners had emphasized the backwardness of Mexico and awakened local political
ambitions. The ease with which the Californians had expelled
Victoria and Chico further emboldened them to act independently.
But the *Californios* did not yet feel strong enough to walk alone.
Hence the first phase of their struggle was to secure recognition
for California as a free state within the Mexican Republic, with
autonomy in its internal affairs.

Alvarado and Home Rule

A leader anxious to leap into the fray was at hand. By late 1836
the twenty-seven-year-old Juan Bautista Alvarado had by virtue of
his talents, education, and powerful family ties made himself
prominent in the politics of the province. In particular, his opposition to centralism placed him before the public as a local patriot.
He was a member of the *diputación* and an *hijo del país*, or native
son, endowed with personal magnetism and eloquence. After
Chico's overthrow, Alvarado and José Castro assembled a force of
about seventy-five men, armed with such antiquated muskets as
were available. At Monterey the revolutionists recruited Isaac Graham, an American fur trapper and hunter of unsavory repute.
Graham had abandoned his legitimate trade for the easier and

more profitable one of running a whiskey distillery on the Rancho Vergeles. A backwoodsman from Tennessee, he was a reckless person with a following of men of similar character. Graham was probably induced to join the revolutionists by promises of land and other favors. Though momentarily grateful for the American's loyalty, Alvarado was to rue the day when he availed himself of his services.

A little "army," made up of Graham's band of about fifty riflemen—Indians, Americans, and renegade Mexicans—together with one hundred Californians under José Castro, quietly appeared at Monterey on November 3. Without bloodshed they took possession of the fort. One cannon ball, fired by a lawyer who had to look in a book to find out how, struck the house of the governor. This so terrified Gutiérrez that he surrendered immediately. Once again a governor appointed by the Mexican government was put aboard a homeward-bound ship, the third such official to be expelled from California.

Alvarado thereupon wrote his relative Vallejo: "It is wonderful, Uncle, with what order our expedition has been conducted. Everybody shouts *vivas*, for California is free." Recent repudiation of the Mexican constitution of 1824, which had been considered a basic guarantee of provincial rights, had angered the Californians. On November 7, 1836, California's *diputación* issued a proclamation declaring her a "free and sovereign State"—at least until Mexico should restore the Federalist Constitution of 1824 as a sort of conditional "Declaration of Independence." Alvarado was named governor by the *diputación*; Vallejo was designated military chief, and Monterey again became the capital. Despite the fact that Alvarado had led a successful revolt, he was still sufficiently fearful of Mexican authority to keep the Mexican banner floating in public places. Also, California was, of course, still a part of Mexico. When news of the uprising reached the central government it issued a swarm of proclamations, threatening dire punishment to the participants. The Californians, meanwhile, governed themselves.

Nevertheless, their inclinations toward local patriotism and independence again were overshadowed by internal quarrels and sectional jealousies. In the extreme south the pueblo of San Diego had a special grievance. It had long wanted the provincial custom house to be located within its municipal confines, but had been unable to wrest that distinction from Monterey. Such disagreements resulted in an armed encounter between Californians; this took place near San Buenaventura, with Castro at the head of the northerners and Carlos Carrillo in command of the southerners.

Only one man was killed. After another skirmish at Las Flores, in which the two factions met in "a battle for the most part of tongue and pen," Alvarado was able to persuade Carrillo to disband his troops, thus ending active opposition to the Monterey government.

Alvarado, in August, 1838, was confirmed as governor of California by Mexico. Some expressed surprise that the central government should confer this honor upon a man lately in rebellion against it. Actually the authorities probably cared little who was governor of California so long as he was loyal and did not ask for money or troops to defend his position. Once more, Alvarado was established as governor, Vallejo as military commander, and Monterey as the capital.

A few years of respite from internal dissension followed, permitting Governor Alvarado to devote attention to affairs that had been sadly neglected. The missions continued to deteriorate, however, in spite of his effort to save something from the wreck by appointing the honest and hard-working William E. P. Hartnell as a government inspector. The ruinous state of the missions, it was discovered, was not altogether due to dishonest administrators. The mission Indians were at least partly responsible; they had in many cases carelessly disposed of the little property that had been distributed to them. In addition, with some encouragement from the former neophytes, the non-Christianized, semiwild Indians of the interior were conducting raids on the exposed and disintegrating missions, running off horses and mules, and killing unguarded cattle.

Another problem of the Alvarado administration was the continuing sentiment for insurrection, especially in the south. Among the leaders of this movement was Pío Pico, who still sulked at the refusal of California's junta to locate the capital at Los Angeles. In the north, the fear of foreigners remained evident. The composition of California's permanent foreign residents had changed somewhat since the arrival of the earliest traders, merchants, and rancheros. Most of these pre-pioneers were greatly respected; among them were such honored names as those of Hartnell, Cooper, Fitch, Spear, Davis, Spence, Stearns, and Robinson. In the 1830's a few troublemakers, however, had come into the province, many via Santa Fe, New Mexico, where American trappers and traders congregated. In California some of these refused to settle down. Among them Isaac Graham, in particular, was distrusted by Alvarado, who considered that ruffian foolhardy enough to attempt seizure of California's government. (Partly because of Graham's participation in the revolt of 1836 which Alvarado had led against Gutiérrez, Alvarado had good reason to know the American's adventurous turn of mind.) Graham, who, as noted, had settled near Monterey, made his cabin a center for a rabble-rousing group of former fur trappers and sailors, as well as other restless spirits. Through a local priest, Alvarado got wind of an alleged plot to overthrow him, a conspiracy whose origin he traced to Graham's cabin. Texas had become independent in 1836 largely through the efforts of ambitious Americans who had infiltrated the territory; remembering this, the governor could easily imagine that Graham's ilk had similar hopes for California.

In April, 1840, Alvarado began to round up various suspects. Out of a total of 120 foreigners that he arrested, he sent Graham and forty-five of his "dangerous" associates, in irons, to San Blas. The governor was subsequently accused of trumping up a false charge of conspiracy against these foreigners, as a pretext to rid the province of them. Yet many "respectable" foreign residents approved of Alvarado's clamping down upon Graham and his followers. They believed these restless men posed a definite menace to the stability of life in California. Ultimately the British consul at Tepic, in Mexico, took up the exiled Graham's cause with the Mexican government; the old hunter was acquitted of charges of conspiracy, ordered released, and even given free ship passage back to California. This was something of a rebuke to Governor Alvarado by higher Mexican authority. In July, 1841, the citizens of Monterey were astounded to see Graham and two dozen of his ragged companions disembarking from a ship in that port, as insolent as ever. So ended the "Graham Affair," to which more importance has possibly been ascribed than it deserves.

More Visitors by Sea

In addition to the foreigners who came to California to stay, a number continued to arrive on "inspection tours." Mention has been made of the visits of La Pérouse, Vancouver, Beechey, and Du Haut-Cilly; in the thirties and forties, increasing numbers of such travelers appeared in the California ports. The French naval frigate *Venus*, under the command of Captain Abel du Petit-Thouars, in 1837 remained for a month at Monterey after a trip to the principal ports of the west coast of Latin America. The elaborate official report of the expedition is of particular interest on account of its superior descriptions of the Alvarado Revolution and and of California politics. Another visitor, also on a trip of observation for the French government, arrived in California three years later; this was Eugène Duflot de Mofras, whose voyage was rumored to have imperialistic overtones. These trips were obviously more than pleasure tours. Interest in California was mounting, and foreign governments were eager to obtain information about the province.

The United States, as concerned as any other outside power over the future status of California, sent its first naval expedition to the Pacific Coast in 1841. The leader of this enterprise, Commodore Charles Wilkes, though dour and pessimistic elsewhere in his report, wrote enthusiastically about what he called the greatest natural harbor in the world, San Francisco. His account, like the others, gives invaluable glimpses of California's social, economic, and political climate during this critical period in her history.

The Return to Mexican Rule under Micheltorena

Only for short periods of time during the Mexican era did California escape being an asylum, indeed a dumping ground, for unemployed Mexican officials. The joint native rule of Alvarado as civil governor and Vallejo as *comandante-general* ended late in 1842, although these men continued prominent in California affairs. In August of that year a newly-appointed executive, Manuel Micheltorena, a former soldier with Santa Anna in the Texas campaign and now a general of brigade, arrived quite suddenly at San Diego. In appearance he was attractive, with an erect, military bearing, and in manner gracious. But Micheltorena came handicapped by a military company of three hundred tough *cholos*, or half-breed ex-convicts. In a state of near destitution, these "troops" had been sent with Micheltorena by the Mexican government partly for the purpose of restricting the further entry of foreigners into California. As irregulars, they had not received pay in a long time, and could not resist the temptation to steal kettles, pots, chickens, jewelry, and even clothing. Their depredations upon outlying ranchos also included the molesting of local señoritas. At San Diego, where the governor was first welcomed to California, local residents soon became anxious to speed him and his *rateros*, or scamps, northward to the capital of Monterey.

Before his arrival at Monterey, Micheltorena was met by a startling piece of news. Hostilities between Mexico and the United States seemed on the verge of breaking out. Commodore Thomas Ap Catesby Jones, in command of the American Pacific squadron, was under the mistaken impression that war had already been declared and he had made a hurried run from Peruvian waters to raise the flag of the United States prematurely at Monterey. Convinced of his great error within only a few hours, Jones restored the Mexican flag and the difficulty was composed, for the moment, in a friendly manner. California would have further experiences with forceful United States military commanders.

Governor Micheltorena eventually encountered more serious troubles. The old quarrel between Monterey and Los Angeles about the location of the capital kept cropping up. Outbreaks of the Indians continued, too, to cause anxiety. As for foreigners, Micheltorena tried to secure their loyalty by granting tracts of land in the Sacramento Valley to a number of them, including the Americans Job Dye, Dr. John Marsh, William Knight, P. B. Reading, and A. G. Toomes. As a consequence he was decidedly popular with some foreigners; yet he feared them, as did others of his countrymen.

Micheltorena's Expulsion

Micheltorena made every effort to win the favor of all Californians. He made up out of his own pocket losses resulting from the thievery of his men. He pleased the friars by restoring certain properties to their care, even though this action came too late to save the moribund mission system. Micheltorena also was the first governor to give education real attention; he established better schools in the province than had ever existed. But the Californians regarded the presence of his convict troops as a bitter insult, one of many heaped upon them by the Mexican government. It became evident that Micheltorena too had to go. The only question was when.

In November, 1844, another revolt broke out, again under the leadership of Alvarado and José Castro. Vallejo held aloof from the conflict, attempting to keep the peace by urging Micheltorena to send his soldiers home to Mexico. On November 22, however, the governor marched against the rebels. After an encounter near San Jose, in which argument took the place of fighting, a treaty was concluded. Micheltorena agreed to send his *cholos* out of the country within three months, but the harassed governor had no authority from Mexico to carry out this promise. It soon became evident that he was not even making any attempt to do so, and was using the time gained to win over local foreigners in order to resist further revolts. Micheltorena thereby lost the allegiance of many Californians. By now there was a fixed determination to drive him out of the province.

Foreign residents were aligned on both sides in the quarrel with the governor, depending on their personal motives. Isaac Graham joined Micheltorena's forces chiefly to avenge himself upon Alvarado, whom he never forgave for his arrest and exile in 1840. Stearns took sides with the localists Alvarado and Castro to gratify his hatred of Mexico and the rancor which he still nursed for his treatment by Governor Victoria. Sutter, a German-Swiss adventurer who had come to California in 1839 to build a fort at New Helvetia on the Sacramento River, contracted to aid Micheltorena in consideration for a large grant of land, in addition to that which he had already obtained from Alvarado. Graham and Sutter, however, did not long remain on the governor's side. They were persuaded by fellow foreigners (among them the American frontiersmen William Workman and B. D. Wilson) that they could best serve their own interests by joining Alvarado. In all, about fifty foreigners enlisted against Micheltorena, whose own forces, congregating near Los Angeles, included a hundred drilled Indians from the interior armed with guns, bows, and arrows.

On February 20, 1845, the opposing armies, each four hundred strong, met at Cahuenga Pass and engaged in a two-day artillery duel, at such long range that there was little danger of anyone's being hit. The foreign contingents on both sides then awakened to the folly of shooting at each other over a quarrel in which they had relatively little to gain whatever the outcome might be. At Los Angeles the foreigners held a conference and resolved to withdraw from the conflict, an action that caused the fighting between Micheltorena and Alvarado virtually to cease. On February 22 Micheltorena, having perceived that his foreign support had vanished, agreed to be deported from California. He also sensibly consented to take his unpopular jailbird army with him. With his departure, Mexico's direct rule over California came to an end. The province thus achieved, before the American conquest, what amounted to independence.

Following these events, Pío Pico finally attained his long-sought goal, recognition as civil governor by Alvarado and other native sons. José Castro, as powerful at Monterey as Pico was in Los Angeles, became military *comandante*. California was determined to govern itself, but it soon found that self-rule posed pitfalls. Almost immediately the old rivalry between the north and south flared up. Pico used his position to remove the capital to Los Angeles again. Meanwhile, Castro and his northern cohorts almost literally latched onto the Monterey custom house as a center of power. California was a house divided. The finances of the government became hopelessly involved: there were constant disagreements about the allocation of revenues; debts piled up; salaries were seldom paid. Pico was in a position to control legislation, but Castro had possession of the funds. This damaging quarrel between *comandante* and governor, between north and south, between custom house and local officials, dragged on fruitlessly during 1845–1846. There seems little doubt that this factionalism, which constantly threatened to erupt into actual warfare, helped reconcile the Californians to United States rule. Vallejo and other prominent native sons became convinced that Americanization would and should occur. This growing attitude is sometimes forgotten by historians. It is true that many Californians later remembered with nostalgia the peaceful, unprogressive pastoral era that was supplanted by a driving, ambitious, pushy American period. But other Californians had actually looked forward to this change of rule as the best hope for California's future tranquillity and progress.

Russian Abandonment of California

The increase in the number of Americans coming into California was accompanied by a general Russian exodus. American settlers had already moved closer and closer to Fort Ross. The Russians, instead of expanding their small settlement eastward to the Sacramento River, had found their way largely blocked by Yankees; among these was John B. Cooper, who, by 1837, had taken possession of a rancho in the upper part of the Russian River Valley. Furthermore, the Russian establishment at Ross had become a heavy financial burden. In its last four years of operation, the fort had lost 45,000 rubles for its owners. The Russians were discouraged also, as early as December 2, 1823, by American President James Monroe's historic message in which he stated that lands in the Western Hemisphere were "henceforth not to be considered as subjects for future colonization by any European powers." During the next year the Russians abandoned their claims to the Oregon country. They finally withdrew from California in 1842. The news was received with great joy at Monterey.

Before their departure the Russians carefully disposed of both property and equipment. Since they had gone through the form of buying the lands from the Indians (although the price paid was a mere bagatelle), the Russians claimed that they should be reimbursed for the territory. The Californians believed that, in view of the long, and illegal, occupancy by the Russians, all buildings, lands, and other property should be turned over to the provincial government without charge. A Russian commissioner who came to California from Alaska to oversee the withdrawal, however, threatened to burn Ross rather than give it away. In the autumn of 1841 the Russians concluded a sale with Sutter that solved this problem. Although the Swiss was heavily in debt, he arranged to purchase all movable property at Fort Ross—including a glass hot-house, farming implements, a small vessel, a few cannon, some old French flintlock muskets, and various military supplies and muni-tions—for $50,000.

So ended thirty years of Russian occupancy of their outpost in California. Today the only relics of their tenure are a few partially preserved buildings and some archival records. In addition, there remain various place names—among them Fort Ross itself, the Russian River, and Mount St. Helena, named for the Empress of Russia. The Russian withdrawal occurred on the eve of American rule as a new day was dawning for California.

SELECTED READINGS

Fragmentary aspects of the last days of Mexican rule are portrayed in such local studies as J. J. Hill, *History of Warner's Ranch and Its Environs* (Los Angeles, 1927), and George William and Helen Pruitt Beattie, *Heritage of the Valley: San Bernardino's First Century* (Pasadena, 1939). Other books that reflect the era almost tangentially are Stephenson's *Yorba*, William D. Phelps, *Fore and Aft, or Leaves from the Life of an Old Sailor* (Boston, 1871), and Henry A. Wise, *Los Gringos, or an Inside view of Mexico and California* (New York, 1849). The Davis, Robinson, and other memoirs also help fill the gaps in accounts written specifically about the Gutiérrez, Alvarado, and Micheltorena regimes. Another eye-witness account is the already mentioned *Diary of Faxon Dean Atherton*.

The report of the *Venus* is entitled *Voyage autour du monde sur le frégate Vénus pendant les années 1836–1839 . . . par Abel du Petit Thouars* (11 vols., Paris, 1840–1855). A selected translation by Charles N. Rudkin, covering the California portion of the expedition, is *Voyage of the Venus: Sojourn in California* (Los Angeles, 1956). Eugène Duflot de Mofras' original narrative, *Exploration du territoire de l'Orégon, des Californies et de la Mer Vermeille . . .* (Paris, 1844) has been translated, edited, and annotated by Marguerite Eyer Wilbur, as *Duflot de Mofras' Travels on the Pacific Coast . . .* (2 vols., Santa Ana, 1937). See also the descriptions by Charles Wilkes in his *Narrative of the United States Exploring Expedition during the years 1838, 1839,*

1840, 1841, 1842 (5 vols., Philadelphia, 1844), as well as the popularized biography of Wilkes, *The Hidden Coasts,* by Daniel M. MacIntyre (New York, 1953).

The Russian departure from California is discussed in the standard biographies of Sutter mentioned as readings for the next chapter.

The emergence of California, particularly the southern counties, into an American pattern of life is the theme of Robert Glass Cleland's substantial *The Cattle on a Thousand Hills: Southern California, 1850– 1870* (San Marino, 1941, 1951); the economic and social processes described in that volume began to occur at a date considerably earlier than Cleland's subtitle suggests. Supplemental are various books that give one an insight into the last days of the Mexican era. Among these is Thomas Jefferson Farnham, *Travels in the Californias, and Scenes in the Pacific Ocean* (New York, 1844). See also Myrtle M. McKittrick, *Vallejo: Son of California* (Portland, 1944), several biographical sketches in Rockwell D. Hunt, *California's Stately Hall of Fame* (Caldwell, Idaho, 1950), and Richman's *California Under Spain and Mexico.* Literary aspects of the shift from a Hispanic to an Anglo-Saxon orientation are the subject of a brochure by James D. Hart, *American Images of Spanish California* (Berkeley, 1960).

13

Trappers, Traders, and Homeseekers

The overland movement to California pioneered by Jedediah Smith was soon joined by a number of other adventurous American trappers, among them James Ohio Pattie, Ewing Young, William Wolfskill, the Sublette brothers, Kit Carson, and George Nidever. Many of these, and dozens of less renowned traders and homeseekers—including the obstreperous Isaac Graham referred to in the preceding chapter—were to remain in California and help transform the province into an American outpost.

The Patties

Prominent among the "mountain men" was the Kentuckian James Ohio Pattie, who in 1824 set out with his father, Sylvester—then a widowed resident of southern Missouri—on a trapping expedition southwestward from the Missouri River frontier. On June 20 the little party, consisting of five persons, crossed the Missouri some sixty miles above St. Louis. There they joined a larger party en route for New Mexico. Not all of these persons accompanied Sylvester and James Ohio Pattie into the unexplored Southwest, however; some struck off in other directions. For several years the Patties trapped for beaver along muddy and unattractive streams which no white men had even seen before. They reached the Mohave villages on the Colorado by March 16, 1826, some six months before Jedediah Smith, thus becoming the first Americans to trap along the California and Arizona frontier. As they made their way throughout the uncharted Southwest they took many furs, and the future prospects of the party seemed excellent when marauding Indians stole their pack animals and compelled them to cache the unwieldy furs, most of which they never recovered. Still worse, another cache was confiscated by the Mexican governor at Santa Fe, who pocketed the proceeds himself, on the ground that the Americans had been trapping without a license. Thus began a series of hardships which, in the end, brought death to the elder Pattie and disappointment and poverty to the younger man.

Late in September, 1827, the Patties, with about thirty companions, continued westward from Santa Fe to trap on the Gila. By the first of December they reached the junction of that river with the Colorado. Repeated misunderstandings caused the party to divide, until the Pattie group numbered but eight persons. These wandered haphazardly through what is today southern Arizona. At one campsite a band of Yuma Indians, under cover of a heavy storm and the blackness of night, stampeded their horses. This left the Patties no choice but to build canoes from nearby cottonwoods for transport down the Colorado. Floating down that river, they set traps all along the banks, and their store of beaver skins again increased daily.

As the Patties approached the Gulf of California they abandoned their small handmade canoes, due to the "tumultuous commotion of the water." Burying their stock of furs, they set out on a grueling journey farther westward across Lower California, in the hope of reaching some sort of Mexican settlement. The fierce sun and scorching sand, the almost total lack of moisture, and their own extreme fatigue brought a sense of desperation to the little company.

With the assistance of friendly Indian guides, they came finally to the Dominican mission of Santa Catalina; but instead of being accorded needed relief by its padres, they were thrown into the guardhouse. After a week of scanty fare, they were sent under guard to San Diego, then the seat of the California governor's residence. Like Jedediah Smith, they were amazed at the harsh treatment accorded them by Echeandía and further dismayed when he remanded them to separate prison cells. The governor was especially suspicious of the trappers as a result of Smith's recent expedition. The impaired health of Sylvester Pattie was not equal to the poor food and execrable physical tratment, and he was seized with an illness that proved fatal.

After the death of his father, the younger Pattie was given a chance to serve the governor. To translate English language documents, and to deal with foreign visitors, the governor needed an interpreter. Also, Echeandía relaxed his extreme rigor when a small-pox epidemic began to rage in the upper part of the province and casualties multiplied alarmingly, especially after he learned that Pattie had brought along some scarce vaccine. The governor promised him a passport for a year if he would vaccinate the people on the coast, at the same time agreeing to compensate him for the service and to grant him his liberty. Pattie eventually accepted these terms, and traveled up and down the coast for Echeandía vaccinating some ten thousand Indians and other California residents. For his efforts he was dubbed by another trapper "sometime surgeon extraordinary to his Excellency, the Governor of California."

Upon completion of his task, Pattie was thunderstruck when confronted with the demand that he become a Catholic before receiving the favors promised him by the governor. He refused to change his religion and left California early in 1830 by sea. Making his way overland to Mexico City and then to Vera Cruz, he disappeared from the pages of history. Pattie was significant not only because he pioneered the Gila River route to California, but also because he left for posterity one of the most exciting of all records of Western adventure. His colorful *Personal Narrative*, first published in 1831, is a mine of often unreliable but always fascinating information.

Ewing Young

Among the fur traders of the Southwest perhaps none was more active than Ewing Young. For more than a decade he trapped along the streams of the southern Rocky Mountains as well as the San Joaquin and the Sacramento Rivers in California. Although he organized and led an impressive number of trapping parties during this period, he remains one of the last heralded of California's "mountain men." He learned his trade early in life, trapping first mainly in the waters of the Pecos. In August, 1829, he headed a party of twenty-nine men from Taos toward California; they went by way of the Zuñi villages and the Salt River, traveling down the Gila and the Colorado, after which the party divided. Some of the men, among them Young's protégé Kit Carson, decided to cross the Mohave desert with Young to the settlements of southern California. Following Jedediah Smith's trail, the party moved through

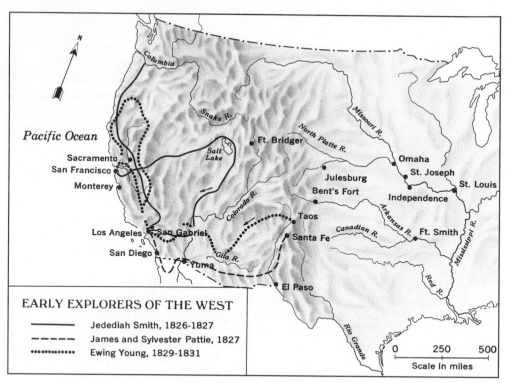

EARLY EXPLORERS OF THE WEST

———————	Jedediah Smith, 1826-1827
– – – – –	James and Sylvester Pattie, 1827
••••••••••••	Ewing Young, 1829-1831

Scale in miles
0   250   500

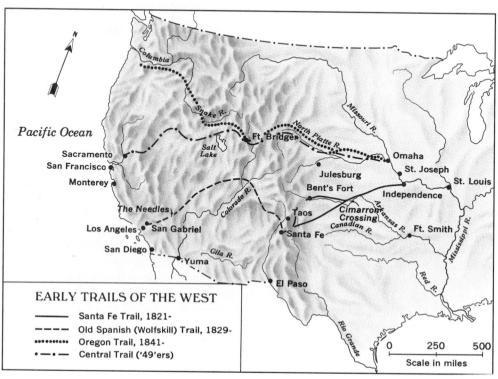

EARLY TRAILS OF THE WEST

———————	Santa Fe Trail, 1821-
– – – – –	Old Spanish (Wolfskill) Trail, 1829-
••••••••••	Oregon Trail, 1841-
•–•–•–	Central Trail ('49'ers)

Scale in miles
0   250   500

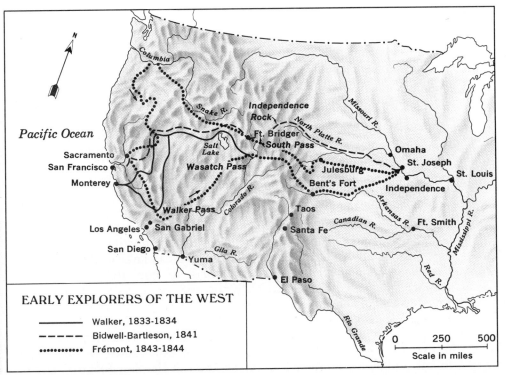

EARLY EXPLORERS OF THE WEST

———————— Walker, 1833-1834

– – – – – – Bidwell-Bartleson, 1841

••••••••••• Frémont, 1843-1844

0   250   500

Scale in miles

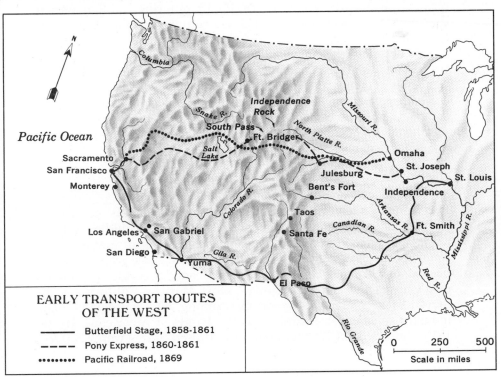

EARLY TRANSPORT ROUTES
OF THE WEST

———————— Butterfield Stage, 1858-1861

– – – – – – Pony Express, 1860-1861

•••••••• Pacific Railroad, 1869

0   250   500

Scale in miles

Cajon Pass and, early in 1830, reached San Gabriel Mission. Hardy, and inured to physical danger, Young attained a great reputation as a trail blazer as a result of such treks.

In 1831 Young took thirty-six men to California along the old Pattie route. Among the members of this group were Isaac Williams, Jonathan Trumbull Warner, Isaac Sparks, and Kit Carson's brother, Moses. All would leave their mark on California. On this expedition Young engaged in otter and beaver trapping, both along the coast and in California's northern interior. After trapping along the Kings River and wide stretches of the San Joaquin, he proceeded to the Sacramento, coming upon a Hudson's Bay Company brigade a few miles south of the American River. American trapping competition with that English company was already under way. Early in 1833, Young moved farther northwest, passing along the southern and western shores of Clear Lake and reaching the coast about seventy-five miles north of Fort Ross. Then he followed the seashore in search of beaver as far as the Umpqua River in Oregon. He proceeded along Smith's trail to the northern limit of Klamath Lake, before moving back southward to cross the Klamath and Rogue Rivers and then the Pit, to the headwaters of the Sacramento. Young next made his way down the Sacramento Valley to the American River, then to the San Joaquin, and onward beyond the Kings River, finally entering the San Bernardino Valley in December of 1833. He returned to Los Angeles the following summer.

This detailed itinerary may convey some idea of the scope of the travels, made under frightful conditions, of trappers and traders like Ewing Young. Unfortunately Young left little in writing, and the complete record of his life can never be written; but even the scraps that have been pieced together mark him as one of the significant forerunners of the overland movement to California.

Other Early Trappers

Part of the early fur trade in the Southwest was carried on clandestinely, since as a rule only Mexicans (including Californians) possessed licenses to trap legally in Mexican territory. Milton Sublette, a brother of William Sublette, was granted such a license, but only on condition that he teach "a certain proportion of Mexicans the art of trapping." Most Mexican Californians displayed little interest, however, in trapping, and consequently this industry fell almost entirely into the hands of Americans. By the 1830's hundreds of trappers from the United States were scattered all over the Southwest, and sooner or later they ended up in California.

In 1824 William Wolfskill had joined Young and others to trap along the tributaries of the Colorado, collecting about $10,000 worth of furs. The legendary "Pegleg" Smith was a member of Young's party that trapped on the Gila in 1826. Another visitor to California at about this time was George C. Yount, a pioneer for whom the town of Yountville, in Napa County, was named. In 1829–1830, Christopher (Kit) Carson was, as already noted, a member of Young's expedition to California. And many other fur men also became prominent in the future state. Among these trappers was J. J. Warner, whose southern California ranch became a rendezvous for old-timers. Others were David E. Jackson, of Jackson Hole and Grand Teton fame, and Job F. Dye, who later wrote his valuable *Recollections of a Pioneer of California*. Thomas Fitzpatrick, often known by his Indian name of "Broken Hand," was renowned as one of the most dependable of all the guides of his day. Joseph Reddeford Walker is remembered as the discoverer of Walker Pass, and Louis Robideaux, trapper of French descent, as the man for whom Mount Robidoux in southern California is named. Other colorful figures among the fur men were "Uncle Billy" Waters, "Old Bill" Williams, Ceran St. Vrain, Isaac Slover, and Nathaniel Pryor. Each in his own way helped expand American influence in the Far West.

Sutter's New Helvetia

As California steadily accommodated to foreign influence, a prominent and unique role was taken by Johann Augustus Sutter. Born in the Grand Duchy of Baden, Sutter left Switzerland for America in 1834, to escape a debtor's prison and an angry wife. After tarrying in Indiana and Missouri, and visiting parts of Mexico along the Santa Fe Trail—as well as Honolulu and the Russian colonies in Alaska—he arrived on the Pacific Coast. Called "a dreamer with a gifted tongue," Sutter achieved a distinctive place in California's history; he was shrewd and wily, as well as visionary.

Sutter brought with him to California Hawaiian, or Kanaka, laborers, hoping to build a self-sustaining colony and fort in the Sacramento Valley. In 1839 he obtained permission from Governor Alvarado to occupy a virtually unexplored 50,000-acre tract of land near the junction of the Sacramento and American Rivers, after convincing Alvarado that he could act as a semiofficial representative of the government in the interior. Impressed with the proposal, the governor also promised Sutter Mexican citizenship. The early American trader William Heath Davis, Jr. first guided Sutter's party to the site of the future city of Sacramento, where Sutter planned to build his fort. Fearful of Indians, Sutter took two pieces of artillery with him into the wilderness. When, after eight days, the company reached their destination, they found some seven or eight hundred Indians awaiting them. Sutter prepared his party to resist attack, but the Indians were more curious than hostile and large numbers of them ventured out on the river to greet the foreigners in *tule balsas* (fibrous raft floats). Reassured, Davis and Sutter landed at a convenient anchorage along the Sacramento and pitched tents, only to pass the first night in the company of swarms of gigantic mosquitoes which attacked without mercy. Davis later recounted how he took leave of the group the next morning, Sutter firing a salute in honor of his departing guide. Upon hearing the noise of the cannon, hundreds of Indians crowded into Sutter's encampment. Large numbers of deer, also startled at the sound, ran crazily out of the nearby woods; "the howls of wolves and coyotes filled the air, and immense flocks of water fowl flew wildly about over the camp."

At the site of California's future capital, then in the midst of this primitive wilderness, Sutter began construction in 1840 of a defense outpost, although the work was not completed on it until several years later. He had, it will be recalled, purchased from the Russians at Fort Ross the bulk of their property. Sutter now constituted himself as guardian of the Sacramento frontier, setting up appropriate fortifications. His fort, when finished, featured an adobe wall eighteen feet high by three feet thick, enclosing a rectangular space approximately 500 by 150 feet. Sutter named his colony New Helvetia, in honor of his homeland.

Once naturalized as a Mexican citizen, and clothed with Mexican authority to administer justice, Sutter took steps to prevent robberies, to repress Indian hostilities, and to check illegal trapping and fishing. The new leader won the respect of the local Indians, many of whom he employed along with the Hawaiians he had brought with him. On his vaguely bounded grant of eleven square leagues, Sutter combined the occupations of trapper, trader, farmer, stock raiser, merchant, military ruler, and feudal magnate. He assumed an attitude of real independence, threatening on one occasion to raise the French flag and to march on the government garrison at Sonoma. At another time he broadly intimated that he would brook no interference with his plans and purposes by Mexican officials.

Sutter's marked friendliness for Americans coming into California over the Sierra passes naturally irritated California leaders. In his *Autobiography* he wrote: "I gave passports to those entering the country, and this they did not like. I was friendly with the emigrants, of whom they were jealous. I encouraged immigration, while they discouraged it. I sympathized with the Americans while they hated them." Within a short time Sutter, in effect, established a barony at New Helvetia, consisting of Indian workers who also tended thousands of sheep, cattle, horses, and hogs that roamed at will over his principality. He also developed a profitable trade in beaver skins and other agricultural products and acted the role of lord of all he surveyed.

Because New Helvetia was located on the main line of overland immigration, it came to be recognized not only as a logical trade center, but also a rendezvous for newcomers winding down the trails from the heart of the Sierra Nevada. The name of Captain Sutter became commonplace to these immigrants, to whom it stood for generosity and goodness of heart. Later, by a strange fate, the gold discovery which enriched others proved to be the undoing of Sutter. His laborers were lured away from his workaday operations by the glamor and higher wages that were associated with gold. The validity of his land titles under American law were inevitably questioned as squatter riots occurred on his lands in the 1850's. By such misfortunes, Sutter was eventually reduced from affluence and power to a position of bankruptcy.

Bidwell and the First Overland Migrants

Sutter was not the only foreigner to settle in the interior of California with Mexican permission. "Doctor" John Marsh, a young Harvard graduate, had reached California in 1836 with a company of Santa Fe trappers, and had settled on a rancho in northern California near the base of Mount Diablo. The publication of some of Marsh's letters in Missouri newspapers stimulated considerable Midwestern interest in California. Then the trapper Louis Robideaux, upon his return from California in 1840, also started a campaign of publicity on behalf of the Pacific province, arousing a fever of excitement in the little frontier town of Weston, Missouri. The trapper claimed he had found "a perfect paradise, a perpetual spring" out West. During that year almost every inhabitant of Weston and the surrounding countryside planned to migrate to California; hundreds banded themselves together into a Western Emigration Society.

Local businessmen threw cold water upon the plan, circulating unfavorable news concerning California, and before spring zeal for the great migration had cooled. The Western Emigration Society went to pieces. One spirited member, however, a twenty-year-old school teacher named John Bidwell, had become irrevocably imbued with the idea of seeing the great West and California. Accordingly, he helped to ready a migration party, though he "had barely means to buy a wagon, a gun, and provisions." By May 1, 1841, Bidwell's company was organized, consisting of forty-seven emigrants, three trappers, a group of Catholic missionaries and their wagon freighters (eleven in all), a lone Methodist minister, and various adventurers. Fifteen women and children were in the party. Paul Geddes was elected its president, John Bartleson captain, and Bidwell secretary. Thomas Fitzpatrick ("Broken Hand"), who had trapped in the Rocky Mountains and was headed for that area again, was the only person familiar with the country to be traversed. The group of missionaries, headed by the renowned Jesuit Peter De Smet, were making the westward journey in order to establish a mission among the Flathead Indians; De Smet had already wandered extensively throughout the West among the Pottawatomie, Sioux, and Blackfeet, but had not yet visited the northern Rocky Mountains, the region which was the destination of the missionaries as well as of Fitzpatrick.

On May 19, 1841, the motley caravan, known popularly as "the first emigrant train to California," started on its dusty way from Sapling Grove, Missouri. First came the missionaries, with four carts and one wagon. Next in line of march were eight wagons drawn by horses and mules. Then came the last unit, consisting of five wagons drawn by seventeen yoke of oxen. As clerk, Bidwell kept a journal, especially valuable for its account of daily life in a wagon train. He also recorded such less routine matters as the creation of "a new family" en route, an event that occurred on June 1, 1841, when one Isaac Kelsey married a Miss Williams. A week later Bidwell wrote that eight or ten buffalo were killed, their bones giving the camp the appearance of "one complete slaughter yard." On the twenty-second the party reached Fort Laramie, moving on to Independence Rock, near the Sweetwater River, well within present-day Wyoming. The emigrants next crossed South Pass toward the Bear River Valley and on July 11 reached the turn-off point of the Oregon Trail near Soda Springs. There Father De Smet, the guide Fitzpatrick, and about half of the original party departed the caravan for Fort Hall, fifty miles to the north. The rest of the party, thirty-two in number, proceeded on toward California.

Staggering through the alkali flats near the Great Salt Lake, with constant mirages ahead, the travelers jettisoned more and more of their heaviest possessions, including furniture, washpans, butter churns, baggage, and even cumbersome wagons. By September 16, Bidwell wrote that "All hands were busy making pack-saddles and getting ready to pack." No one in the party had experience in packing animals; one can only imagine a caravan of loose packs, frightened horses, kicking mules, and bellowing oxen accompanied by their footsore owners. Inexperienced and trail-weary, the group wandered for days through the Humboldt Valley and Carson Sink, in today's western Nevada, most of their provisions gone. Then one night Bartleson, a blundering and selfish person, with eight of the other men took the best horses and abandoned the party of which he was ostensibly leader. Several days later these nine deserters shamefacedly returned to camp near the Walker River, having failed to find a better route toward the Sierra crest. By that time Bidwell had calmly taken command.

After slaughtering their remaining oxen, and jerking and drying the meat for the trip ahead, the group began the ascent of the High Sierra mountain mass. As they traveled through deep snows, they carefully kept together. Bidwell's diary reports, of the twenty-eighth of October: "We ate the last of our beef this evening and killed a mule to finish our supper. Distance six miles." Two days later, to their great relief, the travelers "beheld a wide valley," and on the last day of the month they killed two antelope and some wild fowl. They had come to the edge of the Sacramento–San Joaquin Valley, which they estimated incorrectly as some hundreds of miles wide. A large stream which they now saw proved to be the Stanislaus River. They reached Marsh's ranch on November 4, 1841, almost six months after setting out from Sapling Grove.

John Bidwell quickly found employment under Sutter at New Helvetia. With each succeeding year he became more closely identified with the development of California; the qualities that had made him a trustworthy leader at a moment of crisis on the overland trail brought him renown, in time, as a prince among California pioneers.

Other American Homeseekers of the 1840's

During the early forties hundreds of Americans entered California by various overland routes; many of these came in small parties from Missouri and Arkansas, with Independence, Missouri, being the most usual gathering point for the caravans. One of these groups, which departed for California at about the same time as

Bidwell's party, was known as the Workman-Rowland company from the names of its leaders. About half of these emigrants were in quest of homes in the West, while others sought adventure or were attracted by the lore of unexplored territories. The Workman-Rowland group encountered comparatively little hardship, partly as a result of their decision to take the Santa Fe Trail rather than the lesser-known northern route. They also wisely drove along flocks of sheep for daily sustenance and were in good physical shape when they came through Cajón Pass in California and arrived at Mission San Gabriel—only a little after Bidwell reached "Doctor" Marsh's ranch. Promptly upon their arrival John Rowland sought out the local Mexican authorities, presented them with a list of the names of his party, and declared his intention of obeying all legal requirements for settlers. Notwithstanding a previous warning by the Mexican minister at Washington against emigration to California, these Americans actually were given a sort of welcome by local residents. The ease with which some of them also received large grants of land encouraged others to immigrate. However, it must not be inferred that during those disturbed years there existed any well-defined official policy of inviting American settlers into California.

Still another expedition across the mountains into California was that of the Chiles-Walker party in 1843. This was led by the old trapper Joseph Reddeford Walker and by Joseph B. Chiles, who had been with Bidwell's 1841 expedition. The main party came out from Missouri by way of Fort Boise, and proceeded southwestward across the Sierra toward the Owens Valley. After encountering many obstacles, the company reached the Walker River and Walker Lake, and then Owens Lake. At that point, because of the weakened condition of the animals, the travelers were compelled to abandon their wagons, the first ever brought into California by overland homeseekers. About Christmas they reached the headwaters of the Salinas River, and continued on to John Gilroy's ranch in the lower Santa Clara Valley. This party and such other pioneer groups as that of Lansford W. Hastings, which entered California from Oregon in 1843, scattered to different points as individual homeseekers soon after their arrival.

In May of 1844, another party, this one known as the Stevens-Murphy group, left the Missouri River and proceeded along the emigrant trail to Fort Hall. About half of them decided to go to Oregon. The remainder—including about twenty women and children—headed toward California; they reached the Humboldt Sink about the first of November, to enter the High Sierra region. Before they could complete preparations for crossing the Sierra Nevada, the first snow had made its appearance. Taking a westerly course, instead of pursuing the southerly route along Walker River, they broke a new path into California. So great were the difficulties encountered, however, that three of the men were left at Donner Lake. Not until the middle of the following March did the last members of the company finally reach the California rancho settlements.

During 1845, half a dozen more of such sizable groups traveled overland from the Missouri frontier to Sutter's Fort. These companies included the Grigsby-Ide party, consisting of fifty men with their families, and the Hastings-Semple party, which reached Sutter's Fort on Christmas Day. In the latter group was Robert Semple, a six-and-a-half-foot Kentuckian who was to become editor of California's first English-language newspaper and president of its first constitutional convention.

By word of mouth, and through newspapers, magazines, and pamphlets, an effective though uncoordinated publicity campaign developed, coaxing immigrants from all parts of the United States over the Western trails by the hundreds. Frequently small parties, meeting on the plains, joined forces to travel in long trains together for weeks on end. Once in California they could count, as previously noted, on Sutter to protect them from hostile California authorities. Early in 1846, the master of New Helvetia predicted the arrival of more than a thousand Americans that season. When Sutter wrote to an acquaintance about California's officialdom, including its military commandant, he hinted sarcastically that if "this Rascle of Castro" should undertake to interfere with his activities, "a very warm and hearty welcome is prepared for him." Sutter could not afford to be more explicit, lest his message be captured. In a letter to Jacob P. Leese, an American trader, the Swiss referred to the ten guns and two field pieces he kept in readiness to protect his fortress; Sutter added significantly, if not grammatically: "I have also about 50 faithful Indians which shot their musquet very quick."

It is impossible to trace the movements of the numerous parties of overland immigrants of 1846, or even to record the names of all their leaders. Vivid portrayals of the experiences of these homeseekers are to be found in such books as Edwin Bryant's *What I Saw in California* (1848) and Jessy Thornton's *Oregon and California* ... (1849). During 1846 a number of Americans also reached California by water. Conspicuous among these was the party headed by the Mormon leader Samuel Brannan, who entered the Golden Gate with a company of young colonists on the last day of July. Part of the group had intended to go on to Salt Lake City, where Brigham Young planned to build a new Zion of Mormonism. During the voyage two children were born on board the *Brooklyn*, the ship which Brannan had chartered—one, a boy, named Atlantic; the other, a girl, christened Pacific.

Out of a total of 7,000 persons who migrated to the Pacific Coast during the years from 1843 to 1846, the number of immigrants who actually entered California probably did not exceed 1,500. The early settlers were generally more attracted by the Oregon territory. So many Americans, in fact, came to the Northwest that the Hudson's Bay Company began to fear for British commercial control over the region. Company representatives actually sought to divert Americans coming through Fort Hall away from what is today Oregon and Washington by persuading them of California's superiority.

Frémont

By 1842 the days of the mountain men had begun to wane. As many independent trappers settled down to a life of trading, an era of exploration increasingly shaped by government survey parties began. In this new period the United States Army's Topographical Engineers played a large role. The year 1843–1844 saw the arrival in California of John C. Frémont, naturalist-explorer-scientist, on his second expedition to the Far West. Frémont's guide on this expedition, as well as on the one he had made the year before, was Kit Carson. It was not the direct purpose of the Frémont expedition to induce homeseekers to emigrate toward the Pacific; nevertheless, Frémont, working in the tradition of his mentor, the French geographer Joseph Nicollet, produced a number of maps of the western territory which had precisely that effect.

Frémont reached Fort Hall on September 19, 1843. From there his party proceeded by way of the Snake River to Fort Boise, down the Dalles, and via the Columbia to Fort Vancouver, where provisions for three months were laid in. Then Frémont returned to the Dalles. His intention was to explore Klamath Lake and to search for "a reported lake called Mary's, at some days' journey in the great basin; and thence still on southeast to the reputed Buenaventura River." Moving boldly through northwestern Nevada, Frémont continued to the Truckee and Carson Rivers. He originally had no plans to cross the Sierra Nevada into California, but on reaching the mountains rashly decided to take his weary men over them. While ascending the eastern slope of the Sierra, on January 29, 1844, he found it necessary to discard a twelve-pound brass howitzer which his party, ostensibly a scientific venture, had lugged along.

After an icy crossing of the Sierra Frémont's men reached Sutter's Fort, or New Helvetia, via Carson Pass, early in March. Frémont rested several weeks at New Helvetia, then moved southward along the San Joaquin Valley to the Kings River. He next crossed Tehachapi Pass toward the Great Salt Lake and returned to Saint Louis. The explorer's official report, thousands of copies of which were printed and eagerly read, brought Frémont new fame. Historians, however, continue to differ over whether he was truly "the West's greatest adventurer," "a man unafraid," the "pathmarker of the West"—as his biographers have called Frémont—or whether he was merely a follower of other men's trails under government auspices. While his first entry into California was almost accidental, and scarcely a new venture, its importance for later events is obvious. Frémont mapped, surveyed, and charted the trails of the trappers, publicizing their routes and thus attracting more overland travelers to the West. He also stirred up a hornet's nest of controversy over his third expedition, in 1845–1846, and came to embroil himself deeply in the American conquest of California.

The Donner Party

In the spring of 1846 James F. Reed of Springfield, Illinois, with two friends, George and Jacob Donner, formed one of many emigrant companies to depart for California that year. Their party was doomed to play a fateful, indeed tragic, role in the history of the American West. The struggles of this first overland train from Illinois were due in part to the ineptness and lack of force of George Donner, who became nominal head of the group. Bad luck as well as bad judgment plagued the whole enterprise, although some of its participants displayed notable heroism in the midst of disaster. Included in the party were well-to-do farmers and poor families, persons of learning and ignorant folk, native Americans and Irish and German emigrants. A disproportionate number of elderly people, women, and youngsters were among them, and the group as a whole was particularly shy of able-bodied men.

The Donners prepared to join an Oregon caravan, proceed with it to Fort Hall, then branch off via Frémont's route into central California. The company's outfit included seed and implements to be used in farming, and bolts of bright cotton cloth, handkerchiefs, flannels, beads, earrings, laces, and silks for use in trading with the Indians. The most important equipment consisted of several large, strongly constructed wagons, whose curved frames were covered with tent cloth. The party also brought along necessary livestock, as well as more than $10,000 in cash "stitched between the folds of a quilt for safe transportation."

The group was astir before dawn on April 15, and by noon the emigrants were well started on their trip. They reached the Mississippi within a few days; on May 11, in the best of spirits, they made camp at Independence. During early June all continued to go well. From a point near the junction of the North and South Platte, Mrs. George Donner wrote:

We are now four hundred and fifty miles from Independence. . . . I could never have believed we could have traveled so far with so little difficulty. The prairie between the Blue and the Platte rivers is beautiful beyond description.

The travelers celebrated the Fourth of July in patriotic style, with songs, a reading of the Declaration of Independence, and an address by one of the men in the party. Not the slightest hint of misfortune had yet occurred.

At Fort Bridger the leaders of the caravan made their first mistake. They decided to follow the amateurish advice of Lansford W. Hastings, who had published *An Emigrants Guide to Oregon and California* (1845) describing a new route to California, allegedly two hundred miles shorter than the one by way of Fort Hall. This route, "Hastings Cut-off" (which Hastings had never seen), originated on the Overland Trail and terminated about eight miles west of today's Elko, Nevada. It ran south of the Great Salt Lake via Fort Bridger and joined the California Trail on the Humboldt River. The illusory cut-off turned out to be a nightmare for the Donner party.

On July 20, the Donners broke camp and plunged into an unknown wilderness. Along an almost impassable route, they fought their way through the Wasatch Mountains. At times the party was compelled to use ten yoke of oxen to draw a single wagon up the sides of a steep gulch. Despite their fortitude, the emigrants were a month—instead of a week, as they had planned—in reaching the shores of the Great Salt Lake. The loss of time proved costly. West of Salt Lake it became apparent that the supplies would give out before the group could reach California. Two members of the party, Charles Stanton and William McCutcheon, volunteered to proceed on horseback to procure food from Sutter's Fort. The frustrating hardships the travelers were obliged to face during those September days of 1846 almost defy description. Because of lack of water they left thirty-six head of cattle on the desert. A mirage, revealing the waters of a lake, turned disappointment into anguish. Return to Fort Bridger was impossible; there was no alternative but to continue desperately onward.

The situation got more tense after an argument that resulted when a member of the party, John Snyder, inadvertently struck the wife of another member, James F. Reed, with a bull whip. Reed, enraged, stabbed Snyder to death; he then used the boards from his wagon to make a coffin for the dead man. The Donner party passed a severe judgment on the murderer, who claimed he had acted in self-defense. There on the remote desert floor of Western America, miles from the nearest habitation, Reed's companions forced him to leave the train. With his gun and a few provisions he set out alone for California. Each day thereafter Reed's wife and children looked for traces of him along the way— the feathers of a bird killed, or an occasional note pinned onto a bush. They wondered whether he might be scalped by Indians, or whether he would ever make it alone to some frontier outpost. The Donner party had banished one of its most needed members.

As they slowly moved toward the Sierra, the Donner leaders made another mistake. Winter was coming on fast. Instead of pressing forward, the party tarried four days for a badly needed rest. Truckee Meadows, near the present city of Reno, Nevada, was covered with grasses and clover of good quality. It was difficult to leave such security behind and proceed on toward the unknown. On October 19, Stanton returned from Sutter's Fort with two Indian guides, seven mules, and limited amounts of beef and flour. He had left his sick companion, McCutcheon, behind with Captain Sutter. Three days later the party crossed the winding Truckee River "for the forty-ninth and last time in eighty miles." They next went up Prosser Creek and followed it northward through barely passable canyons to the mouth of Alder Creek. Clouds high on the mountain crest gave a clear indication of approaching winter, and there was a nip in the air. Finally alarmed, the emigrants found as they moved into the higher elevations that their wagons could not be dragged through the early snows that fell in the Sierra that year. One wagon broke its axle and tipped over onto little Eliza Donner, three years old, and Georgia, age four; the children were almost crushed by the avalanche of household goods that fell upon them. There was further delay as the party repacked provisions onto cumbersome oxen.

Full-scale winter descended upon the Donners almost a month ahead of time in the vicinity of upper Alder Creek. The snow became so deep that one part of the train was snowbound near Donner Lake, at an elevation of 7,150 feet, while another group holed up under brush, pine branches, and inadequate canvas shelters about six miles from the first entrenchment. The party was forced to wait thus for the four months until early spring, inadequately sheltered by the snow-covered pines on one of the Sierra's windiest and coldest passes. The snow that winter eventually reached a depth of twenty-two feet. No one knows the full extent of the harrowing experiences endured during the continuous battle against freezing and starvation. Writers sympathetic to the Donner party later denied allegations of cannibalism, but it is probable that desperate conditions caused almost all of the marooned pioneers who survived to eat the flesh of dead trailmates.

During the winter the group made repeated efforts to get out of the mountains. They improvised snowshoes out of oxbows and strips of rawhide. In mid-December, 1846, a party known as "The Fifteen" left the rest. After weeks of severe suffering, dazed and stumbling about in the snow, seven survivors emerged from the Sierra via Emigrant Gap onto a California rancho. On the nineteenth of February, 1847, the emigrants back up on the Sierra crest were startled by shouts. The strongest of them, climbing to the top of a huge snow bank, witnessed the "most welcome sight of their lives"—a reconnaissance party of seven men, which had been provisioned by Sutter, composed of some of the formerly snowed in survivors. Each man bore a pack of provisions. Even Reed, banished earlier from the party, arrived with a second relief party to save some of the very men who had cast him out. He was overjoyed to find his wife and four children still alive, despite their grotesque privations. A third rescue group also appeared to offer help to the emigrants. George Donner, however, leader of the train, was now too weak and sick to travel. His wife, though able to make the journey, refused to leave her husband, allowing her little daughters to be taken from her to safety. When the fourth and last relief party arrived in the spring they found that Mrs. Donner too had died. Forty-five of the seventy-nine persons in the original Donner party had survived.

A Western World

American westward pioneers were an independent lot, and they faced their problems accordingly. The absence of binding precedent or tradition in the frontier life, and the restless energy prodding these people to become trappers, miners, and ranchers, was inevitably allied with a common sense that helped them struggle through their adversities. Along with American practicality, these pioneers had a faith which, though not carefully defined or paraded publicly, was insurmountable. A mixture of individualism, religious conviction, and incurable nationalism led many of them to believe it was their "manifest destiny" to build a new Western world beyond the mountains in California. There was also conspicuous among these men a sense of justice—of the direct and immediate variety. The Westerner, quick to defend himself against any attack, resented the law's delays, and restrictions of government were irksome to him. Though nobody was more ready to show himself a friend to one in need, nobody was more swift to rebuke the perpetrator of an action that was considered dishonorable. The "popular tribunal," sometimes full of excess zeal for hoisting the hangman's noose, exemplified one of the less attractive characteristics of this new Western world.

Despite its inherent drawbacks, however, the West exerted a generally emancipating influence on those who came into contact with it. The man on the trail, concerned as he was with simple survival, saw things large; generally the environment forced him into action rather than thought. And, as he marched into California, it was the land that he most wanted. It lay about him in inviting abundance. "Here was a country," wrote Walter Colton in 1846, "where furlongs stretch into leagues." If only all this land could soon become a part of the United States! In an age when tension between their country and Mexico mounted, American settlers naturally harbored such thoughts. Furthermore, the rate of American migration to California in the 1840's seemed almost to forecast its future control by *Yanquis*.

The studious "Doctor" Marsh's estimate of California's population for 1845 included 7,000 persons of Spanish blood and 10,000 domesticated Indians. In addition, Marsh calculated that foreigners in the province numbered 700 Americans; perhaps 100 English, Scotch, and Irish; and another 100 Germans, French, and Italians. The number of Americans may seem small by modern standards, but it is significant that of the foreign population of California during the Mexican regime, the American group far outnumbered all other groups combined. And more settlers continued to enter the province from the United States.

SELECTED READINGS

The literature of the overland fur trade, already huge, is still multiplying. Basic to its California phase are Hiram Martin Chittenden, *The History of the American Fur Trade of the Far West* (3 vols., New York, 1902), and Paul C. Phillips, *The Fur Trade* (2 vols., Norman, Okla., 1961). Southwestern aspects of the subject are described in

Robert Glass Cleland, *This Reckless Breed of Men* (New York, 1950). References concerning Jedediah Smith are cited among the readings for Chapter 11. Other works on individual pioneer trappers include Joseph J. Hill, "Ewing Young in the Fur Trade of the American Southwest," *Oregon Historical Quarterly*, XXIV (March, 1923), 1–35; T. D. Bonner, *Life and Adventures of James P. Beckwourth* (New York, 1856); Charles L. Camp, ed., *James Clyman: American Frontiersman* (San Francisco, 1928); William Henry Ellison, ed., *The Life and Adventures of George Nidever* (Berkeley, 1937); Alpheus H. Favour, *Old Bill Williams, Mountain Man* (Chapel Hill, 1936); and the incomparable *The Personal Narrative of James Ohio Pattie of Kentucky*, edited by Timothy Flint (Cincinnati, 1831). Pattie's narrative seems almost purposefully vague at times. This characteristic is clarified in Stanton A. Coblentz, *The Swallowing Wilderness* . . . (New York, 1961), a biography of Pattie which, regrettably, has no index, bibliography, or scholarly apparatus. See also Clifton B. Kroeber, ed., "The Route of James Ohio Pattie on the Colorado in 1826: A Reappraisal by A. L. Kroeber," *Arizona and The West*, VI (Summer, 1964), 119–136. Iris Wilson, *William Wolfskill, 1798–1866: Frontier Trapper to California Ranchero* (Glendale, 1965), is a detailed account of how one mountain man refound himself in a new setting. The lives of many others are examined in LeRoy Hafen, ed., *The Mountain Men and the Fur Trade of the Far West* (6 vols., Glendale, 1965–1968). W. J. Ghent has written a life of Thomas Fitzpatrick entitled *Broken Hand* (New York, 1931). Doyce B. Nunis has dealt with Andrew Sublette in *Andrew Sublette: Rocky Mountain Prince, 1813–1835* (Los Angeles, 1960).

Other rewarding volumes on the fur trade are Bernard De Voto, *Across the Wide Missouri* (Cambridge, 1947), and Lewis H. Garrard, *Wah-to-Yah and the Taos Trail* (Cincinnati, 1850). George F. Ruxton, *Life in the Far West* (New York, 1859), is a novel which reproduces quite accurately many aspects of the fur trade. As their titles indicate, not all of these books bear directly upon California, but almost all of them deal with the Far West. See also, especially for an account of the Hudson's Bay Company in California, Alice Bay Maloney, *Fur Brigade to the Bonaventura* (San Francisco, 1945), and her earlier article, "Peter Skene Ogden's Trapping Expedition to the Gulf of California, 1829–30," California Historical Society *Quarterly*, XIX (December, 1940), 308–316. More on the Hudson's Bay Company in California is in Dorothy Blakey Smith, ed., *James Douglas in California, 1841* (Vancouver, 1965). A good personal view of the fur trade, touching also upon California, is in Sir George Simpson, *Narrative of a Journey Round the World, During the Years 1841 and 1842* (2 vols., London, 1849). A. C. Laut, *The Story of the Trapper* (New York, 1902), is an informative discussion of the topic. Stanley Vestal's *Mountain Men* (Boston, 1937) is, like other books by that author, a popularization resting upon the work of other historians as well as upon first-hand accounts.

The colorful Sutter has attracted much attention. His autobiography, in German, is entitled *Neu-Helvetien: Lebenserinnerungen des Generals Johann Augustus Sutter* (Frauenfeld, Switzerland, 1944). Consult also Erwin G. Gudde, *Sutter's Own Story* (New York, 1936). Secondary accounts are James Peter Zollinger, *Sutter: The Man and His Empire* (New York, 1939); the less valuable work by Julian Dana, *Sutter of California* (New York, 1938); and Marguerite Eyer Wilbur, *John Sutter: Rascal and Adventurer* (New York, 1949). See also John A. Hawgood, "John Augustus Sutter: A Reappraisal," *Arizona and the West*, IV (Winter, 1962), 345–356.

A biography of Bidwell has been written by Rockwell D. Hunt under the title *John Bidwell: Prince of California Pioneers* (Caldwell, Idaho, 1942). Bidwell's own *Echoes of the Past*, ed. by Milo M. Quaife (Chicago, 1928), and reprinted as *In California Before the Gold Rush* (Los Angeles, 1948), also gives one a picture of the first overland emigrant party to California. There are many books depicting the trail records of other expeditions. Two of the best are Edwin Bryant, *What I Saw in California* (New York, 1848), and J. A. Thornton, *Oregon and California in 1848* (2 vols., New York, 1849). An excellent account of an overland expedition of 1843 is that by Overton Johnson and William H. Winter, *Route Across the Rocky Mountains* (Princeton, 1932). Marsh's role in receiving these overland parties is discussed in the standard biography by George D. Lyman, *Dr. John Marsh, Pioneer* (New York, 1930).

Books concerning Frémont are listed among readings for the next chapter.

Thomas F. Andrews, "The Controversial Hastings Overland Guide: A Reassessment," *Pacific Historical Review*, XXXVII (February, 1968), 21–34, restores to that controversial source some of the influence denied it by later historians.

A mine of information about the Donner tragedy, including diaries and correspondence of various survivors (among them Patrick Breen and James F. Reed), is in Dale Morgan, ed., *Overland in 1846: Diaries and Letters of the California-Oregon Trail* (2 vols., Georgetown, Calif., 1963).

The Donner party has also been dealt with in the following books: C. F. McGlashan, *History of the Donner Party: A Tragedy of the Sierra* (Stanford, 1940, 1947); George R. Stewart, *Ordeal by Hunger: The Story of the Donner Party* (New York, 1936, 1960); and Walter M. Stookey, *Fatal Decision: The Tragic Story of the Donner Party* (Salt Lake City, 1950). A first-hand account, written later in life, is Eliza P. Donner Houghton's *The Expedition of the Donner Party* (Los Angeles, 1920). See also Virginia Murphy Reed, "Across the Plains in the Donner Party," *Century Magazine*, XLII (May–October, 1891), 409–426—a highly interesting account by the daughter of James F. Reed, who was banished from the party; she infers that virtually every family "was forced to eat human flesh to keep body and soul together." An interesting recent commentary on the Donner route is David E. Miller, "The Donner Road through the Great Salt Lake Desert," *Pacific Historical Review*, XXVII (February, 1958), 30–44. A fictionalized treatment is Joseph Pigney, *For Fear We Shall Perish* . . . (New York, 1961).

An extremely useful set of overland trail maps, with a skillful accompanying narrative, is provided in J. Gregg Layne's *Western Wayfaring: Routes of Exploration and Trade in the American Southwest* (Los Angeles, 1954). Consult also George R. Stewart, *The California Trail* (New York, 1962).

14

American Conquest

American sentiment for the acquisition of California had deep roots. Even before the appearance of the first trappers, traders, and homeseekers in the Western province, the United States had expressed official interest in purcasing it. In 1829 President Andrew Jackson had sent Anthony Butler as his envoy into Mexico to negotiate for extensive territory in the American Southwest. Butler was an unfortunate choice; his suggestion of a bribe which would lead to the acquisition of California, Texas, and New Mexico offended the Mexicans, and he returned home in diplomatic disgrace. The idea of adding California to American territory, however, was never abandoned by Jackson, nor by his successors, Presidents Van Buren, Tyler, and Polk. The strategic location of San Francisco Bay alone, with its matchless harbor and rich surrounding country, greatly impressed all of these presidents.

Furthermore, the laxity of Mexican control over the province made it obvious that California might well fall into the hands of some outside power. The Russians had, of course, by 1842 withdrawn from their trading post in California, but other countries continued to take a keen interest in the future of the province. Even Prussia, as historians have recently discovered, had an acquisitive eye on California. French interest in the territory had been whetted by the previously mentioned voyages of La Pérouse and De Mofras. In 1841 Vallejo wrote Governor Alvarado: "There is little doubt that France is intriguing to become mistress of

193

California." De Mofras, as a matter of fact, had expressed his explicit opinion that "a French protectorate offers to California the most satisfactory way of escape from the dangers that threaten its future." The account of his explorations made careful note of the number of Frenchmen residing at different points in the territory, emphasized the essentially foreign character of Sutter's New Helvetia, and called to mind the identity of French and Spanish religion and temperament.

England's interest in California and the West (including Texas and Oregon) was even stronger than France's, and deepened with British suspicions of French designs on the coast after the De Mofras visit. From the time of Vancouver onward, the commanders of English vessels along the Pacific Coast, as well as James Alexander Forbes, British Consul at Monterey, had sent strong suggestions to the British Foreign Office that California be acquired by the Crown. Although hindsight indicates that an English invasion of California was never really imminent, one can, nevertheless, understand the anxiety of the Californians. In 1846, they became apprehensive at the news that Father Eugene McNamara, a Catholic priest, proposed to plant a colony of one thousand Irish and English Catholic families in the San Francisco Bay region. Supposedly this scheme had official English backing. McNamara's purposes were stated to be those of advancing the cause of Catholicism and of preventing usurpation of California by the United States—"an irreligious and anti-Catholic nation." Father McNamara never fulfilled his plan, and it has never been fully explained how English imperial aspirations were supposed to have been reconciled with these Irish Catholic ambitions. We know today that fears of British designs upon California were greatly exaggerated. Nevertheless, such fears had some bearing upon the development of United States policy, particularly during the era of President James K. Polk.

Deepening United States Involvement

Two of the events that had occurred in California in 1839 and in 1840 were to prove especially significant in terms of the American position there—the founding of Sutter's fort at New Helvetia, and the arrest of the former fur trapper Isaac Graham. Sutter's presence astride the overland trails has already been discussed as a definite threat to Mexico's authority in the interior of California. Graham's internment, along with that of his various rough associates, preceded the stationing of permanent United States naval forces in California waters. Under President Tyler a movement for purchase of the province became more definite. A United States diplomat, Waddy Thompson, pointed out the particular advantages of possessing San Francisco Bay, calling it "capacious enough to receive the navies of all the world." He contended: "It will be worth a war of twenty years to prevent England from acquiring it."

In 1842 the Stars and Stripes had already momentarily supplanted the Mexican eagle in California; Commodore Jones had, as previously noted, raised the American flag over Monterey in the mistaken belief that the United States was at war with Mexico. This was a great embarrassment to Jones, to the Navy, and to the chagrined United States government. Although Secretary of State Daniel Webster tendered the Mexican government a formal apology, the episode revealed that the United States did not intend to be caught unprepared in any race between the great powers to acquire California. California officials were understandably antagonized and remained on their guard against future American designs.

President Polk was elected on a platform favoring the annexation of Texas and settlement of the Oregon boundary with England. Implicit in the platform was strong interest in California also. In 1845, when Polk came into office, foreign governments began to understand that the United States was committed to an expansionist policy. Any interference by a European power with American plans might cause war. To the English especially, it became clear that an inevitable result of war between the United States and Mexico would be American rule over California. But there is evidence that the British foreign secretary, Lord Aberdeen, felt powerless to prevent this, since he was unwilling to risk the consequences of a war in order to keep California from falling under United States control.

Polk sent the alert Thomas Oliver Larkin to Monterey as his consul and confidential agent, to report in detail on conditions there. The president wanted Larkin to prepare the groundwork for peaceful American penetration. Even before Americans in large numbers settled in California, it had been clear that the province could not long remain under Mexican rule. Mexico was too weak administratively to cope with the foreign challenge.

Polk first hoped to attempt the purchase of California. If he should fail, there were three other possibilities: (1) a revolt instigated by leading Californians against Mexico, aided also by American residents there who could be expected to seek admission into the Union; (2) patient delay, while the province was occupied by more Americans who would inevitably seek their independence; and (3) forcible seizure in a war with Mexico. Polk's undeniably aggressive policy involved the appointment of John Slidell as his official representative in Mexico, partly to explore the possibility of purchasing or annexing Texas and obtaining California and New Mexico, as well. United States failure in negotiations for the Southwestern territories was due as much to disturbed internal Mexican political conditions as to Mexico's unwillingness to sell, although the Mexicans did regard the very suggestion of giving up these territories to Yankees as demeaning.

After the failure of the Slidell mission in October, 1845, and the American annexation of Texas that year, Mexican-American diplomatic negotiations deteriorated steadily. Mexico greatly resented this "seizure" of one of its provinces although, since 1836, the Texans had proclaimed themselves independent. On April 25, 1846, following various border quarrels, Mexican forces entered the disputed territory between the Nueces and the Rio Grande Rivers. General Zachary Taylor had already moved United States troops up to the Nueces as early as July, 1845 to protect the new state. President Polk's administration now called the Mexican action an invasion of American territory and requested a declaration of war from Congress. This was forthcoming on May 12, 1846. When General Taylor crossed the Mexican border, the action inflamed the entire southwest from Texas to California.

Frémont and the Hawk's Peak Incident

Frémont, well aware that war with Mexico over the annexation of Texas and other territorial conflicts in the Southwest was possible, had left St. Louis in May 1845 with his third Western expedition. Its professed purpose, further exploration of the Great Basin and of the Pacific Coast, was not likely to relieve the tension between the two countries. With a party of sixty-two soldiers, scouts, topographers, and six Delaware Indians, Frémont again crossed the Sierra to Sutter's Fort, reaching California December 9, 1845. This time he traveled as far south as Monterey, where he held a conference with Consul Larkin. José Castro, who commanded the garrison at the capital city, was suspicious of the motives which had brought Frémont there. Frémont explained that his expedition was purely scientific and peaceful, and that he had come to Monterey only to purchase needed supplies. Castro thereupon gave the expedition permission to winter in California, with the understanding that Frémont would keep his men away from the coastal settlements. The California officials obviously suspected ship-to-shore American contacts.

In early March, 1846, after rejoining the main body of his force in the Santa Clara Valley—under temporary command of the trapper Joseph Reddeford Walker—Frémont demonstrated his flair for the dramatic. He withdrew toward a bluff named Gavilan, or Hawk's Peak, where he built a log fortification overlooking the Salinas Valley, only twenty-five miles from Monterey. He raised the American flag and seemed about to entrench himself when he received the news that Castro, in protest against his conduct, was about to order him from the province. At first Frémont ignored the possibility of trouble. Then a warning letter from Larkin, and the realization that Castro seemed to be preparing a force to dislodge him, persuaded Frémont to vacate Hawk's Peak "slowly and growlingly" and move his men northward toward the Oregon wilds. Although he had, perhaps, meanwhile thought over his indiscreet conduct, Frémont's rashness seriously embarrassed Larkin and those other established American residents who hoped for peaceful annexation of California by quiet diplomacy and behind-the-scenes contacts. The feelings of California officials toward the United States, furthermore, were outraged by the incident at Hawk's Peak.

On his way north the young commander was overtaken by Lieutenant Archibald H. Gillespie, a United States Marine Corps officer who had crossed Mexico in disguise. He produced a packet of secret messages from United States officials in Washington, including Secretary of State James Buchanan, as well as from Frémont's wife, Jessie Benton, and her father, Thomas Hart Benton, the expansionist chairman of the United States Senate Committee on Territories. Verbal instructions from President Polk may well have been given him as well. In the absence of documentary evidence, historians will never be able to determine the precise orders given Frémont—at this time or earlier. Whatever the content of the communications he received, their effect was to turn him back toward northern California. Gillespie's dispatches probably warned that war with Mexico was inevitable and, in effect, directed Frémont to hold himself in readiness to cooperate with land and naval forces of the United States. Concerning the messages from Benton, Frémont later wrote: "His letters made me know distinctly that at last the time had come when England must not get a foothold; that we *must be first*. I was to *act*, discreetly but positively."

Frémont's decision to return to the Sacramento Valley, an act which he subsequently declared to have been "the first step in the conquest of California," transformed him from an explorer into a soldier, and almost into an imperialist. He has since been strongly criticized for his conduct, and it is generally conceded that he was wanting in tactful approach at this time. Yet, the vague governmental instructions under which he was acting hardly specified what his relationship should be with the aggressive little group of Americans that had settled in California's Central Valley. His return was "to the fears of the settlers as a spark to powder." As he approached the Marysville (now Sutter) Buttes, sixty miles north of Sutter's Fort, the Americans flocked into his camp. All were disturbed and excited by the rumors of approaching war between the United States and Mexico, but they were wholly in the dark regarding United States governmental intentions and even regarding the appointment of Larkin as President Polk's confidential agent. They imagined that a strong band of Californians, intent upon expelling all foreigners, planned to take over Sutter's Fort, their rallying point. It is for this reason that they so enthusiastically welcomed the arrival of Frémont. The explorer, however, placed himself in an extremely difficult and delicate position. He had no official instructions to support or to instigate a revolt among American settlers in California. Apparently, however, he did not want to see an incipient uprising dissolved, with Americans driven out of the disputed province for lack of his support.

The Bear Flag Revolt

The fears of the disturbed settlers near Frémont's camp continued to mount. Even the conservative Consul Larkin wrote Secretary of State Buchanan that he refused to predict the course of events: "I shall be in continual expectations of hearing of some outbreak from one or the other, in one or two years, perhaps in less time." Encouraged, albeit passively, by Frémont, some of the Americans were spoiling for a fight. One group, under the leadership of Ezekiel Merritt, seemed almost anxious for outright hostilities to begin; these men were rough, leatherjacketed frontiersmen, part of a "floating population" of Americans in California whose behavior was considered distasteful and uncouth by many of their compatriots. The more substantial foreign residents, including Sutter and Larkin, were appalled by the conduct of these ruffians who saw themselves in the role of American patriots. Yet, neither Sutter nor Larkin would have accused them of lacking courage; instead, they considered them lacking in good judgment.

Early in June, 1846, the frontiersmen heard that a large *caballada*, or band of horses, which José Castro had obtained from

Vallejo, was being driven from Sonoma to the Santa Clara Valley by Mexican officials, via Sutter's Fort. Merritt's men thought these horses destined for use against the American settlers, as part of a movement for their expulsion. With the knowledge, if not the sanction, of Frémont, Merritt and his followers intercepted the horses and took them to Frémont's camp. Sutter, anxious to avoid open hostilities with the Californians, was disgusted over Frémont's support of these quarrelsome Americans in what appeared to be a warlike act.

A few days later, Merritt joined forces with another local American leader, William B. Ide, in the capture of General Vallejo's headquarters in northern California, at Sonoma. This event, occurring even before news of the large confiscation of horses had reached the Mexican commander, was especially surprising since Vallejo was known to be a strong supporter of Americans in California. In fact, Larkin had counted upon Vallejo's unusual prestige with both the native population and the settlers to help in smoothing the possible annexation of California to the United States. At dawn on June 14, the followers of Merritt and Ide burst into Vallejo's home and routed the general from his bed. By their behavior, which included gulping down his brandy, they offended and confused his family and personal entourage. "To whom shall we surrender?" asked the general's wife, unable to comprehend the commotion. The Americans forced the humiliated Vallejo to sign vague articles of surrender and placed him under arrest. Also arrested were Lieutenant Colonel Victor Prudon and Captain Salvador Vallejo. The members of Vallejo's Sonoma garrison were taken in a body to Sutter's Fort, much to the chagrin of the old Swiss.

As a result of his boldness at Sonoma, Ide emerged as the leader of the American revolt. His followers had already provided themselves a flag with which to dignify their movement. They would have liked to use the American Stars and Stripes, but Frémont would not authorize them to do so, however much he sympathized with them. Therefore, Ide and his men had improvised a red and white flag, on which a grizzly bear faced a red star. They selected the bear because the grizzly was the strongest animal in California. The framers of this crude ensign wrote about it: "A bear stands his ground always, and as long as the stars shine we stand for the cause." On the day they captured Sonoma, the Bear Flaggers raised their standard over its plaza. They spoke of themselves thereafter as representatives of the "California Republic," and made Sonoma their base. On June 24 they engaged in a relatively bloodless skirmish with the Californians between the pueblos of

San Rafael and Sonoma. The engagement somehow received the name "Battle of Olompali" but it was clearly unimportant, except in consolidating the position of the Bear Flaggers. Neither they nor the Californians whom they fought had yet heard that an official state of war existed between Mexico and the United States.

Ide's men desired to be known as something other than a band of filibusters. He therefore issued a proclamation giving his "inviolable pledge" that all persons "not found under arms" should remain undisturbed. The anomalous and extra-legal situation of the Bear Flaggers had become daily more evident. This independent group had excited themselves into staging a revolt far more severe than the Graham Affair half a decade before. To what lengths this revolution might have gone will, however, never be known. The Bear Flag movement came to a sudden halt when the American flag was officially raised at Sonoma, after the capture of Monterey on July 7, 1846, by the naval forces of Commodore John Drake Sloat. (Sloat had heard of the outbreak of war early in June while anchored at Mazatlán, on the west coast of Mexico, and had quietly slipped out of that harbor and proceeded to California.) When the American ensign replaced the short-lived Bear Flag, the "California Republic" was thereby terminated. Late in July the American military command formally nullified the actions of the Bear Flaggers, and Vallejo and his fellow prisoners were ordered released.

Provincial pride and historical romanticism created the legend that the Bear Flag Revolt produced an independent California, which then became part of the United States. Actually, the Bear Flag uprising was of limited significance in the acquisition of California; it reflected the attitude of only a few disgruntled and irresponsible settlers in the province, and it accomplished little. The conquest of California would have occurred without it.

Early Success

One American who played a significant, though not spectacular, part in the conquest of California was Consul Larkin. He had come to the province as early as 1832, and had developed a thriving trading business along the coast. Following his appointment as United States consul in 1843, Larkin had dutifully kept his government informed as to conditions in California, with which he became thoroughly familiar. Larkin's policy was always conciliatory but by no means unfaithful to his country's interests. His consular dispatches constitute a rich source of information about a confusing period in California history. And his personal contribution to its American conquest was more significant than generally acknowledged.

Commodore Sloat, as commander of United States naval forces in Pacific waters, had been instructed to seize various California harbors in the event of war with Mexico. He had learned from Larkin of the Hawk's Peak incident involving Frémont; believing hostilities to be imminent, he had, early in June, 1846, ordered naval forces to proceed toward Monterey to establish American control there. He set out immediately with them, in the flagship *Savannah*. Admiral Sir George Seymour, commander of the British squadron in the Pacific, was also in the area, keeping a close watch upon the movements of the American fleet. At Monterey, Sloat received official dispatches and held extended conferences with Consul Larkin. These concerned revolutionary sentiment in California, the capture of General Vallejo, the Bear Flag uprising, and the latest activities of Frémont. Since Sloat did not at once raise the American flag, he has been charged with indecision and inaction. However, he was in a delicate position; he had no idea by what authority Frémont had been acting, nor had he been informed as to the import of the messages that Gillespie had brought that commander. Yet it is evident from the proclamation Sloat issued to the inhabitants, as well as from his correspondence, that he had positive knowledge of hostilities in Texas along the Nueces River, even though he had not been officially notified of any "formal declaration of war" by Washington.

At 10 A.M. on July 7, 1846, Sloat landed some 250 marines and seamen at Monterey under Captain William Mervine. They marched directly to the custom house, where the commodore's proclamation was read, the United States flag raised and cheered, and a salute of twenty-one guns fired from each American vessel. Sloat's proclamation referred to the state of war between the two nations but announced:

I declare to the inhabitants of California that, although I come in arms with a powerful force, I do not come among them as an enemy of California; on the contrary, I come as their best friend, as henceforward California will be a portion of the United States, and its peaceful inhabitants will enjoy the same rights and privileges as the citizens of any other portion of that territory . . . together with the privilege of choosing their own magistrates and other officers for the administration of justice among themselves; and the same protection will be extended to them as to any other state in the Union. . . .

A week later the flag of the United States was flying at Yerba

Buena, at Sutter's Fort, at Bodega, and at Sonoma, headquarters of the Bear Flaggers. Sloat's landing came just in time to prevent that group from further military action, which might well have proved disastrous.

On July 15, 1846, Commodore Robert F. Stockton arrived at Monterey on the *Congress*, to replace Sloat. The new commander's vigorous actions were in striking contrast with Sloat's moderation. On July 23, Stockton issued a more belligerent proclamation than Sloat's. This one announced that Stockton would not confine his operations "to the quiet and undisturbed possession of the defenseless ports of Monterey and San Francisco," but that he planned to march "against these boasting and abusive chiefs" of the interior and southern districts. Stockton reorganized the forces of Frémont, which included some of the Bear Flaggers, on a wartime footing. Although himself a naval officer, Stockton promoted Brevet Captain Frémont to the rank of major. Frémont then enlisted volunteers from the American settlers into a unit called the California Battalion of Mounted Riflemen, and, acting under orders, joined Stockton in a spectacular initial capture of much of the province. "We simply marched all over California, from Sonoma to San Diego," wrote John Bidwell afterward, "and raised the American flag without protest. We tried to find an enemy, but could not." This early success was possible because the Californians had no organized army worthy of the name; Castro's immediate forces numbered scarcely a hundred men, largely disaffected and almost without arms. But Castro threatened that if Americans marched on Los Angeles they would find their grave.

Reversal

On the afternoon of August 13, 1846, American naval forces entered Los Angeles and raised their flag without opposition. Stockton issued several more proclamations and concluded what may be called the first conquest of California. Gillespie, the courier who had met Frémont with messages from Washington, now a captain, was left in command of Los Angeles with a garrison of but fifty men. In enforcing an unrealistic local curfew imposed by Commodore Stockton, he unfortunately displayed an attitude of intolerance toward the Angeleños. Tact and friendliness would have been more powerful weapons. Resentment at Gillespie's arbitrary actions and threats of punishment stirred up the natives. With the encouragement of their firebrand leaders, they proceeded from irritation to exasperation, and from exasperation to insur-

LOS ANGELES, 1857. (From a contemporary print.)

rection. On September 23, Gillespie's small garrison was attacked, and Gillespie's men found themselves surrounded on a hilltop in the middle of Los Angeles by several hundred excited citizens determined to hold onto southern California. Besieged and short of water, Gillespie was in a perilous situation. Under cover of darkness he sent a courier on the long journey northward for aid from Commodore Stockton. The daring ride of an American soldier, reputedly Swedish-born, whom the Americans knew as John Brown but the *Californios* as Juan Flaco, has become almost legendary. This "Lean John"—the Paul Revere of California history —covered the more than five hundred miles between Los Angeles and San Francisco in about four and one-half days. The dispatch he carried was written on cigarette papers and concealed in his long hair. He was pursued for miles by unfriendly California horsemen, but kept riding. Despite lack of sleep, and difficulty in securing fresh horses, he finally delivered Gillespie's message of distress to Commodore Stockton.

That commander immediately ordered aid to Gillespie, and Captain William Mervine set sail for southern California with three hundred and fifty men. On October 7, 1846, his vessel, the *Vandalia*, dropped anchor at San Pedro, outside Los Angeles. He was almost too late. Captain Gillespie's hilltop position had become untenable even before Flaco could deliver his message. Gillespie had already virtually surrendered to the Californians but had been allowed to retreat with his men under a flag of truce to San Pedro, with the provision that the Americans would depart by sea when they reached that port. Gillespie, however, promptly set aside the hasty agreement with the Californians when he saw the new American military forces, which Captain Mervine placed under his command.

There followed an engagement, known as the "Battle of the Old Woman's Gun," on the nearby Domínguez Rancho. In this conflict the Californians fought under the command of José Antonio Carrillo. They were mounted on horses and armed with sharp willow lances and smooth-bore carbines; their most damaging weapon, however, was a four-pound cannon. This antique firearm, which had been hidden by an old woman during the first American assault on Los Angeles, was tied with leather *reatas*, or thongs, to the tongue and wheels of a mud wagon. Thus made ingeniously mobile, the cannon was whipped up and down a hillock facing the Americans, with great effectiveness. The Americans were forced to retreat to their ships, having suffered five killed and a number wounded. They buried their dead on a small island near San Pedro, thenceforth known as "Dead Man's Island."

Anti-American opposition spread, and for a brief time the territory from Santa Barbara to San Diego was again in the hands of the Californians. On July 29, 1846, Frémont had landed at San Diego from the U.S.S. *Cyane*, raised the American flag, and taken possession of that pueblo; he had then returned to Monterey. Further resistance soon broke out in southern California, however, and Stockton proceeded south to occupy San Diego. While Frémont was raising reinforcements in Monterey to assist Stockton, a skirmish took place on November 16, 1846, in the Salinas Valley—the only actual engagement fought by American forces north of Los Angeles during this phase of the hostilities. Known as the Battle of Natividad, this conflict resulted in four Americans killed and as many more wounded, the Californians sustaining a similar loss.

After landing at San Diego, Stockton began planning an attack on the "horse-covered" hills toward the north. Suddenly an important message arrived which modified not only his plans but the entire course of events in California. This was a desperate dispatch from General Stephen Watts Kearny. In June, 1846, the War Department had ordered Kearny, a veteran of the War of 1812, and an experienced army officer, to proceed overland with an "Army of the West" from Fort Leavenworth, Kansas. He was to seize Santa Fe in the province of New Mexico, then to move toward California, where he was to cooperate with Commodore Stockton. On Kearny's westward march of more than a thousand miles from Sante Fe, he was accompanied by three hundred men of the First United States Dragoons. These troops were followed by another company of dragoons and five hundred members of an enlisted Mormon Battalion.

En route, General Kearny met the celebrated scout Kit Carson near Socorro. Carson, originally attached to Frémont's forces, had taken part in the first stage of the conquest of California. At the time of his encounter with Kearny, the scout was taking official dispatches from Stockton eastward to Washington. These optimistically phrased dispatches informed President Polk that Stockton had extended American control over the whole of Mexican California. Carson himself, who had left before the renewed fighting in southern California broke out, and hence did not know of it, also told Kearny that the American flag was flying from every important position in California, that the war had ended, and that Mexican control of that province was over. Kearny therefore decided to send a large share of his force back to Santa Fe, while he continued on toward California with about two hundred dragoons and two small howitzers. Because Carson was such an experienced guide, Kearny literally turned him around and took him west with him. The general sent Stockton's dispatches eastward with one of his own scouts, the mountain man Thomas Fitzpatrick.

The Battle of San Pascual

On December 5, 1846, northeast of San Diego, General Kearny ran into an unexpected hornet's nest of opposition. More than 150 armed Californians, under Andrés Pico, were encamped at the Indian village of San Pascual (near present-day Escondido). Kearny rashly ordered an attack before dawn, in a cold rain. At first the Californians seemed to retreat from the field. Suddenly, however, they wheeled about and charged Kearny's scattered, water-soaked forces with muskets and long, sharp willow lances. The Americans, their carbine ammunition wet, tried to beat off the onslaught by hand-to-hand combat, but they were at a marked disadvantage in the melee. Eighteen Americans lay dead in the mud before Kearny's rear guard could bring up howitzers to repel the attackers. Nineteen other soldiers were wounded and one was missing. Most of the fatalities resulted from lance thrusts rather than from gun wounds. The total number of Americans who ultimately died was twenty-two. General Kearny himself received two ugly lance wounds. The Californians suffered only minor injuries.

Kearny composed a message to Stockton urgently pleading for help; he described how the battle had been fought with valor against heavy odds, how his cumbersome, tired and bony mules were no match for the quick California ponies, and how his short sabres offered practically no defense against the long lances of his mounted opponents. He sent this dispatch to San Diego by Kit Carson and Lieutenant Edward F. Beale, early on the day following the battle. He then resumed his march toward San Diego, hoping that Stockton's reinforcements would soon reach him. Kearny's progress was slow and his position precarious. After he made his next camp on a hill near the San Bernardo Rancho, he was virtually surrounded by hostile forces. His powder was damp, and supplies were dangerously low; the tired dragoons were forced to subsist for four days on mule flesh and a scanty water supply. But their spirits were heartened when almost two hundred sailors and marines arrived from San Diego, in response to the appeal Kearny had sent to Stockton. The siege was soon lifted and Kearny resumed his march, reaching San Diego on December 12, 1846. The Battle of San Pascual, despite the relatively small number of casualties it involved, has taken its place in history as perhaps the largest armed conflict ever to occur within the boundaries of California.

The Reconquest of Los Angeles

Worn by privation and embarrassed by his near-defeat at San Pascual, Kearny reported the incident to the War Department as a victory. He reasoned that he had fought off a superior enemy under great odds. The general considered that it was his mission to establish the supremacy of the United States over California, and he behaved accordingly toward Stockton and other Americans who were already there. Actually, of course, prior to his arrival the "first conquest" had occurred under Stockton, as commander in chief and acting governor. Kearny soon let it be known that the army was taking over, but Stockton understandably declined to relinquish full command of his land forces and his position as military governor. Nevertheless, the two combined their resources into a task force numbering about six hundred army dragoons, marines, and sailors, and left San Diego on December 29 to attack

Los Angeles. Officially, during their march northward, Stockton bore the title of commander in chief of the expedition, while Kearny was named commander of troops. Frémont, now a lieutenant colonel, was also about to approach Los Angeles, from the north. He moved southward from Monterey with four hundred men, and, after a week's delay to obtain supplies at Santa Barbara, entered the San Fernando Valley near Los Angeles on January 11, 1847. Kearny was to have trouble with Frémont, who had Stockton's backing.

In their march on Los Angeles from the south, Kearny and Stockton met no real opposition until they reached the banks of a muddy little stream, the San Gabriel, near the present town of Montebello. There they encamped on January 7. General José María Flores was hoping to surprise the Americans with a last-ditch cavalry stand along the north bank of the river. Kearny and Stockton, however, forded the stream in the form of a square, and this strategy enabled them to capture the opposite bank quickly from the skirmishers. Two days later, in the *Cañada de los Alisos*, near the Los Angeles stockyards, the forces under Kearny and Stockton fought the final conflict of the war in California. Known as the Battle of La Mesa, this was of slight importance as a military contest but it did confirm the victory at the San Gabriel River and permit the actual reoccupation of Los Angeles. The Californians abandoned the field, scattering in different directions; this was in effect the end of resistance to the invading Americans, whose army and navy had triumphed together. On January 10, 1847, American troops entered the City of the Angels and marched to its plaza, where Gillespie hoisted the flag he had been compelled to haul down the previous September. The Stars and Stripes have never since been lowered in California.

Conclusion of Hostilities

It was, however, Frémont, tardily arriving on the scene from the north, who received the surrender of the last armed forces in California. Andrés Pico may have feared that Kearny and Stockton would place him before a firing squad; apparently, he preferred to surrender to Frémont, and did so on January 13, 1847, in the outskirts of Los Angeles. His brother, Pío Pico, last Mexican governor of California, had already fled to Sonora. José María Flores, hotspur leader of the government in its last days, had also escaped. Frémont, fully confident as to his own authority to conduct official negotiations, now entered into a truce with Andrés Pico. Although, in effect, he was acting over the head of Kearny, a brevet brigadier, Frémont personally pardoned Pico and other local leaders; the peace treaty he concluded with them, known as the Cahuenga Capitulation, was in fact a generous document in all respects. Pico's preference for surrending to Frémont, rather than to Kearny or Stockton, embroiled these American commanders in a three-way fight. An unfortunate conflict in orders from both the Navy and War Departments led to a savage quarrel over which of California's conquerors was actually commander in chief of the thousand or more men assembled under them at Los Angeles. On January 16, 1847, Stockton relinquished his post as governor of California in favor of Frémont and traveled to the East Coast. Stockton thereby left Kearny and Frémont to fight it out over who was the real United States commander of California. Ultimately Kearny clearly established his authority over Frémont, against whom he prepared court-martial charges.

Some lesser American commands reached California too late to participate in the actual conquest. The Mormon Battalion, under Lieutenant Colonel Philip St. George Cooke, had followed General Kearny westward, reaching San Diego only on January 29, 1847—however, its members took great pride in having served the United States in California. In July this unit marched to Los Angeles to be honorably discharged, after building a fort, Fort Moore, on the hill where Gillespie had been besieged. On the sixth of March another unit, consisting of 250 members of Colonel Jonathan D. Stevenson's regiment of New York volunteers, arrived in San Francisco. Within a few months their discharge was also completed and many of these men were absorbed into the California population. By March, 1848, nearly all volunteers were discharged from active service.

The war between the United States and Mexico formally came to an end with the signing of the Treaty of Guadalupe Hidalgo on February 2, 1848. A new southwestern boundary now gave the United States all of Upper California as well as New Mexico and Texas. Residents in these areas had the option of becoming American citizens or of leaving former Mexican territory. The United States agreed to pay Mexico the sum of $15,000,000 for the land it took, and it politely disregarded the fact that American forces had partly conquered Lower California, encountering considerably stiffer opposition there than in Upper California. This treaty accomplished one of the major objectives which President Polk had set for himself upon entering office. California had become an indisputable part of the United States.

SELECTED READINGS

Literature concerning the conquest of California by the United States is sizable. Numerous books depict the subject in terms that are heroic and patriotic. The first sober study of the background of Americanization was Robert G. Cleland, *The Early Sentiment for the Annexation of California* . . . (Austin, 1915), originally a Princeton University doctoral dissertation. More recent appraisals are John A. Hawgood, "The Pattern of Yankee Infiltration in Mexican Alta California," *Pacific Historical Review*, XXVII (February, 1958), 27–37, and, in the same journal, Norman A. Graebner, "American Interest in California, 1845," XXII (February, 1953), 13–27. The role of President Polk in developing official interest in California is made clear in E. I. McCormac, *James K. Polk: A Political Biography* (Berkeley, 1922). Polk's personal diary has been edited by Allan Nevins as *Polk: The Diary of a President* (New York, 1929). The last days of Mexican rule are the subject of George Tays' article "Pio Pico's Correspondence with the Mexican Government, 1846–1848," California Historical Society *Quarterly*, XIII (March, 1934), 99–149. A perceptive but dull analytical study is Frederick Merk's *Manifest Destiny and Mission in American History* (New York, 1963).

British interest in California is discussed in Ephraim D. Adams, "English Interest in California," *American Historical Review*, XIV (July, 1909), 744–763. Prussian interest is treated in John A. Hawgood's "A Projected Prussian Colonization of Upper California," *Southern California Quarterly*, XLVIII (December, 1966), 353–368. The controversial Jones is the subject of George B. Brooke, "The Vest Pocket War of Commodore Jones," *Pacific Historical Review*, XXXI (August, 1962), 217–233.

Frémont's activities in California have, of course, been much debated. A useful starting point is the collection of Frémont's own reports, in an accessible modern edition by Allan Nevins, entitled *Narratives of Exploration and Adventure* (New York, 1956). Nevins has also contributed two standard Frémont biographies, the latest of which is *Frémont: Pathmarker of the West* (New York, 1939). An early biography is John Bigelow's *Frémont: Memoir of Life and Public Services* (New York, 1856). One should also consult less adulatory books, including Cardinal L. Goodwin's *John Charles Frémont: An Exploration of His Career* (Stanford, 1930); though dated, this is still a valuable authority. Consult likewise Richard R. Stenberg, "Polk and Frémont, 1845–1846," *Pacific Historical Review*, VII (September, 1938), 211–227. Jessie Benton Frémont's two books, *Souvenirs of My*

Time (Boston, 1887) and *Far West Sketches* (Boston, 1890), are interesting but unreliable as to the events of the conquest era. She, like her husband, in his "The Conquest of California," *Century Magazine*, XLI (April, 1890), 917–928, and *Memoirs of My Life* (New York, 1887), argues *ex post facto*, justifying each detail of his conduct. Thomas Hart Benton, *Thirty Years View* (2 vols., Boston, 1854–1856), is a book with a wider scope by Frémont's noted father-in-law. Filled with important data on the conquest of California is the account of the *Proceedings of the Court Martial in the Trial of (J. C.) Frémont* (Washington, D.C., 1848).

An early interpretation of the American era in California by a professional philosopher is Josiah Royce, *California: From the Conquest in 1846 to the Second Vigilance Committee* (Boston, 1886), reprinted in modern format with an introduction by Robert Glass Cleland (New York, 1948). Aspects of the Bear Flag revolt are treated in Fred B. Rogers, *Bear Flag Lieutenant: The Life Story of Henry L. Ford* (San Francisco, 1951) as well as in William B. Ide's first-person narrative, *Who Conquered California* (Claremont, 1880). A reprinted version of Simeon Ide's rare *A Biographical Sketch of William B. Ide*, with an introduction by Benjamin F. Gilbert, has been published (Glorieta, N. M., 1967). A wealth of information exists in John A. Hussey's "The United States and the Bear Flag Revolt," Ph.D. dissertation, University of California, Berkeley (1941). A compact study of yet another member of that generation of Americans in California is Doyce Nunis, Jr., *The Trials of Isaac Graham* (Los Angeles, 1967).

A contemporary account of the conquest is James Madison Cutts, *The Conquest of California and New Mexico . . .* (Philadelphia, 1847). Kearny's march west is discussed in William H. Emory's *Notes of a Military Reconnaissance . . .* (Washington, 1848). Another contemporary description is Joseph Warren Revere, *A Tour of Duty in California . . .* (New York, 1849). Various articles in the *Pacific Historical Review* have dealt with participants in the conquest. Recent examples are William H. Ellison, "San Juan to Cahuenga: The Experiences of Frémont's Battalion," *Pacific Historical Review*, XXVII (May, 1958), 245–261, and George Tays, "Frémont Had No Secret Instructions," IX (June, 1940), 159–171. The war in Lower California is described in Peter Gerhard, "Baja California in the Mexican War, 1846–1848," *Pacific Historical Review*, XIV (May, 1945), 418–424. Consult also John A. Hawgood's very critical treatment, "John C. Frémont and the Bear Flag Revolution," *University of Birmingham Historical Journal*, VII (1959), 80–100. On the Battle of San Pascual see Arthur Woodward's *Lances at San Pascual* (San Francisco, 1948), and Philip St. George Cooke, *The Conquest of New Mexico and California* (New York, 1878). A general history of the war, including the Far Western phase, is Justin H. Smith's *The War with Mexico* (2 vols., New York, 1919). Useful also is Walter Colton, *Three Years in California* (New York, 1950), a personal narrative by the first United States *alcalde* at Monterey. A persuasive revisionist view of the Mexican War as a shameful event in our history is Glenn W. Price's *Origins of the War with Mexico: The Polk-Stockton Intrigue* (Austin, 1967).

There is a very biased life of Sloat by Edwin A. Sherman, *The Life of the Late Rear Admiral John Drake Sloat* (Oakland, 1902), but modern biographies of most other participants in the conquest, except Frémont, have yet to be written. See, however, *A Sketch of the Life of Com. Robert F. Stockton* by Samuel J. Bayard (New York, 1856). Consult also Robert J. Parker, "Larkin, Anglo-American Businessman in Mexican California" in *Greater America* (Berkeley, 1945), the best short estimate of Larkin's career and importance. Examine also John A. Hawgood, ed., *First and Last Consul, Thomas Oliver Larkin . . . A Selection of Letters* (San Marino, 1962). Recent books touching on the American conquest of California are Fred B. Rogers, *Montgomery and the Portsmouth* (San Francisco, 1959) and Werner H. Marti, *Messenger of Destiny: The California Adventures, 1846–1847, of Archibald H. Gillespie* (San Francisco, 1960). Dwight L. Clarke, *Stephen Watts Kearny, Soldier of the West* (Norman, Okla., 1961), is a recent biography. A careful discussion of the military regimes that followed the conquest is Theodore Grivas, *Military Governments in California* (Glendale, 1963).

15

Gold

Like the American conquest, James Wilson Marshall's discovery of gold on January 24, 1848, was one of those events that influenced United States history as well as California's. Marshall's discovery occurred at Coloma, located on the south fork of the American River. This was not the first discovery of California gold. Minor finds had been made long before 1848, principally by mission Indians who brought the metal to the padres; but the friars reputedly cautioned the natives not to divulge the location of the gold, lest the province be inundated by money-mad foreigners. In 1841, one Baptiste Ruelle had uncovered a small cache of gold he had deposited near Los Angeles.

Better known was the finding of gold in 1842 at San Feliciano Canyon, in southern California about eight miles from modern Newhall. On an uncertain date in that year Francisco López, a ranchero, stopped to rest in the canyon after searching for some stray horses. With a "sheaf knife" the hungry López dug up a few wild onions. When he noticed some bright flakes and nuggets clinging to their roots, he excitedly uprooted more of the plants. Hearing of López' find, several hundred men went up San Feliciano Canyon to seek gold. On November 22, 1842, the American trader Abel Stearns "sent to Alfred Robinson, Esq., 20 oz. California weight of placer gold to be forwarded by him to the U.S. mint at Philadelphia for assay." Unfortunately the San Feliciano lode was shallow; it "played out" within a few months. At about the same time another American trader, William Heath Davis, saw bits of gold ore in the possession of the California padres. However, until the arrival of the Americans, the Californians generally lived free from the gold fever that had afflicted the Spanish conquerors of Mexico and Peru.

Marshall's Discovery

The "gold rush" of 1842, if it can be called that, was purely local. It was Marshall's later discovery that focused the attention of the entire world on a new El Dorado. Equipped with a modest education, a flintlock rifle, and his father's trade as a coach and wagon builder, Marshall had come to California from his native New Jersey by emigrant train in 1844. First he had gone to work for Sutter, subsequently buying two leagues of land nearby on Little Butte Creek where he built and repaired spinning wheels, plows, ox yokes, and carts—in short, he was self-employed as a general utility man around Sutter's Fort. In 1846, after participating in a campaign against the hostile Mokelumne Indians, he joined the Bear Flag group and then enlisted in Frémont's California Battalion, continuing in military service until after the American conquest. Marshall then returned to Sutter's Fort, "barefooted and in a very sorry plight," to find that nearly all his livestock had strayed from his ranch or had been stolen. Like many another California combatant, Marshall had received no compensation for his volunteer war services. With virtually no resources, he was glad to find employment again with Sutter.

The community around Sutter's Fort was growing rapidly with the influx of immigrants, and the demand for lumber was increasing accordingly. Sutter therefore agreed to supply the necessary capital for a community sawmill, in return for one-fourth of its future production. He sent Marshall to search for good accessible timber and a suitable location for the mill. The site chosen was in a small valley, about 1,500 feet in elevation, on the south fork of the American River some forty-five miles northeast of Sutter's Fort. Local Indians called the place Cullomah.

In January, 1848, when Sutter's mill was practically completed, his men cut some timber; but the tailrace, or artificial flume channel which turned the main water wheel, was too shallow to turn the wheel fast enough. Water was therefore channeled into the race by means of a wing-dam, or diversion, from the river and allowed to run each night to deepen the bed. What happened is best told in Marshall's own words:

When the channel was opened it was my custom every evening to raise the gate and let the water wash out as much sand and gravel through the night as possible; and in the morning, while the men were getting breakfast, I would walk down, and, shutting off the water, look along the race and see what was to be done. . . .

One morning in January—it was a clear, cold morning; I shall never forget that morning—as I was taking my usual walk along the race after shutting off the water, my eye was caught with the glimpse of something shining in the bottom of the ditch. There was about a foot of water running then. I reached my hand down and picked it up; it made my heart thump, for I was certain it was gold. The piece was about half the size and of the shape of a pea. Then I saw another piece in the water. After taking it out I sat down and began to think right hard. I thought it was gold, and yet it did not seem to be of the right color. . . . Suddenly the idea flashed across my mind that it might be iron pyrites. I trembled to think of it! . . . Putting one of the pieces on a hard river stone, I took another and commenced hammering it. It was soft and didn't break: it therefore must be gold, but largely mixed with some other metal, and very likely silver; for pure gold, I thought, would certainly have a brighter color.

When I returned to our cabin for breakfast I showed the two pieces to my men. They were all a good deal excited, and had they not thought that the gold only existed in small quantities they would have abandoned everything and left me to finish my job alone. However, to satisfy them, I told them that as soon as we had the mill finished we could devote a week or two to gold hunting and see what we could make out of it.

Soon afterward another of Sutter's laborers, Henry W. Bigler, formerly a member of the Mormon Battalion, found gold outside the tailrace of the mill. While hunting fresh venison meat for the camp Bigler detected particles of the shining metal along the river banks. Sutter, at first incredulous about the flakes and grains of gold, many the size of wheat grains, tried to keep the find secret. It would have been better for him if he could have done so. After the discovery of gold on his property, the baron of the Sacramento began to undergo a whole series of misfortunes. His diary tells how in early March a party of Mormons working for him "left for washing and digging Gold and very soon all followed, and left me only sick and lame behind." He complains that many other workmen thereafter left his service, hurting every branch of his interconnected business operations. Even the Indians, wrote Sutter, were "impatient to run" to the gold streams, and he was compelled to leave a year's wheat crop ungathered in the fields around New Helvetia. Moreover, he had spent large sums on the Coloma sawmill and on a flour mill at Brighton which he could find no one to operate.

The Irresistible Magnet

Marshall's and Sutter's secret had proved too great to keep. Not long after the discovery Sam Brannan, now a prominent merchant at New Helvetia, galloped down from Sutter's Fort to San Francisco with dust and nuggets from the new gold fields. As he rode along its streets he shouted "Gold! Gold! Gold from the American River!" swinging his hat wildly with one hand and in the other waving a medicine bottle full of bright dust. Soon a stampede started as people, singly and in bands, deserted their homes for the icy streams of the Sierra in quest of riches.

Labor costs in towns near the coast rose rapidly. Almost all business, except the most urgent, stopped. Seamen deserted ships in San Francisco Bay, soldiers departed from barracks, and servants left their masters, forfeiting accumulated wages in a frenzy of excitement. Threats, punishment, and money were equally powerless to stem this human tide. Forgetting to collect debts or to pay their bills, gold seekers rode, walked, and even hobbled on crutches toward the Sierra. Amidst the hysteria San Francisco's early newspaper, the *Californian*, suspended publication on May 29, 1848, announcing: "The majority of our subscribers and many of our advertisers have closed their doors and places of business and left town. . . . The whole country, from San Francisco to Los Angeles and from the seashore to the base of the Sierra Nevada, resounds with the sordid cry of 'gold! Gold!! GOLD!!!!' while the field is left half planted, the house half built, and everything neglected but the manufacture of shovels and pickaxes . . ." Thomas Oliver Larkin bitterly lamented the depopulation of his beloved Monterey, where buildings fell into disrepair and stores closed down. He wrote of the local scarcity of supplies: "Every bowl, tray, and warming pan has gone to the mines. Everything in short that has a scoop in it and will hold sand and water." "The gold mines," wrote Walter Colton, "have upset all social and domestic arrangements in Monterey; the master has become his own servant, and the servant his own lord. The millionaire is obliged to groom his own horse, and roll his wheelbarrow."

Within a few months news of California gold had found its way to every part of the globe. Exaggeration of the riches was so prev-

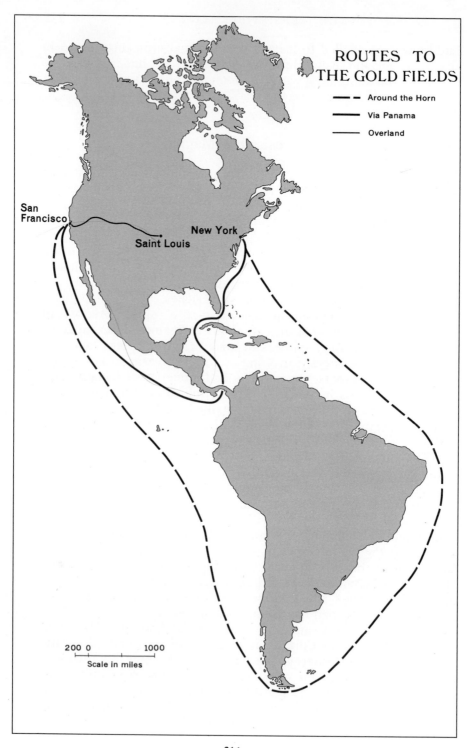

ROUTES TO
THE GOLD FIELDS

- - - Around the Horn
—— Via Panama
—— Overland

San
Francisco

Saint Louis

New York

200 0   1000
Scale in miles

alent that one writer remarked: "A grain of gold taken from the mine became a pennyweight at Panama, an ounce in New York and Boston, and a pound nugget at London." Marshall's discovery occurred almost at the moment of the signing of the Treaty of Guadalupe Hidalgo between the United States and Mexico. By May, 1848, gold had been found at distances of thirty miles surrounding Sutter's Mill. By the first of June, two thousand men were already digging for gold, and in another month that number doubled. Before the end of the year California's gold yield had reached $10 million. The gold hunters of 1848, however, constituted but the vanguard of a human avalanche soon to descend upon California.

After President Polk mentioned the discovery of gold in his presidential message of December 5, 1848, even wider publicity was given the event. At the beginning of 1849 there were, exclusive of Indians, only some 26,000 persons in California. Before midsummer the number had reached 50,000. By the end of the year it was probably 115,000, notwithstanding the official but inaccurate census report of 92,597 for the year 1850. Possibly four-fifths of the population were Americans and most were men. Approximately half of the adult population was engaged in some branch of mining. Among the 20,000 foreign immigrants were sizable contingents from Mexico, Great Britain, Germany, France, and Spain; and lesser numbers from Chile, Peru, and the Hawaiian Islands. Few nationalities were wholly unrepresented. The Chinese were among the most numerous of the foreigners; by 1852 more than 20,000 had come to California. As a result, California's towns and cities seemed notably international, especially when compared with those of other Western territories.

The speed with which the settlements in California grew was altogether remarkable. Still sometimes known as Yerba Buena, the future San Francisco became the most rapidly growing city in the world. From only 812 persons in March, 1848, it came to contain upwards of 5,000 by early summer of 1849 and by 1850 it was a boom town of 25,000 people. Upstream, Sacramento's embarcadero, or waterfront area, to the west of Sutter's Fort, also took on intense activity. Sacramento, on the route to the inland mines, became another headquarters or rendezvous for throngs of adventurers who headed for the diggings from San Francisco.

Some immigrants moved into California southward from Oregon; others made their way northwest over the Sonora Trail from Mexico; numbers of them came via Hawaii. The overwhelming majority of Americans who reached California during those hectic

days, however, selected one or another of three main routes —
"around the Horn," "by way of the Isthmus," and "across the
plains."

The Routes of the Gold Seekers

The route around Cape Horn to San Francisco required six and
sometimes nine months of travel. It was fraught with peril. Sailing vessels were of light tonnage, and not all of them were seaworthy. Though passengers complained about food and fare, they
usually kept their humor and made the best of both monotony
and seasickness. They amused themselves with banjo, fiddle, and
varied games aboard ship; and at landfalls en route, such as at
Rio or Callao, there were bullfights, cockfights, donkey rides, and
the *fandango* for their entertainment. On one ship, the *Rising Sun*,
the Fourth of July was celebrated during the passage around Cape
Horn by the blowing of bugles, the playing of martial music, a
mass reading of the Declaration of Independence, speech making,
and a sumptuous dinner of roast goose, plum pudding, mince pie,
figs, and nuts. The actual passage through or around Cape Horn
was particularly disagreeable and hazardous. It might take a vessel many days to break through the choppy Strait of Magellan,
which was usually enveloped by strong currents and dense fogs.
Yet thousands made it to California in this way, via what became
known as the "white-collar route" because lack of exercise soft-
ened up most passengers after they had spent several seasick
months on shipboard.

Even more Americans, by the thousands, reached California via
the Isthmus of Panama during the late forties and early fifties.
Figures on travel to California in those years are slippery and
unreliable. The following table, however, indicates the numbers of
persons who journeyed to San Francisco by way of both Panama
and Nicaragua.

YEAR	PANAMA	NICARAGUA
1848	335	
1849	6,489	
1850	13,809	
1851	15,464	1,931
1852	24,231	10,563
1853	17,014	10,062
1854	18,445	13,063
1855	15,412	11,293

Travelers crossing the Isthmus, in this day long before the construction of the Panama Canal, were cautioned to limit their personal effects to about seventy-five pounds. They frequently used a watertight bag to transport such articles as clothing, and many took along a carbine, some camping equipment, and a small chest of medicines. Under favorable conditions, the Isthmus route was the shortest and quickest way to California. The voyage from New York to the Panama Coast was 2,500 miles and the trip across the Isthmus 60 more; from Panama to San Francisco it was 3,500 miles. But travel conditions were seldom favorable. Passengers crowded together into vessels like proverbial sardines.

Fully as dangerous as the occasional shipboard epidemics was the necessity of crossing the Isthmus of Panama. Malarial fever was prevalent; amid unsanitary conditions there were many victims of cholera, dysentery, and yellow fever. The typical American gold seeker, ambitious and curious, was not, however, easily swayed from his purpose, and the stifling sixty miles he had to traverse was full of interest. Part of the journey was made by water, in long canoes poled and paddled by native boatmen. Then, the journey overland on muleback proceeded through a vast tangle of luxurious greenness; one saw exotic varieties of birds among the cocoanut trees and tropical ferns, as well as whole forests of orange, crimson, and scarlet flowers. A rough overland ride on muleback finally brought the traveler to Panama. A shortage of coastal vessels, especially during the first half of 1849, sometimes stretched the traveler's stay into months, though later passenger service was better organized.

On arriving at Panama, especially at the beginning of the rush, the gold seeker faced a long and sweaty delay before a ship to California might appear. Then came the uncomfortable, hazardous journey to San Francisco Bay. Most ships had wretched accommodations and their food and water were vile. Following the organization, in April, 1848, of the Pacific Mail Steamship Company, ships powered by steam began gradually to supplement the sailing vessels, then to supersede them; but during the late forties most passenger service to California continued to be carried on in wooden sailing vessels, many of them old, worm-eaten, and leaky.

The covered wagon, or "prairie schooner," symbolizes the vast population movement during the Gold Rush as much as does the clipper ship or steamer. Fortunately the principal routes across the Great Plains were marked out before the rush. Two of these routes were most commonly followed by the "forty-niners." The favorite was a northern route leading directly west from St. Louis,

Independence, St. Joseph, or Council Bluffs, through South Pass in the Rocky Mountains. This was probably taken by 30,000 gold seekers in the year 1849 alone. A southern route proceeded first over the Santa Fe Trail, which ran from Westport (later called Kansas City), to Sante Fe for 775 miles; then it followed the Gila River to the Colorado; and finally crossed the desert into southern California. A party could trundle along some eighteen miles per day on this trail. Caravans averaged twenty-six wagons, each drawn by five yoke of oxen, or a span of ten mules.

With luck, the 2,000 miles to the gold fields over either of these routes could be covered in a hundred days. Many circumstances, however, could cause delay. Rivers had to be forded, food supplies conserved, the trains guarded against Indian attack. Not infrequently wagons had to be unloaded and reloaded several times in a single day due to the difficulty of crossing rough terrain or streams. Many of the larger overland companies had to subdivide when more grass was required for the livestock than could be found in any one place.

Some Argonauts, or gold seekers—though few in comparison to those traveling by way of the Horn, the Isthmus of Panama, or the Great Plains—selected other routes to California. One of these routes required a difficult journey across Nicaragua (see table, p. 218). Perhaps 10,000 persons chose yet another route, which began with a voyage of about eighteen days from New Orleans to Vera Cruz, Mexico. A horseback trip of 280 miles to Mexico City consumed another nine days; then one had to continue to Mazatlán, some 900 miles, or twenty days, of additional travel. The journey was concluded by a voyage to San Francisco taking thirty-five days. Total travel time from New York was frequently four months. The specified travel times, however, often proved theoretical. As one traveler remarked: "All routes were the quickest when the company started, but apt to be the slowest when they arrived."

Death Valley in '49

Among the most tragic of all pioneer experiences were those encountered by the overland gold hunters whose fate led them into Death Valley. Comparatively few persons entered this "seventy-five mile strip of perdition," and those who did so usually went there unintentionally. Many of these unlucky travelers underwent sufferings similar to those of the Donner party in intensity, if not in kind. Death Valley, about one hundred and ten feet below sea level, stretches along California's southeastern Inyo County, east of the Sierra Nevada. Its atmosphere is almost wholly without moisture. During many months of each year the heat is relentless. Constant hot winds blow across the sands, and the blinding glare of the sun parches the skin and induces a feverish, half-crazed state in anyone obliged to endure it for long.

The story of one pioneer group will illustrate the horrors of America's most desolate valley. During the winter of 1848–1849 William Lewis Manly, a native of Vermont, accompanied a large and slow overland party westward over the California Trail. Innumerable delays during that season made it impossible for his party to reach the Sierra in time to avoid the fall snows. Manly and six companions were convinced that the Green River (actually a tributary of the Colorado) flowed in a generally westward course, perhaps to the Pacific. At the Green they discovered a small ferry boat, possibly built by Mormon pioneers, and, after emptying some sand out of the boat, they attempted to navigate the treacherous stream. "We untied the ropes," wrote Manly, "gave the boat a push and commenced to move down the river with ease and comfort. . . ." Soon, however, the stream became a rapid, roaring torrent, dotted with dangerous rocks and shoals. The voyage down the Green came to a sudden halt when the clumsy boat became jammed against a huge rock, pinned so tight that it could not be budged.

Now the party took to walking westward again. After days of travel, Manly's little band was overjoyed to come upon another party near the Great Salt Lake. This group was headed by Asabel Bennett, an acquaintance of Manly's; they joined forces to plot a common strategy. Because it was now late in the season, and they were aware of the plight of the Donner party in the winter snows of the Sierra Nevada, the Bennett-Manly group decided on a somewhat longer but supposedly safer route southward into southern California. From there they planned to move north to the California mines.

The party, however, became trapped in the endless wastes that led toward Death Valley. After wandering aimlessly in a sea of sand, they decided that, instead of trying to retrace their steps, they should travel generally toward the west. In the distance the party could see the Panamint Mountains, their summits white with snow, and these became a landmark for the travelers. Thirteen men, three women, and six children hopelessly moved through the forbidding wastes of Death Valley, unsuccessfully trying, again and again, to escape from Furnace Creek, their main camp. Canyons that led nowhere faced them at every turn. They were able to find a few brackish wells, but food supplies were running out. One after another the oxen were killed for food. As the pioneers dipped into their last sacks of flour and meal, Manly confessed to a morbid despair. He thought he could escape by himself, but resolved that "all must be brought through or perish." As conditions became more desperate, Bennett proposed that Manly and John Rogers, the youngest and strongest men, go ahead on foot to seek help. The main party was to await their return from the California settlements with supplies.

Manly and Rogers struck out toward the Panamints across uncharted desert sands, then made their way over Walker Pass in the southern Sierra. After fourteen days they reached Mission San Fernando, where they obtained flour, beans, three horses, and a mule. Following a short rest, the two men dutifully started back toward Death Valley. Twenty-six days after having departed from their friends they finally found the camp once more, but they came back to a dreadful sight. The survivors were huddled in the meager shade under their wagons, the covers of which they had taken off to make protecting tents for themselves and their animals. Weakness had so reduced the party that Manly and Rogers moved within one hundred yards of the wagons without seeing a sign of life. A shot fired from Manly's rifle brought a man from under a wagon. "Then," Manly wrote in his narrative, "he threw up his arms high over his head and shouted—'The boys have come! The boys have come!' . . . Bennett and Arcane caught us in their arms and embraced us with all their strength, and Mrs. Bennett when she came, fell down on her knees and clung to me like a maniac, in the great emotion that came to her, and not a word was spoken." By their unselfish devotion and loyalty Manly and Rogers won the everlasting gratitude of their forlorn party.

About the first of February, 1850, the little band finally left Death Valley. They abandoned their wagons and all other equipment that could be spared, and packed their meager belongings on the few remaining animals. The party crept along the eastern slopes of the Sierra, passed through Red Rock Canyon, crossed the Mohave River, and finally arrived at Rancho San Francisco over four months after leaving the Salt Lake trail. They had spent an entire year on their journey west, and they were still more than five hundred miles from the mines. The story of the Bennett-Manly party, as told by William Lewis Manly in his *Death Valley in '49*, has become one of the classic accounts of Western history.

FLOOR OF DEATH VALLEY. (From the author's collection.)

223

Life in the Diggings

The California placer camps hardly resembled the paradise envisioned by most gold seekers as they made their difficult way west. Mining was tiring work, accommodations were few, and conveniences were practically nonexistent. Most "claims" lay along the banks of streams where thousands of persons, using every imaginable tool and method, tried to strike "pay dirt." There was little subterranean work, or sinking of shafts, until later years, when the production of gold became heavily capitalized. "Dry diggings," found in flats and gullies where there was no water supply, were worked as eagerly as "wet diggings" along sand bars or stream beds. In California probably more rich ore was found near the surface than in any comparable mining region in the world. Lucky persons also struck it rich in "bench diggings," located on narrow tables along the hillsides, or in the innumerable "bars" (accumulations of sand and rock) opposite the bends of streams.

At first, miners had little experience or knowledge that would help them go about finding gold. As a result, they brought a wide variety of gadgets and equipment with them. Some prospectors achieved marvelous dexterity in simple "panning out" operations. Of all the instruments for washing gold ore, the pan was the simplest. It was made of tin or sheet iron, with a flat bottom about a foot in diameter and sides six inches high—rising at an angle of forty-five degrees. Other miners utilized the washing rocker, or "cradle," one of the most widely known contrivances of the time, and used especially during the first few months in the California mines. This was essentially a machine that extracted loose particles of gold from gravel by a washing operation. Gold-bearing sand dropped toward the bottom also of the "long tom" rocker, an elongated movable trough which supplemented gold pan or cradle. The "gold borer" was employed as one would use an auger or cork-screw, while the "water wheel" had shaft, arms, and crossboards resembling the paddlewheels of a steamboat. The "board-sluice" was a long wooden trough, used where there was a plentiful supply of water. The larger these gravel-washing machines became, in fact, the more water was required for their operation. Sizable mining ventures often involved extensive sluice and waterwheel systems, including "flumes," open ditches usually constructed of heavy boards, and later of expensive iron pipe. Nearly all of the devices just described caused the relatively heavier gold sand to remain in the bottom of whatever vessel was being used. Lighter gravel was washed away by the action of the water.

"Coyoting" was a unique form of mining in which each miner dug his own small separate hole, a backbreaking task. In an area where this operation was prevalent, it was a curious spectacle when red-shirted miners, diligently at work out of sight, suddenly reacted to an unusual noise—their heads popping out of the ground all over a hillside. But this was merely an interesting variation, not the typical method of early California mining. The lonely prospector, equipped with gold pan, with canvas-covered supplies loaded haphazardly on the back of his sure-footed mule, became the symbol of the Gold Rush era, and of the thousands who moved from place to place in search of the precious metal.

The remarkable metalliferous vein which the miners worked, California's principal gold quartz belt, was known as the Mother Lode. It ran northwest and southeast, along a line between Mariposa and Amador, for approximately seventy miles. The lode was characterized by its length, thickness, uniformity, and close proximity to large companion veins. This extensive ore-bearing region came to be divided into the Northern and the Southern Mines, with the watershed separating the Cosumnes and Mokelumne Rivers as the line of demarcation. The many camps above the Mokelumne belonged to the Northern Mines; this region included the American River, with its forks, the Cosumnes, the Bear, the Yuba, and the Feather Rivers, and several smaller streams. Sacramento was the chief depot for provisions. The Southern Mines, whose headquarters was Stockton, included camps lying below the north fork of the Mokelumne, the principal rivers being the Calaveras, the Stanislaus, the Tuolumne, the Merced, and the mountainous portion of the San Joaquin, with its many tributaries.

A number of picturesque place names came to be applied to the towns that mushroomed in the mining regions. These included Git-Up-and-Git, Lazy Man's Canyon, Wildcat Bar, Skunk Gulch, Gospel Swamp, Whisky Bar, Shinbone Peak, Humpback Slide, Bogus Thunder, Hell's Delight, Poker Flat, Ground Hog Glory, Delirium Tremens, Murderers Bar, Hangtown (later Placerville), and Agua Fria ("cold water"). Placerville was first named Hangtown because of a hanging there in 1849 by lynch law; it has had the distinction of longevity, when as a rule mining towns appeared and disappeared astonishingly fast.

The suddenness with which a mining town might spring into being is illustrated in the delightful letters which Louise Clappe wrote home to her sister in Massachusetts from the California mines (her missives were later published as *The Shirley Letters*). Speaking of Rich Bar, she described how two men turned over a stone, beneath which they found a large chunk of gold:

A SUNDAY'S AMUSEMENTS

OCCUPATION FOR RAINY DAYS

"SUNDRY AMUSEMENTS IN THE MINES," 1848–1849. CONTEMPORARY PRINTS.

A DAILY PLEASURE

A PLEASANT SURPRISE

They washed a small panful of dirt, and obtained from it two hundred and fifty-six dollars. . . . they commenced staking off the legal amount of ground allowed . . . and, the remainder of the party having descended the hill, before night the entire bar was "claimed." In a fortnight from that time, the two men who found the first bit of gold had each taken out six thousand dollars. Two others took out thirty-three pounds of gold in eight hours, which is the best day's work that has been done on this bench of the river. The largest amount ever taken from one panful of dirt was fifteen hundred dollars. In a little more than a week after its discovery, five hundred men had settled upon the Bar for the summer. Such is the wonderful alacrity with which a mining town is built.

California's gold-bearing areas were the property of the United States, unsurveyed and legally open neither to occupation nor to settlement. The first claimant of a piece of property, however, was conceded to have the best right to it. Claim jumping, which did occur, has been exaggerated, as has the lawlessness of life in the diggings. Most people who went into the area of the Mother Lode were law-abiding, and eager to establish some system of order. While they awaited the arrival of a regular legal system, the miners organized drumhead courts which meted out such penalties as ear cropping, whipping, and even branding and hanging to convicted transgressors. This system of extralegal justice obviously involved abuses. Almost certainly it did help to discourage crime, however. The regulations that each mining area made and enforced served, in fact, as a practical alternative to anarchy.

Despite the generally rowdy environment, genuine fellowship and hospitality were found in the tents and dugouts of the miners. On Sunday, observed by most gold seekers as a day of rest, the men did their week's washing, baking, or mending, and, remembering wives and children back home, wrote letters. Sunday afternoons and evenings were enlivened by horse racing, yarn swapping, or gambling. A few miners had the hardihood to abstain from drowning their troubles in drink. Prostitutes were in great demand in the predominantly male society.

The bleak days which the miners spent out of doors grubbing for wealth made them especially appreciative of traveling performers, among them Lotta Crabtree, Edwin Booth, and the flaming international celebrity Lola Montez. A more frequent means of entertainment for the lonesome men was singing in groups from a paperback booklet entitled *Put's California Songster*. The lyrics of mining-camp songs were usually set to such well-known airs as "Pop Goes the Weasel," or "Ben Bolt." No song quite equaled "The California Emigrant" in popularity. The chorus of one version, set to the tune of "Oh! Susannah!" was especially popular:

Oh! California!
   That's the land for me,
I'm going to Sacramento,
   With my washbowl on my knee!

A somewhat naughtier air, sung to the tune of "New York Gals," was entitled "Hangtown Gals":

Hangtown gals are plump and rosy,
Hair in ringlets mighty cosy;
Painted cheeks and gassy bonnets;
Touch them and they'll sting like hornets.

CHORUS

Hangtown gals are lovely creatures,
Think they'll marry Mormon preachers;
Heads thrown back to show their features—
Ha, ha, ha! Hangtown gals.
They're dreadful shy of forty-niners,
Turn their noses up at miners;
Shocked to hear them say "gol durn it!"
Try to blush, but cannot come it.

CHORUS

Hangtown gals are lovely creatures, &c.

Boom or Bust

As they churned up the ground, looking for nuggets, the majority of gold seekers averaged earnings of about a hundred dollars per month — a small return considering the conditions of extreme hardship and the cost of living in the mining towns. There were, of course, those who really struck it rich. One man scooped up two and a half pounds of gold in fifteen minutes. Gold at that time sold for $16.00 per ounce. But this was a notable exception, and many miners quickly used up their savings, instead of being able to show a profit for their efforts.

Prices charged for luxuries, and even essential supplies, were fantastic, especially in an age when money in the Eastern United States had several times the purchasing power of today. Copies of Eastern newspapers were grabbed up at $1 apiece. A loaf of

bread, which cost 4 or 5 cents on the Atlantic seaboard, sold for
50 or 75 cents at San Francisco. Kentucky bourbon whiskey
leaped to $30 a quart; apples sold for $1 to $5, eggs for $50 a
dozen (one boiled egg in a restaurant cost as much as $5), and
coffee $5 a pound. Sacramento merchants sold butcher knives for
$30 each, blankets for $40, boots for $100 a pair, and tacks to
nail flapping canvas tents for as much as $192 a pound. Medicine
cost $10 a pill, or $1 a drop, and certain hotel accommodations
$1,000 per month.

Heaps of gold dust, kept in neat doeskin bags, piled up in San
Francisco stores. The traveling Eastern journalist Bayard Taylor
complained: "You enter a shop to buy something; the owner eyes
you with perfect indifference, waiting for you to state your want;
if you object to the price, you are at liberty to leave, for you need
not expect to get it cheaper; he evidently cares little whether you
buy it or not." Another observer described the merchant firm of
Mellus & Howard as "so surrounded with piles of gold dust" and
as receiving "such enormous rents from their landed property, it
is said 400 to $500,000 per annum, that they consider 10 to 12
thousand dollars for discharging a ship a mere flea bite." Persons
who lost both their grubstakes and their courage quickly returned
eastward whence they had come. The most strong-willed and
fortunate miners persevered. Many others wondered whether the
gold boom could possibly be permanent.

After much of the loose ore had been panned out of California's
stream beds in the late 1840's, relatively pure gold became more
and more difficult to discover and to isolate. No longer could penniless miners hope to wrest fortunes from California's rocks and
cliffs with primitive tools and by the sweat of their brow alone.
The required technological changes in mining were to affect inevitably both prices and wages. By the 1850's these changes required
heavy capital outlays from mining operators for new equipment.
In employing the technique of hydraulicking, for example, which
became common, miners used canvas hoses and nozzles to wash
down weathered lodes on the sides of canyons into mechanized
troughs, whose riffles caught free-floating gold particles. At Murderer's Bar and elsewhere whole rivers were diverted so that their
beds could be worked. Intricate paddlewheels operated bucket
pumps that drained the diggings. Hundreds of miles of canals and
flumes carried water through riveted sheet-iron pipes, thus moving
large deposits of ore to devices which could extract the gold.
Stamp mills were also constructed, huge affairs weighing as much
as eight hundred pounds each that clattered away deafeningly as

GOOD NEWS

FOR

MINERS.

NEW GOODS,

PROVISIONS, TOOLS,

CLOTHING, &c. &c.

GREAT BARGAINS!

JUST RECEIVED BY THE SUBSCRIBERS, AT THE LARGE TENT ON THE HILL,

A superior Lot of New, Valuable and most DESIRABLE GOODS for Miners and for residents also. Among them are the following:

STAPLE PROVISIONS AND STORES.

Pork, Flour, Bread, Beef, Hams, Mackerel, Sugar, Molasses, Coffee, Teas, Butter & Cheese, Pickles, Beans, Peas, Rice, Chocolate, Spices, Salt, Soap, Vinegar, &c.

EXTRA PROVISIONS AND STORES.

Every variety of Preserved Meats and Vegetables and Fruits, [more than eighty different kinds.] Tongues and Sounds; Smoked Halibut; Dry Cod Fish; Eggs fresh and fine; Figs, Raisins, Almonds and Nuts; China Preserves; China Bread and Cakes; Butter Crackers, Boston Crackers, and many other very desirable and *choice bits.*

DESIRABLE GOODS FOR COMFORT. AND HEALTH.

Patent Cot Bedsteads, Mattresses and Pillows, Blankets and Comforters. Also, in Clothing—Overcoats, Jackets, Miner's heavy Velvet Coats and Pantaloons, Woolen Pants, Guernsey Frocks, Flannel Shirts and Drawers, Stockings and Socks, Boots, Shoes; Rubber Waders, Coats, Blankets, &c.

MINING TOOLS, &c.; BUILDING MATERIALS, &c.

Cradles, Shovels, Spades, Hoes, Picks, Axes, Hatchets, Hammers; every variety of Workman's Tools, Nails, Screws, Brads, &c.

SUPERIOR GOLD SCALES.   MEDICINE CHESTS, &c.

Superior Medicine Chests, well assorted, together with the principal Important Medicines for Dysentery, Fever and Fever and Ague, Scurvy, &c.

N.B.–Important Express Arrangement for Miners.

The Subscribers will run an EXPRESS to and from every Steamer, carrying and returning Letters for the Post Office and Expresses to the States. Also, conveying "*GOLD DUST*" or Parcels, to and from the Mines to the Banking Houses, or the several Expresses for the States, insuring their safety.——The various *NEWSPAPERS,* from the Eastern, Western and Southern States, will also be found on sale at our stores, together with a large stock of *BOOKS* and *PAMPHLETS* constantly on hand.

Excelsior Tent, Mormon Island,
January 1, 1850.   ALTA CALIFORNIA PRESS.   **WARREN & CO.**

BROADSIDE ADVERTISEMENT OF THE MORMON ISLAND EMPORIUM, IN THE CALIFORNIA MINES, 1848–1849. SUCH STORES ALSO SERVED AS MAIL, EXPRESS, AND BANKING CENTERS. (By courtesy of The Huntington Library, San Marino, California.)

as they reduced tons of rock to manageable powder ore. The first stamp mills were crudely made of vertical logs shod with iron, but these unimposing structures housed expensive imported machinery. The days of pick, shovel, pan, and burro were over.

Along with the numerous technological changes in California mining there occurred a decline in gold productivity. After the mid-1850's production never again reached that of the peak year of 1852, when gold worth $81,294,700 was taken out of California's mines. By 1854 the "easy pickings" of placer mining had practically disappeared and miners looked elsewhere for new diggings. Only much later, in 1880, after other placers were developed in the Trinity-Klamath area of northwestern California, did gold production again soar. But it was mining companies, rather than individual miners, that raised the necessary capital for shaft tunneling and timbering through bedrock, in the case of quartz mining, and for heavy machinery and hoses in the case of hydraulic operations.

Once the gold bonanza drew to a close, prices declined rapidly. Traveling theater troupes that had been able to charge as much as $55 for private stall seats now played to almost empty houses. Merchants found it difficult to sell the expensive "Long Nine" Havana cigars that had once commanded high prices. Shopkeepers threw sacks of spoiled flour into the streets of Sacramento and San Francisco to help fill muddy holes; unsalable cast-iron cookstoves were dismantled and used as sidewalks. No longer did a man need to send his laundry as far as Hawaii, and even China, to be washed. Discouraged miners, returning empty-handed from the diggings, left ghost towns behind them as they flocked back into the cities, anxious to find any sort of work. Others moved into the countryside. Some wisely bought farm lands after the rush and lived to amass the fortunes they had not found in the placers. Nearly all eventually settled down to workaday pursuits that would be important to the state of California in the future.

One observer considered the Gold Rush "the most portentous event in the history of modern mining because it gave an immediate stimulus to worldwide migration." It is also possible to agree with a modern historian of the state who believes that gold represented the very cornerstone upon which California's future was built. Because the events involved with the precious metal had quickened economic expansion and made dramatically evident the need for greater political stability, the Gold Rush had indeed done much for California.

SELECTED READINGS

Basic modern works on the Gold Rush include Rodman W. Paul's *California Gold* (Cambridge, 1947), which explains the principal techniques of mining, and John W. Caughey, *Gold Is the Cornerstone* (Berkeley, 1948), a general analysis of the era. The initial discovery is treated in Erwin G. Gudde, *Bigler's Chronicle of the West: The Conquest of California, Discovery of Gold, and Mormon Settlement As Reflected in William Henry Bigler's Diaries* (Berkeley, 1962). One of the best of many contemporary accounts by a California gold seeker is Alonzo Delano's *Life on the Plains and Among the Diggings* (Auburn, N.Y., 1854). Another volume that discusses conditions along the trails to the gold camps is the vivid narrative by William Lewis Manly, *Death Valley in '49* (San Jose, 1894; New York, 1924). See also Manly's *The Jay Hawker's Oath and Other Sketches*, edited by Arthur Woodward (Los Angeles, 1949). An appraisal of the makeshift governmental arrangement adopted in the diggings is Charles H. Shinn, *Mining Camps: A Study of American Frontier Government* (New York, 1885). Authentic descriptions of life in the mines appear in Bayard Taylor, *Eldorado, or Adventures in the Path of Empire* (2 vols., New York, 1850; repr. 1949).

Valeska Bari has edited some flavorful contemporary accounts in *The Course of Empire* (New York, 1931), and Walker D. Wyman has compiled numerous letters written from the diggings in his *California Emigrant Letters* (New York, 1952). Under the pseudonym "Dame Shirley," Louise Amelia Knapp Smith Clappe wrote *The Shirley Letters from the California Mines* (see the edition with introduction and notes by Carl I. Wheat; New York, 1949). Other first-hand accounts include E. Gould Buffum, *Six Months in the Gold Mines* (Philadelphia, 1850); Carolyn H. Ross, *The Log of a Forty Niner* (Boston, 1923); James H. Carson, *Early Recollections of the Mines* (Stockton, 1852); and Franklin A. Buck, *Yankee Trader in the Gold Rush* (Boston, 1930). A worthy descriptive volume of a more general nature is Thomas Jefferson Farnham, *Life, Adventures and Travels to California* (New York, 1849).

Other representative diaries include David M. Potter, ed., *Trail to California: The Overland Journal of Vincent Geiger and Wakeman Bryarly* (New Haven, 1945), and the remarkably illustrated *Gold Rush: The Journals, Drawings, and Other Papers of J. Goldsborough Bruff* (2 vols., New York, 1944), edited by Georgia W. Read and Ruth Gaines. The passage around South America is described in Rydell's *Cape Horn*

Route, while that via Panama is discussed in John H. Kemble, *The Panama Route, 1828–1869* (Berkeley, 1943). Consult also Oscar Lewis, *Sea Routes to the Gold Fields* (New York, 1949). A melancholy tale concerning a group of belated gold hunters who came to California by sea is Robert Samuel Fletcher, *From Cleveland by Ship to California* (Durham, 1959).

Recent accounts include also Archer B. Hulbert, *Forty Niners* (Boston, 1931), a synthetic job, and Owen C. Coy, *The Great Trek* (Los Angeles, 1931), as well as Irene D. Paden, *In the Wake of the Prairie Schooner* (New York, 1943). See also Ralph P. Bieber, *Southern Trails to California in 1849* (Glendale, 1937). The travails of a group of forty-niners known as "The Sand Walking Company" are recounted in James Edsall Severn, "The Ill-Fated '49er Wagon Train," Historical Society of Southern California *Quarterly*, XLII (March, 1960), 29–40.

A series of essays about the Gold Rush by modern interpreters is presented in John W. Caughey, ed., *Rushing for Gold* (Berkeley, 1949). Popularizations include a book of pictures by Joseph Henry Jackson, *Gold Rush Album* (New York, 1949), and his *Anybody's Gold* (New York, 1941). Carl I. Wheat, *Books of the California Gold Rush* (San Francisco, 1949), discusses promotional literature, guide books, narratives of travel, and scholarly studies relating to the Gold Rush.

Two articles that feature the Gold Rush as more than a California phenomenon are Ralph J. Roske, "The World Impact of the California Gold Rush, 1849–1857," *Arizona and the West*, V (Autumn, 1963), 187–232, and Ralph P. Bieber, "California Gold Mania," *Mississippi Valley Historical Review*, XXXV (June, 1948), 3–28. See also Charles Bateson, *Gold Fleet to California: Forty-Niners from Australia and New Zealand* (East Lansing, Mich., 1964), an account of the rush from the Antipodes from 1849 to 1850. Colorfully written but incomplete is the description of medical practices during the rush in George W. Groh, *Gold Fever* (New York, 1966). Appraisals of the actual discovery are Rodman W. Paul, *The California Gold Discovery: Sources, Documents, Accounts, and Memoirs . . .* (Georgetown, Calif., 1966) and James S. Holliday, "The Gold Rush in Myth and Reality," Ph.D. dissertation, University of California, Berkeley (1959).

16

Approaches to Statehood

After the short-lived Bear Flag Republic ceased to exist, Commodore Stockton, adding to Sloat's initial proclamation to the people of California, had on August 17, 1846, declared a state of martial law. During the Mexican War, therefore, California was treated as conquered territory, subject to military rule. Under international law, such territory ordinarily retains its prior municipal institutions, while the conqueror issues temporary laws and regulations. This was the case in California, where military rule and the civil administration of justice were combined to provide government for the conquered province.

The *alcalde*, a remnant of Mexican bureaucracy, remained the major judicial officer of California at this period. His traditional functions were maintained, but his authority became variable, the *alcalde* at Monterey, for example, having more influence than any of the others. Walter Colton, an American who became *alcalde* of that city, referred to his position as embracing the manifold responsibilities of "guardian of the public peace." Naturally, nearly all the native California *alcaldes* were in time succeeded by Americans, who superimposed upon the Mexican institution the notions of common law they had brought west with them. That law, then, began gradually to supplant the procedures of the past, providing, with the sanction of the military governor, such legal safeguards as trial by jury.

Military Government

In 1847, American rule over California was confused by the controversy between Commodore Stockton and General Kearny over their relative authority. Stockton, as previously noted, regarded himself as possessing precedence; and, when Kearny stoutly asserted his own authority, Stockton refused to recognize it completely. As the controversy deepened, Kearny awaited the instructions from Washington that were eventually to place him in full charge. Meanwhile Stockton continued to be recognized as military commander and territorial governor until, following the Cahuenga Capitulations, he resigned in favor of Frémont, whom he commissioned as governor. Frémont acted as governor for some fifty days, during which Kearny continued to assert his claims.

Meanwhile instructions from Washington had reached Kearny directing that, as the senior officer of the land forces, he should be the governor of California. Then followed the Frémont-Kearny controversy, the upshot of which was the court-martial of Frémont, his conviction, and his subsequent pardon. Frémont was was found guilty of disobedience, conduct prejudicial to military discipline, and even mutiny; but President Polk approved only part of the verdict, and he allowed Frémont to resign gracefully from the army. General Kearny assumed the governorship of California jointly with Commodore William B. Shubrick, Stockton's successor as commander of the naval forces, and he designated Monterey as the capital. Kearny declared it the intention of the United States "to provide for California, with the least possible delay, a free government similar to those in her other territories," indicating that for the time being those laws not in conflict with the United States Constitution would continue in force.

The forming of a new civil government would take time. Local politics remained uncertain. The populace complained about the continuance of Mexican laws, which had been and continued to be enforced without benefit of courts. Frequent murmurings were heard over infringements upon the right of self-government. On May 31, 1847, Kearny was succeeded as governor by Colonel Richard B. Mason. Mason recognized the popular discontent over government, but was obliged to rule under military restrictions, lacking any real authority to establish new civil institutions. Nevertheless, a few days before he received news of a peace treaty with Mexico, he had prepared for publication a new code of laws for California. This code unfortunately was not immediately issued, and, as American immigration into California increased, discontent among the settlers grew. The Treaty of Guadalupe Hidalgo, ratified May 20, 1848, concluded the Mexican War and resulted in the cession of California to the United States. Disgruntled Americans rejoiced, feeling that military rule came to an end on that date.

Mason himself hoped that Congress would soon confer upon Californians their constitutional rights as United States citizens. Unfortunately the political machinery for a civil territorial government was slow to be authorized. In the somewhat exaggerated words of Josiah Royce, California was "to be morally and socially tried as no other American community ever has been tried." Mason continued to administer military rule, in daily expectancy of new congressional instructions about territorial organization. Much to the disgust of Californians, however, Congress adjourned on August 14, 1848, leaving the political future of the territory undecided.

It became ever more difficult for the residents of California to comply with Secretary of State James Buchanan's exhortation "to live peaceably and quietly under the existing government." Californians only grew in the conviction that some kind of self-government should be initiated with the least possible delay. The first preparations toward that goal were made at an enthusiastic mass meeting at San Jose on December 11, 1848. Similar gatherings followed at San Francisco and elsewhere, adopting by acclamation resolutions to the effect that a convention should be held to nominate a candidate for governor. A public meeting at San Francisco, on February 12, 1849, even established temporary municipal government for that city.

The military commanders in California were cautious about handling such civilian activities. When General Persifor F. Smith superseded Mason as commander of the Army Division of the Pacific, he followed the example of his predecessors from Sloat onward. Most of the military commanders sent to the region had been instructed to accommodate to civilian desires, and they had all allowed a wide degree of local autonomy. Smith, too, carried out military rule as best he could, but did not directly interfere with civilian gatherings. By this time Californians were living politically almost as much in a civilian environment as in a military one.

General Bennett Riley, California's next military governor was a mature, amicable leader, who knew both how to obey orders and how to deal with an upset population. Although he originally had no intention of supporting local agitation for a civil government, he changed his mind after learning that Congress had once more adjourned without having provided for statehood. On June 3, 1849, Riley issued a proclamation that called for the selection of delegates to a general convention. Held at Monterey beginning on September 1, 1849, this would form a state constitution and plan a territorial government.

In spite of his sympathies with American residents in California, General Riley had difficulty in putting up with the San Francisco "Legislative Assembly," a fifteen-member body that had assumed extended powers. This group refused to recognize civil power as residing in a military governor, and championed a temporary civilian government for the protection of life and property near San Francisco. It also interfered with California's already inadequate judiciary system and deposed a corrupt *alcalde*, creating and filling other offices as well. The Assembly recommended that a general convention be held at San Jose on the third Monday in August to form a state constitution, for subsequent submission to popular vote. Finally Riley issued a proclamation denouncing the "men styling themselves the 'legislative assembly of the district of San Francisco.'" He called them unauthorized usurpers of the powers vested in Congress and warned Californians not to countenance the organization "either by paying taxes or by supporting or abetting its officers."

As if in reply to the military governor, Senator Thomas Hart Benton, still smarting from the court-martial of his son-in-law, Frémont, championed the rights of California's United States citizens. He and other senators claimed that the moment the treaty of Guadalupe Hidalgo went into force the United States Constitution was extended over California. Congress, in failing to provide a territorial government, had indirectly encouraged the people to legislate for themselves. This "settlers' theory," furthermore, assumed that both congressional authority and the military government of California derived their power from the consent of the people. Therefore, any military governor was subordinate to and held office by the sufferance of the people. Californians had backed the Legislative Assembly of San Francisco because of alleged grievances resulting from the policies of administration leaders in Washington, D.C. These conflicts of interest would have to be reconciled.

Early in 1849, President Taylor had sent a congressional leader, Thomas Butler King, to California as his personal agent. King was to acquire the fullest possible information regarding California's desire for statehood, an issue in which Taylor was greatly interested, and to encourage subtly whatever sentiment he found for the territory's admission into the Union. Such encouragement was not necessary; California was more than ready for statehood. King was so impressed with California that he stayed on, becoming in 1851 collector of the port of San Francisco and later a senatorial candidate.

Meanwhile, the United States military officials in California continued to administer the laws proclaimed by Congress at the conclusion of peace with Mexico; Californians kept clamoring for a constitutional convention. Fortunately for the peaceful settlement of differences, the troublesome San Francisco Assembly recommended that all citizens follow the suggestion of Riley that such a convention meet in September of 1849.

The Constitutional Convention of 1849

The constitutional convention at Monterey could be said to have opened even before its first session convened, so great was the enthusiasm of California residents for their political future. This enthusiasm made itself widely felt during the period when delegates were being elected, a process completed without accusations of regional or partisan advantage. The convention met on September 3, 1849, on the upper story of Colton Hall, a long, newly constructed white building overlooking the town of Monterey and the Pacific Ocean. Forty-eight earnest delegates, the majority of American birth, were sworn in as members of the convention. The huge and angular Dr. Robert Semple of Sonoma, who, as previously noted, had come to California as a covered-wagon pioneer, was elected president of the gathering. William G. Marcy, formerly captain of Stevenson's volunteer regiment, was named secretary, and J. Ross Browne, an itinerant author, reporter. While none of the delegates were nationally known, they proved to be competent and devoted. The document they wrote was not the sudden creation of untutored gold hunters. It was the work of men with a purpose, men who had profited from their residence in California and who were deeply interested in the future of the territory.

Nevertheless, the framing of this constitution was undertaken amid extraordinary difficulties. Native Californians, earlier American settlers, and forty-niners reflected such divergent backgrounds that it seemed an almost impossible task to bring them to full agreement. Perhaps no similar constituent body had ever been quite so unacquainted with each other and so devoid of preconceived plans or policies. The task, however, fell to young and flexible men. The average age of the delegates was thirty-six; the oldest, José Antonio Carrillo, was fifty-three. There were few physical resources, such as libraries, to which they could refer for precedent; probably not more than fifty volumes of law and history were to be found in the locality of Monterey. These, however, included copies of some state constitutions, among them those of Iowa and New York, both of which were heavily drawn upon by the framers.

The native Californians, who numbered seven out of the forty-eight delegates, were shown special courtesies, at least superficially. Perhaps the most distinguished of these was General Vallejo. Dignified and popular, he was well acquainted with American institutions and laws; after the transfer of government Vallejo was to render valuable services to the United States as a member of the first California senate. His personal fortunes suffered severely under American rule, with the loss of the practically unlimited lands on which he had employed hundreds of Indian laborers. Yet such was his personal magnanimity that he wrote in his memoirs: "The inhabitants of California have no reason to complain of the change of government, for if the rich have lost thousands of horses and cattle, the poor have been bettered in condition." Another native delegate to the convention, Pablo de la Guerra of Santa Barbara, had much in common with Vallejo: he too was tolerant and well educated, had been a prisoner of American troops during the conquest, and subsequently became a state senator. Even better known was Carrillo, a Castilian of strong character and intelligence. Antonio M. Pico, Jacinto Rodríguez, Manuel Dominguez, and J. M. Covarrubias were other native California convention members. A very few of the delegates, among them Miguel Pedrorena, had come originally from Spain.

Another foreign-born delegate was John A. Sutter, who by now was regarded almost as an American. Clearly the most influential of the native American delegates was William M. Gwin, a Southern professional politician of wide experience. He had openly come to California for political reasons, and soon sought election to the United States Senate. His knowledge of parliamentary procedure gave him a distinct advantage at the convention; his ability in debate, added to his powers of leadership, marked him as the ablest politician of the group. Another assiduous political talent was that of Captain Henry W. Halleck, Riley's secretary of state. Thomas O. Larkin, as the "first and last American consul to California," also lent his authority to the deliberations, as did several men who had served in the San Francisco Legislative Assembly.

Debates of the Convention

Should the convention proceed at once to form a state constitution, or should it be content to establish a territorial government? This was a basic question. A few native Californians, and conservative settlers from the South, opposed state organization. By an overwhelming majority the convention, however, voted to proceed at once with forming a state constitution. This decision gave California the distinction of seeking admission into the Union without passing through the stage of being an organized American territory.

Next the Committee on the Constitution reported a Declaration of Rights, of sixteen sections. After slight changes had been made, a delegate moved to insert an additional section: "Neither slavery nor involuntary servitude, unless for the punishment of crimes, shall ever be tolerated in this State." This vital proposal was, almost without debate, unanimously adopted. Because the miners did not want slaves working beside them, public sentiment was unquestionably in favor of a free state; but the unanimous vote was rather surprising, since fifteen delegates had emigrated from Southern slave states. California, entering the Union as the sixteenth free state, was to destroy forever the equilibrium between North and South. The convention's vote, however, did not put an end to the slavery question. There was lively discussion about possible prohibition of the entrance of free Negroes into the future state. Slaveholders, it was urged, might bring their slaves to California and free them in great numbers. In such a case the Negroes would be likely to seek service in the mines, and thus compete with white labor to the detriment of the latter. These arguments, however, did not prevail. From the beginning California became a completely free state.

Fiscal and monetary matters also occupied much of the delegates' attention. The convention voiced extraordinary opposition to banks, based chiefly on suspicion of outside wealth and the interference in California affairs it might involve. Providing a satisfactory system of taxation was difficult because the large landholders of southern California naturally objected to a land tax, which they feared would fall heavily upon them while a shifting population farther north and in the mines would enjoy the full benefits of a government they did little to support. Another issue attracting widespread interest was that of separate property rights for married women; this provision, finally adopted, was one of the first such guarantees embodied in the constitution of any state. The convention's debates also revealed strong interest in education. Because of the unanimity expressed in favor of a well-regulated system of common schools, liberal arrangements were made for public education, and the income from certain state lands was set apart for eventual establishment of a state university.

By far the most animated debate of the convention concerned California's boundary. The contest was sectional in character, and imperiled the work of the convention. When California was ceded to the United States by Mexico, its vast territorial extent had not been strictly defined. The 42nd parallel of latitude, however, was generally conceded to form a definite boundary on the north, the Pacific Ocean on the west, and the treaty line between Upper and Lower California on the south. The point in dispute was the eastern border, which perhaps embraced the great desert east of the Sierra Nevada, and even the basin inhabited by the Mormons. In the opinion of the Committee on the Boundary, Mexican California, estimated at nearly 450,000 square miles, was too vast for one state. It recommended as the eastern boundary the 116th parallel. This would have placed the boundary at approximately the eastern border of today's state of Nevada. On this score disagreement was strong. Gwin took a leading part in favoring a large state, reminding the convention that it had met to frame a constitution for the whole of California. It should not dismember the future state, he felt. Semple argued that it was "not desirable that the State of California should extend her territory further east than the Sierra Nevada," a real natural boundary. A larger territory would prove administratively unwieldy. Moreover, the Mormons, who would certainly be affected if the boundary should be moved eastward, were not represented in the convention. Southerners also felt that Congress, already reflecting sectional discord, would never permit one state to settle by itself the question of slavery in so large a territory. The convention, therefore, agreed upon a relatively narrow state area, drawing its line of demarcation east of the Sierra crest, along the desert floor. It was hoped that this decision to restrict the size of California would make the new California constitution more acceptable to the United States Congress. That body was soon to debate California's prospective statehood.

Despite the widely divergent views on these and other matters, the desire to secure California's immediate admission into the Union prompted the delegates to bring their deliberations to an end. The closing ceremonies of the constitutional convention took place on Saturday, October 13. As the delegates affixed their signatures to the constitution, a salute of thirty-one guns was fired at the Monterey presidio just over the hill from Colton Hall, in honor of the states then in the Union (though California itself, the thirty-first, had not officially achieved that distinction). After the cannonade ended, the crowd assembled outside Colton Hall cheered, and men tossed their hats in the air as California's newly adopted Great Seal was displayed publicly for the first time.

This seal bears thirty-one stars, representing the states. Minerva, sprung from the brow of Jupiter, is the foreground figure, symbolic of California's admission to the Union without passing through territorial probation. A grizzly bear crouches at her feet; a miner, with rocker and bowl, illustrates "the golden wealth of the Sacramento"; and beyond the river, whose shipping typifies commercial greatness, rise the Sierra Nevada Mountains. At the top of the seal is the legend "EUREKA," the state motto.

A New Government and Statehood

California's constitution of 1849 had illustrated once again the capacity for self-government under primitive conditions. Despite numerous defects, it endured for thirty years as the fundamental law of a growing state. Nevertheless, more was required to begin a new civilian government in California than the mere writing of a constitution. It had to be disseminated and ratified before it could even begin to be put into effect. Copies of the constitution, printed in English and in Spanish, were quickly sent by messenger to virtually every town, camp, and ranch in California. On November 13 it was ratified by an almost unanimous vote of California's white males. Peter H. Burnett was elected governor, and San Jose was selected as temporary capital. On December 20, the state government was actually established and Burnett was inaugurated, as General Riley gracefully resigned his powers as governor. Whatever legal objections might be raised to putting a state government into operation before congressional approval of its status, Riley judged that these must yield to the "obvious necessities of the case." California was in almost every respect a state, even though it had not yet been admitted to the Union.

Governor Burnett and the other new officials set to work carrying out the provisions of the constitution. The legislative body, consisting of a senate and an assembly, proceeded to convene in a lengthy session lasting until April 22, 1850. This first California legislature, as one of its earliest acts, named two senators to be sent to the federal Congress. One of these was Frémont, who had returned to California as a civilian after his court-martial in order to supervise gold-mining operations on his tract of land at Mariposa. The other was Gwin. In January, 1850, the two men had set out for Washington, and in March they laid copies of the new state constitution before Congress. In long speeches before that body they requested the admission of California into the Union.

The issue was one that excited much interest in Congress. Southern senators and congressmen were considerably agitated at the prospect of the admission of a free state occupying so vast a portion of the recent Mexican cession. The balance of power between North and South seemed irretrievably slipping away. Daniel Webster asserted that slavery was virtually excluded by nature itself from the arid territory acquired from Mexico. The problem was rendered more complicated by its necessary involvement with the national North-South struggle, culminating in that crucial mid-century year, which saw one of the stormiest sessions ever experienced by the United States Congress. It seemed possible that Congress, which had repeatedly disappointed the people of California in the matter of a provisional government, would now delay its admission to the Union.

Finally, after weeks of deadlock, Senator Henry Clay's compromise plan for national union was adopted. This complicated "Omnibus Bill" assuaged the feelings of the South by allowing the future territories of New Mexico and Utah to decide for themselves their slave or free status; California was to be admitted as a free state. On September 9, 1850, President Millard Fillmore affixed his signature to the admission bill; and California's senators and representatives, who had been standing by for months, immediately took their seats in Congress. News of California's admission reached San Francisco on October 18. For both that city and for the state this was a dramatic moment. All business was suspended, and the people poured into Portsmouth Square to celebrate and to hear local orators boast of the fact that California was finally a full-fledged member of the Union.

Locating the Capital

Several cities eagerly vied for the privilege of being selected as California's permanent state capital. In addition to the long-standing claims of Monterey and San Francisco, considerable support also arose for San Luis Obispo, Benicia, Stockton, and Santa Barbara. San Jose was eliminated as a possibility because the legislators were not satisfied with the accommodations available there;

they were familiar with the town as the site of the first session of the legislature, dubbed after a trivial but highly publicized incident the "Legislature of a Thousand Drinks." A proposal by General Vallejo to lay out a new city between San Francisco and Sacramento along the Carquinez Straits received northern support and in June, 1851, Governor John McDougal actually moved the government archives from San Jose to this bleak site named Vallejo after the general. No suitable accommodations for legislative business were in existence there either. Thus the state government was soon moved again to still another site. In February, 1853, a resolution was adopted by the legislature establishing Benicia as the capital. That town, which offered state officials the dubious advantages of a two-story brick building in the middle of some river mud flats, was hardly more suitable than San Jose or Vallejo.

Meanwhile, nearby Sacramento made such a strong bid for the capital that the legislature convened there in 1854. By that time it had become one of the most populous cities in the state, and local pride ran high. A noisy procession marched through the principal streets, addresses of welcome were delivered, and Sacramento proved itself such a congenial and suitable place that it became firmly established as California's seat of government. It remains a city of considerable beauty, and though today rather remote from large centers of population, it has retained its position as the capital for more than a century.

SELECTED READINGS

The Frémont-Kearny-Stockton controversy over the governorship, which came to a head with the court-martial of Frémont, is clearly portrayed in *Proceedings of the Court Martial in the Trial of (J. C.) Frémont* (Washington, D.C., 1848).

Basic to an understanding of California's struggle for statehood are William H. Ellison, *A Self-Governing Dominion: California, 1849–1860* (Berkeley, 1950), and Cardinal L. Goodwin, *The Establishment of State Government in California, 1846–1850* (New York, 1914). Joseph Ellison's *California and the Nation, 1850–1869* (Berkeley, 1927) tells the story of the state's early relations with the country as a whole. A brief but useful article dealing with politics in a Western setting is Earl Pomeroy, "California, 1846–1860: Politics of a Representative Frontier State," California Historical Society *Quarterly*, XXXII (December, 1953), 291–302.

Events at the constitutional convention are related in J. Ross

Browne, *Report of the Debates in the Convention of California on the Formation of the State Constitution* (Washington, D.C., 1850). Later treatments include Rockwell D. Hunt's *The Genesis of California's First Constitution* (Baltimore, 1895). Other accounts of these early years include Samuel H. Willey, *The Transition Period of California* (San Francisco, 1901), James A. B. Sherer, *Thirty-first Star* (New York, 1942), and articles by Joseph and William H. Ellison as well as by Bayrd Still, Grace E. Tower, and Hallie M. McPherson, in the files of the *Pacific Historical Review*, the California Historical Society *Quarterly*, and the Historical Society of Southern California *Quarterly*.

The *Journals* of California's assembly and senate for 1850 have also been printed and are useful, as is the state constitution; a modern printing with an introduction by Robert G. Cleland is *Constitution of the State of California* (San Marino, 1949).

Notable also are Governor Peter H. Burnett's *Recollections and Opinions of an Old Pioneer* (New York, 1880), and William Day Simonds, *Starr King in California* (San Francisco, 1917).

17

Social Ferment

California society remained in a turmoil after the Gold Rush, an unsettled culture without the sort of foundations needed to give it stability. Discordant, brawling, and lawless elements had entered the new state and they were bound to alter its future. The sheer numbers of California's new immigrants created a formidable problem of assimilation. By 1850, only about eight per cent of the white populace of over 100,000 were native Californians. Nearly one-fourth of these had come from foreign countries; the rest came from throughout the United States. Negroes numbered fewer than one thousand persons. Thousands of uncounted Indians, confused and bewildered by the American conquest, were everywhere to be seen. Among the whites, men predominated over women at a ratio of about twelve to one, few of the women and many of the men being unmarried. Nearly three-fourths of the state's residents lived in the Sacramento and San Joaquin Valleys and along the lower slopes of the Sierra mountain barrier. With so divergent a population pattern, California understandably faced a grave period of social unrest.

Vigilantism and Its Roots

Frontier cultures have historically attracted a varied population such as that just described; and, when legal justice has been unable to cope with the special problems inevitably arising, "popular

tribunals" have taken the place of established law. California
proved no exception. In the absence of order each man substituted
his own notions of justice. "Respectable citizens" called with particular fervor for greater public morality; they were especially
concerned with stamping out corruption at San Francisco, the
state's first real city. But Californians did not always rid themselves gracefully of their social nuisances. In an atmosphere of
legal amateurism, vigilantes sometimes devised relatively callous
legal remedies. The failure of duly constituted authorities to pros-
ecute criminal offenders often led to vindictive punishment of
such persons at the hands of vigilantes.

Nevertheless, it would be inaccurate to speak of the activities of
the vigilance committees as being synonymous with mobocracy or
lynch law. The vigilantes arose because the signing of the new
constitution—and even the achievement of statehood—did not
solve the problem of crime in California. Most vigilance committees considered themselves constituted as "the champions of
justice and of right." A mob, in contrast, is a tumultuous rabble
animated by a common passion, subversive to both order and
reason. The vigilantes did not usually operate where there was

effective prosecution of the law. Yet sometimes, in the name of
justice, excessively zealous groups did take over existing legal
processes.

After the discovery of gold, the sudden influx into San Francisco
included hundreds of youths, some of whom formed "gangs" with
the purpose of defying the norms of society. Among them were
adventurous social parasites, criminals, and others simply intent
upon asserting their own rights at whatever cost. Together they
paralyzed the already weak municipal organization of San Francisco. In 1849 a band, calling themselves the "Hounds," or "Regu-

lators," terrorized the city with repeated acts of violence. These
young men were partly composed of remnants of Stevenson's
Volunteers; since their discharge at the end of the Mexican War,
they had been roaming San Francisco's streets as though they
owned them. A similar group of hoodlums had their headquarters
in Sydney Town, a particularly notorious section of the city.
Known as the "Sydney Ducks," this band was composed of former
members of Great Britain's prison colony in Australia, newly arrived in California. Honest residents noted their troublesome
activities by saying: "The Sydney Ducks are cackling."

Meanwhile, in a near-criminal atmosphere of juvenile violence,
antiforeign sentiment flourished in California's new cities. This

nativism, a form of racial hatred, became entwined with the

sordid activities of San Francisco's gangs. On Sunday, July 15, 1849, a crisis occurred which aroused its citizenry as never before. During that afternoon a large and rowdy crowd of Regulators held a "patriotic" parade. After touring various saloons, where they demanded liquor and smashed windows, they began to assault brutally some Chilean families in tents on the city's sand dunes. They ruthlessly beat, kicked, and fired upon these foreigners, several of whom were seriously wounded. As news of these outrages spread, excitement in the town rose to a high pitch. Sam Brannan and other indignant city elders and property owners speedily arrested and prepared to try the offenders. Forming a citizens' court, Brannan's men found the leader of the Regulators guilty of disturbing the peace on eight counts, and they banished him from San Francisco along with a score of his cohorts.

After the routing of the Regulators, many citizens thought that antiforeign violence and criminality lay in the city's past. Soon, however, a veritable delirium of criminality broke out—a state that was to plague San Francisco for several years. As murderers and thieves again went unpunished, and the city government

FLOOD AT SACRAMENTO IN JANUARY, 1850. (From a contemporary print.)

showed no signs of acting against the open vice and corruption, moral indignation mounted.

Vigilance Activity in the Early 1850's

Suddenly the civic conscience shook off its lethargy. In February, 1851, a prominent merchant named Jansen was assaulted in his store and his safe burglarized. The need of the hour seemed to be for a strong organization to enforce the law. Rising to the occasion, "The Committee of Vigilance of San Francisco" finally organized itself on June 10 with about two hundred members pledged "to watch, pursue, and bring to justice the outlaws infesting the city, through the regularly constituted courts, if possible, through more summary course, if necessary." The members determined that "no thief, burglar, incendiary, or assassin, shall escape punishment, either by the quibbles of the law, the insecurity of prisons, the carelessness or corruption of the police, or a laxity of those who pretend to administer justice." At the head of the committee to purge the city of vice was William T. Coleman, then a successful young merchant and later one of the nabobs of San Francisco society.

Scarcely had the organization been formed when two sharp peals of the city's fire bell brought the members to its headquarters, the Monumental Fire Engine House. One John Jenkins, a former convict from Sydney, Australia, had burglarized a shipping office on Commercial Street, boldly carrying off its strongbox. Jenkins made the mistake of brazenly defying anyone to stop him. When several vigilantes sought to do so, he threw the strongbox into San Francisco Bay in an act of further contempt. When he was finally apprehended, the viligance committee showed little hesitation or mercy in dealing with him. They brought Jenkins to their headquarters, where the merchant Sam Brannan acted as his judge. Within a few hours, almost at the stroke of midnight, Jenkins was pronounced guilty. In the early morning hours the condemned man was taken to Portsmouth Square; a scaffold was hastily erected, a noose draped round his neck, and he was hanged. Although a coroner's jury charged Brannan and the other vigilantes with a rather hasty, indeed harsh, execution, San Francisco's "best citizens" approved the sentence heartily. The work of the vigilance committee continued until both the audacity and the power of the Sydney Ducks, and other criminal elements, were forever broken.

On the morning of July 11, 1851, the bell on the firehouse summoned the vigilance committee to consider a case involving another Sydney Duck. This was "English Jim" Stuart, a confessed criminal. Earlier, through mistaken identity, the committee had been about to execute an innocent man; but they discovered their mistake and found Stuart guilty instead. Stuart was led to the Market Street Wharf, where he was hanged aboard the deck of a ship anchored nearby. Two other men, Samuel Whittaker and Robert McKenzie, were soon afterward brought to trial for various crimes. Although they confessed and were condemned by the vigilantes to die, these prisoners were suddenly seized by the legally appointed sheriff and placed in jail. On Sunday afternoon, August 24, they were re-abducted by a party of vigilantes, who took the men to their headquarters. The bell that summoned committee members soon sounded its plaintive death knell. Six thousand men witnessed in silence the execution of Whittaker and McKenzie.

The record of sentences imposed by the vigilance committee of 1851 is as follows, in addition to the four hangings: whipped, one man; deported, fourteen; ordered to leave the state, one; handed over to the "authorities," fifteen; discharged, forty-one. The final entry in the secretary's book is dated June 30, 1852. Even then the association was not formally dissolved, its members standing ready to resume their activities.

The local press endorsed the vigilante movement from the beginning, with the exception of one newspaper. Eastern newspapers, however, were inclined to condemn the committee's activities. The standard justifications given for such "do-it-yourself" justice have included the remoteness, weakness, or corruption of existing law courts, and have often cited the vigilantes for their nobility and heroism. Until recently, most historians have supported this view. A re-examination of the record, insofar as evidence is available, reveals that the distinction between vigilance activity and lynching was often lost sight of and that in some instances grave abuses were committed. Walter Van Tilburg Clark's *The Ox Bow Incident* is one of the few literary treatments to split sharply with that tradition which once glorified vigilantism. Historians, too, have generally criticized the institution with reluctance.

During the early 1850's San Francisco's vigilante activities encouraged related movements in the interior and in the mining camps. Vigilance in a setting of rural isolation sometimes took even more spectacular forms than it did in the cities. The pages of the *Alta California*, the state's most important newspaper of the period, record many instances of the arbitrary administration of justice—again a natural phenomenon in the environment of social disorganization that followed extensive migration into the newly opened mining areas.

Whenever a mob got out of hand, foreigners were likely to bear the brunt of its fury, as in the lynching of Juanita, an "evil" Mexican woman. On the evening of July 4, 1851, at Downieville, a town on the north fork of the Yuba River, a group of American Independence Day celebrants smashed in the door of her shack. In the ensuing turmoil, Juanita knifed one of them. A vigilante jury speedily sentenced her to be hanged, although several of the miners who composed the jury were repelled by the idea of dealing so harshly with a woman. Juanita was "strung up" from a wooden bridge that spanned the Yuba.

Much of the persecution of foreigners, however, had an economic motivation. Immigrant miners, among them Chileans, Frenchmen, and Hawaiian Kanakas, were frequently chased out of select diggings. Yet these foreigners were too valuable a source of cheap labor to exclude permanently from the employment market. After 1850 Mexican labor could be obtained in the mines for as little as $1 per day. Thus, when restrictions, legal or extralegal, got so severe as to drive foreigners permanently out of California, some employers bridled. Groups of them sought to protect foreign laborers against insulting mobs of jealous competitors and to repeal the legislature's "foreign miners' tax" of 1850. When this oppressive nativist tax failed to produce more than $30,000 in its first year of operation (instead of a predicted $2,400,000), pressure for its repeal began to make sense on financial as well as humanitarian grounds.

In the early fifties foreigners were not the only target of amateur law enforcers and guardians of middle-class respectability, who also turned their wrath upon suspected Caucasian miscreants, whether prostitutes, thieves, or aimless drifters. In many towns vigilantes organized for activity, sometimes with ample provocation. At Sacramento 215 citizens formed themselves into a committee in order to police the city more efficiently. At Marysville, after seventeen murders had occurred within a week, another vigilance committee took "prompt steps in the premises." Because robberies were a particularly "frequent and alarming occurrence" around Mokelumne Hill, a scapegoat was once executed in the presence of nearly one thousand witnesses to satisfy the populace there. Presumption of guilt was in general equivalent to conviction, and ordinarily resulted in execution, ear cropping, or whipping.

San Francisco's Second
Vigilance Committee

Only five years after San Franciscans had dissolved their first
vigilante brigades, another committee of vigilance came into being
at that city. This was the most reputable and orderly of all such
groups. As the vision of the hangman's noose faded from popular
memory, criminal activity again increased. About a thousand unpunished homicides occurred in San Francisco from 1849 to 1856.
In this period also, through the stuffing of ballot boxes and the
use of bullying "shoulder strikers," or city toughs, at polling
places, corrupt officials became entrenched in municipal posts.

In this atmosphere the murder of James King of William, gadfly
editor of the *Daily Evening Bulletin*, brought the city's corruption
and lawlessness to still another climax. King had not hesitated to
attack vitriolically prominent personalities, including James P.
Casey, a local politician and an unsavory business opportunist.
After King bluntly stated that his newspaper "would make certain
parties writhe under the agony" of his exposures, Casey marched
into the *Bulletin's* editorial room to demand an apology for various accusations against him that had already appeared in the
paper. When ordered out of the building, Casey vowed he would
kill the editor. King scoffed at this threat in his columns of May
14, 1856.

That evening, about five o'clock, Casey approached the newspaperman on the street, speedily drew out a revolver, aimed it, and
pulled the trigger. King fell to the ground, mortally wounded.
Shortly thereafter Casey was locked up in the city jail. Three days
later a crowd of several thousand vigilantes, enraged over this
latest in a succession of homicides, seized Casey and another accused murderer, Charles Cora, from the city jail and sentenced
them to death before a drumhead tribunal. As King's solemn funeral cortege moved through the city streets, the vigilantes executed
Casey and Cora. Seldom had a swifter, more determined vigilance
movement been organized.

Within a fortnight almost 10,000 men had joined the vigilantes,
with veterans of the 1851 group being among the first to enroll.
Of these, 6,000 were ready to fight. Each member, after taking a
solemn oath, was known only by his assigned number. This San
Francisco Vigilance Committee of 1856 again chose William T.
Coleman as its head. After the election of officers, Coleman formed
an executive committee and an examining committee, and ap-

THE CAPTURE AND EXECUTION OF CASEY AND CORA, 1856. CONTEMPORARY
PRINTS. (H. G. Hills Collection, by courtesy of The Bancroft
Library, University of California, Berkeley.)

pointed a vigilante chief of police and twenty-five policemen to
supplement local law-enforcement officers. The motivating spirit
of the 1856 committee was revealed by its constitution, which described the association as existing "for maintenance of peace and
good order of society." To this end Coleman organized the membership into groups of one hundred men each, with ten companies
to a regiment. A letter from the vigilantes served notice upon San

Francisco's Sheriff David Scannell and his deputies that they would be held strictly accountable for the future custody of accused prisoners.

Mass meetings at Sacramento, Stockton, and other points, as well as at San Francisco, gave the vigilante movement added momentum. There was also opposition to the movement. A Law and Order Party stoutly objected to the activities of the San Francisco committee on the ground that there was no real need of organized vigilance. State Supreme Court Justice David S. Terry of Sacramento went to San Francisco to lend his support to this countermovement of the Law and Order faction. Unfortunately for Terry and his cause, he became involved in a knifing fracas with one of the vigilantes, and was subsequently indicted by the vigilance committee for this violent activity. The judge's behavior, in fact, ironically helped to discredit his argument that duly constituted law and order could cope with crime and public violence. Fortunately the man he had stabbed did not die, and after almost a month of embarrassing hearings Terry was acquitted. Few other public officials opposed the vigilance committee of 1856.

Meanwhile, Governor John Neely Johnson, an antiforeign Know-Nothing Party leader, had taken cognizance of the problem of municipal crime in California, but he was inconsistent in suggesting a solution for combating it. On June 2 Governor Johnson tardily asked Major General William Tecumseh Sherman, then commander of the second division of the California militia, to aid him in the enforcement of state law—a purpose that would naturally entail suppression of vigilante activity. By this time, however, the San Francisco vigilance committee was able to call upon 6,000 armed partisans, and had firmly fortified its headquarters building, now known as Fort Gunnybags. General Sherman, convinced of the military force, enthusiasm, and broad popularity of the committee's activities, did little to stem its power. He wrote, in defense of his unwillingness to oppose the vigilantes, "I do not doubt that six thousand armed men will obey their decrees quickly, energetically, and cheerfully." Protected by a breastwork of bags of sand, piled ten feet high and six feet thick, the committee stationed volunteer guards at all key points. A great alarm bell was suspended on the roof, where several cannon were also placed in readiness.

In its executive chamber, a spacious room in which were hung the flags of different nations, the vigilance committee continued to conduct its trials. Although the executive committee had a "black list," no action was taken except on the concurrence of at least two-thirds of all vigilantes present. The first deportations occurred on June 5, when three men were sent to Hawaii and three others to Panama. Persons so banished were warned not to return to California on penalty of death. There is no doubt that in a number of instances undesirable characters preferred to depart rather than to risk unknown but probably rigorous penalties.

Despite its arbitrary acts in the name of law and order, this vigilance committee of 1856 achieved results of indisputable merit. For several years after the committee ceased its "defense of justice," San Francisco was a relatively well-governed city. Coleman's leadership, plus general public indignation, the desire for clean government, and the impotence of both state and local officials, all had helped produce the atmosphere in which such a committee could function. When its work seemed to be done, on August 18, 1856, the committee voluntarily dissolved itself, ending three months of virtual control over the city. Its last act was to publish its verdicts in a spirit of pride, in expectation of the approval of posterity.

Filibustering

It is natural for historians to treat vigilante activities and filibustering together. Both were typical of mid-nineteenth-century life on an unpoliced, relatively isolated frontier. The term "filibuster," today usually applied to prolonged speech-making that has the primary purpose of delaying legislative procedures, had another, and more brutal, connotation in that era. Filibusters then were men who went abroad in groups to "free" unprotected, exposed territory from foreign control. The residents of such areas naturally considered the invading filibusters to be land thieves if nothing else. When successful the filibuster might be acclaimed a hero at home. When he failed he was branded an unprincipled outlaw.

Filibustering was a phenomenon of a restless, youthful America, convinced of its Manifest Destiny to expand toward the country's "natural frontiers." This expansionist enthusiasm had not abated with the acquisition of Texas and California, and rootless adventurers anxious for new experiences continued to be attracted to pursuits that would extend American rule over still more territory. During the 1850's it was frequently as unpopular for a Westerner to be opposed to filibustering as it was for a Southerner to be against slavery. In fact, the two were not unrelated. Southerners among the filibusters were particularly attracted to projects for spreading slavery into lands farther south. Apologists for filibustering professed admiration for the courage of adventurers willing to shoulder rifles in foreign fields, seeing them as patriotic soldiers of fortune working in the cause of an expanding America. From the White House on down, the federal government had rarely discouraged filibustering. Yet clearly lawless aggression by military forces was sometimes involved in this activity.

The unsettled conditions in California in the 1850's stimulated the phenomenon of filibustering; as dreamed-of riches vanished and doors of opportunity closed, disillusioned gold seekers who feared a humdrum life looked covetously beyond American territory for adventure. However, the filibustering expeditions that originated from California after its admission to statehood were uniformly unsuccessful. The first one occurred in 1851 under the leadership of Alexander Bell, who had once fought Governor Micheltorena at Los Angeles. Bell foolishly planned to reinstate a deposed president of Ecuador; but before he reached Quito, rival factions in that country had composed their differences and united to rid Ecuador of Americans. Bell retreated to Panama, where his party was stranded; the expedition proved a fiasco. That same year Sam Brannan, by then an apostate from Mormonism, led a party of adventurers to Hawaii aboard the vessel *Game Cock*. In his abortive attempt to capture those islands Brannan was lucky to escape the incensed Hawaiian pikemen, who threatened to run their spears through him. Joseph C. Morehead's plan to take the spiny peninsula of Lower California, also in 1851, proved equally futile. After most of Morehead's men deserted, he was fortunate to escape Mexican imprisonment. Though ineffectual, these crude filibusters encouraged attempts by other armed expeditions to seize foreign territory in the Western Hemisphere by force.

French Expeditions from California

Not only Americans were stirred by the possibility of filibustering. California's sizable foreign population included other footloose elements as well, among them a number of Frenchmen who had taken leave of their native country as a result of the revolutionary movements of 1848. These men too craved a life of adventurous treasure seeking. The leaders of these French immigrants, who were in some cases of aristocratic birth, were especially interested in plans to colonize Mexico. Three such persons have left their mark upon the history of both California and northern Mexico: the Marquis Charles de Pindray, Lepine de Sigondis, and Count Gaston de Raousset-Boulbon.

De Pindray was a nobleman of considerable personal strength, skilled also in handling weapons. In 1851 he accepted an offer from the Mexican government to raise a company of volunteers to protect the Sonoran mines against Apache Indians. This recruiting he did in California, where restless adventurers were then in great supply. For their service his men (all French immigrants) were to receive valuable lands, which Mexico hoped would serve as an effective buffer colony facing the United States. On the day after Christmas that year De Pindray landed on the Mexican west coast at Guaymas with a force of 140. Their reception was at first enthusiastic. Adding some natives to his band, De Pindray proceeded inland to Arispe; then he and his men began an arduous march across the desert toward the gold mines of the interior. The task presented unsuspected difficulties; internal dissension developed, complicated by the growing ill-feeling between De Pindray's forces and the Mexicans through whose territory they passed. Finally, illness of the leader halted the expedition. Suddenly De Pindray was mysteriously shot through the head. He may have been murdered by Indians, or by one of his men. The survivors of his party straggled back to the coast, where they made a hasty departure from the country.

The expedition of Lepine de Sigondis, another expatriate Frenchman, resembled that of De Pindray in many ways. Both men were promised land in Mexico and both organized parties to settle this land. Both met political and economic conditions in the Mexican northwest that proved their undoing. De Sigondis's enterprise, enlisting some sixty men, was even more narrowly conceived than that of De Pindray; treasure was its only object. De Sigondis was fortunate to escape death. Future filibusters would not always be so lucky in the enterprises they launched from California.

The most renowned of all its French filibusters was Count de Raousset-Boulbon, nicknamed "Little Wolf." He was characterized by marked versatility, abounding energy, and great personal courage. Well-educated and not entirely without idealism, he was at the same time prodigal and self-indulgent. He came to California in 1850 to seek his fortune, but met with only slender success in numerous jobs. Then, with an eye on the rich mines of Sonora, he turned to the promotion of a colonization enterprise in which Patrice Dillon, French consul at San Francisco, was much interested. Dillon, himself a sort of filibuster at heart, became enthusiastic over the prospect of forming a buffer colony in northern Mexico to checkmate the further advance of the United States. In 1852, after De Raousset-Boulbon obtained concessions in the area, actually underwritten in part by an anonymous banking house, both the French minister in Mexico and the governor of Sonora became financially interested in the filibuster's operations.

In high hopes, De Raousset-Boulbon sailed for Guaymas, on the Mexican west coast with 260 men, on May 19, 1852. He received a warm welcome at that Mexican coastal town, but this was followed by a month's irksome delay due to political road blocks. The count ignored local warnings that he must carefully placate rival Mexican political factions. Also, he refused to proceed to the interior by a circuitous route to avoid both local Indian and Mexican opposition to him. When he received peremptory orders from one Mexican faction to report in person at Arispe, more than a hundred miles away from the seacoast, the Frenchman haughtily sent two underlings instead. These men returned with terms under which the party was warned to operate while in Mexico; but De Raousset-Boulbon rejected the demands *in toto*, thereby making his company an armed enemy of local Mexican officialdom. There followed a period in which De Raousset-Boulbon was justly accused of organizing a rebellion in Mexico. He indiscreetly offered to "liberate" northwestern Mexico and was actually able to capture Hermosillo. The count, however, soon realized his hopelessly isolated position in a foreign land, and, after seventeen of his men were killed and twenty-three wounded, he agreed reluctantly to retreat toward Guaymas on the seacoast and then to return to San Francisco.

During the next few years the count was in and out of Mexico, repeatedly seeking from the government there land grants in Sonora upon which to settle numerous French, German, and Irish adherents. On the eve of a second expedition, however, by means of which De Raousset-Boulbon was about to attempt again the planting of the proposed colony in northern Mexico, his hopes were dashed by a report that President Santa Anna had sold part of Sonora to the United States. The count was unwilling to believe the report, but it alarmed his financial backers, who refused to advance further funds. Actually, the rumor had a firm basis in the negotiations then being conducted between Mexico and the United States over a strip of land on the south side of the Mexican boundary. This territory, extending from the Gulf to the Rio Grande and embracing more than 45,000 square miles, was to be known as the Gadsden Purchase; it became a part of the United States in 1854.

That same year De Raousset-Boulbon, undaunted, led another expedition into Mexico. This time, when the Frenchman reached Guaymas on the vessel *Challenge*, with about five hundred men, he met unified resistance instead of the partial welcomes of the past.

After part of his force had been killed, the remnant became demoralized, and he was compelled to surrender. Tried on a charge of conspiracy, he was convicted and executed on August 12, 1854. At his own request the indomitable count faced a firing squad unblindfolded. His men were allowed to escape. This marked the end of French expeditions from California to gain a foothold in Sonora.

"The Gray-Eyed Man of Destiny"

A rival of De Raousset-Boulbon and the best known of all California filibusters—indeed, one of the most melodramatic figures in United States history—was William Walker. A restless native of Tennessee, Walker completed his medical studies at the University of Pennsylvania, went to Paris for further study, then spent a year in visiting various European cities. He did not find the practice of medicine to his liking, and, after further wandering, arrived at San Francisco in June, 1850. Following a short venture into journalism there, during which a caustic pen sent him to jail, he entered into law practice at Marysville.

Accounts of French colonization in Mexico fired Walker with a passion to venture into a new field, a passion that eventually led him to be called "the gray-eyed man of destiny" and "the archfilibuster of California." In 1854, just as Walker was forming his own expedition, misfortune struck De Raousset-Boulbon's last filibustering attempt. Both men had competed for the limited funds that were available for such risky ventures. Walker's ambition was to bring about the independence of Sonora and Lower California for ultimate annexation to his own country, thus affording a new arena for the extension of slavery. He possessed an unquestioning belief in his own destiny. Yet his personal physique was far from impressive. He is described as a slight, red-haired, gray-eyed man, freckle-faced and slow of speech, below medium height, and weighing scarcely more than a hundred pounds. Walker opened a recruiting office in San Francisco, where hundreds bought scrip, or land certificates, from him to be redeemed in Sonoran lands.

Walker, eluding United States government officials who did not want him to sail, left the Golden Gate on the ship *Caroline* with forty-eight followers, and landed at La Paz, where he was reinforced by some two hundred Mexicans. He then proclaimed the free and independent "Republic of Lower California." This short-lived "government" he quickly abolished, however, to launch the "Republic of Sonora," consisting of the states of Lower California and Sonora, with himself as president. Reports of his activities brought him immense popularity in California. While Walker campaigned in Mexico the flag of the new republic waved over his San Francisco enlistment office and his bonds found a ready market there.

But soon there were reverses for Walker. Native Mexicans began to feel increasing patriotic resentment toward these California-launched foraging expeditions; also some of his men deserted. Walker's harsh punishment of deserters added to his unpopularity. When he was ready to start for Sonora from Lower California, he had only a hundred men left; the force was reduced to thirty-five by the time they reached the Colorado River. This remnant, necessarily abandoning the project, finally reached the United States boundary near Tia Juana in May, 1854, and there surrendered to American authorities. Tried at San Francisco on a charge of violating United States neutrality laws, Walker was acquitted and resumed the practice of law, though not for long. Filibustering had become a permanent obsession with him.

Walker's next objective was Central America—Nicaragua in particular. One of the revolutionary factions in that country conceived the idea that, with Walker's aid, success would be certain, and Walker lent a willing ear. On May 3, 1855, he set sail for Nicaragua with sixty enlisted men. After landing, he declared himself to be the President of Nicaragua. Although he gained temporary power by this bold act, Walker overreached himself when he proclaimed a reversal of the Nicaraguan antislavery laws that had been in existence for a generation. A series of revolts followed, and Walker was compelled to surrender to native leaders in May, 1857. Walker fled back to the United States, where he undertook the planning of various other expeditions, despite his arrest on several occasions for violating American neutrality laws. His last enterprise involved a landing in Honduras, undertaken in hopes of returning to Nicaragua. The Hondurans, however, objected violently to the invasion, and Walker was shot as a foreign interloper on September 12, 1860.

Henry A. Crabb and the End of Filibustering

One of the last California filibusters was Henry A. Crabb, who had been a schoolmate of Walker's in Tennessee. A resident of Stockton after 1849, Crabb, like Walker, was intrigued by the possibility of spreading slavery abroad. In 1855 he enlisted a following of assorted swashbucklers and adventurers for his own expedition to Nicaragua; the exploit soured and he returned, a year later, to enter California politics. Soon he was plotting a second enterprise.

Following his marriage into a prominent Sonoran family, Crabb, in 1857, organized the Arizona and Gadsden Colonization Company with the ambitious purpose of taking over part of the Mexican state of Sonora. "General" Crabb outfitted his expedition in Los Angeles and El Monte, and proceeded overland via the San Gorgonio Pass in southern California, past Yuma, and on to Sonora. There various Mexican leaders of rival factions again united to prevent foreign inroads into their territory. His forces shattered, Crabb surrendered to the Mexican commander; he and his men were brutally executed.

This tragic episode ended filibustering expeditions from California. Though abounding in color and excitement, these ventures hardly induced Mexico's border states to break their feeble ties with the central government of the country. Instead, the filibuster came to be considered an invader, personifying pillage, rape, and the destruction of property. From another point of view, the California filibusters were victims of insufficient financial backing, poor planning, and bad leadership. Their decline can only be considered fortunate. During the negotiations that led to the Gadsden Purchase, the filibusters had proved a particular embarrassment to United States officials; and in general they had lost the United States much good will. Filibustering, in fact, had proved itself an outmoded stepchild of Manifest Destiny. California, once free of such unwholesome and blatant nationalism, proceeded to display a new maturity, as well as greater respect for law and order—paradoxical legacies of its period of social ferment.

SELECTED READINGS

A starting point, as yet not superseded, for the study of California's vigilante activities is Hubert Howe Bancroft, *Popular Tribunals* (2 vols., San Francisco, 1887). An account of the 1851 vigilance movement, edited by Mary Floyd Williams, is entitled *History of the San Francisco Committee of Vigilance of 1851* (Berkeley, 1921); she also edited the *Papers of the San Francisco Committee of Vigilance of 1851* (Berkeley, 1919). Consult also Shinn's *Mining Camps*. William T. Coleman wrote the story of the Vigilance Committee of 1856 in an article entitled "San Francisco Vigilance Committees" in *Century Magazine* XLIII (November, 1891), 133–150. James A. B. Scherer's biography of Coleman, *The Lion of the Vigilantes: William T. Coleman and the Life of Old San Francisco* (Indianapolis, 1939), includes extensive commentary on Coleman. A popular work on the subject is Stanton A. Coblentz,

Villains and Vigilantes: Story of James King of William and Pioneer Justice in California (New York, 1936). See also George R. Stewart, *Committee of Vigilance: Revolution in San Francisco* . . . (Boston, 1964).

General Sherman's troubles with the vigilantes were reported in a series of his letters in *Century*, XLIII (December, 1891), 296–309, entitled "Sherman and the San Francisco Vigilantes." There is a quasi-history of the 1856 movement, *San Francisco Vigilance Committee of '56* (San Francisco, 1883), written by one of its members and edited by Frank M. Smith. Another treatment is James O'Meara's *The Vigilance Committee of 1856* (San Francisco, 1887). Government reports are in *Senate Executive Documents*, 34th Congress, 1st and 2nd sessions, Volume XV (Washington, D.C., 1857) and 3rd session, Volume VII (Washington, D.C., 1857). Also consult, for the flavor of the period, Jerome Hart, *A Vigilante Girl* (Chicago, 1910), a popular novelette.

Condemnations of vigilantism appear in the previously mentioned novel by Walter Van Tilburg Clark, *The Ox Bow Incident* (New York, 1942), in Ellison's *A Self-Governing Dominion*, and in John W. Caughey, *Their Majesties the Mob* (Chicago, 1960). Leonard Pitt, "The Beginnings of Nativism in California," *Pacific Historical Review*, XXX (February, 1961), 23–38, discusses the relationship of intolerance to the breakdown of law and order in the California mines. Shinn's *Mining Camps* is helpful on this subject also.

Writers have treated filibustering as both a national and local phenomenon. Among the older works are James Jeffrey Roche, *By-Ways of War: The Story of the Filibusters* (Boston, 1901), and *The Story of the Filibusters* (London, 1891) by the same author; W. V. Wells, *Walker's Expedition to Nicaragua* (New York, 1856); and Walker's own *The War in Nicaragua* (Mobile, 1860). Also useful for a study of Walker's career is William O. Scroggs, *Filibusters and Financiers* (New York, 1916). Laurence Greene, *The Filibuster* (New York, 1937), is a biography of Walker.

The best work on De Raousset-Boulbon and the French expeditions from California is Rufus K. Wyllys, *The French in Sonora, 1850–1854* (Berkeley, 1932). See also Wyllys' articles in the *Pacific Historical Review:* "The Republic of Lower California, 1853–1854," II (June, 1933), 194–214; "Henry A. Crabb—A Tragedy of the Sonora Frontier." IX (June, 1940), 183–194; and "An Expansionist in Baja California, 1855," I (December, 1932), 477–482.

A note on Crabb by H. D. Barrows is "Crabbe's [sic] Filibusters," *Historical Society of Southern California Quarterly*, VIII (March, 1911), 193–195.

The Brannan expedition to Hawaii is treated in Andrew F. Rolle, "California Filibustering and the Hawaiian Kingdom," *Pacific Historical Review*, XIX (August, 1950), 251–263; and some last manifestations of filibustering are described in Rolle's "Futile Filibustering in Baja California, 1888–1890," *Pacific Historical Review*, XX (May, 1951), 159–166.

18

A New Culture at the Golden Gate

San Francisco—historically and culturally—deserves to be called California's first city. After the Gold Rush the old Spanish hamlet of Yerba Buena grew out of its sand hills, its flapping canvas tents, lean-tos, and rickety frame shacks to become a city. In the twenty years between 1850 and 1870, San Francisco also exchanged its cultural primitiveness for a cosmopolitan diversity of tastes and ideas. This transformation of a makeshift pueblo and polyglot trading post into a confident metropolis sometimes seemed to have occurred even more rapidly than it did. The German traveler Friedrich Gerstäcker, who returned to a new gaslit San Francisco after only a year's absence in the mines, wrote:

I really did not know where I was, did not recognize a single street, and was perfectly at a loss to think of such an entire change. Where I had left a crowded mass of low wooden huts and tents, I found a city in a great part built of brick, houses, pretty stores.

By the time the rancho days of the "splendid idle forties" were past, San Francisco's harbor had become a forest of masts. In 1851 a visitor counted six hundred ships there. Sailors, traders, and miners had displaced rancheros in the city's life, and "flush times" had come to the village by the Golden Gate. The weight of gold nuggets helped push open doors once gently closed to all but a few *Yanquis* by California's native society. Thousands of invading foreigners ushered out a sleepy Mexican past.

The Aftermath of the Gold Rush

Although the citizens of San Francisco voted themselves a charter in 1850, few early residents expected to remain there permanently. Some American pioneers spoke of staying in California for only five years and, therefore, showed little interest in investing in such long-term projects as durable housing. During the decade following the Gold Rush, a spirit of chance pervaded the city. Yet pressing civic problems demanded action. The fire hazard grew because of the large number of flimsy wooden structures that had been constructed instead of adobe dwellings. Housing became even more of a problem as the need for it increased drastically during the early fifties. In 1850 more than 36,000 immigrants arrived in San Francisco by sea alone—representatives of every race, creed, and culture. Among them were spendthrifts, future

NORTH BEACH, SAN FRANCISCO, CA. 1860. (H. G. Hills Collection; by courtesy of The Bancroft Library, University of California, Berkeley.)

soldiers of fortune like William Walker, bankers, bandits, and gamblers. "The very air," journalist Bayard Taylor wrote, "is pregnant with the magnetism of bold, spirited, unwearied action." In his book about the new El Dorado, Taylor sensed that the success of this new land would depend upon the sort of political, economic, and cultural system which Californians shaped.

San Francisco actually consisted of a series of interconnected settlements, a circumstance that made the administration of law and order most difficult. A sheltered little enclave called "Happy Valley" still contained about 1,000 makeshift tents during the winter of 1850. "Pleasant Valley" opened onto an open beach front from the middle of town. "Sydney Town," around the base of Telegraph Hill to the north, became a hangout of convicts and "ticket of leave" men, castaways from Australia. This district had been a particular target of the committee of vigilance in its drive against crime. There were other outlying settlements, "Little Chile," "Spring Valley," and "St. Ann Valley," in which criminal activity could easily be hidden. All of these areas eventually merged into the larger municipal unit of San Francisco.

Before its consolidation San Francisco underwent a prolonged baptism by fire. Six conflagrations swept over the city in a period of eighteen months. The first took place in December, 1849, when a million dollars' worth of canvas structures and the merchandise stored in them were consumed. A second great fire, even more disastrous, occurred in May of 1850. After an interval of scarcely a month came a third fire. Following this, further erection of inflammable tents and cloth structures was prohibited. But lumber, so extensively used in local building, proved scarcely less combustible. Another serious fire occurred the following September. Most damaging of all was the disaster of May 4, 1851, which destroyed a large part of the town. San Francisco would eventually rebuild itself in brick and stone, but until it did the city was subjected seasonally to full-scale fires.

The young city also had its economic problems. The air of uncertainty after the Gold Rush was reflected in the San Francisco commercial market, where prices, long subject to violent fluctuations, dropped sharply. Pickled beef and pork went from $60 to $10 per barrel; wheat flour decreased in price from $800 to $20 per barrel. Merchants could only guess what new changes to expect in supply and demand. At least one storekeeper actually used surplus merchandise for filling ruts along the city's streets. Others dumped spoiled flour and unsalable cast-iron stoves into mud holes. Imports piled up at the wharfs and few items remained difficult to obtain.

The Gold Rush boom had coaxed bankers, and traders, as well as merchants, away from unspectacular business pursuits and into speculations that were to prove their undoing. The goal of most newcomers was to build themselves granite and marble mansions on Nob Hill. Unfortunately for their plans, the unprecedented production of gold in the interior, which exceeded half a billion dollars in the period from 1849 to 1855, had confused the economic fabric of California's largest city. After 1853, the downward swing of the financial pendulum and the declining yield of gold from the placers decreased the influx of population, causing an abrupt reversal in property values. Rents quickly fell, as did the prices of city lots. Housing sites that had cost $15 before the rush reached $8,000 during its height, only to plummet to less than $100 later.

Among the more profitable business enterprises of the time, though it too had its risks, was the operation of saloons and gambling establishments. Gerstäcker described the *Cafés Chantants*, usually kept by Frenchmen, as "common drinking rooms," in the back part of which there was often a stage and a piano. Their function, he reported, was to encourage "loud laughter, riotous conversation," and to distract patrons from workaday responsibilities. Gambling also took place there, as well as in the bona-fide gambling houses. Among the latter, Denison's Exchange, the Parker House, the St. Charles, and the Bella Union all featured numerous games of chance. Some gambling parlors were elegantly decorated with plush furniture, chandeliers, and mirrors; the El Dorado, with its eight gaming tables, velvet upholstered chairs, and spacious bar, attracted perhaps the greatest crowds. Upstairs in these establishments there were also prostitution cribs. In the plushier spots customers were expected to keep their derringers out of sight, unless attacked. Nowhere in the world were there so many billiard tables in proportion to the population as in San Francisco. A few of the wealthiest citizens of the town during this period got their start as professional faro dealers or card men.

Another popular pursuit, in San Francisco as in the rest of the masculine American West, was the practice of dueling. Only after years of public criticism were these avenging "affairs of honor" abolished. San Francisco was predominantly a city of young men, far away from home and removed from family restraints. As a result, gambling, dueling, attending theatrical performances and other forms of rather ostentatious living, had more general appeal than did churchgoing. For some men gambling became a mania. This, however, was not the whole story. The Reverend

Albert Williams, an observant clergyman, paid the frontiersmen this tribute: "Though the Church and religion received not from all the heed which was desired, neither the one nor the other was spoken against; both were commended." In 1849, Williams organized the First Presbyterian Church of San Francisco. Other churches were founded by street preachers like the popular William Taylor. Mission Dolores served as a place of worship for Catholics of the town until 1849, when their first city church, named for Saint Francis, was organized.

Cultural Growth

Regardless of its unsteady economic and social conditions, San Francisco was concerned with culture. From the beginning, education was one of its major interests. In September, 1847, the first city public school committee met. In 1849 John C. Pelton arrived from Boston to open a municipal school on Portsmouth Square, based upon New England traditions of instruction; and in 1851 the city added a superintendent of schools and regular board of education. (In 1850, to implement the legal provisions of California's Constitution of 1849, John G. Marvin was sworn in as the state's Superintendent of Public Instruction.) In addition, San Francisco early became known for its outstanding museums and libraries. By 1853 the first Academy of Science in the West was located there. Later, this cultural impetus developed substantially, supported by the mining fortunes of Nevada's Comstock Lode and by the riches of California's railroad kings.

San Francisco also quickly achieved dominance in the journalistic activity of the new state. California's first English-language newspaper, the *Californian*, had appeared at Monterey, on August 15, 1846. Actually, this four-page weekly was only half in the English language, with the other side being printed in Spanish. Because of the local scarcity of paper, it had to be printed on any stock available, and even on wrapping and tissue paper. In May, 1847, the *Californian* moved to the future San Francisco. Only a few months after this paper appeared, Sam Brannan founded the *California Star*. The Gold Rush temporarily stopped publication of these pioneer journals, but in 1849 the two papers merged to become the weekly *Alta California*, which became a daily the next year.

Mid-century California, with San Francisco as its cultural center, nourished considerable literary activity. Especially characteristic of this early writing are travel accounts and books of reminiscence and recollection, some written by pioneers who had originally come to California by sea. A few examples of these works follow. Richard Henry Dana's classic *Two Years Before the Mast* (1840) was one of the first books to introduce the pastoral California of hide and tallow days to a wide reading public. Dana's views on California, however, reflect a New Englander's bias against a Hispanic society. A less well known but similar pioneer sea chronicle by a Yankee maritime trader was Richard J. Cleveland's *A Narrative of Voyages and Commercial Enterprises* (1842). Cleveland, a native of Salem, Massachusetts, admired the physical beauty of California, but, like Dana, was not favorably impressed by its early government and society. Both books represent what Professor Franklin Walker has called "gringo views of hidalgo culture." Another early work, called forth in part by Dana's writing, was Alfred Robinson's *Life in California* (1846). Robinson, long a resident of the Mexican province, wrote from the viewpoint of one who wished to refute the inaccuracies of the ordinary traveler. After Dana, Cleveland, and Robinson, the production of books about California continued unabated.

Valuable accounts that treat the period following the hide and tallow trading era include Edwin Bryant's *What I Saw in California* (1848), Bayard Taylor's *El Dorado* (1849) and Walter Colton's *Three Years in California* (1850). Joseph Warren Revere's *A Tour of Duty in California* (1849) is a superior description by a young lieutenant in the United States Navy of his tour of both Lower and Upper California, including the "gold region," ports, and "Indian areas." Colton, in a later book, *Deck and Port* (1850), further describes pioneer Americanization. Such books, published in the East, helped give California new national prominence, both before and after she became a state.

Lonely Americans within the new state clamored for every sort of literary fare, from travel descriptions to pseudophilosophical writing to straight reporting. Most of this early writing appeared not in nationally printed books but in local journals; and most of the journals were spawned in San Francisco and its tributary regions. The *Golden Era*, founded in 1852, was California's first weekly of any literary pretension. It was followed by the *Pioneer* (1854), *Hutchings' California Magazine* (1856), and the *Hesperian* (1858). Such magazines, though perhaps unsophisticated by today's standards, were entertaining and informed organs of expression which generally enjoyed a successful, if brief, career. The *Golden Era*, longest-lived of the early journals, continued to be published until 1893.

The real distinction among the journals, however, belongs to the *Overland Monthly*, a little brown-covered magazine with a grizzly bear on its masthead. The *Overland*, which began publication in July, 1868, and continued intermittently until 1883, compared favorably with some of the best Eastern literary journals. Bret Harte was its editor during the first few years. Harte had come to California in 1854, and had started out as a typesetter on the *Golden Era*; after he left that job, he wrote for the *Californian*. During his editorship of the *Overland Monthly*, in association with Noah Brooks, Ina Coolbrith, and Charles Warren Stoddard, he achieved national status as a writer of short stories. As editor, he encouraged numerous other authors to write for the *Overland* and thereby gained Eastern audiences for them too. Harte had first attracted attention in the *Golden Era* by the publication of *"M'liss,"* and went on, in August, 1868, to write "The Luck of Roaring Camp." This was followed by other local-color stories in the *Overland*, including "Plain Language from Truthful James." Harte's "The Outcasts of Poker Flat," published in that journal in January, 1869, reaffirmed and strengthened the reputation created by his earlier stories, leading him to wider audiences. More than any other writer, Harte created a stereotype of the Western miner as an unkempt, bearded, red-shirted rowdy. In romanticizing this symbolic figure, he did for the miner what Owen Wister later did for the cowboy. Mark Twain's descriptions of miners and mining camps in his *Roughing It* are more realistic than Harte's, but Twain's *Roughing It* is still considered primarily a humorous book, not ordinarily taken seriously. Although modern readers usually find Harte's work overly sentimental, even mannered and forced, he nevertheless imparts much of the flavor of the colorful events that he saw in California's mining camps, cow towns, and wild interior.

A rugged and sometimes crude literature of burlesque was fashionable at the time Harte and his fellow writers were turning out their more craftsmanlike work. One of the exponents of this jokester style was an army officer stationed in California, Lieutenant George Horatio Derby, known under two pen names, "The Veritable Squibob," and "John Phoenix." In 1856 he wrote a salty and humorous book, *Phoenixiana*, which became immensely popular. Its readers roared at such Derby remarks as "Absinthe makes the heart grow fonder," and "They came to cough and remain to spray." The latter was adopted as an advertisement by a San Francisco druggist. Lieutenant Derby regularly lampooned and chided men and institutions with his coarse humor.

This tendency also characterized the writing of another forty-niner, Alonzo ("Old Block") Delano, a perennial favorite of the miners. Delano's *Pen Knife Sketches* (1853), his *Life on the Plains and Among the Diggings* (1854), and his melodramatic play, entitled *A Live Woman in the Mines* (1857), were widely read. Educated and uneducated alike reveled in the horseplay and humor which this writing brought into lonely and obscure camps. "Old Block" was the proud possessor and exploiter (in the Jimmy Durante manner) of what was considered California's largest nose. His appearance and activities, as well as his writing, made him widely known throughout the West. As captain of an immigrant party that had crossed the plains, and later as speculator, merchant, and banker, he was a vigorous participant in the Gold Rush. Delano's realism was rooted in his own vivid experiences; thus his exaggerations, sentimentality, and rustic humor were particularly attractive to his readers. Illustrated by Charles Nahl ("The California Cruikshank"), Delano's books, in their time, became virtual best sellers. Other Gold Rush favorites included John R. Ridge, a writer of half-Cherokee extraction who used the sobriquet "Yellow Bird"; Prentice Mulford, who took the name "Dogberry" as his pseudonym, and who became a spiritualistic hermit; and William H. Rhodes, who wrote under the name "Caxton."

Local colorists and frontier satirists continued to be popular in California in the period that followed the scramble for gold. Among them were J. Ross Browne, Rollin Daggett, and Dan de Quille. They were not great writers, yet they mirrored the unformed, innocent, and excitable society in which they lived. They boasted interminably about the achievements of a proud generation, and wrote high-flown, grotesque, deliberately facetious exaggerations. Their fanciful writings help the historian to understand an environment in which large numbers of restless readers were emerging from the primitiveness of the mining camps. This Southwestern group of writers effectively used dialect, nostalgia, audacity, and extravagance to entertain their readers. Their hilarity and exuberance delighted literary audiences. For their readers such authors brought to life again, mainly by their skillful anecdotal vernacular, common experiences from their past mining activities. This writing consisted largely of ironical plays, short stories concerned with outdoor life, and an occasional sermon or heated discussion of local politics. San Francisco's journals printed in profusion the prose and poetry of these writers, who won for themselves a place that few California authors today enjoy.

Mark Twain

A then obscure writer, whose sketches reflected the best characteristics of Western literature, became a literary immortal. This was Samuel Langhorne Clemens, or Mark Twain. From the beginning he wrote with distinctive craftsmanship and humor. Twain had come West with his brother, Orion, following a brief and irritating period of military service with a Confederate Missouri home guard unit during the first months of the Civil War. (Years before, Twain had been a river pilot.) Twain went into mining in Nevada, and when bad weather kept him from work in the diggings, he amused himself by writing burlesque and caricature sketches. These he signed "Josh" and sent to the *Territorial Enterprise*, the main newspaper of Virginia City; this town was located in what is now Nevada, but then was dominated by California culture. In 1862 he walked 130 miles from a lonely mining site to Virginia City to take a job on the *Enterprise* for twenty-five dollars per week. Two years later Twain left Virginia City and drifted into California proper, where he became a reporter for the San Francisco *Morning Call*. He also wrote shrewd drolleries for the *Golden Era* and the *Californian*.

Twain's employment on the *Call* proved rather too grinding, providing him little of the freedom he had enjoyed on the *Territorial Enterprise*. Yet at San Francisco he met some stimulating fellow writers, among them Prentice Mulford, Bret Harte, Charles Warren Stoddard, and Joaquin Miller. Together they contributed pieces to the *Golden Era* and other journals. Twain once called the *Golden Era* "The best weekly literary paper in the United States—and I suppose I ought to know."

Twain was always an individual among individuals. In 1863, he got into trouble with the San Francisco police because of certain letters he sent his old paper, the *Enterprise*. In these he assailed the corruption of San Francisco's police force, naming names, and at the same time made other strong accusations of political venality. Because of local reaction to these charges, Twain decided to get away, at least until the feeling against him blew over. A friend, James N. Gillis, suggested that he take refuge at a cabin retreat that Gillis owned on Jackass Hill, near Angel's Camp in the Tuolumne uplands. Twain lived almost a hermit's existence there. He relaxed, read, wrote, and mined for gold, returning each night to sleep in Gillis's log and slab-sided cabin. In the barroom of a dingy hotel at nearby Angel's, Twain heard one Ben Coon—a former Illinois riverboat pilot—tell an interesting, sprightly story about a rigged frog-derby. The story intrigued Twain. Although it had already been printed in different versions in the California press, it was new to him. Twain took down this and other local stories he heard. He stayed on at Angel's that winter and, on a plain table in front of his cabin's rough stone fireplace, he wrote the first version of "The Celebrated Jumping Frog of Calaveras County." At some time between March and October he rewrote the story, making it his own; for one thing, he added a beguiling twist to the ending. This work was done at the request of the humorist Artemus Ward, who wished to include the piece in a collection of tales to be published in New York. Without Twain's permission, the piece got submitted, via Ward, to an Eastern journal, the *New York Saturday Press*. First printed there on November 18, 1865, it made Twain famous almost overnight, and on December 16, the *Californian* republished it. In May, 1867, it was published once again, as the title story in Twain's first book, *The Jumping Frog of Calaveras County and Other Sketches*.

During the long winter at Angel's Camp Twain had done much to develop his natural art of storytelling. He set himself the goal of writing well-embellished, incredible tales in exactly the same manner as he told them to the lonesome miners around him. Returning to San Francisco, he wrote a few more sketches for local journals, but the national publicity he achieved from the story of the jumping frog launched him on a greatly expanded career. In 1866, at the age of thirty, he sailed for the Sandwich Islands as a correspondent of the Sacramento *Union*. Upon his return, Twain gave a series of comical lectures on Hawaii in various California and Nevada towns. These started him on his way as a popular public speaker. Then, after four months, he headed East.

Twain had made his mark in California and the West, and it had provided him with much material. His book *Roughing It* grew out of his experiences in the Nevada mines. Eventually he also assembled his reports from abroad to the San Francisco *Alta California*, Sacramento *Union*, and New York *Tribune* in book form, as *The Innocents Abroad* (1869). These writings helped him gain the considerable international stature he came to enjoy. His realistic and satirical examination of society's shortcomings and hallowed beliefs was at the heart of his success. Out West, where conditions were crude, Twain was encouraged to write with directness and imagination; and his work continued to show the humor and loose narrative style he had developed there.

Early Artists

San Francisco nourished from its earliest days, in addition to its varied and prolific writers, a notable artistic colony. Among the many foreign-born craftsmen associated with the area was the German etcher and print maker Edward Vischer. Vischer traveled throughout California making numerous sketches of the missions, which, after the Gold Rush, had been reduced to a state of "noble ruin." Another significant artist was the Scottish painter William Keith, sent West by the publishing house of Harper and Brothers in 1858 to execute some romantic engravings of the missions. The celebrated bear symbol on the masthead of the *Overland Monthly* is said to have been the work of Keith, who became a fast friend of Bret Harte. In 1866 Keith also painted an Overland Stage Coach poster which became well known all over the nation. His water colors of the Yosemite, as well as his oils depicting other scenes from the California landscape, grew popular among the rich of San Francisco and he became one of the most appreciated artists in the West, and surely the most renowned of California's landscape painters. Regrettably, most of Keith's best canvases were lost in the San Francisco fire of 1906.

Wealthy patrons also were much attracted to the paintings of Charles Christian Nahl. Nahl, a German, had come to California in 1848. Taken with the grandeur of its scenery, he began painting landscapes, and soon was producing as well a series of lighthearted sketches for San Francisco publishers. These sketches were printed on lithographed stationery on which the miners wrote home their news from the gold fields, and were later reproduced as etchings illustrating books, principally those of Delano. Nahl's oils became especially popular on Nob Hill, and until his death in 1878 he was busy with numerous commissioned canvases. For the most part these were executed in a markedly romantic style. Critics admired his work and he was acclaimed, like Keith, a major local artist.

John W. Audubon, youngest son of the noted naturalist, met with considerably less luck. He toured the California diggings after the Gold Rush making hundreds of realistic pencil and water-color sketches of what he saw. Audubon then decided to ship many of these paintings and sketches to the East Coast. Because they were too bulky to go overland, he entrusted them to a close friend who was traveling eastward in 1857 on the ship *Cen-*

RESIDENCES OF MRS. MARK HOPKINS AND GOVERNOR STANFORD, SAN FRANCISCO.
(H. G. Hills Collection; by courtesy of The Bancroft Library,
University of California, Berkeley.)

COLTON AND CROCKER MANSIONS, SAN FRANCISCO.
(H. G. Hills Collection; by courtesy of The Bancroft Library,
University of California, Berkeley.)

tral America. The vessel was sunk, and Audubon's friend and the bulk of his work went down with the ship. Audubon did little artistically after this disaster. Today only a few of his sketches survive.

Albert Bierstadt, like Vischer and Nahl a German artist, first came to San Francisco in 1858; he had traveled by way of the Rockies with a government exploring expedition. Bierstadt's canvases found a ready sale throughout the United States and Europe. In particular, his exquisite paintings of the animals in the mountains, plains, and forests of North America grew very popular. His chief interest, like that of his contemporaries, lay in idealizing such natural wonders as the Yosemite Falls, the giant Sequoias of the Sierra, and California's coastline. Later in life Bierstadt returned East and continued his work in his New York studio near Irvington-on-Hudson. He died in 1902 at the height of his success. Some of his best oils, like those of Keith, were destroyed in the fire of 1906.

In part, the artistic production of San Francisco, and indeed its cultural and social life in general, was based on wealth. The tastes of the city's affluent citizens naturally were reflected in the various forms of art they subsidized. Contemporary descriptions of the city of the "golden fifties and champagne sixties" uniformly stress its opulence, particularly as revealed in architecture and allied arts. The popularity of certain styles produced a special uniformity in the buildings constructed by the rich during that period. The same Italian artists who painted the interiors of Mark Hopkins' three-million-dollar baroque castle on Nob Hill also decorated theaters, hotels, saloons, and brothels along what came to be known as the Barbary Coast. Gilt-edged Victorian residences like that of Charles Crocker, with its ornate carvings, rococo bell towers, and intricate verandas, overlooked hilly lawns sprinkled with cast-iron animals. Popular legend has it that in the vicinity of the Hopkins mansion there were so many brass fences that one man was kept busy just polishing them. The Flood mansion, across the street from Hopkins', had such a fence as a memento of the days when its owner, James C. Flood, was a barkeep who prided himself on his brass bar rail.

The Theater

A prominent part of San Francisco's cultural scene has traditionally been its drama. Immediately after the Gold Rush its Jenny Lind Theater was a favorite haunt of theater fans, who flocked there to see such performers as the notorious Lola Montez. Lola, whose name was linked with many lovers, including King Ludwig of Bavaria, had been treated as a strumpet in the large cities of the Eastern United States. At San Francisco, however, her reception was an ecstatic one, even as compared with that given the great Shakespearean troopers Junius Brutus Booth and his son Edwin. Lola capitalized on the title given her by Ludwig—Countess of Landsfeld. But it was her beautiful figure, flashing eyes, and raven-black hair that captivated audiences. Her "Tarantula Dance," in which she shivered and trembled, was a particular lure for the huge crowds that assembled to see her. Although some San Franciscans called her dancing a disgrace, Lola remained wildly popular. In 1853 she married Patrick Hull, an editor of the San Francisco *Whig*. But the footlights proved to be a stronger lure than merely another romance, and Lola continued her theater engagements. At the primitive mining camp of Grass Valley her husband, with whom she had quarreled violently, suddenly died. In response to the earnest entreaties of miners, Lola agreed to resume performing, at a charge of one hundred dollars per admission. Even at this rate, she never lacked for customers. Brandishing a whip on stage, Lola both defied and wooed male audiences to a point of frenzy. After reputedly selling her jewels for $20,000 to the madam of a fashionable brothel, she left California behind for new conquests in Australia.

Lola Montez, however, was only one of the performers warmly received by early San Francisco audiences. In the two decades from 1850 to 1870 there was a great deal of interest in classical drama, and the Booths, among other actors, also enjoyed tremendous popularity. Despite the crudity of the environment in which *A Midsummer Night's Dream* or *Romeo and Juliet* might be staged, audiences took these performances most seriously, hurling both praise and maledictions at actors on stage. The number of performances staged and cast at San Francisco was staggering. One authority has uncovered the fact that 1,100 different dramatic pieces were produced there from 1850 to 1859. Many of these were under the sponsorship of Thomas Maguire, an impresario and gambler who came to be known as the "Napoleon of the drama." It was this early theatrical monopolist who opened the Jenny Lind Theater and who attracted the most spectacular "stars" to the city.

Whether a performer was in a legitimate stage play or in a minstrel show, or a melodrama, or was a dancer in an extravaganza, the star system, in fact, emerged at an early date. A yearning for identification with individual performers characterized

San Francisco's audiences. Players, of course, were amazed when gold nuggets and diamond brooches were thrown onto the stage by frontiersmen who had struck it rich in the back country. One of the artists on whom attention was showered was the flaming redhead Adah Menken. Clad in flesh-colored tights, she was probably the first woman to play the title role in *Mazeppa*, a play based on a romantic poem by Lord Byron. During 1863, at the Tivoli Theater, the shapely Miss Menken showed such consummate talent that the St. Francis Hook and Ladder Company made her a member of its fire-fighting brigade. This popular actress was wooed by international figures, including Alexandre Dumas and his son, as well as Dante Gabriel Rossetti. In later years Miss Menken was to be followed in popularity by Lillian Russell and Sarah Bernhardt.

Writers, artists, and actors thus all found San Francisco a congenial place in which to work. Thousands of talented, creative persons crowded into a bohemian quarter that stretched from North Beach across Telegraph Hill. Following the primitiveness of the Gold Rush years, an increasingly cosmopolitan culture seemed to be developing and flourishing. If California did, indeed, reshape its culture from about 1850 to 1870, San Francisco was the place where this occurred.

SELECTED READINGS

Among contemporary descriptive narratives of early San Francisco are Bayard Taylor, *Eldorado, or Adventures in the Path of Empire* (New York, 1850; repr. 1949), and Friedrich Gerstäcker, *Narrative of a Journey* . . . (New York, 1853), as well as T. A. Barry and B. A. Patten, *Men and Memories of San Francisco* (San Francisco, 1873). Useful for descriptive sketches of a later period is Robert E. Cowan, *Forgotten Characters of Old San Francisco* (Los Angeles, 1938). For a visual impression see John H. Kemble, ed., *San Francisco Bay* (Cambridge, Md., 1957), a superb pictorial maritime history. Julia Altrocchi, *The Spectacular San Franciscans* (New York, 1949) and William M. Camp, *San Francisco, Port of Gold* (New York, 1947) also set the scene for uninitiated readers, though rather gaudily. In this same romantic vein is Samuel Dickson, *San Francisco Is Your Home* (Stanford, 1947). Similarly impressionistic are Julian Dana, *The Man Who Built San Francisco* (New York, 1936); George D. Lyman, *Ralston's Ring* (New York, 1937); and Amelia R. Neville, *Fantastic City* (Boston, 1932), and Miriam Allen de Ford, *They Were San Franciscans* (Caldwell, Idaho, 1941). James J. Corbett, *The Roar of the Crowd* (New York, 1925) mirrors a part of the life of the city at a somewhat later time. See also Felix Riesenberg, *Golden Gate* (New York, 1940) and Charles Caldwell Dobie, *San Francisco, A Pageant* (New York, 1943) as well as Helen Throop Purdy, *San Francisco As It Was* (San Francisco, 1912).

Cultural growth, as measured by educational advance, is discussed in William G. Cain, *John Swett: The Biography of an Educational Pioneer* (Santa Ana, 1933) and in John C. Pelton, *Origin of the Free Public Schools of San Francisco . . .* (San Francisco, 1865). See also the somewhat more obscure *Act to Establish a System of Common Schools . . . introduced by John G. Marvin* in *California Laws and Statutes* (Sacramento, 1852). A basic interpretation of early journalism and literature is Franklin Walker, *San Francisco's Literary Frontier* (New York, 1939). The theater is treated in G. R. MacMinn, *The Theater of the Golden Era* (Caldwell, Idaho, 1941). The literary production of individual authors, especially Twain and Harte, was so great that any attempted list of even their best writings would become voluminous. Notable biographies include Bernard de Voto, *Mark Twain's America* (Boston, 1932), Justin Kaplan, *Mr. Clemens and Mark Twain* (New York, 1966), and Ivan Benson, *Mark Twain's Western Years* (Stanford, 1938). Most useful in identifying the sources of Twain's earliest writing is Edgar M. Branch, *The Literary Apprenticeship of Mark Twain* (Urbana, 1950). Regarding Harte, perhaps the best general book is George R. Stewart's *Bret Harte: Argonaut and Exile* (Boston, 1931). Stewart has also written about George Derby in *John Phoenix, Esq.: The Veritable Squibob* (New York, 1937). On Browne, see David Goodman, *A Western Panorama, 1849–1875: The Travels, Writings and Influence of J. Ross Browne* (Glendale, 1966). Francis P. Weisenburger has written a biography of Rollin Daggett entitled *Idol of the West* (Syracuse, 1965). Concerning all these authors, consult Walter Blair, *Native American Humor* (New York, 1937).

Useful bibliographical aids to the location of early California literature are Joseph Gaer, ed., *Bibliography of California Literature* (SERA Project, 1935), and Edgar J. Hinkel, ed., *Bibliography of California Fiction, Poetry, Drama* (3 vols., Oakland, 1938). For nonfiction titles, see Robert E. Cowan, *A Bibliography of the History of California and the Pacific West* (3 vols., San Francisco, 1933; Columbus, Ohio, 1952). Focusing attention on San Francisco is *The Western Gate: A San Francisco Reader*, edited by Joseph Henry Jackson (New York, 1952).

Accounts of the innumerable artists attracted to California are harder to come by. One of the few biographies is Eugen Neuhaus, *William Keith: The Man and the Artist* (Berkeley, 1938). Another biography, copiously illustrated, is Brother Cornelius's *Keith, Old Master of California* (New York, 1942). Helpful sketches of John W. Audubon, Albert Bierstadt, William Keith, Charles C. Nahl, and Victor Prevost are in *California Centennials Exhibition of Art* (Los Angeles, 1949). See also *The Drawings of John Woodhouse Audubon*, intro. and notes by Carl S. Dentzel (San Francisco, 1957). No genuine history of California art, early or late, yet exists.

19

Post Gold Rush Commerce and Industry

After the gold rush, California's commercial growth was sometimes erratic. In a period of rugged frontier individualism, marked by the exploitation of natural resources, economic expansion was bound to be wasteful. But, eventually, a more orderly, settled, and balanced pattern began to emerge. As the hide and tallow traffic, the overland fur trade, sea-otter hunting, and other early exploitative "industries" receded into history, Californians turned toward more permanent means of livelihood.

One of the declining occupations, of course, was gold mining, because the most precious deposits of ore were rather quickly exhausted. As already indicated, individual miners moving from one rich lode to another gave way to organized mining companies, which could provide the machinery and technical personnel required to engage in deep-shaft quartz operations. The percentage of the population engaged in mining continued to decrease. According to the 1850 census reports, 50 per cent of California's working population was engaged in gold mining. By 1860, the percentage of persons so occupied had dropped to 38. Of these, many were employed in large-scale gold operations, either in the quartz and stamp mills or in smelters and foundries. Some miners turned from gold to silver mining. A few entered the professions that depended for much of their activity at that time upon the mining industry — law, engineering, and banking. Former red-shirted miners also settled down to running hardware stores, liv-

ery stables, and saloons. Henceforth labor would become more
skilled in the refining and manufacture of raw materials and in
the production of mineral and agricultural products. Greater
numbers of people also began to earn their living by retailing,
wholesaling, warehousing, and processing goods. To the occupations represented by the rancher and the miner were added such
new trades as those of the gunsmith, tanner, collier, butcher, jew-
eler, cabinetmaker, and baker.

There were many other changes in the state's economy. Immigration, though reduced from Gold Rush days, was still heavy, and
the increase in population brought new markets. Regularly scheduled stages and freight vehicles took the place of overland covered wagons. Farmers, merchants, and settlers all encouraged an
atmosphere of economic growth — as did Eastern investment
capital.

Whaling and Fishing

By mid-century the Yankee sea captains had extended their whaling operations beyond the waters of Alaska to the Bering Sea,
even to the coast of Japan, and as far south as Peru. Along with
Honolulu, the California ports continued as major centers for the
whalers. In 1855 alone some five hundred whaling vessels visited
the Pacific Coast, though not all of these were American. Seventeen Portuguese firms at Monterey, as an example of the size of
the operations, obtained 24,000 barrels of whale oil in a three-
year period, the average yield from one gray whale being 20 barrels. The industry's center of gravity was still the Atlantic Ocean,
but in the quarter-century after 1850 it slowly shifted to the
Pacific, where San Francisco became its principal base. Yet whaling was destined to falter. By 1881, the California whaling fleet
had dwindled to only forty vessels, though it lingered on into the
twentieth century. (The vessel *Wanderer*, at the time she was lost
on the rocks of Buzzard's Bay, August 26, 1924, was the last
active American whaling bark to operate under sail.) The significance of the whaling industry should not be estimated in terms
of monetary returns to investors alone. Like the fur trade, whaling illustrated the growing interest of Americans in the Pacific in
general and in California in particular.

As new markets reflected the growth of population out West,
the Pacific whaling industry was supplemented by the expansion
of commercial fishing. After the Gold Rush, fleets of fishing boats
regularly swarmed in and out of the harbors of California. Sal-

mon fishing had begun early in the state's northern waters. In 1855 at least three firms were already engaged in smoking and salting salmon in the vicinity of Sacramento. By 1880 the federal census would show a capital of $1,800,000 invested in salmon fisheries, including 850 boats. The annual catch that year was about 12,000 tons. The next year canned salmon production on the Pacific Coast amounted to $5,000,000 annually. As the fishing industry expanded operations, Monterey emerged as a terminus for the anchovy and sardine fleets, while San Pedro became a tuna-packing center. Other southern ports, too, were well known for their tuna catches, while the state's central ones handled sole, sand dabs, and other smaller fish. After the 1880's California fishermen added large catches of mackerel, skipjack, albacore, rockfish, and barracuda to their wares in order to meet increasing demands for fish. Shellfishing, especially for clams, crabs, and abalone, also grew into a significant industry.

Continued Mining: The Comstock Lode

From 1851 to 1855 the United States produced 45 per cent of the world's gold, and most of this came from California, despite the great decline that followed its Gold Rush. Through the 1860's mining still employed as many persons as were engaged in any other single occupation in California. Even in the 1870's, with an annual production usually in excess of $15 million, California still surpassed other Western states in mining activity. Furthermore, the production of gold in these other states never matched that of California's peak years. The replacement of hard-rock and placer miners by large commercial firms greatly increased production in the state. As pan and cradle gave way to quartz crushing and ore pounding machinery, the chemist became a virtual partner of the miner. The pulverizing of quartz, which was then treated with mercury or quicksilver to form an amalgam, was a big technical advance in mining procedures. By 1857 more than one hundred and fifty quartz mills had been erected in California.

The new technological developments in mining were accompanied by the discovery of rich silver deposits beyond the eastern boundary of California, in the Washoe region. The story of the Comstock Lode belongs properly to the history of Nevada. Yet the financial dependence of that region upon San Francisco and the effects of this discovery in California were pronounced. Without California capital the Comstock would never have been developed. Even the miners who worked the lode came from Califor-

PLACER MINER ON THE COLORADO RIVER, CA. 1890.
(C. C. Pierce Collection; by courtesy of The Huntington Library,
San Marino, California.)

nia. As early as 1853 various hard-rock prospectors had poked about the brush-strewn slopes of Mt. Davidson, east of the Sierra. They had dug up a bluish-tinged ore which interfered with washing operations and which they cast aside as "that blasted blue stuff." In 1859 an assayer found that this "waste" was basically rich sulfide containing almost $4,800 per ton in silver as well as $1,600 per ton in gold.

Virtually overnight some ten thousand persons moved eastward on hastily constructed wagon roads that wound precipitously down the Nevada side of the Sierra. Although a Sacramento stage made the trip every three days, reservations were needed long in advance. Freighting into the Washoe mines became a big business and toll roads grew to be as valuable as certain mining claims. Until rail facilities could be built, supplies had to be hauled by mule and ox teams to Virginia City, center of the boom. That community quickly transformed itself from a tent mining camp into a proud town of frame and brick buildings whose male population was almost exclusively employed in the nearby mines. In one year alone almost two thousand men were added to the payroll of one company, the Gould and Curry Mine and Mill.

This and other mining firms worked the Comstock for more than fifteen years, during which the area around today's Carson City, Reno, and Virginia City was gripped by a fever of speculation. By the 1860's thirty mills were in operation, and as many companies floated mining stock on national security markets. William C. Ralston and his Bank of California invested heavily in the Comstock, transporting thousands of feet of timber as well as machinery and other equipment over the Sierra—items essential in order to shore up friable earth along the deep tunnels that led to veins of silver fifty feet or more in width. Utilizing a unique German method of mine-timbering, known as Philip Deidesheimer's Cribbing Technique, the San Francisco financiers who made up "Ralston's Ring" turned the Comstock into a honeycomb of crisscrossing channels, tunnels, conduits, and shafts. The Comstock swallowed up 80 million feet of lumber a year, aside from the thousands of cords of wood necessary to operate its mills. Peak annual requirements reached the equivalent of 1,200 miles of 12" x 12" timber. The lode was, therefore, justifiably called the tomb of the nearby eastern Sierra forests.

Hard-rock miners were lowered into the perilous shafts to dig in the damp, hot underground. The Comstock was an interconnected series of volcanic and metallic fissures, a complex, jumbled mass of veins that provided high excitement for those who sought to fathom its mysteries. It took some fourteen years to reach and to strip bare the richest ore pocket, known as the "Big Bonanza." In 1873 the epicenter of the lode was finally tapped and the silver boom approached its peak of production. That year a venturesome mill owner and future San Francisco mayor, Adolph Sutro, began to build an expensive new tunnel into the heart of the Comstock's ore bodies. This impressive engineering feat provided the hot sumps below the ground with ventilation, better access, and vital drainage facilities. The tunnel also connected the vast network of existing "squirrel holes," as J. Ross Browne called the Comstock diggings. Completion of Sutro's tunnel in 1878 came many years too late, however, to reap for its stockholders the benefits promised by its builder. Yet Sutro wisely sold his own stock in the tunnel for a profit of a million dollars.

In addition to Sutro, a number of other Western millionaires got their start in the Comstock. The combined efforts of George Hearst, E. J. ("Lucky") Baldwin, John W. Mackay, James Fair, James C. Flood, William S. O'Brien, John P. Jones, and Alvinza Hayward were needed to exploit the ganglia of ore bodies that lay hidden beneath the surface. Calculating and bold, these men belonged to the same aggressive generation as the Goulds, Vanderbilts, Fisks, Carnegies, and Rockefellers. In an age of rugged individualism and laissez-faire economics, these tough-minded, sometimes ruthless, tycoons created dynasties and monopolistic economic empires, in the West as in the East. The Western barons boasted that half the mansions in San Francisco were constructed, prior to 1906, with Comstock silver and gold earnings.

By 1870, "The King of the Comstock," William Sharon—who controlled vital lumber and rail interests—had coaxed William C. Ralston into overcommitting both himself and the bank he headed in the "Washoe Madness." Ralston, Sharon, and Darius Mills, by the mid-1860's, had created the Union Mill and Mining Company, a syndicate which sank millions into a vigorous fight for control of the Comstock, in opposition to their archrivals, Flood, Mackay, and O'Brien. A national panic in 1873 resulted in slumps in both the production and the marketing of silver, signaling the beginning of trouble for investors in the lode. Not all these were business tycoons. In California everyone from draymen to barkeeps had invested heavily in a mania of speculative irresponsibility. When Ralston's Bank of California failed in 1875, the event set off a string of financial bankruptcies. For a time almost every bank in the state closed its doors, and serious unemployment added to the dark financial picture. Ralston himself (unlike some of his close associates) was unable to save his own fortune. Distraught at the prospect of ruin, he met his death either by suicide or by accident in the icy waters of San Francisco Bay. As Comstock mining securities continued to plunge in value, a number of persons who were suddenly faced with drastic losses took their own lives.

The mines of the Comstock nevertheless enriched those few who were lucky enough to hold onto their interest in its estimated total production of $350,000,000 in bullion and $130,000,000 in dividends. The lode achieved its maximum output in 1877—almost $50 million—and afterwards slumped badly. By 1880, the Comstock had permanently failed. All things considered, it is possible that as much capital was put into developing the Comstock Lode as was ever taken out in dividends or earnings. The major developers of the Nevada mines, however, had for the most part built up sizable profits that enabled them to go on to new ventures. Once the "blue stuff" of Six-Mile and Gold Canyons gave out, and the Ophir and Crown Point mines closed down, many of these speculators returned to San Francisco. They used their salvaged treasure to build a new city. Sutro became its mayor and bequeathed to it a noted library, still in existence. Mackay lent his energies and capital to an international cable and telegraphic system that long bore his name. Flood and Fair had their family names perpetuated in San Francisco by other prominent landmarks, including today's Fairmount Hotel.

Freight, Stage, and Mail Service

California's economic development was especially closely related to the growth of transportation at this time. The Far West's two earliest mining rushes—that to the California gold areas after 1848 and that to the Comstock a few years later—greatly accelerated progress in transportation. Staging and freighting in particular were stimulated, even though good roads were not in existence in much of the West during the nineteenth century. In some localities toll roads were, however, maintained in fair condition.

During the 1850's slow-moving mule and pack trains operated over regular routes in California, gradually extending their services eastward and northward into the territories of Utah and Oregon. Freight outfits often used three loaded wagons per unit, with a hitch of eight mules or oxen; as a rule, one animal pulled about a thousand pounds of weight. The grueling toughness of freighting produced a breed of hardy "bull whackers" and "mule skinners" who, like the stagecoach drivers of the same era, were known for their consummate skill in profanity.

The May 30, 1849, issue of the San Francisco *Alta California* announced the establishment of what was probably the first stage line in California, Maurison and Company's service from Stockton to the Stanislaus mines.

In midsummer, 1849, James E. Birch established a stage line which operated over a fifty-mile stretch from Sacramento to Coloma and also to such spurs off the main route as Mormon Island, a mining center. Miners who were anxious to reach the placers in the mountains, but who preferred to go by other means than on horseback or on foot, paid Birch a stage fare each way of two ounces of gold, or $32. John Whistman inaugurated in 1850 a regular stage service between San Jose and San Francisco, taking nine hours to make this forty-five mile run. His fare was also two ounces of gold. By the middle 1850's there were a dozen lines, mostly servicing the state's mining centers. One stage ran twice a month between San Francisco and Los Angeles. From 1854 onward the California Stage Company operated a profitable statewide integrated service. This firm grew out of a merger of five local lines, eventually running stages over routes 1,500 miles long.

A monthly mail delivery had begun between Salt Lake City and Sacramento by 1851, utilizing mule-drawn relays over a 750-mile route. The Great Salt Lake Carrying Company hauled passengers from Sacramento to the Mormon settlements for $300 and freight for $250 per ton. From Sacramento this route passed through Folsom, Placerville, Hope Valley, and Carson Valley, along the Humboldt River, into southern Idaho, then back around the north side of the Great Salt Lake. In 1854, because the road across the Sierra was impassable during winter months, the route was changed, its terminus becoming San Diego, via the Mormon Trail. George Chorpenning, a pioneer freighter, carried the mail over this route for several years thereafter.

Passengers on the early stages were warned that the trip might be a bone-jarring experience. The stage routes were often treacherous, crossing both arid wastes and rapid streams. Crude ferries over the latter only gradually gave way to permanent bridges. Few stages traveled at night, for fear both of Indians and of dangerous potholes. Drivers were well paid for their arduous work. It was no easy job to drive the large teams of mixed mustangs, hitched to heavily loaded stages, along the rough and stony roads and over the steep grades of the Sierra. Drivers were expected to do their utmost to keep on schedule and they had to know how to handle nervous teams of animals carefully. A good driver communicated with his mules or horses through gentle movements of the reins. If he sometimes gave a dramatic crack of his whip as he got his wagon underway, it was more to impress spectators and passengers than the animals.

Numerous tributes have been paid to these picturesque "knights of the rein." Among them were some famous California drivers: Hank Monk, immortalized by Mark Twain, George Monroe, Baldy Hamilton, Buffalo Jim, Buck Jones, Curley Bill, "Old" Jim Haworth, "Uncle" Billy Mayhew, and "Charley" Parkhurst. Only after Parkhurst's death in 1879, incidentally, was "he" found to be

GOING INTO THE SOUTHERN CALIFORNIA MINES BY STAGECOACH, 1904. DIGGINGS ARE IN THE CANYON IN THE BACKGROUND. (C. C. Pierce Collection; by courtesy of The Huntington Library, San Marino, California.)

a woman named Charlotte. Tough as saddle leather and inured to the dust and heat of the trail, these "whips" raised stage driving to an art and won the affection, or, in certain cases, the hatred of travelers. Apart from their other functions, in the single one of carrying the mail to remote outposts they rendered an invaluable service to California and the West.

In 1851 there were few stage stations and only thirty-four post offices in all of California. So poor was delivery service that for six weeks during the harsh winter of 1852–1853 Los Angeles received no regular mail. The employment of dependable drivers and the establishment of new stage stations inevitably forced postal and parcel rates upward. In spite of the progress being made, however, service remained so defective that a clamor went up in California during the fifties and sixties for improved schedules. As a result two Eastern staging firms, the Adams and Company Express, and later (beginning in 1852) Wells, Fargo and Company, absorbed much local mail service, including the shipment of gold and other valuables. Both companies established branches in the mining camps and towns of the new state. With their system of national connections by land and water, they came to be regarded as more dependable than the patchwork of local stage operations. It was said about Wells, Fargo, with only moderate exaggeration, that its representatives were to be found at every turn of the road. In a five-year period Wells, Fargo transported $58,000,000 worth of gold into San Francisco alone. In time both companies also took on banking functions.

Nevertheless, local lines continued to provide the bulk of passenger service, as well as to transport a considerable proportion of the mail, both within California and overland from the Midwest. Gradually more stage stations were constructed, so that there was one every forty or fifty miles. At these, drivers obtained fresh horses, enabling some stages to run by day and night, and passengers could rest briefly but primitively from their journey. Although faster stages were shrinking travel time considerably, they still offered only a rugged alternative to walking. In fact, when a route was hilly or muddy, passengers sometimes had to get out and push. Travelers called Jared B. Crandall's notoriously slow Sierra stage firm "the line of Foot and Walker." A week of travel through clouds of dust and in the rain and snow upset many a passenger. In a few cases travelers were driven insane; in others they stopped the stages to duel with one another over some minor matter.

The best stage lines used Concord carriages, manufactured by Abbott, Downing and Company in New Hampshire. The cabs of these coaches rode on a leather cradle of thorough braces that cushioned passengers against the buffetings of the road. Strongly constructed of light New England ash and well-seasoned oak wood, and of iron from Norway, the Concord coaches were sometimes ornately paneled with clear poplar. One of these 2,500-pound carriages sold for as much as $1,500, and required three spans of good horses, costing up to $1,000 a span. Not until Phineas Banning began to manufacture carriages at Wilmington in southern California were similar coaches built in the West. Banning began operation in 1867 of a stage connection between Los Angeles and Wilmington, which proved especially popular because of the quality of his coaches. Most stage lines simply adapted old mud wagons such as were to be seen on almost every ranch in California during the 1850's. These springless vehicles, fitted out to carry twelve passengers (as compared with fourteen to twenty-two in a Concord coach), were rather slow. Any driver who could cover sixty miles in six hours, handling six reins at one time, was considered a hero by youngsters along his route.

Stage lines, however, steadily improved their service, anticipating the coming of the railroads. They eagerly sought federal subsidies to help defray their expensive operations. In 1855 a bill was introduced in the United States Senate which would have authorized the Postmaster General to contract for a weekly mail service from Missouri River points to the Pacific Coast. Over two more years passed, however, before Congress voted through an overland mail bill. Part of this delay was caused by tension between North and South over future transportation routes. With the Pacific railroad project also hopelessly involved in this sectional discord, Californians were at the mercy of Congress as to the hauling of mail and freight. The bill was finally approved in March, 1857, requiring "the service to be performed with good four-horse coaches or spring wagons, suitable for the conveyance of passengers, as well as for the safety and security of the mails." The selection of a route through Texas, running in a semicircle from St. Louis to San Francisco, produced a storm of Northern criticism. Known as the Ox Bow Route, this had the advantage of being an "all-year route," whereas other trails westward were seasonal.

Hard-driving John Butterfield, successful bidder for the franchise to carry the mails over the designated course, started his cross-country stages moving toward California in September, 1858. Butterfield demonstrated that, by using relays of horses, his coaches could cover the 2,800 miles between Tipton, Missouri, and San Francisco in twenty-four days, eighteen hours, and twenty-six minutes. The schedule called for an average speed of five miles an hour, day and night, with fresh horses waiting at ten-mile inter-vals. As basic equipment the more than one thousand men em-ployed by Butterfield used two of the most famous vehicles of the mid-nineteenth century: Concord coaches and Troy carriages—or Celerity wagons. The passenger fare from St. Louis to San Fran-cisco was $200. Overland travelers, however, were a secondary

L. LICHTENBERGER'S CARRIAGE FACTORY, 147–149 MAIN STREET, LOS ANGELES, 1883. (C. C. Pierce Collection; by courtesy of The Huntington Library, San Marino, California.)

cargo in comparison to the mails; they had the option of either preparing meals en route themselves or purchasing inferior, and usually cold, food at stations. Passengers received scant attention at the hands of busy station men and preoccupied drivers.

As the Civil War approached, the Northern states became increasingly concerned with rerouting the overland stages to California so that the Union could be sure of maintaining the mails. For economic and strategic reasons this service was vital. Even before the outbreak of war, Butterfield, as operator of the route for the federal government, therefore, began to transfer movable equipment northward piece by piece. In 1861 the Butterfield Overland Mail's Southern course was abandoned in favor of a direct connection from St. Louis to California via Salt Lake City. Had not sectional tension continued to keep the nation from settling upon a clear-cut railroad route, as recommended by various congressional surveys, overland staging probably would have disappeared before the Civil War. Staging remained highly subsidized by the national government throughout that conflict.

Ships of the Desert

A picturesque episode in the story of Southwestern transportation began in 1855 with the authorization by Congress of a "Camel Corps," as recommended by Secretary of War Jefferson Davis. He and other backers of this innovation believed that if camels could successfully be used in Africa and Asia, they might also flourish in the "Great American Desert." The projected "lightning dromedary express" made its first experimental trip westward to California from Arizona in only fifteen days, with the camels swimming the Colorado River on their way. On the eighth of January, 1858, the population of Los Angeles turned out to witness the appearance of this first camel caravan. The camels had come from Fort Defiance in northeastern Arizona and were on their way to Fort Tejon, where Lieutenant Edward F. Beale maintained his headquarters. Beale supervised several subsequent trips between that fort and Albuquerque, the camels being used principally to transport freight.

Because the camel experiment gave promise of success the Army planned a regular caravan system. This project proved short-lived, partly because of Beale's recall eastward for Civil War duty. Also, the "ships of the desert" developed sore legs and feet from the Arizona and Nevada trails, which were covered with cacti, prickly pear, and sagebrush. Exasperated mule drivers, furthermore, wanted nothing to do with the smelly "humpbacked brutes." Two particularly hard drivers, "Greek George" Caralambo, and an Arab, Haiji Ali ("Hi Jolly"), managed the stubborn camels with considerable success. The project was abandoned in 1864 when the last of the animals were sold at San Francisco, after which they were used for pleasure riding and in circuses. There is a story that others were turned loose in the desert and that for years thereafter unbelieving travelers reported having seen their ghostly profiles in the shadowy night.

The Pony Express

Still another novel experiment in Western transportation was to be tried out. This was the use of fast relays of horses to carry mail more efficiently between distant points than was possible by stage service. The first "pony express" was actually that of Major George Chorpenning, who headed a firm that, in 1858, delivered a message from President James Buchanan in Washington to Sacramento, California, in only seventeen days. The Pony Express proper, however, began operations in 1860 under the aegis of the Central Overland California and Pike's Peak Express Company. This firm, founded by experienced transportation men, had for some time been running a passenger and freighting business; it had acquired, incidentally, a number of ready critics, who, angered by its failure to maintain both its schedules and equipment, had dubbed the C.O.C. & P.P.E. the "Clean Outa Cash & Past Paying Expenses" line. The idea for a widespread mail operation originated with one of the line's officials, William Russell, who organized the subsidiary firm of Russell, Majors and Waddell to operate the new service. The Pony Express began to function on April 3, 1860, with the departure of a rider from St. Joseph, Missouri, for California. At the same time a packet of letters was conveyed eastward from San Francisco to Sacramento by river boat, then forwarded by rail to Folsom, and next, by stage or pony via Placerville to Genoa in present-day Nevada where it began the long day-and-night journey to St. Joseph, Missouri.

The westward route was, in general, the same as that taken by overland wagons—as far as Folsom, then on to Sacramento. Both rider and horse went on from the capital by steamboat down the Sacramento River and across the bay to San Francisco. The run of 1,966 miles was completed in nine days and twenty-three hours, or less than half the time required by the best stages; these usually took about twenty days to reach California from St. Joseph. By means of this impressive record, Russell, Majors and Waddell attracted national attention to their Pony Express.

Full equipment of the Pony Express comprised 80 riders, 190 stations, 400 stationmen, and 400 fast horses. More than $700,000 was invested in the enterprise by its owners. Young, light riders were selected to deliver the mail, at salaries averaging from $100 to $200 a month. These boys were armed only with a six-shooter and a knife, and were required to take an oath against using profane language and intoxicating liquor. Each man rode about thirty miles, changing horses every ten miles, though emergencies sometimes called for more strenuous riding. "Buffalo Bill" (William F. Cody) is credited with a continuous ride of 384 miles. Jim Moore, another Pony Express employee, once rode 140 miles, and then, after a stopover of ten minutes, leaped again into the saddle, because of his partner's illness, for the return trip of 140 miles.

The letters that these men transported in their leather pouches were written on the thinnest of paper; the rate of postage was at first $5 per half ounce, later reduced to $1.50 and finally to $1. Only one trip was completely missed and one mail lost, out of 650,000 miles ridden. Operating conditions were sometimes arduous. For example, riders found it necessary, during winter storms, to use pack animals under difficult conditions, particularly along the Sierra trails. The Pony Express, carrying its weekly mails without government subsidy, proved unprofitable despite its high postage rate. During its first eight months of service Californians sent east only one hundred and seventy-two letters, and less than a dozen were submitted to the company for westward transportation. Completion of a transcontinental telegraph line in 1861 ended the Pony Express. It was officially discontinued on October 7, 1861. Though it had operated for only sixteen months, its demonstration of the practicality of a central route, which would serve as a forerunner of the Central Pacific Railroad, made the Pony Express famous as a national institution. By 1862 Russell, Majors, and Waddell, who had run the Pony Express only as a sideline to their other business, were in such dire financial straits that they sold out their stage operation to a corporation headed by Ben Holladay.

Holladay, almost compulsively ruthless and tough, was an uneducated but shrewd former mule skinner with financial interests in stagecoach, steamboat, and, later, railroad transportation. He purchased and united various shaky remnants of the West's stage lines. By obtaining also numerous franchises, toll roads, and ferry rights in California and elsewhere, he briefly presided over the

West's greatest transportation empire. Holladay, called the "King of Hurry," made staging a big business, eventually dominating 3,300 miles of stage routes. For a time he boasted that he operated his overland stages to California at a loss, in part because of the personal request of President Lincoln. After 1862, he provided triweekly service westward at a cost of $225 per passenger over the 1,900 miles from Atchison, Kansas, to Placerville, California. Once the Civil War broke out, this was a vital supply line. By 1865, through wartime inflation, the price of tickets had risen to $500. In October of the next year, anticipating the building of a national railroad system, Holladay sold his overland staging operations to Wells, Fargo and Company, which rapidly gained control of still other independent stage companies, including the old Butterfield Overland Mail Company interests.

Outlaws

Whether they worked for Ben Holladay or Wells, Fargo, Western riders and drivers ran the risk of encountering road agents of all descriptions. All together, the Wells, Fargo stages were robbed 313 times. Outlaws focused particularly upon the principal stage routes. They would appear suddenly at a coach door, masked and armed, quickly relieve passengers of their valuables and the stage of its strong box, then make off before the law arrived. Resistance meant instant shooting. Nor were the outlaws' activities restricted to harassment of the stages. The lone horseback traveler might fall prey to a skillfully thrown lariat, or there might be wholesale horse stealing, or even murder.

Chief among the California banditti was Joaquín Murieta, the notorious brigand, elusive and adroit. His name struck terror from one end of the state to the other. He has been called a cavalier as well as an outlaw. But even if one rejects as untrue some of the innumerable stories about his misdeeds, Murieta remains the superbandit of California's past. The Texas ranger Harry S. Love, an experienced manhunter, was hired by the state legislature to track him down. Captain Love finally captured and killed a man supposed to be Murieta; the head of the victim was later exhibited in a jar of alcohol. The sight of this token contributed to the development of a certain sympathy for Murieta among viewers.

One of the highwaymen that infested the area around Los Angeles in the fifties was Juan Flores, another expert with the pistol who was also "uncannily clever with the knife." But most feared of all in the southern part of the state was Tiburcio Vásquez, who was captured only in 1874, after he had evaded the law for many years. A sheriff's posse blasted him out of a hideout in the Cahuenga hills, and he surrendered after a volley of buckshot caught him in the left arm and leg as well as the side of his chest and head. To the jury that ultimately condemned him Vásquez testified that early in life "I got my mother's blessing and told her I was going out into the world to suffer and take my chances." When asked what he meant, he stated: "That I should live off the world and perhaps suffer at its hands." After twenty years of living off the world Vásquez was hanged until dead at San Jose.

In northern California Black Bart, a taciturn and gentlemanly road agent who wore a long linen duster, and a flour sack over his head, achieved legendary renown because of the invariability of the four words he used upon stopping a stage: "Throw down the box!" In the eight years between 1875 and 1883 twenty-eight drivers ultimately did throw down their express boxes for Black Bart. After nearly every robbery he left behind a taunting verse signed "Black Bart, the PO-8." To confuse his pursuers further, Bart's poetry was written in varying hands. One such poem, possibly apocryphal, was printed in a California mining paper:

> "So here I've stood while wind and rain
> Have set the trees a-sobbin'
> And risked my life for that damned stage
> That wasn't worth the robbin'."
> Black Bart, the PO-8

Bart inadvertently dropped a handkerchief at one robbery; its laundry mark led detectives to San Francisco, where he turned out to be a respected mining engineer named Charles E. Bolton. He was sent to San Quentin Penitentiary for five years, served his sentence, and then disappeared forever.

Many other stages were looted by bandits such as Dick Fellows, Tom Bell, and Rattlesnake Dick. As time passed, however, gold shipments became smaller and less frequent, and the incentive to pursue a life of crime diminished accordingly. The increasing pressure of public opinion also helped improve the processes of law and order. The railroad made the stage less attractive and those coaches that continued to operate employed armed express guards and detectives whose job it was to spot stage robbers. But for the most part after 1860, the outlaws had become a romantic legend.

The Telegraph

In his engaging book, *A Tour of Duty*, published in 1849, an early California visitor, Joseph W. Revere, predicted "the extension of the *Magnetic Telegraph*, with all convenient speed, from St. Louis to San Francisco." Local service, of course, came first, beginning with the completion on September 22, 1853, of a connection between the lighthouse at Point Lobos and San Francisco. This line was primarily employed to convey important maritime and weather data. Later that year San Francisco and San Jose were also connected telegraphically, and other lines were established shortly thereafter. A message to the interior on October 24, 1853, was sent to Marysville, a distance of 210 miles; it went via stations at San Jose, Stockton, and Sacramento. By October 8, 1860, Los Angeles was connected telegraphically with San Francisco, and thereafter dispatches received via the Overland Mail could be telegraphed northward. In the 1860's local telegraphers merged themselves into the pioneer California State Telegraph Company, which gradually extended its service along the entire Pacific Coast.

In June, 1860, a congressional act was passed "to facilitate communication between the Atlantic and Pacific states by electric telegraph"; an annual subsidy of $40,000 was provided for this purpose. Coast-to-coast telegraphic communication came into actual operation almost before the public grasped its full significance. On October 24, 1861, the first telegraphic message was sent to the east coast from California; addressed to President Lincoln, this communication forecast a new bond between the Atlantic and Pacific states. The first throb of current sounded the death knell for the Pony Express.

Banking and Finance

Related to the development of both mining and staging was banking. The earliest frontier bankers sometimes began as saloon keepers, express and stage operators, or as businessmen with strong safes in the back of their stores. Into their crude repositories, miners poured treasure for safekeeping on festive visits to town. In that day of the double-eagle twenty-dollar gold piece, and of two- and four-bit silver slugs, merchants charged as much as five percent interest a month for their banking service. As contrasted with modern banks, which lend out the money of depositors and are consequently glad to have their accounts, these early banks considered keeping a miner's doeskin bag of nuggets or "poke" of dust quite a chore. Storage of another man's worldly goods might prove a touchy business should so much as a sneeze occur as gold dust was being handled.

The first banker at the mining camp of Mokelumne Hill, Gallant D. Dickinson, operated according to arrangements that were probably typical. The vault of his "bank" was, according to an early source, "an excavation a yard square, under the bed occupied by himself and Mrs. Dickinson. Its compartments were buckskin bags, and the revolver of large caliber which he kept always near him served as a time-lock. The buckskin bags were tied with string, and none was received unless labeled with the name of the owner." Dickinson offered his clients no guarantees against theft.

Gradually banking operations became somewhat better organized. By storing money, lending it, transporting it, and manipulating both gold and other media of exchange, local hardware merchants, commissary owners, and mill operators transformed mediocre businesses into flourishing banks. On occasion several such merchants might join together to form a new bank. Yet only the large national express companies possessed the facilities for the safe transportation of money.

Adams and Company and Wells, Fargo and Company were joined in time by other firms that made the handling of money a major enterprise. By 1855 there were nineteen banks and nine insurance companies located in San Francisco. That year a financial panic was blamed on the haphazard business methods of these firms. The first of the banks to close its doors was Page, Bacon and Company, one of California's most prominent institutions. After depositors had begun their run on this bank, the panic snowballed. Most other San Francisco banks also had to cease operations when their gold resources were depleted by the demands of frantic account holders for specie payment of their deposits. The Wells, Fargo interests weathered the storm, but among the banking houses which failed that year was Adams and Company. This firm had offices in almost every California commercial center. Since the company owed almost $2,000,000 to depositors when it failed, charges of dishonesty were, perhaps naturally, levied against the Adams personnel by an irate public. Other insolvent companies met with similar accusations.

The banking panic of 1855 ushered in a decade of depression, during which most Californians showed little faith in the stability of their banks. This skepticism was justified by the banks' continuing loose practices. In 1862, however, the state legislature passed an act stipulating new conditions for the incorporation of savings and loan societies. Even earlier, some savings banks had reorganized themselves under more responsible auspices. These institutions included (in 1857) the Loan Society of San Francisco and (in 1859) the Hibernian Savings and Loan Society. There was still no ironclad guarantee against either personal chicanery or banking errors, but most San Francisco banks did their best to clean up operations and to recoup tarnished reputations in an age when a national bankrupt law did not exist. In 1864, William C. Ralston's Bank of California was rechartered under a plan that fortunately guaranteed payment to worried depositors when, in 1875, both Ralston and the bank suffered serious losses as the result of overspeculation in the Comstock Lode.

By the 1860's, Los Angeles emerged as a banking center, catering to the prosperous ranchers and farmers who populated in increasing numbers the southern city's outlying districts. Prominent among the earliest banks established there was Hellman, Temple and Company, formed in 1868. Isaias W. Hellman was a Los Angeles merchant who at first simply accepted for safekeeping the surplus funds of his customers. A scuffle with a drunken Irishman convinced Hellman that he should keep more careful accounts in order to protect himself, and he was thus led into legitimate banking. Hellman's original firm was organized as the Farmers and Merchants Bank and, later, as the Farmers and Merchants National Bank. Another company, the Commercial Bank, began operations in 1876; it developed into the First National Bank of Los Angeles, and subsequently became one of the strongest financial institutions on the Pacific Coast.

The history of banking in California was similar to the economic history of the state. At the start of the American era there was an early exploitative stage with both difficulties and opportunities that tempted men to become corrupt. Then came a restoration of confidence. In time, bankers became indispensable to the progress of California's commerce and industry. Without the assistance of bank loans, small farmers could not have planted fields and orchards, built their homes, purchased livestock, financed the building of irrigation systems, or put up boundary fences. The need for banks in the world of commerce was even more obvious.

Early Manufacturing

Large-scale manufacturing in California appeared tardily on the scene. This fact can be partly explained by the unstable conditions of a new frontier and by its immense distance from large Eastern cities. Supplies with which to engage in manufacturing were often scarce. For the first few years following the American conquest, consumer needs continued to be met by imports. Then the market for manufactured goods became great enough to stimulate the development of industry. As early as 1849, the Union Iron Works of San Francisco, a pioneer firm, was founded by James and Peter Donahue to meet local needs for wire, pipes, and machinery. The business expanded rapidly, and similar works began to appear at Sacramento and Stockton. In 1865, following a period of depression, Irving M. Scott took over the Union Iron Works; his energy and ability caused the products of this firm to become known around the world.

During the Civil War, the interruption of the flow of goods from Eastern states not only encouraged local infant industries; it also converted California's major port of San Francisco into an export center whose docks, warehouses, and piers were piled high with freight. Increasing numbers of ships entered the Golden Gate in ballast to load grain, flour, lumber, wool, mineral ores, quicksilver, and other products. More and more, these commodities were processed as well as produced in California. Such exports, which continued to mount by both overland and maritime transportation facilities, provided the means by which the state could purchase other goods it required from outside its borders.

Even before the war, in 1860, California had 3,505 manufacturing establishments. Nearly a hundred flour mills were then in operation, as were scores of lumber and textile mills, foundries like the Risdon and Pacific Iron Works, the San Francisco chocolate factory of Domenico Ghirardelli, and later the sugar-beet refineries of the Oxnard Brothers and Claus Spreckels, grist mills, cigar factories, tanneries, cotton manufacturing plants, ship repair yards, brick and tile yards, potteries, gunpowder works, and boot factories. That year San Jose, Stockton, Sacramento, Marysville, and Merced each possessed a woolen mill. Almost every town of similar size had a brewery or distillery and a metal or iron shop, and soon canneries would make their appearance. After the Gold Rush a flourishing wagon and carriage industry had begun with the early shops of John Studebaker at Placerville, and Phineas

Banning at Wilmington. In spite of the increases in production, California needed still more blacksmiths, harness and saddle makers, wheelwrights, carpenters, shoemakers, and numerous other craftsmen to meet its many wants.

In short, the period after the 1850's saw a great advance in California's commercial development. Eastern capital, which skipped over parts of the Middle West to invest in California, was responsible for much of the expansion of productive capacity. The completion of a transcontinental railroad in 1869 also contributed, by making vital raw materials more accessible and by further widening the export market. San Francisco alone, by 1876, was the site of forty-seven foundries and machine works. Such manufacturing plants profited, too, from California's mild climate, which made year-around employment both pleasant and profitable. As a consequence of all these factors, California was outgrowing the primitive economy of its frontier days. In general, it had avoided domination by one particular industry. Diversified, reasonably self-sufficient, and endowed with remarkable natural resources, the state was on its way toward economic maturity.

SELECTED READINGS

California's growing economy after the Gold Rush, including developments in mining, is described in John S. Hittell's books *The Resources of California* (San Francisco, 1863) and *Mining in the Pacific States of North America* (San Francisco, 1868), as well as in J. Ross Browne, *Resources of the Pacific Slope* (San Francisco, 1869).

The Comstock Lode is the subject of two books by George D. Lyman: *The Saga of the Comstock* (New York, 1934) and *Ralston's Ring: California Plunders the Comstock Lode* (New York, 1937). The Washoe region, and the men who developed it, are further discussed in G. B. Glasscock, *The Big Bonanza* (Indianapolis, 1931), and Lucius Beebe and Charles Clegg, *Legends of the Comstock Lode* (Oakland, 1950). Oscar Lewis, *The Silver Kings* (New York, 1947), tells what became of the Comstock fortunes. Julian Dana, *The Man Who Built San Francisco* (New York, 1936), is, in part, a biography of Ralston. Earlier accounts of the Comstock include Dan De Quille's *History of the Comstock Mines* (Virginia City, 1889) and Charles H. Shinn, *The Story of the Mine* (New York, 1896). Salting with fake gems during Comstock days is described in Asbury Harpending, *The Great Diamond Hoax* (San Francisco, 1915). A fictionalized treatment of the Comstock is to be found in Mark Twain's *Roughing It* (Hartford, 1872). Probably the best general history of the lode is Grant H. Smith, *The History of the Comstock Lode, 1850–1920* (Reno, 1943). A superior personal recollection of the "Comstock Kings" is George L. Upshur, *As I Recall Them* (New York, 1936). See also Robert E. Stewart, Jr., and Mary Frances Stewart, *Adolph Sutro: A Biography* (Berkeley, 1962). Rodman W. Paul, *Mining Frontiers of the Far West* (New York, 1963) carefully compares California and Nevada mining.

Books that depict the early staging and freighting history of California include Oscar O. Winther, *Express and Stagecoach Days in California* (Stanford, 1936), and Le Roy R. Hafen, *The Overland Mail, 1849–1869* (Cleveland, 1926). Winther has published numerous articles on the subject, with attention also to California's connections with Oregon and other parts of the West. Frank A. Root and William Elsey Connelley, *The Overland Stage to California* (Topeka, 1901), is an older but standard treatment. Useful also is William Tallack, *The California Overland Express: The Longest Stage Ride in the World* (Los Angeles, 1935), a reminiscence. The story of staging within California is entertainingly presented in William and George H. Banning, *Six Horses* (New York, 1930). See also Ernest A. Wiltsee, *The Pioneer Miner and Pack Mule Express* (San Francisco, 1931), as well as Roscoe P. and Margaret B. Conkling, *The Butterfield Overland Mail, 1857–1869* (3 vols., Glendale, 1947). Walter B. Lang, ed., *The First Overland Mail* (2 vols., East Aurora, New York, 1940–1945), offers the reader contemporary accounts of stagecoach journeys over the Butterfield routes. See also M. H. B. Boggs, *My Playhouse Was a Concord Coach* (Oakland, 1942).

Regarding Holladay's overland staging see Ellis Lucia, *The Saga of Ben Holladay: Giant of the Old West* (New York, 1959). The standard work on this subject is J. V. Frederick, *Ben Holladay the Stagecoach King* (Glendale, 1940). Also consult Edward Hungerford, *Wells Fargo: Advancing the American Frontier* (New York, 1949).

The Pony Express experiment is described in Glenn D. Bradley, *The Story of the Pony Express* (Chicago, 1913). A popularized treatment is Samuel H. Adams, *The Pony Express* (New York, 1950). Also concerned with the drama and lore of this subject is William Lightfoot Visscher, *A Thrilling and Truthful History of the Pony Express* (Chicago, 1908). On the connection between the Pony Express and overland freighting see Raymond W. Settle and Mary Lund Settle, *Empire on Wheels* (Stanford, 1949), and, by the same authors, *Saddles and Spurs* (Harrisburg, 1955), as well as their *War Drums and Wagon Wheels: The Story of Russell, Majors and Waddell* (Lincoln, Nebr., 1966), and W. Turrentine Jackson, "A New Look at Wells Fargo, Stagecoaches and the Pony Express," California Historical Society *Quarterly*, XLV (December, 1966), 291–324. The short-lived camel experiment is described by Lewis B. Lesley in *Uncle Sam's Camels* (Cambridge, Mass., 1929) and by Harlan Fowler in *Camels to California* (Palo Alto, 1950).

The activities of a noted stagecoach builder and operator form part of an imperfect biography by Maymie Krythe, *Port Admiral: Phineas Banning* (San Francisco, 1957). Descriptions of travel in California are offered in William H. Brewer, *Up and Down California in 1860–1864* (New Haven, 1930). Government road-building activities are the subject of W. Turrentine Jackson's *Wagon Roads West* (Berkeley, 1952). A superior account of the extension of telegraph service to California is in the book by Robert L. Thompson, *Wiring a Continent* (Princeton, 1947).

Joseph Henry Jackson wrote two perceptive books about California outlaws: *Tintypes in Gold: Four Studies in Robbery* (New York, 1939) and *Bad Company* (New York, 1949). These can be supplemented by Ben C. Truman's *Life, Adventures and Capture of Tiburcio Vásquez, the Great California Bandit and Murderer* (Los Angeles, 1874). A popularized biography of Murieta is Walter Noble Burns, *The Robin Hood of El Dorado* (New York, 1932). Dane Coolidge, *Gringo Gold* (New York, 1939), is a novel about this famous bandit.

California's early banking history is recorded in Ira B. Cross, *Financing an Empire* (4 vols., Chicago, 1937). Consult also Robert G. Cleland and Frank B. Putnam, *Isaias W. Hellman and the Farmers and Merchants Bank* (San Marino, 1965); Robert G. Cleland and Osgood Hardy, *The March of Industry* (Los Angeles, 1929). Harris Newmark's *Sixty Years in Southern California* (New York, 1916, 1930) tells the story of southern California's early economic development. So do two books by J. A. Graves, *My Seventy Years in California, 1857–1927* (Los Angeles, 1929) and *California Memories* (Los Angeles, 1930).

20

The Land Problem

For the Spaniards, land always held a particular fascination and importance. Indeed, it was their very basis for measuring both wealth and status. Under the Spanish land system, newly discovered terrain belonged solely to the King, who did, however, authorize a few private grants to California colonists, as trustees of the Crown. Later, the Mexican colonization law of 1824 (discussed in Chapter 9) increased the number of California land grants to more than eight hundred. By the time of the American conquest, almost fourteen million acres in all had been granted by Spanish and Mexican officials, with some of the grants overlapping each other. A few claims existed that were gargantuan, 133,000 to 1,775,000 acres in size. The average expense to early grantees for sometimes handsome properties had seldom exceeded twelve United States dollars.

The American Clamor for Land

Although the Treaty of Guadalupe Hidalgo, ending the Mexican War, had guaranteed resident Californians protection and security in the "free enjoyment of their liberty, property and religion," increasing dissatisfaction over the large land grants was expressed by the settlers who had arrived more recently, especially the Americans. Two distinctly different land traditions—the Spanish and the Anglo-American—were at loggerheads. For perhaps too long the rural Hispanic populace had clung to its silver-trimmed saddles and other symbols of the past. After 1850, old-time California residents, with many herds of stunted cattle on their hands, which had to be offered for sale at a prohibitive price because of the high cost of raising them, faced increasing imports of stronger Texas longhorns. Many rancheros fell into debt, finding themselves caught in a fatal net of rising costs, falling income, and heightened competition. Unfortunately for them, more and more land-hungry American farmers were streaming into this cattle frontier. Almost all of them sought land.

Ranchos located near a creek or on lake frontage were especially exposed to poachers. Overland cattle drovers often stopped at such places to water their stock. American homesteaders who liked what they saw frequently became squatters, challenging the right of rancheros to hold their large land grants intact. Some incoming Americans justified seizures of land by pointing out that, unlike other areas of the United States, California had made available to the public almost no arable free land. Other squatters, who knew nothing of the history of Spanish or Mexican land claims, looked upon unoccupied lands as government property legitimately subject to private occupation, sometimes claiming the produce of the land and even stray cattle. Still other newcomers roamed about the country, living in their wagons and using up a free water supply and grazing areas; these nomads, too, often picked up unbranded calves and other range animals.

In 1849 the Secretary of the Interior appointed William Carey Jones, like Frémont a son-in-law of Senator Benton, to investigate the validity of California's land grants. Jones was to determine precisely which lands fell under congressional jurisdiction. His report of May, 1850, was quite out of harmony with the wishes of the squatters. Jones found the majority of the Mexican grants in conformity with the law; in short, the titles were "mostly perfect," and "equivalent to patents from our own government." Even where technical evidences of ownership by grant were insufficient, continuous occupation was held to have established title.

A previous report on land titles, filed by Henry Wager Halleck on March 1, 1849, had reached a different conclusion. Halleck, an army captain, was then serving as California's secretary of state under Colonel Richard B. Mason, acting military governor. His report, thus made under army auspices, highlighted the spurious basis and doubtful validity of many land claims granted in the Mexican era. Halleck found unsurveyed tracts particularly ill defined, both as to origins and as to boundaries. In the last year of the Mexican era, 1846, eighty-seven grants had been made by Governor Pico; some of these were to his personal friends. Such grants, many with no well-established boundaries, were the most questionable of all.

Viewed from the standpoint of the American pioneer, it was intolerable that "a few hundred despised Mexicans" should control vast tracts of the most fertile and desirable lands to the exclusion of American farmers. What right had the Vallejos, the Argüellos, or the Swiss Captain Sutter to regal estates of eleven or more leagues? Did not the land rightly belong to "the hardy men who faced the dangers of desert and sierra" and brought American institutions and laws to California?

The Federal Government and California Land

Ultimately, the most important phase of the land question concerned how much land might be opened up within the state by the federal government: which parts of California would be declared public lands for sale? After 1851, it took several decades to answer this question. The United States land survey of California was begun that year. Thereafter large tracts of federal land became available for sale and for pre-emption purposes, especially after the Homestead Act of 1862 was passed by Congress. California itself became a gigantic land dealer. The state was eventually granted 500,000 acres of land by the federal government for distribution, in addition to two sections in each township for school purposes. Many individual purchasers were attracted by the low prices of these federal lands, and some pressure was thereby taken off private landholdings that might otherwise have been subject to squatting.

As a preliminary step in the land survey, a congressional act of March, 1851 ("to ascertain and settle the private land claims in the State of California") created a Land Commission to receive petitions from private land claimants and to pass upon the validity of their titles. Landholders failing to present claims within two years would forfeit all rights to their lands, which would thenceforth be considered "a part of the public domain of the United States." This Land Act was mostly the handiwork of Senator Gwin, whose sympathies lay with American landseekers. The constitutionality of the act was cogently questioned by Justice John Currey of the California Supreme Court in his judgment in the case of *Boteller et al.* vs. *Dominguez*. This case concerned a defendant who, at the time of the Mexican cession, had a perfect title to a tract known as Las Virgenes, but who had had his land confiscated because of his failure to submit his claims to the United States land commissioners. When the case was taken to the United States Supreme Court, however, that body upheld the constitutionality of the Land Act.

It is true that during the re-examination of grant titles by the Land Commission, which convened in San Francisco early in 1852, many native landowners were subjected to embarrassment and perhaps, in some cases, to unfair legal treatment. (The subject is discussed later in this chapter.) On the other hand, a few fraudulent claims were uncovered. One of the most astounding of such cases was that of José Y. Limantour, a French resident of Mexico. In 1853 he asserted ownership of 600,000 acres, including a number of important islands and four square leagues both within and adjoining the boundaries of San Francisco. A decade previous to this time the Frenchman had given aid to Governor Micheltorena, who had, according to Limantour, signed his land-grant documents. Local residents, whom he suddenly asked to move off their lands or to pay him quitclaims, regarded Limantour's action as attempted blackmail. When his claims were upheld by the federal Land Commission, genuine alarm spread through San Francisco, especially since his claim included the lands on which the presidio, the custom house, the mint, and other government property stood. Finally a federal District Court established forgery and adjudged Limantour's claims fraudulent. Arrested and pending trial for embezzlement, Limantour deposited a $30,000 bond. This he quickly forfeited, fleeing the country for Mexico. In high dudgeon, the Attorney-General of the United States pronounced his claims "the most stupendous fraud—the greatest in atrocity as well as in magnitude—ever perpetrated since the beginning of the world."

Comparable in its audacity was the Santillan claim to three square leagues at the heart of San Francisco, allegedly awarded in 1846 to a mendicant parish priest named José Santillan. A company of Eastern buyers, called the Philadelphia Association, had later purchased this claim. The organization planned to develop the land for business expansion, as soon as the claim was confirmed by the Land Commission. However, to its consternation, local residents whose holdings were threatened appealed to the United States Supreme Court, and in 1851 the Santillan claim was invalidated. This reversal of legal title contributed to an atmosphere of grave skepticism over the authenticity of such claims. As late as 1886, however, the deluded trustees of the old Santillan claim had not yet abandoned hopes of compensation for their loss.

Continued Squatter Activity

American squatters were especially numerous around the bustling new city of Sacramento. When Sam Brannan and other business-men took measures to oust them, squatter leaders promptly responded that the land was presumed to be public and that any settler would be protected by law. Nothing but superior force could dislodge the resolute squatters, who continued to seize vacant lots in the middle of the night, build weak "ribbon fences" around them, and erect flimsy shanties in the enclosures. Further conflict was inevitable. On August 14, 1850, forty armed squatters attempted to regain possession of a lot which one of their party had recently occupied, but from which he had been evicted. Sacramento's mayor, who asked the aid of all citizens in suppressing the riot, ordered the squatters to give up their arms and to disperse. They refused to oblige, and in the riot that followed the mayor was wounded. Martial law was then declared and an extraordinary police force of five hundred men summoned for duty. In the hectic days that followed, Sacramento Sheriff Joseph McKinney was shot and mortally wounded, and several squatters were killed. Not until two military companies arrived from San Francisco were the squatters removed and order restored.

Squatting had also begun at an early date in and about San Francisco, and the practice was not discontinued until land titles were authoritatively settled by court decisions. Stopping the squatters, however, took years to accomplish. Scarcely any part of the city or county was exempt from seizure at some time by squatters. Some of the victims of the San Francisco fire of 1851 even fenced in their city lots while the ashes were still hot, in order to prevent their property from being "jumped" by American newcomers to the area.

Sometimes squatting was done for speculative purposes. There were, in fact, "professional squatters," who hired themselves out to hold possession of coveted land. The usual equipment of such operators consisted of blankets to keep warm at night and fire-arms to fend off other poachers in the daytime. This system was especially common in mining regions. A prospector could not leave his claim untended for so much as a week and expect to find it unoccupied on his return—especially if he had not set up on his property a clear, written notice of ownership, with boundary stakes. "Claim jumping" sometimes occurred precisely because adequate notice of site ownership had not been made.

Not all squatters, however, were scoundrels. Many honestly believed that the grants on which they had settled were not actually the possession of others. Thus they took on in good faith the backbreaking job of land development. Accurate surveys of grants generally did not exist, and most original boundary marks had disappeared or become unrecognizable. The original title to Rancho San José read: "A large oak was taken as a boundary, in which was placed the head of a beef and some of the limbs chopped." Sometimes an owner's cattle brand was burned into a tree. Such marks were quickly obliterated by nature and their existence was hard to prove. Further confusion arose because of numerous duplications and conflicts in the names and boundaries of grants. The *Californios* had built few fences and had almost never quarreled over boundaries. There had been no reason for disputes over land, which had been plentiful and of slight value until the coming of Americans.

As squatters increased in numbers, their votes were eagerly sought by politicians. In 1854, Governor John Bigler's annual message referred glowingly to "that enterprising and useful portion of our people"—the squatters. Even the judiciary evinced increasing solicitude for their welfare. In 1856 an astounding statute, entitled an "act for the protection of actual settlers and to quiet land titles in this state," was passed by the legislature. It provided that "all lands in the state were to be deemed and regarded as public until the legal title should be shown to have passed to private parties." In short, it was a piece of squatter legislation. This act was, however, pronounced unconstitutional by the state Supreme Court.

The Effects of the Land Act of 1851

The Land Commission had opened its hearings in San Francisco on January 2, 1852; it finally adjourned on March 3, 1856, having undergone a complete change of personnel during its existence. During that four-year period rancheros searched their homes for original grants from Mexican governors, ferreted maps out of the Surveyor General's San Francisco archives, called upon friends and relatives to testify to their long tenure on the land, and consulted lawyers—all to justify their titles. The burden of proof remained on them. They were at a disadvantage in other respects, too. None of the land commissioners either spoke or read the Spanish language. Claimants in southern California were further handicapped by their distance from the place of sessions. Rancheros mortgaged their lands at high interest rates to pay legal fees, made trips to appeal to Washington officials and agencies, and waited hopefully for confirmation of their titles.

The seemingly unending series of legal clashes provided much work for specialized law firms, among them Halleck, Peachy and Billings at San Francisco. These attorneys required large fees for their intricate unraveling of land-title problems, especially those involving vaguely defined, poorly surveyed, or overlapping boundaries; still other properties posed complex tax-delinquency problems. Supposedly "final" decisions of the Land Commission were repeatedly contested in both lower and upper courts. Numerous cases culminated in appeals to the United States Supreme Court. Legal delays ran into many years. Confirmation of the patent to the San José de Grácia de Simi Rancho, as an example, took fourteen years, or until 1865; and this was the first grant to be patented in what is now Ventura County after the Land Grants Act of 1851 became operative. In another case a claimant had to wait thirty-five years before he could call his land his own. From 1865 to 1880 alone, the owners of Rancho Palos Verdes underwent seventy-eight law suits, six partition suits, a dozen suits over the ejection of squatters, three condemnation proceedings, and other legal controversies outside the courts. Some titles were fortunately settled more quickly.

Litigation over pueblo land claims retarded the municipal settlement of both San Francisco and Los Angeles. The city of San Francisco answered several lengthy suits by claiming that, under Spanish legal tradition, it was, like every pueblo, entitled to four square leagues of land. The city received final federal title to its lands only after clearing up the already mentioned Limantour and Santillan claims. At Los Angeles, the city fathers voraciously staked out claims to four leagues square (considerably larger than four square leagues), but these claims were whittled down. In 1866, President Andrew Johnson finally confirmed that city's title to a tract of 17,000 acres. In the case of San Luis Obispo, and other small towns, the federal land commissioners disallowed claims to four square leagues.

Confusion over titles was compounded when squatter settlements were "platted" upon lands claimed by several owners. In several such cases squatters tore down fences, built makeshift shacks, and ripped out boundary and ownership markers. Knifings, shootings, and other forms of bloodshed and personal violence occurred whenever squatters were threatened with ejection from lands on which they had made improvements. When they received adverse court decisions, settlers organized themselves to influence the nomination of judges. Squatters, indeed, sought to form a new Settlers' Party to safeguard their right to land on which they had made improvements. They also tried to gain pre-emption legislation, both in the Congress and in the state legislature. Americans in California insisted upon the free public lands that their compatriots in Oregon were receiving.

There were prominent politicians on both sides of the squatter-versus-rancher issue. Among those who championed the rights of squatters were Governors J. Neely Johnson and John Bigler, as well as Senator Gwin, who had drafted the Land Act of 1851. On the other hand, Frémont, when a senator, and later, in 1856, his brother-in-law William Carey Jones lobbied actively for speedy confirmation of outstanding undecided land grants, some of them of a questionable and even fraudulent nature. Frémont and Jones, however, were principally motivated by self-interest. Jones claimed one huge grant and Frémont another, the latter of which was confirmed by the Land Commission in 1855. This claim of Frémont's, in the Mariposa region, was so debatable that its confirmation raised some question as to the commission's fairness.

Most historians, with the notable exception of Professor Paul Wallace Gates, have judged the Land Act of 1851 an unwise document. Professor Gates, however, points out that the United States government acted in consonance with "half a century of experience" in land decisions handed down in American frontier areas. Other historians remain critical of the government's failure to accommodate itself to conditions in a newly acquired territory. Some accommodation, one may argue, might have been expected of a supposedly superior system of law and order. Instead, the United States foisted rigid land-title examinations upon California's befuddled residents, who had only recently became citizens. Without knowledge of either American law or language, these native Californians were understandably irritated. They accused Congress, 3,000 miles away, of catering to voters who lived elsewhere than in the West. Congress was, indeed, preoccupied with the increasing tension between North and South; it still saw California as far, far out on the frontier, and considered Western problems only sporadically.

The fact that Congress could be pressured into rigorously sifting hundreds of land titles raised an unnecessary barrier between American claimants and the *Californios*. The sense of security once felt by the natives gave way to despair. Threatened sometimes by violence over land seizure or cattle rustling, the rancheros, unused to moving about with revolvers strapped around their waists, generally yielded. Law enforcement was not, incidentally, well organized in rural areas, and an influx of frontier "bad men," who could be enlisted by squatters, made rural areas dangerous.

Though the *Californios* theoretically had recourse to the courts, the law was often interpreted by squatter judges and squatter juries and administered by squatter sheriffs. The formidable array of power on the side of the squatters at times led to "squatter compromises" by which squatters could buy land which they frequently already controlled with barbed wire and revolver. Though such land sales radically altered the economic unity of a rancho, this was frequently the only way to accommodate self-invited squatters without actual violence.

A fairly contemporary assessment of all this confusion over land, that of Henry George's *Progress and Poverty* (1871), stated:

> If the history of Mexican grants of California is ever written, it will be a history of greed, of perjury, of corruption, of spoliation, and high-handed robbery, for which it will be difficult to find a parallel. . . .

The self-justification of the squatters does not seem to alter what Robert Glass Cleland once called a policy that "penalized legitimate landowners, often to the point of ruin, played into the hands of speculators, discouraged settlement and immigration, retarded agricultural progress, and by creating a resentful and disaffected landless element, served to produce a large measure of social instability."

The 1860's were the years of the locust on California's ranchos and farms. Land sales brought only temporary relief to the insolvent. Furthermore, a series of physical disasters combined to produce unfortunate results. In addition to a crop-destroying grasshopper invasion, came floods and then, in the middle of the decade, a period of bone-dry aridity. (Five thousand head of cattle were marketed at Santa Barbara in these years for only thirty-seven cents each, and the annual income of even wealthy American land barons like Abel Stearns fell to only $300.) Desperate rancheros tried to raise vegetables, to sell out corrals of horses, to rent them for plowing, to cut up cordwood for sale in nearby towns— anything to recoup losses.

All their misfortunes, sometimes magnified, cannot, of course, be blamed upon United States land policies. Personal improvidence, falling farm prices after the Civil War, and a mechanized agricultural system were also responsible. New and oppressive property taxes likewise reduced the fortunes of landowners, encouraging concentration of vast holdings in the hands of lawyers and bankers. Mobilizing their credit effectively, California's *nou-*

veaux riches formed relatively tax-free and tight land monopolies from whose deleterious effects the state took decades to rid itself.

In short, both native residents and incoming Americans were hurt by the confusion over land ownership in California. Public confidence in land titles was so shaken that for years buyers were well advised to exercise caution. No genuine title to land could be established in some cases until after the 1870's. This situation, incidentally, led to the founding of flourishing state title-insurance businesses. Californians, however, weathered the many frustrations over land titles. And their descendants have made real-estate development a major economic activity. But their success would not have been possible, at least to the same degree, if California's great ranchos had remained intact. The struggle over dissolution of these old Spanish and Mexican land claims is, in that sense, related to the growth of a more modern California.

SELECTED READINGS

An introduction to the land problem is W. W. Robinson's *Land in California* (Berkeley, 1948). Another book by the same author, though of more limited scope, is *Ranchos Become Cities* (Pasadena, 1939), basically a history of the development of municipalities in and around Los Angeles. Caughey's *California* and Cleland's *Cattle on a Thousand Hills* contain statements of the pro-California position in regard to the land struggle. An almost diametrically opposite interpretation is Paul W. Gates, "Adjudication of Spanish-Mexican Land Claims in California," *Huntington Library Quarterly*, XXI (May, 1958), 213–236. See also Gerald D. Nash, "Problems and Projects in the History of Nineteenth Century Land Policy," *Arizona and the West*, II (Winter, 1960), 327–340, Gates's "Pre-Henry George Land Warfare in California," *California Historical Society Quarterly*, XLVI (June, 1967), 121–148, and his *California Ranchos and Farms, 1846–1862* (Madison, Wisc., 1967). R. H. Allen, "The Influence of Spanish and Mexican Land Grants in the Agricultural History of California" (University of California, Giannini Foundation ms., 1932) maintains that the Spanish land grants did not establish a pattern for California's agriculture in the American era.

Earlier treatments are William M. Gwin, *Private Land Titles in the State of California: Speech in Reply to Mr. Benton* (Washington, D.C., 1851), and John Currey, *Treaty of Guadalupe Hidalgo and Private Land Claims . . .* (San Francisco, 1891). Indispensable to any student of the problem is Ogden Hoffman, *Reports of Land Cases, Determined in the United States District Court for the Northern District of Cali-*

fornia (San Francisco, 1862). Of similar importance is William Carey Jones, *Report on the Subject of Land Titles in California* (Washington, D.C., 1850). See also Henry W. Halleck, "Report on California Land Grants," in *California Message and Correspondence, 1850* (United States Congress, House Executive Document No. 17; Washington, D.C., 1850), and Royce's *California from the Conquest in 1846 to the Second Vigilance Committee in San Francisco: A Study of American Character* (New York, repr. 1948), 367–387. A general account of the land problem in the United States is Thomas C. Donaldson, *The Public Domain: Its History, with Statistics* (Washington, D.C., 1881). Numerous and sometimes polemical private and governmental pamphlets were issued during the uncertain period of land litigation. An interesting example is *Letters of William Carey Jones in Review of Attorney General Black's Report to the President of the U.S. on the Subject of Land Titles in California* (San Francisco, 1860). Central to this controversy is Henry George, *Our Land and Land Policy: National and State* (San Francisco, 1871).

The land problem and related historical events have also been treated in fictional form. A novel of conflict, reflective of land differences between the old Hispanic heritage and the new American way, is Muriel Elwood, *Against the Tide* (New York, 1950). Similar in theme is William MacDonald, *California Caballero* (New York, 1936).

21

California and the Union

California was one of the few states (Vermont, Kentucky, and Texas were others) that skipped the interim territorial stage of political organization. Its enormously rapid growth was partly responsible for its movement directly into statehood, and its population continued to increase at a prodigious rate—310 per cent by the end of its first decade as a state. At that time, in 1860, California had a population of 380,000, of which residents born outside the state outnumbered the native-born by two to one.

California's growth created an open field for ambitious Eastern and Southern politicians willing to migrate westward to fill a political vacuum. With President Zachary Taylor's election to the Presidency in 1848 the Whig party took over many Eastern governmental positions, thereby releasing a flood of unemployed Democrats. Some of these headed West. Among them was New York's Irish Tammany regular David C. Broderick, who subsequently sought to transfer that city's political ward system to San Francisco. Other shrewd politicians, bringing with them years of political experience, helped tie the new state more closely into the Union, although full "economic statehood" was not achieved until the railroad truly linked California with the nation.

Another of California's new political leaders was William M. Gwin, a native of Tennessee who became one of the Western state's first two senators. Both Gwin and Broderick developed small but loyal followings. In an atmosphere of relative political simplicity such men attained power partly because of the prevailing popular disinterest in state politics. In frontier areas the struggle for existence did not leave the ordinary man much time for political activity or public service. Most settlers were absorbed in the processes of daily life, mending leaks in their cabin roofs, lining wells with bricks, and fencing property boundaries. Nor were old-time *Californios* inclined to make politics their profession; not many were trained in public oratory, so essential in those days to political victory.

The New State's Government

After California's constitution was ratified, the first legislature met at San Jose in December, 1849, and Peter H. Burnett was sworn in as governor. He was an affable pioneer from Oregon, and, in politics, a Democrat. Burnett remained in office until January, 1851, when succeeded by another Democrat, John McDougal. Few of the early California governors were sufficiently outstanding to merit special attention. They performed their duties for the most part ably but perfunctorily and did not generally possess unusual capacity or color.

Among the earliest tasks to which California's early politicians turned their attention was the organization of her new counties. The former military governor, General Bennett Riley, had divided the state into ten districts to be represented at the constitutional convention of 1849. These districts were subdivided by the first California legislature into twenty-seven counties, through an act of February 18, 1850. There were certain changes made later in the counties: Branciforte County was changed by amendment to Santa Cruz, Yola came to be spelled Yolo, and Colusi became Colusa. Also, in response to growth of county population, a law was enacted in 1851 creating the counties of Nevada, Placer, and Klamath. Sierra, Siskiyou, and Tulare were added the following year. The boundaries of other counties continued to be redefined, until, in 1907, the separation of Imperial from San Diego brought the number of counties in California to fifty-eight.

Equally important, and somewhat more obscure, were the beginnings of party organization in California. The functioning of the Democratic Party in the state dates from a meeting of its stalwarts at the temporary capital of San Jose during March, 1851. Later that year a Democratic convention, meeting at Benicia, nominated a candidate for governor; this was John Bigler, who had worked at Sutter's Fort before the discovery of gold. The Whigs, too, were naturally eager to capture the governorship. Bigler's opponent, nominated by a Whig convention at San Francisco, was Pierson B. Reading, a former participant in the Bear Flag revolt who had worked his way up from the gold placers into political life. Bigler received the strong backing of his fellow Democrat, Senator Gwin, won the election, was inaugurated governor January 8, 1852. The legislative practices of the time, on the part of both parties, were often venal. Corruption generally went unquestioned. For more than a decade there was but slight change in the relative strength of California's major parties, the state usually continuing Democratic.

In 1851 the legislature failed, after 142 ballots, to elect a successor to United States Senator Frémont, leaving Gwin for the better part of a year the only accredited representative at Washington. Frémont, who had drawn the short senatorial turn by lot, had served as senator less than a month. It is not strange, therefore, that Gwin came to look upon California as "his particular preserve." The proslavery Southern viewpoint that he represented stood in contrast to California's "free state" admission into the Union back in 1850. Sooner or later Gwin's supremacy was bound to be challenged.

The Growing Democratic Split

Under Gwin's tutelage the next session of the state legislature was marked by persistent efforts to promote sentiment in favor of slavery. The resultant passage both of a fugitive slave act and of discriminatory laws against the Negro seem strangely out of harmony with the antislavery record of California. Meanwhile, David C. Broderick, one of the most remarkable personalities in the political annals of California and a Democrat vigorously opposed to these pro-Southern measures, was stirring up statewide opposition to Gwin.

The campaign of 1853–1854 brought a definite split in California's Democratic Party, Broderick now entering into alliance with Governor Bigler and denouncing the "Southern democracy" of Gwin. It was a sordid campaign, eventually resulting in the re-election of Bigler. (Bigler was also a political import, having been schooled in politics in Pennsylvania—where his brother became, like himself, a state governor.) Perhaps the most salient feature of the intraparty controversy was Broderick's cutting rhetoric, which was especially evident at the Democratic state convention of July, 1854, in Sacramento. There his faction faced Gwin's cohorts head on. Delegates of both groups wore concealed pistols and bowie knives, although no blood was shed. When the factions could not settle their differences, two conventions emerged out of the one, with each selecting its own candidates. By 1855 this rivalry between the two wings of California's Democratic Party had almost wrecked it entirely; not until the threat posed by the new Know-Nothing Party made cooperation necessary for survival did the two wings of the party extend token cooperation to one another.

In the middle fifties the strong Know-Nothing sentiment against foreigners, manifested first in California's mining days, spread with rapidity to almost every town and mining camp in the state. The controversial Know-Nothings concealed their tactics and kept some of their principles known only to a few. This secrecy was a far cry from the usual methods employed by political parties to gain votes, but it proved highly effective in keeping the Know-Nothing principles veiled. Not to have done so would have lost the party votes, for the Know-Nothing motivation was anti-Catholic as well as nativist. When asked what they stood for, they stated that they "knew nothing." Operating largely behind the scenes, this little-understood party, which used secret handclasps, signals, passwords, and a ritual which emulated the Masons, pumped for Oriental exclusion and for delays in the naturalization of aliens. It was also anti-liquor and Bible-quoting, persisting in its power in California long after its strength dwindled elsewhere.

The Know-Nothings had first been successful in a San Francisco local election. Although the party had not in 1851 openly participated in any state campaign, it did wield influence behind the scenes. Its strength increased so rapidly that by 1856 the Know-Nothings caused California's Whig Party virtually to disband. That year the state's tide of "Americanism," plus the promise to reform the efficiency of state government, swept a Know-Nothing, J. Neely Johnson, into the governor's mansion. For a few years the Know-Nothing movement was potent in California.

The governorship, however, was by no means the highest political prize in California. Far above this office was the United States senatorship, and the real center of controversy during 1855–1856 was the contest for California's senatorial posts. Again, Gwin and Broderick held the spotlight.

The Gwin-Broderick Rivalry

The political rivalry of Gwin and Broderick, both of whom had come West in 1849 full of ambition, has probably never been exceeded in intensity in California. Their differences on national issues and the clash of their personalities made cooperation by these two Democrats difficult. Gwin, standing more than six feet in height, was the picture of the dignified and courtly southern gentleman. He was both a physician and a lawyer, as well as a politician. Dr. Gwin's followers in the Democratic Party, who held strong proslavery views, were known as the Chivalry Wing, or "Chivs"; Gwin himself was called (by his opponents) the "arch-champion of the slave-holding interests in California." Broderick, a bold and bitter fighter, was schooled in the politics of Tammany Hall. A self-made man, he had worked in New York as an apprentice to a stonecutter, as a stonemason, as a saloon keeper, and as a volunteer fireman. At San Francisco he became a smelter of gold and silver, as well as a merchandiser of these precious metals. Broderick was unequivocally opposed to slavery and its extension; without actually buying their allegiance, he succeeded in getting key legislators to follow his lead in this and other issues. His consuming passion was to become a United States senator.

Broderick first made himself political master of San Francisco and then built up a powerful machine in the state, ruling political underlings by a combination of methods — some reprehensible, some respectable. The Sacramento *Union*, which opposed Broderick, once called him a "Field Marshal" of politics, a tribute to his political skills. In 1854–1855 Broderick attempted to force the election of a successor to Gwin—a year before the normal date—and almost succeeded. Beaten back only temporarily, he soon renewed the struggle for supremacy with Gwin. The Know-Nothings, calling themselves a "reform" group, sought to take advantage of the serious rift in the Democratic Party created by the Gwin-Broderick fight. With a Know-Nothing elected governor in 1856, their next goal was to persuade the legislature to name a Know-Nothing senator. They almost succeeded in doing so that year, but did not have quite enough votes.

In the next few years the Broderick-Gwin feud literally dominated California politics. In March, 1857, both Gwin and John B. Weller, who had succeeded Frémont as senator in 1851, would end their term of office. Both sought re-election. Besides Broderick, other aspirants to the senatorial posts included Milton S. Latham, James A. McDougall, Joseph McCorkle, and Stephen J. Field, all men of importance. The political situation at Sacramento was tense. After Broderick had captured the approval of the legislature for one of the senatorial seats, he held himself arrogantly aloof from the deadlock over the other one. Then, after extorting from Gwin a promise that Broderick would have a virtual monopoly of the federal patronage (or the awarding of official positions only after consulting California's senators), he grudgingly agreed to support his rival's re-election. Gwin was finally elected three days after Broderick, but only because the Irishman had given the signal. Broderick returned to San Francisco a conquering hero. By sheer determination, Broderick had attained the office he had sworn to capture. Because of a political bargain he had become California's major senator, or so he thought.

Gwin's "Chivs" were, however, vehement in their denunciation of Broderick. The old feud between the two men and the factions they represented soon re-opened. Practical politics in California descended to a new low, and the state Democratic Party was split more widely than ever before. Broderick ran into opposition from other quarters, too. President Buchanan disagreed with him politically, disliked him personally, and refused to honor Broderick's bargain with Gwin concerning patronage. Instead, the President showered his attentions on Gwin. On the floor of the Senate, Broderick was discredited by his own sharp tongue. He charged Gwin, in speech after speech during 1859, with graft and the misappropriation of government money. Furthermore, Broderick was one of four senators on the national scene (including Stephen A. Douglas) who strongly opposed President Buchanan's pro-Southern views on the future territorial organization of Kansas. The national Democratic administration put strong pressure on the gritty Broderick to bring him to heel.

As charge followed countercharge, Broderick found allied against him the President, his fellow legislators, and a large segment of his own party, even back in California where he had been so strong. These all condemned him for repeated disobedience to the party and failure to cooperate with other Democrats. Despite close support from Senator Douglas, and despite William H. Seward's reference to him as "the brave young senator," Broderick's star had begun to set. He wanted to be a good party man, but on his own terms. Almost regretfully he announced on July 25, 1859: "During the first session of the last Congress I attended all the caucuses of the Democratic party, until the door was shut in my face. . . ." When Broderick went so far as to accuse the Buchanan administration of corruption, he was virtually ridden out of the Democratic Party.

The Terry-Broderick Duel

In the summer of 1859 Judge David S. Terry, a close friend of Gwin's and an unsuccessful candidate for renomination to the state Supreme Court, became incensed with Broderick and the

"Douglas Democrats." Terry was particularly irritated by Broderick's personal abuse of Gwin. Broderick read an account of Terry's subsequent vituperative descriptions of him, and responded with several similarly unflattering public statements about Gwin and Terry. These led to a demand for "satisfaction" by Terry. Broderick at first declined the challenge. Terry thereupon resigned from the bench and demanded a retraction from Broderick. Broderick refused; and a duel was almost inevitable in that age when "affairs of honor" were in vogue. Early on the morning of September 13 the principals of the most memorable duel in California politics met outside San Francisco, in the presence of about seventy spectators. Broderick's pistol went off accidentally and the bullet struck the ground from six to ten feet in front of him before he could take aim. Terry's shot lodged in his adversary's breast. Broderick fell to the ground, mortally wounded. Three days later he died, in his fortieth year.

Broderick's faults were now forgotten, and the duel in which he had lost his life began to have serious political repercussions. True, the Democrats at Washington and in California were rid of one of the most uncompromising personalities of California history. But because Broderick had been so out of sympathy with his party, his death caused many admirers to surrender their votes to the Republicans. Personally friendly with such Republican stalwarts as Edward D. Baker, Broderick had held views close to those of many Republicans and had been called a "Black Republican" by fellow Democrats, in an effort to stamp him with the label of disloyalty. Partly as a result of Broderick's posthumous influence, the presidential campaign of 1860 held more than ordinary significance for the political history of California. One might even say that the bullet which spared Broderick total exclusion from his party also contributed to the triumph of Lincoln in 1860 in California. At the national level tension between North and South continued to create a seemingly unbridgeable chasm; Stephen A. Douglas, standard-bearer of the Northern Democrats, became almost as obnoxious to the South as any Republican. In California, too, the Douglas and anti-Douglas Democrats struggled against one another. This bitter conflict, partly an extension of the Gwin-Broderick feud, temporarily wrecked the Democratic Party in California. The November election gave Lincoln and the Republicans California's four electoral votes.

The California legislature of 1860 was the last ever to be dominated by the Chivalry wing of the Democrats. After the Terry-Broderick duel Gwin, whose pro-Southern views grew distasteful in the North, became a political corpse and a liability to the Democrats. In 1861 he was arrested as a disloyal person and in the last years of the Civil War both Gwin and Terry went into exile in Mexico.

California Negroes and the Approach of the Civil War

Except for California's interlude of Know-Nothingism, the state's voting record had been Democratic since its admission to the Union in 1850. In spite of the influence of the Southern Democrats, its constitutional convention had determined that California was to be a free state.

Even before the Gold Rush, antislavery leaders frequently claimed that local conditions made slavery unlikely to succeed as a social system. Relatively few Negro slaves had been brought into California from the South. There were, however, Negroes in the original California pueblos and, later, a few Negro frontiersmen. Among the more prominent Negroes in California were Jacob Dodson, a volunteer with Frémont on his 1842 expedition, James P. Beckwourth, a scout and trapper who came west in 1844 and named Beckwourth Pass, and William A. Leidesdorff, Vice Consul to Mexico at Yerba Buena, who was of Danish-Negro parentage. In 1851 Biddy Mason, a young slave woman, crossed the desert on foot, driving a herd of sheep behind her master's wagon train. She later secured her freedom through the courts. Hard working, frugal, and a shrewd investor, she amassed a fortune in real estate at Los Angeles.

Various Negroes succeeded in striking it rich during the Gold Rush. In Brown's Valley, Fritz Vosburg, Abraham Holland, Gabriel Simms, and several other black miners operated the Sweet Vengeance mine most profitably. Others, among them Alvin Coffey, used gold dust mined in the High Sierra to purchase freedom from their masters. Coffey had to pay $1,000 for his own manumission and equal amounts to free several members of his family in Missouri. After accepting his money, Coffey's Missouri master took him back to St. Louis and sold him to a new owner. In 1854 Coffey, duped and re-enslaved, returned to the California mines; after several more years of hard labor, he earned another $7,000, with which he bought freedom for a second time. While California's 1849 constitution excluded chattel slavery, it did not spell out carefully enough the rights of freedmen. Not until after the Civil War did the federal courts fully guarantee those rights.

The census of 1850 lists about 1,000 Negro residents. By 1852 their number had grown to 2,200. Legally, none of these Negroes were slaves. The terms of California's admission to the Union prohibited slavery, long before Lincoln, in 1863, issued his Emancipation Proclamation. Yet California could not completely escape the side effects of slavery as a national institution. The California Fugitive Slave Act of 1851, passed at Gwin's behest, had provided that slaves brought in before the advent of statehood might be reclaimed and returned to slave states. This law was pronounced constitutional by the state Supreme Court. In numerous instances, however, slaves brought into California before its ban against slavery became effective were given their freedom by masters who wished to remain legally in the state.

The growth of California's Negro population is illustrated by the activities of Darius Stokes, a Negro pastor, who, by September, 1856, had founded fourteen colored churches in California. He claimed that the assessed valuation of property owned by the colored population of San Francisco that year was $150,000, and that three-quarters of a million dollars had been sent home to the South by Negroes to purchase freedom for members of their families. Stokes remarked that "men had paid as high as $2,000 each for their companions who were enslaved, to gain their freedom, and bring them to this State." Among them were the mining engineer Moses Rodger and mine owners Gabriel Simms, Freeman Holland, and James Cousins. One Negro had purchased eight of his own children and had paid $9,000 for them, having earned the money by washing clothes. Another, Mifflin Wistar Gibbs, helped his people with money earned as a San Francisco merchant. Mary Ellen Pleasant, known as "Mammy" Pleasant, in addition to running a hostelry considered notorious by some, fought for civil rights. Recorded in her deeds were $30,000 she donated to buy rifles for the John Brown raid at Harpers Ferry, and for trips south to help Negroes escape the bondage of slavery.

In 1855 the "Convention of Colored Citizens of California" was called in San Francisco to formulate plans for improving the Negro's status. This organization was responsible for repeal of harsh and restrictive laws. A militant newspaper owned and edited by Negroes, *The Elevator*, which was published under the motto, "Equality before the Law," became the voice of the "Colored Convention's" executive committee.

As national disagreement between North and South grew in intensity, a majority of Californians remained loyal to the Union. An antislavery group within the state included such prominent citizens as Collis P. Huntington, Cornelius Cole, Mark Hopkins, Charles and Edwin B. Crocker, and Leland Stanford. California was hardly able, however, to free itself entirely from disloyal influences. Through open act and secret intrigue Southern sympathizers tried to kindle the fires of secession.

Among the Southern residents of California who held fast to their sectional sympathies was Kentucky-born General Albert Sidney Johnston, Army commandant at the presidio of San Francisco. To him and other Southern officers the "coercion" of California into a state of war by the North was clearly unconstitutional; nevertheless, these men confined their protests to the verbal level. As open war threatened the United States, General Johnston's loyalty came into question and he voluntarily gave up his command to join the Confederate Army. Other Southern officers from California's Sixth Army Regiment followed him into the Confederacy.

There was another attitude of opposition to the Union in addition to the Southern one. Before Lincoln's inauguration there was talk of a "Pacific Republic," much of it by Representative John C. Burch. This legislator urged Californians, in case of a fratricidal war, to "call upon the enlightened nations of the earth to acknowledge our independence, and to protect us. . . ." John B. Weller, who became governor in 1858, also advocated that California, instead of siding with either North or South, should found on the shores of the Pacific "a mighty republic, which may in the end prove the greatest of all." In January, 1861, a resident of Stockton hoisted a flag intended to represent the Pacific Republic. This only touched off a general raising of the Stars and Stripes throughout the city. Union feeling remained strong. The dream of a Pacific Republic finally died with a joint resolution of the legislature, adopted May 17, 1861, which declared "that the people of California are devoted to the Constitution and Union now in the hour of trial and peril."

Though sympathy for the South was essentially an unpopular cause, disloyalty continued to appear in a variety of forms. Chief among these was the organization of a number of fiery clandestine societies pledged to aid the Confederate cause. Such secret groups included the Knights of the Golden Circle, the Knights of the Columbian Star, and the Committee of Thirty. The members of these statewide organizations avoided large meetings, only a few key officers quietly coming together to initiate new members and to plot their difficult courses. Advocacy of secession also broke out in newspapers, in public speeches, and in sermons and prayers from the pulpit, as well as at private celebrations of Confederate victories, and during harangues in barrooms. A few local papers heaped vituperation upon President Lincoln and his administration. Newspapers that went so far as to urge independence for California included the San Francisco *Herald*, the Sacramento *Standard*, the Alameda *County Gazette*, the Marysville *Gazette*, the Los Angeles *Star*, and the Sonora *Democrat*. The Tulare *Post*, which changed its name to the Visalia *Equal Rights Expositor* at about this time, printed such inflammatory editorials that the result was the destruction of the paper and its printing plant by the state militia. Federal postal authorities barred several other papers from the United States mails. Five "disloyal" papers were destroyed by mob violence. Pro-Union papers, however, were far more numerous and enjoyed wider circulation. Prominent among these were the *Bulletin* and *Alta California* at San Francisco and the *Bee* and *Union* at Sacramento, the most influential journals in the state.

After the firing on Fort Sumter signaled the beginning of the Civil War, Californian interest in the conflict grew especially intense. Though Californians were spared actual warfare at home, impressive pro-Union demonstrations took place in all parts of the state, with resolutions of loyalty being adopted at mass meetings in many towns and counties. San Francisco grew into a virtual citadel of loyalty. Its Home Guards, a sort of new committee of safety, conducted propaganda for the North, promoted enlistments in the Union Army, kept an eye out for conspiracy, and worked vigorously for the election of a war governor who would unstintingly support Lincoln. The citizens of California, having cast their vote for Lincoln in 1860, the next year chose the Republican Leland Stanford as their governor. Assuming office on January 10, 1862, Stanford achieved prominence as California's Civil War governor.

The War Period

During the war, to counteract secessionist sentiment by settlers from slaveholding states, the California legislature enacted numerous emergency measures. A new law made it a misdemeanor "to display rebel flags or devices." Illegal behavior also came to include "adherence to the enemy" either by "endorsing, defending, or cheering" the subversion or destruction of United States authority. Punitive state laws were likewise enacted "to exclude traitors and alien enemies from the courts of justice in civil cases." Secessionist dissension after 1861 at El Monte, Visalia, San Luis Obispo, Santa Barbara, San Bernardino, and Los Angeles was summarily discouraged by federal troops.

Meanwhile, Californians were being moved to new heights of

sentiment for the Union cause by such orators as Thomas Starr King, a vigorous Unitarian preacher, and Myron C. Briggs, a Methodist editor and minister. As many as 40,000 persons came to hear these clergymen at mass meetings held in San Francisco.

Although King lived in California less than four years, he was an extraordinary figure in the history of the state. His reputation as minister, author, and lecturer in Boston was so great that the members of the First Unitarian Church in San Francisco had invited him from a distance of 3,000 miles to fill their vacant pastoral position. After his arrival in California in April, 1860, King's philanthropic efforts and magnetic platform manner quickly swelled the church's membership and endeared him to the populace of San Francisco. But his most notable achievements occurred after the outbreak of the Civil War. King became a major spokesman for the Union cause. He contributed time and money to raise funds for the Sanitary Commission, forerunner of the Red Cross. Over one fourth of the money donated to this organ. ization throughout the entire country came from California. King's eloquence was so great that his supporters said of him: "King saved California for the Union." His lecture tours throughout the state also led King to a love of the Sierra Nevada. He had written books on the scenic beauty of New England and was planning to do a similar work on the Sierra when he died of diphtheria in 1864 at the age of thirty-nine. The state legislature and courts adjourned that day in tribute to King and flags flew at half-mast throughout the state. In 1931, King was chosen, along with Father Junípero Serra, to represent California in Statuary Hall in the Capitol Building in Washington, D.C.

King, of course, was not alone in promoting the interests of the Union in California. An equally significant figure, his friend Colonel Edward D. Baker, boldly affirmed that the state would be true to the Union "to the last of blood and treasure." Baker and President Lincoln had been fellow lawyers in Illinois in the 1830's, and both had represented the Springfield district in Congress. Lincoln, in fact, had named his second son Edward Baker Lincoln out of respect for this good friend. After he came West, Baker had joined forces with Cornelius Cole, editor of a small newspaper in Sacramento, to help publicize the Republican Party; the two men had campaigned especially actively for Lincoln as President and for Stanford as governor. Baker rode in Lincoln's carriage in Washington at the presidential inauguration ceremony in 1861, introducing the President on the occasion of his inaugural address. Later, as a Union colonel, Baker headed the California Battalion. He died in action at the Battle of Ball's Bluff.

Other state leaders, too, as well as many private citizens, enlisted in various military units. The "California Hundred," for example, sailed through the Golden Gate on December 11, 1862, leaving loudly cheering crowds behind at dockside. Five weeks later, after a trip around Cape Horn, these troops reached Boston for service in the Union Army. Earlier, another company, consisting mainly of native-born Californians, was organized at San Jose; its members were equipped with lassos, in the use of which they were expert. On April 28, 1862, the "California Column," a unit of volunteers under the command of Colonel James H. Carleton, marched to Yuma and then via Tucson into New Mexico Territory, too late to carry out their mission of forestalling a Confederate invasion of the Southwest. Despite the enthusiasm of these individual units, relatively few Californians saw active service. Conscription was never enforced within the state. California furnished the Union, in all, with a few regiments of cavalry and infantry, which served in Masachusetts and in Washington Territory. A total of about 15,000 men in California enlisted in the Union Army; many troops drilled at home-town armories and remained stationed where their military units were mustered into service.

Although only a negligible military contribution toward the winning of the war can be claimed for California, her gold provided indispensable financial strength. As a "hard-money" state, however, she did not at first gracefully accept national laws designed to increase the supply of money by making paper greenbacks legal tender for the payment of debts. Californians, reared in a mining economy and accustomed to gold and silver, did not trust greenbacks as a stable currency. Because of this feeling, the state legislature in 1862 actually declared null and void the federal government's Legal Tender Act. A remedy for California's embarrassing failure to cooperate in using paper money was finally found in the Specific Contract Act of 1863, a technical compromise between the state and the nation that made possible the use of paper money. In part because of this measure, California gold in considerable amounts flowed into the federal treasury, bolstering the nation's economy during the wartime period of unprecedented financial stress. The state also helped greatly to supply the Union armies with wool, wheat, and other materials. Most requests for aid from the federal government were quickly met, as was not always the case with other states.

The war hastened California's integration into national life in other ways also. In particular, passage of the Pacific Railroad Bill of 1862 by Congress was facilitated by the absence of those Southern legislators who had traditionally blocked adoption of a Northern railroad route. During 1863 work on the Central Pacific Railroad was begun at Sacramento, and a San Francisco and San Jose Railroad was opened for operation. On the political scene, both wartime governors, Stanford and Frederick F. Low, joined national party leaders in temporarily abandoning the name Republican; instead, they sought the support of all citizens under a Union Party label. Also, both endorsed measures championed by the national administration for the purpose of winning the war. Anyone at the state capitol who deviated from such loyalty was apt to feel the whip of censure. Lincoln's popularity remained so great in California that in 1864 he again received the state's votes for the Presidency. Once the war ended, the Union Party was dissolved and a more normal Democratic and Republican party structure emerged as the basic political framework.

The Postwar Political Scene

It is unnecessary to discuss in detail the year-by-year history of California politics following the Civil War. In an age of excessive materialism many voters still demonstrated colossal indifference to politics. At the rural level, ignorance of political issues often accompanied this indifference; the result was social lethargy. Only after 1875 did the picture change somewhat. Then a relatively few reform-minded voters turned from the two major political parties to new splinter groups. Denis Kearney's Workingmen's Movement, for example, began strong agitation for a greater share in political decision making. (This will be discussed in detail later.) Constitutionalists, nativists, vegetarians, grangers, prohibitionists, greenbackers, and even a Pro-Irrigation Party also emerged to make demands upon the legislature at Sacramento.

Few California governors and senators achieved national stature in the period from the end of the Civil War to the turn of the century. One of the exceptions to this general rule was former Governor Stanford, who represented California in the Senate. He served a full term from 1885 to 1891, and was re-elected, but he died in office on June 21, 1893. Railroad builder, politician, and philanthropist, Stanford had risen from humble origins to create one of the largest fortunes, political and economic, in the West. A legislator of relatively similar stature, repeatedly re-elected to the Senate, was George Hearst, father of the well-known publisher. Senator Hearst, too, died in office, on February 28, 1891. Still one other politican deserves mention, at least as a geriatric won-

LELAND STANFORD, CA. 1875. (By courtesy of The Bancroft Library, University of California, Berkeley.)

der. This was Senator Cornelius Cole—political fixture par excellence. Beginning with his work with California's antislavery leaders before the war, Cole served in both houses of Congress. He outlived practically every opponent in his remarkable 102 years of life, from 1822 to 1924. He had actually lived during the lifetime of every United States President except Washington. President John F. Kennedy had already been born when Cole died.

In the years before the turn of the century the Republicans were in the ascendancy; the Democrats captured the governorship and senatorial posts only occasionally. Both parties remained basically conservative and voters seemed satisfied to follow national trends rather than to create significant local ones. Except for the anti-Chinese issue, most public concerns were those of the nation as a whole. Among the prevalent attitudes were absorption in the free-silver and other monetary controversies, belief in a high tariff, distrust of labor agitators, and widespread apathy toward reformers. Hubert Howe Bancroft has written of this indifference to the idea of reform, that "To judge California by the history of the state and municipal politics would be to misjudge her." Bancroft was referring mainly to corruption, mediocrity, and bossism, but also, in part, to one of the dullest periods in California's political life. Not until the era of the Progressives, spurred by the dramatic leadership of Theodore Roosevelt, would Californians be decisively moved by the spirit of reform. That particular development, however, belongs to a later chapter in the state's political history.

SELECTED READINGS

For an understanding of politics in California after the Gold Rush see the previously mentioned William H. Ellison, *A Self-Governing Dominion*. The Gwin-Broderick-Terry fracas is described in A. R. Buchanan, *David S. Terry of California: Dueling Judge* (San Marino, 1956). Another biography of Terry is A. E. Wagstaff, *Life of David S. Terry* . . . (San Francisco, 1911). Donald E. Hargis, "The Issues in the Broderick-Gwin Debates of 1859," California Historical Society *Quarterly*, XXXII (December, 1953), 313–325, emphasizes that principles, as well as personalities, were crucial to the rivalry of the two men. L. E. Fredman, "Broderick: A Reassessment," *Pacific Historical Review*, XXX (February, 1961), 39–46, reaches a different conclusion. Scheduled for publication in 1969 is David Williams, *David C. Broderick: A Political Portrait*. Valuable early works are Winfield J. Davis, *History of Political Conventions in California, 1849–1892* (Sacramento, 1893); Jeremiah Lynch, *A Senator of the Fifties: David C. Broderick of California* (San Francisco, 1911); and James O'Meara, *Broderick and Gwin* . . . *A Brief History of Early Politics in California* . . . (San Francisco, 1881). A studious volume in the University of California "Publications in History" series is Joseph Ellison's previously cited *California and the Nation*.

Other articles that deal with California's political history of this period include William H. Ellison, ed., "Memoirs of Hon. William M. Gwin," California Historical Society *Quarterly*, XIX (1940), 1–26, 157–184, 256–277, and 364–367; and Philip G. Auchampaugh, "James Buchanan and Some Far Western Leaders, 1860–1861," *Pacific Historical Review*, XII (June, 1943), 169–180. Ellison has also written on "The Movement for State Division in California: 1849–1860," *Southwestern Historical Quarterly*, XVII (1914), 101–139. See, too, Walter R. Bacon, "Fifty Years of California Politics," Historical Society of Southern

California *Annual and Pioneer Register*, V (1900), 31–43, and Earl Pomeroy, "California, 1846–1860: Politics of a Representative Frontier State," California Historical Society *Quarterly*, XXXII (December, 1953), 291–302.

The career of John McDougal, California's first American lieutenant governor and its second governor, is examined in H. Brett Melendy, "Who Was John McDougal?" *Pacific Historical Review*, XXIX (August, 1960), 231–243. McDougal is sometimes confused with James A. McDougall, another but later important politician. Regarding the latter see Russell Buchanan, "James A. McDougall, A Forgotten Senator," California Historical Society *Quarterly*, XV (September, 1936), 204–205.

Civil War California is discussed in Percival J. Cooney, "Southern California in Civil War Days," Historical Society of Southern California *Annual*, XIII (1924), 54–68, and, in the same historical series, Imogene Spaulding, "The Attitude of California to the Civil War," XII (1912–1913), 104–132; John J. Earle, "The Sentiment of the People of California with Respect to the Civil War," American Historical Association *Annual Report*, I (Washington, D.C., 1907), 125–135, and Horace Davis, "The Home Guard of 1861" in *The Pacific Ocean in History* (New York, 1917), pp. 363–372; Helen B. Walter, "Confederates in Southern California," Historical Society of Southern California *Quarterly*, XXXV (March, 1953), 41–55. A Civil War Centennial commemorative issue of the California Historical Society *Quarterly*, published in December, 1961, contains Benjamin F. Gilbert, "California and the Civil War: A Bibliographical Essay"; see also Gilbert's "The Confederate Minority in California," California Historical Society *Quarterly*, XL (June, 1941), 154–170.

A general but rather unsophisticated account of the Western phases of the Civil War is Jay Monaghan, *Civil War on the Western Border* (Boston, 1955). Not much stronger is Oscar Lewis, *The War in the Far West, 1861–1865* (New York, 1961). See also Aurora Hunt, *The Army of the Pacific* (Glendale, 1951), as well as the same author's *Major General James Henry Carleton: Western Frontier Dragoon* (Glendale, 1958), which tells the story of the California Column's march toward the Rio Grande. Consult, too, Leo P. Kibby, "Some Aspects of California's Military Problems During the Civil War," *Civil War History*, V (September, 1959), 251–262. Relations with the federal government are discussed in Milton H. Shutes, *Lincoln and California* (Stanford, 1943). See also Edward A. Dickson, "Lincoln and Baker: The Story of a Great Friendship," Historical Society of Southern California *Quarterly*, XXXIV (September, 1952), 229–242; Shutes, "Colonel E. D. Baker," California Historical Society *Quarterly*, XVII (December, 1938), 303–324; and C. J. Stillé, *History of the United States Sanitary Commission* (Philadelphia, 1866).

The late-nineteenth-century political scene emerges from a number of books. Richard Frothingham, *A Tribute to Thomas Starr King* (Boston, 1865); E. R. Kennedy, *The Contest for California in 1861* (Boston, 1912); and George T. Clark, *Leland Stanford* (Palo Alto, 1931). Consult also such reminiscences as Cornelius Cole, *Memoirs* (New York, 1908), and Stephen J. Field, *Personal Reminiscences of Early Days in California* (San Francisco, 1880). See, too, Lauren E. Crane, ed., *Newton Booth of California* (New York, 1894). An account of the career of Governor Frederick F. Low is Robert H. Becker, ed., *Some Reflections of an Early California Governor . . .* (Sacramento, 1959). Regarding King see also Ann Casey, "Thomas Starr King and the Secession Movement," Historical Society of Southern California *Quarterly*, XLIII (September, 1961), 245–275, and Russell M. Posner, "Thomas Starr King and the Mercy Million," California Historical Society *Quarterly*, XLIII (December, 1964), 291–307. An account of the activities of the American Party, which originated in California, is John Higham, "The American Party, 1886–1891," *Pacific Historical Review*, XIX (February, 1950), 37–46.

The Negro, whose presence in California has been obscurely documented, is the subject of Delilah Beasley, *Negro Trail Blazers of California* (Los Angeles, 1919), as well as Rudolph M. Lapp, "The Negro in Gold Rush California," *Journal of Negro History*, XLIX (April, 1964), 81–98; Lapp's "Negro Rights Activities in Gold Rush California," California Historical Society *Quarterly*, XLV (March, 1966), 3–20; Sue Bailey Thurman, *Pioneers of Negro Origin in California* (San Francisco, 1952); Lionel U. Ridout, "The Church, the Chinese and the Negroes in California, 1849–1893," *Historical Magazine of the Protestant Episcopal Church*, XXVIII (June, 1959), 115–138; William E. Franklin, "The Archy Case," *Pacific Historical Review*, XXXII (May, 1963), 137–154; and Mifflin Wistar Gibbs, *Shadows and Light: An Autobiography* (Washington, D.C., 1902). See also Clyde A. Duniway, "Slavery in California After 1848," *Annual Report*, American Historical Association (Washington, 1906).

A view of politics at the turn of the century and afterward is available in Frank Hamilton Short, *Selected Papers* (San Francisco, 1923), and George Lyttleton Upshur, *As I Recall Them: Memories of Crowded Years* (New York, 1936). Gerald D. Nash, *State Government and Economic Development: A History of Administrative Policies in California, 1849–1933* (Berkeley, 1964) recounts how government agencies have stimulated economic activity.

22

Ships and Rails

America's first transcontinental rail system, when finally completed in 1869, became largely responsible for the modern economic development of California. Yet the construction of this transcontinental railroad was delayed through the efforts of its many opponents, among them various Eastern shipping interests. These sought to keep the nation's attention, and consequently congressional subsidies, focused upon the advantages of steamship service; they wished to encourage the impression that Western railroad building had little potential as the best form of large-scale transportation.

Transportation to California via Panama

After the settlement of the Oregon question in 1846, and in particular after the beginning of the California Gold Rush in 1848, thousands of persons had sought cheap transportation to the American West. Travelers on the East Coast were told that, for their fare of $380, they could reach California in a matter of weeks via Panama. Rather than spend the long time required to go around Cape Horn or to undertake the dusty, uncomfortable trip on the overland trails, thousands of persons chose this Panamanian route. In 1849, regular ocean mail service began over the same route. From New York to the Isthmus of Panama the mail was carried aboard vessels of the government-subsidized United States Mail Steamship Company, and from Panama to San Francisco by the Pacific Mail Steamship Company, also under government contract. These two firms and other steamship companies, including the Aspinwall and Vanderbilt maritime interests, clamored increasingly for government aid. They argued that the United States, in a strategic as well as economic sense, should look to the sea as its avenue to California, that the ocean routes were the best ones, and that ports like San Francisco could be fortified and made into unsurpassed gateways to the Orient as well as logical entry points to the American West Coast. These maritime interests, of course, had a considerable stake in maintaining intact their early supremacy over the sea routes to California.

They were not alone, however, in their concern over communication between the United States and her new Pacific territories; the issue had become a matter of national interest as well. In 1846 the Polk administration had attained from Colombia the right of transit over the Isthmus, whose neutrality was guaranteed as part of the agreement. A trans-Isthmian railroad was frequently suggested in Congress as stopgap measure until a canal could one day be built. The Eastern steamship companies, whose link with the Pacific would be improved by such a project, voiced no objection to that kind of railroad construction. Indeed, they lobbied in favor of a railroad through Panama at midcentury. Californians, too, took a strong interest in a Panamanian railroad

During 1848, a syndicate headed by John L. Stephens, William H. Aspinwall, and Henry Chauncey petitioned Congress for a subsidy to build the railroad. Although they failed to obtain this United States government help, the Colombian government made a route available and the American company began work in May, 1850. The route ran from an Atlantic Isthmian port named Aspinwall, after the major shipping firm that had lobbied for this road, to the Pacific port of Panama. Construction was difficult and hazardous; workers, victimized almost incessantly by insects, were exposed to malaria and other diseases. Progress in cutting a road bed through mangrove stumps and tangled vines proved incredibly slow. Nevertheless, by the following May, the road had been completed as far westward as the interior village of Gatun. The next phase of construction carried the railroad from there to Gorgona, about the middle of the Isthmus. Construction obstacles increased to such an extent, however, and the ranks of the workers were so thinned by sickness and death, that progress faltered. For a time, during 1853, work was discontinued altogether. Nevertheless, construction crews of the company, which employed a total of 7,000 men drawn from all parts of the world, reached a summit ridge by January of 1854; the remainder of the route led downward toward the Pacific side of the Isthmus of Panama. Near midnight on January 27, 1855, in a pouring rain, the last rail was laid. On the next day the first locomotive traveled from the Atlantic to the Pacific Oceans. The construction cost of the project had been $8,000,000.

The railroad trip across the Isthmus of Panama at first required six hours to complete, but was later reduced to three. Frequently as many as 1,500 passengers were carried westward by rail in a single half-day. More than 400,000 passengers and upwards of $750,000,000 in precious metals were transported over the road during the thirteen years ending in December, 1867. The bulk of this traffic was either headed for or returning from California. Upon the arrival of passenger steamships on the Atlantic coast of Panama, trains were dispatched at almost any hour in order to meet connecting steamships on the Pacific side. The same was true for travelers and goods going in the opposite direction. The regular fare for adults was $25. For a time the Panama link between Atlantic and Pacific, later only a minor rail connection, served Californians moderately well.

Completion of a more direct transcontinental line, however, eventually ended much of the need for this Isthmian route to California. Smooth operation of the railroad was also impeded by sanitary and financial problems. Its American directors eventually sold their equipment to a French company that later began to build an ill-fated canal, the precursor of the modern Panama Canal.

Inland Water Transportation

Once passengers had been brought to California by the Pacific Mail Steamship Company, they frequently continued their journey by other forms of water transportation. The P.M.S.S. Co. operations extended also to inland transportation. Along the San Francisco water front, riverboat captains corralled many of the new arrivals, taking them up the inland streams to their ultimate destination within California. This service fanned out from the Golden Gate to key interior ports, including the growing communities of Marysville, Sacramento, and Stockton. Utilizing a splendid system of natural waterways, graceful steamboat fleets and single muddy scows alike ascended the San Joaquin, the Sacramento, and the American.

At first a haphazard, independently operated traffic, this nevertheless important activity was bound to become systematized and better regulated. Individual operators were besieged by problems. The owners of the largest and best-known Sacramento steamboats, for example, including the *Senator*, the *Cornelia*, and the *New World*, found their vessels difficult to operate and maintain. Repair was often impossible due to shortages of parts. Because of the unfortunate and dangerous practice of racing, numerous disastrous accidents occurred. Under high steam pressure, iron boilers exploded and decks buckled, causing the bodies of passengers to be strewn over the surface of the water. In 1854, a number of independent owners of river steamers joined to form the California Steam Navigation Company. Until the railroads challenged its dominance, and hydraulic mining silted up its waterways, "California Steam" virtually controlled traffic in San Francisco Bay and along the inland rivers. From 1849 to 1855, the *Senator* alone reputedly earned her owners a fortune of $1,500,000. Her first year of operation netted receipts of $600,000. Shippers had to pay $50 or more per ton to have freight transported from 'Frisco to distant Red Bluff, the head of Sacramento navigation.

Some smaller competitors of the California Steam Navigation Company found it so powerful in prescribing freight and passenger rates that they actually welcomed the monopoly-breaking transcontinental railroad. In 1871, the company was, in fact, sold to the railroad interests. Thus, eventually, the Southern Pacific Railroad Company's sternwheelers competed with those owned by the California Transportation Company and the California Navigation Company. Together, these firms provided continuing mail, passenger, and freight service to the interior in the later nineteenth century.

Planning an Overland Railroad

The dream of a railroad across the North American continent had existed almost since the first railways were constructed in America. As early as 1836 an article advocating such a project appeared in the *American Railway Journal* under the title "An Atlantic and Pacific Railroad." The prophecy of Asa Whitney in 1845 that a transcontinental railroad would "change the whole world, [and] allow us to traverse the globe in thirty days. . . ." was not an idle utterance, but a statement based on careful calculation. This self-appointed spokesman for the project presented before Congress that year a scheme for a railway from Lake Michigan to the mouth of the Columbia. Whitney spent much time and money to promote his proposal. During the 1840's others came forward with various plans to connect the Missouri River towns with the new American settlements along the Pacific Ocean.

By the midcentury year of 1850 the expense of getting to California by sea averaged $400, and the trip sometimes took 120 days or even longer. Overland stage service also remained expensive, slow, and uncomfortable. Advocates of a transcontinental railroad pointed out that such a trip might be made by rail for as little as $150 and in only 20 days' time. This argument was made the basis of an appeal by Californians for congressional action. Obviously federal money would be needed in large quantities to complete so vast a project. Objections were widely raised, particularly in those sections of the country that stood to benefit least from a connection between East and West. Critics of the railroad maintained that the cost of construction would be prohibitive, with huge government land grants and loans being required to compensate the builders, due to the large financial risks involved. Others frankly doubted that a railroad could ever be constructed over the crest of either the Rockies or the Sierra.

Nevertheless the idea of a Pacific railroad gained increasing acceptance in Washington. The various deeply rutted and confusing trails to the West were by now clearly inadequate. It became obvious that both for purposes of hauling mail, passengers, and freight more quickly, and for defense of the West Coast, a good rail route was seriously needed. There was generally no disagreement that such a route should traverse the shortest possible distance, because of the tremendous costs involved. Also, a decision was reached rather early that the terminus should be in California, rather than in Oregon. But the question of the exact route westward was debated for years. Numerous routes were favored, the most heavily traveled trails tending to be considered most seriously for the ultimate choice.

During the 1850's debates in Congress over Western railroad legislation were interminable and baffling. Legislators had had little experience with the colossal problems involved; congressmen, perhaps inevitably, mingled passion and interest with reason and judgment. Many questions arose to block passage of a railroad bill. Should construction and operation of the road be administered by the government outright? Or should the railroad be built and operated privately? If the latter, should the project be under close government control? How far should federal and state governments go toward financial encouragement and direct subsidies? What kind of land grants would prove most advisable? As Congress wrestled with these issues, its debates were further complicated by the constant infusion of regional considerations.

As early as 1852, a route that swung generally southward through Texas, and then proceeded by way of the Gila Valley to Yuma and on to San Diego in California, was strongly advocated by Southern interests. This proposal, however, was quickly followed by others, and became only one of four that survived congressional debate. Finally, an appropriation was voted in 1853 to make explorations and surveys to determine the "most practicable and economical route." Various survey parties of army engineers headed West for this purpose, but months ran on into years, and 1855 the goal seemed as distant as ever. Even after the appearance, in thirteen large illustrated volumes, of the results of the government exploring parties (the compilation presented conclusive evidence of the practicability of several routes), there was further congressional delay.

The railroad cause, however, did not lack spokesmen to maintain public interest in the issue, and some of these were eloquent. The famed journalist Horace Greeley of the New York *Tribune*, who in 1859 made an overland trip to San Francisco, wielded an especially influential pen on behalf of a transcontinental railroad. In 1861, the outbreak of the Civil War pointed up decisively the necessity for the railroad and brought to an end all prospects of a Southern route. Military and political considerations now became paramount. It was evident that the railroad was essential to bind the Pacific Coast safely to the Union.

Organization of the Central Pacific

On June 28, 1861, three California merchants founded the Central Pacific Railroad Company at Sacramento: Leland Stanford acted as president of the company, Collis P. Huntington as vice-president, and Mark Hopkins as treasurer. In a few years these three and Charles Crocker, who had joined them in the venture, came to be called the "Big Four." Originally, their enterprise, however, relied less on their own efforts than on the almost single-handed determination of a young Connecticut-born civil engineer, Theodore D. Judah. In 1855, at the age of twenty-eight, Judah had laid out the rails of the Sacramento Valley Railroad, to serve the mining regions along the slopes of the Sierra Nevada. Although that railway consisted of only twenty-three miles of track, it spurred Judah's ambition to promote a transcontinental system.

By the late fifties Judah was advancing some bold engineering concepts, which he felt would make possible the construction of a railroad over the Sierra. For such efforts he was often ridiculed in both Washington and California, some calling him "Crazy Judah" and others accusing him of promoting the operation purely for motives of personal gain. Judah, however, had attained considerable construction experience, both in the East and in California and this background gave his ideas a certain persuasiveness. By personal lobbying in Washington, he was finally able to bring effective pressure to bear on individual congressmen for passage of a railroad bill. Also, it was actually Judah who, because of the chronic financial difficulties of his existing operations, had interested Stanford, Huntington, Hopkins, and Crocker in the railroad project. Judah's own line ran only from Sacramento to Folsom. Judah became chief engineer of the new Central Pacific Railway Company.

Congress, on July 1, 1862, passed the Pacific Railroad Bill. In addition to the four-hundred-foot right of way, a generous government land subsidy was given the railroad builders. Numerous sections of this terrain stretched off in checkerboard fashion on either side of the track almost as far as the eye could see. In all, the railroad builders were entitled to 1,280,000 acres of public land for every hundred miles of track they laid plus some three million dollars in credit for each of the two railroad construction companies. Both the Central Pacific and Union Pacific railroad companies were obligated to construct at least twenty-five miles of road a year, and the thirty-year government bonds (at six per cent interest) authorized for the railroad could not be redeemed for cash until at least forty miles of road had been constructed. Although the transcontinental railroad would be built by these two separate corporations, Congress stipulated that the entire road should be operated "as one connected, continuous line." Actually this was to be done only theoretically. The Central Pacific and Union Pacific companies remained separate entities. Both companies were empowered to and did issue the contracts for construction of their section of the transcontinental railroad. On the western end of the line the Central Pacific remained supreme.

Judah and his partners had also induced Congress to grant them, in the bill, a federal loan subsidy of $16,000 per mile for track laid across level land, $32,000 a mile in the foothills, and $48,000 per mile across mountain areas. Judah's partners, who were more adaptable morally than he, devised a plan to collect, for part of the construction, twice the subsidy they were entitled to. Their strategy was simply to convince Congress that the foothills of the Sierra Nevada began further west than was the case. This reasoning, which was duly written into the bill, in effect "moved" the mountains to Arcade Creek so that they extended within only ten miles of Sacramento—near the center of the great valley of California!

These young men, indeed, were shrewd, bold, and effective. Stanford was a 36-year-old dealer in groceries and provisions when the partnership was formed; Judah was then 35. Crocker, at the age of 38, was the owner of a dry-goods store; and Huntington, at 39, and Hopkins, at 47, were partners in a hardware business. In a few years all except Judah were multimillionaires. Judah, the true originator of the enterprise, died prematurely in 1863. He was reputedly en route to seek Eastern capital with which to buy out his avaricious partners when he was stricken with a fatal attack of yellow fever, which he had contracted on a previous trip to the East Coast via the Isthmus of Panama.

It seems likely that the original intention of Judah's partners was to amass the lucrative federal subsidies by laying down the road bed and track as quickly as possible. Crocker, who supplanted Judah as construction engineer, wanted ultimately to sell the company to others, who would operate the road. Crocker admitted in 1883: "We built that road for the profits we could make in building it, and when we got it done we didn't know what in the devil to do with it." Stanford too stated, years later, that he and his colleagues would gladly have sold their railroad in 1869 for ten cents on the dollar. Judah had apparently fought some bitter battles against his partners' desire to substitute rapid construction for sound engineering. Due perhaps to his efforts, the construction actually proved to be quite enduring.

The provisions of the Pacific Railroad Act of 1862, generous as they were, were increased in 1864. In that year the Central Pacific officers, together with the backers of the Union Pacific, achieved passage of an amendatory act which doubled the land grants and increased financial inducements. The credit of both these companies was thereby greatly strengthened, enabling them to find a market for their mortgage bonds. The personal enrichment of the "Big Four" was, thus, made possible by the government's generosity. Yet some sort of subsidy was inevitable. The clearly apparent fact that the enormous obstacles to construction of the railroad could be overcome only by vast sums of money, the pressure created by the war, and the inexperience of Congress in dealing with such a gigantic project—all help explain why the legislation of that era was so loosely written. It was natural, in an age of untrammeled business expansion, that construction of the first transcontinental railroad should have been left to private initiative.

Construction of the Railroad

Actual building operations were begun by the Central Pacific in 1863, antedating by a year and a half the first track laying by the Union Pacific Company. Building eastward from Sacramento, the Central Pacific had to ship its machinery and supplies from the East around Cape Horn, or via Panama, at great expense. Union Pacific crews, on the other hand, moving west from Omaha, were able to transport heavy supplies over the track they had already laid. The Sierra Nevada presented an even more formidable obstacle to the engineers of the Central Pacific than the Rocky Mountains were to offer to those of the Union Pacific. The California mountains, however, did supply timber for ties, trestles, and the long stretches of snow sheds required in midwinter—a resource at first lacking to the Union Pacific as it worked its way across the relatively treeless Great Plains.

In order to cut a roadway through the rock walls of the Sierra,

CHINESE CONSTRUCTION WORKERS ON THE CENTRAL PACIFIC RAILROAD AT "CAPE HORN," A STRATEGIC POINT IN THE CROSSING OF THE SIERRA CREST. (From a contemporary print.)

Central Pacific construction crews used quantities of picks, shovels, black blasting powder, mortar, axes, ladders, wheelbarrows and dumpcarts, in addition to thousands of laborers. Not only was mechanical equipment commonly employed today simply nonexistent, but also workers were handicapped by the fact that little was known about some of the wilderness to be traversed. For a labor force, the Central Pacific relied chiefly on 15,000 Chinese, whom Crocker had imported for this purpose. Crews of these expendable "Celestials," a name taken from "the Celestial Empire" of China, tied by ropes around their middles, chipped at the sides of Sierra cliffs seven thousand feet high for wages of less than $2 per day. After they had chiseled out a crude footing along the steep canyon walls, other Chinese would make use of this toehold in blasting out a roadway for the track. By September, 1865, the Central Pacific extended fifty-six miles eastward from Sacramento—that is, some distance into the Sierra Nevada. During the winter of 1865–1866 the only work possible in that area was construction within the tunnels. It was then that Crocker undertook to haul and sledge three locomotives, forty railroad cars, and material for forty miles of track forward across almost thirty miles of winding, unfinished roadbed, blasted out previously, into the canyon of the Truckee River. There lighter snow made possible grading and track work on the eastern side of the Sierra. Despite irksome delays, due largely to financial difficulties, the Central Pacific crossed the Sierra Nevada summit in December, 1867, at an elevation of 7,047 feet; and from there, the work of the crews was speeded by the less rugged terrain and the previously completed section of the road. They soon crossed the state line and began construction in Nevada.

The Union Pacific relied mainly on Irish immigrants for its construction crews. There was a lively sense of rivalry between the two companies, and it became especially intense when Crocker announced a schedule of a mile of track for every working day. His Chinese—known as "Crocker's Pets"—responded wholeheartedly to every new demand made upon them. By June, 1868, they had reached Reno, but it was not until early in 1869 that the most feverish construction occurred. On one day the Union Pacific's "Paddies" laid six miles of track; Crocker's Chinese countered with seven miles. The latter ultimately set a record with ten miles and fifty-six feet of track laid in just under twelve hours. That day Crocker reputedly won a bet of $10,000 because of their labor.

The national press contributed to the excitement over this competition. The following contemporary account depicts graphically the track-laying activities:

A light car drawn by a single horse gallops to the front with its load of rails. Two men seize the end of a rail and start forward at a run. At the word of command, the rail is dropped in its place, right side up with care, while the same progress goes on at the other side of the car. Less than thirty seconds to a nail for each gang; and so four rails go down to the minute. . . . The moment the car is empty it is tipped over on the side of the track to let the next loaded car pass it, and it is tipped back again; it is a sight to see it go flying back for another load, propelled by a horse at full gallop at the end of 60 or 80 feet of rope, ridden by a young Jehu, who drives furiously. Close behind the first gang come the gaugers, spikers, and bolters and a lively time they make of it. It is a grand Anvil Chorus that these sturdy sledges are playing across the plains . . . 21,000,000 times are those sledges to be swung, 21,000,000 times are they to come down with their sharp punctuation, before the great work of modern America is complete.

The government subsidy was, of course, based upon mileage of track laid, and each railroad was on that account alone eager to cover as much ground as possible. As the distance between the rival construction crews lessened, their competition became ever more keen. For a time grading crews worked within a few hundred yards of each other along parallel lines, since they could not agree as to where the tracks should join. Early in May, 1869, government railroad commissioners ruled that the two lines should meet at a little summit in northern Utah Territory called Promontory, 56 miles west of Ogden, 1,086 miles from Omaha, and 689 miles from Sacramento. There the gap was closed, finally fulfilling the edict of Congress that "the rails shall meet and connect, and form one continuous line."

Driving the Golden Spike

It remained only to drive the last spike. On the tenth day of May, 1869, on desolate Promontory Point, the formal ceremony was performed, uniting Atlantic and Pacific with bands of steel. Two bonnet-stacked, wood-burning locomotives faced each other, on the new tracks, one headed east, the other west. Several hundred witnesses were present, including four companies of the Twenty-first Infantry Regiment from Fort Douglas, officials of both railroads, a photographer, and nearby settlers. Following the driving of Arizona's spike of gold, silver, and iron, and Nevada's spike of silver, California's polished laurel tie was put in place and her spike of gold produced. President Stanford of the Central Pacific and Vice-President Thomas C. Durant of the Union Pacific proceeded to drive this last spike while the locomotive whistles screamed. Each blow of the silver sledge was announced via telegraphic connection to Eastern cities, where the event was celebrated by the ringing of bells. Stanford was the only member of the "Big Four" to put in an appearance at the ceremony.

It was a memorable day for California, as for the nation as a whole. San Francisco gave itself up to three days of celebration. The telegraph announced: "The last rail is laid! The last spike is driven! The Pacific Railroad is completed!" At Sacramento the bells and whistles of thirty different locomotives joined in a chorus with the bells of the city's churches and fire houses. Bret Harte, envisioning a future burgeoning trade with the Orient, wrote a poem to celebrate the driving of the last spike:

> *What was it the Engines said,*
> *Pilots touching, head to head*
> *Facing on the single track,*
> *Half the world behind each back?*
>
> *You brag of the East. You do.*
> *Why I bring the East to you.*
> *All the Orient, all Cathay,*
> *Find thru me the shortest way;*
> *And the sun you follow here*
> *Rises in my hemisphere.*
> *Really—if one must be rude—*
> *Length, my friend, ain't longitude.*

Now it took only seven days to travel the 3,167 miles, over numerous separate railroad lines, from Sacramento to New York. Successful completion of the largest engineering job yet undertaken in North America was a decisive event in California history. In 1869, one hundred years after the settlement of the Pacific province by the Portolá-Serra expedition of 1769, California's frontier isolation had finally come to a close.

Development of the Southern Pacific

As previously noted, the builders of the Central Pacific had not intended to become the operators of it. But they later found their greatest fortunes in the hauling of both freight and passengers. Not only did their gaudy Silver Palace Sleeping Cars carry thousands of excursionists and settlers West, but also, long lines of boxcars transported lucrative cargo. Large shipments of wheat, gold, silver, lumber, and dozens of other commodities brought the "Big Four" wealth undreamed of by Judah. In 1865, while still building the Central Pacific, they chartered the Southern Pacific Railroad Company and, by acquiring smaller branch lines, constructing several others, and closely consolidating all their enterprises, they eventually created a railroad system covering hundreds of miles from San Francisco and Los Angeles to termini as far away as New Orleans and Portland. Its auxiliary steamship connections would also link California with New York and Havana.

After the completion of the Central Pacific, the "Big Four" first extended their activities into the San Francisco Bay region, then established north-south routes through California's Central Valley and along the coast from Oregon to Southern California. The name under which the firm now operated was the Southern Pacific Railroad Company; the state legislature had chartered this company on December 2, 1865. To run its Sacramento line into Oakland, via Stockton and Niles Canyon, the Southern Pacific took over the construction rights of the Western Pacific Railroad and also began rail-ferry service from Oakland to San Francisco. The existing lines that were absorbed by the new Southern Pacific combine included the San Francisco and Oakland Railroad Company; the San Francisco and Alameda Railroad Company; the New Orleans, Mobile and Texas Railroad; the Carson and Colorado Railroad; the Oregon and California Railway; and the Sonora Railroad.

For a time the national panic of 1873 kept the company from building eastward outside the state. But, in 1877, it reached out from Los Angeles to Yuma, via Colton and Indio. Instead of joining the Texas and Pacific Railroad at Yuma, as was once planned, the fiercely competitive Southern Pacific pushed on southeastward until it reached Tucson in 1880. It took quick advantage of the Texas and Pacific's construction and financial difficulties to lay its own track over some of the proposed route of the rival road. In some cases only one possible route existed, and the first company to lay down its tracks gained the right of way. The Southern Pacific did carry out its agreement to join the Atchison, Topeka and Santa Fe Railroad; the lines were connected at Deming, in New Mexico Territory, on March 1, 1881, thus opening up a second transcontinental line. A third such route came into being when the Southern Pacific met the Texas and Pacific at Sierra Blanca, Texas, January 1, 1882; and another extension of the Southern Pacific's "Sunset Route" led from New Mexico eastward, absorbing the Galveston, Harrisburg and San Antonio Railway. This line reached New Orleans on February 5, 1883.

Behind all this expansion, of course, was the intense rivalry between railroads for the large amounts of federal land which were at stake. The Central and, later, Southern Pacific systems received over eleven million acres within California alone. Because railroad construction was so costly, the railroad claimed that this subsidy was absolutely necessary. And since the line considered a city privileged to be on its route, it also demanded county and city lands; the extent of a city's favors helped the "Big Four" decide what communities they would service. Enticement of the railroad required money, with which a community would buy the construction bonds the railroads demanded as security. They were openly accused of extorting funds from towns along prospective railroad routes; the Southern Pacific retorted that it needed this money for building bridges and overpasses, and for grading track beds. Scores of new towns came into being largely because the inhabitants of country crossroads and former sheep and cattle camps were able to persuade the railroad builders to lay their tracks through these settlements. Without railroad connections with the outside world a potential city was "as good as dead." Among the key interior towns that mushroomed because the railroad ran through them were Fresno, Merced, Tulare, Modesto, and Bakersfield. Some communities were simply by-passed and left to slumber. Los Angeles, today the largest city in California, almost met such a fate. However, after the city fathers allowed the Southern Pacific in 1876 to acquire an already existent 22-mile line to Wilmington, Los Angeles was ultimately joined to the railroad's network.

As the first major railroad in the state, the Southern Pacific clung tenaciously to its monopoly. Not until the eighties was that hold seriously challenged by the Atchison, Topeka and Santa Fe. Building westward, the Santa Fe reached El Paso in 1881, then (as previously noted) crossed New Mexico and Arizona, sending its woodburning locomotives into Needles, where it bridged the Colorado River. Next the Santa Fe purchased and rented various short lines west of that point. It entered Los Angeles by way of San Bernardino in 1887, then ran a new track northwest from Barstow to San Francisco. The Santa Fe had built, bought, and negotiated its way into California, but heavy construction costs, fierce competition with the Southern Pacific, and a general depression in 1893, led to its bankruptcy and later reorganization. In California the Southern Pacific was to reign supreme for many more years.

SELECTED READINGS

Early passenger transportation by ship to California is described in A. H. Clark, *The Clipper Ship Era, 1843–1869* (New York, 1910). In *The Panama Route*, already cited, Kemble relates the story of the Panama steamers. The difficulties of traffic over the Isthmus of Panama are treated in F. N. Otis, *Illustrated History of the Panama Railroad* (New York, 1861). There is no general maritime history of California, though inland water transportation is discussed in Jerry MacMullen's *Paddle-Wheel Days in California* (Stanford, 1944).

Basic to an understanding of Western railroad building are the *Pacific Railroads Reports* (13 vols., Washington, D.C., 1855). A one-volume condensation is George Leslie Albright, *Official Explorations for Pacific Railroads* (Berkeley, 1921). Among the earlier books on the railroad builders are Creed Haymond, *The Central Pacific Railroad Company: Its Relation to the Government* (Washington, 1888), a defense; Grenville M. Dodge, *How We Built the Union Pacific Railway* (Omaha, 1903); Lewis Henry Haney, *A Congressional History of Railroads in the United States* (2 vols., Madison, 1908–1910); and John Moody, *The Railroad Builders* (New Haven, 1921), a volume in the "Chronicles of America" series. Also useful is Robert E. Riegel, *The Story of the Western Railroads* (New York, 1926). A popularized account of building the transcontinental railroad is Wesley S. Griswold, *A Work of Giants* (New York, 1962). More specific is Carl I. Wheat, "A Sketch of the Life of Theodore D. Judah," California Historical Society *Quarterly*, IV (September, 1925), 219–271. An interesting sidelight is John H. Kemble, "The Big Four at Sea: The History of the Occidental and Oriental Steamship Company," Huntington Library *Quarterly*, III (April, 1940), 339–358. See also C. B. Glasscock, *Bandits and the Southern Pacific* (New York, 1929).

Other important works include John D. Galloway, *The First Transcontinental Railroad* (New York, 1950); Stuart Daggett, *Chapters on the History of the Southern Pacific* (New York, 1922); and Oscar Lewis, *The Big Four* (New York, 1938), an only partially satisfactory account of a subject for which the documentation has been destroyed or is missing. The Southern Pacific Company's *Southern Pacific's First Century* (San Francisco, 1955) falls within the category of authorized history, as does Neill C. Wilson and Frank J. Taylor, *Southern Pacific: The Roaring Story of a Fighting Railroad* (New York, 1952). Glenn C. Quiett, *They Built the West: An Epic of Rails and Cities* (New York, 1934), and Gilbert H. Kneiss, *Bonanza Railroads* (Stanford, 1941), are informative. On the Santa Fe three books are helpful: Glenn D. Bradley, *Story of the Santa Fe* (Boston, 1920); James Marshall, *Santa Fe: The Railroad That Built an Empire* (New York, 1949); and L. L. Waters, *Steel Trails to Santa Fe* (Lawrence, 1950).

23

Agricultural and Urban Growth

The economy of many agricultural states depends heavily on some single crop, such as corn, cotton, dairy products, or beef. California, however, as the nation's leader in agricultural output, produces more than two hundred farm commodities in sizable quantities. This agricultural diversity is due in part to a varied climate, and also to the work of the generations of Spanish padres who cultivated their lands carefully and introduced European methods of artificial irrigation. The garden and field planting that went on at the missions was, as previously seen, later complemented by cattle ranching, which for a time became the most characteristic of California's agricultural activities.

By the mid-nineteenth century California's agricultural pattern had become genuinely diversified. The consumption within the state of its beef, wheat, and later citrus and wine production, steadily increased. California's needs were not confined to food alone. An insatiable demand for lumber led to the development of a forest-processing industry along with planing mills and lumber yards. California's forest reserves, thus, constituted yet another of its natural assets. Her forest lands lay chiefly in the Sierra Nevada and along the northern coast counties. They contained large timber stands of Ponderosa pine, Douglas fir, spruce, redwood, piñon-juniper woodlands, and widespread chaparral and mesquite. California was, nevertheless, not self-sufficient in its needs for wood and came to draw heavily upon nearby Oregon and Washington.

As to farm products, the population increase after the discovery of gold set the pattern for California's future agricultural growth. The already-mentioned rising consumer demands determined what California's farms and ranches would grow. The early scarcity of agricultural products encouraged farmers to raise more basic foodstuffs, especially cattle and wheat. Two decades later, the completion of the transcontinental railroad not only created new markets for almonds, peaches, pears, oranges, cherries, walnuts, grapes, and olives, but also provided a large labor supply for ranches, orchards, and vineyards. The flood of newcomers that descended on the state from 1870 to 1890 became their own best customers. California's agricultural expansion ever since has, like her commercial progress, been rapid and flexible.

Cattle and Sheep Ranching

Before the close of the eighteenth century there were probably 100,000 head of cattle in California, and the numbers were sharply increased during the Gold Rush boom. Ranching, which had long been California's main business, shared this distinction only with mining during the middle years of the nineteenth century. From 1849 onward large numbers of both cattle and sheep were driven overland to California from settlements in the Mississippi Valley, the New Mexico pueblos, Salt Lake City, and other parts of the West. In 1849 the price of beeves reached $500 at Sacramento; by 1851 cattle were still bringing from $50 to $150 per head. These were the flush years for California's rancheros. By the early 1860's more than 3,000,000 cattle roamed the hills and the valleys of California. The influx of population had similarly accelerated the growth of sheep herding, which profited from the demand for wool as well as from that for meat. By the 1850's several hundred thousand sheep grazed on the state's ranges, and in the decade from 1850 to 1860 the number of these animals rose to over a million.

When sheepmen erected sheds and fences, and their lambs overcropped the ranges, trouble flared up between them and sensitive cattlemen. Fences impounded roaming cattle in search of free grass. With their ranges overstocked, cattlemen were in no mood to see the easy movement of their animals checked by barbed wire. In this conflict, which occasionally reached the stage of violence, the sheepmen seldom emerged victorious. The cattlemen

VICENTE LUGO RANCH HOUSE AND SOME OF ITS LANDLORDS AND NEIGHBORS, 1892.
(C. C. Pierce Collection; by courtesy of The Huntington Library,
San Marino, California.)

were more powerful and better organized. A few dry summers and
a few severe winters drove small ranchers out, leaving behind the
large cattle outfits, backed by Eastern, and sometimes English or
Scottish, capital. Sheepmen often fell into the category of small
operators, and as such suffered especially from the control of
water by the large cattle baronies. Nevertheless, some sheepmen
were able to form large sheepfolds or even corporations, and
these prospered.

It was, however, cattle that claimed the loyalty of most Western stock growers. A cattle range was sometimes even more valuable than a gold mine. But, in the middle sixties, a combination of dispiriting adversities arose to plague rancheros. New methods of farming and ranching were beginning to displace the old system. The pressure of the large cattle outfits made itself felt more strongly each year. Weakened by years of land-title litigation with squatters and with the federal government, they now had to cope with the problem of nationally depressed agricultural prices. Also, a series of oppressive state property taxes made it necessary for some rancheros to mortgage their lands, and high interest rates on farm mortgages drove them still further to the wall. Feeling the hostility of squatters and the pinch of poverty, they sold out their lands, to become day laborers for others or to join the unemployed in California's towns.

Complicating the plight of cattle owners during the sixties was a further factor, one that had been traditionally friendly to them —the weather. A devastating drought in 1863–1864 kept the California skies cloudless for months on end. The dust on the ranges in those years was so dense that it clogged the nostrils of dying cattle. The bleached skeletons of thousands of animals dotted the valleys and hillsides. Many hundreds of thousands of cattle, starved for green grass and water, perished in southern California. Abel Stearns alone lost 30,000 head on his various ranchos near Los Angeles. Sheep too died like flies. The price of land slumped, with southern California range lands selling for as little as ten cents per acre by the late 1860's. The lure of cheap lands, however, brought new settlers, and by the mid-seventies population pressure drove the price of land upward again—but too late to benefit the old rancheros.

In addition to the favorable price of Western land, occasional crop failures and the harshness of life on the wide and treeless prairies of Illinois and Iowa encouraged farmers to leave their sod cabins behind and to head for Oregon and California. A piece of their popular balladry recorded the appeal which California had for these Western migrants:

> *Since times are so hard, I'll tell you, sweetheart,*
> *I've a mind to leave off my plow and my cart*
> *And away to California my journey I'll go*
> *For to better my fortune as other folks do.*

These American successors to the rancheros set about to change California's agricultural life forever. They were men with an eye for new markets, close cooperation with the railroads, and improved beef-production methods. Over the years, California's cattle herds, roaming the ranges without supervision, had markedly deteriorated. As a result of inbreeding, they had become scrawny, mangy, and bony, and their numbers had been drastically reduced on account of the drought. Heavier, meatier strains began to be imported; new techniques of stock feeding and breeding were introduced from the United States and England, and fenced-in ranges became increasingly common.

The activities of some of the new landowners, in spite of their ranching skill, were not beyond reproach. Some of these men were of a type whose avarice and opportunism were described with loathing by the economic critic Henry George. Powerful combinations or individual land barons took over wide stretches of choice pasture lands, which they jealously guarded from encroachment. The cowhands of the Miller and Lux enterprises could boast that they rode over range—either owned or leased by the company—stretching from Oregon to Mexico. At the Rancho Tejón in Kern County, General Edward F. Beale ran cattle, after 1862, on some 200,000 acres of land. His operations resembled the highly integrated, efficient techniques of modern times and stood in great contrast to the leisurely ways of the California vaquero.

The improved methods of cattle raising which rescued that industry were applied also to sheepherding, with similar effectiveness. California's sheep flocks had reached almost 3,000,000 head by 1870 and 7,000,000 five years later. The breeding of California stock with imported Merino strains produced a superior quality of wool, for which the demand increased markedly. In the 1870's large profits from wool, which sold on the California market at twenty-five cents per pound, made it possible for sheep owners to build fine residences at both San Francisco and Los Angeles. Many of these men hired experienced Basque and Mexican sheepherders to tend their flocks while they lived in town. Although another drought in 1877 weakened the California flocks somewhat, the sheep industry remained relatively stable until the growth of population so increased land values that ranchers could make more money in other ways.

Dairying, Hog Raising, and Cereal Production

Little use had been made of either butter or milk during the Mexican period of California's history, the chief value of cattle being in hides and tallow. In a new era there gradually developed about the San Francisco Bay district and in Humboldt County a considerable production of dairy products, in response to the demands of the growing population. The state's output of butter for 1867 was 6,000,000 pounds, and of cheese half that amount. By the 1880's and 1890's skilled Swiss-Italian dairymen from Switzerland's Canton Ticino helped significantly to increase California's production still further, especially along the coast near San Luis Obispo.

Toward the close of the century, the existing dairies—which were then neither sanitary nor efficient—began to be supplanted by establishments that used labor-saving devices and modern methods. Some of the world's finest Holstein and Jersey herds were bred in California. Butter, milk, cream, casein, cheese, milk powder, and ice cream rapidly increased in demand, and dairies became widely distributed throughout the state. Stanislaus, San Joaquin, and Los Angeles Counties were dairy zones of special importance. Those dairies close to large centers of population, as at Norwalk, helped make Los Angeles County first in the nation in dairy production.

Part of the success of the dairy industry, as well as that of stock raising in general, depended upon the availability of feed for animals. A mechanical revolution in agriculture provided cast-iron and steel plows, mowers, reapers, hay rakes, and threshers; and horsepower was substituted for oxen to pull the new machinery. The introduction of commercial fertilizers also increased the efficiency and productivity of farms. Before the mechanization of California farming took place, Philip D. Armour, titular head of the national meat-packing house that still bears his name, actually left the California agricultural scene because of inadequate feed stocks. Armour had raised hogs in the Mother Lode area during the Gold Rush, but, finding that the warm summer climate and consequent shortages of water limited his supplies of corn fodder and pasturage, had moved to the Middle West. In the years following Armour's exodus, however, the tremendous expansion of corn acreage in California which was made possible by mechanization resulted in a corresponding increase in the hog population. In 1850 the hogs in California numbered only 2,700 head. By 1860 the figure had increased to 456,000 and by 1880 to 603,000.

After the Civil War the cultivation of crops for both human and animal consumption gradually superseded cattle ranching in value of operations. Among the most important of such crops were various kinds of grain, which often could be grown successfully without the expensive irrigation equipment required for certain other commodities. Wheat and corn, furthermore, were in demand on international markets and therefore had the advantage of being only partially dependent on local economic changes. California's climate and soil were splendidly suited to growing these and other grains in volume. Whereas the state had imported most of its grain during the Gold Rush, within a few years vast new ranches in California's Central Valley made it more than self-sufficient as a producer of oats, barley, corn, and other cereals.

By the 1870's California wheat in particular had become an important export crop. The state produced an unusually hard, dry, white grain, especially popular with British millers. Much of the trade to England, with Liverpool's busy Corn Exchange as its destination, was controlled by Isaac Friedlander, California's "Grain King." Friedlander managed his own means of production, shipping terminals, and global marketing arrangements. With the aid of the San Francisco financier William Ralston, Friedlander displayed real genius in marshaling credit. Aboard sailing vessels he shipped his hard durum wheat in burlap bags to Australia and China also, as well as to the wheat-short Mediterranean countries. Italians, for example, milled California's wheat into *pasta*, while the French made it into their distinctive breads.

In 1870 California's wheat production was already more than six times the combined total of the states of Oregon and Washington. Annual production grew from 6 million bushels in 1860 to 40 million bushels in 1890. By the latter year, during a period of extensive national expansion of wheat acreage, California ranked second among all the states in wheat production. A reorganization of California agriculture had made this increase possible. Large-scale, exploitative commercial farming was widespread. "Small-time farming," dependent upon the hazards of weather, price fluctuations, and market saturation, had become excessively risky. In fact, too many novices had turned to farming, and failure was inevitable for some of these—just as, earlier, many inexperienced forty-niners had tried their luck at mining without success. The individual farmer possessed few of the resources at the command of a Friedlander. In that age an increasing amount of capital was required for the purchase or rental of land, and for the new farm machinery that had become necessary for profitable operations. Many small farmers were forced to borrow money at crushing interest rates.

In the 1870's and 1880's, especially fierce competition—which the local farm Granges proved incapable of abating—developed between the large fruit, cattle, and wheat growers and these small farmers. In the case of the wheat producers this rivalry touched off a "grain war" over the shipping of wheat abroad. By cooperating with Friedlander, large producers could make more favorable

HARVESTING IN THE SAN FERNANDO VALLEY, CA. 1900 (C. C. Pierce Collection; by courtesy of The Huntington Library, San Marino, California.)

deals with middlemen, and railroad and steamship owners than could small growers. The big landowners, therefore, were able to show much larger profits. They bought out farmers who could not meet the competition, and their operations often came to resemble those of a corporation. Such agricultural combines eventually turned to raising new commercial crops, including rice, cotton, and hay, some of this production being in response to demands from markets outside California. The development of specialized irrigation techniques also encouraged crop diversification.

Not all large landowners were monopolists, however. William S. Chapman, in the 1870's the largest landowner in California, on several occasions actually encouraged the growth of small farms. Although there is evidence that he was also a corrupter of land-office personnel in the Fresno area, Chapman sold part of his million acres of terrain to settlers for less than $2 per acre and experimented with new techniques of cultivation. He introduced new crops, too, including alfalfa as a "cover crop" to be used in the feeding of cattle. By 1872, along with Friedlander, Charles Lux, and William C. Ralston, he was active in irrigation development in the lower San Joaquin Valley.

In this period the federal government also indirectly encouraged the growth of small farms, by making available millions of acres of public land for private agricultural use. Many parcels of government land, of course, ended up in the hands of the large agricultural speculators, sometimes in violation of the law. These speculators, who often set up agricultural communities with the hope of profiting from the efforts of the farmers who held land under them, usually did little to encourage crop diversification. There was a great risk involved in such operations, because of the heavy capital outlays required to begin them. The colonies were often badly managed and sometimes poorly located; and when they failed, both the individual farmers and the speculators were ruined.

Cotton and Silk

Although experiments with the growing of cotton had been conducted from time to time since California's Spanish period, the crop did not attain commercial importance until much later. It could seldom be cultivated without irrigation. Attention to cotton cultivation increased during the Civil War, but in the early 1870's only about 2,000 acres were planted in cotton in all California. The ordinary yield then varied from 250 to 500 pounds per acre. Cotton was cultivated on a somewhat larger scale in the late seventies. In that decade a short-lived "plantation" of about eighty acres actually existed within the Los Angeles city limits. But the production of this commodity was still quite limited. The raising of cotton depended upon favorable weather conditions, cheap irrigation, ample transportation, and the finding of large markets. These conditions did not exist, in combination with one another, much before World War I. Not until the second decade of the twentieth century did cotton production boom in California. Then new irrigation projects in the Imperial and southern San Joaquin Valleys greatly increased the acreage suitable for the crop. Cotton was being grown on 138,000 acres in the Imperial Valley by 1918, and on 90,000 acres of the once-arid stretches of the San Joaquin by 1924. The quality of this cotton was superior even to some grown in the American South, and yield per acre was frequently higher. Eventually, relocation of large automobile-tire factories close to the sources of cotton supply greatly boosted production. (Before the introduction of nylon, cotton was heavily used in tire manufacturing.) As a result of these developments, California became a major cotton state.

No such success story can be told concerning silk raising in California. In 1854 a French immigrant botanist, Louis Prévost, introduced sericulture to California at San Jose. Several years later the experimental production of silk spread to southern California, and in 1862 the legislature offered a relatively handsome bounty for cocoons. Sericulture, however, never really became more than a passing fad among a handful of growers; conditions in the state were just not favorable for the industry. Advertising brochures designed for tourist consumption continued to speak of California's silk farms, but few of these remained in existence after 1890.

Early Development of the Citrus Industry

From the days when the padres had introduced fruit trees into the mission gardens, horticulture was continually expanded throughout California, albeit at a slower pace than the raising of cattle or the planting of wheat and cotton. Fruit growers were long held back by the lack of transportation facilities. Remote from large markets, they found it commercially impossible to ship perishable crops eastward until the development of the refrigerated railroad car. Then, however, some growers began to prosper spectacularly by raising and marketing one unique crop—citrus fruit. This crop is still one of the most important in California.

California's citrus fruits include lemons, tangerines, and grapefruit. But the real symbol, and overwhelming source of strength, of the citrus industry is the orange. In the mission period orange groves were relatively small and undeveloped, producing pithy, thick-skinned, and often sour fruit. One of the earliest orange groves in California was that planted at San Gabriel Mission in 1804. It consisted of six acres—about four hundred trees—some of which were still bearing as late as 1885. About 1834, a Frenchman, Luís (or Louis) Vignes, successfully transplanted some thirty-five of these mission trees to his Aliso Street residence in Los Angeles, near the present Union Station. Other growers experimented sporadically with planting them around what is now the plaza area.

In 1841 one of these Los Angeles growers, William Wolfskill, a former Kentucky trapper, replanted a weed-wild two-acre orange grove that he had recently acquired. His operations became so successful that he eventually expanded his holdings to seventy acres. Other Los Angeles growers also expanded and, by 1872, there were 35,000 orange trees in that county. Wolfskill's son sent the first trainload of oranges eastward to Saint Louis in 1877, soon after the Southern Pacific Railroad made its services available to Los Angeles. The freight charges for the shipment were $500. The fruit arrived in good condition and, because Wolfskill made a good profit, he sent other carloads to the East. His "export approach" to orange marketing, of course, depended heavily on the new rail facilities. The possibilities of advertising, which were just beginning to be realized, also proved a boon to orange growers. Wolfskill disposed of one crop for $23,000, a fact that induced other growers in southern California to expand their acreages considerably.

The most substantial experimentation in the large-scale cultivation of oranges occurred at Riverside. There in September, 1870, Judge John Wesley North, who had served as President Lincoln's Surveyor General and who, as a New York speculator, had later been chased out of Tennessee by the Ku Klux Klan, bought four thousand acres of barren land on credit. Some of this hilly terrain was virtual desert, covered only by occasional cacti, agave plants, and blooming yucca. North carried on a vigorous promotional campaign to attract settlers to the sandy tract. His project resembled in many ways the shepherded migration arranged almost simultaneously by Nathan C. Meeker and Horace Greeley to Greeley, Colorado, also a planned agricultural colony. In cooperation with the transcontinental railroads, which arranged special low fares, North was successful in bringing many immigrants to California from Michigan and Iowa. Most of them, however, decided that they liked the greener portions of California. A few undiscouraged settlers nevertheless settled at Riverside, and these began, in the spring of 1871, to plant thousands of orange seedlings. By cooperative irrigation, they hoped to make their desert land bloom like a rose. Among the settlers in North's agricultural colony were an Eastern couple whose activities would, indeed, drastically alter the course of California's still-infant orange industry.

To the agricultural pioneer Luther Calvin Tibbets and his wife Eliza belongs the credit for introducing, in 1873, the new Washington Navel variety of oranges to California. This stock had originally been sent from Bahia, Brazil, to the United States Department of Agriculture in Washington—hence its name. Under the care of Mrs. Tibbets, the tiny cuttings she and her husband had brought to California grew to maturity and produced a meaty, juicy, flavorful, seedless orange. The fruit attracted immediate attention at the first of a series of annual citrus fairs at Riverside. The two Tibbets trees became the parent stock for whole orange groves, as heavy demands for these oranges resulted in frenzied planting throughout the 1880's. California's climate and soil seemed especially suited to the Washington Navel, and growers won an increasing number of state, national, and even international prizes for the quality of their fruit.

Eventually orange growing spread widely throughout Los Angeles, Riverside, Orange, San Bernardino, San Diego, Ventura, and Santa Barbara Counties. Trees were also planted in the Imperial, Coachella, and Sacramento Valleys, as far northward as Oroville and Chico. The fruit of northern trees, however, was usually not so sweet as that grown in sunnier southern counties.

In the early days of the orange industry there was no adequate crop-inspection or fruit-quarantine system. As a result, a number of destructive insects were introduced through nursery stock imported from various parts of the world. The "cottony cushion scale," for example, came to California from Australia in 1868. In the next twenty years it spread throughout the orchards of southern California. So serious was the effect of this pest that the orange industry in Los Angeles County was at one point threatened with extinction. In 1888 the United States Department of Agriculture sent a special investigator to Australia to study the habits of the cottony cushion scale in its native land. The following year a small ladybird beetle (*Novius cardinalis*), which vigorously attacked the scale, was introduced into California. This Australian ladybug, as it is popularly called, not only checked the spread of the cottony cushion scale but in some localities almost exterminated it. As a consequence, in 1891 orange shipments from Los Angeles County increased spectacularly from 781 to 2,212 railroad carloads.

A second disease, black scale, also seriously damaged the citrus industry. In addition, sooty mold caused great decay among individual trees. To fight both the mold and the black scale, growers had to wash tree trunks thoroughly. About 1901, they turned toward a relatively inexpensive new technique—the spraying of orchards with distillate oil. This proved less effective, however, than fumigation, then considered to be the best protection against diseases affecting orange trees. Growers have found no better remedy to this day.

Another hazard to the orange industry, and one of the largest, was frost. In the winter months temperatures sometimes fall below freezing in California's orange groves. Protection against frost was found in the form of oil heaters burning cheap crude oil. Nearby city dwellers, however, whose house furnishings, draperies, and rugs were sometimes covered with soot from the oil burners, complained bitterly. Eventually, the orchards were protected against cold damage by wind machines, which keep air currents in motion to prevent frost.

The Increasing Success of Citriculture

Oranges soon came to be planted on such a scale by many growers that operations the size of Wolfskill's were considered small. One of the industry's primary concerns was the quest for larger markets. To absorb increased production, new consumers had to be found, inside as well as outside California; more efficient means of servicing these customers were another necessity. As long as each grower attempted to market his own fruit, he remained easy prey to commission agents and speculators who secured rebates from railroad companies. The larger the grower's crop, the more indebted he became to these middlemen and to packers by the end of a growing season.

After 1893 growers formed a loose cooperative. marketing organization. Though not entirely satisfactory, this was a great improvement over old methods of marketing. It prepared the way for still another organization, founded in 1895 as the Southern California Fruit Growers Exchange. Immediately this exchange began to handle 32 per cent of California's total orange shipments eastward. In time the exchange was shipping most of California's annual citrus crop. On March 27, 1905, an even more important cooperative was incorporated as a successor to the Southern California Fruit Growers Exchange. This was the California Fruit Growers Exchange, which proceeded to make cooperative marketing general throughout the state, rather than only in southern California. Its trade name "Sunkist" was now used in the most vigorous advertising campaign the orange industry had yet attempted.

The California citrus industry, in fact, now set about to change the American breakfast diet. Specially decorated trains, which dispensed oranges at whistlestops in the Middle West, gaudy advertising billboards, free orange wrappers and spoons, and essay and poetry contests all helped carry the message of California's "golden fruit" eastward. As a result of this campaign a glass of orange juice, or sliced oranges or grapefruits, were being widely adopted as partial substitutes for such starch and fat staples as buckwheat cakes, bacon, ham, porridge, and waffles. The orange became identified with California, as the slogan "Oranges for health; California for wealth" attested. The song "It's Always Orange Day in California," from Oliver Morosco's musical "Canary Cottage" (1914), runs:

California, you were a Golden Country
  Long before a man set foot on you.
California, you had your Golden Poppies
  When Cabrillo came in fifteen forty-two.

California, you had your Golden Mountains
  Back in eighteen forty-nine.
And you've still a Golden plume,
  For you wear a Golden bloom of oranges all the time.

CHORUS

It's always orange day in California,
  Forget your winter snow,
  Come out and see them grow
The Golden sun is here to warm you
  For every Golden fruit there's a Golden Heart to boot

Become a Booster—We'll make you used to the Golden climate.
So hop a train, gol darn ya, and come out to California
  On Golden orange day.
It's always orange day in California.

California's chambers of commerce, the Los Angeles All-Year Club, and dozens of other booster organizations soon joined in the advertising campaign begun by the citrus industry.

The California Fruit Growers Exchange also experimented with new methods of production as a means of aiding the growers who belonged to it. Many improvements resulted from Exchange encouragement of individual enterprise in this respect. Success with the Valencia orange variety can be ascribed, in large part, to a Fullerton grower, C. C. Chapman. He found that his trees were such heavy bearers that they almost tore themselves to pieces by their production of fruit. Other growers who faced the same problem had disgustedly sunk much of their profits into propping up the overloaded limbs of their Valencia trees. Chapman worked out a system of pruning that checked rank growth and enabled

ORANGE GROVES IN THE 1920's. (From the author's collection.)

his trees to carry a greater burden without damage to each tree.

Chapman was responsible for other innovations as well. It was a general custom among growers to pay pickers and packers by the box. To forestall hurried and careless handling of his oranges, Chapman stationed himself among his men and began to pay crews by the day. His presence among them set high fruit-grading and packing practices. He inaugurated fruit-inspection techniques that were a forerunner of the modern packing-house assembly line. Prevention of the bruising of fruit not only enriched Chapman; it also led to the discovery that blue mold could be controlled by wrapping oranges in paper, which meant greater profits for the entire orange industry.

Commercial introduction of the Eureka and Lisbon varieties of lemons further rounded out the development of California citriculture. The Eureka lemon, native to Sicily and introduced into Los Angeles about 1870 by C. R. Workman, is comparatively free from

363

thorns, and has a tendency to early bearing, continuous blooming, and the "setting" of the fruit on the very tips of its branches throughout each year. The Lisbon lemon bears fruit uniformly throughout the tree, and its heavy foliage protects the fruit from sunburn. Maturation of its largest crop in the winter also makes this tree attractive. Because of the superiority of these two species of lemons, and because of their particular climatic needs (warm days and cold nights), California has long produced almost 100 per cent of the lemons grown in the United States.

Grapefruit production, however, experienced steadily increasing competition from Florida and Arizona. In recent years California has done well to produce 15 per cent of the total United States crop. Unlike the lemon, the grapefruit tree requires a warm, uniform night temperature; in the Texas and Mexican Gulf Coastal regions the climate approximates the desired tropical conditions more closely than is the case in California.

California thus owes its success in citriculture to the development of specialized growing and marketing methods, to favorable climatic combinations, and to alert, cooperative growers. Among those attracted to become growers were numerous retired business or professional people from the East and Middle West. Prominent people who had lost their health seemed especially attracted to the management of orange groves. A few also became amateur, and later professional, beekeepers. A new life in California's sunshine and dry air often proved restorative and rewarding. Such folk brought needed capital to the state's agriculture, along with their business abilities. Not infrequently they created a second financial fortune out West. Many of these "retired" city dwellers, who built fine residences amid their orange groves, typified in their very persons the slogan "Oranges for health; California for wealth."

Varied Crops in Varied Places

Within the rolling spurs of the Coast Range and between the Sierra and the sea lie many of the most fertile valleys of California. Among these garden spots are the Napa, Livermore, Santa Clara–Santa Rosa, Salinas, San Luis, Santa Maria, Santa Inez, Santa Clara of the South, San Bernardino, and San Fernando Valleys. In such fertile coastal areas some of California's most characteristic crops are grown. One of these is olives, whose cultivation dates from the Spanish period. After José de Gálvez saw to it that cuttings from olive trees and crude farm implements were shipped to California from New Spain, the production of both black and green olives began to flourish. By the end of the eighteenth century San Diego Mission alone had an olive grove consisting of more than five hundred trees. Olive oil, once called locally *aceite de comer*, which means edible oil, has been produced in California uninterruptedly for at least 150 years. La Mirada became an olive grove center, as did Sylmar in the San Fernando Valley, where a 2,000-acre grove was advertised as the largest in the world. The state's current output of olives is more than 50,000 tons per year.

Like olives, walnuts were first cultivated in California by the Spanish padres. Rancheros were not ordinarily growers of tree crops. Vallejo's estate at Sonoma—"Lachryma Montis"—was an exception to the relatively tree-barren ranchos elsewhere; and the Camulos Rancho near Ventura also grew numerous fruits and vegetables before the American conquest. Following secularization of the missions, the groves of those establishments fell into disuse, and many trees died. Pruning, cultivation, and irrigation later restored a few mission trees to their former vigor, but it was basically a new fruit industry that emerged under American rule. In 1854 French prunes were successfully introduced into the Santa Clara Valley, which also became the world's chief producer of Italian prunes. In 1867 at Santa Barbara the soft-shell walnut was planted commercially, and at Los Angeles, in 1873, William Wolfskill and Luís Vignes replanted the English walnut on a similar scale. This walnut, once called the Madeira nut, or Persian walnut, forms the basis of California's present nut crop, which accounts for almost 100 per cent of the nation's walnuts. California still also produces virtually all the almonds grown in the United States.

Enthusiasm over the size and quality of the state's agricultural products sometimes led Californians into rapturous descriptions that seemed unbelievable to outsiders. In his book, *The Resources of California* (1863), John S. Hittell wrote of a field of one hundred acres which, in 1853, produced 90,000 bushels of barley. He described potatoes that weighed four to seven pounds each, cabbages seven feet wide, and onions twenty-two inches in circumference. Hittell also claimed he saw a three-year-old red beet that weighed 118 pounds and was five feet long, in addition to a tomato twenty-six inches in circumference. Eastern readers were justifiably skeptical.

As previously noted, however, it is a fact that California is without a close rival in horticultural production among the states. In addition to such fruit crops as peaches, cherries, apples (principally at Sebastapol and Banning), apricots, pears, grapes, and plums, in the production of most of which California ranks first nationally, a number of vegetables have been grown in significant quantities since the late nineteenth century. One of the factors in this agricultural development has been the work of such pioneer botanists as Luther Burbank, who from 1875 until his death in 1926 carried on valuable experiments with novel garden crops at Santa Rosa. Burbank's efforts, the details of which are recounted in his autobiography, *The Harvest of the Years* (1927), made possible the increased production of many vegetables. Tomatoes, lettuce, cauliflower, carrots, alfalfa, sugar beets, celery, and potatoes found new farmers and new markets. Accompanying California's burgeoning agricultural productivity was the development of a large canning industry; such trade names as Del Monte, Iris, and (in the case of sugar packaging) Spreckels became and have remained familiar in thousands of households. The growth also of a hatchery industry at Petaluma and in the San Fernando Valley near Los Angeles (until twentieth-century tract-housing developments began to eradicate chicken farms) occurred during this period. Following the example of the orange industry, cooperative marketing and packing exchanges were established by a variety of livestock, vegetable, and fruit producers. But these developments characterized California agriculture even more after the turn of the century.

"Vines in the Sun"

An important and colorful part of the agricultural history of California has been the development of its wine industry. A fortunate combination of climate and soil, particularly in northern California, gave viticulture a propitious start. And Europeans skilled in the care of vines arrived early in the region. The work of these patient vineyardists and wine makers has resulted in a considerable contribution to the state's economy. Today, more than 90 per cent of the United States grape crop and most of the wine production comes from California.

The industry has a long and honorable history, not only in California. In the Bible the Apostle Paul offers Timothy the following advice: "Drink no longer water, but use a little wine for thy stomach's sake and thine often infirmities." In 1770, the year after the first Franciscans arrived in California, the missionaries, following this advice, set out a small patch of grape cuttings at San Diego. Vines of the European *vitis vinifera* stock were also planted at Missions San Gabriel, Santa Barbara, and San Luís Obispo, where they bore grapes for over a hundred years. The first vineyard planted at San Gabriel contained three thousand such vines. This stock, known as the *Vina Madre* (Mother Vine) or the "Mission variety," provided cuttings which became the basis of many of California's earliest vineyards. Although the Spanish padres also planted orchards, wine, used in the celebration of the mass, was for them even more of a necessity than fruit. But their methods were crude and, by today's standards, their product was inferior.

Thus the California wine industry was started by Spaniards; other foreigners, however, later participated in its development. In 1857 a group of Germans formed the Los Angeles Vineyard Society on lands which they had bought about thirty miles southeast of Los Angeles, not far from the ocean. They gave their tract (one and a half miles by one and a quarter miles in size) the name Anaheim, from its location in the Santa Ana Valley and the German word for home, *heim*. Around their property the Germans built a fence five and a half miles long, consisting of 40,000 willow poles, each eight feet long, of which six feet projected above the ground. They defended their fence by a ditch four feet deep, six feet wide at the top, sloping downward to a breadth of one foot at its bottom. The willow poles took root to form a living wall around the colony. Such "fortifications" were constructed mainly to keep out roving herds of cattle.

With water from the Santa Ana River, the Germans irrigated numerous twenty-acre vineyards. The colonists lived in a central plot. Among these settlers only one man originally understood the art of wine making, but they all went about the new work with patient industry. In ten years the value of their property had increased from five to ten times its original worth. The year after the colony was begun the Los Angeles *Star* (on April 18, 1858) printed the news that the colonists were planting more than 400,000 vines. Almost twenty years later, on December 11, 1877, the same paper announced one of the less desirable side effects, in the view of the California law, of all this planting: "Internal Revenue Collector Hall swooped down on an illicit distillery at Anaheim one day last week and captured the still and one thousand gallons of grape brandy spirits."

Also among the early wine makers was Agoston Haraszthy, a Hungarian of noble birth who is credited with the introduction, in 1851, of Zinfandel grapes at his Buena Vista vineyard at Sonoma. Others included Etienne Thée and Charles Lefranc, two Frenchmen who were the founders of the Almadén Vineyards at Los Gatos. In 1858, Charles Krug, editor of the *Staats Zeitung*, first German newspaper on the Pacific Coast, bought land from Haraszthy and planted twenty acres of vines in the Sonoma Valley. Two years later he moved to the Napa Valley and founded the distinguished winery that still bears his name. Europeans who settled in California following the Gold Rush produced dry burgundies, clarets, sauternes, and even champagnes of excellence in the state's northern valleys. They also began a tradition of hospitality and graceful living amid their vines—one of the most enjoyable aspects of a modern tour of California's "wine country."

Truly large-scale production of wine in California, however, had to await the arrival of good vine cuttings from Europe. As early as the spring of 1862 the state legislature sent "Count" Haraszthy there to bring back 100,000 cuttings of three hundred different varieties of select grapes. These he divided among the wine growers of the state. In spite of the impetus that such help gave the industry, the early wine producers encountered difficulties that resembled those of the orange growers. In the 1870's a dreaded enemy of the vine, the phylloxera, an almost microscopic soil-inhabiting aphid, practically wiped out California's struggling wine industry. There were also marketing problems. By 1879 some 150,000 acres of California land was planted in vines, 90 per cent of which were of the wine-growing varieties. At first growers could secure only a limited market outside the state. In 1880, however, their stock of stored wines was exhausted because of a poor vintage year and the supply suddenly became insufficient to meet the demands of the market. A fall in European production, due to the ravages of the phylloxera, had also occurred. Then grapevine planting began to expand beyond the limits of the northern valleys. Perhaps no crop was so well adapted to the climate of almost every California county. In the mid-1880's wine-growing became quite fashionable, especially among the rich. One of the largest vineyards in the state belonged to Senator Leland Stanford, who owned 3,060,000 vines near Mission San Jose. Senator James Graham Fair, a forty-niner and Comstock millionaire, built a winery near Petaluma. Senator George Hearst owned a vineyard in Sonoma County, and E. J. "Lucky" Baldwin grew grapes at Santa Anita in sandy and hot southern California.

By the 1880's no organization planted quite so many grapes as did the Italian-Swiss Agricultural Colony at Asti. It was founded principally by northern Italians from Genoa, Turin, and the Lombard vineyard towns, who had settled in considerable numbers in the Napa and Sonoma Valleys. The workers of this semi-utopian colony were to receive free all the wine they could drink, in addition to a basic wage—an arrangement that they chose in preference to receiving stock in the colony. After a few lean years this colony, like the German one at Anaheim, prospered. Its 1897 vintage was so large that there was insufficient cooperage in all California to hold the wine. A reservoir had to be chiseled out of solid rock, which became the largest wine tank in the world; when empty this huge vat could accommodate a dance floor for two hundred persons.

As California wines began to win national and foreign prizes for their excellence, many new wineries appeared, not only in the Sonoma Valley but at Napa, in the Livermore Valley, and in the San Joaquin–Sacramento Valley. At Cucamonga, in southern California, the Secondo Guasti family owned the largest (and probably the sandiest) vineyard in the world; their operation specialized in the production of such fortified dessert wines as ports, sherries, and muscatels. At Fresno, Modesto, Madera, and other interior towns, Italian and French immigrants established vineyards that were to increase still further California's international reputation in wine production. The Inglenook Cellars at Rutherford, the Paul Masson winery at Saratoga, and the Beaulieu vineyards of Georges de Latour, also at Rutherford, became important in the history of viniculture after the turn of the century. A tradition both for improved production and for wines of high quality grew out of patient techniques which were learned in Europe and transplanted to California. The total land devoted to the state's vineyards increased from 70,000 acres in 1880 to more than 250,000 acres by 1924. Although the Prohibition era of the 1920's temporarily put an end to wine making, the industry flourished again as soon as Prohibition was repealed. Two notable new operations, those of Louis M. Martini and the Christian Brothers (the latter a religious order), began to produce creditable wines near St. Helena on a large scale during this period.

The art of wine making is a fascinating one. In the early years of the California industry the equipment needed to make wine cost less than one hundred dollars. It generally consisted of several tubs to receive the juice of the grapes, a small lever or cider press, and half a dozen French "claret casks." Wine making takes place from about the middle of September to the first of October, according to the maturity of the grapes. Grapes must be picked only when fully ripe, and when there is no dew or other dampness on them. Upon their arrival at the press, all leaves and unripe or decayed fruit must be eliminated before the crushing process begins. Care must also be taken not to crush the seeds, which impart a bitter taste to the wine. If the wine is to be red, the pulp is left with its juice after the grapes are pressed. If the wine is to be white, the skins must immediately be separated from the juice.

In either case, the juice flows into large casks, where it is exposed to the air to hasten fermentation. Fermentation begins in three or four days; temperature now plays an important part. If the fermenting grape juice is not kept at 65° F. the wine either will be poor in quality or will spoil, sometimes by souring. The liquid becomes "quiet" in a few days; then impurities are strained out, barrel bungholes are sealed, and the wine is left undisturbed for several months. In the next process, called "racking off," the wine is transferred into smaller oak casks for aging, which should improve it in mellowness. In the case of the best wines, aging, especially important for the red varieties, often occurs in corked bottles rather than in barrels and casks. Generally, fifteen pounds of grapes are needed to make one gallon of wine—along with considerable skill, generosity and patience on the part of the vintner. Many California wine makers have built wide reputations on the tradition of a long, expensive, and honorable process.

A sizable part of the grapes grown in California are dried for sale as raisins. The beginnings of the state's raisin industry antedate the Civil War, but as late as 1880 raisin production amounted to only 75,000 lug boxes (the standard unit of measurement) annually. Ten years later California's annual raisin output had increased to 1,600,000 boxes. Since 1900 the growth of the industry has been considerable. From 1937 to 1941 California produced almost 75 per cent of all the raisins grown in the United States. This proportion has generally been maintained.

Reclamation and Irrigation

In recent years an increasingly large part of California's agricultural production has consisted of vegetables. Their cultivation was once restricted to those areas where good surface water existed and could be tapped readily by artesian wells; but extensive reclamation of swampy land and irrigation of dry terrain have opened up vast new areas for farming operations. All sorts of crops, from artichokes to watermelons, can now be grown in almost every one of California's fifty-eight counties.

One of the first regions to undergo reclamation was the large triangle of land lying within the fork formed by the Sacramento and San Joaquin Rivers. This area of more than 500,000 acres, once consisting of a group of islands and swampy plains, had begun to be transformed by the end of the nineteenth century, along with other low-lying delta land. Both individual farmers and the state built dykes, canals, conduits, and check dams to protect farms from floods. The delta has since become known for its output of deciduous fruits, rice, sugar beets, asparagus, spinach, celery, and other vegetables.

Irrigation of California land on a large scale, as opposed to the modest achievements of the mission padres in this respect, was greatly facilitated by the passage of the Wright Act in the state legislature during 1887; this measure provided for the organization of irrigation districts by farmers. Without specifically allotting funds for the assistance of farmers, this act was an encouraging agricultural milestone. Irrigation is always expensive and sometimes dangerous, but its importance in developing agriculture throughout California has been virtually incalculable. The Imperial Valley is a notable example. Sometimes called the "American Nile" area, this valley is located in the dry and hot southeast part of the state. Much of the soil there is sandy and alluvial. Up to 1891, the land under irrigation in the Imperial area was only 90,344 acres. This figure was more than doubled in ten years' time, and acreage was to expand even more dramatically in the twentieth century. In fact, the Southeastern corner of California has been transformed from a waterless, sandy basin into a garden of abundance since the last decade of the nineteenth cntury.

George Chaffey, a Canadian who in the mid-1880's had successfully built a self-sustaining irrigation colony at Ontario, near Los Angeles, planned this transformation of the Imperial Valley. By diverting the waters of the Colorado River, which ran unchecked into the Gulf of California, Chaffey made it possible for the Imperial Land Company to bring a large number of settlers into the valley by 1900. However, the opening up of the area nearly proved catastrophic. In 1905 a serious flood began that lasted almost two years, and created the still-existing Salton Sea. This torrent, caused by the miscalculations of Chaffey's inexpert successors, could not be stopped until the dangerous breach in the banks of the Colorado River was sealed. The area was below sea level and the river threatened to inundate the whole valley. On February 10, 1907, with the help of Southern Pacific Railroad crews, rampaging flood waters were finally turned back after many months of effort. Once the flood damage was repaired the Imperial region grew into an almost model agricultural community. The novelist Harold Bell Wright's mediocre but popular novel, *The Winning of Barbara Worth*, made the valley well known throughout the United States. Letters written to the East by enthusiastic settlers there lauded the fertile soil and caused hundreds of curious persons to visit Imperial, first as tourists, then as settlers.

By 1909 more than a thousand miles of main and lateral canals had been constructed in the Imperial Valley. In 1913 this canal system covered more than half a million acres, extending even below the border into Mexico. The California operation was, for its time, the largest irrigation project, private or public, in the United States. Barley, alfalfa, and other farm acreage rapidly expanded, and the valley became known as the "Winter Garden of the World." Its lettuce shipments in 1924 reached a total of 9,489 carloads—more than half the lettuce shipped from the entire state. Imperial became equally famous for its cantaloupes and other melons.

Farther northward, due east of Palm Springs, the Coachella Valley proved to be another marvel of productivity with the assistance of artificial irrigation. Crops in this valley have the particular advantage of early maturation. In the Coachella the annual harvest of table grapes, dates, melons, strawberries, and orchard fruits begins about May 25. Temperatures quickly climb to above 110°, making the area especially notable as a producer of Red Emperor, Tokay, Ribier, and Thompson Seedless grapes. Before 1900, at the end of spring each year, carloads of early fruits and vegetables began to leave the Coachella Valley for Eastern depots. Since then the region has remained an important one in the state's farming economy.

The Founding of Towns

Closely connected with artificial irrigation and the resultant development of agriculture was the emergence of numerous small towns. Ranching—indeed an entire way of life—began to be supplanted by an agricultural-urban society that preceded the California of today. Often, as rancho holdings were broken up by controversies over legal titles, the lands fell into the hands of urban promoters and lot venders, and communities sprang up on these sites which took the names of the former ranchos. Even rancheros themselves founded such towns. For example, William Heath Davis converted part of his Rancho San Leandro (acquired by marriage from the important Estudillo family) into the central California community of San Leandro. He urged a neighboring native family, the Peraltas, to do likewise with their grant. The Peralta claims, however, which covered part of the present sites of Berkeley, Oakland, and Alameda along San Francisco Bay were disputed in the courts for years; and the Peraltas profited but little from the ultimate urban development of their rich terrain.

Davis continued to pursue his interest in town founding, becoming one of a number of typical entrepreneurs who risked their capital to create a new urban order in California. At first these "towns" were little more than country crossroads, that ultimately became farm supply centers. In the 1850's, long before railroad connections with the outer world had been provided, Davis and his associates also bought up parts of various ranchos in the area of the old Spanish-Mexican village of San Diego. Though dogged by lack of wood and water, such town founders strained their resources to the breaking point. Admittedly, personal profit was their motive. They built houses, paved streets, constructed wharfs for visiting steamers, provided hotels for dusty overland travelers

SAN DIEGO, CA. 1852. POSSIBLY SKETCHED BY JOHN RUSSELL BARTLETT. (Reproduced from his *Personal Narrative* . . . [1856].)

—in short, tried to transform a community of crumbling adobes and rude shacks into a city. Davis' project, however, was doomed to failure. Later, in the 1860's, the real estate promoter Alonzo Erastus Horton constructed yet another "New San Diego," only to lose his fortune also.

In contrast to Davis and Horton at San Diego, some town developers succeeded from the start. Among these was Phineas Banning, founder of Wilmington. This community was fortunately situated on an estuary providing easy maritime access to the expanding pueblo of Los Angeles. Banning's Wilmington wharf and warehouses were built, in the period 1851–1858, on a harbor sheltered by a rock jetty between Terminal and Dead Man's Islands, near what was to become the town of the "New San Pedro." The harbor's channel was dug deep enough to float in barges and steam tugs carrying freight and passengers from ocean vessels anchored offshore. During the Civil War the United States Army established Camp Drum and Drum Barracks near Banning's home at Wilmington. This government installation helped to assure the future of Wilmington as a new port for Los Angeles.

One further example of town founding will help illustrate how ranchos became cities, once the litigation over land titles was clarified in the late nineteenth century. Also in southern California, the city of Pasadena mushroomed out of Rancho San Pasqual, formerly the site of an Indian village located near the banks of the San Gabriel River. Throughout the 1850's Manuel Garfias, who held the grant to the rancho, had faced grave economic problems. Repeated borrowing, at ruinous rates of interest, finally forced Garfias to sacrifice the rancho property. In 1859 he sold San Pasqual for $1,800 to Benjamin W. Wilson, who had come to California with the Workman-Rowland party. During the following year Wilson deeded a half interest in the land, for $4,000, to Dr. John S. Griffin, chief medical officer in California with the United States Army. In 1867 the two men built the Wilson Ditch, to bring water from the nearby Arroyo Seco to their mesa lands. Next, having taken Judge Benjamin S. Eaton into their enterprise, they succeeded in interesting D. M. Berry, representative of a group of colonists from Indiana, in the lands they had for sale to settlers. Although the national financial panic of 1873 depleted the resources of the Indiana colonists, Berry quickly incorporated the San Gabriel Orange Grove Association to buy the developers out. Before the end of that year he had sold $25,000 worth of stock in the enterprise, handing the whole of this amount over to Griffin for his four thousand acres—which had originally cost Griffin only one dollar per acre. By early 1874 hundreds of Eastern colonists had driven their horses and buggies to the site, receiving fifteen acres of land for each $250 share of stock they purchased in Berry's land enterprise. Two years later Wilson sold his holdings too at a handsome profit.

The new Hoosier colony at San Pasqual provided itself with a reservoir holding 3,000,000 gallons of water, and with vital irrigation conduits leading into new orchards and grain fields. In 1875 the settlers chose the name Pasadena from the Chippewa Indian language, a name touristically, and probably inaccurately, translated as "Crown of the Valley." In the twentieth century this town, once dotted with clumps of oak and fields of poppies, was to transform itself into a winter playground of millionaires who would build mansions along its Orange Grove Avenue. Pasadena has profited handsomely from its invaluable, almost prodigal, land inheritance. Sadly, in the development of such "rancho towns," it was the native Californians—the former owners of the land—who gained least, if at all.

Various factors contributed to the rapid growth of towns like Pasadena: the low cost of land, the drastically increasing population pressures caused by the railroads, and the remarkable energy of town founders and developers in establishing irrigation and water facilities as well as local transportation. These speculators turned an arid countryside into prosperous cities. San Leandro, Pasadena, Wilmington, and San Diego are examples of their pioneering enterprise and willingness to take risks.

The Railroads and the Land Boom of the Eighties

The boom in California's urban growth toward the end of the nineteenth century, like that in agriculture, was closely connected with the railroads. The new flood of population that descended on the state from 1870 to 1890, seeking to substitute harsh winters with sunshine, of course contributed to California's overall urbanization. It also helped determine where some of its future cities would be located. To southern California, in particular, there flocked unemployed cowboys and fruit pickers, dispossessed wheat farmers from the Middle West, engineers, health seekers, real estate promoters, and a variety of tradesmen, artisans, and merchants. Whether they settled down as town dwellers or farmers, these new residents became their own best customers and created a boom that fed on itself.

The movement of population reached its peak in 1887. It will be recalled that the Atchison, Topeka, and Santa Fe Railroad first arrived at Los Angeles that year. This event touched off a bitter rate war with the Southern Pacific. At the height of the rivalry, passenger fares from the Middle West to southern California dropped from $125 to as little as $1, encouraging unprecedented travel. More than 200,000 persons came to California in 1887 by railroad and many of these stayed on, thereby helping to cause the real estate boom. Dozens of towns sprang up immediately in Los Angeles County, for example, and colleges, banks, and other institutions were also founded. Within less than two years a hundred communities with 500,000 lots had been "platted" inside the borders of the county. Though lacking in coal and metals, and isolated on the far side of North America without a fully developed harbor, Los Angeles had embarked on a period of prodigious growth—the result of skillful realty advertising and the lure of climate, as well as of the railroad competition.

The land-boom advertising campaigns, often abetted by the railroads, were a considerable phenomenon in themselves. In particular, promoters who were familiar with Italy attempted to exploit the similarities between California and ancient Tuscany or Campania. They pointed out especially vivid resemblances along the Golden State's coastline, and knowing tourists agreed that the terraced bluffs around Santa Barbara and Carmel were reminiscent of the Riviera's Santa Margherita and Rapallo. Blue skies, olive trees, and craggy cliffs took some observers back to Posilippo on the Bay of Naples. Even the California rainfall resembled Italy's, in that the least rain fell in the south. California's Hispanic past also contributed to the Mediterranean similarity. The resemblance even became the subject of books, including Peter C. Remondino's health-stressing *Mediterranean Shores of America* (1892) and Charles Dudley Warner's *Our Italy* (1902). Writer Grace Ellery Channing and artist Ernest Peixotto published articles entitled respectively "What We Can Learn from Rome," in the magazine *Westways*, and "Italy's Message to California," in *Sunset*. An endless stream of such literature appeared from 1880 onward. One visitor, Oscar Wilde, referred to Los Angeles as "a sort of Naples." On a subliterary level, the Mediterranean theme formed a definite part of the publicity in the rivalry between towns. An illustration in the *Golden Era* of May, 1888, reminded readers that San Diego, instead, wanted to be called the "Naples of America," and Long Beach claimed to be still another Naples. One California county emblazoned its 1905 *Sunset* magazine advertisement with the banner heading: "The Italy of California, Glenn County." Both the San Diego and Riverside chambers of commerce issued brochures that advertised "their" Italy of America.

The comparison, which stressed the ancient and the romantic, was carried over enthusiastically into the naming of new towns; California soon had its Hesperia, Rialto, Tarragona, Terracina, and Verona. At one such namesake, Venice, the real estate boom of the eighties even saw the building of imitation lagoons and terraced piazzas along an open beach. Architecture and formal garden design later added to California's Mediterranean coloration. At Senator James D. Phelan's Villa Montalvo, near Saratoga, Italian-inspired rococo porticoes, manicured cypress hedges, stone gryphons, and classical statues sustained the mood. Similar in style was Henry E. Huntington's estate at San Marino. Educational institutions, too, were affected by the trend. The façade of Stanford University's chapel framed a mosaic similar to that of the Rome church called St. Paul Outside the Walls. The new Occidental College campus was classical in its inspiration, while a future U.C.L.A. campus was to use red-brick Romanesque construction. Later, also, Scripps College bowed toward Italianate architectural design, as did countless churches.

By the turn of the century, virtually all aspects of the California scene reflected the boom which had come with the railroad. The hordes of new residents had helped wipe out forever the Far Western frontier in California. A strong agricultural economy had been established, and the increasingly urban society with which it was interrelated had entered its period of greatest development.

SELECTED READINGS

Three early books that discuss agriculture as a factor in California's material growth are John S. Hittell, *The Resources of California* (San Francisco, 1863), Titus F. Cronise, *The Natural Wealth of California* (San Francisco, 1868), and J. Ross Browne, *Resources of the Pacific Slope* (San Francisco, 1869). A later pioneer authority, Edward J. Wickson, discussed agricultural progress in several books: *The California Fruits and How to Grow Them* (San Francisco, 1900), *Nurserymen and the Plant Industry* (Los Angeles, 1921), *Dairying in California* (Washington, 1896), *One Thousand Questions in California Agriculture Answered* (San Francisco, 1914), and *Rural California* (New York, 1923). Consult also the agricultural chapters of Cleland and Hardy's *March of Industry*. One of the best recent histories of American agriculture is Paul W. Gates, *The Farmer's Age: Agriculture, 1815–1860* (New York, 1960). This book devotes pp. 387–397 to the status of farming in California up to the Civil War. A general symposium, edited by

Claude B. Hutchison, is entitled *California Agriculture* (Berkeley, 1946). Persons interested in gardening may wish to read Victor Padilla, *Southern California Gardens* (Berkeley, 1961).

Regarding California citriculture, an early work is John E. Colt, *Citrus Fruits* (New York, 1915). On the founding of the orange center at Riverside, see Merlin Stonehouse, "The Michigan Excursion for the Founding of Riverside, California," *Michigan History*, XLV (September, 1961), 193–209. Articles concerning citrus and other tree crops grown in California appear in the files of *The California Cultivator*. See also E. Bartholomew and W. B. Sinclair, *Lemon Fruit: Its Composition, Physiology, and Products* (Berkeley, 1953). The "orange culture" of California is placed in its characteristic historical setting by Oscar Osburn Winther's "The Colonial System of Southern California," *Agricultural History*, XXVII (July, 1953), 94–103. The course of the navel-orange industry in California is the subject of the article by Minnie Tibbets Mills, "Luther Calvin Tibbets, Founder of the Navel Orange Industry of California," Historical Society of Southern California *Quarterly*, XXV (December, 1943), 127–161. Basic to an understanding of Burbank's agricultural experiments is a book by his sister, Emma Burbank Beeson, *The Early Life and Letters of Luther Burbank* (San Francisco, 1927). Weak as to history, but comprehensive in other respects, is Herbert J. Webber and Leon D. Batchelor, eds., *The Citrus Industry: History, Botany, and Breeding* (2 vols., Berkeley, 1943).

The principal contemporary authority on sheep in the nineteenth century was Henry Stephens Randall, whose *The Practical Shepherd* (Rochester, 1863) and *Fine Wool Sheep Husbandry* (New York, 1863) contain much material applicable to conditions in California. See also Edward N. Wentworth, *America's Sheep Trails: History, Personalities* (Ames, Iowa, 1948). An account of a sheep drive from Kern County to the Green River in Wyoming is Earle Crow, *General Beale's Sheep Odyssey* . . . (Bakersfield, 1960). See also L. T. Burcham, "The Advent of Sheep in California," *California Livestock News*, XXXIII (May, 1957), 13–15.

Useful for an understanding of the California cattle industry are Cleland's *Cattle* and Edward F. Treadwell's biography of Henry Miller, *The Cattle King* (New York, 1931; repr. Boston, 1950), which contains a valuable chapter on politics. Two other general books are Edward Everett Dale, *The Range Cattle Industry* (Norman, Okla., 1930), and Ernest Staples Osgood, *The Day of the Cattleman* (Minneapolis, 1929), the latter a classic that has been reprinted in various modern editions. Though both of these books say little about California in particular, they offer essential information concerning the cattle industry. More specific is L. T. Burcham, "Cattle and Range Forage in California: 1770–1880," *Agricultural History*, XXXV (July, 1961), 140–149, and the same author's earlier *California Range Land* (Sacramento, 1957). See also James M. Jensen, "Cattle Drives From the Ranchos to the Gold

Fields of California," *Arizona and the West*, II (Winter, 1960), 341–352, as well as Dane Coolidge, *Old California Cowboys* (New York, 1939). An article that combines an apologia of early agricultural land speculation with developments in ranching and farming is Gerald D. Nash, "Henry George Reexamined: William S. Chapman's Views on Land Speculation in Nineteenth Century California," *Agricultural History*, XXXIII (July, 1959), 133–137.

Early books about the wine industry include George Husmann, *The Cultivation of the Native Grape and Manufacture of American Wines* . . . (New York, 1866), and his *Grape Culture and Wine Making in California* (San Francisco, 1888). Another such work is Edna Eunice Wait, *Wines and Vines of California* (San Francisco, 1889). Early contemporary discussions include also Arpad Haraszthy, "Wine Making in California," *Overland Monthly*, VII (1871), 489–497, and a book by the same author, *California Wines and Grapes* (San Francisco, 1883); a superior series of articles on the Haraszthy family by Paul Frederickson appears in *Wines and Vines* (July–October, 1947). On the Anaheim colony see Mildred Yorba MacArthur, *Anaheim: The Mother Colony* (Los Angeles, 1959), and Lucile E. Dickson, "The Founding and Early History of Anaheim, California," *Historical Society of Southern California Annual Publications*, XI (March, 1919), 26–37. Consult also Iris Ann Wilson, "Early Southern California Viniculture, 1830–1865," *Historical Society of Southern California Quarterly*, XXXIX (September, 1957), 242–250. A helpful work, especially on the economic and political aspects of California wine production, is Vincent P. Carosso, *The California Wine Industry, 1830–1895* (Berkeley, 1951). Useful also is John Melville, *Guide to California Wines* (New York, 1955), as is M. F. K. Fisher, *The Story of Wines in California* (Berkeley, 1962).

Particularly rewarding and unique early descriptions of the wine and orange industries were printed in the Los Angeles *Star* for January 30, 1858; April 8 and 18, 1858; April 21, 1870; November 19, 1870; December 11, 1877; and April 12, 1892. See also the San Francisco *Alta California*, January 15, 1858, and the San Francisco *Chronicle*, December 19, 1879. Two articles by Rodman W. Paul give one a penetrating view of California as a grain-producing state. These are "The Great California Grain War. The Granger Challenges the Wheat King," *Pacific Historical Review*, XXVII (November, 1958), 331–349, and "The Wheat Trade Between California and the United Kingdom," *Mississippi Valley Historical Review*, XLV (December, 1958), 391–412. Earlier useful accounts include Horace Davis, "California Breadstuffs," *Journal of Political Economy*, II (September, 1894), 517–535, and, also by Davis, "Wheat in California," *Overland Monthly*, I (November, 1868), 442–452.

The struggle of the farmers against flood-carried hydraulic mining debris is the topic of Robert L. Kelley, *Gold vs. Grain: The Hydraulic Mining Controversy in California's Sacramento Valley* (Glendale, 1960). Experiments with agricultural irrigation are treated in Frederick

D. Kershner, Jr., "George Chaffey and the Irrigation Frontier," *Agricultural History*, XXVII (October, 1953), 115–122. See also J. A. Alexander, *The Life of George Chaffey: The Story of Irrigation Beginnings in California and Australia* (Melbourne, 1928).

A good recent article on the growing of silk is Nelson Klose, "California's Experimentation in Sericulture," *Pacific Historical Review*, XXX (August, 1961), 213–227.

The rural-to-urban transformation of California, which still continues, is a vast subject, best explored by reading local histories. Some of the best recent ones are Gordon S. Eberly, *Arcadia: City of the Santa Anita* (Claremont, 1953); William Martin Camp, *San Francisco: Port of Gold* (Garden City, 1947); Works Progress Administration, *Berkeley: The First Seventy-Five Years* (Berkeley, 1941); Chester G. Murphy, *The People of the Pueblo: or The Story of Sonoma* (Portland, 1937, 1948); Clara H. Hisken, *Tehama: Little City of the Big Trees* (New York, 1948); Hallock F. Raup, *San Bernardino, California: Settlement and Growth of a Pass-Site City* (Berkeley, 1940); Donald H. Pflueger, *Glendora—The Annals of a Southern California Community* (Claremont, 1951) and his *Covina: Sunflowers, Citrus, Subdivisions* (Claremont, 1964); Katherine M. Bell, *Swinging the Censer: Reminiscences of Old Santa Barbara* (Santa Barbara, 1931); and L. J. Rose, Jr., *L. J. Rose of Sunny Slope, 1827–1899* (San Marino, 1958). Regarding San Diego, there are six volumes by Richard F. Pourade that span the period from its origins to World War II. These are *The Explorers* (1960); *Time of the Bells* (1961); *The Silver Dons* (1963); *The Glory Years* (1964); *Gold in the Sun* (1965); and *The Rising Tide* (1967). Also see Andrew F. Rolle, *William Heath Davis and the Founding of American San Diego* (San Diego, 1953) and Max Miller, *Harbor of the Sun: The Story of the Port of San Diego* (New York, 1940). Regarding the state capitol, see Joseph A. McGowan, *History of the Sacramento Valley* (3 vols., New York, 1961). The same author has published *The Sacramento Valley: A Students' Guide to Localized History* (New York, 1967).

Representative histories of ranchos that become cities include Joseph J. Hill, *The History of Warner's Ranch and Its Environment* (Los Angeles, 1927); Robert G. Cleland, *The Irvine Ranch of Orange County, 1810–1950* (San Marino, 1952); and Ruth Waldo Newhall, *The Newhall Ranch: The Story of the Newhall Land and Farming Company* (San Marino, 1958). The comprehensive work on this subject is W. W. Robinson, *Ranchos Become Cities* (Pasadena, 1939), a most suggestive book. See Hallock F. Raup, "Rancho Los Palos Verdes," *Historical Society of Southern California Quarterly*, XIX (March, 1937), 7–21, and Andrew F. Rolle, "Wagon Pass Rancho Withers Away: La Ballona, 1821–1952," in the same journal, XXXIV (June, 1952), 147–158. Consult also R. Louis Gentilcore, "Ontario, California and the Agricultural Boom of the 1880's," *Agricultural History*, XXXIV (April, 1960), 77–87.

The basic work on the large migration that came mostly by rail after 1887 is Glenn S. Dumke, *The Boom of the 'Eighties in Southern California* (San Marino, 1944). Development of a port at Los Angeles before the "free harbor" fight is discussed in Richard W. Barsness, "Iron Horses and an Inner Harbor at San Pedro Bay, 1867–1890," *Pacific Historical Review*, XXXIV (August, 1965), 289–304.

24

Problems of Race

Many immigrant strains have contributed to the development of California. As we have seen, the railroad to the East was built largely with Chinese labor. California's growth was furthered, too, by the efforts of Japanese farmers in the Central Valley, of Italian and French wine growers in the north, and of Swiss and German dairymen along the Coast Range. The combined presence of these immigrants made California relatively receptive, especially in comparison with other Western states, to foreign ideas, food, styles of clothing, and patterns of life. Yet it is true that California's history includes some discreditable episodes of suspicion, harshness, and violence toward foreigners and minority groups. During the nineteenth century, Orientals faced an especially tough battle for acceptance. Their mistreatment is perhaps best summed up in the phrase, "He doesn't have a Chinaman's chance."

Early Chinese Immigration

In 1844, Caleb Cushing, minister plenipotentiary from the United States, went to China to negotiate for the opening of Chinese ports to American trade. Partly as a result of a treaty of trade and friendship which Cushing signed with China, contact between California and the Orient began to increase. In 1847, the first small band of Chinese immigrants found their way into the state. By

1852 some 20,000 had arrived, attracted by stories of its great mineral wealth and of high wages paid in its mines and work camps. In 1860 there were 34,933 Chinese in California and, by 1870, 49,277.

California's first Chinese immigrants were treated with consideration. In 1850 they were given a prominent place in San Francisco's memorial service on the occasion of President Zachary Taylor's death. In the same year they were invited to help celebrate the admission of the state to the Union. Governor McDougal once called the Chinese "one of the most worthy classes of our newly adopted citizens,"and he even expressed a desire for further Oriental immigration. This general attitude of welcome was in part due to California's need for a dependable supply of common laborers. Orientals showed themselves to be particularly adaptable and faithful workers. In the mines, on railroads and ranches, in laundries and hotel kitchens, in cigar factories, and in private homes, they seemed to have a passion for work and, furthermore, were content with meager wages.

The first serious dissatisfaction with the Chinese appeared in the mines where, in spite of their small daily earnings, the Chinese through perseverance and frugality sometimes accumulated more gold than did extravagant whites. With the particular purpose of handicapping the Chinese, Californians in 1850 enacted the Foreign Miners' License Law, which imposed a monthly tax of twenty dollars on immigrant miners. This measure had the effect of driving a horde of penniless foreigners away from the mines to San Francisco. The law was eventually repealed, and a milder tax substituted, to be followed in 1855 by an immigration head tax of fifty dollars to be paid by each foreigner upon entry in the state. As to the personal characteristics of "John Chinaman," as the individual Chinese came to be called, he was usually a patient, peace-loving, hard-working miner. He paid his bills promptly and was prudent enough to leave the richest mining claims to Americans. Neverthless, when he got in the way of aggressive whites, he often became the victim of sharp accusations and violence. Some diggings were frankly closed to Chinese and other foreigners.

"California for the Americans!" was a cry increasingly voiced by nativists in the cities as well as in the mining camps. Influenced by heightening public antipathy, Governor Bigler, who in 1852 succeeded McDougal, stigmatized the Chinese as scum "coolie" laborers. In a special message he called upon the state legislature to prohibit contract immigration, thus becoming the first important official to display anti-Chinese prejudice. When the financial

CHINESE BUTCHER SHOP IN SAN FRANCISCO, CA. 1890.
(Wyland Stanley Collection, photograph by I. W. Taber;
by courtesy of The Bancroft Library,
University of California, Berkeley.)

panic of 1854 brought prices down with a crash, ruining business houses and causing grave unrest, feeling against the Chinese reached new heights. Miners by the thousands drifted back to San Francisco, only to find the labor market glutted. The presence in that city of large numbers of Chinese was held chiefly responsible for its distressing unemployment. White workers complained bitterly that the Orientals, by undercutting wages, deprived them of work—that they were, in fact, human leeches "sucking the very life-blood of this country." Governor Bigler, again capitalizing on the prevailing public temper, rebuked the legislature in 1854 for its negligence in not voting for strong exclusion and deportation laws.

Prejudice among whites extended even to little children, who were encouraged by some of their elders to practice public disrespect and insult against the Chinese. Mistreatment of the "pig-tail," or "almond-eyed Celestial," was of daily occurrence by the late 1850's. Sharply set apart by their physiognomy, dress, religion, mores, and exotic food habits (they ate bamboo shoots, salt ginger, dried duck liver, and seaweed), the Chinese were in no position to retaliate. The nadir of indignity may be said to have been reached in San Francisco's notorious 1855 "Pig-Tail Ordinance." This regulation required Chinese men convicted of breaking the law to have their queues cut off one inch from the head. The ordinance, suspended for a time and then reinstated, both reflected and contributed to the belief that the Orientals were unassimilable.

Meanwhile, in spite of prejudice and persecution, from 1850 to 1900 a "Little China" was steadily growing in San Francisco. This was located on upper Sacramento Street and along Dupont Street. The mysteries of Chinatown held a great attraction for the curious —especially tourists. Smoke-filled gambling dens flourished, and back-room saloons, secret passages, deep basements, and hidden recesses teemed with hivelike activity, day and night. Opium smoking in filthy dens both fascinated and revolted Americans. The Chinese were also accused of importing prostitutes for the use of whites and of keeping these women in bondage.

The mass of the Chinese who continued to come to California did so not of their own initiative, but under conditions only slightly removed from servitude. When the Central Pacific railroad was being built, Mark Hopkins supervised the founding of the "Six Companies" to recruit, transport, and utilize Chinese labor on a large scale. This enterprise, operated by Hopkins' agents, was responsible for much of the immigration in the early 1860's— about 9,000 Chinese in all. Included among "Crocker's Pets," as these railroad workers were often called, were not a few moral delinquents and other undesirables, in contrast to the Chinese who had come earlier as miners. Impoverished, undernourished, sometimes sickly, the laborers bound to the "Six Companies" by contracts came chiefly from southern China, where devastating poverty and ignorance existed. They were in no sense free laborers, but rather tools of ruthless speculators who paid them a few pennies per hour. Shrewd human brokers cooperated with railroad and steamship agents to exploit the Orientals. Governor Stanford once called the Chinese "peaceable, industrious and economical, apt to learn and quite as efficient as white laborers." Since their labors made a vast fortune for him, he would have been deficient in grace if he had said anything less.

Increased Anti-Chinese Sentiment

At San Francisco and at other places where the Chinese came into economic competition with laborers in various trades, resentment mounted until it eventually exploded into violence. In 1859 the feeling reached such a pitch that Governor Weller sent a company of state militia into Shasta County to put down riots instituted by northern miners. By 1867 "anti-coolie clubs" had grown strong enough to dictate punishment for the misbehavior of Orientals, and sheriffs, courts, and juries were generally passive in the face of such action. In December of 1867 various Chinese were brutally driven out of French Corral in Nevada County and their cabins destroyed. Out of a total of twenty-seven Caucasians arrested for this mob violence, one was tried and the rest set free. The guilty man was fined only $100. On October 23, 1871, nearly a score of Chinese were massacred in a Los Angeles race riot, originating in a quarrel between two Chinese factions. This episode, one of the bloodiest in the history of the state, was ignored by the law. Los Angeles soon earned a notoriety based on protracted

CHINESE FORTUNE TELLER, SAN FRANCISCO, CA. 1890. (H. G. Hills Collection, photograph by T. E. Hecht; by courtesy of The Bancroft Library, University of California, Berkeley.)

lawlessness both in its Chinatown and in nearby "Nigger Alley."

The explanation of this racial hostility is complex, involving economic, social, political, moral, and religious considerations. The daily press contributed to the inflammation of sentiment by charging the Chinese with intolerable competition, especially in mining, construction work, cigar making, and in the lesser trades. Moreover, critics accused the Orientals unjustly of draining the countryside of substantial sums of money, supposedly sent to China. The Chinese were regarded as the "Yellow Peril," unprogressive, living on inferior food in crowded, unsanitary dwellings, a threat to "Christian values and Republican government." They were said to be pagan, depraved, and vicious. It was commonly believed that they practiced a mysterious quasi-government among themselves which somehow tended to encourage internecine wars. At the same time, their accusers, with characteristic racist logic, found the Chinese lack of interest in assimilation particularly inexcusable. Xenophobes, or race haters, called for national exclusion laws.

Although the majority of Californians probably favored exclusion, a treaty negotiated in 1868 by Anson Burlingame further eased the passage of Orientals into the state and allowed the railroad kings to flood its labor market with still more Chinese immigrants, who proved to be valuable as railroad laborers for many years after the railroad was built. Agitation against the Chinese continued at both local and state levels. In 1871, Governor Newton Booth was elected to office on an anti-Chinese platform. Almost every time the state legislature convened, nativists proposed an "immigrant tax." By 1876, a total of 116,000 Chinese were living within the state's borders. There was strong feeling for repeal for the Burlingame Treaty, which had guaranteed free migration. Such pressures were bound to affect legislation at the national level. In 1878, a resolution of the United States House of Representatives requested President Rutherford B. Hayes to seek a change in all treaties that permitted unlimited Chinese immigration into the country. Congress that year passed the "Fifteen Passenger Bill," restricting the immigration of Orientals to fifteen passengers on any ship entering the United States. Although President Hayes vetoed this legislation, an inflamed public, especially in California, pressed for a Chinese treaty with stronger exclusionist provisions.

A new treaty of 1880 with China was the result. Under this, the United States could "regulate, limit, or suspend" the entry or residence of its laborers but it could not absolutely prohibit their immigration. California laboring groups kept up the anti-immigrant pressure, and in June, 1882, the Democratic state convention passed a sweeping resolution against further Oriental immigration. Both major parties were, in fact, anti-Chinese—on a national as well as a state level. In 1882, President Chester Arthur signed a bipartisan exclusion bill which suspended Chinese immigration for ten years and aroused much anxiety in China. The Scott Act of 1888 further enraged Chinese officials by providing that foreign laborers who had left United States shores could not return. The Geary Act of 1892 extended the prohibition against Chinese immigration for another ten years. Despite vigorous complaints from Peking, both the Geary and Scott Acts were held to be constitutional by the United States Supreme Court.

By the mid-1890's, the country was definitely moving toward a policy of absolute exclusion. In December, 1901, as the Geary Act approached termination, China's minister to the United States suggested an adjustment "more in harmony with friendly relations of the two governments." But this plea was ignored. A deluge of petitions from California, continually pouring in upon Congress, helped to bring about the passage of bills providing for further restriction. On April 30, 1902, despite a stiff note of complaint from Chinese Minister Wu Ting Fang to Secretary of State John Hay, a new federal bill, "to prohibit the coming into and to regulate the residence within the United States . . . of Chinese and persons of Chinese descent," was passed and approved by President Theodore Roosevelt.

California can take little pride in its part in the history of Chinese exclusion. Widespread bigotry, race prejudice, and political chauvinism were prime factors in both local and national agitation against Orientals. On the other hand, the United States, unlike leading European powers, refrained from carving up the Chinese Empire after the Boxer Uprising of 1900, and returned an indemnity fund levied against China so that it might be used to educate young Chinese in America. But such a tardy manifestation of good will, even when it accompanied the inauguration of America's Open Door Policy, could not immediately eradicate American guilt for the treatment of the Chinese.

California still has a sizable Chinese population. Large colonies exist at both San Francisco and Los Angeles, though those in the smaller towns have declined. At the turn of the century, Fresno's Chinatown boasted 5,000 inhabitants, and had its own Chinese opera house. By the 1960's the Chinese population of Fresno had been cut in half. Except for the celebration of the Chinese New Year and the annual moon festival each fall, Chinese activity in California's interior towns is not to be compared with that of earlier times. Yet, a former joss house in Weaverville functions not only as a state historical monument but also as a bonafide Taoist temple. Its altar, imported from China during the Gold Rush, is ancient. In a slightly lingering anti-Oriental atmosphere, the Chinese tongs, or welfare and fraternal organizations, continue strong, however, at Los Angeles and San Francisco. The Chinese in these large centers have remained a relatively homogeneous group, largely as a result of the success of their restaurants and shops, in artificially created "Chinatowns" rigged for tourists.

The Japanese Influx

The history of the Japanese in California has from the first been colored by the facts and attitudes regarding Chinese immigration, though their experience has also differed in many respects from that of the Chinese. Significant numbers of Japanese began to enter California in the late nineteenth century. Like the Chinese, they experienced reasonable treatment at first. A Japanese trade delegation that visited the state legislature in 1872 received courteous attention; the number of Japanese entering California did not yet pose an economic threat.

Not until 1891 did the Japanese immigration into the United States for a single year exceed one thousand, but from that time on it increased markedly. Acquisition of Hawaii in 1898 was followed by a heavy two-year influx of both Japanese and Chinese from these Islands, and public opinion was, therefore, aroused anew against all Orientals. Nevertheless, they still came. In 1900 alone, 12,626 Japanese entered the United States. The federal census for that year, admittedly incomplete, shows that a total of 24,326 Japanese then resided in the country. By 1910 the number had grown to 72,157, and strong opposition to the Japanese was being voiced in California.

To a degree, agitation against Orientals had subsided during the Civil War. After the war, however, industrial discontent produced renewed hostility toward foreigners. "The front door has been off its hinges long enough," one California xenophobe of the 1870's declared. In this atmosphere, the Japanese posed a new cheap labor threat, and Californians applied the term "yellow peril" to them. In the 1880's another "American Party" was formed, in the tradition of the Know-Nothings, partly for the purpose of attacking Orientals. Both anti-Japanese and anti-Chinese sentiments were voiced at a mass meeting in San Francisco in 1900, when there was great public discussion of the Chinese Exclusion Act.

The first specifically anti-Japanese exclusion meeting was held in May, 1905, at San Francisco, resulting in the organization of an Asiatic Exclusion League.

In 1906, the San Francisco Board of Education recommended the establishment of special schools for Chinese and Japanese, separate from those for Caucasians. Based on a state statute, which the city had been violating, this recommendation was, thus, tardy. Before final action on this proposal could be taken the city experienced the great earthquake disaster of 1906, which for a while disrupted all civic activities except those devoted to recovery. When a "separate school order" was at length issued, requiring the transfer of a majority of San Francisco's ninety-three Japanese pupils to the existing Oriental school, great indignation was aroused in Japan, and diplomatic protests were promptly lodged with the American government. The Japanese objected as much to the inclusion of their children in a separate school with the Chinese as to any other discrimination. President Roosevelt insisted that the national government was a party to the controversy, stating: "As soon as legislative or any other action in any state affects a foreign nation, then the affair becomes one for the Nation, and the state should deal with the foreign power purely through the Nation."

In accord with the President's view, the order of the San Francisco school board was rescinded. But anti-Japanese sentiment was not so easily appeased. Following a recommendation by a newly organized Japanese and Korean Exclusion League, the San Francisco school board passed a second resolution, on October 11, 1906, again announcing that Japanese children would be received only at an "Oriental" public school, along with the Chinese. Once more the order was received in Japan as a genuine affront. This time the federal government's view was expressed by Secretary of State Elihu Root, who stated that the United States government "would not allow any treatment of the Japanese people other than that accorded the people of other nations." In January the Attorney General of the United States brought two legal actions in California to enforce treaty immigration agreements with Japan. However, since a legal decision (Plessy vs. Ferguson) had become the law of the land, the Federal suit could affect only alien Japanese children, who had treaty rights, but not the native born who, of course, did not. Meanwhile the mayor of San Francisco and members of the school board journeyed to Washington to confer with President Roosevelt. On March 14, 1907, the suits were dismissed, but only after the local Board of Education rescinded the objectionable order. By Roosevelt's prompt and decisive action a diplomatic crisis was happily averted.

The unabated arrival of Japanese laborers in large numbers, however, led to continued agitation against them. In 1908 hostile demonstrations were such as to cause Ambassador Aoki to protest once more to the President, who telegraphed Governor James N. Gillett that restrictive measures then before the California legislature would strain relations with Japan at a time when the Roosevelt administration was already negotiating for the exclusion of labor immigrants. Accordingly, the bills were withdrawn.

Most of the problems, however, remained. By 1910 the Japanese population in California had reached more than 40,000. These immigrants seemed most prolific in bearing children. Also, in contrast to the Chinese who as a rule seemed placidly uninterested in material success, the Japanese were often ambitious and enterprising. Farmers among them, for example, worked impressively long hours, expecting the same of all the members of their families. The morale and drive of the Japanese at this time, both as a nation and as a people, according to one authority, may have been due in part to pride over their victory in the Russo-Japanese War of 1905. Regardless of their circumstances, many of their troubles in California were due to the fact that they were both alert and acquisitive in business matters. The newspapers which campaigned steadily against the Japanese never accused them of stupidity or apathy—characteristics popularly ascribed to the Chinese. Rather, the press depicted the Japanese as efficient, shrewd, and conniving; in fact, they seemed to possess almost to excess the enterprise admired most by some of their Caucasian neighbors, with whom they had come into economic competition.

Obviously the major way to cut down further Japanese immigration was by diplomatic means. In order to avert an international crisis with Japan, Roosevelt called for further negotiations, which resulted in the well-known "Gentlemen's Agreement"; this was actually part of the Root-Takahira accords, which became effective in 1908. Under these new provisions Japanese and Korean laborers who surreptitiously entered from Mexico, Canada, and Hawaii were legally excludable from the United States. Furthermore, the Japanese government agreed to issue passports, valid for the continental United States, only to nonlaborers, or to workers resuming residence there, or joining a parent, wife, or children. California officials hoped this agreement would effectively prevent the smuggling of Japanese into the United States. It did not. Immigrants subsequently entered the country illicitly in large numbers, especially from Mexico.

The institution of Japanese "picture bride" marriages further offended exclusionists. A Japanese laborer in America, unable to go home to be married, often made the acquaintance of his future wife through a go-between who arranged an exchange of photo-graphs. After the couple agreed to become man and wife, the wed-ding ceremony was largely a matter of legal documents. This procedure allowed numerous potential immigrant mothers to be brought into the United States by an essentially evasive technique. In October, 1919, the Japanese Association of America, keenly aware of current criticism, passed a resolution proposing the abo-lition of such marriages. As of February, 1920, passports were no longer issued to "picture brides" by the Japanese government. Data on illicit entry are very vague for obvious reasons, but it probably amounted to only a small percentage of the total Japa-nese population.

New agitation against the Japanese led in 1913 to the proposal by the state legislature of a California Alien Land Act, known as the Webb Act. This bill sought to prevent Oriental aliens ineligible for citizenship from holding land. The measure seemed about to pass when the Japanese ambassador remonstrated with Secretary of State William Jennings Bryan. So pressing was the issue that a new President, Woodrow Wilson, dispatched Secretary Bryan to Sacramento to urge state legislators to draw up another bill, one "which would meet the views of the people of the state and yet leave untouched the international obligations of the United States." The intercession of the federal government resulted in removing some verbiage from the Webb Act, but its most drastic clauses, unpalatable to the Japanese, remained intact. The mea-sure, which became effective in August, 1913, provided that "Aliens not eligible for citizenship may inherit or devise real estate only as prescribed by treaty," that real property acquired by such aliens would eventually be returned to the state, and that agricul-tural lands could not be leased to such aliens for periods to ex-ceed three years. The Japanese government understandably lodged another series of formal protests at Washington, contending that the act was irreconcilable with accepted treaty principles, because it embodied unjust and obnoxious discrimination.

The Japanese Problem after World War I

The Webb Act remained on the books, but there were ways in which the Japanese could evade its provisions. One of these was to gain control of land by registering it in the name of another land-owner who was a citizen. By the leasing and subleasing of land, the Japanese came to control increasingly large truck-farm acreages of crops such as lettuce, celery, tomatoes, beans, and strawberries. The more land the Japanese acquired, the more they were feared as an economic threat.

Laws resembling California's Webb Act were passed against Orientals in nearby Oregon, Idaho, and other Western states, but California's legislation was the harshest. After World War I, Secretary of State Robert Lansing wrote to California legislators from the peace conference at Versailles that any further anti-Japanese legislation would seriously affect a settlement of peace terms. Once again California was urged to moderate its uncompromising attitude toward exclusion. But by 1920 the Japanese population in California had reached 72,000 (an increase of over 30,000 in ten years), because of loopholes in both the "Gentlemen's Agreement" and the Webb Act. Popular feeling resulted in the legislature's Anti-Alien Initiative Measure of 1920, which utterly prohibited the owning of land by Japanese or the leasing of farm land to them. Under its terms the Issei, or Japanese born in their native homeland, were forbidden even to hold an interest in any company owning real property.

Californians still feared the efficiency of the Japanese and the possibility that they might come to dominate the state's economic life. In 1917 Senator James D. Phelan charged that "because they work unremittingly—man, woman, and child, and participate in none of the activities of the community, they are capable of crowding out, and do crowd out the white population, until today the greatest production of potatoes, garden truck, beans and berries is controlled by them." Further resentment was caused because some Japanese refused to work for wages, preferring to bargain for a share of the crops. In this they differed from the Chinese laborers, as they did also in their quick adaptation to varied industries and in their apparent land hunger. Nevertheless, the two groups together did much of California's farming. In some districts the Japanese and Chinese occupied up to 75 per cent of the total irrigated area. They were strongly entrenched in the rice-growing region of Glenn, Colusa, and Butte Counties, in the asparagus, berry, vegetable, fruit, and vineyard sections of the Sacramento–San Joaquin delta, in Sutter and Placer Counties, in the grape, raisin, and fruit districts of Fresno, Kings, and Tulare Counties, in the vegetable and fruit districts of Los Angeles and Orange Counties, and in the cantaloupe and vegetable districts of the Imperial Valley. The numbers of Japanese engaged in California fishing increased 168 per cent during the four-year period preceding 1920.

After World War I, the Native Sons of the Golden West, the California State Grange, and various other labor and patriotic organizations banded together in opposition to this Oriental immigrant group. These Californians regarded the possible intermixture of Caucasians and Orientals as a grave danger. Accordingly, as thousands of young Japanese women began to come to the United States, California's exclusionists demanded a tighter federal immigration law. This demand led to the provisions in the Immigration Act of 1924 which abruptly put an end to the "Gentlemen's Agreement." Henceforth scarcely any Oriental alien ineligible to citizenship could be admitted into the country. Certainly the later deterioration of relations between Japan and the United States was in part caused by attitudes related to such immigration difficulties. In California the anti-Japanese agitation was to reach its most extensive proportions during World War II, when the rights of citizens of the United States of Japanese descent would be sorely tried. This aspect of Japanese-American relations will be treated in a later chapter.

Other Foreigners and Their Influence

The Orientals in California doubtless absorbed some of the nativist antagonism which might otherwise have been directed toward other immigrants. The French, Germans, Italians, and Irish, for example, encountered far fewer barriers to social acceptance and economic success. It seemed that these foreigners cast off the traces of their immigrant origins more quickly in the West than in the large cities of the East. In appealing rural environments especially, the folkways and customs of Basque sheepherders, Swiss dairymen, and Armenian fig growers often merged easily with those of their neighbors. As the immigrant's native language fell into disuse, and his connections with the "old country" became more remote, he was, perhaps by virtue of separation from other foreigners, definitely encouraged to put down permanent California roots.

Many foreigners were particularly attracted by the California countryside, and prospered there. As the population of cities grew, harvesters of prunes, tomatoes, cucumbers, grapes, and strawberries were needed in greater numbers. Europeans who came to California to pick crops frequently became owners of the very land they once were hired to work. Their skills brought forth harvests from hillside farms, too rocky and poor of soil for their original owners. The industry and achievement of such groups as the French and Germans have been discussed in the preceding chapter.

Other foreigners headed instinctively for the cities. The versatile Irishmen Denis Kearney and Frank B. Roney became labor organizers, and James McClatchy achieved prominence as a newspaper publisher. Less numerous in California than in a state like Massachusetts, the Irish nevertheless made their mark.

In the cities, the Italians and French were often found in the restaurant trades, or along with the Portuguese, in the fishing industry. Numerous foreign-language newspapers enjoyed a wide circulation among the immigrants. While usually slanted toward issues and personalities of the nationality involved, this foreign press contributed to California's cosmopolitan flavor. By the 1870's the San Francisco Italians regularly published as many as five journals. At San Francisco's North Beach, in fact, the Italians formed the majority of the population after 1890. One Italian leader was Amadeo Pietro Giannini, founder of the modern Bank of America. In its earlier stage as the Bank of Italy, this organization contributed much to the rebuilding of the city after the fire of 1906 had destroyed banking and credit facilities. Another product of the Italian section was Angelo Rossi, a florist who later became mayor of San Francisco.

While some foreigners modified their customs in accordance with the new environment, others were either more independent or more traditional. The Irish and Germans seemed particularly reluctant to give up native folkways. The Germans often pointedly sought to remain masters of their own fate, and one of the results of this attitude was that the tradesmen, merchants, and farmers among them were admired for their thrift and industry. Among the prosperous leaders of California's German element were Adolph Sutro and Henry Teschemacher, both mayors of San Francisco. Theodore Cordua and Charles Weber became founders of Marysville and Stockton, just as the German-Swiss Sutter had, earlier, founded Sacramento. Heinrich Virmond was an outstanding merchant and trader. Already mentioned have been Claus Spreckels, who became the "sugar king" of California, and Edward Vischer and Charles Christian Nahl, artists. For the most part, however, separate immigrant strains in California's past are not readily identified. That part of its history has been quite effectively obliterated. One reason is that few issues of the foreign newspapers published at San Francisco and Los Angeles have been preserved. Also, foreigners frequently anglicized their names, in an attempt to gain greater social acceptance. Many institutions and colonies that were founded by particular immigrant groups for their own protection quickly proved to be unnecessary and rapidly disappeared. Little remains of the French utopian colony of Icaria Speranza, organized in 1881 near Cloverdale, or the German colony at Anaheim. Further north, above San Francisco, the Italian-Swiss colony at Asti still exists, but in a commercialized form markedly different from that of its founding.

The paucity of records, together with the lack of systematic research into foreign influence in the American West, has caused the racial homogeneity of the population to be exaggerated. Actually, what documents are available—census statistics, travel accounts, corporation records, newspapers, and local annals—all suggest that a conspicuous foreign element has historically existed. This element participated in the shaping of life on many California cattle and sheep ranches, as well as in logging camps, mines, railroad construction camps, and fruit orchards. And the immigrant contribution in the arts, trades, and agriculture, sometimes achieved in a climate of social duress, lingers on.

SELECTED READINGS

Older works that deal with Chinese immigration include Mary R. Coolidge, *Chinese Immigration* (New York, 1909); G. F. Seward, *Chinese Immigration: Its Social and Economic Aspects* (New York, 1881); and William Speer, *China and California: Their Relations Past and Present* (San Francisco, 1853). A more recent appraisal is Elmer C. Sandmeyer, *The Anti-Chinese Movement in California* (Urbana, 1939). Articles that treat the problem include Rodman W. Paul, "The Origin of the Chinese Issue in California," *Mississippi Valley Historical Review*, XXV (September, 1938), 181–196; Helen R. Goss, "The Fourth Estate in Old Tuolomne," Historical Society of Southern California *Quarterly*, XL (June, 1958), 125–137; and, in the same journal, Mildred Welborn, "Events Leading to the Chinese Exclusion Act," X (January, 1914), 49–58. A later issue of this *Quarterly* contains a discussion of a closely related subject, David V. Dufault's "The Chinese in the Mining Camps of California: 1848–1870," XLI (June, 1959), 155–170. This can be supplemented with Richard H. Morefield, "Mexicans in the California Mines, 1848–1853," California Historical Society *Quarterly*, XXXV (March, 1956), 37–46. See also the interesting study by Robert F. G. Spier, "Food Habits of Nineteenth Century California Chinese," California Historical Society *Quarterly*, XXXVII (March–June, 1958), 79–84, as well as, in the same *Quarterly*, Henryk Sinkiewicz, "The Chinese in California," XXXIV (December, 1955), 301–316, and Ping Chiu, *Chinese Labor in California, 1850–1880: An Economic Study* (Madison, 1963). Consult also Gunther Barth, *Bitter Strength: A His-*

tory of the Chinese in the United States, 1850–1870 (Cambridge, Mass., 1964); Kian Moon Kwan, "Assimilation of the Chinese in the United States: An Exploratory Study in California," Ph.D. dissertation, University of California, Berkeley (1958); and Kwang Ching Liu, Americans and Chinese (Cambridge, Mass., 1963).

Useful for an understanding of other foreign influences in California in general are The Commonwealth Club, The Population of California (San Francisco, 1946), and Doris M. Wright, "The Making of Cosmopolitan California—An Analysis of Immigration, 1848–1870," California Historical Society Quarterly, XIX (December, 1940), 323–343, and XX (March, 1941), 65–79. The books of Carey McWilliams contain many thought-provoking generalizations about foreigners. These include California: The Great Exception (New York, 1949); Factories in the Field (Boston, 1939); Southern California Country (New York, 1946); and Prejudice: Japanese-Americans, Symbol of Racial Intolerance (Boston, 1944).

Works concerning the Japanese include Yamato Ichihashi, Japanese Immigration: Its Status in California (San Francisco, 1915); T. Iyenaga and K. Sato, Japan and the California Problem (New York, 1921); K. K. Kawakami, Japan in World Politics (New York, 1917); H. A. Millis, The Japanese Problem in the United States (New York, 1915); and Sidney L. Gulick, American Democracy and Asiatic Citizenship (New York, 1918). Representative of a vast government literature on the subject of Oriental exclusion is "California and the Oriental, Japanese and Hindus," Report of State Board of Control to Governor William D. Stephens (Sacramento, 1922). A helpful article is Thomas A. Bailey, "California, Japan, and the Alien Land Legislation of 1913," Pacific Historical Review, I (March, 1932), 36–59. Books that deal with later abuses against the Japanese include D. S. Thomas and R. S. Nishimoto, The Spoilage (Berkeley, 1946); D. S. Thomas, The Salvage (Berkeley, 1952); Jacobus ten Broek, Edward N. Barnhart, and Floyd W. Matson, Prejudice, War, and the Constitution (Berkeley, 1954); and Roger Daniels, The Politics of Prejudice: The Anti-Japanese Movement in California and the Struggle for Japanese Exclusion (Berkeley, 1962). See also Robert E. Hennings, "James D. Phelan and the Woodrow Wilson Anti-Oriental Statement of May 3, 1912," California Historical Society Quarterly, XLII (December, 1963), 291–300. More anti-alien agitation is described in Gladys H. Waldron, "Antiforeign Movements in California, 1919–1929," Ph.D. dissertation, University of California, Berkeley (1956).

Regarding California's non-Oriental nationalities, see Andrew F. Rolle, "Italy in California: A Mediterranean America," Pacific Spectator, IX (Autumn, 1955), 408–419. See also Rolle's "Success in the Sun: the Italians in California," Westerner's Brand Book (Los Angeles, 1962), and his The Immigrant Upraised: Italian Adventurers and Colonists in an Expanding America (Norman, Okla., 1968), as well as Hans C. Palmer, "Italian Immigration and the Development of Cali fornia Agriculture," Ph.D. dissertation. University of California, Berkeley (1965).

Frederick G. Bohme, "The Portuguese in California," *California Historical Society Quarterly,* XXXV (September, 1956), 233–252 treats another important immigrant group. Erwin G. Gudde, *German Pioneers in Early California* (Hoboken, 1927), and Charles G. Loomis, *The German Theater in San Francisco, 1861–1864* (Berkeley, 1952), are among the few works on the Germans. Excellent is Raup's *The German Colonization of Anaheim.* On the French see Gilbert Chinard, ed. and trans., *When the French Came to California* (San Francisco, 1944), an English version of "Treny's" *La Californie Devoilée* (Paris, 1850), an early book that explains how the French emigration companies operated. Useful also is Abraham P. Nasatir, *French Activities in California: An Archival Calendar Guide* (Stanford, 1945). See also Daniel Levy, *Les Français en Californie* (San Francisco, 1884), and Edouard Auger, *Voyage en Californie* (Paris, 1854), as well as Olympe Audouard, *A Travers L'Amerique: Le Far-West* (Paris, 1869). More chauvinistic than critical are the two following books on the Irish in California: Hugh Quigley, *The Irish Race in California and the Pacific Coast* (San Francisco, 1878), and Thomas F. Prendergast, *Forgotten Pioneers: Irish Leaders in Early California* (San Francisco, 1942).

A start on the history of California's Jews is Justin G. Turner's "The First Decade of Los Angeles Jewry: A Pioneer History, 1850–1860," *American Jewish Historical Quarterly,* LIV (December, 1964), 123–164. Regarding Negroes, see the bibliographies of Chapters 21 and 37.

25

Crushing the Indian

Even in comparison with the Chinese and Japanese, the minority that suffered most during the late nineteenth century in California were the Indians. As hordes of settlers Americanized California, assaults on the Indians by white traders, cattlemen, miners, merchants, and the military increased in number and gravity. Indian lands were overrun and tribal ways were challenged. As elsewhere in the American West, invading Caucasians, instead of accommodating themselves to Indian prerogatives, demanded that the Indian change his way of life to suit them. Indians in general seemed to be characterized by cultural remoteness from the whites. Yet physical proximity, although imposed, exerted a great will to survive.

Unfortunately, longstanding friction between California's diverse Indian groups prevented them from taking a united stand against the technologically superior whites, and they were able to launch only sporadic and generally ineffective attacks. In contrast, the Americans, who seemed bent upon Indian extermination, demanded and received the protection and aid of their government. In the period after the Mexican War, the United States War Department ordered infantry and cavalry units to patrol pressure points and to deal sternly with Indian outbreaks. The practical result of white infiltration was gradual decimation of the Indians; they had already suffered a decrease in numbers under Spain and

Mexico, but their losses during the American era were appalling.

Starvation, disease, and liquor conspired with bullet and knife against the Indians. Pulmonary and venereal infections, smallpox, and other Caucasian imports wiped out even the marginal well-being that the Indians had enjoyed under Mexican rule. As indicated previously, there were more than 100,000 Indians in California when Commodore Sloat raised the United States flag at Monterey in 1846. Then came the Gold Rush; in the period from 1849 to 1856 alone California's Indian population was reduced to about 50,000.

Rarely had the Indian's land tenure been disturbed in pre-American times; the prevailing practice from the early Spanish period had offered legal protection against such action. But when the United States took over California from Mexico, the aggressive Americans would not concede the Indians usufructuary or other rights to the lands they had formerly held. "Gringo" newcomers, refusing to accommodate their civilization to the Indians, commonly paid no more attention to their presence on "government lands" than if they were so many coyotes. Pioneers who had been shot at by warriors while crossing the Plains were scarcely in a conciliatory mood. To most settlers an Indian was an Indian, and well-armed whites usually had their way in the struggle over land.

Driven from their homes and from the land of their fathers during the 1850's, the Indians for the most part fled to inaccessible and desolate spots. But although the majority were of this peaceable and submissive inclination, quite devoid of the fierceness of the Plains Indians, some northern California Indians were more resentful. Their occasional spirit of resistance, resulting in attacks upon the property and livestock of settlers, was swiftly met with American armed might. An Indian might revenge any outrage suffered at the hands of Caucasians by killing the first white man he met thereafter. In turn, the Americans reacted with measures that sometimes included the wiping out of entire Indian villages. Such conflicts made up California's so-called "Indian Wars," or skirmishes.

In this pre-reservation era, the Indians in the towns and cities fared perhaps worst of all. Their wages were miserable—only half those paid to whites—while the conditions under which they worked were unspeakably bad. Even worse, however, were the disastrous effects of their immoderate gambling and addiction to firewater.

MOHAVE INDIAN FAMILY ON THE COLORADO RIVER, FIVE MILES NORTH OF NEEDLES. THE UNCLOTHED MAN IS THE CHIEF. (By courtesy of The Huntington Library, San Marino, California.)

Developing a Government
Reservation Policy

After the Gold Rush, frequent Indian raids on outlying ranches increased demands by harassed ranchers and settlers that the natives be controlled. Beyond the organization of posses to pursue marauders, some sort of permanent reservation system, throughout the country, seemed indicated. Travelers in California and elsewhere out west also demanded protection. As a result, the federal government authorized the negotiation of treaties with Indian tribes, by which they were to vacate their traditional hunting grounds in favor of life on reservations promised them by Indian agents.

As early as 1849 the federal government took steps to develop a reservation system in California. That year Thomas Butler King was sent to the state to study conditions and to collect data, and Adam Johnston was made Indian sub-agent, under a new Department of the Interior, for the Sacramento–San Joaquin area. In 1850 a United States Indian Commission, armed with an appropriation of $50,000, was appointed to negotiate California's reservation system. This commission, consisting of Redick McKee, George W. Barbour, and Oliver Wozencraft, arrived in California in January, 1851. Its members encountered numerous difficulties in persuading the Indians to move out of their mountain homes onto the flat lands of the Central Valley. The Indians interfered with gold mining operations in the Sierra, but finally their hunger and need forced them to negotiate with the commissioners.

Eighteen treaties were concluded with the leaders of 139 native bands, representing practically the total Indian population of the state. The Indians agreed to recognize the sovereignty of the United States, to keep the peace, and to refrain from acts of retaliation. More important, they accepted eighteen reservations, aggregating 7,500,000 acres, and promised at the same time to quitclaim and cede old land rights to the government. The commissioners, in turn, agreed to pay the Indians certain sums in agricultural implements and other goods, to retain the new reservations for the Indians' use in perpetuity, and to provide skilled instructors and supervisors in farming, blacksmithing, and woodwork.

These California treaties were transmitted by President Millard Fillmore to the United States Senate. Much to the chagrin of the conscientious commissioners, the Senate failed to ratify the treaties. Fulfillment of the agreements was considered too costly; the commissioners had contracted claims of $716,394.79, at which most legislators balked. These stillborn treaty documents of the California Indian commissioners lay forgotten in federal archives for over half a century. The Indians claimed they had promptly complied with the terms imposed, but the compensatory acreages promised them had, for the most part, not been forthcoming.

A few Indians had been herded onto marginal strips of land after the federal government, nevertheless, began to criss-cross their former preserves with roads. In a corrosive environment of shacks and shanties, they lived a life that was neither Indian nor white. "Never in the poorest huts of the most poverty-stricken wilds of Italy, Bavaria, Norway, and New Mexico," protested Helen Hunt Jackson, had she seen anything "so loathsome as the kennels in which some of the San Diego Indians are living." It is a grievous truth that for years almost nothing was done to help these outcasts. In other words, only half a reservation system existed in California during the 1850's—and a mismanaged half system at that. Some writers have referred to this phase of the Indian story as one of virtual extermination.

Worsening Indian-White Relations

The management of California's Indian reservations, from their inception in 1853 up to relatively recent times, is hardly a matter for pride. Especially during the 1850's and 1860's, many of the Americans placed in charge of Indian affairs were clearly unfit for their posts, and in the case of some of them, personal venality accompanied inexperience. Too often, whenever a reservation contained valuable land, avaricious whites were permitted to swoop in and the Indians were driven onto rocky or sandy terrain. There they almost literally competed with squirrels for the acorns that fell from the oaks. Some Indians voluntarily left the reservations to become unskilled laborers on ranches and farms, but these were often considered a shiftless and irresponsible element to be exploited by the whites. Early municipal ordinances encouraged a system of virtual peonage under which a rancher, by paying the fine of an Indian arrested for drunkenness, picked up a laborer, who was required by law to work off the amount of his fine. Indians seldom understood the white man's regulations, under which they too, perforce, lived. Whenever land titles were transferred, permission given Indians to remain on certain lands was often disregarded and the Indians finally evicted.

In general, the federal policy of dealing with the Indians was as unsuccessful in California as elsewhere—with one notable exception. In 1853 Edward Fitzgerald Beale, the naval officer whose activities at the time of the conquest of California have already been mentioned, became the first superintendent of Indian affairs within the state. On a tract of 75,000 acres at Fort Tejón, south of the Tehachapi Mountains, Beale attempted to convert a wild, mountainous region into a model preserve for a remnant of 350 Tejón and Cas-take (Castaic) Indians. He believed that this relatively small group could become permanently self-sufficient and that such an experiment, if successful, might be influential throughout the West. Work at Tejón proceeded so well that Beale gave his Indian wards a voice in their affairs—an almost unheard-of innovation in Indian relations. He met frequently with selected chiefs to discuss such matters as the disposal of crop surpluses. Beale never hesitated to criticize white citizens, or to take ruthless disciplinary action against his own subordinates, when either treated the Indians unjustly. This policy resulted in complaints to Washington about his administration. After a change of Indian policy officials at the national capital, political pressure and the charges of malfeasance lodged against Beale forced him, in 1855, to relinquish his superintendency. His cherished Fort Tejón was subsequently whittled down to 25,000 acres, and its federal appropriation was cut in half. What was left of the Tejón reservation remained intact for several years after Beale's dismissal, but its effectiveness had been hobbled. Finally, in 1863, Tejón was abandoned.

California's other Indian preserves were soon reduced to marginal plots of unwanted land, where tribe after tribe deteriorated and became obscure. The grubby reservations that continued to exist at Nome Lackee in the Sacramento foothills, at the mouth of the Noyo River on the Mendocino Coast, and on the Klamath River south of Crescent City, were utterly inadequate. Neither natives nor whites benefited from a system that settled the Indians in a cramped, stagnating environment. Such mismanagement of Indian affairs had occurred partly because two agencies of the federal government, the War Department and the Department of the Interior, frequently quarreled over how to handle the Indian. "Pacification by feeding," or a closely-regulated life on the reservation, was long the general policy of the Interior Department. When, however, the Indian escaped from inhospitable reservations, the War Department ordered the Army after him in hot pursuit, either killing him outright or driving him back. The Army insisted that, unless it was given complete control of the Indian, it could not shoulder responsibility for the safety of whites. Whenever the lives of Caucasians were at stake, the Army usually got its way.

Under the circumstances, it is perhaps remarkable that the Indians displayed so little open hostility toward the settlers. In the south there had been only one significant uprising, that which took place near Warner's Ranch in 1851, under a subchief named Antonio Garrá. In the 1850's and 1860's skirmishing took place with some frequency in northern California, especially along the Humboldt, the Eel, and the Rogue Rivers. For the most part, the whites (civilian and military) wanted to drive Indians into remote locales where they would be rendered relatively harmless to white settlements. Another solution was to confine them to prescribed reservations. In one case, an expedition against retreating Indians led to a remarkable geographical discovery. Possibly the first whites to look upon the Yosemite Valley were members of Joseph Reddeford Walker's 1833 trapping expedition. But the effective discovery of the Yosemite was made in 1851 by Major James D. Savage. That year Savage, volunteer leader of a group of whites known as the Mariposa Battalion, was deputized by Governor McDougal to pursue marauding Yosemite and Chowchilla Indians. Savage's posse chased about 350 Yosemites into their rugged Sierra hiding place, above the south fork of the Merced River. Here the whites stumbled upon one of the world's most exquisitely beautiful valleys. Soon thereafter Savage's men received the surrender of some of Chief Tenieya's warriors, but the Indians slipped away one night while their guard slept. This made necessary another stubborn military campaign. Only after Chief Tenieya's favorite son was killed did the old warrior himself finally surrender. Most of the Indian bands had capitulated by the time the Civil War had ended, though a few continued to hold out for many more years.

The Modoc War

The last and most dramatic of California's Indian conflicts was the Modoc War, the culmination of two decades of Modoc-white difficulties. The first bloodshed had occurred in 1852, when the Indians attacked an unsuspecting immigrant train en route to California, killing nearly half of this relatively small party. Nearby miners demanded the extermination of the savages who had participated. With one of their number, Ben Wright, as leader, they formulated a plan for outwitting the Indians. Throwing the Modocs off their guard by proposing a peaceful settlement of differences, the Americans launched their retaliatory "Ben Wright Massacre" against the offending Indians. The surviving Modocs never forgot what they considered an infamous butchery, and for the next ten years hostilities continued intermittently.

In 1864 most of the Modoc tribe—seriously reduced in number —were persuaded by United States Indian agents to go to the Klamath Reservation in southern Oregon. But this northward migration caused the Modocs to trespass on the hunting lands of the Klamath Indians. The Klamaths resented the presence of the Modocs and restricted their freedom of movement. Chief Kiente-poos (Captain Jack) of the Modocs quickly led his people back southward to their ancestral preserves. Late in 1869, Alfred B. Meacham, superintendent of Indian affairs for Oregon, persuaded Captain Jack to return to the Klamath Reservation with two hundred Modocs. When, however, the Klamath Indians were as overbearing as before, the chief and his band returned again the following spring to their old camping grounds in northeastern California, along the Lost River in what is present-day Modoc County.

By coming back to California the Modocs defied United States authority as vested in its Indian agents, an act that usually invited military intervention. Disturbed settlers, in an atmosphere of confusion, spoke of organizing a force to protect themselves against the Modocs. By the winter of 1872 the Army moved in an observation force. On a November day in that year a Modoc girl named Wi-ne-ma caught sight of the military strength of the whites. Anxious to prevent bloodshed, she mounted a bay mare at Yreka and rode seventy-five miles to warn her people and to urge them not to resist. She thereby became a heroine of her tribe. An unfortunate clash, however, occurred when an Indian known as Scar-Faced Charley refused to give up his pistol to United States authorities. In the aftermath of this incident eleven settlers were killed by marauding Modoc bands, and the American cavalry closed in on the Indians. The Modocs, at the order of Captain Jack, retreated with their ponies and other property toward the contorted lava beds to the southwest of Lake Rhett. There they sought the safety of caves guarded by jagged rocks and ledges. Though cut off from food supplies, the Indians could subsist by eating field mice and bats found in the caves, and by drinking water from underground springs. Captain Jack announced that he would not molest settlers unless they entered his winter camp, claiming that he desired only peace and that it was the whites who were warlike. Nevertheless, the Army was determined to force the Modocs back onto the reservation. The cost of dislodging the small band of Indians, secure in their lava fortress and supplied with old muzzle-loading rifles and other antique arms, was to prove high.

On January 17, 1873, Colonel Frank Wheaton, U.S.A., advanced on the Modocs, ordering volley after volley of cannon fired into the lava. This attack had little effect upon the Indians. Concealed behind their natural rock breastworks, they returned a deadly fire against the charging Americans. The Army's losses compelled quick retreat. At this critical juncture the Quakers and other pacifist elements persuaded President Grant to create a peace commission. General E. R. S. Canby, commander of the Modoc operation, Superintendent Meacham, and two other commissioners made arrangements to meet Captain Jack. Both sides agreed that during these peace councils no further shooting would take place.

With one thousand men surrounding the Modocs, General Canby moved his camp to the edge of the lava beds, one and a half miles from the Modoc stronghold, and pitched a council tent between the opposing camps. However, at the Indian war council, Captain Jack was goaded by his fellow tribesmen, despite his earnest protestations, into a treacherous promise. After the Modoc warriors had placed a squaw's hat upon Jack's head and taunted him as a coward and a fish-hearted woman, he was placed in the position of having to prove his bravery by murdering the white general. Although Wi-ne-ma made a passionate plea to Meacham and Canby to remain in their own camp, a fatal peace conference was held on Good Friday, April 11, 1873. Both the Indian and the white emissaries had agreed to be unarmed. Actually, not only did the Modocs bring along concealed pistols and knives, but several young warriors lay hidden in the nearby bushes, armed with rifles. After Captain Jack gave the signal for attack, he shot General Canby. Meacham was also stabbed and shot, though not fatally.

General Canby's troops determined to chastise the killer of their commander by pursuing Captain Jack through the lava beds. They were, however, frustrated time after time, and lost the greater part of a detachment of soldiers under Lieutenant Thomas Wright. Nevertheless, there could be but one end to the unequal struggle between the Modoc Indian remnant and the Army. When Captain Jack's warriors finally could hold out no longer, they escaped from their caves, separating into two groups. One band then surrendered, and along with various Klamaths eventually became government scouts. The other Modocs fought on until Captain Jack was captured. He and two of his accomplices were tried by court-martial and hanged at Fort Klamath. Before it ended, the Modoc War had cost the United States government half a million dollars, plus the lives of a general and about seventy-five men. All this might have been avoided if the Modocs had been allowed to remain occupants of a few relatively worthless and geographically remote lava beds and some marginal grazing land.

Befriending the Indian

The swift and relentless disappearance of the California Indians, especially in the latter half of the nineteenth century, is both tragic and pathetic. It seems incredible that between the beginning of the American period and the opening of the twentieth century their number declined from 100,000 to 15,500. In these few decades a proud people were utterly broken in health and morale.

After General Grant became president in 1869, he replaced all of California's Indian agents, and those in most western states, with army officers. The new Superintendent of Indian Affairs there was Major General J. B. McIntosh, a man of unusual ability who was anxious to help the Indians. He found the condition of the former Mission Indians pitiable, scattered as they were over a wide region and living in small villages or rancherías. In 1870 General McIntosh succeeded in getting four townships of land at Pala and San Pasqual set aside for these Indians. Because of pressure from white citizens in San Diego County, these reservations were, however, abolished during the next year and McIntosh, as well as other army officers in the Indian Service, were replaced. Next, various churches were allotted Indian agencies to supervise, and the Mission Indians were assigned for a time to the Methodist denomination. The policy of appointing church agents, however, also gave way, as had the military superintendencies, to appointees named by the Commissioner of Indian Affairs. One of these, Charles A. Wetmore, a special commissioner to the Mission Indians, attracted widespread sympathy for their landless plight. As a result of public support of Wetmore's pleas on behalf of the downtrodden natives, President Grant in 1875 established nine small reservations in San Diego County and later created additional reserves by executive order. These lands were, however, generally arid, brush strewn, and unfertile.

Wetmore's good work was followed by that of Helen Hunt Jackson, a highly emotional champion of Indian rights. Along with Abbot Kinney, she was appointed a special government commissioner to investigate Indian conditions. Her two influential books, *A Century of Dishonor* (1881) and *Ramona* (1884), focusing upon California, called attention to the mistreatment of the Indian. Mrs. Jackson decried the history of the nation's reservation policy in such words as these:

President after president has appointed commission after commission to inquire into and report upon Indian affairs, and to make suggestions as to the best methods of managing them. The reports are filled with eloquent statements of wrongs done to the Indians, of perfidies on the part of the government; they counsel, as earnestly as words can, a trial of the simple and unperplexing expedients of telling truth, keeping promises, making fair bargains, dealing justly in all ways and all things. These reports are bound up with the Government's Annual Reports, and that is the end of them.

Other humanitarians then began, somewhat tardily, to press for reform. Late in the nineteenth century Charles Fletcher Lummis, Southwestern author, editor, librarian, and an acquaintance of Theodore Roosevelt at Harvard, joined Mrs. Jackson's campaign; he solicited funds with which the displaced Indians of the Warner's Ranch area in southern California were eventually settled on more fertile lands near Pala. In 1902 Congress appropriated $100,000 for the purchase of lands for the Warner's Ranch Indians and any other homeless local natives; part of this money could be spent to relocate them, or for subsistence and the purchase of agricultural implements, building materials, and farm animals. Hundreds of Indians were thereby resettled upon 3,438 acres of land bought for them at Pala. By 1903, as a result of growing public sympathy, the Indian Bureau set aside twenty-seven reservations for the Mission Indians, ranging in size from 280 to 38,600 acres. This was in addition to a reservation of 45,000 acres at Tule Lake.

Largely as the result of the widespread influence of such reformers, the Dawes Act of 1887 had acknowledged federal responsibility for the care and sustenance of Indians. The legal fiction that the Indian population of the country was composed of separate nations, each with its own sovereignty, had long since ended. Under this congressional law Indians were given many of the privileges of white citizens, including the right of each family head to own 160 acres of land. This land was, however, to be held in trust for twenty-five years, after which time the Indians were to receive full ownership of their holdings, and full American citizenship.

Only a few reservations in California were, however, altered by the Dawes Act. The only significant reservation to be so affected was Fort Mohave, with some public domain allotments made also to the Washoe Indians. Otherwise, allotments, mostly of from five to ten acres, were made under separate acts passed from 1890 to 1910. Remaining non-allocated tracts were held in tribal trust, as they are today. The Bureau of Indian Affairs was able to persuade Congress to renew trusteeship annually after the initial twenty-five-year period specified by the Dawes Act had expired. Indian opposition to the allotment of lands for whites remained strong in

California, where they were successful in preventing wholesale allotments from Indian reserves, except in one or two instances.

The decline of tribal autonomy throughout the state came long before the allotment process began. Allotment, however, did mean the demise of some villages; yet abandonment of the land and dispersal of many tribelets occurred mostly before the major allotment procedures got underway. Indians who remained on reservations came to rely heavily upon the extensive government ration system. As a result these Indians increasingly got into the habit of refusing to support themselves by work.

In allocating them land, the poorest plots often went to them and the best were sold to white settlers. Even when the Indians were lucky enough to be awarded good land, they were so inexperienced with matters of legal ownership that they were frequently tricked into selling their best holdings. But, worst of all, the Indians, with little experience in cultivating or managing land, made but a poor adjustment to a white environment. The Dawes Act came almost too late to benefit a people who, by then, needed charity as much as government definition of their status. Some who claimed that the Indian functioned best in his own environment—as a member of a tribal group rather than as an individual—lived to see the Dawes Act repealed by the Indian Reorganization Act of 1934. From that date onward to 1953, the government restored tribal life, a handicraft culture, and a reservation society to the Indian. By the time of this change in official policy, of course, great numbers of Indians had left the reservations for good. Despite continuing public interest in their welfare, only about a dozen bands out of four dozen in the state registered with Indian Reorganization Act authorities. Indian opposition to that law seemed to center around rejection of continued governmental intervention.

Most of today's California Indians (who, in fact, are typically of mixed descent) have been assimilated into the general population, though some linger on in the confining atmosphere of those tiny reservations that still exist within the state. Varying in area, resources, and population, these reservations usually lack good soil and a sufficient water supply with which to carry on agriculture successfully. Recognizing the problems besetting a long-neglected people, through the years certain private, state, and national organizations, among them the Northern Indian Association, the Indian Rights Association, the Sequoia League, the Indian Board of Cooperation, and the California League for American Indians, have made a generous contribution to the betterment of Indian conditions in California. One testimonial to their efforts is the Sherman Institute, near Riverside; this unique school was privately founded in 1901 with government encouragement to afford the Indian children of southern California practical industrial and handicraft training.

With a few such exceptions, however, Caucasian efforts to help the California Indian have failed. The Indian himself has at times seemed to resist progress, at least in the sense that whites define the term. In recent years some Indian tribal groups have won favorable land-tenure court decisions, both federal and state. Beginning in the 1930's, two California attorney generals, Earl Warren and later Robert Kenny, sought to obtain payment of $1.25 per acre from Washington for lands allotted the Indians as their property. As a result of Case K-344, the rights of various groups of "treaty Indians" came to be appraised at $17,500,000. But, in 1944, after some fifteen years of litigation, the Indians were finally awarded only $5,165,863.46. This sum, furthermore, was placed in the United States Treasury—to be made available by congressional appropriation under extremely confining terms. Governmental niggardliness had once again characterized United States-Indian relations.

After World War II a series of legal claims against the federal government were lodged by Indians throughout the nation, in which professional historians became involved as consultants. Pursuant to the notable Ute case, won outside California, the United States Supreme Court from 1948 to 1950 awarded 3,337 acres of Palm Springs land to seventy-one surviving members of the Agua Caliente band of the Cahuilla Indians. Because these Indians remained unsatisfied with that allotment, Congress in 1959 passed an additional law of equalization on their behalf. They thereby achieved virtually a commanding position in real estate ownership at the popular resort town, receiving in excess of 30,000 acres. The Palm Springs Indians held about 2,000 acres of this land in "tribal tenure," including the land on which their spa is located.

In addition, extensive hearings before a federal Indian Claims Commission during the 1950's and 1960's led to a federal decision that California's Indians held an aboriginal title to at least 64 million acres of land for which they were to be paid approximately 45½ cents per acre, totaling $29 million. The Indians had claimed 100 million acres at one dollar per acre.

Such legal victories have come rather too late in the history of the Indian, and have scarcely proved useful in salvaging his tribal homogeneity. Instead, the Indian has more frequently had to make an awkward adjustment to the society which succeeded in overwhelming him.

Stilted in befriending the Indian, his white masters first made up the fiction that he was a member of a "nation," and later treated him as a ward of the federal government, rather than as a resident of the "nations" with which government treaties had been signed. A white policy of tardy accommodation and Caucasian confusion seemed inescapable. We are, indeed, still divided as to how we should solve "the Indian problem." The roots of failure to manage their plight are sunk deep in the American past. Furthermore, expiation of guilt late in the Indian record seems impossible. Yet today's society requires a better image of the Indian and his origins if any sort of justice, albeit belated, is to be done to his record.

SELECTED READINGS

Sources concerning the origins, ethnology, and folkways of the California Indians have been cited in the readings for Chapter 2. A basic work on the California Indians is R. F. Heizer and M. A. Whipple, eds., *The California Indians: A Source Book* (Berkeley, 1951). Cook, *The Conflict Between the California Indian and White Civilization* and Helen Hunt Jackson, *A Century of Dishonor* (New York, 1881), recount the devasting pressures exerted on the Indians by the whites. Consult the Harper Torchbook reprint edited by Andrew F. Rolle (New York, 1965). See also George W. Manypenny, *Our Indian Wards* (Cincinnati, 1880), and a more specific article concerning Indian relations with the federal government by William H. Ellison entitled "The Federal Indian Policy in California," *Mississippi Valley Historical Review*, IX (June, 1922), 37–67. An unpublished doctoral dissertation of importance is Charles B. Leonard, "Federal Indian Policy in the San Joaquin Valley: Its Application and Results," University of California, Berkeley (1928). Another significant dissertation is Imre Sutton's "Land Tenure and Changing Occupance on Indian Reservations in Southern California," University of California, Los Angeles (1964). Consult Sutton's "Private Property in Land among Reservation Indians in Southern California," *Yearbook*, Association of Pacific Coast Geographers, XXIX (1967), 69–89. Richard Thomas discusses Indian leadership in "The Mission Indians: A Study of Leadership and Cultural Contact," Ph.D. dissertation, University of California, Los Angeles (1963). Useful chapters on Indian administration are in Edward Everett Dale's *The Indians of the Southwest* (Norman, Okla., 1949). See also C. E. Kelsey, "The Rights and Wrongs of California Indians," Commonwealth Club of California *Transactions* for 1909–1910 (San Francisco, 1910), and

C. C. Painter, *Condition of Affairs in Indian Territory and California* (Philadelphia, 1888). A more general treatment is Charles C. Royce, *Indian Land Cessions in the United States* (Washington, D.C., 1899).

On Beale's reservation system see Stephen Bonsal, *Edward Fitzgerald Beale: A Pioneer in the Path of Empire, 1822–1893* (New York, 1912), and Helen S. Giffen and Arthur Woodward, *The Story of El Tejón* (Los Angeles, 1942), as well as Richard E. Crouter and Andrew F. Rolle, "Edward Fitzgerald Beale and the Indian Peace Commissioners in California, 1851–1854," Historical Society of Southern California *Quarterly*, XLII (June, 1960), 107–132. J. Ross Browne, *The Indians of California* (San Francisco, repr. 1944), and John W. Caughey, ed., *The Indians of Southern California* (San Marino, 1952), treat the general condition of the California Indian in the nineteenth century.

On the Indians and the discovery of the Yosemite see Lafayette H. Bunnell, *Discovery of the Yosemite and the Indian War of 1851* (Los Angeles, 1911), and Annie R. Mitchell, *Jim Savage and the Tulareno Indians* (Los Angeles, 1957), as well as C. Gregory Crampton, ed., *The Mariposa Indian War, 1850–1851: Diaries of Edward Eccleston* (Salt Lake City, 1958). A little-known revolt is described in William Edward Evans, "The Garra Uprising: Conflict Between San Diego Indians and Settlers in 1851," California Historical Society *Quarterly*, XLV (December, 1966), 339–349.

Regarding the Modoc War, Jeff. C. Riddle—son of Wi-ne-ma, the Modoc heroine—and Frank Riddle, an American miner, together wrote *The Indian History of the Modoc War and the Causes That Led to It* (San Francisco, 1914). More recently, Keith A. Murray has produced *The Modocs and Their War* (Norman, Okla., 1959). See also Max Heyman, *Prudent Soldier* (Glendale, 1960), a biography of General E. R. S. Canby, the general who lost his life commanding U.S. troops in the Modoc War. A contemporary account of that conflict by an officer who participated in it is C. T. Brady, *Northwestern Fights and Fighters* (New York, 1907). Another first-hand account is A. B. Meacham, *Wigwam and War-path, or The Royal Chief in Chains* (Boston, 1875).

Anyone who has ever been involved in the defense of Indian rights will appreciate Kenneth Johnson, ed., *K-344, or the Indians of California vs. the United States* (Los Angeles, 1966). Descriptive non-anthropological scholarship about the Indian has been a kind of patchwork. Beginning with Helen Hunt Jackson's above-mentioned epochal but controversial tract to William T. Hagan's moderate but skimpy *American Indians* (1961), this field of writing has been, at turns, polemical, exhortatory, and filiopietistic. Traditionally respected authorities in the field—Grant Foreman, Clark Wissler, George E. Hyde, and John Collier—are gone.

26

The Workingmen and the New Constitution

The origin of the Workingmen's movement in California is best understood in the light of the social discomfort—in some cases positive suffering—that was widespread during the period following the Civil War. Economic conditions were increasingly disturbed. Recovery from the devastating national panic of 1873 was slow; and the dry winter of 1876–1877 ruined California's grain harvest and added to the travails, already described, of ranchers. As a result, numerous farm hands were unemployed, and many of those who were not were discontented. Such workers frequently slept in barns, were not permitted to eat with their employers, and lacked common sanitation facilities. Bands of tramps infested California's dusty roads. Unemployed workers flocked to the cities, with several thousand seeking public relief in 1876 at San Francisco alone. Hordes of the unemployed were anxious to work for wages of $2 per day. Labor riots in large Eastern cities also encouraged discord out West. Workingmen renewed demands for unionization, and demonstrated vigorously for the eight-hour day as one means of sharing jobs more widely. By 1877 the general discontent had assumed a decidedly threatening aspect.

414

Kearney and the Organization
of the Workingmen

An unusually forceful labor leader in San Francisco arose to give direction to this dissatisfaction. Denis Kearney, a native of County Cork, Ireland, had arrived in California during 1868, having followed the sea from boyhood. In personal habits he was industrious and frugal. In appearance he was short and stout, with coarse features and dark eyes. Usually clothed in a low-cut waistcoat, as a speaker he was forceful, even fervid, displaying a crude epigrammatic skill and possessing the power to sway his hearers with intemperate language. A San Francisco freight-draying business, which he purchased in 1872, prospered until Kearney's incendiary utterances caused merchants to withdraw their patronage.

Unfortunately, Kearney found it to his purpose to inject the race issue into labor agitation, thus keeping anti-Chinese prejudice to the fore. With telling effect, he harangued large crowds of workers, reiterating the popular slogan, "The Chinese Must Go!" As unemployment increased, Kearney charged ever more heatedly that the Chinese were competing unfairly. The fact that 22,000 Chinese immigrants arrived in California's ports in 1876 added fuel to the flames Kearney had helped to light. The San Francisco papers of the period, which except for the *Chronicle* were usually antilabor as well as anti-Chinese, were filled with reports of disturbances. They graphically reported that Kearney's "shoulder-striking hoodlums," recruited among disgruntled workers, increasingly tormented edgy Chinese. In particular, the city's anti-Chinese labor riots of July, 1877, posed an emergency which the police proved inadequate to meet. Kearney's men threatened even to seize control of the state. Consequently, another Committee of Safety was formed by aroused citizens, under the presidency of William T. Coleman, "The Lion of the Vigilantes." This group equipped itself with 6,000 hickory pick handles with which to quell rioting workers along the waterfront. Below the palaces of the Nob Hill millionaires, irate workers continued to prowl the streets looking for hapless Chinese, newly landed from Canton. At the Pacific Mail Steamship Company docks, one July night, the situation grew acute. A brisk two-hour fight occurred before Coleman's vigilantes could subdue workers who sought to prevent the landing of more Chinese from ships in the bay. Coleman's committee restored peace and order, prevented the rioters from damaging municipal and private property, and stood by for further service.

On September 21, 1877, several months after these violent labor conflicts, Kearney and various other militant organizers officially founded the Workingmen's Party of California. Previously, labor had been organized into several disparate and ineffective sub-groups, among them an amorphous San Francisco Trade and Labor Union. With 15,000 men unemployed within that city, Kearney determined to dramatize their plight by making his protests felt at the municipal and state levels of government. His basic strategy was to accuse existing political groups of corruption and to demand more representation for labor's interests. On the day he announced the founding of the party, Kearney delivered one of his characteristic harangues to a meeting of the unemployed. He declared that every Workingman should add a musket to his household effects, and predicted that within a year at least 21,000 laborers would be "well armed, well organized, and well able to demand and take what they will, despite the military, the police, and the 'safety committee.'"

Kearney, who had by then muscled the softer-spoken J. G. Day out of the leadership of San Francisco's laboring ranks, delighted the workers with his oaths and threats of violence. The open-air meeting held on Sunday afternoon, September 23, 1877, in a vacant lot in front of San Francisco's new City Hall, was the first of a series of sessions at that location in which Kearney pleaded eloquently for the support and active cooperation of the laborers in the Workingmen's movement. Kearney proposed "to wrest the government from the hands of the rich and place it in those of the people," as well as "to rid the country of cheap Chinese labor." He hoped "to destroy land monopoly," and "to elect none but competent Workingmen and their friends to any office whatever." On one occasion the fiery Irishman suggested that "a little judicious hanging" would be the best course to pursue toward "robber-capitalists."

With a decade of previous labor activity in the area to build on, the work of organizing the new labor party proceeded swiftly. As its dominating spirit, Kearney also held nightly affairs in different parts of San Francisco, and his speeches grew ever more inflammatory. One of the largest meetings took place in late October, 1877, at the sand-lot location, with 3,000 persons attending. A few days later, Kearney and six associates were arrested and put in the city prison. The Irishman was thereby virtually assured of martyrdom; the event significantly increased his following by the high pitch to which it raised public excitement. After nearly two weeks in prison, Kearney was released, and he resumed his unrestrained attacks upon public officials. Under his leadership, new labor demonstrations were organized. In January, 1878, a group of 400 unemployed Workingmen set out for San Francisco's City Hall to demand "work, bread, or a place in the county jail." Before they reached their destination the number of marchers had swelled to 1,500. When the mayor pleaded that he was powerless to help them, another mass meeting was held, in which discretion was thrown to the winds. The workers threatened to "blow up the Pacific Mail Steamship Company's dock and steamers," to bomb the Chinese quarter, and to use firearms and "infernal machines" to destroy "marked men." In this violent and charged atmosphere Coleman's militia re-formed once more, a United States Navy man-of-war arrived to protect the government mail docks, and some of Kearney's firebrand followers were thrown into prison. An alarmed legislature passed an act making it a felony to incite a riot, or to encourage or commit acts of violence against persons or property.

On January 21, 1878, the Workingmen's Party held its first state convention. The assembly made Kearney its permanent chairman and adopted a platform inveighing against a government that "has fallen into the hands of capitalists and their willing instruments." The party also railed predictably against Chinese labor as "a curse to our land, a menace to our liberties," and against the corruption of land monopolists, those "enemies of the Workingmen." Exercising its earliest influence in municipal elections, the Working-men's Party soon became a powerful force in state politics. In 1878–1879 it elected various state Supreme Court judges, eleven state senators, and sixteen assemblymen. Despite Kearney's voluble oratory and compelling vigor, disintegration began to appear in the party ranks after a rumor spread that he had accepted railroad money and was personally corruptible. Kearney's integrity, motives, and loyalty to his workers continued to be impugned by his enemies within the movement in a half-truthful whispering campaign that led to his temporary removal from office at the end of 1878. Kearney's opponents hoped, by his ouster, to combat the mounting charges of labor recklessness with which his leadership had been tarred by the press and by conservative bankers and merchants. Another group within the Workingmen's movement, however, stuck by Kearney.

Despite his sand-lot excesses and the various charges brought against him, Kearney's personal political influence was undeniably considerable. He was the spokesman of a labor movement that, though relatively naïve, was significant as the first organized attempt to rally the forces of labor in California. Many of the reform measures he advocated, progressive and advanced for their time, ultimately were adopted within the state. These included the now-familiar eight hour day, a statewide public school system, particularly for industrial and vocational education, reform of the banking system, and restrictions upon business profiteering and land monopoly. Kearney's Workingmen were more antimonopolistic than anticapitalistic. Yet, in an age when business still felt little urge to apologize for its abuses, they were considered dangerous radicals and their leader reprehensible. Furthermore, Americans, especially on the frontier, were often strongly individualistic and not prone to organize collectively as laborers.

California's Second Constitutional Convention

During this period when the Workingmen's movement was gaining rapidly in size and strength, California was moving toward a revision of its constitution. The constitution of 1849 had endured long beyond the expectation of its framers. It had been formed to meet the needs of a frontier area anxious for admittance to the Union without delay, and its inadequacy in the face of multifarious new problems was increasingly apparent. Indeed, the legislature had several times recommended the drawing up of a new constitution, but its proposals had been sidetracked. Among the defects of the old constitution were its outmoded provisions for public finance, the lack of a system for safeguarding the public lands, an unrealistic tax-apportionment system, and the absence of machinery for improving labor conditions. Also, it provided no effective control over railroads and public utilities. Discontent with the railroads in particular was rising sharply.

On September 5, 1877, the electors which California normally sent to the national electoral college voted on the question of holding a convention for the purpose of revising the state constitution. After Governor William Irwin declared that a majority had voted affirmatively, an act for calling such a convention became law on April 1, 1878. The state committees of the Republican and Democratic Parties met together in San Francisco immediately afterward, in an effort to nominate a joint ticket of nonpartisan delegates. Although they had difficulties in attaining agreement, partly because they differed over what reforms were required, the two parties finally made joint recommendations at local conventions in most of the counties of California. The Workingmen, of course, also drew up a slate of candidates, in spite of their internal dissension.

The statewide election of delegates took place on June 19. When the successful candidates convened at Sacramento, on September 28, 1878, seventy-eight registered as nonpartisan delegates, fifty-one as representatives of the Workingmen's Party, eleven as Republicans, ten as Democrats, and two as independents. Of the one hundred and fifty-two delegates only two—both Workingmen from San Francisco—were natives of California. Indian residents and those of Spanish background were not represented at the convention. The largest occupational group was made up of lawyers, with fifty-nine of the delegates being members of the bar. Farmers had the next largest representation, thirty-six in all. Thirty-five delegates were of foreign birth. As compared, however, to the delegates of the Constitutional Convention of 1849, these men were not nearly so cosmopolitan as to background.

In general, the delegates spoke for three main power groups. In descending order of influence these were: (1) capitalists and corporations, including large land-holders, represented at the convention by expert legal counsel and various incumbent state legislators; (2) aggrieved farmers eager to reform existing railroad, water, and monopoly practices as well as what they felt to be unfair taxation; (3) city laborers, who owned even less property than heavily mortgaged farmers, and whose anticonservative interests were similar to those of that group. As the convention got under way, much time was taken up with relatively trivial points of order, appeals from the chair's decisions, and questions of personal privilege. There was even prolonged discussion of whether to admit "phonographic reporters." As for the actual business of the convention, propositions for constitutional provisions were put forth in an almost endless procession. The discontent of the farmers and laborers found frequent expression; nearly every Workingman had a separate motion to present. One of them, Dr. C. C. O'Donnell, reflected his party's most extreme views in his definition of the term *corporation* as "a corrupt combination of individuals, formed together for the purpose of escaping individual responsibility for their acts."

Taxation and the Railroad Issue

A topic of major importance at the convention was that of taxation, including assessment, collection, and the exemption of property from taxes. Various proposals were advanced in favor of a poll tax, an ad valorem tax on all property, an income tax, a graduated tax on large estates, and suspension of taxes for citizens who were already in debt. Most of these measures, of course, were proposed by advocates of heavier taxation of the rich; and it became obvious that conservative interests would seek to block extensive tax reforms. Some accommodation between these conflicting viewpoints over the raising of state revenues would have to be made within the convention.

The two convention delegates representing an Independent Taxpayer's Party assumed a prominent position in the debates over the taxation issue, alleging that the bulk of future taxes would be shouldered by the poor unless some sort of constitutional reform were devised to equalize the tax burden. This party had, indeed, previously come into being with the announced object of backing legislators "who would command the confidence of the whole people, and who would be free from the control of rings and corrupt combinations." Those who opposed this generally nonpartisan, reformist group dubbed it the Dolly Varden Party, after the soft-hearted and yet wily coquette in Charles Dickens' novel *Barnaby Rudge*. During the deliberations of the constitutional convention, the Independent Taxpayer delegates were able to marshal such support from the Workingmen and other reform groups that they achieved passage of their principal proposal: California's State Board of Equalization (which had actually been in existence since 1870) was empowered by the convention to assess the value of *all* property taxable by the state government. The board henceforth was to consist of one member from each congressional district, and its duty would be "to equalize the valuation of taxable property in the several counties, and also to assess the franchise, roadway, road-bed, rails and rolling stock of all railroads operated in more than one county in the state."

This latter provision, intended to increase the taxes levied on the railroads, reflected the widespread discontent with those corporations. Too often Californians had heard their legislative sessions called the "legislature of a thousand steals," because of alleged extensive collusion between politicians and railroad officials. Further, the railroads were responsible, in the opinion of many, for fulminating an explosive racial and labor conflict by their importation of thousands of Chinese. The farmers at the convention were particularly anxious that control of the Southern Pacific should be a prominent part of the agenda. They charged that the railroad fraudulently influenced local elections, artificially rigged high freight rates, and unfairly favored large shippers through the use of secret rebates. In particular, the Southern Pacific's quarrels with farmers who had settled on railroad lands in the state's Central Valley blackened the reputation of the railroad. California's farmers, highly individualistic and sensitive to economic coercion, were united in the belief that they owed deference to no one—least of all to the railroad.

Since California was predominantly an agricultural state, the constitutional convention was bound to reflect the pressures of its farm groups. By the 1870's, most of the numerous local "farmer clubs" had been absorbed by the national Patrons of Husbandry, or the Grangers, who stood solidly for the reduction of freight rates and for the lessening of public expenditures. The Grangers, in fact, aided by such influential reformers as Henry George (to be discussed at length in Chapter 27), succeeded within a few years in making the railroad magnates the whipping boys of late-nineteenth-century life. George claimed that such monopolies were damaging the poor and rewarding the rich. Dissatisfied farmers were quickly joined in their protests by equally discontented laborers, who also felt that California's economy, dominated by railroad interests, was at the service of the rich and powerful. More and more, this opposition to the railroads was a factor that the major political parties had to recognize. The Democrats, reflecting this sentiment sooner than the Republicans, officially came to favor the reduction of railroad rates, the prohibition of railroad discriminations, and the revocation of special privileges enjoyed by corporations and large landowners. In time Republican governors and senators, too, would have to state publicly that they were not opposed to an antimonopoly stand.

Railroad regulation at the convention, however, proved difficult to achieve. Although a State Railroad Commission was created, to consist of three members elected at the same time as governors, its powers were not extensive. Furthermore, those it had were only partially enforced. Long before the federal government's Interstate Commerce Commission was formed in 1887, California's Railroad Commission had become virtually ineffectual. Individual commissioners bowed regularly to the blandishments of the railroads. Whenever the state's "tax bite" was considered to be onerous, railroad attorneys appealed to the courts; working with sympathetic judges, the railroad could keep tax liens against it tied up in legal proceedings for years. The state, unable to collect these assessments, was forced to accept whatever the railroad chose to pay. About this state of affairs Henry George once complained: "Astute lobbyists and manipulators are kept in the constant pay of the Central Pacific Railroad, which has organized corruption into a perfect scheme." Government reforms, particularly at the state level, did not yet cut deeply, and the hardships that the farmers suffered on account of railroad prerogatives and abuses continued for many years after the constitutional convention.

In 1880, at Mussel Slough, near the town of Hanford in Kings County, a bitter dispute between farmers and the railroad even resulted in the loss of several lives. Various settlers, after improving individual plots of land along the slough—"sold" to them by the railroad—were confronted with a delay in the conveyance of their land titles by the Southern Pacific Company. The enraged homesteaders claimed they had been tendered the land under specified and irrevocable conditions, only to have railroad officials change these terms. The law was, nevertheless, technically on the side of the railroad, and Southern Pacific representatives tried to evict the settlers. A bloody battle ensued between the two groups, in which seven persons were shot to death and an eighth badly wounded. A number of settlers were then tried because they had resisted the law, and were convicted and sent to prison for protecting what they believed to be their property.

The railroad's land-management policies, as dramatized by this incident, and its further struggles with farmers, caused tension against it to mount steadily in California. One has only to read Frank Norris' dramatic book, *The Octopus*, to realize how central the railroad was to the late-nineteenth-century history of California and how powerfully public opinion turned against it as the chief symbol of malevolent wealth. Another novel, Josiah Royce's contemporary account, *The Feud of Oakfield Creek*, trenchantly criticized the railroad's practices. Despite the tide of emotion that rose against the railroad, however, full regulation of it would have to await the reforms of the Progressive movement just prior to World War I.

Other Major Issues at the Convention

Although reform-minded delegates at the constitutional convention were united in their opposition to the railroad, they split over proposals made to control banks. Opposition to banks had been voiced publicly for years. Local bankers, however, were essential to the farmer, and rural bank stockholders and directors represented interests identified with agriculture. Consequently, the Grangers sided with the country bankers against measures for the reform of banking practices, while nonpartisans joined the Workingmen's Party in attacks aimed principally against city banks. Prolonged debate developed over a constitutional revision, proposed by David S. Terry, that bank directors or trustees should be

liable to creditors and stockholders for moneys embezzled or mis-
appropriated by bank officers. Numerous banks actively pro-
pagandized their clients against this proposal. In fact, during the
convention Sacramento's building and loan associations as well as
its banks sent out circulars opposing the constitution in general.
Hoping that their clients would pressure delegates before it was
voted upon, some San Francisco banks also circularized their depositors against controls on credit firms of all sorts. They charged
that discrimination against banks and other financial institutions
was implied by Terry's proposed constitutional amendment. When
a convention vote was forced, however, the measure was carried
by a considerable majority. A prediction that bank owners and
directors would leave the state because of this burdensome regulation proved false.

An issue as prominent as California's anti-Chinese agitation was
also bound to be a feature of the constitutional deliberations. In
fact, on the convention floor the Chinese question seemed to afford a unique opportunity for histrionics. Spokesmen for the
Workingmen were almost unanimous in their denunciation of
Chinese immigration, repeatedly urging the exclusion of Orientals
from the nation. One labor delegate in particular clamored for the
insertion in California's new constitution of clauses embodying
Kearney's slogan, "The Chinese Must Go!" The most surprising
convention speech hinging on the racial issue, however, was a
vigorous protest against engrafting a single anti-Chinese section
onto the constitution. This futile address was delivered by Charles
V. Stuart of Sonoma, who for two months had said nothing from
the floor and to whom politics was positively distasteful. Despite
Stuart's effort, the majority of the delegates were uncompromising in their hostility to Chinese immigration. A number of anti-
Chinese clauses were adopted almost unanimously as provisions
of the new constitution. Section II (later held to be in conflict
with the United States Constitution, and therefore void) prohibited the employment of Chinese by corporations. Section III
forbade Chinese employment "on any state, county, municipal, or
other public work, except in punishment for crime." Condemnation of Asiatic "coolieism," or debased contract labor, as "a form
of human slavery" also became part of the state constitution.

All party lines disappeared when the convention considered
educational matters. These were treated with dignity and fore-
sight. A limitation against teaching any language but English was,
after spirited discussion, stricken out of the proposed constitution. California's public school system was given what remains its
basic shape, though it has, of course, been modified by numerous

amendments from time to time. The University of California, already created by a legislative act of March 23, 1868, was accorded the higher legal status of a constitutional corporation. Other matters determined by the constitutional convention of 1879 concerned the granting of divorces, the state's rights of eminent domain, and the definition of its water rights. In connection with this last topic, the section of the new constitution formulated to safeguard California's public waters and shoreline would long thereafter be cited in support of her claims to oil tidelands. Minor alterations were made in the organization of the state's executive and legislative branches of government, while the judiciary was reorganized. The convention also had brought before it the issue of woman suffrage, by delegates who pleaded for the political equality of the sexes. Champions of the measure, however, met with little success; although Wyoming had enacted woman suffrage as early as 1869, California was not to achieve it until 1911.

Public Reception of the Constitution

The constitutional convention continued its deliberations for one hundred and fifty-seven days. Numerous influential pressure groups, including the Workingmen, nonpartisans, banks, the Grange, and the railroads, had confused and slowed down the work of the convention. Indeed, by their incessant lobbying they had clearly hindered its reform potentialities. Yet no one doubted that each group had a right to have its claims fully heard. On March 3, 1879, an engrossed copy of the constitution finally emerged. The document was adopted at the convention by 120 to 15 votes. Two months later, in spite of considerable local opposition (a majority of nearly 16,000 were against it in San Francisco alone), the constitution was ratified in a statewide election by almost 71,000 votes.

In the balloting over ratification, both the Republican and Democratic Parties officially supported the constitution, although some individual Republicans opposed its adoption on the grounds of its antirailroad features, which were actually mild. Many conservatives, of course, felt differently. Former Governor Low, a lifelong Republican, deplored, in his reminiscences given to historian Hubert Howe Bancroft in 1883, the fact that both the San Francisco *Bulletin* and *Call* accepted money from the railroads to fight the constitutional convention's railroad reforms. Republican Governor Booth, too, believed a measure of railroad reform necessary. The opinion of such leaders was undoubtedly an influential factor in the election. Another feature of the public debate over the constitution was the organization of a Constitution Party, its purpose being to support the new charter. Despite its prolabor façade, its advocacy of free compulsory education, and its opposition to monopoly, however, working people felt that both the new party and the constitution itself were guilty of excessive conservatism. The Constitution Party died quickly when it failed to win general support away from other factions.

Although the constitution was ratified by a majority of California's voters, little public enthusiasm was shown for the new fundamental law of the state. In the main, the constitutional convention had failed to achieve its most pressing objectives. Its restraints upon corporations proved especially disappointing, and relations between capital and labor continued as unhappy as before. Henry George considered the power of California's largest land monopolists unbroken. And no satisfactory solution had been reached to the problem of revenue and taxation.

California's current unwieldy constitution consists of the document produced by the convention of 1879 plus more than three hundred amendments. It is seven times as long as the Constitution of the United States. Many of the amendments are statutory, having a debatable place in the organic law, and they often present serious difficulties in the interpretation of the constitution. Actually this constitution is a code of laws assembled together in catalogue-fashion, rather than a frame of government. Yet its unwieldy defects have fortunately been minimized.

The Dissolution of the Workingmen

Closely connected with the constitutional convention were the fortunes of Kearney's Workingmen's movement. Although Kearney was not personally a delegate, his party's representatives at the proceedings pushed for the reforms which he had repeatedly suggested. Some of these were eventually incorporated as basic provisions of the new document, in spite of the fact that the Workingmen delegates were unskilled in political maneuvering. Conscious of their inexperience, Kearney's men put forth their views with such vehemence that they doubtless scared off potential supporters, including the farmers who guarded their freedom with an equal amount of conviction. On the other hand, sometimes the Workingmens' blunt tactics were effective. Their proposal for an eight-hour day on public works projects was the signal for especially warm debate. Here was the essence of radicalism! Yet, after one Workingmen delegate's statement that he was laboring at the convention "pretty nearly fifteen hours a day," the majority voted in the eight-hour day as a just demand.

Actually, the Workingmen may be said to have reached the peak of their political power at the time of the constitutional convention. Soon thereafter they began figuratively to slide downhill. The men elected by the party as public officials were as a rule unsuccessful officeholders, on account of their political inexperience. In the legislature, Workingmen assemblymen and senators were repeatedly blocked by representatives of opposing parties. The failure of these labor legislators to secure basic reform measures made workers increasingly dissatisfied both with the movement and its leaders. By February, 1880, when Kearney was again arrested for his vociferous sand-lot speeches, the split between him and various other party stalwarts had widened. He favored affiliation with the national Greenback-Labor Party; his opponents wanted the Workingmen to form an attachment with the Democrats. A few months later, in July, the Democratic wing of the Workingmen deposed Kearney, and thereafter the movement fell apart.

As a matter of fact, only three Workingmen candidates had been reelected to the state assembly in 1879, and these had run on the Democratic ticket. In a newspaper interview two years later, Kearney stated: "There is no Workingmen's Party now, and it would take a telescope larger than Lick's to find a vestige of the giant that shook not only the state but the nation." By 1882, the party had passed out of existence. The wily Irish labor leader retired from politics and became first a real estate agent, then a stockbroker, and later the operator of an employment office. He inherited a large fortune and seemingly "went soft" in the years until his death in 1907.

Kearney had staunchly pioneered a movement that was most important in the history of American labor. The Workingmen, less than a year after their formal organization, had been able to elect one-third of the delegates to the constitutional convention of 1879. Although they were unsuccessful in achieving their whole reform program, they did make labor's wishes publicly known. The new constitution's restrictions against land monopoly, against the railroads, and against the power of corporations had been gained in part because of the Workingmen's agitation. One authority believes that the Workingmen at the convention were responsible for the dubious accomplishment of transforming the Chinese issue into a national one: by making Easterners more fully aware of that problem, they contributed to the Federal Exclusion Act of

1882. Finally, the Workingmen's political platform, which advocated the eight-hour day, a fixed salary scale for government jobs, and the establishment of a bureau of labor affairs, gave considerable impetus to the organization of labor. Agitation for all these goals rubbed off onto the two major parties, influencing the Democrats especially. Into the state's political balance of power had been thrown a potentially strong force—one which, though temporarily deterred, would rise again to demand a more specific program for the betterment of labor.

SELECTED READINGS

Books and articles dealing with the early development of the labor movement in California are notably scant in number and quality. A seminal article is Ralph Kauer's "The Workingmen's Party of California," *Pacific Historical Review*, XIII (September, 1944), 278–291. Henry George wrote an article entitled "The Kearney Agitation in California" for *Popular Science Monthly*, XVII (August, 1880), 433–453. James Bryce's noted *American Commonwealth* (New York, 1891) also discussed "Kearneyism," though Kearney objected to Bryce's description. Regarding early labor organization see, in addition, Lucile Eaves, *A History of California Labor Legislation* (Berkeley, 1910); J. C. Stedman and R. A. Leonard, *The Workingmen's Party of California* (San Francisco, 1878); and two books by Ira B. Cross, *Frank B. Roney: Irish Rebel and California Labor Leader* (Berkeley, 1931), and *History of the Labor Movement in California* (Berkeley, 1935). There is more material on Denis Kearney in George H. Tinkham, *California Men and Events: 1769–1890* (Stockton, 1915). An admirable biographical study that includes an account of social unrest in the late nineteenth century is Charles Albro Barker's *Henry George* (New York, 1955). See also Arthur N. Young, *The Single Tax Movement in the United States* (New York, 1916), and Henry George, Jr., *Life of Henry George* (New York, 1900).

The following books about the constitutional convention of 1879 are helpful: *Debates and Proceedings of the Constitutional Convention of the State of California* (3 vols., Sacramento, 1880); Winfield J. Davis, *History of Political Conventions in California* (Sacramento, 1893); and Carl B. Swisher, *Motivation and Political Technique in the California Constitutional Convention, 1878–1879* (Claremont, 1930). The latter is easily the best study of the convention to date. Representative newspapers of the time are also useful for an understanding of the constitutional convention, though most reflected a strong partisan bias. The

San Francisco *Chronicle* was the only journal to support the Workingmen, for example, and the Sacramento *Record-Union* was commonly considered a railroad organ. The *Chronicle* referred to the *Record-Union* as the "Stanford organ, circulation about 1750." The San Francisco *Examiner* represented the farmers' viewpoint, while the *Alta California*, San Francisco's best-edited paper, tried to remain neutral.

Regarding California tax problems before the turn of the century, see C. C. Plehn, "The Taxation of Mortgages in California," *Yale Review*, VIII (May, 1899), pp. 35ff. Criticism of the railroads, which led to constitutional attempts to control them, is highlighted in Gordon W. Clarke, "A Significant Memorial to Mussel Slough," *Pacific Historical Review*, XVIII (November, 1949), 501–504. In the same journal, consult also Irving McKee, "Notable Memorials to Mussel Slough," XVII (February, 1948), 19–27.

27

California Culture, 1870-1918

California's culture represents a fusion of two traditions—the Spanish and the Anglo-American. Writers and artists have drawn heavily on the rural and picturesque Spanish heritage. They have also sought to recapture the vanished world of frontiersman and miner. This rediscovery, though often of a past no more than legendary, has infused color into California's cultural atmosphere. At the same time, a self-conscious pride in the new state's achievements characterized the work of its first American chroniclers. As concern with materialistic matters grew, there also developed in California literature a trend toward more realistic description and a bitterly critical, almost explosive sense of protest. Each of these characteristics will presently be discussed.

By 1870 the pioneer phase of California's history had generally ended. No longer an outpost of civilization, California was ready to build a more refined culture. Popular enjoyment of artistic performances was continually increasing, especially at San Francisco, where an enthusiastic theater movement flourished. A growing number of wealthy patrons were now in a position to encourage prose, poetry, art, and learning. These persons founded museums and galleries and financed opera houses and symphony orchestras. Furthermore, native creative impulses, though frequently transplanted from the East, were becoming sufficiently strong to give Californians a measure of cultural independence.

By far the most numerous of the creative groups active in California during the late nineteenth and early twentieth century were the writers. Actually, it is not always easy to determine precisely what literature is native to a locale. Many of California's outstanding authors have been born elsewhere, though their writing is set in the state of their adoption and their style has been influenced in various ways by their experiences in California. Thus they are in a very real sense "California writers." Helen Hunt Jackson, for example, whose literary efforts on behalf of the California Indians were discussed in Chapter 25, was originally a New England writer of children's stories. Mark Twain, the author of several narratives set in the Far West, came from Hannibal, Missouri, and wrote much of his best work not in California but in Hartford, Connecticut. Bret Harte, many of whose writings became cherished Californiana, was a transplanted native of New York who spent the latter part of his life in England. Joaquin Miller, hailed as "Poet of the Sierra," came from Indiana by way of Oregon, while three of California's most trenchant critics of the nineteenth century, Frank Norris, Henry George, and Ambrose Bierce, were also born outside the state.

Although only a handful of the most outstanding writers about California were native sons, the influence of the state in various ways upon their style was such as to qualify many of them as Californian, if not "pure Californian." In any case, the state's rich literary heritage rekindled the enthusiasm of numerous authors from elsewhere.

Critics and Reformers

The earliest "California School" of writers had tended either to concentrate on the geographical wonders of the state or to caricature its raw society in a spirit of horseplay, sometimes evoking humor by the crude use of dialect and bad grammar. By the 1870's their writing had become somewhat less flamboyant, more realistic and sophisticated. Some writers had begun to deal with matters of pressing social reform, and the opulence and occasional vulgarity of the post Civil War period was soon to bring forth further criticism from Californians as well as from other Americans. In particular, the writing of Henry George, Frank Norris, and Jack London subjected the capitalistic order to strong attack, while such other reformers as Josiah Royce, Ambrose Bierce, and Helen Hunt Jackson were publishing influential works on related social, political, and economic problems. One of the most provocative economic thinkers, creator of a "theory of the leisure class,"

Thorstein Veblen, taught at Stanford University from 1906 to 1909. After a period of residence in the East, he returned to California in 1926 and lived there until his death.

Henry George, restless and unorthodox, had held half a dozen jobs along the San Francisco waterfront before he turned to the career of economic analysis that made him world-famous. He had been a seaman and a printer and he had even tried to support himself by prospecting for gold. George once reminisced: "I was, in fact, what would now be called a tramp. I had a little money, but I slept in barns to save it and had a rough time generally." Then, in an atmosphere of grave labor turbulence and high unemployment, George became a newspaper reporter and editor with an intense ambition to voice the complaints of the working people. While developing his ideas in San Francisco, he wrote for the *Californian* and four other journals. Despite the fact that he had almost no formal schooling, his writings, among them tracts supporting the movement for an eight-hour working day in the 1870's, attracted wider and wider attention. George personally set the type for some of these highly original activist tracts.

Moving on to more extended efforts, he evolved with painstaking care an appealing "single-tax" theory in his book *Progress and Poverty* (1880). In this volume George protested against the presence of poverty and wealth side by side in so rich a land, and charged that large absentee land monopolists and speculators were collecting an "unearned increment"—which he regarded as a malicious form of rent—from their vast properties. Thus, George felt, at the height of the labor unrest of the late nineteenth century the wealthy were further enriching themselves at the expense of the downtrodden. George was almost obsessed with the significance of land-use in human history. In California, idle land was everywhere before his eyes, and he may well have exaggerated the importance of the issue in larger terms. His book nevertheless sold three million copies, making George a champion of the landless "laboring masses" and winning him the respect even of persons who opposed his socialistic ideas. Having attained national prominence, he moved to New York and became a professional pamphleteer, lecturer, and propagandist for liberal causes; in 1886 he ran against Theodore Roosevelt for mayor of New York City.

Another original California thinker who wrote in a reformist vein was Josiah Royce. Born in 1855, at Grass Valley, Royce had little in his pioneer background to suggest that he would one day sail out of San Francisco to teach and to write books about philosophy at Harvard. After graduating from the University of California in 1875, Royce studied in Germany, at Leipzig and Göttingen, and then returned to the United States for further instruction at Johns Hopkins University. Like Henry George, he conceived and published his initial writing in California. He too was incensed, perhaps a bit more objectively, at the abuses of the land monopolists and of the railroad. In 1875, Royce sent his first essay to the *Overland Monthly*. By 1882, he was on the Harvard faculty, and he was named a full professor there ten years later. Though sometimes prolix in expressing himself, Royce became, along with William James, one of the most influential American philosophers, basing his theories on the principle of individuality and human will rather than upon the role of intellect. An idealist and nonconformist, Royce rejected the notion of any monopoly in state or national politics; he expressed his distaste for railroad domination with particular effectiveness in a novel entitled *The Feud of Oakfield Creek* (1887). Royce's most important book about his native state was *California . . . A Study of American Character* (1886), but his writing about California actually forms only a small part of his bibliography. As a reformer, Royce, unlike Henry George, tended to concern himself more with politics than with economics, and his criticisms of society were generally philosophical rather than explosive.

A spiritual ally of Royce and George was Charles Howard Shinn, who, although trained as a political scientist, became a forceful anti-monopolist and conservationist. His *Mining Camps: A Study in American Frontier Government* (1885) is a minor classic. Shinn wrote in the tradition of what Daniel Boorstin has called "the great amateurs," among them Francis Parkman, Hubert Howe Bancroft, Hiram M. Chittenden, and, later, Bernard De Voto. Shinn's *The Story of the Mine* (1897) and his *Graphic Description of Pacific Coast Outlaws* (1958) combine industry, accuracy, and a sense of the dramatic in history.

Like Royce and George, a somewhat later writer, Frank Norris, also became a bitter critic of monopolies in general and the railroads in particular, but he used primarily the medium of fiction to launch his attacks. Born in 1870, Norris grew up in California. He turned to the realistic techniques of the French novelist Emile Zola in his quest for the most powerful literary style with which to present his views, and thus became a leader in the movement toward realism in American writing. Shortly before his death at the age of thirty-two Norris wrote about his work: "I never truckled. I never took off the hat to fashion and held it out for pennies. I told them the truth. They liked it or they didn't like it." Norris' most famous work was, of course, *The Octopus* (1901). It etched in pitiless detail the clash between the railroads and the farmers, describing the rails over which the latter had to transport their wheat as oppressive steel tentacles. *The Octopus*, together with Norris' other novels *McTeague* (1899), *The Pit* (1903), and the posthumous *Vandover and the Brute* (1914), won him wide critical acclaim as a pioneer "romantic realist" and as an important figure in the history of American social protest.

The writing of Frank Norris exerted a deep influence upon Jack London. London's realism also, at first, combined a strong romantic strain with a sense of social conscience. In such popular works as *The Call of the Wild* (1903) and *The Sea Wolf* (1904), London celebrated the untamed savage brutality and primitiveness of nature, displaying both his skill as a storyteller and his sensitive feelings for his fellow men. He lacked restraint and finish, but showed a genuine talent for characterization, particularly of the passionate egos of his almost superhuman heroes. London was strongly influenced by his early environment. He was born at San Francisco and grew up in Oakland; the region had a marked effect upon his writing. In a recently discovered letter, London related how, from boyhood onward, his life became intimately associated with San Francisco Bay:

It is worthless to give the long sordid list of occupations, none of them trades, all heavy manual labor. . . . At 15 left home and went upon a Bay life. . . . I was a salmon fisher, an oyster pirate, a schooner sailor, a fish patrolman, a longshoreman, a boy in years but a man among men.

London described this type of life in *The Cruise of the Dazzler* (1902) and in *Tales of the Fish Patrol* (1905). His early struggle to make a living as a writer is the subject of the autobiographical *Martin Eden* (1909), which emphasizes his dissatisfaction with society. His later works, reflecting growing feelings of tension over the shortcomings of the American industrial order, led him to champion socialism as a means of righting the wrongs of mankind. Both *The Iron Heel* (1908) and *The Revolution* (1910) reveal how strongly London was attracted to Marxism as an economic and political alternative to democracy. Although he donated considerable money to Socialist groups (including one which projected an I.W.W. "invasion" of Lower California as late as 1911), London eventually became discouraged with revolutionary causes. By the year of his death, 1916, at the age of forty, he was no longer a Socialist Party member. London's total literary production was astounding: in seventeen years, he had turned out some fifty books filled with adventure, primitive violence, and

THE POET GEORGE STERLING, JACK LONDON, AND PORTER GARNETT, BOHEMIAN GROVE, CALIFORNIA, 1909. (By courtesy of The Bancroft Library, University of California, Berkeley.)

class struggle. In 1960, long after his death, California dedicated a Jack London State Park to his memory. It is located in the Valley of the Moon in Sonoma County, where he did much of his last writing while battling against melancholia and alcoholism. There one can still see the ruins of Wolf House, which was built on his earnings, but which burned before he could occupy it.

A writer of quite a different sort, the brilliant, acid-tongued, and vindictive Ambrose Bierce, had the distinction of dominating the California literary world for decades with his witty and opinionated diatribes. His journalistic targets were many, from disreputable politicians to untalented young authors. The following couplet on the garrulity of one enemy is typical:

The more he rocks the cradle of his chin
The more unruly grows the brat within.

Bierce delivered his contemptuous judgments with gusto, and his satire was sometimes gruesome and amusing at the same time. But he produced works of such differing standards of excellence that critics conflicted violently in assessing his writings.

Bierce's fundamental point of view was aristocratic. He saw himself as a sensitive man in a corrupt age, against which he jeered. Bierce also doubtless considered himself the censorious figure, par excellence, of California letters. By the use of derision, irony, and cynicism, this complex and deeply pessimistic man pummeled his readers unceasingly. From the late 1880's onward his criticisms of society appeared in the columns of young William Randolph Hearst's San Francisco *Examiner*; and like Hearst, Bierce gained as many enemies as adherents. Hearst was then a militant progressive who, by hiring this "Devil's Lexicographer," launched some devastating attacks against the Southern Pacific railway interests. Later Bierce went on to other forms of journalism and to fictional writing. The largest number of his readers were attracted by his tales of sardonic humor, horror, and mystery, which resemble those of Poe. Bierce included, in popular collections of his own, such especially admired stories as *A Horseman in the Sky* and *The Damned Thing*. *The Dance of Death* (1877), a literary hoax in the writing of which Bierce was a collaborator, and *The Monk and the Hangman's Daughter* (1892), a short novel, went through many printings. In his *Can Such Things Be?* (1893) Bierce included such disparate elements as the Civil War, California, and his pet horror plots. Perhaps his most famous book was *The Devil's Dictionary* (1911), composed of a series of ironic definitions. Bierce's career ended at the pinnacle of his success. His disappearance in 1913, when he was seventy, is as mysterious as his most controversial writings. It is assumed that, dissillusioned and tired, he went to revolution-torn Mexico and that he died there. He was never again heard from.

Another of the California critics with a wide reading public was Helen Hunt Jackson, who first visited the state in 1872. She combines an early interest in the mistreatment of Indians with a concern for the decay of the old Spanish tradition. Exploiting these themes nationally, Mrs. Jackson published a number of articles in *Century Magazine*. These and her book *A Century of Dishonor* (1881) stirred up considerable interest in the Indian. However, her *Ramona* (1884) did not achieve the desired effect of arousing the public's indignation for the Indian cause; readers instead took *Ramona* to be a true picture of California's idyllic and peaceful Arcadian past. Nevertheless, Mrs. Jackson deserves to be viewed as a social critic of considerable influence.

Writers of Reminiscence and Nostalgia

Not all California writing during these "middle years" of the state's cultural development was of the critical variety. Many authors were more concerned with chronicling the romantic past or with describing the present in favorable terms than with analyzing the shortcomings of society. Some who had come as visitors to California in its early years stayed on and, as later residents, wrote their reminiscences. Several of their books are basic. Among these was William Heath Davis, whose *Sixty Years in California* (1889) and posthumous *Seventy-Five Years in California* (1929) give one a personal view of the society that grew to maturity with Davis at San Francisco. Usually such chroniclers looked at the past with uncritical pride. They highlighted the drama and heroism of pioneer hardships and drew heavily on their own experiences in the American conquest, the Gold Rush, and other eras crucial to the development of the state. Their accounts are a valuable repository of historical data, sometimes entwined with sentimentality, legend, and folklore, but rooted mostly in fact.

In southern California in particular there were several gifted writers of reminiscence. Major Horace Bell's *Reminiscences of a Ranger* (1881), the first English-language book printed in Los Angeles, deals with the period following the 1850's. Harris Newmark's *Sixty Years in Southern California* (1916) presents a view of the social and commercial life of the same area, through the eyes of a successful Jewish merchant. These accounts can be supplemented by Sarah Bixby Smith's memories of life on a sheep ranch in the 1870's and 1880's, entitled *Adobe Days* (1925), and Jackson A. Graves, *My Seventy Years in California* (1927).

There were also a number of writers who glorified the Hispanic heritage of California. Representative of this nostalgic tradition was the New Englander Charles Fletcher Lummis, eccentric but brilliant editor and Harvard acquaintance of Theodore Roosevelt.

His work on behalf of the Indians has already been noted. Lummis' *The Land of Poco Tiempo* (1893) and *The Spanish Pioneers* (1893) set the trend for other books of adulation about the *dolce far niente* existence that supposedly prevailed during that earlier period in California history. Bizarre in his personal mannerisms, Lummis characteristically wore a green corduroy suit, with a Spanish sombrero on his head and a red sash wrapped around his middle. He paid little attention to convention and lived out his own distinctively bohemian interpretation of Spanish colonial life in El Alisal, the house which he constructed from boulders on the edge of Los Angeles' Arroyo Seco. Infatuated with the cult of Spain and with the majesty of Indian remains, Lummis also dedicated himself to the restoration of the missions and the saving of Indian-Spanish folk traditions. From 1895 to 1902 he edited *The Land of Sunshine*, which later became *Out West*, a journal extolling the beauties of life "at the right hand of the continent." On its pages appeared the first English translations of Father Serra's diary, Costanso's journal, and Benavides' memorial. Contributors included David Starr Jordan, Joaquin Miller, Edwin Markham, Mary Austin, Jack London, Eugene Manlove Rhodes, Frank Norris, Mrs. John Charles Frémont, Mrs. George Custer, George Parker Winship, Washington Mathews, T. S. Van Dyke, Charles Frederick Holder, Frederick Webb Hodge, Gutzon Borglum, Maynard Dixon, Edward Borein, Ina Coolbrith, and William Keith.

Headquartered at his boulder-hewn home, El Alisal (now State Monument No. 531), Lummis entertained John Muir, John Burroughs, Theodore Roosevelt, Ernest Thompson Seton, John Collier, Mary Garden, Mme. Schuman-Heink, Mme. Modjeska, Will Rogers, Douglas Fairbanks, Harold Lloyd, Blasco Ibañez, the Duke of Alba, Frederick Remington, William Keith, Thomas Moran, Nicholas Murray Butler, Stewart Edward White, William Allen White, Charles Francis Saunders, Charles Dudley Warner, and most contributors to *Out West*. Among his protégés were Mary Austin, Maynard Dixon, Eugene Manlove Rhodes, Harry Carr, and University of California President David Prescott Barrows. All such persons were in one way or another distinguished in the arts or public affairs.

Also writing prior to World War I were two authors whose works, highly popular among Californians, were rooted broadly in the ethnology, folklore, and natural history of the state. These were George Wharton James and Charles Francis Saunders. James was for years employed by the Southern Pacific Railroad, and the books he wrote for publicity purposes kept romantic memories alive, praised the wonders of nature, disseminated Indian lore, and actively promoted California as a place to live. Among James' most widely read books were *In and Out of the Old Missions* (1905), *Through Ramona's Country* (1907), and *The Heroes of California* (1910). After 1912, as editor of Lummis' magazine *Out West*, James exerted further considerable influence in attracting tourists to southern California. Saunders, a Quaker naturalist from Pennsylvania who sought the fascination of the southern California back country, and who settled in Pasadena, wrote such charming books about the state as *Under the Sky in California* (1913), *With the Flowers and Trees in California* (1914), and *Finding the Worthwhile in California* (1916). Saunders' deft pen and simplicity of expression won him an appreciative audience among readers of all ages.

The books and articles of Mary Austin were often of a more fictional nature. In 1899 this arch-feminist had traveled west from Illinois with her family to homestead land near Bakersfield. Until 1905 she taught school in various Owens Valley towns. During these lonely but fruitful years, she grew deeply attached to the land and its people. Her writings reveal a fascination with the effects of physical environment upon human beings, and, in particular, an intuitive feeling for the Indian and the stark wilderness in which he was forced to live. Miss Austin wrote incisive stories and articles for Lummis' magazine and produced a particularly penetrating early volume, *The Land of Little Rain* (1903). The latter remained her best known book; it consists of fourteen quiet but penetrating sketches of the people, animals, and land lying to the south of Yosemite and to the north of Death Valley. It is this southern Sierra country to which Mary Austin devoted many years of personal observation. She also published historical romances like *Isidro* (1905), a work which was almost venerative in its description of this region. In other books, including *The Basket Woman* (1904), *The Flock* (1906), and *California, Land of the Sun* (1914), she transmitted to readers a sense of the West's sagebrush and sand and a feeling for desert symbols in general. After 1911 she lived at Carmel, Paris, London, New York, and finally, at Santa Fe, but her interest in the West and California remained constant.

Various other women celebrated the glories of California's past. Among these was Gertrude Atherton, who spent most of her life in the San Francisco region, where she was born in 1857. A wealthy woman, she traveled widely, and her immensely popular novels ranged in background from ancient Greece, France, and Germany to the West Indies and California. Among her California best sellers were *The Splendid Idle Forties* (1902), the work for which she is chiefly remembered, and *The Californians* (1898); the latter is a rather thin re-creation of Spanish California's society as it met the tests of Yankee invasion. One of her most poignant books was *My San Francisco* (1932), an intensely felt retrospective work. Kate Douglas Wiggin, whose works were also popular at this period lived in California during the 1880's, writing and organizing free kindergartens for poor children. Her specialty was in writing moralizing books for girls, among them *A Summer in a Cañon* (1889). In a similar vein was Kathleen Norris (sister-in-law of Frank Norris), a native San Franciscan who, after 1910, wrote dozens of sentimental books of special interest to young women.

Stewart Edward White, another prolific author, had spent his boyhood in California but had later moved away. After publishing his first book, *Westerners* (1901), he resettled in California and produced a steady succession of volumes whose locale was the Far West. Among White's books, which were frequently serialized in the *Saturday Evening Post* and other Eastern journals, were *The Blazed Trail* (1902), *The Cabin* (1910), *Gold* (1913), and *The Forty Niners* (1918). His *The Saga of Andy Burnett* (1947), along with his *The Long Rifle, Ranchero, Folded Hills,* and *Stampede,* tells the story of a young man's trek across the mountains to Carmel and of the friction between the Hispanic and Anglo-Saxon ways of life. In general, one would have to classify the work of Mrs. Atherton, Mrs. Wiggin, Mrs. Norris, and White as insubstantial but entertaining, reflecting the national taste for the Western environment, its deserts, mountains, and its adventurous but moral heroes and heroines.

The production of literature designed to gratify this taste continued until World War I and even after. A late example was Walter Nordhoff's book *The Journey of the Flame,* which appeared in 1933 but which belongs to an earlier era in its style and inspiration. Written under the pseudonym Antonio de Fierro Blanco, it was a fictional reminiscence of life in Spanish Baja California by the son of a prominent old-time resident, German-born Charles Nordhoff. The elder Nordhoff had written publicity pieces for the railroads, including *California for Health, Pleasure and Residence* (1874) and *Peninsular California* (1888). Between the publications of the father and the son, other romanticized treatments of California's past and current glories, half fiction and half truth, maintained the sentimental tradition of Lummis' *Out West.* One book glorifying the California farmer was even imported from the British Isles: this was a novel by the Englishman

Sidney H. Burchell, entitled *Jacob Peek, Orange Grower: A Tale of Southern California* (1915). In spite of the volume of such writings being created and consumed, relatively few of California's descriptive writers after the middle of the nineteenth century were major artists. Incurably romantic and obsessed with the picturesque, they achieved widespread popularity precisely because these qualities suited the reading public of their times.

Poets

Among the best-known poets of California in this period was Joaquin Miller (Cincinnatus Heine Miller), dubbed by himself and his admirers "Poet of the Sierra." Miller first went to San Francisco in 1870, where he soon came to be included in the circle of Bret Harte. That year he published at his own expense *Pacific Poems*, a romantic celebration of California and the West which circulated widely and made him nationally famous. Acclaimed also in England as a "frontier poet," he capitalized upon his popularity by touring both that country and the European continent. The English poet William Michael Rossetti introduced Miller at Pre-Raphaelite literary soirées, where Miller read his long-winded poetry dressed picturesquely in chaps and sombrero, a red shirt, baggy trousers complete with suspenders, cowhide mining boots, and sealskin coat. Miller loved to play the part of a bearded, almost uncouth Western rustic—in short, to simply act out Harte's stereotype of the miner. After he returned from his European excursion he built "The Hights" (as he spelled it), a quaint, lofty cliffside home in the Oakland hills. For years, until his death in 1913, he was one of California's most prominent literary figures. Although Miller achieved both respect and adulation in his own day, despite his exaggerations and eccentricities, today he is ranked as a literary mediocrity.

The theme of California as a pastoral paradise was not limited to fiction; it also dominated, for example, the thin poetry of Ina Coolbrith, the almost-forgotten first poet laureate of California. Like Miller, she wrote emotional verses that evoked high praise from the sentimental audiences to which she catered. For them her "meadow larks never ceased to warble." In a similar vein were the writings of Ella Sterling (Cummins) Mighels, whose *Story of the Files* (1893) and *Literary California* (1918) caused the state legislature to award her the title "Literary Historian of California." The writings of another official poet laureate, John Steven McGroarty, particularly his *Mission Play*, staged annually at San Gabriel after 1912, were in this same glamorized historical (or, more exactly, legendary) tradition.

Two other California poets who achieved widespread fame were Edward Rowland Sill and Edwin Markham. The Connecticut-born Sill graduated from Yale in 1861, then came to California by sea via Cape Horn. He held a variety of jobs, including the position of post office clerk at Sacramento, and from 1874 to 1882, that of English professor at the University of California. Then he forsook teaching for full-time writing. A man of wide intellectual attainments, Sill stressed the California locale in much of his poetry and prose, including *Venus of Milo* (1883) and *Christmas in California* (1890). One of his poems, "The Fool's Prayer," was to be found in almost every American anthology of the day.

Although born in Oregon, Edwin Markham grew to manhood on a ranch in California. He also gave up teaching, in 1899, to write poetry. Markham remained in California for over forty years, from 1857 to 1901, and bespoke its praises in his book, *California the Wonderful* (1914). His best-known work, of course, is *The Man with the Hoe and Other Poems* (1899). Admittedly Markham's major inspiration for the title poem of the volume came from the French painter Jean François Millet; but this protest against the brutalization of downtrodden farmers, composed in striking blank verse, may well have been suggested to him also by his years spent in a ranching environment at a time when economic conditions were acute. The poem catapulted him to international fame. Enigmatic as to the precise symbolism of "The Man with the Hoe," Markham saw his poem translated into forty languages, and it reputedly earned him more than $250,000. Like Sill, who was a close friend, Markham ultimately moved away from California but was fondly remembered almost as a native son.

Little humor accompanied the many late-nineteenth-century paeans to California's past glories and natural wonders. An exception was the doggerel verse of Bret Harte and, later, of Gelett Burgess. Burgess was briefly a surveyor for the Southern Pacific Railroad before he became an illustrator and minor poet. By the turn of the century his verse "The Purple Cow" was being recited all over the country:

> *I never saw a purple cow*
> *I never hope to see one*
> *But I can tell you anyhow*
> *I'd rather see than be one.*

Just as Harte deplored the popularity of his poem "The Heathen

Chinee," the work for which he was perhaps most widely known, so Burgess came to regret the renown this verse attained:

> Oh, yes, I wrote the Purple Cow
> I'm sorry now I wrote it
> But I can tell you anyhow
> I'll kill you if you quote it.

This zany piece had originated in *The Lark,* a whimsical publication which Burgess published from 1895 to 1897 with Porter Garnett and other San Francisco literati. After the turn of the century Burgess moved to New York, where he continued his career as illustrator, writer, and playwright.

Historians

By the end of the nineteenth century two amateur compilers of history, Zoeth Skinner Eldredge and Theodore H. Hittell, had made use of the autobiographical accounts of the first generation of pioneers to produce multivolume histories of the state. These men, in spite of their lack of professional training, wrote fully and sometimes quite capably concerning the major events of the past. Clearly the best of California's amateur chroniclers, however, was Hubert Howe Bancroft, San Francisco bookseller and publisher, who between 1875 and 1890 painstakingly compiled a series of books about the Pacific Coast from Alaska to Latin America. His books eventually numbered thirty-nine stout volumes, whose 30,000 pages were only partly written by himself. In fact, he set up a virtual "history-factory" production system, with an able staff of paid assistants to interview numerous early residents.

At the heart of the Bancroft series were seven heavily footnoted volumes on California. Like Charles Lummis, Helen Hunt Jackson, Mary Austin, and Gertrude Atherton, Bancroft was highly romantic about California, as his *California Pastoral* (1888) especially demonstrates. Although Bancroft was an untrained historian, his books on the whole were comprehensive if not well integrated. Also strongly rooted in detail, they once dominated California historiography and they still provide us with a mine of distinctive information. Bancroft's invaluable manuscript and book collection, assembled in the West, in Europe, and in Mexico, was ultimately sold to the University of California at Berkeley for $250,000, less $100,000 donated by Bancroft. His collection, which also includes newspapers, maps, diaries, and memorabilia, forms the core of the university's Bancroft Library.

After World War I, a band of academically trained scholars took on the task of structuring the history of California in a more objective and authoritative manner. At the state university in Berkeley anthropologist Alfred L. Kroeber turned his attention to the Indian past. Historians Herbert E. Bolton, Charles E. Chapman, and Herbert I. Priestley dealt with the Spanish period. In southern California, interpretation of the American era received the attention of Robert G. Cleland and, later, of John W. Caughey. In addition to the academic historians there were many able laymen. Among these were Henry R. Wagner, a retired mining engineer who made himself a specialist upon Spanish voyages and travels in Western America, and Carl Wheat, an authority by avocation on the California Gold Rush and early trails into the Far West.

Miscellaneous Commentators on the California Scene

A number of writers of nonfiction were attracted particularly by California's natural wonders, and by its plant and animal life. John Muir was easily the most popular of these naturalists. No writer has shown such feeling for the majesty of the Sierra peaks and for the natural treasures of the great valley of the Yosemite. Scottish-born, but educated in the United States, Muir spent much of his life out of doors, tramping all over the California back country; he became an influential defender of its forests, mountains, and wildlife against human encroachment. President Theodore Roosevelt listened with special care to Muir's advice about the preservation of America's native flora and fauna. One result of this was considerable government action on behalf of wilderness areas. Muir died in 1914, leaving behind numerous books that are still widely read, among them *The Mountains of California* (1894, revised 1911), *Our National Parks* (1901), *Stickeen* (1909), *The Yosemite* (1912), and *Steep Trails* (1918). Because of such writings Muir came to be cherished by readers above all other California naturalists.

Other prominent naturalists included the brothers Joseph and John Le Conte, who produced their best-known geographical writings and mountain sketches in California. The Le Contes were joined in time by David Starr Jordan, later president of Stanford University, whose *Alps of the King and Kern Divide* (1907) testi-

THE NATURALIST JOHN MUIR. (Photograph by Bradley and Rulofson, San Francisco [no date]. By courtesy of The Bancroft Library, University of California, Berkeley.)

fied to his skill as a writer-naturalist. This work ranks in importance with Clarence King's *Mountaineering in the Sierra Nevada* (1872). King, a brilliant Yale-educated geologist, included John Muir in a circle of close personal friends that also numbered John Hay and Henry Adams.

On occasion, visiting foreign celebrities turned their attention to California. In 1882 the English aesthete Oscar Wilde included the state in his nationwide lecturing tour. Perhaps the most renowned visiting Englishman was Robert Louis Stevenson, who in 1880 published an essay entitled "The Old Pacific Capital" in *Fraser's Magazine* in London. This dealt with Monterey and, along with Stevenson's *The Silverado Squatters* (1884), it recalled his idyllic stay in California during 1880. Despite his poor health he had a pleasant and productive visit, and that year he was married there to an American woman whom he had followed from Europe. Stevenson's account of a subsequent sojourn at Monterey was included in *Across the Plains, With Other Memoires and Essays* (1892). This piece is a vivid portrayal of the charming, sleepy pueblo which Stevenson saw as about to be overcome by an avalanche of tourists whom he called "millionaire vulgarians of the Big Bonanza." Stevenson's unpublished manuscript *Arizona Breckonridge, or A Vendetta of the West* was also probably written in

California. He made one final nostalgic trip through San Francisco in 1888 on his way to the South Seas, where he died.

Before and after the turn of the century a host of well-known native American writers were also drawn to the California locale. Typical of such authors was Charles Warren Stoddard. He arrived in San Francisco as a boy in 1855, grew up there, and became a world traveler who wrote books on the South Seas, Hawaii, Egypt, and the Holy Land. Stoddard was primarily a descriptive essayist, though on occasion he wrote poetry; his volume of *Poems* was edited in 1867 by Bret Harte, with whom he had been associated in contributing pieces to San Francisco's *Golden Era* and in working on the *Overland Monthly*. His best-known California book was *In the Footprints of the Padres* (1903). After a worldwide career, during which he was for a time secretary to

BROADWAY, LOOKING SOUTH FROM SECOND STREET, LOS ANGELES, JUNE 8, 1889, AT THE OPENING OF THE CABLE CAR ROUTE. (C. C. Pierce Collection; by courtesy of The Huntington Library, San Marino, California.)

Mark Twain, he died at Monterey in 1909, having written dozens of minor pieces about California for a variety of journals.

Journalism

Mention has been made of San Francisco's pioneer literary journals and of California's earliest newspapers, the *Californian*, the *California Star*, and the *Alta California*. By 1854, San Francisco had twenty-two newspapers and journals. In southern California the San Diego *Herald* and the Los Angeles *Star* were the two main papers of the 1850's. In 1853 the humorist George Derby for a time took over the editing of the *Herald*, converting it into a satirical sheet that lampooned the imitativeness of other California newspapers. The San Diego *Herald* eventually gave way to the *Union*, as at Los Angeles the *Star* made way for the *Times*. The *Times* and the *Union* then became the major papers of southern California's two largest cities.

California newspapers of the late nineteenth century were in the main four-page affairs, with five to seven columns of small type. On the front page they usually ran several columns of advertisements, including patent-medicine claims, notices by quack doctors who promised to alleviate the severest bodily aches and pains, and ads for such motley merchandise as high-buttoned shoes, canvas sails, pink velvet vests, ten-penny nails and "long-nine" cigars. The rest of the front page was generally devoted to news from the outside world. Before the completion of the transcontinental telegraph in 1861, this news was frequently weeks, even months, behind the times. Eventually the California newspapers were modified in content and format to fit changes in public tastes. They began to print reasonably up-to-date national and international news dispatches along with the feature prose material that had previously been their stock in trade. Weeklies increasingly became dailies, and by the 1870's were generally published six times a week, with no edition on Mondays.

Meanwhile, new papers were being founded, and existing ones transformed. In 1865, at San Francisco, Michael and Charles De Young established the *Chronicle* as a theatrical journal. In the next year it dropped the word "Dramatic" from its masthead and, by printing "telegraphic news," was soon on its way to becoming an important general paper. Another journal that emerged at San Francisco was also rooted in the arts. This particularly vigorous newspaper, the *Argonaut*, was founded in 1877 and edited by a brilliant controversialist, Frank Pixley. What the

Overland Monthly had been among monthlies, the energetic *Argonaut* became among weekly papers. The *Argonaut* maintained a standard of workmanship markedly in contrast with those newspapers that existed primarily by pirating Eastern news dispatches and features. A refreshing journalistic alternative, the *Argonaut* featured numerous original literary and descriptive pieces. Another notable San Francisco publisher was William Randolph Hearst, who in 1887 received the San Francisco *Examiner* as a gift from his father, Senator George Hearst. Young Hearst soon revolutionized it, and much of modern journalism too. He created one of the world's great news empires. Although often remembered as a reactionary publicist, in his youth Hearst was, as has been noted, a real progressive.

Elsewhere, too, journalism flourished as population grew. At Sacramento, after 1883, Charles K. McClatchy gave new life to the Sacramento *Bee*, founded in 1857 by his father. For several generations it was to remain, along with the Fresno and Modesto *Bees*, other members of the same hive, an authoritative voice in the Sacramento Valley. At Los Angeles, General Harrison Gray Otis acquired the *Times* in 1881. This paper, whose ownership subsequently passed into the hands of Harry Chandler and his descendants, played a vital role in the growth of Los Angeles; it became embroiled in a number of important civic issues (discussed elsewhere), among them what came to be known as the Free Harbor struggle, the Owens River water controversy, and union difficulties. At Santa Barbara after the turn of the century Thomas Storke's *News Press* also grew to be the oracle of that community. After 1900 centralization of control increasingly characterized California journalism, with the established "newspaper families" extending their domain over most of the major California dailies. The political philosophies of the De Youngs, the Hearsts, the McClatchys, the Storkes, and the Chandlers were sometimes different, but they all built substantial and influential newspapers vigorously involved with the dominant issues of their time.

Music and Drama

California has long provided a receptive audience for a variety of musical performances. San Francisco's opera season, in particular, came to be among America's most celebrated by the end of the nineteenth century. From 1879 onward, the Tivoli Theater and Opera House in that city offered a year-round schedule of operatic performances. In fact, the Tivoli holds a record in the history of American opera for the number of years it maintained a twelve-month season, as it did until 1904. Within the walls of this theater many distinctive events were staged, including the reputed first performance of Pietro Mascagni's one-act opera *Cavalleria Rusticana* in 1890. At the last musical performance to be held in the Tivoli, on November 23, 1913, another Italian composer, Ruggiero Leoncavallo, conducted his *I Pagliacci*.

In the meantime, at the Tivoli and at other theaters all over the state, Californians attended musical events with such enthusiasm that impresarios frequently sold out every theater seat. In 1911 the symphony orchestra of San Francisco became the first in the nation to be assisted regularly from public funds. Prior to World War I no native Californian was a musical personality of national prominence, but many such performers were attracted to the state, along with those of international fame. Among them was Adelina Patti, the most celebrated soprano from the end of the Civil War to the turn of the century. Others, such as Ernestine Schumann-Heink and Lotte Lehman, liked California so much that they settled there. Mesdames Nellie Melba, Luisa Tetrazzini, and Amelita Galli-Curci were other famous divas feted in California. Tetrazzini, who made her North American debut at the Tivoli

MARKET STREET FROM THIRD STREET, SAN FRANCISCO, LOOKING EAST, BEFORE THE EARTHQUAKE AND FIRE OF 1906. (H. G. Hills Collection; by courtesy of The Bancroft Library, University of California, Berkeley.)

in 1905, became the darling of San Francisco's opera fans and, incidentally, had a gourmet recipe for chicken named after her— probably at San Francisco. Still other popular stars, operatic and symphonic, were Beniamino Gigli, Geraldine Farrar, Theodore Chaliapin, Giovanni Martinelli, Ignace Jan Paderewski, Artur Schnabel, and Arturo Toscanini. On the very night of the San Francisco earthquake and fire of 1906 the great Italian tenor Enrico Caruso sang the role of Don José in Bizet's *Carmen,* while elsewhere in the city the young Shakespearean actor John Barrymore was giving one of his earliest San Francisco performances.

One of the most exciting aspects of California's cultural life has been the development of its drama, which, like music, was in the late 1800's warmly supported by increasingly affluent Californians. Thus, long before Hollywood became a thespian center, numerous actors and actresses were drawn to California. San Francisco was the first Western city to support a professional theater on a large scale. Only New York, in fact, surpassed its record of literally hundreds of performances each year. Dozens of Shakespearean plays were produced in San Francisco after 1870, including *The Merchant of Venice, Richard III, Hamlet, Othello,* and *Macbeth.* Sheridan's *School for Scandal, The Rivals,* and *Pizarro* were also frequently performed, as were the plays of Bulwer-Lytton. In addition to these were such dramas dealing with local scenes as Augustin Daly's *Horizon,* Bret Harte's *Two Men of Sandy Bar,* and Joaquin Miller's *Danites in the Sierras.* Minstrel, variety, and vaudeville shows charmed other patrons of theatrical productions.

In the 1850's Lotta Crabtree, a star of melodramas, had drawn national attention. The scarcity of women had helped make her immensely popular in the California mining camps, through which she had trouped with the actor Edwin Booth. At this time a child prodigy, she had, in fact, warmed the hearts of lonesome migrants throughout the West. She remained a perennial favorite in California, to which she returned frequently in the course of a career that lasted until 1891. In 1876 "La Petite Lotta," as she had been billed as a child, presented a fountain to San Francisco. This gift, standing in Market Square, symbolized her attachment to the city—a feeling that was reciprocal, as the San Francisco *Argonaut* later pointed out:

San Francisco took her to its heart as it has few show people in the city's history. Although she acted on occasion, it was her singing, banjo-playing, and clog-dancing which endeared her to the miner's heart and showered her with gold.

Without question the most outstanding male actor to appear in California during this period was Edwin Booth, whose name was almost synonymous with that of Hamlet in the minds of theater goers throughout the country. In 1876 Booth, this time without his father Junius, came back to San Francisco for an eight-week engagement. He smashed all attendance records for the dramatic stage in the United States, with hundreds being turned away each night from the theater in which he played. That season a young San Francisco boy managed to get a walk-on part alongside Booth. His name was David Belasco. With San Francisco as his base, Belasco soon afterward began to troupe the Pacific Coast as actor, director, and manager of several theatrical companies. During the 1870's he played more than 170 parts in 100 plays. In 1882 Belasco headed East to new prominence on the New York stage, where he produced, incidentally, some of the plays in which Lotta Crabtree appeared. He went on to become one of the great impresarios of theatrical history.

The citizens of San Francisco could seemingly never get enough entertainment. In 1876 the Polish actress Helena Modjeska accompanied her husband and the author Henry Sinkiewicz to California, where they planned to settle in the previously mentioned utopian colony of Anaheim. After this experiment, Madame Modjeska, at the suggestion of Edwin Booth, went to San Francisco to perform. There she achieved a new American prominence in the roles of Lady Macbeth, Ophelia, and Cleopatra. An entirely different type of performer, Lillian Russell, also came to California in 1881, the year after she began her career. By that time the city supported twelve different theaters. In one of these blond Miss Russell appeared in the revue *Babes in the Woods* attired in a blouse, purple tights, and high-buttoned shoes. Although female tongues wagged, hundreds of males applauded her performances vigorously. After the turn of the century the Western-born actress Maude Adams packed large audiences into San Francisco's theaters to see her incomparable performances of J. M. Barrie's *Peter Pan* and *The Little Minister*, while the native San Franciscan David Warfield pursued a successful career under the guidance of Belasco. Warfield and Oliver Morosco, author, impresario, and theater owner, joined forces to present a number of productions in San Francisco and elsewhere along the Pacific Coast.

A few of San Francisco's earliest theatrical traditions have been maintained up to the present time. Since 1872 San Francisco's Bohemian Club has carried on a sometimes half-serious but significant thespian tradition. In that year, the club, originally founded by newspapermen looking for a quiet refuge after hours, began to admit actors and artists. Shortly thereafter, Henry Edwards, English actor and member of the stock company at the California Theatre on Bush Street, became the second president of the club. In 1878, when Edwards departed for New York City, an overnight farewell picnic was held for him at Paper Mill Creek in Marin County. Because it was so successful, the next year the Bohemians traveled to Duncan's Mills on the Russian River. That outing was notable as the occasion for the first al fresco performance of Shakespeare's *As You Like It*—an event that became, so the Bohemians claim, the model for subsequent open-air presentations at English country estates. The Bohemian Club acquired, and owns today, some 2,700 acres along the Russian River, in a redwood forest known as the Bohemian Grove, still the scene of some of the club's productions. Its early Grove entertainments included what club members called "House Jinks," consisting of the reading of papers and speeches, and individual musical performances.

Higher Education

Aside from literary, musical, and dramatic activity, the cultural growth of California during the late nineteenth century can be measured partly by its educational advances. Mention has already been made of the establishment at San Francisco of the first public municipal school system in California. This development was followed in the post Civil War era by the growth of hundreds of public schools throughout the state. Compulsory attendance of grammar school students was first instituted in 1874, and later came to be applied to all persons between the ages of eight and eighteen.

The first institutions of collegiate rank were founded by church endowment, and they almost all suffered heart-breaking handicaps such as shortages of money and difficulties in obtaining adequate faculty staffs. The Catholics established various institutions before the turn of the century, the first of which was Santa Clara University, founded in 1851 as a preparatory school. Later Loyola University, the University of San Francisco, Saint Mary's, and Immaculate Heart College were established by various Catholic religious orders. In contrast to the colleges and universities begun by Protestant denominations, Catholic institutions have remained under church auspices.

Among the early colleges established by Protestants was the College of the Pacific; today located in Stockton, it was begun at San

Jose by the Methodists in 1851 as the University of the Pacific, the name it has recently re-adopted. In 1879 the same denomination founded the University of Southern California, later to become an independent institution. Mills College, situated in the Oakland suburbs, traces its history to 1852; it is now the oldest women's college in the Far West. At nearby Palo Alto Stanford University was founded in 1890 by Leland Stanford as a memorial to his only son, and became the most richly endowed of all the private universities and colleges of the West. Stanford gained early prominence through the writings and manifold activities of its first president, David Starr Jordan, who has previously been mentioned as a nationally known scholar and naturalist.

In southern California, Occidental College was founded in 1887, and Pomona College only a few months later. The Associated Colleges of Claremont (including Pomona, Scripps, Claremont University College, Mudd, and Claremont Men's College) grew out of this founding of Pomona College in 1887. In 1901 the Quakers established Whittier College, and in 1909 the Baptists founded a college at Redlands, later called Redlands University. By the early twentieth century, most of these colleges achieved intellectual independence and voluntarily gave up their sectarian connections but retained many of the philosophic traditions under which they had been founded.

The privately endowed institutions in California, meanwhile, had come to be supplemented by a vigorous state university and college system. In 1868, the University of California was formally created by a bill of the state legislature. Henry Durant was its first president, followed two years later by Daniel C. Gilman. When Gilman resigned in 1875 to accept the presidency of Johns Hopkins University, he was succeeded by the scientist John Le Conte. The most renowned of the subsequent heads of the university was Benjamin Ide Wheeler. These presidents, all conservatives, established a notable humanistic academic tradition.

Symbolic Faith in Progress

Californians, like other Americans, have traditionally commemorated their pride in human progress, cultural and material, through state exhibitions, county fairs, and other public celebrations. The Panama-Pacific Exposition of 1915 was a symbolic highlight of California's pre-World War I era. Although half the world was plunged into war as its exhibits neared completion, this exposition (and another held the same year at San Diego's spacious

Balboa Park) proclaimed the state's progress since the turn of the century. On October 14, 1911, President William Howard Taft had turned the first spadeful of earth for the building site in San Francisco. Public enthusiasm for the exposition was tremendous at the time of these ground-breaking ceremonies, and it remained unabated. At the exposition, beginning early in the summer of 1915, crowds exceeded all expectations. Much attention was given to the new communication with the East Coast made possible by the opening of the Panama Canal, and the first telephone connection between San Francisco and Chicago was established at this time. Although it consisted of an uninspired conversation between Secretary of the Interior Franklin K. Lane and his assistant, Stephen T. Mather, in Chicago, it contributed to an atmosphere of high hopes for California's future. Displays of art, books, agriculture, machinery, food, and other hallmarks of progress were paraded before 19,000,000 duly impressed visitors. Mirror pools, potted palm trees, amusement facilities, and a great central promenade completed the effect of the eleven large plaster-of-paris palaces in which the exhibits were housed.

A different kind of symbol of the state's progress was the very city of San Francisco, which had firmly established its leadership in cultural aspiration and achievement. Its citizens could take particular satisfaction in their theaters, libraries, churches, and the growing university across the Bay, as well as in a continuously strong press that published more newspapers than the city of London. San Francisco also was becoming well known for its unusual hotels and restaurants. At various times, Presidents Grant, McKinley and Roosevelt all enjoyed gold-service banquets in the Palace Hotel's Palm Court on Market Street. In that same hostelry Diamond Jim Brady once downed six dozen oysters for the edification of numerous astonished onlookers. Such prominent visitors were merely symptomatic of the growing importance of the state and of its first city.

After 1900, in a golden age of *gourmandiserie*, it was possible to obtain a delectable meal, with the best Napa claret, at Papa Coppa's for less than fifty cents. In an atmosphere reminiscent of *la bella Italia* his restaurant offered *tortellini al brodo, lasagne,* and *zabaglione* for dessert. Continuing onward for entertainment, visitors could find still another brand of hospitality at Leveroni's Cellar, the Bella Union, or the Bank Exchange Saloon, the latter located in the historic Montgomery Block. The Cliff House, near the city's Seal Rocks, offered an incomparable view of the Pacific.

Before the great fire of 1906 absorbed its energies in material reconstruction, and before prohibition and civic reform chastened

San Francisco, it was one of the most amazing cities in North America. Much of its charm has, furthermore, lingered on until today. In part, this comes from the hospitality it has always extended to cosmopolites, including writers, actors, singers, musicians, and other creative folk. The city's faults are America's faults but San Francisco's virtues are its own.

The generation that came to maturity between the Civil War and World War I possessed an unshakable faith in progress. Though condemnation of the railroads, labor strife, and political corruption caused some public concern, California's basic optimism remained predominant. The reformist criticisms of George, Norris, and London were not allowed to trouble the state's self-possessed tranquillity. California's romantic chroniclers and prophets of success proved more attractive than her peddlers of gloom. Californians could and did justifiably take pride in both their material and cultural accomplishments.

SELECTED READINGS

An incomplete but useful anthology of California writing is Joseph Henry Jackson's *Continent's End: A Collection of California Writing* (New York, 1944), and a helpful bibliographical essay is Lawrence Clark Powell, *Land of Fiction* (Los Angeles, 1952). The transition of California literature from its nineteenth-century past into the twentieth century is skillfully charted, for the southern part of the state, by Franklin D. Walker's *A Literary History of Southern California* (Berkeley, 1950). His *San Francisco's Literary Frontier* deals with the first generation after the Gold Rush.

Charles Barker's book on Henry George has become the standard treatment of that important economist. Recent analytical scholarship is found in Kenneth M. Johnson, "Progress and Poverty—A Paradox," California Historical Society *Quarterly*, XLII (March, 1963), 27–32. In addition to Charles Shinn's *Mining Camps* (repr. New York, 1948, with an introduction by Joseph Henry Jackson), he wrote *The Story of the Mine* (New York, 1896) and *Graphic Description of Pacific Coast Outlaws* (New York, 1958).

John Muir left behind an unfinished autobiography, *The Story of My Boyhood and Youth* (Madison, Wisc., 1965). Ambrose Bierce is the subject of several biographies, among them Walter Neale, *Life of Ambrose Bierce* (New York, 1929); Paul Fatout, *Ambrose Bierce: The Devil's Lexicographer* (Norman, Okla., 1951); Richard O'Connor, *Ambrose Bierce: A Biography* (New York, 1967); and Edmund Wilson, *Patriotic*

Gore (New York, 1962), which includes a particularly perceptive section on Bierce. Frank Norris is treated in Franklin D. Walker, *Frank Norris* (Garden City, 1932), and Ernest Marchand, *Frank Norris: A Study* (London, 1942). On Jack London, consult Joan London, *Jack London and His Times* (New York, 1939); William McDevitt, *Jack London's First* (San Francisco, 1946); the fictionalized biography *Sailor on Horseback* (Boston, 1938) by Irving Stone; and Richard O'Connor, *Jack London* (New York, 1964).

A few of California's descriptive authors of this transition period have rated full-scale biographies and biographical studies. Regarding Mary Austin, consult Thomas M. Pearce, *The Beloved House* (Caldwell, Idaho, 1940), and her own autobiography, *Earth Horizon* (Boston, 1932), as well as Helen M. Doyle, *Mary Austin: Woman of Genius* (New York, 1939). Other useful treatments are Ruth Odell's *Helen Hunt Jackson* (New York, 1939); Edwin Bingham, *Charles F. Lummis, Editor of the Southwest* (San Marino, 1955); Dudley Gordon, "Charles Fletcher Lummis, Cultural Pioneer of the Southwest," *Arizona and the West*, I (Winter, 1959), 305–316; Gordon's "The West's Incomparable Don Carlos," *Harvard Alumni Bulletin* (October 14, 1967), 16–23; and Martin S. Peterson, *Joaquin Miller: Literary Frontiersman* (Stanford, 1937). Informative as to Stevenson's stay in California is Anne Roller Issler, *Our Mountain Heritage, Silverado and Robert Louis Stevenson* (Stanford, 1950), and Katharine D. Osbourne, *Robert Louis Stevenson in California* (Chicago, 1911).

More than a glance at historiography is afforded in a biography by John W. Caughey, *Hubert Howe Bancroft: Historian of the West* (Berkeley, 1946). Also suggestive of developments in historical scholarship is *Greater America: Essays in Honor of Herbert Eugene Bolton* (Berkeley, 1945). Newspapers are examined in Edward C. Kemble, *A History of California Newspapers* (New York, 1927), reprinted from the Sacramento *Union* of 1857. John P. Young's now-dated *Journalism in California* (San Francisco, 1915) and John Bruce's *Gaudy Century: The Story of San Francisco's Hundred Years of Robust Journalism* (New York, 1948), are more general surveys. Journalism and other literary forms are treated uncritically by Ella Sterling (Cummins) Mighels in *The Story of the Files* (San Francisco, 1893), which is nevertheless a valuable compendium. There is a *History of the Los Angeles Star* by William B. Rice (Berkeley, 1947). A newspaperman's autobiographical memoir of Fremont Older's San Francisco *Bulletin* days is R. L. Duffus, *The Tower of Jewels: Memories of San Francisco* (New York, 1960). See also Mrs. Fremont Older, *San Francisco, Magic City* (New York, 1961), by the widow of one of the most brilliant newspaper editors in the city's history. She re-tells, in scrapbook-anecdote form, the story of some of the city's most exciting moments.

Early-twentieth-century drama forms a part of *Memories and Impressions of Helen Modjeska: An Autobiography* (New York, 1910). This can be supplemented by *Portrait of America: Letters of Henry*

Sinciewicz, translated and edited by Charles Morley (New York, 1959). Consult also William Winter, *The Life of David Belasco* (2 vols., New York, 1918); Constance Rourke, *Troupers of the Gold Coast: or The Rise of Lotta Crabtree* (New York, 1928); Parker Morell, *Lillian Russell: The Era of Plush* (New York, 1940); and Eleanor Ruggles, *Prince of Players: Edwin Booth* (New York, 1953).

Developments in higher education are charted in university and college histories, among them William W. Ferrier, *Origin and Development of the University of California* (Berkeley, 1930). See also his *Ninety Years of Education in California* (Berkeley, 1937) and Robert G. Cleland, *The History of Occidental College* (Los Angeles, 1937); building on Cleland's earlier book is Andrew F. Rolle, *Occidental College: The First Seventy-Five Years, 1887–1962* (Los Angeles, 1962). Consult also Charles W. Cooper, *Whittier: Independent College in California* (Los Angeles, 1967), and Helen Raitt and Bernice Moulton, *Scripps Institution of Oceanography: First Fifty Years* (Los Angeles, 1967). Edith R. Mirrielees, *Stanford: The Story of a University* (New York, 1959), and Charles Burt Sumner, *The Story of Pomona College* (New York, 1914), are informative histories.

Regarding educational leaders, Ferrier's *Henry Durant* (Berkeley, 1942) deals with the first president of the University of California, while an appreciative biography of Stanford's first president is Edward M. Burns, *David Starr Jordan: Prophet of Freedom* (Stanford, 1953). Consult also the unfinished *Memoirs of Ray Lyman Wilbur,* edited by Edgar Eugene Robinson and Paul Carroll Edwards (Stanford, 1960). The accounts of Jordan and Wilbur are paralleled, for the University of California, by Benjamin Ide Wheeler's reminiscences in *The Abundant Life* (Berkeley, 1926).

A biography of a leading cleric of this period is John B. McGloin's *California's First Archbishop: The Life of Joseph Sadoc Alemany, 1814–1888* (New York, 1966).

28

Twentieth-Century Progressive Politics

In California, as throughout the nation, the period between 1900 and the outbreak of World War I stands out strongly as one during which public opinion clamored for a new morality in business and government. The discontent of Western farmers was directed primarily at the large railroad and meat-packing monopolies and secondarily at banking, finance, and manufacturing trusts. City workers especially opposed the influence of Big Business over government, and focused their anger upon corrupt machine politics at the municipal level. A group of energetic reform-minded journalists, who came to be known as "muckrakers," joined these agrarians and city workers in publicly exposing corrupt big-business practices and in championing close control of large trusts, or industrial combinations. In California the combined forces of the progressives, as those bent on reform called themselves, concentrated particularly on the fight against railroad monopoly and bad politics.

The beginning of the new century had seemed to augur no spectacular political or economic changes such as those that were actually to take place. No state or national leader had yet arisen to head the crusade for reform. In the presidential campaign of 1900, California calmly voted for the conservative William McKinley over William Jennings Bryan, as did the nation as a whole. California also elected a complete slate of Republican congressmen. By 1904 the national mood had shifted somewhat toward liberalism, however, and the state again followed the prevailing political pattern. It supported Theodore Roosevelt, who had become the standard bearer of reform. But in the ensuing gubernatorial campaign, it elected Republican James N. Gillett, a machine candidate, and generally the state remained a Republican stronghold. The great mass of the populace attached little significance to the question of which party was in office. The popular belief was that the control of the state lay behind the scenes, rather than with either of the major parties. The real power, most people thought, was the Southern Pacific Railroad.

Combating the Railroad

For half a century, indeed, beginning with the construction of the railroad, its political activities were closely involved with the course of California history. At first the probable purpose of the railroad's founders in entering the field of practical politics was to maintain their monopoly as to rates and services. Railroad lobbyists and emissaries—principally William F. Herrin of San Francisco and Walter Parker of Los Angeles—were adroit dispensers of money on behalf of their cause. At Sacramento, when the legislature was in session, Herrin, as chief counsel of the Southern Pacific, saw to it each week that a round-trip ticket to San Francisco was left on the desk of every member. Annually the railroad did bribe a sizable number of the forty members of the state senate and even more the members of the assembly. The railroad also regularly subsidized newspaper editors with monthly payments. It hoped thus to obtain favorable publicity in a state where a kind word for the railroad was a rarity, and where, in fact, in scores of agricultural communities the railroad could be denounced with little fear of offending anyone, except perhaps the local ticket agent.

The Mussel Slough tragedy had added an increased burden of ugliness to the railroad's reputation. As previously noted, George, Norris, and Royce had complained in their books that the great power of the railroad was virtually free from regulation and control. Even before the development of the Southern Pacific, the Central Pacific had been charged with being the "third party" in state politics, with having "its leaders, its managers, its editors, its orators, its adherents" everywhere, and with bearing no allegiance to the people of the state. Especially resented was the notion that the railroad, somehow, was outside the law. The constitution of 1879, as we have seen, had made provision for a Board of Railroad

Commissioners; but this measure had been ineffective so far as actual regulation of freight and passenger rates was concerned. Other sincere attempts at reform, too, achieved nothing. The railroad had gained so powerful a grip on the state, and was able to maintain it to such an extent because of its considerable control over the press, that opposition seemed futile. Meanwhile, such critical independent newspapers as the Sacramento *Union* were subjected to relentless opposition.

Nevertheless, public concern over the situation continued inevitably to grow. As has been noted, farmers had long been hostile to the railroad because of its discriminations against small customers and its under-the-table rebates for favored shippers. Ranchers and fruit growers also resented the failure of the state to take decisive action to control the railroad's power. A series of exposés worsened the popular opinion of the railroad still further. The most damaging of these disclosures included the public airing in 1883 of the incriminating Colton letters. David D. Colton, a retired brigadier general of volunteers, had been a close associate of Huntington, Stanford, and Crocker during the period after 1874 when they were lobbying for government bills and subsidies to establish the Southern Pacific network from Yuma into Arizona and New Mexico. Although General Colton possessed only a minor interest in the company, Huntington wrote him frankly and frequently. His letters provided a cumulative picture of Huntington's manipulation of men and events as chief political agent for the company in Washington. After Colton died suddenly in 1878, his widow was highly dissatisfied with the financial settlement (slightly in excess of half a million dollars) which she received from her husband's former colleagues. Her protests to them were especially poorly received because General Colton, who had been seeking a steadily larger share in the Southern Pacific, had had a falling out with Huntington before his death. Five years later the still unhappy Mrs. Colton publicly released several hundred of the personal and business letters Huntington had written to her husband, and in subsequent litigation these letters were also read into the court record.

Long lists of corruptible state and national officeholders came out of the correspondence, in the course of which Huntington had indiscreetly discussed the actual costs of obtaining passage of certain bills that would favor the railroad. When the letters were published by the San Francisco *Chronicle* and the New York *World* he tried, in vain, to defend himself through the editorial pages of the San Francisco *Argonaut*, which piously reported: "All through these letters runs the idea of serving the people of

California. . . . After reading these letters we find in them nothing
. . . that any business man in America would not have done under
like conditions." The Colton letters, however, by providing an inside view of Huntington's cynical use of power to influence legislation, merely supported the popular conviction that the railroad
had established a virtual government within a government. In
1887, when Huntington was called to appear before the United
States Railway Commission, he even admitted that he would have
considered it perfectly proper to pay the salaries, fees, and expenses of the entire Arizona territorial legislature in order to get
legislation passed. He apologized neither for his methods nor for
his objectives. As Huntington put it: "I've been in business fifty
years, and practiced the usual methods known among business
men to accomplish certain objects. . . . My record as a business
man is pretty well known among business men and there is nothing in it I am ashamed of."

After the revelation of the sensational Colton letters, Huntington came in for still further notoriety in connection with the issue
of repayment of the government advances which had made possible the original construction of the Central Pacific. Although the
Big Four had voted themselves huge dividends, they had made no
attempt during the period of their greatest prosperity to pay off
these government loans. Congress had begun in 1878, with the
passage of the Thurman Act, to consider legislation designed to
compel the railroad company to retire ·the thirty-year bonds on
schedule, but Huntington had used every means at his command
to prevent such measures. Within a few years he was left alone to
carry on both this fight and that against the building of rival
transcontinental systems; Hopkins died in 1878, Crocker in 1888,
and Stanford in 1893.

Each of the four men had amassed a fortune in excess of $50
million. Toward the end of the century a financial writer estimated
Huntington's fortune to be $70 million. He owned enough railroad
trackage to connect the North and the South Poles, and he literally
could travel from Newport News, Virginia, to San Francisco without ever riding on anyone else's rails. He also owned timber
stands, sawmills (in which he employed his nephew, Henry E.
Huntington), steamship lines, and coal mines. During the 1880's
and 1890's, Huntington continued, nevertheless, to maintain that
the railroad had performed primarily a public service. He thought
that the thirty-year debt bonds (at 6 per cent interest) which the
railroad was obligated to repay should be withdrawn and replaced
by ninety-nine-year obligations at 1½ per cent interest. He re-
stated his conviction that no impropriety had occurred in his lob-

bying, and that he had operated entirely within the business ethics allowable in an age later labeled as one dominated by "Robber Barons."

The national press, however, charged that Huntington wanted what amounted to cancellation of the railroad's debts to the government. And the San Francisco *Examiner*, under young William Randolph Hearst, kept up a particularly vigorous barrage of criticism against Huntington. In 1896 Hearst sent Ambrose Bierce to Washington to cover Huntington's activities. Bierce wired his paper devastating daily descriptions of Huntington's testimony before congressional committees. Bierce's trenchant reports, republished nationally, not only aroused anew the wrath of Californians, but also exposed to wider public view Huntington's questionable respect for honesty, his vindictiveness, and, above all, his lack of concern for any interests other than those of the railroad. These articles, accompanied by cartoons that showed Huntington leading the governor of California around on a leash, proved instrumental in defeating his refunding proposals.

Another public controversy that dogged the last days of Huntington's career was the free-harbor fight. By 1890 Los Angeles had achieved a population of over 50,000 persons; the figure was to reach 100,000 in the next decade. The city was clearly on its way toward becoming the largest in California. Only one deficiency threatened to halt this expansion—the lack of a suitable harbor. Ships still docked at the windy and badly exposed roadstead of San Pedro–Wilmington which was surrounded by mud flats, sand hills, and dank sloughs. It was clear that federal funds alone could build the expensive docks, sea walls, slips, and passages necessary for a modern harbor, although some persons maintained that private interests should manage the actual construction of the harbor. Since two sites, San Pedro–Wilmington and Santa Monica, were available, a bitter fight also developed over the future location of an expanded harbor. Once federal funds seemed to be forthcoming, the controversy as to location sharpened, with Congress remaining undecided about this choice through the mid-nineties. The Huntington interests favored construction of a deep harbor at Santa Monica, principally because the Southern Pacific controlled all the railroad approaches to that location. It is still arguable which site was actually better for Los Angeles. Angelenos, however, knew that if Congress should select Santa Monica, their future harbor would, in effect, be a port constructed for the benefit of Huntington and his company.

Determined to forestall the awarding of federal funds to Santa Monica, an aroused Los Angeles citizenry organized a Free Harbor League whose object was to secure the appropriation for San Pedro. The term "free harbor" sprang from the feeling that the new port should not be dominated by the railroad. The Terminal Railroad, a minor competitor of the powerful Southern Pacific, had access to San Pedro, a fact that gave Los Angeles at least some assurance that access to its future harbor would not be the exclusive province of the Huntington monopoly. Otherwise, critics of the Southern Pacific felt, it would set whatever freight rates it wanted, and thus govern the loading and unloading of harbor cargo. Senator Stephen M. White allied himself with the Free Harbor Leaguers, as did the Los Angeles *Times* and the city's Chamber of Commerce, under its energetic secretary, Charles Dwight Willard. Senator White, a vigorous and persuasive orator, battled for three years, from 1893 to 1896, to prevent Huntington from achieving his goal of having the federal funds allocated to Santa Monica. In fact, catering to independent and rural voters, White launched an attack upon all attempts to make state or federal government the agent of large corporations, with special emphasis on the railroad. The free-harbor fight ended with San Pedro being designated as the site of Los Angeles' port, again epitomizing the distrust of the Southern Pacific that had been built up in the public mind.

In 1900, the tough and flinty Collis P. Huntington reached the end of his life. Shortly after his death, his nephew, Henry, sold the control of the Southern Pacific to E. H. Harriman. Henry formed out of seventy-three existing local lines a new and improved interurban railway system to serve the Los Angeles area, known as the Pacific Electric Railway Company. But the nephew was never quite able to rid himself of the stigma of his uncle's primitive capitalism. Only when the magnificent Henry E. Huntington Library and Art Gallery was founded in San Marino, after the turn of the century, did the memory of the Huntington name begin to mellow in public esteem.

One should not, however, conclude that the power of the railroad was significantly weakened by the death of the last of the Big Four. Professor George E. Mowry has suggested that when the Harriman interests took over the Southern Pacific at the opening of the century "the railroad machine was, if anything, politically stronger than at any time in the past." On the whole, company officials maintained their traditional policies. William F. Herrin, the chief counsel of the Southern Pacific under the Big Four and afterwards vice president, survived every reorganization of the company through World War I. He remained a strong power in state politics, a power that even the progressive movement found hard to challenge. Yet the new tide of reform was rising ever higher in California and nationally, gaining particular impetus from the presence of a reform-minded President, Theodore Roosevelt, in the White House.

It has been traditional for historians to berate the railroad builders as venal schemers against the public interest. Quite another case could be made on their behalf, as Allan Nevins has done in his studies of John D. Rockefeller, Sr. In an age of industrial buccaneering each represented the mores of untrammeled individualism. To charge what the traffic would bear was a natural state of affairs in the nineteenth century. Long unheard was the notion that a regulatory public commission should decide passenger and freight rates according to costs and a "fair" profit. In 1910 the railroads capitulated to precisely such regulation, drafted by John M. Eshleman, a confidant of Hiram Johnson who was elected to the state railroad commission that year.

The Attack on Municipal Corruption

The American people now seemed ready to clean up the country, including all levels of government. In an era when Charles Evans Hughes was exposing insurance scandals in New York, the regime of Governor Robert M. La Follette of Wisconsin was meticulously investigating the corruptive power of lumber and rail interests in that state. Meanwhile, the best-known of the muckrakers, Lincoln Steffens, strongly interested in "good government," systematically exposed the corrupt alliance of business and politics in city after city, in the series of articles later collected as *The Shame of the Cities*. Steffens, who had spent his boyhood in Sacramento and who returned subsequently to become a resident of the state, devoted part of his concern to cities in California. Other civic reformers also cried out for a municipal clean-up campaign in California.

San Francisco was particularly ripe for an investigation. From 1897 to 1901, the city had enjoyed a moderately reformist administration under Mayor James D. Phelan, a prominent young financier of inherited wealth and somewhat liberal persuasion. Then, on January 8, 1902, a labor-backed political machine, the Union Labor Party, captured the city administration and installed a theater musician, Eugene E. Schmitz, as mayor, with Abraham Ruef, an extremely clever attorney with a handle-bar mustache, as the power and brains behind the throne. He was a reformer turned opportunist. Ruef had once been idealistic about politics.

With Schmitz, however, Ruef collected bribes, blackmailed legitimate businesses, and extorted graft through a variety of protection rackets—with all these payments under the guise of attorney's fees to Ruef. In particular, they forced the purchase of liquor, cigars, and special licenses on gambling establishments, and bilked French restaurants that were known to have hidden prostitution cribs upstairs. The Ruef-Schmitz team levied tribute, too, upon municipal employees, the Pacific Gas and Electric Company, the Home Telephone Company, and the city's streetcar system. Ruef saw himself as a future senator, and Schmitz planned to run for governor.

In 1905 the San Francisco *Bulletin* began publishing a series of articles by Fremont Older, its reformist editor, excoriating the city regime. Older, former mayor Phelan, and sugar magnate Rudolph Spreckels were about to begin a full-scale campaign to overthrow Ruef and Schmitz when physical disaster struck San

EARTHQUAKE DAMAGE, SAN FRANCISCO, CITY HALL FROM LARKIN STREET, APRIL 23, 1906. (H. G. Hills Collection, photography by T. E. Hecht; by courtesy of The Bancroft Library, University of California, Berkeley.)

Francisco. This catastrophe was to throw new light on the city's administration.

The San Francisco Earthquake and Fire

At 5:16 A.M. on April 18, 1906, a massive earthquake shook the ground along the San Andreas Fault from Salinas in the south to Cape Mendocino in northern California. A loud, rumbling noise awakened thousands at San Francisco. Then came a terrifying creaking and grinding sound as flimsy buildings were suddenly twisted off their foundations. More substantial multistoried brick structures cascaded into the streets. Yawning fissures opened up in the earth. Almost every chimney in the city was so badly cracked that passersby were in constant danger. Short-circuited electric wires, which fell into the city's streets, set off fires that

EARTHQUAKE DAMAGE, SAN FRANCISCO, VALENCIA STREET, BETWEEN 17TH AND 18TH STREETS, APRIL 23, 1906. (H. G. Hills Collection, photograph by T. E. Hecht; by courtesy of The Bancroft Library, University of California, Berkeley.)

swept through block after block of apartments and residences. When volunteer firemen attached their hoses to hydrants, no water came out of the mains. Not only were pipes broken, but in some instances it was discovered that the city's fire hydrants had never even been hooked up to its water system. This gross neglect, which had been tolerated by the corrupt government of San Francisco, cost the city dearly.

Firemen fought fanatically, even without water, to stamp out the advancing flames. But the fire moved relentlessly from the downtown area toward Powell, Polk, and Van Ness Streets. At O'Farrell, Geary, and Sutter, panic-stricken property owners stood on the roofs of their buildings with strips of carpet, beating out the flames. Many persons who refused to heed the warnings of police and firemen not to stand too close to the fireline lost their lives when debris fell on them.

As the fire continued to spread, General Frederick Funston, commandant of the Presidio of San Francisco, charged into the city and proceeded to dynamite more than a quarter mile of wooden and stone mansions along Van Ness, one of its most beautiful streets. Explosion as well as burning therefore took an awesome toll in the fire, which raged for three days and two nights before it burned itself out. Both Nob Hill and Chinatown were left in ruins; almost the entire northeastern part of the city, for an area of four square miles extending from the Southern Pacific Depot on the south to Telegraph Hill on the north side, lay in debris. Over five hundred city blocks had been destroyed, and along with them most of the city's business houses, banks, churches, and newspaper offices. The total property loss in San Francisco was placed at $200,000,000, and 452 people had lost their lives. At nearby Palo Alto, Stanford University's newly constructed buildings were also largely demolished.

Despite massive relief shipments sent from all over the world, 300,000 homeless people were forced to live for weeks in Army tents pitched on vacant lots, along the streets, and in Golden Gate Park. Campers, some clad in their best Sunday clothes, munched on rations of shredded-wheat biscuits and drank beef tea. Hundreds of tins of corned beef were also distributed by the Red Cross, and by standing in lines several blocks long children could get free oranges and milk.

The much maligned Southern Pacific Railroad Company was most helpful in the aftermath of the 1906 earthquake. Its workers laid temporary tracks through burned and dynamited areas, hauling away rubble and debris with emergency train-wreck equipment, cranes, and handcarts.

Reform

Even as the work of rebuilding the devastated city began, and a new and wider Market Street rose from the ashes, definite plans for the destruction of the brazen Ruef-Schmitz machine were being formed. At this point Older, Phelan, and Spreckels were joined in their clean-up efforts by an able young attorney, Francis J. Heney, who, as a special United States prosecutor, had successfully indicted fraudulent timber operators in Oregon. Older persuaded President Roosevelt to lend to the California reform group, along with Heney, the ace detective William J. Burns, whose close cooperation with Heney in the timber-fraud trials had resulted in the convictions of a number of prominent Oregon politicians, including a United States senator. Now these men were ready to proceed with their strategy that was ultimately to bring the San Francisco political ring to trial.

After months of secret detective work, the great "San Francisco graft prosecution" publicly began in November, 1906, with the indictments of Ruef and Schmitz for extortion. Masses of incriminating evidence were soon piled up, in addition, against several leading executives of the city's public utility corporations. Patrick Calhoun, president of the United Railroads of San Francisco, and his company's chief counsel, Tirey L. Ford, were indicted on charges that they had paid almost a quarter of a million dollars to Ruef, part of it to bribe the San Francisco Board of Supervisors for the privilege of substituting elevated trolleys for cable cars. Whereas the bribe takers, Ruef and Schmitz, were widely condemned for their crookedness, the bribe givers, Calhoun, Ford, and other indicted officials of such firms as the Parkside Realty Company and Pacific States Telephone and Telegraph Company, were regarded quite differently by a large part of the public and some of the newspapers. It was argued in their behalf that the respectable business community had been blackjacked into making deals with the thieving Union Labor politicians who ran the city. Although this logic could hardly acquit the bribe givers of dishonesty, a number of legal technicalities were produced at the trial of Calhoun and Ford in defense of the two men; and they finally escaped conviction for bribery on the grounds that the "attorney" to whom they had paid a "fee," Ruef (although known to be the political boss of the city), was not a public officeholder. This outcome of the trial only revealed further the extent of "underground government" in San Francisco.

THE DEFENSE IN THE GREAT SAN FRANCISCO GRAFT PROSECUTION OF 1906–1907 HENRY ACH, ONE OF ABRAHAM RUEF'S ATTORNEYS, IN WHISPERED CONVERSATION WITH RUEF. SAN FRANCISCO POLICE CHIEF BIGGY AT LEFT. (Carl Hoffman Papers; by courtesy of The Bancroft Library, University of California, Berkeley.)

During the long graft trials Fremont Older and his fellow re-formers not only were subjected to numerous indignities, includ-ing social ostracism by many of their peers, but on several occa-sions even experienced near-violence. Older was kidnaped and forcibly taken by train to Santa Barbara. He believed that there was a plot to kill him, and that this failed only because a hired gunman lost his nerve. After being "found" Older was returned to the trial by police officials. Next, the house of the principal wit-ness, a San Francisco city supervisor, was blown up. Documents intended for use in the graft prosecutions were stolen out of pri-vate homes and offices. On November 13, 1907, a prospective juror who had been challenged by the prosecution because of a criminal record arose in the courtroom during Ruef's trial, drew a gun, strode forward, and shot Chief Prosecutor Heney in the head, wounding him almost fatally. Though the motive for the shooting was probably resentment at the exposure of the man's prison rec-ord, when he subsequently committed suicide it was charged that he had done so to avoid testifying about whether he had been hired to murder Heney.

The San Francisco graft trials lasted more than two years. Of all the defendants, only Abe Ruef finally went to the penitentiary. He was sentenced to 14 years for bribery, but after 4 years and 7 months at San Quentin, he was freed. Ruef may have benefited from public concern over anti-Jewish activities. He owed his freedom mostly, however, to the man who had fought hardest to see him condemned—Fremont Older. In 1911 that crusader, troubled by qualms of conscience over the use of Ruef as a scapegoat by others as guilty as he, launched a campaign on the pages of the *Bulletin* to free Ruef. Older now considered the broken Ruef fully repentant. The editor's compassion may have been partly traceable to a speech of Theodore Roosevelt's in which the President had warned the public to be careful about attacks on public servants. "Especially should we beware," Roosevelt had cautioned, "of attacking the men who are merely the occasions and not the causes of disaster." As for Ruef's political associate, Mayor Schmitz, the state Supreme Court had reversed his conviction. Members of the Schmitz family, who regarded Ruef as an unmitigated liar, resented the fact that their reputation was tarnished by questionable evidence against Mayor Schmitz.

The spirit of municipal reform, meanwhile, was resulting in action elsewhere, particularly at Los Angeles. In that city a "good government" movement took shape under Dr. John R. Haynes, a wealthy physician and an especially severe critic of the influence of the Southern Pacific. Haynes was concerned about the consistently favorable stand which United States Chief Justice Stephen J. Field, a Californian, took toward large corporations. He also criticized business influence over state courts. But Haynes was primarily interested in local government. As early as 1895 he had fathered a Direct Legislation League to help move power out of the hands of the city bosses into those of the electorate. His ideas gave shape to the strongly moralistic, middle-class crusade that was already under way against corruption. Haynes, and men like him, led the fight in denouncing municipal and state "boodlers" and seeking to replace them in public office with honestly elected, responsible citizens. Their ideal was, in essence, to make government responsive to public sentiment, to limit both the power of corporations, especially the Southern Pacific, and that of money-grabbing, wheedling legislators. One of Haynes' acts was the establishment of a foundation bearing his name, with the goal of raising the moral standards of public life. This Haynes Foundation still exists.

Through the influence of Dr. Haynes and his civic-minded fellow citizens, Los Angeles became one of the first cities in the nation to adopt the measures of initiative, referendum, and recall as part of its charter. During 1907 the electorate recalled Mayor Arthur C. Harper after he became involved in a sugar company stock speculation, the first use of the recall technique in the United States. Harper had incidentally received the support of the Southern Pacific machine while running for office, a fact that did not help the mayor's general popularity. Los Angeles' success in using these new and imaginative techniques for strengthening the power of voters provided an influential example for other California cities, as did the San Francisco graft trials—even though many culprits remained unpunished after the latter. Soon indignant reform elements sought the resignation of graft-tainted officials at Sacramento, Oakland, Fresno, and Santa Barbara, for example. The attention of the people of California had been called to the need for political reform, and a strong impetus had been given to a statewide progressive movement.

THE "BIG FOUR" OF THE GRAFT PROSECUTIONS. LEFT TO RIGHT: FRANCIS J. HENEY, WILLIAM J. BURNS, FREMONT OLDER, AND RUDOLPH SPRECKELS. (Carl Hoffman Papers; by courtesy of The Bancroft Library, University of California, Berkeley.)

The Lincoln-Roosevelt League

On August 1, 1907, the California progressives, having won a municipal election at Los Angeles, formed the Lincoln-Roosevelt League. The founders of the League were liberal Republicans, who used the names of both of their greatest party leaders, living and dead, to symbolize their aim of freeing the Republican Party in California from domination by corrupt interests. The President himself gave his early blessing to the group, which was made up generally of well-educated, independent-minded business and professional men. The platform of the Lincoln-Roosevelt League pledged in particular to free the state from domination by the Southern Pacific, reflecting the changing national mood regarding government regulation of business.

In 1910 the League ran Hiram W. Johnson—a stocky little man in a tight vest with the gleam of reform in his eye—as its candidate for governor. Johnson had already achieved fame in the last days of the San Francisco graft prosecutions, which he had taken over after Heney was shot. Now forty-four, a stubborn and steel-nerved politician, Johnson knew how to put the diffuse talents of his supporters to best use. In all parts of the state friends expounded his views. During his 20,000-mile automobile campaign, over rocky, unpaved roads, two powerful newspapermen, Edward A. Dickson of the Los Angeles *Express* and Chester A. Rowell of the Fresno *Republican*, proved to be of especially great service to Johnson. With their help he won the governorship against four other candidates and led numerous progressive Republican legislators to Sacramento.

Seemingly overnight, the Lincoln-Roosevelt League succeeded in an objective that neither the Republicans nor the Democrats alone had been able to accomplish in a generation—the overthrow of one of the nation's most entrenched political systems. The California progressives were now in a position to introduce fundamental reform measures before the legislature. And the legislature of 1911 enacted these with unparalleled expedition, racking up a record that was the envy of progressives in every state of the Union, and receiving praise from Theodore Roosevelt for its accomplishments. Measures providing for statewide initiative, referendum, and recall were among the first to be adopted. Then came bills designed to cut down further on the prerogatives of political machines and bosses. Previously, for example, the parties had nominated senatorial candidates within politically safe conventions. The Direct Primary Law, originally passed in 1909, and significantly amended in 1911 and again in 1913, now secured the nomination of candidates by the voters themselves.

The state legislature of 1911 also added a total of twenty-three amendments to the constitution, and all of these were subsequently adopted by the voters. These amendments represented tangible progress on such vital issues as control of public utilities, workmen's compensation, the regulation of weights and measures, conservation of natural resources, income-tax provisions, and women's suffrage. Other progressive measures included a "blue-sky" law designed for the protection of the securities investor, a comprehensive civil-service law, laws providing for mothers' pensions, and the establishment of a legal minimum wage for women and minor children. There were also bills providing for nonpartisan elections in counties, and permitting cities and towns to adopt the commission form of government. In such instances party organization was to be subordinated to merit.

These reforms seem routine enough today, but in their time the many measures enacted by the California progressives were major innovations. A black spot in the record of these reformers, however, was their insistence upon Asiatic exclusion. One writer has called Johnson and his retinue a group of racists whose liberalism did not extend to minority groups. Yet one should remember that both liberals and conservatives throughout the nation before World War I were generally opposed to unrestricted immigration.

The major immediate achievement of the progressive victory in California was undoubtedly the retreat of the Southern Pacific from state and local politics. On its own initiative the railroad thereafter greatly narrowed the scope of its political activities. After belatedly recognizing the disadvantages of its unpopular operations, the corporation professed to welcome the opportunity "to divorce itself from its former relations to politics." As governor from 1911 to 1917, Johnson and his progressive associates in the state legislature helped make sure that the railroads would be the servants and not the masters of the people.

The California progressives devised one final self-serving governmental change—cross-filing. After 1913, by the use of this technique their candidates could become the nominees of more than one party for a political office. Indeed, a candidate's party affiliation need not even be identified on primary ballots. This special convenience allowed progressives to retain their Republican registration and, thereby, to influence the regular Republican Party structure.

The Progressive Party and Its Decline

By 1912 the California progressives had become deeply involved in the movement to found a third national political group, the Progressive Party, under the leadership of Theodore Roosevelt. The purpose of this organization, which came to be known as the "Bull Moose" Party, was to provide an alternative both to the Old Guard Republicanism represented by Roosevelt's successor, Taft, and to the allegedly machine-led Democratic Party structure. Roosevelt was nominated for the presidency on this ticket, with California's Governor Johnson as his running mate. The pair carried the state by a narrow margin that year, but lost the national election. Johnson's unsuccessful excursion into national politics retarded his reform program in the next session of the state legislature. Disorganized by defeat, the California progressives lost much of their drive. By 1913 these former fire-eaters had declined into "tired reformers," according to Professor George E. Mowry. In 1914, Johnson was, nevertheless, returned to the governorship under the Progressive banner. His second administration was primarily concerned with shoring up the processes of government, reorganizing inefficient departments, enforcing long-dormant regulations, and invigorating the state's creaky political machinery. Outside California, however, the defeat of the Progressive Party in 1914 had been almost a total one.

The confusion engendered in the national election of 1912 made itself felt again in the presidential campaign of 1916, when Republican Charles Evans Hughes ran on the party ticket against President Woodrow Wilson. In theory the Republican Party was reunited. Johnson ran for the United States Senate. Wilson's victory in 1916, by only 3,700 votes, was due partly to Johnson's personal antipathy to Hughes. Although both men came from the same political tradition, they stood aloof from one another. Each warily took the measure of the other from a distance, as though they were antagonists. The evidence, however, suggests that the theory of Johnson's responsibility for the defeat of Hughes is an oversimplification of a complex piece of state and national political history.

In August, 1916, Hughes visited California with a group of campaign advisers. His retinue kept in poor contact with Governor Johnson. Moreover, a feud had broken out between the Republican Party's central committee and Johnson. Hughes did nothing

HIRAM JOHNSON (REPUBLICAN), GOVERNOR, 1910–1917; UNITED STATES SENATOR, 1917–1945. (California State Library.)

to heal the breach while he was in California. Not only did Hughes offend labor-union members by eating in a San Francisco club that displayed an open-shop sign; he also scarcely realized the extent of Johnson's egotism and of his power in his home state. Both men were momentarily in the same hotel, the Virginia of Long Beach, without meeting. Whether justly or not, Johnson felt snubbed by Hughes. With Republican victory ostensibly the goal of both, it may be considered that their advisers were at fault in having allowed such a tense situation to develop. Years later Edward A. Dickson, an associate of Johnson's, wrote about this unfortunate disharmony as follows:

But personal resentments and long-standing feuds are not easily forgotten. The bitter political quarrels during the stormy presidential campaign back in 1912 . . . had left wounds among the leaders that were slow to heal. Highly important results not infrequently are caused by trivial events.

Many persons knew that Johnson, resentful toward Hughes, had failed to campaign vigorously for his fellow Republican. Had he done so any more than half-heartedly, he could, some believed, have easily swung the state for Hughes. The voting was so close that Hughes retired on election eve in the belief that he had been elected. The next morning he learned that California's vote was still in the balance. Two days later its electoral votes finally went to Wilson, leaving Hughes twelve votes short of the presidency. Some still assert that it was the California vote, which came in last, that lost Hughes the election. But he also lost Ohio, Montana, Nebraska, Kansas, Maryland, Missouri, and Oklahoma; California was reflecting a national pattern. Furthermore, California could then cast only thirteen electoral votes—in contrast, for example, to Ohio's twenty-four. California's contribution to Wilson's "gallon of victory" was not necessarily the vital fourth quart.

Johnson's race for the Senate in the election of 1916 had been a worrisome undertaking in view of recent Progressive defeats. He was anxious not to alienate potential Democratic voters, and this may be one reason why he had not worked hard for Hughes or criticized Wilson very strongly. Johnson won the seat (with both the Progressive and Republican nominations) by almost 300,000 votes. He kept the senatorship for nearly thirty years until his death in 1945. With his departure for Washington, in 1917, one could say that the Progressive movement in California was really over. Its last official gathering had been held at San Francisco's Palace Hotel the previous July.

The state's political pattern thereafter reverted to one with a more clearly national orientation. Like other states, California ratified the Eighteenth Amendment to the federal Constitution by vote of its legislature in January, 1919, thus becoming the twenty-fifth of the states to approve Prohibition. Numerous towns in southern California had already adopted local prohibition; but, chiefly because of its large vineyards and wine interests, California in general—and particularly the cities of the north—had previously been considered a stronghold of "wet" forces.

In the crucial postwar election year of 1920, as President Wilson's internationalist policies crumbled into ashes, Johnson hopefully believed that he might capture the Republican presidential nomination. Like Theodore Roosevelt, who had died in 1919, Johnson vigorously opposed United States entry into the League of Nations—a position popular in California as in the nation as a whole. Johnson won the state primary, however, only to see his hopes dashed in the Republican national convention by the nomination of Ohio Senator Warren G. Harding. Johnson came home to California an embittered man, and thereafter the Progressive program was overshadowed by straight Republicanism. Indeed, Republicans dominated the state from the 1920's through the 1930's, with California giving its electoral votes to Harding, Coolidge, and Hoover. Not until the New Deal era of Franklin D. Roosevelt was there any significant change in this voting trend.

Meanwhile, the old progressives had to campaign under other labels.

Despite their eclipse in the period after World War I, the progressives had made an ineradicable mark on the history of California. They not only had cleaned up state and local government but had also improved its efficiency. Without seeking to destroy the capitalistic economic structure they had called attention to its weaknesses. Although seemingly self-righteous at times, their criticisms of society occurred within what they considered a patriotic framework. They generally operated in an atmosphere of reasonableness, believing it possible to eradicate the evils of society by the use of common-sense reform measures. Their chief California goal, "to kick the Southern Pacific out of state politics forever," was definitely attained. Had the Republican Party in 1912 not split into conservative and reform wings, the progressive campaigns might have gone further toward achieving their goals. Nevertheless, they succeeded in increasing the responsibility of government, an accomplishment that was to have far-reaching salutary effects both upon state politics and upon the business community.

SELECTED READINGS

In addition to Lewis, *The Big Four,* and Daggett, *Chapters on the History of the Southern Pacific,* numerous other works also treat the struggle between the reformers and the railroad. Violence in the San Joaquin Valley during the 1880's is described in J. L. Brown's *The Mussel Slough Tragedy* (Fresno, 1958), and in Irving McKee, "Notable Memorials to Mussel Slough," *Pacific Historical Review,* XVII (February, 1948), 19–27. Financial involvements of the railroad are the subject of an article by H. J. Carman and C. H. Mueller, "The Contract and Finance Company and the Central Pacific Railroad," *Mississippi Valley Historical Review,* XIV (December, 1927), 326–341. A strong pro-company apologia is Cerinda W. Evans, *Collis Potter Huntington* (2 vols., Newport News, 1954). More recent scholarship is Ralph N. Traxler, "Collis P. Huntington and the Texas and Pacific Railroad Land Grants," *New Mexico Historical Review,* XXXIV (April, 1959), 117–133. Railroad involvement in the free-harbor controversy is the subject of Charles D. Willard, *The Free Harbor Contest at Los Angeles* (Los Angeles, 1899); and a biography of a major protagonist in that struggle is Edith Dobie's *The Political Career of Stephen Mallory White* (Stanford, 1927).

Ward M. McAfee illustrates the alliance between railroad bribery and local interests but directs attention to certain redeeming characteristics in "Local Interests and Railroad Regulation in California During the Granger Decade," *Pacific Historical Review*, XXXVII (February, 1968), 51–66, and in his doctoral dissertation (Stanford, 1965), entitled "Local Interests and Railroad Regulation in Nineteenth Century California." Local railroad development and politics are also treated in Morley Segal, "James Rolph, Jr., and the Early Days of the San Francisco Municipal Railway," California Historical Society *Quarterly*, XLIII (March, 1964), 3–18.

Particularly useful in understanding the spirit of reform which swept the country and one of the great books of its time is J. Lincoln Steffens, *The Autobiography of Lincoln Steffens* (2 vols., New York, 1931). The leading work on the general reform movement in California prior to World War I is George E. Mowry, *The California Progressives* (Berkeley, 1951). The political origins of the Progressive movement are treated in Donald E. Walters, "Populism in California, 1889–1900," Ph.D. dissertation, University of California, Berkeley (1952). Albert H. Clodius, "The Quest For Good Government in Los Angeles, 1890–1910," Ph.D. dissertation, Claremont Graduate School (1953), is a parallel study. Three more unpublished Ph.D. theses, rooted in the Progressive era, are Alice M. Rose, "The Rise of California Insurgency: Origins of the League of Lincoln-Roosevelt Republican Clubs, 1900–1907" (Stanford, 1942); Miles C. Everett, "Chester Harvey Rowell, Pragmatic Humanist and California Progressive" (Berkeley, 1965); and Edward F. Staniford, "Governor in the Middle: George C. Pardee, 1903–1907" (Berkeley, 1955). Spencer C. Olin's doctoral dissertation (Claremont, 1964) has also been published as *California's Prodigal Sons: Hiram Johnson and the Progressives, 1911–1917* (Berkeley, 1968). Concerning corruption in San Francisco, see Walton Bean, *Boss Ruef's San Francisco* (Berkeley, 1952); an older source on the same subject is Franklin Hichborn, *The System* (San Francisco, 1915). Elements of the graft prosecutions in that city emerge from Fremont Older, *My Own Story* (San Francisco, 1919), and Evelyn Wells, *Fremont Older* (New York, 1916), as well as from Steffens' account. A charming and entertaining popularization is Bruce Bliven, "The Boodling Boss and the Musical Mayor," *American Heritage*, XI (December, 1959), 8–11, 100–104. More flamboyant and recent is Lately Thomas, *A Debonair Scoundrel: An Episode in the Moral History of San Francisco* (New York, 1962).

Vivid photographs of the San Francisco earthquake and fire of 1906 are to be found in William Bronson, *The Earth Shook, the Sky Burned* (New York, 1959). Monica Sutherland, *The Damndest Finest Ruins* (New York, 1959), is a recent popular account, as is John C. Kennedy, *The Great Earthquake and Fire, San Francisco 1906* (New York, 1963). Those interested in the technical nature of earthquakes should consult H. O. Wood and N. H. Heck, *Earthquakes of California and Western Nevada* (Serial 609, U.S. Department of Commerce, Coast and Geodetic Survey, Washington, D.C., 1941).

An inside view of the Hughes-Johnson misunderstanding of 1916 is Edward A. Dickson, "How Hughes Lost California in 1916," *Congressional Record* (Washington, D.C., August 19, 1954). One should also read F. M. Davenport, "Did Hughes Snub Johnson?" *American Political Science Review*, XL (April, 1949), 321–332. Informative as to Progressive political techniques and aims is J. Gregg Layne, "The Lincoln-Roosevelt League," Historical Society of Southern California *Quarterly*, XXV (September, 1943), 79–101. Analysis of Governor Johnson's role in national politics is offered in A. Lincoln, "Theodore Roosevelt, Hiram Johnson, and the Vice Presidential Nomination of 1912," *Pacific Historical Review*, XXVIII (August, 1959), 267–283. Consult also Spencer C. Olin, "Hiram Johnson, the Lincoln Roosevelt League, and the Election of 1910," California Historical Society *Quarterly*, XLV (September, 1966), 225–240. Another election is described in H. Brett Melendy, "California's Cross-Filing Nightmare: The 1918 Gubernatorial Election," *Pacific Historical Review*, XXXIII (August, 1964), 317–330. More on cross-filing, which long complicated California politics, is described in Franklin Hichborn, "The Party, the Machine, and the Vote: The Story of Cross-filing in California Politics," California Historical Society *Quarterly*, XXXVIII (December, 1959), 349–357, and XXXIX (March, 1960), 19–34; James C. Findley, "Cross-filing and the Progressive Movement in California Politics," *Western Political Quarterly*, XII (September, 1959), 699–711. See also Robert E. Hennings, "James D. Phelan and the Wilson Progressives of California," Ph.D. dissertation, University of California, Berkeley (1961).

A description of what happened to the reform frenzy is Jackson K. Putnam, "The Persistence of Progressivism in the 1920's: The Case of California," *Pacific Historical Review*, XXXV (November, 1966), 395–411. See too Richard D. Batman, "The Road to the Presidency: Hoover, Johnson, and the California Republican Party," Ph.D. dissertation, University of Southern California (1965), and Russell M. Posner, "The Progressive Voters' League, 1923–1926," California Historical Society *Quarterly*, XXXVI (September, 1957), 251–261.

29

Material Advance

The San Francisco earthquake and fire, the most cataclysmic event in the history of California, sharply set back the growth of the city's population. On the other hand, it greatly stimulated the growth of the neighboring communities, and in San Francisco itself the heavy damage gave years of booming employment to the building trades. Suppliers of plumbing, hardware, roofing, and dozens of similar products prospered. Many civic leaders demanded a rebuilding of the city on a more magnificent and more enduring scale than ever before. Even before the catastrophe, an alert "Association for the Improvement and Adornment of San Francisco" had published elaborate plans for accomplishing its objectives. The Market Street railway and the cable-car system were already under attack as too obsolete and slow. Modernization of these vital facilities could now be incorporated into the city's rebuilding program.

Further south, the same spirit of improvement and expansion was exhibited. Once the bitter struggle over the location of Los Angeles' new harbor had ended with the selection of San Pedro in preference to Santa Monica, Angelenos went on to develop a great port. In 1909, legal consolidation of the coastal towns of San Pedro and Wilmington with Los Angeles occurred as the result of an intricate piece of political gerrymandering, whereby a connecting "shoestring" of land five hundred feet wide, stretching more than fifteen miles to Wilmington, had been annexed to Los Angeles to provide an extended harbor district. This harbor was later ridiculed by northerners as an "irrigated port," but its expansion nevertheless constitutes one of the amazing developments of Pacific Coast history, and it represents a truly significant engineering achievement for its time. Because the harbor was protected only haphazardly from the sea by Point Fermin, War Department engineers had to construct a great angular and elongated breakwater to protect both shipping and wharves. This job had begun in 1899, and by 1912 the breakwater jutted out into the ocean 11,152 feet from the Point. Eventually the breakwaters composing the outer harbor were to extend to Long Beach, and to total more than eight miles in length. This outer harbor came to contain 6,000 acres of channels and anchorages.

These new port facilities, whose construction was followed by formal opening of the Panama Canal in 1914, made Los Angeles one of the world's most important harbor cities. By 1924, Los Angeles had eclipsed San Francisco in total annual tonnage (imports: 1,090,000 vs. 931,920 tons; exports: 3,200,000 vs. 1,870,000 tons) and had become the most important port on the Pacific Coast. Situated on the great circle route to the Orient, Los Angeles harbor continued to enjoy a growth in the 1920's of which the earlier rural residents of the area could scarcely have dreamed. Meanwhile, the city itself was becoming a virtual labyrinth of steel and concrete, expanding rapidly as a population shift occurred from northern California southward. Los Angeles first reached and then surrounded Beverly Hills. Next it pushed its boundaries over the Hollywood Hills toward San Fernando. On the west it came to bound Culver City and northward to adjoin Burbank, Glendale, Pasadena, Alhambra, Vernon, Huntington Park, South Pasadena, Torrance, Inglewood, Gardena, Hawthorne, El Segundo, and Long Beach. From the foothills of the Santa Monica Mountains the city encompassed the Verdugo Hills and eventually included more than 450 square miles of land Though it became the largest metropolis in the world in area, it seemed to lack a central section such as most cities have, and thus "L.A." has been referred to as "a group of suburbs in search of a city."

Urban transportation was a vital factor in the growth of both San Francisco and Los Angeles during this period. Indeed, almost every important step in the development of California has been closely related to improved transportation facilities. (Los Angeles harbor, of course, offers a particularly dramatic illustration of this generalization.) After 1915 in San Francisco, as the northern city increased steadily in size and importance, Francis Marion Smith, "the borax king," developed the Key Route Electric Railway to serve the East Bay area. This line supplemented the city's Peninsular Electric Railway, which found a counterpart at Los Angeles in Henry E. Huntington's methodical expansion of his network of "big red electric cars," the Pacific Electric. At its height the latter transportation web operated 900 cars over 1,100 miles of track. Both rail networks were unifying forces in their respective cities. However, in Los Angeles County, much larger than the city of the same name, transportation continued to be more of a problem than did the more compact metropolitan area of San Francisco. By the mid-1920's Los Angeles County contained more than forty incorporated cities within its limits, and its transport facilities were already strained.

At San Diego similar widespread growth occurred, especially during the decades before and after 1900. That was the era during which John D. Spreckels and Rudolph Spreckels poured millions of dollars into the development of San Diego, including the renowned Hotel del Coronado (1887). After the turn of the century Katherine Tingley and her Theosophists began their colony at Point Loma; William E. Smythe (later a historian of San Diego) cried out against monopoly and Ed Fletcher developed the city's "back country." Both city and county reached a threshold of maturity. As the Horton House of the 1870's gave way to the U.S. Grant Hotel, few even remembered William Heath Davis' shaky attempts to build San Diego in the 1850's. The city's 1908 welcome of President Theodore Roosevelt's "Great White Fleet" ushered in the era of San Diego as a naval center. Its development reached eastward to the Imperial Valley and southward to Tijuana—described in 1905 as "a wide place on a poor road." By 1911 San Diego was the scene also of an armed foray into Baja California, backed by the I.W.W. Four years later saw the appearance of an effulgent Hispanic architecture at San Diego's Panama-California Exposition. There followed the aerial exploits of Glen Curtis and development by the Ryan Aeronautical Corporation of Charles E. Lindbergh's "Spirit of Saint Louis." Among the other forceful personalities who helped to make San Diego better known were E. S. Babcock, Ellen Browning Scripps, and U. S. Grant, Jr., as well as the controversial Charles B. Hatfield, "The Rainmaker."

California and World War I

The prosperity of California as a whole, and especially of its two main cities, was markedly stimulated by World War I. Though the state was geographically remote from the zones of combat, it quickly became involved in the increased demands of the national war effort. For one thing, a few large Eastern factories were beginning to establish offices and branches in California, particularly in the San Francisco Bay area. Eastern capital thus attracted new immigration westward and pulled California closer toward the nation's total economic life.

Before World War I heavy employment had centered around the food-processing industries, including meat packing and fruit and fish canning, as well as lumber, mineral, and oil production. These activities now flourished with renewed vigor, while at the same time the war encouraged diversification and industrial maturation. The number of persons engaged in manufacturing in the state increased from 165,000 in 1914 to over 350,000 by 1929, partly because of the stimulus afforded by the war years. In agriculture the war spurred the production of certain crops in particular. Cotton, for example, grew in demand because of its use in the millions of new uniforms that had to be supplied to soldiers. Taking up the slogan, "Food Will Win the War!" the state also sent huge quantities of grains, fruits, meats, and vegetables into Allied storehouses.

In manpower California contributed more than 150,000 soldiers to the Allied forces, especially to the Ninety-first Division, which saw service in the Battle of the Argonne in France. After the United States severed diplomatic relations with Germany, President Benjamin Ide Wheeler of the University of California obtained from the regents the power to place the university, its entire equipment and all its resources, at the disposal of the federal government. Of the 3,500 men of the university who subsequently went into active service, approximately half became commissioned officers. Stanford University, the University of Southern California, and other institutions of higher learning responded similarly. As she had in the Civil War, California also gave generously to Liberty and Victory Loan drives, in each case exceeding the state quota. After hostilities had come to an end, Californians such as Herbert Hoover and Hugh Gibson played a leading role in promoting the cause of postwar relief activities abroad.

When peace came it was clear that the economy of California had been lifted onto a new plateau of production, distribution, and consumption of both goods and services. Perhaps the most conspicuous economic phenomenon of the 1920's was a housing boom that gave birth to dozens of new towns, some purely residential, others recreational. In southern California these included San Clemente, a distinctive community of red-tile-roof houses on the ocean, the resort center of Palm Springs on the desert, and Lake Arrowhead Village in the mountains. Operating without regard to season, avid realtors developed large tracts of former countryside into sites for thousands of furnace-less plaster palaces and multistoried commercial buildings. The suburbs of cities became dotted with small frame bungalows, which retired Iowa farmers, for example, might buy for as little as $1,000, as well as larger and more expensive homes for those who preferred white "Spanish-style" stucco with palm trees in their yards. Aggressive tourist promotion by numerous local chambers of commerce had been particularly instrumental in creating this boom, which ended, at least temporarily, in 1929.

Developments in Mining

California's traditionally important industry of mining also benefited from World War I. Demands had never been greater for gold and silver, as well as for less glamorous substances such as salt, soda, potash, cement, various clays, and quicksilver. Miners developed new methods of extraction that increased production markedly in almost every county of the state. After the war, however, mining activity again slackened. In 1923 gold production ($13,379,013) was almost exactly what it had been in 1884, and public interest in this once glamorous industry was fading.

Farmers and fishermen, in particular, came to be at odds with the increasingly destructive techniques employed by the mining industry. Hydraulic mining, which necessitated the digging of ditches and the construction of earthen dams, devastated hundreds of square miles of rich agricultural lands. Millions of tons of earth were washed into the Yuba, Bear, and American Rivers, turbulently filling their beds with boulders and yellow mud, known as "slickens." Over the years the bed of the Sacramento was raised several feet, impairing navigation by any except light-draft vessels. When winter rains fell upon rivers filled with mining debris, the result was often torrential floods, which deposited sand and clay over extensive areas and caused almost incredible erosion. Large deposits were carried even to the Straits of Carquinez, and unsightly shoals were formed in Suisun Bay. Only after prolonged litigation, not unmixed with politics, was hydraulic mining finally stopped along the California rivers.

Before the twenties dredger mining had replaced the hydraulic method. In the new operation the dredge, a huge machine, was floated on a scow in an artificial pond fed by a ditch. A chain of heavy buckets brought up sand, rocks, and gravel, from which gold was washed out. Dredge engineers, however, like hydraulic engineers, created desolate wastes by sluicing out great piles of sand and rock; and conservationists intensely disapproved of the use of dredges on the major rivers of the state. Dredger mining too was therefore eventually eliminated in the state. Quartz operations, by means of which gold locked inside rock formations was extracted, then became the predominant mining technique. In spite of the restrictions imposed on methods of mining, California's gold continued to constitute a significant part of United States production.

Sixty other minerals were also produced commercially in California during this period. The state mined increasing amounts of silver, copper, lead, quicksilver, manganese, tungsten, platinum, asbestos, clay, diatomite, marble, and various rock and gravel products. With the development of the automobile prodigious quantities of asphalt and cement were required for highways, creating virtually a new industry. Borax, or sodium borate, had been mined commercially since 1885, when the famed twenty-mule teams began to haul this mineral, used as a cleanser, out of Death Valley. The pioneer freighter Remi Nadeau had hauled ores into Los Angeles from other nearby valleys. By the 1920's California had become the principal supplier of borate products, which found an increasing number of industrial uses. California then ranked second among the states in its total mineral production, despite a lack of large coal and iron deposits.

The Rise of the Oil Industry

California's black gold has, like the yellow variety, played an important part in the history of the state. From the time of the mission padres, petroleum was known to exist in the subsoil. Roaming cattle would sometimes fall into the tar and pitch sumps of southern California, as the animals of prehistoric times had done. Asphalt (which is a form of petroleum) from the Brea beds at Los Angeles was used for roofing from the Mexican period onward. Natural seepages of surface oil and tar existed in numerous other areas as well.

The great oil excitement of 1859 in the East, following the discoveries at Titusville, Pennsylvania, had spread quickly to California, where it encouraged the prospecting for oil. The Pennsylvania strike also greatly influenced extraction and marketing techniques in California. There is some dispute as to where the state's first sizable underground oil deposits were found. The assertion is frequently made, although there is little documentation for it, that oil had first been located in 1857 at Pico Canyon, near San Fernando. The earliest fully verifiable oil well in California, however, was drilled in 1861 in Humboldt County, near the present hamlet of Petrolia. In 1862, a further venture was undertaken in Contra Costa County, near Martinez. Over the next dozen years wildcatters dug shallow wells all over the Santa Susana Mountains near Ventura, as well as at Santa Barbara and further north in the Humboldt Bay region.

Meanwhile, the first actual oil production west of Pennsylvania had occurred in California's Ventura County without the drilling of wells at all. This operation had begun in 1859, after George S. Gilbert, a whale-oil merchant, had investigated oil seepages near Los Angeles. On property belonging to Major Henry Hancock, Gilbert erected a small pot still with which he was producing semi-liquid asphaltum when Hancock drove him off the ranch. Gilbert then moved north and erected another small still in the canyon of the Ventura River. Although minute and crude by the standards of today, Gilbert's production of kerosene for lighting and of lubricating oil was a genuine pioneering venture. His still burned down, however, and he became a merchant at Ventura.

In 1864, the price of crude oil in Pennsylvania advanced from $3 to $14 per barrel between January and August, due to growing consumption. At about the same time a touring professor of chemistry from Yale College, Benjamin Silliman, Jr., after seeing the oil seepages in Ventura County, wrote glowing reports on their commercial possibilities. The result of his account was the formation of two companies in Philadelphia and New York to exploit California oil resources, both firms being controlled by Thomas A. Scott of the Pennsylvania Railroad. A combine, the Philadelphia & California Petroleum Company, drilled the first oil well in southern California, located near the Camulos Ranch, and seven other wells in the Ojai region between 1865 and 1867. One of the latter (Well No. 6 on Sisar Creek) was the first known gusher in California. These wells, however, were not able to sustain production; and even if they had been, they would not have been a notable commercial success. Not until after the turn of the century were techniques developing for making a truly satisfactory illuminant from California crude oil, which is heavy and asphaltic-based. At the time of Scott's enterprise, crude oil was sold as fuel, without refining, as it came from the well heads. After this initial frenzy of the 1860's died away, the California oil industry entered a dormant period that was not interrupted until the mid-1870's, when the California Star Oil Company, whose operations did not become fully developed until even later, began drilling in southern California's Newhall Basin.

The organization of scores of other small firms followed that of the California Star Oil Company. In no industry was competition fiercer or more damaging than in oil refining. Less capital was required to build an early refinery than to establish a store or a livery stable. Because so many wells were dug and refineries set up, production soared, the market was glutted, and prices were slashed. It was hard for pioneer producers to restrain the frenzied rush to new sites, a rush reminiscent of the gold mania of 1848–1849. Their efforts to produce oil profitably proved largely unsuccessful, and few survived this experimental, if exciting, period of speculative enterprise. Despite the production of kerosene for illumination, tar for roofing, and oil for lubrication, the petroleum industry in those years before the invention of the internal-combustion engine also suffered from primitive operational techniques. In 1879 California Star became the Pacific Coast Oil Company, corporate ancestor of the Standard Oil Company of California. Functioning successfully by 1880, Pacific was then the dominant oil company of the state. By 1884 many companies had failed or been absorbed by larger operations; only four firms were producing oil throughout California.

The sustained success of California's oil industry dates from the early 1890's, when it was largely revitalized by two men who were to profit greatly from the state's vast underground reserves. These were Lyman Stewart and Edward L. Doheny. Stewart had made his first fortune, as a young man, in the oil rush at Titusville, Pennsylvania. In 1833, after an overproduction of oil occurred in the Eastern United States—where monopolization quickly set in—Stewart headed West to begin a new career at the age of forty-three. Provided with land leases by T. R. Bard and the Pacific Coast Oil Company, Stewart and a partner, Wallace L. Hardison, spent several lean years prospecting for oil. In 1890 the three men formed the Union Oil Company. Two years later they struck a prodigious well (the "Wild Bill") in Adams Canyon, Ventura County, that flowed down the canyon into the Santa Clara River until it could be capped. This gusher alone produced 1,500 barrels of oil per day for the Stewart enterprise. Within a few years the operations of the Union Oil Company had surpassed those of the Pacific Coast Oil Company. Thereafter the latter company confined its drilling ventures to the Newhall Basin. Until at least 1900, the major market for crude oil, illuminants, and lubricants was the San Francisco Bay region. Consequently Pacific opened a refinery there at Alameda, where the Union Oil Company also built its Oleum refinery in 1895.

The story of the career of Edward L. Doheny is one of the most colorful in the history of American capitalism. Born in Wisconsin in 1856, Doheny started work as a government surveyor. In 1876, as a youth of twenty, he drifted into the Black Hills just as Dakota Territory was experiencing a silver and gold rush. Doheny next headed for Arizona and then Kingston, New Mexico, where another rush was under way. He worked as a mucker and hard-rock miner along the Mexican border, then again as a miner in the Mojave Desert of California. With this experience and some money behind him, Doheny came to Los Angeles in 1892. On the streets of the city he noticed the presence of brea, or tarry pitch, which clung to the wheels of passing carriages and carts, and he traced this substance to a center of oil seepage downtown near Westlake Park. With an old prospector friend, Charles A. Canfield, Doheny leased a city lot and began to dig. When they had, by the use of pick and shovel, reached a depth of 50 feet, the pair struck a pocket of gas that almost asphyxiated them. They then employed a driller, who, at 600 feet, brought in a well with a capacity of forty-five barrels per day. This started a frantic oil boom that caused 2,300 wells to be dug in Los Angeles within the next five years.

A strange, new skyline sprang up in the area of the old pueblo, still no more than a formless, sprawling community of muddy and crooked streets. Greasy little refineries were noisily hammered together, most of them shanty-like structures consisting of a few boards, with an iron drum for a still, and a "worm" in which oil vapors could be condensed. Black derricks were erected in both the front and the back yards of numerous residents. Some of these Angelenos became wealthy, but many others got nothing for their trouble except expensive drilling bills, uprooted gardens, and clouds of dry dust which coated their houses. A particularly rich oil field was found to exist virtually surrounding La Brea Pits in Hancock Park (from which local scientific amateurs had been digging up the bones of prehistoric animals since 1875, the year in which asphalt diggers, working in tar seeps on the ranch of Major Hancock, had exhumed part of a saber-tooth cat). By 1897 oil production in the Los Angeles area, including nearby Puente and Fullerton, had risen to 1,400,000 barrels per year. Five years later the figure reached 9,000,000 barrels.

Meanwhile, Doheny and other operators were having considerable trouble in marketing surplus oil. They sold some of it for the spraying of dusty streets and also persuaded various manufacturers of pipe to use an oil coating to prevent rust. In October, 1894, Doheny's competitors, the Union Oil Company, had succeeded in converting a railroad locomotive, fitted with a tender and tank, into an oil burner for demonstration purposes. After successful runs near Santa Paula, the engine was used on the Cajon Pass grade to pull a string of loaded cars. This was, of course, in part an attempt to create a market for excess fuel oil, by converting at least one industry, the railroads, away from the use of imported coal. The saving in adapting locomotive engines from coal to oil amounted to as much as twenty-five percent in daily operations. The Santa Fe Railroad eventually agreed to pay $1 a barrel for oil, a price which seems low today but which was appealingly high then: from 1895 to 1899 oil had fluctuated in price from $1.50 downward to a few cents a barrel. By 1901, to the added jubilation of oil men everywhere, the Southern Pacific Railroad bought five hundred tank cars and built fifty storage tanks, thereby marking its conversion, like the Santa Fe, from coal to fuel oil.

Encouraged by this new market, the oil industry embarked upon expanded operations, particularly at Coalinga in Fresno County, at Bakersfield, and along the Kern River in Kern County. Doheny branched out boldly beyond the San Joaquin Valley to Peru and Mexico, where he not only drilled for oil but also developed the techniques of paving future automobile roads with asphalt. Such development of the industry was accompanied by extensive construction of equipment, especially tank cars and pipe lines—the latter in use since 1882 in California—in order to handle the outpouring of California's oil fields. By 1903, the state's crude-oil production had reached 24,382,000 barrels annually. Once the needs of the automobile were felt, production shot even more markedly upward, reaching 77,697,568 barrels in 1910.

The Oil Boom of the Twenties

In the 1920's California's greatest oil discoveries took place in a variety of locations, particularly in the San Joaquin Valley and in the Midway-Sunset, Lost Hills-Belridge, Elk Hills, Wheeler Ridge, and Kettleman Hills areas. In these zones oil was typically found in synclinal geological formations, usually marked by domes. But prospecting for it was almost as much an art as a science. Expenses were high and risks great, with most wildcat wells turning out to be dry or unproductive. In southern California, too, new wells were brought in, at Whittier, Fullerton, Coyote Hills, Montebello, Richfield, Compton, Torrance, and Inglewood. Along the coast, or near it, wells were drilled at Watsonville, Santa Maria, Ventura, and Newhall. But the greatest strikes were made in 1920 at Huntington Beach, near Los Angeles, and in 1921 at Santa Fe Springs and Signal Hill. These three fields contained such vast pools of oil that their discovery completely upset national prices and outmoded existing storage facilities and marketing procedures. Increasingly greater capital and experience were needed to exploit such vast underground reserves.

Partly through the centralization of management, the large oil companies of today had begun slowly to emerge. The Lyman Stewart interests, having converted themselves into the modern Union Oil Company, continued to emphasize the creation of new markets. Moving away from simple products like kerosene, axle grease, and candle wax, Stewart now encouraged development of a safe oil burner for marine engines. His firm, as well as each of the other leading companies, also commissioned tanker vessels to transport oil to overseas markets, thereby making California's industry a global one. A new company, the Tidewater Associated Corporation, was formed when some fifty small companies in Kern County banded together to take better advantage of the opportunity to supply the new oil-burning railroad locomotives. The Pacific Coast Oil Company, as previously noted, had become the Standard Oil Company of California, which was for a while part of a national producing, refining, and marketing trust consisting of thirty-three subsidiaries. In 1911, however, by Supreme Court decree, the Standard trust group was ordered dissolved. Having resumed its independent status, the Standard Oil Company of California proceeded to develop the Huntington Beach area, which the discovery wells had previously shown to be so promising. Meanwhile, Union Oil concentrated on Santa Fe Springs, while the third major field, that of Signal Hill, was the site of increasing activity on the part of the Shell Oil Company.

The Signal Hill operations are illustrative of the most productive ventures of the California oil industry in the early twenties. In bygone days Indians had used this hillock, some 300 feet high, as a place from which to signal neighboring aborigines on Catalina Island, across the channel from Long Beach; later, during Spanish times, it had served as a beacon for passing ships. In 1920 Shell of California spent $110,000 to lease part of the hill. The next year its Alamitos Well No. 1 there was gushing out 1,200 barrels of 22°-gravity oil per day. Two years later Signal Hill reached a peak production of 244,000 barrels daily from 265 wells. In that year, 1923, the state produced 25 million barrels of petroleum per month. By 1924, California ranked first in the production of petroleum products, with an output worth $333,292,000. This figure represented almost 70 per cent of the dollar value of the state's mineral production that year. Throughout the twenties California clearly led in the field of Western oil production, though new oil centers were to mushroom in Texas, Louisiana, Oklahoma, and Wyoming during the succeeding decade.

In part, California's early oil leadership was due to the dynamic energy and enterprise of the industry's leaders, but these men

OIL FIELD IN THE CENTRAL VALLEY. (By courtesy of the Standard Oil Company of California.)

were not always above suspicion in the methods they used to develop the state's oil resources. Doheny, for example, attracted considerable notoriety through his eagerness to obtain the Elk Hills reserves. This episode, one of those instances in which the history of the state came to be coupled with that of the nation, produced charges of corruption which led into the very cabinet of President Warren G. Harding. It was revealed that, on November 30, 1921, Doheny had secretly dispatched a satchel with $100,000 in it to Secretary of the Interior Albert B. Fall, "an old prospector friend" who officially held control of the Elk Hills reserves and of others at Teapot Dome, Wyoming. Secretary Fall claimed that the money was only a loan, but a tremendous scandal followed the revelation that he planned to lease these oil reserves to Doheny and others. In 1923, both Fall and Doheny were indicted for bribery and conspiracy to corner national resources. In 1928, Fall was convicted and sentenced to prison, although Doheny, surprisingly, escaped punishment; in effect, he was acquitted of giving the bribe that Fall was convicted of accepting. Doheny died in 1935 at the age of seventy-nine. Today his public benefactions, especially in southern California, remain well known.

Doheny and other pioneer oil speculators of his generation lived in an age when California's oil reserves bubbled out of the earth, spilling, uncontrolled, down city streets, over gardens, and across vacant lots. Public interest in the potential riches to be gained from oil naturally ran high, and it was common for promoters to convey prospective buyers of oil stock by the busload to remote auction sites, where retired preachers made fortunes by hawking lots in the shade of tents pitched in a revival atmosphere. Great opportunities for corruption existed. The career of Courtney C. Julian, a Canadian-born oil driller, boomer, and supersalesman, is an excellent illustration. Julian literally advertised for funds in the Los Angeles newspapers. In 1921 he raised $175,000 in one fortnight, and organized the Julian Petroleum Company, known popularly as "Julian Pete," on the basis of a few wells he had leased on the edge of Signal Hill. After Julian had satisfied a few original stockholders with lucrative dividends, he was able to lure new investors with the testimonials of the first group. Then, by selling bogus preferred and common stock in his dummy corporation, he soon made several million dollars. In 1925, Julian's chicanery created a well-reported scandal. After a public audit of his operations was demanded by outraged holders of the worthless Julian Petroleum stock, he fled the state. As for his subsequent activities, Julian entered the mining stock business, bought a radio station to broadcast smears against his enemies, was accused of mail fraud in Oklahoma during 1930, sailed for Shanghai one step ahead of the law, and committed suicide there in 1934.

In spite of the speculative tendency of the oil industry, and an occasional checkered career such as that of Julian, oil development was to play an increasingly important role in California's economy. Oil was more and more widely used for the production of power and heat, virtually revolutionizing industry and transportation as a major source of energy. The industry, however, continued to suffer from wasteful overproduction, from a boom-and-bust psychology, and from poor conservation methods. One should remember that it grew to maturity in the 1920's, when a veritable fever of speculation in real estate and in the stock market afflicted the nation and the state. As new and deeper wells increased production, the need occasionally arose to curtail output by agreements among the major producers, and such arrangements often led to charges of monopoly and price fixing. In later years production was further cut back by other factors, including dwindling reserves and widespread demands for conservation. Drilling techniques that left millions of barrels of unrecoverable crude petroleum below the surface of the earth aroused public opinion to the need for government action. As time passed, regulation and taxation were imposed upon the oil industry as well as upon most others. The industry itself came to favor well-unitization measures in the interest of conservation. It also sought and was able to obtain significant tax deductions based on its high exploration costs and its need for depletion allowances.

After 1929, a peak year of California oil production, few new fields the size of Signal Hill or Santa Fe Springs were discovered. New discoveries that year, a mile or more below the surface, made Santa Fe Springs the state's largest producer of oil. One exception was southern California's Wilmington field, the development of which contributed to a serious problem in the Long Beach area when land adjacent to the field began to subside. Both Texas and Louisiana now were forging ahead of California in oil production, although growing demands encouraged a constant search for new reserves. The average life of the best-producing wells was only twenty-five to thirty years; and, as California's production zones reached a mature phase, most of these wells had to be drilled deeper than 1,000 feet. These circumstances led California drillers to look toward the ocean for new sources of oil, years before ocean wells were sunk elsewhere. In the 1930's they tapped off-shore reserves from rigs anchored into the ocean floor, with considerable success. The development of the port of Long Beach, for example, which was begun in 1938, was financed in large measure by proceeds from the drilling of a rich oil field along its waterfront. Such offshore enterprises created a new legal issue—the question of whether the state or the federal government owned tideland oil resources. Final determination of the control of the tidelands would have to await future legal decisions. California's oil production, in the years following these first decades of the twentieth century, continued to climb until it eventually reached a million barrels per day. Still later, however, it was to slip downward, making it necessary for the state to import increasing amounts of foreign crude-oil supplies, particularly from Indonesia and Saudi Arabia.

From 1900 to 1930, California's oil industry, despite its uncertain origins, had taken a long step toward maturity. It had been dramatically spurred by the discovery of large new pools, by the development of better refining techniques, including the catalytic cracking process, and by new demands for fuel oil and gasoline for factories, automobiles, trucks, and, eventually, airplanes. In a country of long distances and high hills this industry was bound to flourish.

The Coming of the Automobile

The oil industry in California as elsewhere, of course, depended for much of its market on the demands of the new automobile age. The time was coming when the automobile would obliterate long, tiring trips by carriage between California's widely separated cities, but out West this took some years to accomplish. Although Henry Ford had organized his motor company in 1903, there were not many cars on Western highways in the first years of the twentieth century. Even in 1919 there were fewer than 7 million passenger cars registered in the entire United States. Then, in the 1920's, the auto underwent a transformation from a sputtering plaything of the rich, which frightened ladies and horses, to a vital necessity of the working masses. Quantity production of the inexpensive Model T Ford, whose price once dropped to $280, increased the number of cars owned nationally to over 23 million by 1929. Just under 2 million of these were the property of Californians. Numerically, this registration far exceeded that of other Western states (Nevada, 31,915; Arizona, 109,013; Utah, 112,661; Oregon, 269,007). And on a per capita basis, the California registration was the largest in the United States. Meanwhile, as tractors replaced horses on farms, and buses took the place of trolleys in the larger cities, mechanized transportation of all forms became increasingly common in the West as well as in the East.

Like World War I, the auto markedly stimulated California business, especially roadside enterprise. Service stations sprang up everywhere, providing—in addition to gasoline and minor adjustments—free air, road maps, and restrooms for the convenience of dusty motorists. Repair shops and garages to fix stubborn self-starters, inert spark plugs, and faulty brakes were also virtually indispensable to car owners, who were thereby relieved of many pressing anxieties, including the need to know the meaning of such terms as *magneto, differential,* and *generator.* Supply houses were established to install seat covers, batteries, and side curtains. The growth of tourism gave rise to numerous hotels and motels, which tended to be locally owned until the national hotel chains arrived in California. The manufacturers of new windshields, of rubber tires and tubes, and of automobiles themselves, however, remained centered for the most part in the large cities of the East. Only as demands increased did they move assembly and subsidiary facilities to California. Some Californians, as a result, came to fear that the state was functioning almost as a colonial appendage of the East, dependent as it was for so many of its goods and services on large Eastern corporations.

Perhaps nowhere did the automobile change the mode of life more than in the rural West. Along with the phonograph, the radio, and the movies, the auto broke down the isolation of those who lived on farms and ranches. It also emancipated city workers, who came increasingly to use "the machine" for pleasure trips, especially on weekends and during holiday periods. Gradually, too, automobiles stimulated the decentralization of cities by making it possible for people to live at some distance from their work. In the years 1910–1930 California began to pull itself out of the mud, as the state's rutted country lanes were converted into two-laned ribbons of concrete. These, in turn, gave way after the 1930's to four-lane macadamized highways, which remained in use until the advent of still larger freeways in the forties. The increasingly urgent need for roads, in fact, imposed an unending financial strain upon the state. The $18 million voted for road construction in 1910 seemed like a pittance a few years later. Although state and municipal governments have constructed over 135,000 miles of streets and roads since the advent of the automobile, federal aid has also made a major contribution. In particular, highway routes 66, 70–99, and 101, still major arteries, were built in part with federal funds. These highways changed the face of the California countryside, aiding the development of the many raw settlements growing up in formerly wild and empty deserts.

The automobile made for a new type of landscape. Railroad towns were displaced by crossroads with garages, filling stations, hot-dog stands, and wooden tourist bungalows. Gypsy fortune tellers even joined the throngs of concessionaires desirous of doing business with the unwary easterners who drove westward past neon-lighted stucco booths shaped like a half orange. From these glared such highway signs as "All the Orange Juice You Can Drink for 10 Cents" and "Palmistry Will Tell Your Future in California."

Favorable climatic conditions, low gasoline prices, and thousands of miles of paved highways, plus ready access to desert, beach, and mountain, helped make Californians more and more automobile- and vacation-minded. In addition, thousands of tourists were brought to the state each year by persistent advertising, which especially emphasized California's constancy of sunshine. The most popular resorts were the beaches from Santa Barbara to San Diego, Santa Catalina Island, Lake Tahoe, Sequoia and Lassen National Parks, the Yosemite Valley in the High Sierra, the Russian River above San Francisco, Palm Springs on the desert, and Big Bear and Lake Arrowhead in the San Bernardino Mountains. Even Death Valley became a winter tourist attraction. Winter sports in the highest mountains, especially skiing, grew as popular as hunting, fishing, boating, and swimming in the spring and summer.

There were also, of course, a variety of problems that arose along with the growing number of automobiles. The control of traffic became a matter of great importance and complexity, especially at Los Angeles and San Francisco, where the congestion was heaviest. Another result was that public surface transportation suffered a decline. At Los Angeles the interurban trolley system established by the Pacific Electric Company virtually perished in the interwar years. Railroads were forced to close down branch lines in many areas as passenger buses and trucks took advantage of shorter, more rapid routes between cities. Though accidents continued to mount with the increased traffic, so did the demand for new cars. Whole boulevards, notably Figueroa and Alvarado Streets in Los Angeles, and Van Ness Avenue in San Francisco, came to be monopolized by auto dealers. For advertisement and profit Packard dealer Earl C. Anthony operated KFI, for years Los Angeles' largest radio station, and many other car dealers achieved considerable wealth and prominence. The rise of these businessmen was a dramatic testimonial to the fact that the automobile had become virtually a way of life in California.

An Age of Prosperity

In the twenties and thirties, despite a serious national depression, California's domestic and foreign trade expanded. Increases in tourism and the growth of the mining, hydroelectric power, and cinema industries all helped to gain new economic prominence for the state. But without question the automobile, and its subsidiary industries, was largely responsible for this expansion. The assembly plants of Ford, Chrysler, and General Motors, the tire-production establishments of Firestone and Royal, and such firms as Libby-Owens-Ford Glass and Exide Batteries gave employment to thousands. Throughout the depression years, 1930–1937, automobile production remained surprisingly stable. As the number of branch plants and service centers increased, a trend toward economic decentralization was set in motion; first these, and then numerous other Los Angeles and San Francisco businesses, moved toward the outskirts of the cities, especially to Long Beach and Oakland. Accompanying this shift was the steady emergence of residential suburbs, built to house workers in the new manufacturing districts.

To finance California's massive construction needs, a banking industry second to none continued to develop. This was a period in which existing banks were consolidated into large-scale institutions capable of loaning millions of dollars annually. In 1929, a merger occurred between the First National Bank of Los Angeles and the Security National Bank, under bank president Joseph Sartori. This gave southern California one of the country's largest banks. The largest of all, eventually, was the Bank of Italy, later the Bank of America. Founded in 1904 at San Francisco by Amadeo Pietro Giannini, son of an Italian immigrant, it developed a widespread system of branch banking that came to dwarf the activities of other California banks. Geared to the needs of the small depositor, Giannini's system soon spread beyond the boundaries of the state, and even of the nation. Ultimately the Bank of America became the largest bank in the world, thereby helping to gain greater financial status for California and especially for San Francisco, where the institution's headquarters remained.

The growth of California during the interwar period is perhaps best mirrored in the record established by its largest city. In 1925 Los Angeles already ranked first economically among California cities. That year its commercial output reached more than $500 million and its payroll expenditures $86 million. By 1930,

200,000 PEOPLE WALK NORTH ACROSS GOLDEN GATE BRIDGE AT ITS OPENING ON
MAY 27, 1939. (By courtesy of the San Francisco *Chronicle*.)

2,300,000 people lived within a thirty-mile radius of the city (though the population of Los Angeles proper was much less). Only in the early thirties did "L.A." develop a genuine civic center, with its new Spanish-style Union passenger railroad terminal and nearby complex of municipal government buildings. Between 1930 and 1940 the city also celebrated its 150th anniversary, was host to the Tenth Olympiad in a new coliseum, saw the arrival of the first streamlined transcontinental trains, built an observatory at Griffith Park, constructed a metropolitan water system, and laid the groundwork for what was to become an important wartime aircraft industry.

San Francisco's growth, though less spectacular, also remained impressive. By wisely utilizing federal PWA and WPA funds, the city developed further its already notable civic facilities. A maturing community of taste and refinement, San Francisco strengthened its opera, symphony orchestra, and museums, improved Golden Gate Park, and built the remarkable Bay bridges to supplant the colorful ferry boats previously in operation. On May 27, 1939, the day the Golden Gate Bridge opened, 200,000 people walked across the span. That same year San Francisco was host to the Golden Gate International Exposition, the "World's Fair of the West." Exactly 17,041,999 persons paid the entrance fee for this largest exposition ever held west of Chicago. The island in the middle of San Francisco Bay which was the site of the huge fairgrounds was to have become an airport after the fair, but because of World War II it became a naval base instead.

San Francisco has always been a tourist mecca, with its exotic Chinatown, distinctive cable cars, restaurants, Coit Tower, the Giralda Tower atop the Ferry Building, and its Golden Gate, through which ships stream in a constant procession. During the thirties the city's established enterprises such as shipyards, dry-docks, heavy industries, and canneries continued their expansion; but this was also a great period of experimentation. Men like Captain Robert Dollar made San Francisco the home port of numerous steamship companies, while at the same time the city was becoming an air center. On November 22, 1935, Pan American Airways' "China Clipper" soared off to establish the first air link between North America and the mainland of China. Colorful citizens like the banker Giannini and the politician "Sunny Jim" Rolph combined an ebullient yet shrewd attitude toward the future with a reverence for the traditions of the past. This somewhat paradoxical viewpoint is still, in fact, the characteristic way in which the citizens of San Francisco regard their city and its development.

The spectacular growth of California's population during the twenties and thirties was, of course, part of a larger pattern. This increase has gone on virtually unabated in northern California since the days of the Gold Rush, and in southern California since the real-estate boom of 1887. By 1940, on the eve of World War II, the state's population numbered 6,907,387, representing an increase of 1,563,396 during the previous decade; Los Angeles was a metropolis of 1,504,277 persons, and San Francisco one of 634,536. In the case of San Francisco, increasing numbers of commuters found new "bedrooms" in the suburbs of Alameda, Richmond, Oakland, Berkeley, and Burlingame. Both of California's largest cities, and the state itself, had begun to undergo permanent social changes as a result of the population explosion. With the promise of further expansion ahead, the contrast between the nineteenth and twentieth centuries was to become even more marked.

SELECTED READINGS

As one approaches the present, the printed sources concerning California's history become greater in number. The literature on the growth of the state's two largest cities is particularly full. A superior monographic study of the transition of a town to a city is Oscar Osborn Winther, "The Rise of Metropolitan Los Angeles, 1870–1900," *Huntington Library Quarterly*, X (August, 1947), 391–405. The role of climate in this growth is discussed by Winther in "The Use of Climate as a Means of Promoting Migration to Southern California" (San Marino, 1959). Health as a migration factor is the topic of John E. Baur's *Health Seekers of Southern California* (San Marino, 1959). A look at the same generations and environment is in James M. Guinn, *A History of California and of Los Angeles and Environs* (3 vols., Los Angeles, 1915). The transportation system that supported the growth of Los Angeles is the subject of Spencer Crump's *Ride the Big Red Cars: How Trolleys Helped Build Southern California* (Los Angeles, 1962). The phenomenal growth of Los Angeles is examined, too, in W. W. Robinson, *Los Angeles from the Days of the Pueblo* (Los Angeles, 1959), and in Remi Nadeau, *City-Makers* (New York, 1948). Construction of its first water system is the subject of Nadeau's *The Water Seekers* (New York, 1950). A popularized history is Nadeau's *Los Angeles: From Mission to Modern City* (New York, 1960). Construction of the Los Angeles harbor is discussed in Charles A. Matson's *Building a World Gateway* (Los Angeles, 1945).

San Francisco, before and after the fire, has evoked a large and especially colorful literature. Nostalgic accounts include A. R. Neville, *The*

Fantastic City (Boston, 1932), and Charles C. Dobie, *San Francisco's Chinatown* (New York, 1936). More recently, Frank Parker has paid tribute to an important civic symbol in *Anatomy of the San Francisco Cable Car* (Stanford, 1946). The history of the world-famous harbor is described in William Martin Camp, *San Francisco, Port of Gold* (New York, 1947). An entertaining volume, the last section of which describes San Francisco's post-earthquake era, is Samuel Dickson, *San Francisco Is Your Home* (Stanford, 1947). See also Mel Scott, *The San Francisco Bay Area* (Berkeley, 1959), which stresses community planning.

The role of banks in the urban growth of California is developed in an outstanding subsidized history of A. P. Giannini's empire, *The Biography of a Bank: The Story of Bank of America* (New York, 1954), by Marquis James.

The history of recent mining can be traced in the *Bulletins* of the California State Mining Bureau. General descriptions of the oil industry are included in Carl C. Rister, *Oil: Titan of the Southwest* (Norman, Okla., 1949), and in Paul F. Griffin and Robert N. Young, *California, the New Empire State: A Regional Geography* (San Francisco, 1957). More specific are Frank F. Latta, *Black Gold in the San Joaquin* (Caldwell, Idaho, 1949), and, regarding the history of the Union Oil Company, Frank J. Taylor and Earl M. Welty, *Black Bonanza* (New York, 1950). The latter should be used cautiously. A useful brochure, produced by the American Petroleum Institute, is *California's Oil* (New York, 1948). Consult also R. G. Percy, "The First Oil Development in California," *California Historian*, VI (December, 1959), 29–30. Regarding Doheny, see I. F. Marcosson, *The Black Golconda* (New York, 1924). Doheny and Stewart are both treated in Ruth S. Knowles, *The Greatest Gamblers* (New York, 1959). A discussion of the most pressing issue in the recent oil.history of the state is to be found in Ernest R. Bartley, *The Tidelands Oil Controversy* (Austin, Texas, 1953). The most comprehensive history of one of the state's major oil companies is the first volume of a projected series: Gerald T. White, *Formative Years in the Far West, A History of Standard Oil Company of California and Predecessors Through 1919* (New York, 1962). Regarding oil, see also W. H. Hutchinson, *Oil, Land, and Politics: The California Career of Thomas Robert Bard* (Norman, Okla., 1965) and Walker A. Tompkins, *Little Giant of Signal Hill: An Adventure in American Enterprise* (Englewood Cliffs, N.J., 1967).

Two treatments of "the automobile era" are C. B. Glasscock, *The Automobile Age* (Indianapolis, 1937), and David L. Cohn, *Combustion on Wheels: An Informal History of the Automobile Age* (Boston, 1944). Rockwell D. Hunt, *Oxcart to Airplane* (San Francisco, 1929), attempts a transportation history of the state but contains little information on the automobile. More useful is Phil T. Hanna, "The Wheel and the Bell," *Westways*, XLII (December, 1960), 41–56. Two decades are interpreted in Frank L. Beach, "The Transformation of California, 1900–1920," Ph.D. dissertation, University of California, Berkeley (1963).

30

Water, Conservation, and Agricultural Growth

Development of California's water resources, long of great importance to agricultural growth as well as to industry, became an especially crucial issue in the twentieth century. The vast immigration into the state that accompanied the advent of the automobile could not possibly have been supported without an adequate water supply. Larger cities and small farming communities alike were obliged to find new sources of water when local wells and streams began to fail them.

In California's history the connection of water development with both conservation and agriculture is especially direct. As noted previously, large-scale irrigation is comparatively new to California. Only in 1884 did a statewide irrigation convention meet in Riverside to discuss problems of water usage. Not until 1887 did state legislators pass the Wright Act providing for popular elections to organize water-conservation districts. From 1900 onward, however, hundreds of millions of dollars were spent on dams, wells, canals, reservoirs, catchment basins, and aqueducts. Especially in semiarid southern California, irrigated agriculture— once ridiculed by farmers—became widespread. At the same time the new communities of the state's southland were wisely building upon the valuable conservation experiments of George Chaffey, who had led the way toward replenishing the dwindling water supplies of older communities.

Los Angeles and the
Owens Valley Project

Los Angeles displayed particular interest in Chaffey's techniques, which included the diversion of streams, the creation of lakes, and the storage of subsurface water. Located at the center of a dry belt of settlements, Los Angeles faced a genuine water crisis by 1904, when it became apparent that the city reservoirs were barely able to take in enough water to equal their outflow. The city *had* to find new sources of water. Its solution to the dilemma was to tap the Owens River in the far-off southern Sierra — a scheme that became one of the most controversial projects in the history of the state. In 1904, Chief City Engineer William Mulholland, with the support of his predecessor in the office, Fred Eaton, recommended that a bond issue be put on the ballot to provide funds for construction of a $25,000,000 aqueduct that would traverse the 238 miles from the Owens Valley to Los Angeles. Mulholland and Eaton argued that building such an aqueduct was the only way to relieve the shortages created by continued heavy reliance upon the Los Angeles River, an uncertain underground stream which was then the city's major water source.

The issue was passed, and the project duly got under way. Construction of a pipe and flume system across the Mojave Desert, to catch the melted snow of the southern Sierra, began in 1908. Utilizing an army of several thousand workers, Mulholland completed his complex network of tunnels and trenches in less than five years. In November, 1913, to commemorate a feat then considered second only to the building of the Panama Canal, a two-day celebration was held at the San Fernando Valley spillway where the new concrete aqueduct terminated. About these festivities the faraway New York *Times* reported on November 5:

Thousands of citizens went, this morning, to the head of San Fernando Valley, 23 miles north of the city, and saw General Adna R. Chaffey lift the gates which turned into the San Fernando reservoir a flow, assuring to the city 260,000,000 gallons of water every 24 hours.... Field pieces of the National Guard fired a salute, a band played and the crowds waved flags and shouted as the gates were opened. Fifteen thousand automobiles were parked in a neighboring field.

But in spite of the enthusiastic celebration, and the newspaper accounts that described the construction feat in glowing terms, a bitter controversy developed over the project. Violent criticism of Mulholland and the Los Angeles city fathers came from the ranchers and farmers who had been forced to evacuate their Owens Valley homes under threat of eviction. Sportsmen who loved to fish in the remote valley, as well as other outdoorsmen and naturalists, joined in the chorus of protest. So did such public figures as the popular cowboy actor Will Rogers. Two books in particular excoriated Los Angeles for what it had done; their appearance years after completion of the project is some indication of the intense and sustained nature of the controversy. In *The Story of Inyo* (1922), W. A. Chalfant aired charges of corruption and intrigue, while a newspaperman, Morrow Mayo, wrote a book entitled *Los Angeles* (1933) which included a section on "The Rape of Owens Valley." In this Mayo charged:

Los Angeles gets its water by one of the costliest, crookedest, most unscrupulous deals ever perpetrated. . . . The City of the Angels moved through this valley like a devastating plague. It was ruthless, stupid, cruel, and crooked. It deliberately ruined the Owens Valley. It stole the waters of the Owens River.

Although both Chalfant and Mayo exaggerated the facts in dramatizing the plight of the valley residents, their emotional accounts came to be accepted as fact by most historians. The reputation of Los Angeles as a looter of water resources properly belonging to a pastoral paradise has, in fact, persisted to the present day, with many critics being convinced that private interests in Los Angeles benefited most from the Owens Valley Project.

This point of view is largely based on Mayo's charge that an over-stressed syndicate of businessmen, bankers, and real-estate operators, organized to develop the Van Nuys area of the San Fernando Valley, had formed the main pressure group that lobbied for the Owens Valley Project. This group supposedly bought up fallow land in the area, for prices ranging from $5 to $50 per acre, with the purpose of making a financial killing when the San Fernando Valley was irrigated by Owens River water. Mayo's allegation is subject to dispute, especially in view of the involvement of supposedly responsible government agencies, including the United States Reclamation Service, in whose judgment the Owens Valley Project was a vital necessity for the Los Angeles area. Residents of the four Owens River towns of Big Pine, Lone Pine, Bishop, and Independence were, however, led to believe that the land syndicate had profited unfairly at their expense, because the properties of the syndicate were able to draw upon the huge reservoirs set up just outside Los Angeles to store the Owens aqueduct's water.

These citizens of the Owens Valley appealed in vain to the Chief Forester of the United States, Gifford Pinchot, and to President Theodore Roosevelt. Roosevelt sided with Los Angeles. He even provided for further expansion of the Los Angeles aqueduct system in the Owens Valley by ordering the Bureau of Reclamation to extend existing government "forest" lands into the generally treeless valley. These lands were then made available to the city through conservation legislation. The valley residents, hardly soothed by such action, continued to regard the project as an organized swindle rather than as a piece of aggressive vision. A series of pathetic stories appeared in the national press about the privations inflicted upon these people because of the aqueduct. The *Literary Digest*, a popular magazine of the day, ran a number of such articles during 1923 and 1924 detailing the plight of dispossessed Owensites.

Three fruitless demonstrations illustrated how strongly the people of the Owens Valley felt about the expropriation of their property. The first took place on August 17, 1923, when ranchers near Big Pine armed themselves with rifles and stood guard over the headgate of Big Pine Ditch, to prevent diversion of water from the Owens River into the aqueduct. The next attempt to impede the progress of the aqueduct occurred in May, 1924, near Lone Pine. On this occasion a spillway was dislodged by dynamite and large pieces of the aqueduct torn away. A third event, the last in the series of attempts to damage Los Angeles' new water facilities, was the opening of the Alabama wastegates, five miles north of Lone Pine, on November 16, 1924. The protesters were thus able for a short time to turn practically the entire flow of the aqueduct into the bed of the Owens River. When this show of force too, however, was unavailing, concerted opposition by valley residents collapsed.

The Los Angeles *Record* and the Bishop *Inyo Register* continued to lash out against the project, although their attacks increasingly reflected a sense of futility. Throughout the twenties the charge was repeated that Los Angeles had coerced landowners into selling their property for unfair prices. City officials countered these accusations by pointing out that the average price paid was about $145 per acre, as opposed to a normal price of around $100 per acre. Nevertheless, the seizure of the Owens River had given the city a pervasively unsavory reputation in the mountain areas of the state. There the slogan "Remember the Owens Valley" was frequently voiced, reminding northern legislators for years to come of their constituents' views on the seizure of land for water-development purposes.

In 1928 renewed criticism of William Mulholland arose when a dam which he had constructed in San Francisquito Canyon near the town of Saugus, as part of the Owens River Aqueduct, buckled and collapsed. Close to midnight on March 12 of that year, an avalanche of water cascaded down the narrow Santa Clara Valley to Santa Paula, fifty miles away. Houses, trees, telephone poles, fences, bridges, and railroad tracks were swept away, with 385 people losing their lives. Courageously, Mulholland accepted the blame for having built his dam on a weak and friable bedrock and clay substratum, and thus ended his career of public service on an unhappy note. He is, however, generally remembered now as the father of large-scale water development in California.

From the beginning of the Owens Valley Project, of course, it had many staunch defenders who emphasized its positive contributions to Los Angeles, to the state, and even to the valley itself. Such supporters pointed out, for example, the new roads in the Owens Valley area constructed and improved in connection with the building of the aqueduct. As a result of these, valley residents who once sold alfalfa were able to turn to more profitable enterprises serving the Sierra tourist trade, especially selling gasoline and opening other new highway businesses. The city of Los Angeles eventually reimbursed those whose homes and farms had been confiscated, in addition to paying the prices mentioned previously for the lands of owners who had been willing to sell out. The aqueduct was recognized throughout the world as an engineering achievement that would benefit hundreds of thousands of people and insure the future growth of an important city. The new water supply also made feasible the establishment of a municipally operated system of power generation, capable of producing cheap electricity for thousands of homes and factories. With the subsequent addition of Crowley Lake, a large storage reservoir on the eastern slope of the Sierra, Los Angeles was able to garner yet another source of water from the upper Mono basin.

Like Los Angeles, San Francisco too had to cope with a growing water shortage in the early years of the twentieth century. Although located in an area of generally heavier rainfall, the city had an increasing population whose demands for water would soon, it seemed apparent, exceed the supply. Civic leaders had long been eying the Hetch Hetchy Valley near Yosemite National Park as a future source of water. John Muir and other naturalists, however, objected strongly to the San Francisco plan, which would largely inundate the scenic valley by diverting water from the Tuolomne River. Their protests to the United States Department of the Interior helped to retard construction of the proposed dam for years. Federal authorization, however, came in 1913 when Franklin K. Lane, former city and county attorney of San Francisco, became federal Secretary of the Interior. San Francisco finally completed its Hetch Hetchy aqueduct and power network in 1931. Although the project cost the then-phenomenal price of $100,000,000, it has proved less than essential to the city's growth.

The Boulder Canyon Project

By 1923, even while controversy over the Owens Valley Project was still a public issue, Los Angeles faced much the same conditions that had led it to embark on that water-development measure almost twenty years before. The city was adding 100,000 new residents per year to its population, which was rapidly approaching a total of 2,000,000. Existing water supplies were clearly inadequate. To solve the alarming disparity between the daily intake and outflow of the city reservoirs, a series of desperate means were considered. Consultations with occult rain makers, assorted Indian medicine men, cocksure water dowsers, and other "weather experts," however, only confirmed the belief of the city fathers that the construction of huge new dams was the best solution to the water shortage.

As early as 1922 representatives of Colorado, Wyoming, Utah, New Mexico, Arizona, Nevada, and California had met in Santa Fe, New Mexico, to sign a Colorado River Water Compact. This document provided for development of the basin of that river for the common use of the participating states. Although Secretary of Commerce Herbert Hoover cooperated in the allotment of future water rights to these states, it was not until 1928 that a law (the Swing-Johnson Bill) was passed by the United States Congress to permit construction of the dam in Boulder Canyon which was basic to the proposal. The project was to be undertaken jointly by the federal government, the states, and local municipalities. The designated aims of the measure were to protect the Imperial Valley against recurrent threats of flooding, to provide a multistate water reserve, and to generate hydroelectric energy for an expanding Southwest.

A federal bill of 1930 allocated almost $11 million to begin construction the following year. Meanwhile, localities in the areas to be benefited began organizing themselves for their contributions to the project. Most of the major cities of Los Angeles County, for example, formed a Metropolitan Water District to coordinate future water and power distribution for southern California. In 1931 the district floated a bond issue of over $200 million for construction. The depression blunted sale of the bonds, but the federal government's new Reconstruction Finance Corporation ultimately assumed a large share of the financing of the Boulder Canyon Project. In fact, this project became one of the nation's most important public works, heavily supported by the government in an effort to provide new jobs and thus ameliorate the effects of the depression. The enterprise, furthermore, with the massive Hoover Dam in Boulder Canyon as its dominant structure, was, for its time, one of the largest construction jobs in the world. The dam, 1,282 feet high, required the combined efforts of six large construction companies employing ten thousand workers; the latter had to be housed in a new town, Boulder City, built expressly for the purpose. An artificial lake 242 miles long, Lake Mead, was constructed in connection with the dam, as well as a complicated and expensive system of conduits, flumes, reservoirs, and pumping plants to transport water from the lake. The older Owens River Aqueduct was small by comparison with this installation. Despite opposition at different times from private utility companies, from Army engineers, and from the state of Arizona, Hoover Dam, with its accompanying vital storage facility, Parker Dam, was completed on March 1, 1936. On October 25, 1936, the first commercial power began to flow from Hoover Dam. Huge generators pumped electrical energy into homes, farms, and industrial plants throughout the Southwest.

With its tremendous power-generating capacity, and its unequaled water resources, the Boulder Canyon Project has proved to be of special significance to Los Angeles and southern California. Piercing its way through no less than six mountain ranges, the aqueduct provided a veritable lifeline of water to the communities drawing upon it. The Metropolitan Water District, in order to take full advantage of its possibilities, erected a costly diversion dam to deflect water over a spillway. From this dam, water was channeled westward through an aqueduct 242 miles long to Los Angeles. Another local organization, the Imperial Irrigation District, similarly diverted the Colorado River water at Imperial Dam, above Yuma, Arizona, and transported it 80 miles along the 200-foot-wide All-American Canal, to the farms and cities of the Imperial Valley. A 125-mile extension of this canal, to serve the Coachella Valley, was not completed until 1948. Without the Boulder Canyon Project southern California could not have expanded commercially and industrially as it has. Hoover Dam, further-more, safeguards the Imperial Valley and those communities sur-rounding the Gulf of California from damaging spring floods, storing up water to be released later during periods of summer shortage. This water nurtures a booming population and it has helped transform the Colorado basin into a new center of irriga-tion and agriculture.

Water for the Central Valley

Farther north, particularly in the interior of the state, the 1930's saw California's farmers becoming increasingly concerned over the water supplies needed for agricultural growth. The solution seemed to lie in channeling wasted flood waters into the furrows of dry and dusty farms located far from the rivers. One of the most obvious sources of water was the 400-mile-long Sacramento River, with its average annual runoff of 22,230,000 acre-feet. (An acre-foot of water is the amount that will cover one acre to a depth of one foot—or 43,560 cubic feet.) The Sacramento's drain-age area covers almost 30,000 square miles. Its source is a small lake on Mount Eddy, one of the peaks of the Klamath Mountains near the Oregon border. It flows eastward for twelve miles from this point, then turns south for several hundred more to Suisun Bay, fifty miles northeast of San Francisco Bay. Many tributaries help swell it along the way; among the largest are the McCloud, Pit, Feather, Yuba, Bear, and American Rivers, which rise on the rugged sides of the Sierra and Cascade Ranges. Between Redding and its mouth, the Sacramento River drains the valley which, like California's capital city, was named for it.

By the time the courts banned hydraulic mining in 1884, the channel of the Sacramento was so silted that navigation was al-ready closed to all but the vessels of the shallowest draft. The same situation caused extensive flooding, so that in the 1930's flood control and water conservation along the river basin were long overdue. Millions of dollars of damage occurred in the state's Central Valley every time its rivers went on the rampage, with the cities of Stockton, Visalia, Oroville, Yuba City, and Marysville being particularly vulnerable. In addition to the Sacramento, the San Joaquin River, a long, twisting stream that joins the Sacra-mento from the south, then flows into San Pablo Bay (an arm of San Francisco Bay), played an essential part in the history of conservation in the Central Valley. To conserve and to redistrib-ute the flow of both rivers, a new and inclusive plan for harnessing their water resources passed the state legislature in 1933. This scheme, the Central Valley Project, also proposed to generate large quantities of electric power by impounding part of the waters of the Sacramento, the San Joaquin, and various lesser streams. Massive opposition to the measure was posed by private utility companies. These utilities, particularly the Pacific Gas and Electric Company, looked upon the Central Valley Project as unfair government competition with successfully created private enterprise. When these companies sponsored a public referendum in 1933, however, California voters upheld the Central Valley Project.

With this issue decisively settled, there still remained the problem of raising money to build such extensive facilities. When a state bond issue of $170 million could not be sold on account of the depression, the state appealed to the federal government for assistance under the National Industrial Recovery Act. As a result, California's water program in the Central Valley was declared a national reclamation project. Congress, in a Rivers and Harbors Bill of 1935, authorized the expenditure of $12 million for the construction Shasta Dam, north of Redding, as a first step of the Central Valley Project. Begun in the late thirties, along with the Friant Dam near Fresno, the dams of this project were designed to store almost as much water as all the other reservoirs in California (totaling six hundred or more) combined. Shasta Lake, the construction of which was completed in 1945, is capable of storing 4,500,000 acre-feet of water. In addition, two major water arteries, the Friant-Kern Canal and the Delta-Mendota Canal—153 and 120 miles long, respectively—were built to channel water through the San Joaquin Valley. A system of three smaller valley canals was also projected.

Completion of various parts of the Central Valley Project was delayed for many years by the controversy that continued to rage throughout the 1930's and 1940's as to just who should build and control California's water and power facilities. As the need grew for new construction—of powerhouses, dams, canals, generators, and pumping plants—the struggle came to involve the Bureau of Reclamation, the Corps of Engineers, the state Department of Public Works, numerous municipal water systems, and more than a dozen private utilities. These utility companies, of course, maintained their policy of obstructionism in regard to public-works programs, which they branded as socialistic experiments. Further opposition to government participation came from large landowners, who especially fought the 160-acre limit on land for which any one owner could receive water from a federal Bureau of Reclamation project. The advent of World War II also lessened public enthusiasm for federally financed interior-development projects, by focusing attention instead on such pressing requirements as army camps, public housing, war production, and civilian defense. Despite the various forms of opposition to government development of water resources, however, California's steady growth of population made it obvious that a future water supply could not be assured without even more massive government aid than had already been accepted by the people of the state.

Conservation: Water, Forests, and Power

"No state has gained more than California from the artificial application of water, or has more at stake in the extension of its use," once wrote Elwood Mead, the pioneer conservationist after whom Lake Mead was named. Irrigation is essentially a form of conservation, Mead believed, as did Theodore Roosevelt and other early conservationists. Partly through the efforts of these men, the reclamation of water resources early in the twentieth century came to be accompanied by a belated concern over depletion of the timber and mineral wealth of the Far West. Although the idea of conservation had grown through the years of the progressive movement, effective regulatory steps had yet to be taken.

Within only a few generations whole forests had been ruthlessly denuded by fire and ax. A fortunate exception had occurred in the case of the Muir Woods, one of the world's greatest redwood stands, which was spared through the public-spirited efforts of the nature lover William Kent. Located on the southwest side of Mount Tamalpais, this timber was about to be logged in 1903, when Kent selflessly borrowed $45,000 to buy the land and turn it over to the federal government as a national preserve. In general, however, careless lumber companies were permitted to exploit forest resources, with no provision being made for replacement or selective cutting. By the early twentieth century the close connection between overcutting and periodic disastrous floods had become clear. Some of the choicest lands in the state had already been ruined by such man-made erosion. Wild life too was disappearing as industrialism spread, partly as the result of the decimation of protective forest areas. Some species of animals, like the Big Horn Mountain Sheep, had been reduced to a few scraggly specimens in zoos. John Muir and John Burroughs demanded the creation of parks to protect the magnificent Sequoias

SUNBURST FILTERING THROUGH REDWOOD TREES AND GROUND FOG. THESE TREES ARE IN JEDEDIAH SMITH STATE PARK IN DEL NORTE COUNTY. (By courtesy of Redwood Empire Association.)

and coast redwoods, as well as the wild life of the countryside. It seemed to many others also that government action, at federal, state, and local levels, was necessary to stop the squandering of natural resources.

As early as 1889, Major John Wesley Powell had promoted a nationwide study of water sites and had made recommendations for their preservation. In 1911 California created a State Conservation Commission, and, two years later, a State Water Commission. These agencies began to put into operation the latest national conservation practices, especially the notable advances being made in scientific forestry. Lumbering companies, which first resisted controlled management of government forest preserves, came eventually to see the merits of reforestation. During the year 1924–1925 alone, the California Forest Protective Association planted a million and a half young redwoods and Douglas firs, as well as spruce and cedar trees, on the cut-over lands of Mendocino, Del Norte, and Humboldt Counties. The original belt of forest in those three counties had once been about twice the size of Rhode Island. To prevent the further depletion of such areas, private and government projects of this sort became increasingly common. During the depression years of the 1930's for example, the Civilian Conservation Corps (CCC) carried on extensive replanting along the trails that led into the mountains of California.

It was during this period too that the national and state parks systems were developed, with the National Park Service and the California State Division of Beaches and Parks laboring both to preserve the natural beauties of the state and to prepare the recreation sites that would be increasingly needed as the state's population underwent an inevitable growth. In the years between the wars, California came to include within its boundaries 22 national forests, 4 national parks, and 8 national monuments, in addition to a state park system of some 150 recreational areas. Among the national parks and monuments are Yosemite, Sequoia, Lassen, the Devil's Postpile, and Channel Islands. The state system grew to include the areas known as Big Basin Redwoods, Point Lobos, Humboldt Redwoods, and Morro Bay. Several private organizations, notably the Sierra Club, have also made great efforts on behalf of the preservation of natural wilderness areas.

The development of hydroelectric energy is another aspect of the conservation of California's resources. As the population grew, the demands for electrical energy became almost insatiable. From 1900 to 1923 the Southern California Edison Company alone increased its generating capacity from 12,000 horsepower to 500,000 horsepower. By 1928 this huge utility firm was serving

RIO NIDO BEACH IN THE RUSSIAN RIVER DISTRICT IN SONOMA COUNTY. (By courtesy of Redwood Empire Association.)

more than three hundred cities and towns over an area of 55,000 square miles, with a customer population of two million. Meanwhile, the Pacific Gas and Electric Company transmitted power throughout central and northern California, eventually servicing thirty-eight California counties from generators and hydroelectric plants constructed in some of the highest valleys of the Sierra. The total output of electric current in California increased over 62 per cent in the five years from 1922 to 1927, although this rate of growth was temporarily curtailed by the depression. Especially between 1931 and 1934, private construction of powerhouses, transmission lines, and other facilities declined.

But it was during this same period, as previously noted, that public efforts such as the Boulder Canyon and Central Valley

Projects were experimenting successfully with the production of cheap rural hydroelectric power. Other large-scale electrification projects of the federal government in the New Deal period added to the state's growth in electric-transmission capacity. The power vital to the functioning of a modern California is thus supplied by a variety of public and private sources; the two large utility companies (plus many smaller ones), dozens of municipal power systems, and rural-electrification facilities all transmit electricity through a network of powerhouses which blankets the state.

Continued Agricultural Advance

California's agricultural development, of course, reaped intestimable benefits from new water and power supplies, as well as from land-conservation measures. As in other farm areas of the country, agricultural yield in California spiraled upwards while the acreage of the average farm decreased and the value of farm land boomed. In 1850 California's 872 major ranches had averaged 4,500 acres, valued at ony $2 per acre. By 1920 the average farm contained less than 250 acres, but these were worth nearly $120 per acre. By that year the number of farms had increased to 117,670, and by 1935, a peak of 150,360 was reached. (The figures would indicate a reverse trend twenty years later, when the number of farms declined to 123,074, while the average size increased to more than 300 acres.)

The major problem of the interwar years was not agricultural production but, rather, finding the means to increase sales and consumption of the greatly expanded variety of products which California grew. As elsewhere in the country, crops were plowed under during the depression of the 1930's, at the very time when needy refugees from the Dust Bowl regions of the Middle West were going hungry. To sustain a profitable price level, vineyardists, orange-grove owners, and ranchers redoubled their search for new markets to absorb the greater yields that resulted from better knowledge about spraying, fertilizing, and irrigating crops. Prohibition worked a particular hardship upon grape growers and wineries, which tried to market their products in nonalcoholic forms such as "wine bricks" and grape bars.

Carey McWilliams has called California's almost hyperproductive farm-labor system of these years a "factories in the fields" approach to agriculture. The fruit and vegetable farms of the state's Central Valley in particular came more and more to resemble big-business operations, in their impersonality as in their greater efficiency. A cheap, exploitable migrant labor market, widespread unemployment, increasing mechanization, and specialized production combined to boost output still further, although demands were not yet proportional.

Agricultural centers, meanwhile, were discernibly influenced by industrialization. Fresno, in the San Joaquin Valley, a city served by two railroads and various truck lines, reflected the new pattern of growth. An important transportation terminus, Fresno gradually became a clearing center for the distribution of fresh fruits and vegetables, cotton, livestock, wine, dairy products, and such dried fruits as raisins, apricots, and prunes. In addition, it became a supply center for nearby mountain recreation sites and tourist traffic, and a local headquarters for petroleum, hardware, grocery, and appliance firms. Other valley towns such as Stockton, Visalia, Madera, Merced, Modesto, and Bakersfield grew into similarly important market centers.

Whether the times were good, as from 1923 to 1929, or bad, as from 1930 to 1937, California's agricultural establishment was geared to deliver an uninterrupted flow of farm products. As world and national economic conditions improved after the depression, consumption began to rise sharply once more. Then, during the years 1937–1941, the average annual cash receipts from the marketing of California farm products reached $682,629,000—a sum that no other state could match.

SELECTED READINGS

For critical views of the Owens Valley Project see the books by Chalfant and Mayo cited in the text, and Nadeau's already mentioned *The Water Seekers*. An earlier view of the Owens Valley country, before it was despoiled, forms part of Mary Austin's poetic *The Land of Little Rain* (New York, 1903). Her book *The Ford* (New York, 1917) includes a graphic presentation of what she considered the intrigues of both the irrigation and the oil history of California. The 1928 holocaust in the Santa Clara Valley is the subject of Charles Outland's *Man-Made Disaster: The Story of the Saint Francis Dam* (Glendale, 1962).

The continuing search for water has evoked an extensive literature, especially since the 1930's. Regarding the Boulder Canyon Project one can read Ray Lyman Wilbur and Elwood Mead, *Construction of Hoover Dam* (Washington, D.C., 1935), and George A. Pettit, *So Boulder Dam*

Was Built (Berkeley, 1935). David O. Woodbury, *The Colorado Conquest* (Indianapolis, 1941), and P. L. Kleinsorge, *Boulder Canyon Project* (Stanford, 1941), deal with the same subject. Tracing the details of the struggle between various western states for Colorado River water is John Upton Terrell, *War for the Colorado River*, Volume I of which is entitled *The California-Arizona Controversy*, and Volume II, *Above Lee's Ferry—The Upper Basin* (Glendale, 1965). An introduction to more recent developments, though now somewhat dated, is Robert de Roos, *The Thirsty Land: The Story of the Central Valley Project* (Stanford, 1948). Actual construction of a vital part of the Central Valley Project is described in Viola P. May, *Shasta Dam and Its Builders* (n.p., 1945). Continuing the story is Marion Clawson and Mary Montgomery, *History of Legislation and Policy Formation of the Central Valley Project* (n.p., n.d.). Merle Armitage, *Success Is No Accident: The Biography of William Paul Whitsett* (Yucca Valley, California, 1959) deals with the life of one of the developers of the state's water resources. An overall survey is S. T. Harding, *Water in California* (Palo Alto, 1961).

Suggestive as to the earliest trends in water conservation is William E. Smyth, *The Conquest of Arid America* (New York, 1907). A pioneer work which encouraged much further writing was Charles R. Van Hise, *The Conservation of Natural Resources in the United States* (New York, 1910). *The Report of the Conservation Commission* (Sacramento, 1912) is indicative of state concern over conservation. See also C. Raymond Clar, *California Government and Forestry From Spanish Days . . .* (Sacramento, 1959), another state publication. Problems of flood control, and their relation to mining, are discussed in California Department of Public Works *Bulletin No. 26*, "Sacramento River Basin," (Sacramento, 1931); Kenneth Thompson, "Historic Flooding in the Sacramento Valley," *Pacific Historical Review*, XXXIX (November, 1960), 349–360; and Robert Kelley, "Taming the Sacramento: Hamiltonianism in Action," *Pacific Historical Review*, XXXIV (February, 1965), 21–49. The growth of a major utility company that has played an important part in the development of both water and power in California is charted by Charles M. Coleman, *P.G. & E. of California: The Centennial Story of the Pacific Gas and Electric Company, 1852–1952* (New York, 1952).

Conservation of water and timber resources has also given rise to numerous works of protest and advice. An early opponent of the exploitation of the natural resources of California was the naturalist John Muir. From the 1870's onward, in dozens of articles for the San Francisco *Bulletin*, the *Overland Monthly*, and *Harper's*, Muir stressed this theme. See C. R. Bradley, *Reference List to the Published Writings of John Muir* (Berkeley, 1897). *The Life and Letters of John Muir* (2 vols., Boston, 1924), edited by William Frederic Bade, reveals Muir's deep interest in conservation. So do the various biographies about him, as well as his previously unpublished journals, edited by Linnie M. Wolfe as *John of the Mountains* (Boston, 1938). Also significant are Muir's *The Mountains of California* (New York, 1894), and *Our National Parks* (Boston, 1901). Holway R. Jones, *John Muir and the Sierra Club: The Battle for Yosemite* (San Francisco, 1966), is a worthy tribute published by the organization he founded in 1892. It contains a superb bibliography about the Sierra country. Francis P. Farquhar, *History of the Sierra Nevada* (Berkeley, 1965), is the best history of those mountains. A mimeographed biography entitled *William Kent, Independent*, by Elizabeth T. Kent (Kentfield, 1950), honors the conservationist who saved the Muir Woods.

The relationship of farming to water-development projects is touched upon in Clarke H. Chambers, *California Farm Organizations* (Berkeley, 1952). The same topic, with emphasis on the exploitative characteristics of California agriculture, is treated in Carey McWilliams, *Factories in the Fields* (Boston, 1939). Another significant work regarding California's agricultural growth is Marion Clawson, *Longterm Outlook for Western Agriculture* (Berkeley, 1946).

The interest in nature shown by Clarence King's humane *Mountaineering in the Sierra Nevada* (New York, 1905) has been continued to the present day in the Sierra Club *Bulletin* (1897–   ). A useful volume, for those interested in man's historic imprints on the mountains, is Francis P. Farquhar, *Place Names of the High Sierra* (San Francisco, 1926). Regarding the mountain and wilderness areas of the California back country, see also Joseph H. Le Conte, *Rambling Through the High Sierra* (San Francisco, 1899); Roderick Peattie, *The Sierra Nevada* (New York, 1947); and Oscar Lewis, *High Sierra Country* (New York, 1955). The latest in the line of authors to be captured by the majesty of the Sierran Mountain barrier is W. Storrs Lee in *The Sierra* (New York, 1962). Lee discusses not only the mountains but also the men who sought to master them by conquest or exploitation. Concerning the Sequoias, see Norman Taylor, *The Ageless Relics* (New York, 1962).

31

Labor in an Industrial Age

Between 1900 and 1930 the population of California increased from less than 1,500,000 to more than 5,500,000. One cause of this growth was undoubtedly the tremendous volume of infectious advertising the state produced. It stressed California's beneficent climate, easy living, natural wonders, old missions, wild flowers, ostrich farms, orange groves, fiestas, and rodeos. Chamber of Commerce men, and other tourist-minded folk, could also point to numerous reasons why individual success seemed more easily obtainable in California than elsewhere. Because of the state's richness in land and other natural resources, many conscientious newcomers had already seen their efforts yield handsome results. The opportunity to move with rapidity into better jobs, with the accompanying advantage of social mobility, proved to be a highly marketable enticement. The blue-and-gold tourist folders that urged visitors to spend winters in "the golden state" scarcely hinted that serious social problems brewed beneath the surface of its outwardly placid way of life.

Yet California's remarkable growth did not occur without continuing social and political dislocations. The widespread attention to the state's attractions stood in contrast to the underlying discontent of upsetting elements in its society. From the 1870's, when Denis Kearney had harangued the masses on the windy sandlots of San Francisco, California's workingmen had established a reputation for vigorous assertion of their rights. During the years after the turn of the century, tensions between laborers and employers grew constantly more pronounced. San Francisco workers again resorted to noteworthy political activity in 1901, through formation of the Union Labor Party to achieve their goals. One of the foremost of these, as seen in Chapter 28, was opposition to vested railroad interests, as well as to great concentrations of economic power in the hands of utility magnates, financiers, and shipping tycoons. Labor also raised a strong voice of protest during the period of unusual municipal corruption symbolized by the Ruef-Schmitz scandals in San Francisco. That city, in fact, became one of the most effectively organized labor strongholds in the country, a center from which labor agitators operated vigorously in the interior and in the many coastal valleys of the state. Even after labor had proved its power in a number of cases, however, employers were by no means willing to acknowledge its strength; thus the relation between capital and labor in the early twentieth century was characterized by strain, disorder, and frequent clashes. Even today these difficulties have not been wholly forgotten.

The I.W.W.

After 1905 the Industrial Workers of the World, a socialist-oriented group of dissident unionists organized at Chicago that year, turned its attention to the Far West. In particular, the I.W.W. was developing plans—highly incendiary from the viewpoint of the established order—to organize California's many seasonal and part-time workers into "One Big Union." Among these migratory laborers were field hands, lumberjacks, and cannery workers. These were not welcome to join the American Federation of Labor, largely organized along craft or guild lines. Frequently the plight of California's harvest workers was pathetic. The hours of labor on most farms and ranches were very long and pay extremely low, while conditions in farm labor camps were widely considered to be deplorable. Furthermore, increased use of farm machinery annually lessened the need for such workers' services.

These conditions naturally drew the attention of revolutionary I.W.W. leaders. Inspired agitators set to work throughout the state, with their greatest acivity occurring in the years 1908–1912. By 1910, these organizers had recruited about 1,000 migratory farm laborers as members of almost a dozen locals in California. National I.W.W. membership, incidentally, reached no more than 60,000 at its zenith; revolutionary unionism in America has never had a widespread following. However, the I.W.W., urging radical reform of the economy, mightily stirred the souls of young and sometimes illiterate migrant workers. Those who became members of the I.W.W. were referred to contemptuously in rural newspapers and farm journals as "Wobblies," belonging to an "I Won't Work" movement, while local police officials regarded the volatile organization as an outlaw labor group. Soapbox orators were arrested at meetings and rallies sponsored by the I.W.W., fire hoses were turned on its members, and field workers were warned not to join I.W.W. locals. Municipal officials took no action when organization headquarters in various cities were mysteriously burned.

In spite of such harassment, the I.W.W. persisted. It held mass meetings in front of employment agencies, for example, at which orators charged that these establishments had demanded high fees from workers for jobs that were actually nonexistent. Because of the continued I.W.W. agitation most California towns came to set aside certain areas where public speaking was forbidden. After further inflammatory incidents with local police, the most serious of which took place at Fresno and San Diego, various municipalities adopted stiff regulations aimed explicitly against the I.W.W. Leaders of the organization often violated such ordinances, sometimes because of ignorance of the law. In other cases, however, they did so in defiance, conducting demonstrations with the deliberate purpose of testing free speech.

The terror in which municipal officials held the I.W.W. was, of course, based on its radical ideology. Subscribing as it did to the Marxian concept of class struggle and to syndicalist and anarchist ideas, the organization was undeniably a threat to California's status quo. Both organized and unorganized workers also distrusted the "Wobblies," because of their militant attempts to obtain equal status for Chinese and Mexican workers. Employers naturally hated the I.W.W. techniques of on-the-job recruiting and quick strikes—usually unannounced. Though its leaders were jailed, clubbed, driven out of their headquarters, and even killed, the "Wobblies" still continued their activities, at least for a time.

The longstanding I.W.W. campaign to organize migratory workers reached a peak of violence on August 3, 1913, on a large hop farm near Wheatland in the Sacramento Valley. At stake were the conditions under which itinerant laborers—men, women, and children—were forced to live and work on the farm, known as the Durst Ranch. Virtually no provision had been made to house the workers decently or to provide basic sanitation for them. Eight toilets existed for the use of 2,800 persons. The owners of the ranch had advertised for many more workers than they could actually use and then paid the ones they hired wages as low as seventy-five cents per day. A ranch-owned store, furthermore, held back 10 per cent of these meager wages, forcing field hands to purchase food and supplies at inflated prices. The workers, under the leadership of Blackie Ford, head of the I.W.W. local, called a strike. Then, when a sheriff's posse sought to arrest Ford and other ringleaders, a pistol was fired, and a full-scale riot followed. The sheriff and the local district attorney, as well as several workers, were killed. Governor Hiram Johnson called out the National Guard and brought in private detectives to investigate; as a result of the incident, the I.W.W. organization was virtually dismantled in the Sacramento Valley. Ford and a colleague were convicted of murder and sentenced to life imprisonment.

The Wheatland Riot nevertheless led to various attempts on the part of the state to improve the welfare of migratory workers. The California legislature, with its attention drawn to the problem of seasonal labor, passed several bills toward this end, though such measures were not very effective. A new Commission on Immigration and Housing, for example, did what it could to help achieve decent working conditions but was hampered by lack of power. Those ranchers who imported thousands of extra workers each season to pick peaches, grapes, cotton, and hops still claimed they could not afford to furnish individual dwellings to part-time laborers. They pointed out that, because the harvest season lasts only a few days, or a few weeks at most, such housing remains vacant much of the year and is thus impractical to maintain. Labor leaders contended that this reasoning was a poor excuse for the continued inhumanity with which workers were treated.

Certainly the Wheatland Riot did not mark the end of strife involving migrant workers in California. The prewar era seemed to breed discontent. Late in 1913, a disgruntled agitator who called himself "General" Kelley marched an "army" of several thousand unemployed farm workers to Sacramento to demand relief and sustenance. They resembled Jacob Coxey's army of ragamuffins which, in 1895, had marched to Washington from Ohio with similar demands. In an outcome much like that of the earlier demonstration, Kelley's men were driven off by armed guards after attempting to camp on capitol grounds.

In a federal legal decision of 1895 (*Pollock v. Farmers' Loan and Trust Co.*), Justice Stephen J. Field, a Californian, showed his protective alarm over attacks on the capitalist system: "The present assault is," he wrote, "but the stepping stone to others, larger and more sweeping, till our political contest will become a war of the poor against the rich. . . ."

Bombing of the
Los Angeles *Times*

In 1910, several years before the Wheatland Riot and before Kelley's fruitless march to Sacramento, extremist elements in the labor movement had become involved in an especially notorious episode. This ill-conceived event, the bombing of the Los Angeles *Times*, seriously set back the entire labor movement in California for many years. The blast occurred at 1:07 A.M. on October 1, just as the newspaper's mechanical force was getting the *Times* to press. In the explosion, which was heard for more than ten miles, twenty persons were killed and many more injured, while the *Times* building was reduced to a mass of rubble. The disaster influenced deeply the future social and editorial philosophy of the *Times*. Tension between the paper and labor organizers had been of long duration, and after the bombing mutual suspicion increased even more. The owner of the *Times*, General Harrison Gray Otis, blamed irresponsible labor leaders for the bombing, particularly members of the International Association of Bridge and Structural Iron Workers, then involved in a local strike. Conversely, the voices of labor, denying that a bomb had caused the blast, accused the *Times* of criminal negligence in operating a faulty plant, which union spokesmen called a gas-leaking firetrap. It was only after a lengthy and dramatic trial that the incident was definitely established as an act of union violence.

In 1911 three labor agitators—Ortie McManigal and James B. and John J. McNamara—were brought to trial, accused of organizing the bombing. Labor retained the renowned crusading attorney Clarence Darrow, who was known for his vigorous opposition to both violence and capital punishment. The testimony against the McNamara brothers was far too incriminating for Darrow to win their acquittal. Acting on his advice, they changed their pleas from not guilty to guilty and, after a mysterious compromise with both prosecution and judge, they were sent to the state penitentiary. (The good offices of the noted crusading journalist Lincoln Steffens were used to arrange this compromise, by which the McNamara brothers apparently changed their pleas in exchange for the prosecution's dropping the pursuit of other suspects.) James drew a sentence of life imprisonment and John one of fifteen years. McManigal was freed because he had "turned state's evidence," thereby making it possible for government officials to indict his accomplices.

Despite the confusing testimony that came out of this trial, in an atmosphere of violent acts and vituperative overstatement, most people were incensed by what they considered labor's impatience to demonstrate its growing power. Not only was public opinion vociferous in denouncing the audacity of the bombing, but widespread criticism was also voiced over Darrow's suspicious compact on behalf of the McNamara brothers. The belief grew that this may have been Darrow's only way of saving the lives of the McNamaras, who ultimately confessed the *Times* dynamiting.

DESTRUCTION BY FIRE OF THE LOS ANGELES TIMES BUILDING, 1910. (Photograph by C. C. Tarter, C. C. Pierce Collection. By courtesy of The Huntington Library, San Marino, California.)

Darrow himself was indicted for jury bribery in this case, although he was later acquitted. Unfortunately for union leaders, the bombing so blackened their reputation that labor disturbances were often equated, particularly after the outbreak of World War I, with lack of national patriotism. Thus the *Times* bombing probably helped to kill off the militancy that had characterized the American labor movement.

Continued Labor Strife

The advent of war was to have a number of serious effects upon labor. A heavy demand for both skilled and unskilled workers raised wages throughout the state, particularly in urban areas. Prices rose still more, however, and renewed tension between workers and employers was the result. Apprehensive about the spread of union activity, management urged upon labor the open shop as a temporary and patriotic war measure. As public agitation on behalf of the open shop also became pronounced, union leaders grew increasingly discontent. The issue was the source of considerable new irritation between capital and labor in the midst of the greatest material plenty either had yet achieved. In 1916, violence again erupted.

President Wilson had proclaimed July 22 of that year "Preparedness Day," when the nation was to demonstrate its unity and fitness for service in case war were ever declared. At San Francisco militant advocates of the open shop helped organize a patriotic parade as a Preparedness Day demonstration. Meanwhile, a serious longshoremen's strike was under way. The combination was enough to make employers and union organizers especially edgy about their differences. In the midst of this uneasy situation a suitcase containing a bomb, left by someone on a city sidewalk at the corner of Steuart and Market Streets, exploded at 2:06 P.M., killing nine persons and injuring forty others.

Two radical union leaders, Thomas J. Mooney and Warren K. Billings, were arrested and accused of the crime. A few years before, in 1913, Billings had been convicted of carrying explosives. Although he had claimed to be the victim of a "frame-up," he had been sentenced to two years in Folsom Penitentiary. Newspapers joined avidly in the strong public feeling over the Preparedness Day incident and the Mooney-Billings trial, often dealing in rumor and innuendo. The press circulated a story on January 3, 1917, the day the trial began, that Mooney and Billings had been part of a conspiracy of anarchists who had plotted to assassinate Governor

Hiram Johnson. There was also talk connecting the two men with alleged "Reds" from abroad who were supposedly converging on California to spread the new doctrine of Bolshevism. Both Billings and Mooney presented alibis designed to clear themselves of the Preparedness Day bombing. Mooney produced three photos of himself and his wife on the roof of a Market Street building viewing the parade. A streetside clock conveniently located in the background showed the time to be 1:58, 2:01, and 2:04 P.M., just prior to the bombing. Despite this and other evidence for the defense, Mooney was sentenced to be hanged, and Billings received a life term in the state penitentiary.

A large rally in Petrograd, Russia, helped to focus international attention on the case. The White House was deluged by protests from labor leaders. Under these circumstances President Wilson appointed an investigative committee, whose overall conclusion was that there was insufficient evidence to find anyone guilty. As a result of Wilson's intervention, in the interest of wartime unity, Mooney's punishment was commuted to life imprisonment. Nevertheless, the public remembered that during the trial the prosecution had proved Mooney's association with the McNamara brothers—convicted earlier of planning the explosion of the Los Angeles *Times*—and antilabor sentiment continued to run high. The longshoremen's strike was protracted and finally lost.

The issue of Mooney's and Billings' guilt long remained a burning one. Numerous Californians held simply to the feeling that Mooney and Billings were dangerous men: "They may not be guilty of the bomb explosion, but they belong where they are." From the moment Mooney and Billings went behind the bars of San Quentin Penitentiary, however, labor embarked upon a twenty-year campaign to free the two men, calling them martyrs of an "American Dreyfus Case." Labor sympathizers maintained that Mooney and Billings had been adjudged guilty only because of their past radicalism and association with anarchistic antiwar exiles. Their case continued to attract attention all over the world. In contrast to previous hostility on the part of the press, now thousands of lines of newspaper and magazine copy were written on behalf of Mooney and Billings. Grave charges of perjured testimony during the trial were made in their favor by Fremont Older, the reformist San Francisco newspaperman who had attacked the Ruef-Schmitz machine and who himself came to be called an anarchist by antiunion critics. In 1939, after repeated petitions and appeals, Governor Culbert L. Olson pardoned Mooney as the first act of his administration. Mooney died soon thereafter. Billings was pardoned much later by Governor Edmund G. Brown.

Following the Preparedness Day bombing the open shop reigned in San Francisco and most other California cities for a number of years. In 1919, during the repressive atmosphere of the postwar years, the state of California adopted a Criminal Syndicalism Law to control labor leaders. The act, resulting in part from public fear of the spread of communism after the Russian Revolution of 1917, forbade any form of violence in labor disputes. Anyone convicted of "labor violence" could be sentenced to as much as fourteen years' imprisonment. Radical ideas, especially those of foreign origin, were not to be welcomed in postwar California, which gave its full support during this period to Prohibition and "100 per cent Americanism."

The Criminal Syndicalism Law was vigorously enforced, and ultimately caused the arrest and imprisonment of several hundred persons accused of encouraging the overthrow of law and order. It was invoked to discourage union agitators in such tense situations as the 1923 San Pedro waterfront strike, various cannery strikes during the 1930's, and work stoppages in 1933–1934 among vegetable, fruit, and cotton pickers of the Imperial and San Joaquin Valleys. Ordinarily, of course, these repressive measures were administered by local and state police. But at Salinas, in 1936, growers recruited what they called a "citizen's army" to put down a strike by migrant lettuce pickers. Equipped with shotguns and pick handles, the army "got the lettuce picked," broke the strike, and disbanded offending unions—which resumed agitation soon after the incident. The fierceness of California's Criminal Syndicalism Law was illustrated by the arrest of the writer Upton Sinclair, for reading the United States Constitution aloud in public. The major punitive effect of the law, however, fell squarely where its advocates had intended—upon labor leaders. This legislation, as well as municipal ordinances and public pressure, combined in a few years to kill off what remained of the I.W.W. and other radical labor groups in California. Long before the 1930's such militant labor activity had ceased to be a decisive force within the state.

SELECTED READINGS

Carey McWilliams, in his previously mentioned books *California the Great Exception* and *Factories in the Fields,* has written perhaps more fully than anyone else on the labor problems of California. A standard and comprehensive general labor history is the four-volume work, edited by John R. Commons and others, entitled *A History of Labour in the United States* (New York, 1926–1935). Other general histories, in an area where objective sources run thin, are Irving Bernstein, *The Lean Years: A History of the American Worker 1920–1933* (Boston, 1960), and Foster Rhea Dulles, *Labor in America: A History* (New York, 1955, 1960). Also useful is Samuel Yellen, *American Labor Struggles* (New York, 1956).

In the absence of a completely satisfactory modern history of the I.W.W. in California, Carleton Parker, *The Casual Laborer and Other Essays* (New York, 1920) is useful. A primary source is William D. Haywood, *Bill Haywood's Book* (New York, 1929). Consult also Wallace Stegner's novel *The Preacher and the Slave* (Boston, 1950), which presents a literary picture of the "Wobblies." Another literary analysis is that of Robert L. Tyler, "The I.W.W. and the West," *American Quarterly*, XII (Summer, 1960), 175–187. John Dos Passos utilizes the "Wobblies" as part of his criticism of American capitalism in *U.S.A.* (New York, 1939). Yet another novelist, Stewart Holbrook, is somewhat more objective in "The Last of the Wobblies," *American Mercury*, LXII (April, 1946), 467–468. Paul F. Brissenden, *The I.W.W.: A Study of American Syndicalism* (New York, 1920), is an older technical analysis. See also Louis Adamic, *Dynamite: The Story of Class Violence in America* (New York, 1935), and William J. Burns, *The Masked War . . .* (New York, 1913). Burns was a prominent detective in the *Times* bombing case. The most recent and comprehensive study of the "Big Red Scare" is Robert K. Murray, *Red Scare: A Study in National Hysteria, 1919–1920* (Minneapolis, 1955). Specifically dealing with the Preparedness Day incident are Ernest J. Hopkins, *What Happened in the Mooney Case* (New York, 1932), and by Thomas J. Hunt, *The Case of Thomas J. Mooney and Warren K. Billings* (New York, 1929), and the interesting, but not fully reliable, *Frame-up: The Incredible Case of Tom Mooney and Warren Billings* (New York, 1967) by Curt Gentry. Adela Rogers St. Johns' *Final Verdict* (New York, 1962) tells the story of her attorney father, Earl Rogers. He was involved in saving Clarence Darrow from the charge of bribing the jury in the Los Angeles *Times* bombing case and in other dramatic legal instances in California. *The Autobiography of Upton Sinclair* (New York, 1962) is full of details about his involvement in labor struggles that affected California politics.

Books that touch upon the tensions described in this chapter include Bernard C. Cronin, *Father Yorke and the Labor Movement in San Francisco, 1900–1910* (Washington, D.C., 1943); Frederick L. Ryan, *Industrial Relations in the San Francisco Building Trades* (Norman, Okla., 1936); Grace H. Stimson, *Rise of the Labor Movement in Los Angeles* (Berkeley, 1935); and Paul S. Taylor, *The Sailors' Union of the Pacific* (New York, 1923). Articles that cover the same field are Thomas W. Page, "The San Francisco Labor Movement in 1901," *Political Science Quarterly*, XVII (December, 1902), 664–688; Ed Rosenberg, "The San Francisco Strikes of 1901," *American Federationist*, IX

(January, 1902), 15–18; Lillian Symes, "Our American Dreyfus Case," *Harper's*, CLXI (May, 1931), 641–652; E. Guy Talbott, "The Armies of the Unemployed in California," *Survey*, XXXII (August 22, 1914), 523–524; Walter V. Woehlke, "Bolshevikis of the West," *Sunset*, XL (January, 1918), 11–13, 73, 82. A more general useful article is Gerald D. Nash, "The Influence of Labor on State Policy: The Experience of California," California Historical Society *Quarterly*, LXII (September, 1963), 241–257. See also Norris C. Hundley, Jr., "Katherine Philips Edson and the Fight for the California Minimum Wage, 1912–1913," *Pacific Historical Review*, XXIX (August, 1960), 271–286.

Five unpublished M.A. theses and Ph.D. dissertations are also valuable in reconstructing the dramatic labor strife of the early nineteenth century and after in California: Richard C. Searing, "The McNamara Case: Its Causes and Results," M.A., University of California, Berkeley (1935); Richard C. Miller, "Otis and His *Times*," Ph.D., University of California, Berkeley (1961); Hyman Weintraub, "The I.W.W. in California, 1905–1931," M.A., U.C.L.A. (1947); Richard A. Frost, "The Mooney Case," Ph.D., University of California, Berkeley (1960); and Woodrow C. Whitten, "Criminal Syndicalism and the Law in California, 1919–1927," Ph.D., University of California, Berkeley (1946).

32

The Depression Years

After the collapse of the stock market in October, 1929, the nation's economic situation grew increasingly worse and President Herbert Hoover's Republican administration seemed powerless to stop the downward economic spiral. Late in 1932, through the Reconstruction Finance Corporation, the government made numerous emergency loans to financial institutions throughout the country. This money, as well as federal funds allocated to the individual states, was supposed, as Democratic critics said, to "trickle down" to individual citizens through their municipalities. Such aid, however well-intentioned, did not prove effective. New measures of a radically different nature were needed, on both the national and the state levels.

At the local level of politics California suffered from what might be called a transient mentality. Too few people had historically been willing to improve community government. As sojourners, their interest in California was, at first, temporary. Swarms of quasi-residents, in search of jobs and spiritual roots, moved about in the frontier tradition, hardly knowing what level of government authority to obey or to appeal to for help.

As in the rest of the country, unemployment spread throughout the West, and at the same time the strength of California unionism markedly decreased. Not only did its farm labor remain unorganized; unemployed city workers too found themselves in intense competition for jobs. The bargaining power of local union leaders was thus further weakened; labor spokesmen were in no position to demand the closed shop, or to insist upon better working conditions of any sort.

In the presidential elections of 1932, the Democratic candidate was Franklin Delano Roosevelt, governor of New York. Roosevelt's record-breaking campaign took him to the major cities of the Far West, and many thousands of Californians responded to his magnetic personal appeal. Roosevelt also offered genuine hope to those who were down-hearted and discouraged. Many Californians had tired of hearing that speculation in the stock market was the primary cause of the depression. They were more interested in the solution of local problems than in such national issues—which they often found complicated and unfathomable—as the currency, the tariff, and unemployment in Eastern cities.

At the Commonwealth Club in San Francisco on September 23, 1932, the Democratic candidate set forth his political and economic views more clearly than at any other point during the campaign. He described in somber terms the increasing concentration of private enterprise in the United States into a relatively few large business concerns. "Put plainly, we are steering a steady course toward oligarchy, if we are not there already," he said. Roosevelt went on to speak of every man's right to life and to a comfortable living, and declared: "Our government, formal and informal, political and economic, owes to everyone an avenue to possess himself of a portion of that plenty sufficient for his needs, through his own work." When election day came, California voted overwhelmingly for Roosevelt.

But while Roosevelt campaigned, the situation was growing steadily worse. Overproduction of both agricultural and commercial commodities caused unemployment to spread still further as cutbacks were ordered. Once-prosperous industries, farms, and real-estate developments were being mired down by the depression. Within a few months many banks, as the result of repeated runs on their holdings by worried depositors, were threatened with collapse. To allow time for the state legislature to devise protective legislation in the bank situation, California Governor James Rolph, Jr., ordered a three-day bank holiday on March 2, 1933. By March 4, the day of President Roosevelt's inauguration, almost every state governor had declared a bank holiday or had imposed severe restrictions on withdrawals. On the same day Rolph extended the California bank holiday for three more days.

The country faced economic paralysis, with the scarcity of money in some cases reducing business to a barter system. Hope ran high that Roosevelt's "New Deal" would quickly be put into effect in such an emergency. Because Roosevelt demonstrated that he viewed the crisis as far from insoluble, Californians as well as other Americans looked to him for the coordinated leadership that seemed vitally necessary. The new president's answer was to launch a massive program clustered around the "Three R's": relief, recovery, and reform. Initially the most important of these, for California and for every other state, was relief.

The "Okies" and "Arkies"

Although California's relief activities—carried on through a State Relief Administration—were far from adequate to meet emergency conditions, thousands of new migrant farm workers descended upon the state in the depression years to add their needs to those of other citizens. California, fearful of the consequent burden on its economy, issued a publication warning migrants not to come there to seek jobs. However, rumors of high wages and comfortable conditions out West caused many to make a trip that they were later to regret.

Among the newcomers were 350,000 farmers from the parched and unproductive Dust Bowl areas of the Middle West; these were generally known as "Okies" or "Arkies," from their origins in Oklahoma or Arkansas. Their trek overland in rickety flivvers and jalopies, with brooms and pails tied onto running boards, and the tops of the vehicles heaped with mattresses, children, and blankets, has been given vivid literary treatment in John Steinbeck's well-known novel *The Grapes of Wrath*. Most of these migrants arrived in California during 1935 and in the four years thereafter. Because the labor situation was already so gravely depressed, even responsible citizens impatiently threw up their hands in anguish over the new influx of population. State legislation was passed to close the border to indigents, although later, in 1941, the United States Supreme Court declared such laws unconstitutional.

The migrant workers who came to California in the 1930's settled mostly in the farming regions of the Central Valley area. There, job conditions remained more critical than elsewhere in the state—as bad, in fact, as those which the I.W.W. had deplored previously. These immigrants resembled the homesteading pioneers of the nineteenth century, except that they had no homesteads. Housed often in rude tar-paper shacks and in other unsanitary hovels, many of them were in dire need of direct relief. Too many farm owners became accustomed to paying the starvation wages which the newcomers were forced to accept. Themselves faced with bankruptcy, the owners claimed they could not possibly spend money they did not have to improve the working conditions of the refugees. Both the AFL and the CIO battled almost in vain in the pear orchards of Marysville, in the packing sheds of Bakersfield, and in the canneries of Fresno to organize migrant workers during the interwar period. In 1933–1934, after a wave of field strikes, a group of farm owners, the Associated Farmers of California, organized themselves as "an educational agency to inform the public about the type of personnel leading the agricultural strikes." This strike-prevention group came to number 40,000 members, and it proved more than a match for the ineffective United Cannery, Agricultural, Packing and Allied Workers of America, CIO, to which most of the relatively few unionized migrant workers belonged.

After 1930, during the depths of the depression, California's people turned for gubernatorial leadership to James ("Sunny Jim") Rolph, Jr. A long-time mayor of San Francisco, Rolph was a familiar figure on horseback at parades and pageants. Although folksy, colorful, and convivial, "Sunny Jim" was a curious choice to make in a time of great emergency. He had no idea how to cope with massive unemployment and poverty. Furthermore, he opposed almost any reform of California's tax structure and signed legislation which caused taxes to fall unfairly upon persons of the lowest income. A sales tax on food came to be blamed upon Rolph, who also made the mistake of endorsing a brutal, jail-break lynching. When he died in 1934, "Sunny Jim" was succeeded by the lieutenant governor, Frank Merriam, who resembled President Hoover in his conservatism over what must be done to fight the depression.

Folksinger Woody Guthrie, who had an almost magical ability for pithy characterization, mocked the ineptitude of the stuffy Merriam in one of his ballads. He also captured the spirit of confusion and the public intolerance over what to do about the Okies and Arkies. This prejudice was surely born of a combination of insecurity, embarrassment, and shame concerning one's fellow Americans, caught in a tragic social and economic web. California laborers, who were already hard pressed, saw these impoverished invaders as willing to work for low wages, willing to live in ghastly "Hoovervilles," and willing to endure even sluggings and beatings by alleged "deputy sheriffs." Steinbeck portrays the Okie as faced with a choice between slow starvation and criminal prosecution for vagrancy and other heinous offenses. Guthrie, like Steinbeck, embodied the depression years. Born in an Oklahoma oil boom town, he went on the road at thirteen. While moving across the land he spent several years at Los Angeles, where he sang for thirty minutes a day on a local radio station. Guthrie preached optimism, spoke for "the little man" and "the drifting families," and voiced both strength and bitterness in his "talking blues":

We got to old Los Angeles broke,
So dad-gum hungry we thought we'd choke,
And I bummed up a spud or two
And my wife cooked up potater stew . . .
Fed the kids a big batch of it,
But that was mighty thin stew . . .
So dad-gum thin you could pretty nearly
Read a magazine through it . . .
If it had been just a little thinner,
I've always believed,
If that stew had been just a little bit thinner,
Some of our senators could have seen through it.*

Like Steinbeck, Guthrie felt that California was being misused by selfish, scared people:

California's a Garden of Eden
A paradise to live in or see . . .
But believe it or not,
You won't find it so hot
If you ain't got the Do-Re-Mi.†

Guthrie, who composed over a thousand songs, is perhaps best remembered by his "folk national anthem" entitled *This Land Is Your Land.*

This land is your land and this land is my land,
    From California to the New York Island,
    From the redwood forest to the Gulf Stream waters,
    This land was made for you and me.
As I went a walking that ribbon of highway
    I saw above me that endless skyway,
    I saw before me that golden valley,
    This land was made for you and me.
I roamed and rambled, and I followed my footsteps
    To the sparkling sands of her diamond deserts,
    All around me, a voice was sounding,
    This land was made for you and me.
When the sun come shining and I was strolling,
    The wheat fields waving, the dust clouds rolling,
    A voice was chanting and the fog was lifting,
    This land was made for you and me.‡

---

* *Talking Dust Bowl*, words and music by Woody Guthrie. TRO © copyright 1961 Ludlow Music, Inc., New York, N.Y. Used by permission.
    † *Do-Re-Mi*, words and music by Woody Guthrie. TRO © copyright 1961 and 1963 Ludlow Music, Inc., New York, N.Y. Used by permission.
    ‡ *This Land Is Your Land*, words and music by Woody Guthrie. TRO © copyright 1956 and 1958 Ludlow Music, Inc., New York, N.Y. Used by permission.

Mexicans and Filipinos

The problem of providing housing and food for migrants from other parts of the United States was aggravated, for both federal and state relief agencies, by the need to care also for increased numbers of Mexicans. These refugees, who came especially from the Mexican province of Sonora, slipped over the international border to find employment in California's factories and farms, where they came into sharp competition with other common laborers. California was becoming more industrial, but it scarcely needed this additional influx of workers during the depression. Crowding the relief rolls, most of the Mexicans remained in the vicinity of Los Angeles, where they formed one of the largest expatriate Mexican communities in the world.

Serious problems of education, housing, and assimilation developed around California's Mexican minority. Forced to accept unpleasant jobs at low wages or to remain unemployed, they clung to their language, clustered in their own organizations, and retained a strong, unchanged sense of separate tastes and outlook. Later, youthful Mexican gangs—known during and after World War II as *Pachucos*—got into trouble with police because of fights on the streets of east Los Angeles and other communities. Carrying switch-blade knives in their trouser pockets, and razor blades in their long hair, they were a source of chagrin to older and more sober Mexicans, as well as to *Anglos*. Such marginal delinquents posed a particularly acute problem of acculturation both for themselves and for their fellow nationals. In 1943, discharged Navy and Marine veterans, in addition to "white hoodlums," rioted against the "zootsuit *Pachucos*." Such intolerant critics shortsightedly associated the *Pachuco* gangland attitude with Mexicans in general.

The Filipinos in California faced similar problems. Like the Mexicans, they were willing to work long hours for little money, and thus they competed strongly for jobs as houseboys, laundry workers, and restaurant dish washers and fry cooks. During the depression years unemployed whites resented them thoroughly. This resentment led illiterate Caucasian workers to attack the Filipinos on grounds other than economic; they accused them, for example, of being social undesirables. The racial tension sometimes became so pronounced that it led to physical violence. Sentiment against Filipino farm laborers led to the Watsonville riot of 1930, and also to a disturbance at Salinas in 1934, in which they were brutally manhandled.

By the mid-1930's numerous proposals for the exclusion of Filipinos were heard in the California legislature. In the next few years ·thousands of them decided to leave for their native islands. The state offered them free transportation if they promised not to return. When World War II broke out, numerous Filipinos who had remained behind in California enlisted in the United States Navy, where they frequently became mess boys on the staffs of admirals. In general, California's Filipinos, like the Chinese and Japanese, patiently bore the public criticism and efforts at exclusion which they continued to meet in varying degrees. Economically the workers from other countries may have been comparable to the pitiful native minority of which the "Okies" and "Arkies" formed part; but there remained a basic difference between them in the minds of many people. The Dust Bowl refugees were not foreigners; the Filipinos and Mexicans were.

The Vogue of Utopian Schemes

California's mild climate was another factor contributing to depression problems. It attracted thousands of older people, many of them feeble and unable to work. They had given little thought to precisely how they expected to earn a livelihood. The oldsters seemed unconsciously to believe that sunny California would, in one way or another, sustain them. In many cases they were dependent on a modest investment income, now seriously reduced due to the nation's economic difficulties, or they had suffered from the collapse of banks and building and loan associations. These elderly people in particular tended to be attracted by a variety of schemes that promised to alleviate their hardships by redistributing the uneven national and state wealth.

Among such plans was the movement known as technocracy, which drew much support from other segments of the population as well. Technocracy's chief advocate was Howard Scott, an engineer who wanted to create a utopian society in the 1930's by eliminating poverty. With visionary fervor, he urged the harnessing of society's "energy" for the benefit of mankind. To achieve maximum utilization of both human and natural resources, Scott proposed to place technical experts in control of industry and government. A corps of technocracy spokesmen, equipped with blueprints, explained the intricacies of Scott's proposed engineering civilization in almost every sizable California community. Discussion centers sprang up in abandoned drug stores, garages, and unrentable buildings; backers of technocracy have, in fact, continued to argue its blessings at a dwindling number of these discussion centers.

Like technocracy, the other utopian social plans that the depression years seemed to encourage in California were almost always identified with some one personality. One of these was the controversial Upton Sinclair, who had been, since the days of the Progressive era, a well-known crusading author and journalist. A habitual participant in liberal causes, he was also a founder of the American Civil Liberties Union in California. While Sinclair continued his active writing career (which will be discussed in the next chapter), he repeatedly ran for office on the Socialist ticket. In 1920 he unsuccessfully sought a congressional seat for the first time. Two years later he ran for the Senate and in 1926 and 1930 became the Socialist candidate for governor. It should be mentioned that, even before World War I, a significant socialist movement had existed in California. Its leaders included Job Harriman, Gaylord Wilshire, and J. Stitt Wilson, none of whom achieved the prominence of Sinclair.

Sinclair's last attempt at public office was in 1934, when he vigorously sought the Democratic nomination for governor. He won the nomination because the experimental characteristics of the program he proposed appealed to party leaders as the best possibility of ridding the state of long years of Republican rule. Although they proved to be mistaken in this judgment, Sinclair's program did attract many of California's older people as well as its chronically unemployable and indigent folk. His EPIC ("End Poverty in California") Plan was, in fact, tailor-made for the discontented and downhearted, of which California had more than its share. One of the measures Sinclair advocated was a monthly pension of fifty dollars for widows, the aged, and the physically handicapped. In addition, like Henry George earlier, he championed graduated inheritance and income taxes, a tax on idle land, and a massive cooperative program to stimulate employment and business. Sinclair believed that small home owners should be exempt from taxation, and that state ownership and operation of farms and factories would cure unemployment. He also urged the adoption of a novel scrip currency to replace hard-to-get dollars for new state construction.

Although Sinclair's program held much the same appeal for the masses of unemployed as did President Roosevelt's New Deal, then moving into high gear, Sinclair did not gain Roosevelt's endorsement. The President seems to have considered Sinclair's program too radical and idealistically impractical. Others also regarded Sinclair as an extremist—a visionary whose socialistic notions were unworkable and even dangerous. During perhaps the most bitterly contested of California's gubernatorial elections, the conservative press, radio, and movie industry united in a campaign against Sinclair. The very reactionary nature of much of this opposition gained him many supporters he might not otherwise have had, though not enough to secure his election. Sinclair's opponent was a bland traditionalist, Frank F. Merriam, who, as lieutenant governor, had in 1934 succeeded to the governorship upon the death of Governor Rolph. In November Merriam received 1,138,620 votes as against Sinclair's 879,537. After this defeat Sinclair's EPIC plan collapsed like a pricked balloon. He was to remain remarkably active as a novelist, but his office-seeking days were over.

The discontented groups who had fought hard for Sinclair's victory did not easily give up the ideals he championed. Instead, they turned to even more radical messiahs. It was an age when reactionary radio orators and amateur local pundits of every description gained huge followings by advocating a variety of measures to cure the ills of mankind. Among these popular leaders was Dr. Francis E. Townsend, a retired physician who sold real estate at Long Beach. With the slogan "Youth for work and age for leisure," he proposed in 1934 his Townsend Old Age Pension Plan, a supposedly fool-proof scheme that would provide a monthly pension of $200 for every person over the age of sixty—provided all of each payment was spent within one month. A 2 per cent federal tax upon business transactions was to support the plan. To Townsend his plan was actually not so much a pension scheme as a means of eliminating aged workers from jobs which "belonged to younger persons." Principal opposition to the plan came from those who feared it would pyramid taxes and, ultimately, living costs. But Dr. Townsend considered most of his opposition purely political.

Townsend led a national "crusade" through his homey newspaper *The Townsend Weekly* and through the 5,000 clubs organized in his name. From 1934 to 1937, even after a congressional investigation resulted in his conviction for contempt of Congress, his movement flourished among the elderly. Although national Townsend Club membership was estimated at from 3 million to 10 million, Dr. Townsend's plan aroused still wider opposition among those who considered its provisions unsound. Even Sinclair opposed it as economic madness. Faithful subscribers to Townsend's newspaper continued to read it long after his plan had any chance of adoption. Remnants of the Townsend movement exist even today.

In 1938, yet another visionary plan came to the fore—the
"Thirty Dollars Every Thursday," or "Ham and Eggs," proposal.
Its sponsors, who suggested giving a pension to every unemployed
person in the state over the age of fifty, were in some ways even
more radical than Townsend. The scheme was to be financed by
the sale of state bonds and by a 3 per cent gross income tax on
individuals and businesses within California. The purchase of a
two cent stamp (in order to make each $1.00 warrant negotiable
per week) had the appeal of "producing" $1.04 at the end of fifty-
two weeks. The additional four cents "gained" was to be used to
administer the program. Payment of most state taxes would be by
scrip or warrants. Pushed by professional politicians in the state
elections of 1938, the measure came close to adoption, despite the
fact that many well-informed critics labeled it the height of economic irresponsibility. This movement, as well as the cure-all
EPIC plan and Dr. Townsend's pension scheme, can perhaps best
be understood in terms of the despair and confused thinking of
the depression years. The failure of the welfare-minded New Deal
administration to endorse such locally improvised plans doubtless
contributed to their end. Nevertheless, California's welfare agitation of the early 1930's, admittedly demagogic on occasion, helped
speed passage of the Social Security Act of 1935, a more realistic
national approach to security.

Federal Relief and Work Programs

Throughout the nation the pattern of depression relief that was to
become best known was that administered by the federal government. A series of congressional measures, most of which survived
Supreme Court tests of their constitutionality, enabled Roosevelt
to deliver on his campaign promises of a "New Deal" featuring
relief, recovery, and reform. Dozens of new federal agencies, generally known by the alphabetic abbreviations of their titles, were
established to perform a number of functions designed to bring
back prosperity. Often these organizations worked in partnership
with state agencies, so that relief and employment were administered with a particular view to local needs.

Mention has already been made of the use of federal funds to
construct Hoover Dam and of the national government's participation in the Central Valley Project. Other federally financed power,
reclamation, flood-control, and navigation projects were also to
affect markedly the future of California. By the middle thirties the
short-term relief benefits of massive government aid had become

everywhere evident. In California, as elsewhere throughout the nation, destitute people depended upon receiving weekly government checks to sustain them until they could get jobs. In addition to this direct relief, agencies of the federal government provided a variety of employment opportunities to help relieve the situation further. Unemployed young men, for example, were given jobs in the Civilian Conservation Corps (CCC). This particular project pushed through construction of mountain trails and firebreaks on federal forest lands or in the six new state parks established in California during 1933. Other young people in college were aided by National Youth Administration (NYA) money. Their fathers, meanwhile, worked on Works Progress Administration (WPA) or Public Work Administration (PWA) construction projects.

Though criticized as extravagant at the time, and bitterly resisted by conservatives on grounds of principle, these activities were undeniably effective in alleviating conditions of economic hardship. Their cost, moreover, came to seem relatively modest in the light of expenditures during World War II and after. Certainly no state benefited more from the federal relief program than California, where the hundreds of new schools, parks, roads, and beach facilities built during the depression—in addition to the larger-scale projects previously mentioned—contributed materially to its development then and in the years that followed.

The Olson Administration and California's Governors

Despite the popularity of the New Deal—which helped Franklin Roosevelt to sweep the state in four successive national elections —there was only one Democratic state administration in California during the first half of the twentieth century. Until Governor Culbert L. Olson came to power in 1938, Californians had not seated a Democratic chief executive since Governor James H. Budd, who left office in 1899. Only an occasional Democrat had been elected to the legislature.

California's governors have hardly been men of greatness. Most of the later governors came from modest origins; like Olson, few were highly educated. Fewer of them, like Hiram Johnson or Earl Warren, became national figures. No governor of California has gone on to become President of the United States, although two became vice-presidential candidates and one became Chief Justice of the United States Supreme Court. Because of their disparity in background, it is difficult to make comparisons of them, or even to rate their sometimes obscure administrations. As a result, most California historians have simply omitted mention of the state's governors from their writings.

In the Olson years, what stands out is the limited power of the governorship.

The reform movement that had come into prominence in the early years of the century had been largely led by the Progressives, who were of Republican origin. The Republican Party in California, in fact, was then generally more liberal than in the nation as a whole. Conversely, the Democratic Party in the state had never built up a tradition of progressivism and reform. Even regarding the repeal of Prohibition, which wreaked havoc upon a basic California industry, wine-making, the Democrats were politically timid.

Nevertheless, the reaction against Republican President Hoover that accompanied the depression made it possible for William Gibbs McAdoo, former Secretary of the Treasury under President Wilson and director general of the railroads in World War I, to slowly build up a Democratic political machine in California during the early 1930's. McAdoo, who was Wilson's son-in-law, was elected to the Senate from California in 1932. That year President Franklin Roosevelt had a special reason to be grateful to him. The rangy McAdoo had stridden to the platform at the Democratic Party Convention in Chicago to cast California's forty-four votes for F.D.R. With this switch of the Golden State, Roosevelt, within minutes, received the Democratic nomination. By 1938, however, Sheridan Downey defeated McAdoo, then seventy-five years old, for the Democratic nomination to his Senate seat, despite a trip to California by President Roosevelt to endorse McAdoo. Downey went on to win a striking victory in the election also. On the same ticket, Olson, who had previously served a term in the state senate, was elected governor; in this office he followed the placid Republican administration of Governor Merriam, who had defeated Sinclair in 1934.

The Olson regime in California was expected to inaugurate a "New Deal in miniature." Olson was a frank advocate of FDR's ideas and, as a former backer also of Sinclair's EPIC Plan, he was known to stand for reformist policies. But he suffered the misfortune of becoming governor during the last stages of the depression, when public pressure for liberal measures had abated somewhat. Although Olson tried to solve such pressing problems as California's migrant-labor situation, an economy-minded Republican legislature enticed even Democrats into withdrawing support of Olson's reform program. In attacking agricultural problems, Olson also met the determined opposition of such pressure groups as the Associated Farmers, which opposed government "meddling" with the seasonal labor situation. Not only was Olson thus unable to secure passage through the legislature of his principal social measures, but his administration was also wracked by the bungling of inferior appointees. His first official act—the freeing of Tom Mooney in 1939—therefore remained his most dramatic one. Olson, however, did achieve moderate reform of the California penal system and of its mental-hygiene and youth-correction programs. Olson, who died in 1962, was ahead of his time.

Renewed Labor Agitation

In the later New Deal years the organized labor movement in California recouped the losses it had suffered during the depths of the depression and showed surprising new force. As more industries moved to the West Coast the accompanying growth in the numbers of urban workers offered new opportunities for labor leaders to strengthen their power. Especially following the upswing of business after the recession of 1937, the CIO attracted an increasingly large following among previously unorganized laborers, who were encouraged by the industry-wide bargaining techniques of John L. Lewis, the vigorous and effective CIO president. Lewis personally turned his attention to those unskilled laborers in California's fields and factories who had once been the target of I.W.W. organizers. For a time it appeared that Lewis might actually be able to unionize even farm workers. As it turned out, however, he was not able to realize this objective.

Another area of activity ripe for further labor organization was the California waterfront—particularly at San Francisco. Since the 1890's, when Frank Roney had founded the Coast Seamen's Union, San Francisco had been the center of West Coast maritime agitation, which came to be led principally by Andrew Furuseth. Born in Norway in 1846, Furuseth had sailed before the mast for years, and then had come to San Francisco; in the 1880's he became a waterfront organizer there, and soon achieved prominence as a pioneer crusader for seamen's rights. He had dedicated himself to the extermination of such evils as "buckoism," "the crimp," and boardinghouses run by, or for the benefit of, maritime companies. In an atmosphere described as "a purgatory of unending monotony," shipboard "bucko mates" on occasion sadistically beat seamen, while sailors were regularly forced to pay a set fee to the "crimp," a sort of labor broker, in order to obtain employment. Similarly, the operators of certain boardinghouses, attracting seamen by providing them with beds, meals, and even clothing on credit, charged inordinate prices for such services. Then these operators, sometimes with scores of unemployed seamen deeply in their debt, turned such men over to the masters of ships with whom they were in league. The sailors were, of course, in no position to bargain over their wages, and suffered accordingly. Enraged by all these practices, Furuseth also fought allotments and advances to seamen, which, he maintained, helped ultimately to impoverish them. A lobbyist of no mean ability, Furuseth had much to do with the passage of the La Follette Seamen's Act to improve existing conditions. When, at his death in 1938, his ashes were thrown into the sea, the old man was honored by all maritime workers for his devoted service to the cause of the sailors. His work was by no means completed, but the Sailors' Union of the Pacific carried it on, as did various other generally unrelated union organizations.

Waterfront workers at San Francisco, still dissatisfied, considered their Longshoremen's Association not a bona-fide labor body but a company union through which shippers controlled hiring and most other labor conditions. This, they charged, was actually an open-shop situation. The prevailing discontent paved the way for the entrance of radicalism into the maritime labor movement, which now acquired new leaders. Among these was Harry Bridges, a spellbinding, Australian-born longshoreman who operated a hydraulic winch on the Embarcadero, San Francisco's wharfs. He began to attract much attention in the early 1930's by complaining that a speed-up of waterfront operations, enforced by company supervisors to reduce the costs of handling vessels in port, caused many accidents among the longshoremen. The maritime firms countered by stating that San Francisco's total tonnage had declined yearly because of the unrealistic demands of waterfront workers. To combat the shippers, Bridges proceeded to reorganize the International Longshoremen's Association, working at times even against local labor bosses.

Bridges was sharp-faced, nervous, and dynamic. His enemies called him a dangerous alien radical, if not a Communist. But thousands of longshoremen up and down the Pacific Coast stood behind his authoritarian but effective I.L.A. leadership. By 1934 his power was such that he staged a strike which crucially affected shipping from San Diego to Seattle. In addition to what he called "union security," Bridges wanted a minimum thirty-hour week at wages of a dollar an hour. He also objected strongly to the "shape-up" system of hiring longshoremen, which essentially was a procedure by which shipping-company foremen gathered together waterfront workers to select those the company wanted. Bridges charged that, as a result, favoritism and pandering to company demands often determined whether a worker was employed, instead of such union-sponsored criteria as seniority. What Bridges wanted, and ultimately obtained, was a system of hiring halls under union control.

The center of the great maritime strike of 1934, naturally enough, was San Francisco. Beginning on May 9, the I.L.A. tied up traffic in and out of the port for ninety days. In sympathy with the longshoremen, many other workers went out on strike too. Sailors marched off their ships; warehousemen quit their jobs; teamsters abandoned their trucks and lift vans. Hundreds of ships lay idle in San Francisco Bay, while cargoes rotted and rusted on piers and in warehouses.

The bitterness that existed on both sides of this massive labor dispute made arbitration difficult. President Roosevelt tried in vain to achieve a settlement. The attempt by employers to use strikebreakers only aggravated matters. On July 5, "Bloody Thursday," an especially violent episode erupted, in which the San Francisco police moved against picket lines with tear gas. Before it was over, two union pickets had been shot to death, and over a hundred men, including police, had been wounded. On July 14, I.L.A. leaders appealed to all unions not already involved in the sympathy strikes to join in protesting the action of the police. Almost 150,000 workers of all descriptions stopped work for three days. The entire San Francisco area was paralyzed, in the most severe disturbance the city had undergone since the earthquake and fire of 1906. The governor called out the National Guard, 5,000 strong, to protect state property. This move intensified the resentment of riotous strikers, as did the action of "vigilantes" who wrecked "radical" meeting places.

Internal disputes among union leaders themselves finally helped end the strike. The more conservative ones felt that this outbreak, especially the general strike, damaged the long-term interests of unionism; this was too high a price to pay for a short-term victory against management. As allied union members returned to work in the late summer of 1934, only the longshoremen remained out on strike. Eventually these were prevailed upon to "work" specified ships and to submit their demands to the arbitration of a Presidential Longshoremen's Board. (Union leaders had previously refused proposals for federal arbitration.) In October the longshoremen won certain concessions from management, including higher wages and joint control of their own hiring halls. However, fourteen agitators seized or arrested in the strike were later deported as aliens residing unlawfully in the United States. And, though the strike had resulted in a quasi-victory for labor, the public was not to forget that the price had been violence.

Settlement of this strike, furthermore, by no means brought peace to the San Francisco waterfront. A series of shorter labor stoppages occurred throughout the later thirties. A jurisdictional altercation between Bridges and two other labor leaders, Harry Lundeberg and Joseph P. Ryan, continued until Bridges took his longshoremen into the CIO. The Norwegian-born, ambitious Lundeberg and the Sailors' Union of the Pacific which he headed decided to operate within the AFL. Bridges, who came to control a new International Longshoremen and Warehousemen's Union, remained a controversial character; in part because of his great power, demands were made for his deportation from 1936 onward. A congressional committee (the Dies Committee) on un-American activities charged that the ILWU and other CIO unions were under Communist leadership and control. Lundeberg, one of the chief witnesses against Bridges, claimed that Bridges had actually forgotten the waterfront and "moved uptown into the cocktail lounges." Later he accused Bridges of being a Communist whose purpose was to use the unions for the purposes of the Communist Party. Anti-union newspapers joined in denouncing Bridges, but they found it difficult to substantiate the charges of Communism against him. The courts upheld Bridges' radical unionization techniques. While often personally explosive, he retained his power along the Pacific Coast and eventually expanded it to Hawaii.

During the mid-1930's the example of San Francisco's waterfront, as well as the influence of the prolabor administration of President Roosevelt, led to demands for increased unionization in numerous strongholds of the open shop throughout California. One of these places was Los Angeles, the very center of the "American Plan," as the open shop was also known. By 1935, after both Lundeberg and Bridges had effectively unionized the port of San Pedro, union pressures filtered back from the city's waterfront into Los Angeles proper. Next, the plasterers, hod carriers, plumbers, typographers, tire workers, steam fitters, and auto workers became more adamant in their demands upon management.

Along with occasional strife, however, unions and employers came to view each other with increased respect as each grew stronger. By the end of the 1930's, in fact, a new era of cooperation by negotiation had begun in the relations of California labor and management. Harry Bridges called strikes an "obsolete weapon," while Roger Lapham, chairman of the board of the

American-Hawaiian Steamship Company (and later mayor of San Francisco) stated: "I do not believe that employers should organize to break unions." Though still distrustful of one another both sides had, nevertheless, learned to cooperate for their mutual benefit.

Meanwhile, the New Deal encouraged collective-bargaining agreements through federal agencies, particularly the National Labor Relations Board. From 1932 onward, labor looked upon the federal government as a friend who would listen carefully and often respond to its demands, in California and elsewhere. A handful of disgruntled workers, of course, felt that the federal government could do still more than it did to relieve depression conditions. Conversely, many businessmen were convinced that the coddling of labor, accompanied by emergency pump-priming economic measures, could not possibly restore prosperity. But these complaints were in the minority. For the most part, during those depression years, California capital and labor both joined vigorously in the national struggle to find some way out of the prevailing economic darkness.

William Randolph Hearst

Against the background of the grave social dislocations of the depression years the figure of William Randolph Hearst stands out in particular relief. Born into a wealthy family at San Francisco in 1863—his father, Senator George Hearst, had created a mining fortune—young Will attended Harvard and, in 1887, at the age of twenty-four, was handed the San Francisco *Examiner* to manage. Through his personal genius, unlimited energy, and willingness to invest vast amounts of his father's money, Hearst made the *Examiner* the most powerful paper on the West Coast. His reputation as a young and energetic publisher was first made, as mentioned in an earlier chapter, by his attacks on the Southern Pacific in California. In many other respects, too, the young Hearst appeared in the role of a reformist crusader; but by the 1930's he was to bear little resemblance to the liberal of earlier decades. Hearst came to believe that reform had gone quite far enough and that the forces of conservatism must rally to reverse the abusive power of labor unions, of state and national government, and, in particular, of dangerous New Dealers.

Throughout his eighty-eight years of life Hearst was an enigma even to close personal associates. Though outwardly shy, he never lost a basic urge to dominate, and he made his power felt even at the international level through his chain of some thirty newspapers, thirteen magazines, and many radio stations. Hearst came to be associated, usually controversially, with a remarkable number of issues and events. Prominent among these were the Spanish-American War (which he almost surely helped cause); hatred of the two Roosevelts (although by one of the choicest ironies of history he had in large measure obtained the presidential nomination of the second one); antivivisection; opposition to United States entry into both World Wars; suppression of radical minorities; and distrust of the League of Nations as well as of most other forms of internationalism. In promoting his various prejudices, Hearst achieved mixed results. Thinking persons were often offended by his convictions, and nearly always repelled by his taste.

At the heart of Hearst's empire were his newspapers. He bought papers all over the country and applied to them the techniques of reckless spending and reporting that had made the *Examiner* successful. There was a sameness about their sensational reportage, as well as about their shallow feature articles, slanted editorials, and columns calculated to appeal to a less than educated readership. These newspapers, in short, were the archetypes of yellow journalism—and the despair of Hearst's critics. In California's depression decades, as the "Chief" grew steadily more conservative and eccentric, the Hearst press was one of the bulwarks that stood in the way of economic or political reform. Even many conservatives shunned Hearst as he moved toward the extreme right. The Hearst machine spewed hate at both President Roosevelt and Governor Olson, and fulminated against all attempts to "tinker" with the currency, to "coddle" the unemployed, and to "socialize" the country.

The headquarters of Hearst's domain was his San Simeon estate, located along the rocky coast between San Luis Obispo and Monterey. In the interwar years "the Lord of San Simeon" poured $35 million into the construction of an immense castle there. Stocking it with art treasures from all over the world, Hearst made San Simeon a rendezvous for famous guests drawn from the fields of the movie industry, art, music, literature, and public affairs.

Hearst, like his mother, Phoebe Apperson Hearst, was given to subsidizing selected philanthropic and educational institutions. Nevertheless, there were many who felt that, at a time when the state's economy was faltering, he could easily have used more of his annual income (at times $15 million) for other purposes than to gratify his unquenchable acquisitive impulse. In 1935 his far-flung personal empire was valued at $200 million. His holdings included seven castles; warehouses full of antique furniture, hundreds of paintings, and tapestries; ranches on which he raised a total of 10,000 beef cattle; and several zoos, hunting lodges, and beach homes.

Orson Welles' 1940 film entitled *Citizen Kane* drew a skillful picture of the egotism and personal imperialism of the aging genius. As times changed, the anachronism of "Citizen Hearst," as one of his biographers calls him, became more and more apparent in a society where "the greatest good for the greatest number of persons" was increasingly espoused as a public philosophy.

Hearst did not live long enough to see the ultimate decline of his newspaper empire. After World War II the Hearst dynasty, like that of Colonel Robert R. McCormick in Chicago, crumbled. By the mid-1960's his two major papers, the *Examiners* at San Francisco and Los Angeles, gave way to the *Chronicle* and the *Times.* The *Examiners,* both morning papers, had to be merged with the Hearst evening newspapers to meet the new competition of suburban dailies and radio and television newscasts, and to deal with the problems of rising production costs, lowered advertising, and falling circulation.

SELECTED READINGS

There is no book that deals exhaustively with California during the depression years. Competent general analyses are Broadus Mitchell, *Depression Decade* (New York, 1947), and Dixon Wecter, *The Age of the Great Depression, 1929–1941* (New York, 1948). Paul N. Woolf, *Economic Trends in California, 1929–1934* (Sacramento, 1935), covers only economic aspects of the crucial years of the depression. On the Dust Bowl migration see, in addition to the novels of John Steinbeck, the treatment by Dorothea Lange and Paul S. Taylor, *An American Exodus: A Record of Human Erosion* (New York, 1939). The story of the California social crusaders, including Dr. Townsend, is told in Luther Whiteman and Samuel L. Lewis, *Glory Roads: The Psychological State of California* (New York, 1936). A book that is more statistical than descriptive is Abraham Holtzman, *The Townsend Movement: A Political Study* (New York, 1963). Regarding the Prohibitionists see Gilman Ostrander, *The Prohibition Movement in California* (Berkeley, 1957). See also Abe Hoffman, "A Look at Llano: Experiment in Economic Socialism," California Historical Society *Quarterly,* XL (September, 1961), 215–236. Consult also Carey McWilliams, "Pension Politics in California," *Nation,* CLXIX (October 1, 1949), 320–322, for a review of the pension movement. Politics in the 1920's and 1930's are the subject of Robert Pitchell, "Twentieth Century California Voting Behavior," Ph.D. dissertation, University of California, Berkeley (1955); Royce D. Delmatier, "The Rebirth of the Democratic Party in California, 1928–1938," Ph.D. dissertation, University of California, Berkeley (1955), and Ronald E. Chinn, "Democratic Party Politics in California, 1920–1956," Ph.D. dissertation, University of California, Berkeley (1958). Jackson K. Putnam, "The Influence of the Older Age Groups on California Politics, 1920–1940," Ph.D. dissertation, Stanford (1964), ranges skillfully over problems of politics, economics, and psychological motivation. On Sinclair, the basic book is his own *I, Candidate for Governor—and How I Got Licked* (Pasadena, 1935).

H. Brett Melendy and Benjamin F. Gilbert's *The Governors of California* (Georgetown, Calif., 1965), is the only overall study of the state's governors. Arthur M. Schlesinger, Jr.'s *The Politics of Upheaval* (New York, 1960), mirrors political events in California during the 1930's on the national scene.

California's New Deal years are treated in detail by Robert E. Burke, *Olson's New Deal for California* (Berkeley, 1952). John Phillips, *Inside California* (Los Angeles, 1939), is a personal anti-Olson view by a local lawmaker. Oliver Carlson, *A Mirror for Californians* (Indianapolis, 1941), takes a look at the same period. Olson's successor is the subject of Irving Stone's sanguine *Earl Warren: A Great American Story* (New York, 1948).

The references on labor in California given in the Selected Readings for Chapter 31 are pertinent to this chapter. See also Mitchell Slobodek, *A Selective Bibliography of California Labor History* (Berkeley and Los Angeles, 1964). The best biography of a California maritime labor leader is Hyman Weintraub's *Andrew Furuseth: Emancipator of the Seamen* (Berkeley, 1959). This can be supplemented with Robert Knight, *Industrial Relations in the San Francisco Bay Area, 1900–1918* (Berkeley, 1960), and Paul S. Taylor, *The Sailors' Union of the Pacific* (New York, 1923). Alexander Saxton, "San Francisco Labor and the Populist and Progressive Insurgencies," *Pacific Historical Review,* XXXIV (November, 1965), 421–438, discusses labor from 1890 to 1914. Charles Norris, *Flint* (New York, 1940), is a novel that depicts agitation in the San Francisco shipyards during the middle thirties. A fuller glimpse of the same scene is in Camp's *San Francisco: Port of Gold.* San Francisco's crippling strike of 1934 and other labor disturbances are discussed in Ira B. Cross, *History of the Labor Movement in California* (Berkeley, 1935). More specific are Mike Quin, *The Big Strike* (Olema, 1949), and Paul Eliel, *The Waterfront and General Strike . . .* (San Francisco, 1934). Yellen's *American Labor Struggles* also includes a chapter on the 1934 waterfront disturbances.

Concerning Hearst, consult Rodney P. Carlisle, "The Political Ideas and Influence of William Randolph Hearst," Ph.D. dissertation, University of California, Berkeley (1965); Oliver Carlson and Ernest S. Bates, *Hearst: Lord of San Simeon* (New York, 1937); John Tebbel, *The Life and Good Times of William Randolph Hearst* (New York, 1952); John K. Winkler, *William Randolph Hearst: A New Appraisal* (New York, 1955); W. A. Swanberg, *Citizen Hearst: A Biography of William Randolph Hearst* (New York, 1961).

33

Twentieth-Century Cultural
Developments

After 1900, California culture steadily grew in diversity and vitality. The turbulence of an expanding society groping to find itself resulted in many forms of intellectual ferment. Some of this experimentation was misdirected and confused; unfortunately it has helped give California a reputation it only partially deserves for embracing the derivative and the mediocre. In the first part of the present century social improvisation of every form became the vogue. In impressive bursts of energy this tendency was widely reflected in the state's general "culture." The present chapter thus begins with a discussion of some of the strangest aspects of California's society during the early twentieth century, though these by no means constituted the only focus on the cultural scene.

Faddists and Cultists

During the first quarter of the century southern California in particular was descended upon by numbers of migrants armed with solutions to most of mankind's dilemmas, from economics to health. The mild climate and cheap housing helped attract these people, many of whom were members of bizarre social and religious cults who had been discontented elsewhere. With them they brought ideas—undoubtedly sincere for the most part—that even tolerant natives found difficult to accept. Spiritualism and similar beliefs flourished. A few diet faddists went so far as to preach that they could conquer illness by mixing "spiritual power" with such foods as "mushroomburgers" and date milk shakes. Among the new arrivals were also religious fundamentalists like the Rev. Robert P. Shuler of Kentucky and Dr. Billy Sunday, the nationally known radio evangelist. They were joined by Yogi mystics, Swami palm readers, rain makers, Hindu fakirs, and other occultists of every description. Earnest devotees—including sentimental elderly persons and aging former movie queens—joined to venerate their chosen spiritual leaders.

Theosophy, a modern sect following various Buddhistic and Brahmanic theories, gained many adherents in California long before the general arrival of religious experimenters in the 1920's. The theosophists sought knowledge of God by both mystical insight and philosophical speculation. From a "Theosophical Society" founded in New York in 1875 by Mme. H. P. Blavatsky, the theosophic movement spread nationally. Another woman, "The Purple Mother," Katherine Tingley, established a Point Loma Theosophical Community near San Diego about 1900. It lasted until shortly after her death in 1929. In the 1920's the theosophist Annie Besant also came West and settled in the Ojai Valley below Santa Barbara. There she brought "The New Messiah," one Krishnamurti, to preside over her small flock of converts. Until her death in 1933 this rival of Katherine Tingley's looked upon her Ojai community as the cradle of a "new civilization."

Another woman who played a special part in the religious cultism of California was Aimee Semple McPherson, a dynamic, Canadian-born evangelist who founded the Four Square Gospel Church in Los Angeles. Full of verve and loud of voice, Mrs. McPherson, or Sister Aimee as she was called, quickly established herself as the most successful of the lady ministers. She practiced conversion, physical healing, and a kind of therapeutic human redemption through a vigorous and spectacular form of evangelism. On occasion she scattered religious tracts from an airplane; at other times she held prayer meetings in a boxing arena. A talented showman who sometimes wore the white uniform and gold braid of an admiral, Sister Aimee had a potent appeal for the downhearted and the lonely. From the platform of Angelus Temple, she exhorted the multitudes to follow her into mortal combat with the devil. For twenty years she broadcast religious services over radio station KFSG. In 1925 the station wandered off its assigned wavelength. Herbert Hoover, then Secretary of Commerce, ordered the station's license suspended, whereupon Sister Aimee cabled him: "PLEASE ORDER YOUR MINIONS OF SATAN TO LEAVE MY STATION ALONE. . . . YOU CANNOT EXPECT THE ALMIGHTY TO ABIDE BY

YOUR WAVELENGTH NONSENSE. . . ." In 1926 Sister Aimee walked into the ocean and was presumed to have drowned. Eight days later she reappeared with a story that she had been kidnapped, and was given a grand reception at Los Angeles. The story, however, was exposed as highly questionable, if not as absolutely false. As a consequence Sister Aimee came into temporary difficulty with the law, although she did not lose the loyalty of her army of followers. Mrs. McPherson died in 1944. By that time she had accumulated a great deal of property, through cash donations, and had added more than two hundred branch churches to her unique religious denomination. She had offered her followers not only the entertainment of bell ringers and xylophone bands but also friendship and material aid, in an era when the sick and needy that had gravitated toward southern California seemed to crave her unorthodox form of prayer and guidance.

Sister Aimee was a notable individual expression of that occultism for which the area was becoming known over the nation; an institutional expression of the same general phenomenon—still common today—is the "funeral park." These rather stereotyped establishments are to be found in considerable number throughout southern California. They are advertised as happy vales for the departed, and their stock in trade is the glossing over of the facts of death as associated with the mundane cemetery or graveyard of the past. Swaddled in euphemisms, mourners are presented with a glowing vision of the hereafter as a desirable place to go, in happiness and contentment. The crudities of this approach have lent themselves to the lampooning of satiric authors, especially Aldous Huxley and Evelyn Waugh. Writing from a somewhat different point of view and on a broader subject, Carey McWilliams, a sociologically inclined attorney and journalist, has skillfully analyzed the peculiar regional environment that has proved hospitable to such varying forms of occultism. He sees southern California as "an island on the land" which absorbed the frontier, as a place where odd practices and practitioners were encouraged to succeed long after more stable social patterns had become the rule elsewhere. Ideas and movements that embarrassed the rest of the nation were tolerated in southern California, which, regrettably, came to be tarred with a reputation for the bizarre. The southern California of the 1920's did sometimes seem to reflect partly delusional behavior, showing signs of impairment of its public sense of reality. In the individual such behavior is normally associated with mental regression to infantile stages. In their delusions, some persons saw, heard, and even met angels as well as demons.

Literary Trends

During the early twentieth century, writers from all over the nation continued to visit California, as Mark Twain, Bret Harte, Helen Hunt Jackson, and Mary Austin had done. Some of the later California writers, however, were more distinguished by their industry than by their literary finesse. A notable example of the writer who came to California before World War I and made a sizable fortune there was Zane Grey. Prior to settling in Altadena, where he built himself a Zuni-style terraced house, Grey had been an Ohio dentist with experience also as a professional baseball player. In California, Grey soon was writing at least one and sometimes two Western novels per year. The most popular of these was his *Riders of the Purple Sage* (1912). His work was stereotyped and pedestrian, but its exploitation of the color and, loosely speaking, of the history of the West achieved vast popularity for its author. He strongly influenced subsequent "pulp" writers of Western fiction by setting a style which was undeviating as to plot but which was highly marketable. More than sixty of Grey's books were printed in very large editions. His production was far in excess of immediate—as opposed to long-term—demand; and although he died in 1939, Grey's manuscripts continued to be published annually long after his death.

In the same tradition of literary mass production was Harold Bell Wright. First an artist and later a minister, Wright was the author of several dozen novels set in the West. At about the time he moved to California he published his first successful work, *The Shepherd of the Hills* (1907). Wright's *The Winning of Barbara Worth* (1911), focusing upon the reclamation of the arid Imperial Valley from the desert, sold more than a million and a half copies. His other best-selling novel, *The Eyes of the World* (1914), also used southern California as a literary backdrop. Wright's work frequently displayed traces of his earlier vocation as a preacher; for example, his major characters were generally conceived as absorbing inner strength from an environment just on the edge of the wilderness. This theme of nobility springing from the soil never seemed spontaneous, however, and Wright's books are not highly regarded today. Another subliterary arrival in southern California, characteristically concerned with regional themes, was Gene Stratton Porter, author of the popular *A Girl of the Limberlost* (1909). Having made her home at Los Angeles, Mrs. Porter continued to write poems and local fiction until her death in 1924.

Some far more significant American writers also arrived in California during this period. One of these was Hamlin Garland, who had already achieved fame as the celebrator of the "middle border," in a number of works based on the frontier experience in his native Middle West. Toward the end of his life Garland moved to Hollywood with his daughter, and spent his last years there. Little of major importance marked this period, although Garland did produce in California his *Roadside Meetings* (1930), *Companions on the Trail* (1932), and *My Friendly Contemporaries* (1932). He also absorbed some of the local environment, writing a number of studies concerning spiritualism and psychic phenomena. Another prominent author, Theodore Dreiser, spent several years in Hollywood during the 1920's and then settled there in 1938, staying on until his death in 1945. Like Garland, he turned to other interests in these later years, producing *The Bulwark* (1946), a minor work published after his death, which stresses spiritual values in the life of the individual. A laborer in a different area and with a different purpose was Will Durant, a popularizer of great ideas in history, who was engaged with his philosophical studies of the history of mankind.

In recent years various renowned foreign-born writers have also spent considerable time in California. Aldous Huxley, Thomas Mann, and Christopher Isherwood settled in the southern part of the state and produced many books there. In addition to the attacks by Huxley and Evelyn Waugh on what they considered to be the macabre "cemetery culture" of the region, the lampooning of quackery and faddism, in both religion and economics, has been a favorite sport among other visiting writers and lecturers, as well. Satirists, more often than not Englishmen, have depicted in unrestrained fashion the exotic unreality of California, its commercialism, the vapidity of Hollywood, or the harsh realities behind the new fortunes that were being coined there. Conversely, California has been called a boneyard for aging British intellectuals. Some of these writers, especially Huxley, grew quite philosophical about the confusion they saw.

Not all the new arrivals, of course, were critics of the land that welcomed them. Isherwood's writing continued to be focused on the Berlin that he had known between the wars. Mann and his daughter Erika came to California as refugees from the terrors of Nazism, and both dealt with themes far from the safe and lovely land in which they had sought refuge. Sadakichi Hartmann, a little-known Japanese-born historian of art and an aesthete of the first order, in the period between the wars also wrote plays, played bit parts in the movies, and, at San Francisco, produced strangely beautiful and exotic poetry.

Among others of California's best poetic craftsmen was George

Sterling. Influenced in his earlier years by Bierce, Sterling became best known for his romantic sonnets, musical in style and diffuse in theme. He produced most of his work at Carmel on the Monterey peninsula, where he settled after writing his first poetry in a studio of San Francisco's fabled Montgomery Block. Focusing on humanity at large, and the sadness of life in particular, Sterling was a troubled spirit, like his friend Jack London. In London's words, he "looked like a Greek coin run over by a Roman chariot." His volume *Testimony of the Suns* (1903) was imaginative and honest. In 1926, after writing several other books of poetry, Sterling killed himself in San Francisco's Bohemian Club.

Robinson Jeffers, however, is unquestionably the greatest poet California has produced. Jeffers, after graduation from Occidental College, went to live at Carmel and there built with his own hands an imposing stone residence named Tor House. With his wife, Una, and his sons he spent the rest of his life in that house. Jeffers set forth powerfully his feelings about man's depravity and the underlying futility of life, which he contrasted with the unspoiled nobility of the Carmel coastline. Realistic as well as symbolic in his themes, Jeffers made man out to be a relatively insignificant and unworthy child of nature. He once wrote, "Cut humanity out of my being, that is the wound that festers." His respect for the primeval and for the wonders of the universe itself were what first drew admirers to his stark poetry and what kept them reading his works. Jeffers was at his best in such long narrative poems as *Roan Stallion* (1925) and *Be Angry at the Sun* (1925). In his later years, *Medea* (1947), a classic tragedy adapted for poetic drama from Euripides, also brought him great acclaim. Early in 1962 he died in his beloved Tor House.

The reformist writers of twentieth-century California moved in the tradition of Henry George, Frank Norris, and Jack London. Among them was Upton Sinclair, a native of Baltimore who is another in the long line of California's literary imports. Like London and Norris, he had a profound desire to correct social ills, and he used his writings as an effective means of doing so. Sinclair came to California after World War I, having already written his well-known novels *The Jungle* (1906) and *The Money-Changers* (1908). He has had an extraordinary career producing numerous books while at the same time exerting active leadership in countless liberal causes. As we have seen, Sinclair lost the bitterly fought gubernatorial election of 1934; almost everything he stood for was detestable to business interests and his platform, as divulged in his book *The EPIC Plan for California* (1934), was inflammatory in its utopianism. Despite the

worldwide attention his writings have demanded, it is not easy
to measure the effect they have had. There is no question, however, that books such as *The Jungle*, directed at specific evils,
achieved specific reforms. In later years Sinclair wrote a series
of best sellers, published in many languages and generally
known as the Lanny Budd series. In these novels the chief protagonist, an illegitimate son of a munitions manufacturer,
becomes involved in a variety of international plots, intrigues,

JAGGED STRETCH ALONG THE COAST OF SONOMA COUNTY, NORTHERN CALIFORNIA.
(By courtesy of Redwood Empire Association.)

and political maneuvers. The series begins with *World's End* (1940), and continues through nine more novels to *O Shepherd Speak!* (1949), during which time Lanny sees the failure of the Versailles treaty, joins the anti-Nazis, observes the Spanish Civil War, is named a confidential agent of President Roosevelt's, is involved in World War II, and helps to plan the peace that follows it.

Recent California Novelists

In addition to the many writers who have moved to California, the state has produced some native-born authors, especially novelists, of the first rank. The best known of the "California novelists" is John Steinbeck, born at Salinas in 1902. In his early books *The Pastures of Heaven* (1932) and *Tortilla Flat* (1935), Steinbeck discovered himself as a writer through using the people and the setting of the Salinas Valley, much as William Faulkner often relied for his subject matter on a mythical county in his home state of Mississippi. Steinbeck's work portrays vividly both character and terrain, and frequently reflects the author's anger with social injustice; the latter quality gives it a certain kinship with the books of such reformist writers as Sinclair. In keeping with his biological training, Steinbeck also constantly compares human behavior to that of other living organisms. *The Grapes of Wrath* (1939), his most important novel and a Pulitzer Prize winner, displays a sociological and almost a polemical bent. The book, as previously mentioned, chronicles the plight of Oklahoma farmers who are forced by Dust Bowl conditions of the early thirties to move westward and become "fruit tramps" in California. In its poignant, if overdrawn, description of these rootless, deprived hangers-on, Steinbeck achieved a trenchantly dramatic impact. He has since found much raw material for his writing in society's harsh treatment of other "undesirable" minority groups.

For a time, however, Steinbeck's writing seemed to have lost a good measure of its earlier vitality. His long novel *East of Eden* (1952), again set in the Salinas locale, was only moderately effective as a symbolic analysis of evil. *The Wayward Bus* (1947) and *Sweet Thursday* (1954) were even less significant efforts. But critics could never predict the Steinbeck genius; no one could be sure that his next book would not be a minor classic. *The Winter of Our Discontent* (1961) was, regrettably, not such a book. Although he increasingly disregarded California as the setting of novels that were written and conceived in the Eastern United States, Steinbeck's major themes, drawn from his native soil, have remained relatively constant. His *Travels With Charley in Search of America* (1962) was attractive to many readers, but presumably the Nobel Prize for Literature, awarded him in 1962, reflected the merits of his earlier work.

As Steinbeck had done, William Saroyan discovered rich literary lore in the agricultural area where he was born. Saroyan's work is largely set in the countryside around Fresno, and it reflects his Armenian origins in the San Joaquin Valley. His novels and plays, including *My Heart's in the Highlands* (1939), *My Name Is Aram* (1940), and *The Beautiful People* (1942), present a group of rural characters who are rhapsodically individualistic, if not to say eccentric. Saroyan is perhaps even better known for his short stories. In these, as in his other works, an assemblage of warm and attractive people, reflecting the author's kindly assessment of human nature, are depicted as inhabiting a kind of carefree, allegorical dream world.

Following World War II Steinbeck and Saroyan did not fully recapture the youthful audiences that had been their admirers before that catastrophe. At about this time, partially replacing the works of these men in popular favor, much good writing began to come out of the colleges and universities of the state. At Stanford, for example, Wallace Stegner was earning acclaim for his flavorful books, many of which were set in the American West, among them *Mormon Country* (1942) and *The Big Rock Candy Mountain* (1943). Meanwhile, as a professor of English, he encouraged talented students in his creative-writing seminars. At the University of California Mark Schorer (*The State of Mind*, 1947) and Henry Nash Smith (*Virgin Land*, 1950) also successfully combined writing with teaching. Richard Armour, on the faculty of Scripps College, made a name for himself as the "playful poet," with light verse somewhat reminiscent of that of Gelett Burgess.

The academic writers frequently developed historical themes, in both fiction and nonfiction. At Occidental College, historian Robert Glass Cleland produced solid yet entertaining narratives on the fur trade, the California ranches, and the American West in general; and at the University of California George R. Stewart, in such books as *Fire* (1948) and *Sheep Rock* (1950), spanned the twin areas of history and literature in a workmanlike and fascinating way. Stewart's earlier *Bret Harte* (1931) and *Ordeal by Hunger* (1936) fall more definitely within the category of nonfiction, while his *East of the Giants* (1938) and *Storm* (1941) are fictional works. Also writing fiction in a Western setting was Walter Van Tilburg Clark, for a time on the faculty of San Francisco State College. There he taught his students the techniques he had developed in order to write his successful books *The Ox-Bow Incident* (1940) and *The Track of the Cat* (1949). At U.C.L.A. John Espey explored the Pasadena of his youth in his novel *The Anniversaries* (1963). Another professor who wrote popularly in the postwar years was Eugene Burdick of the political science faculty at the University of California. His book *The Ninth Wave* (1956) is a fictional view of California politics as seen by a trained observer. With William J. Lederer, Burdick went on to write *The Ugly American* (1958), a book that created a national stir by its critique of Americans abroad, especially the most bumptious of those government officials administering foreign-aid programs in other lands. Burdick collaborated with another college teacher, Harvey Wheeler, on *Fail-Safe* (1962), a novel which gratified the taste of the macabre-minded by predicting an accidental nuclear holocaust.

In other books, too, California writers have dealt critically with the present. The best-known novel of Niven Busch, *California Street* (1959), concerns a San Francisco newspaper dynasty. He has also written *Duel in the Sun, The Hate Merchant,* and *The Actor.* James Edmiston's *Home Again* (1955) is a poignant criticism of the federal government's forcible removal of Japanese-born Americans from the Pacific Coast area during World War II. A related theme runs through Abraham Polansky's *A Season of Fear* (1956), an indictment of the public attitude toward minority groups. San Francisco Chinese form the backdrop of C. Y. Lee's tasteful *The Flower Drum Song* (1956), which became both a musical play and a film.

The list of prominent postwar writers also includes Jessamyn West, a Quaker educated at Whittier, whose *The Friendly Persuasion* (1945) was transformed into a prize-winning movie script. Her *South of the Angels* (1960), like James M. Cain's *The Postman Always Rings Twice* (1934) and *Mildred Pierce* (1941), is set in southern California (Cain's books were also adapted for the films). Many other California writers, too, share with Steinbeck, Saroyan, and Jeffers a reliance on their state's locale. Max Miller's favorite haunt was San Diego, and his book *The Harbor of the Sun* (1940) is set in that city. Similarly, Judy van der Veer skillfully described the San Diego back country in *Brown Hills* (1938) and *November Grass* (1940). John Fante, in *Wait for the Spring, Bandini* (1938) and *Dago Red* (1940), and Joe Pagano (*Golden Wedding*, 1943) have portrayed an Italian-American background of life in the West.

Another successful literary Californian, at least on a commercial level, was the Massachusetts-born writer Erle Stanley Gardner. Admitted to the California bar in 1911, he began writing about criminal topics as an avocation; only later did he turn to this employment professionally. Gardner is best known as the creator of Perry Mason, a detective-lawyer who as the supersleuth hero of innumerable books and television shows has received something of the popular adulation won earlier by A. Conan Doyle's Sherlock Holmes. Gardner, like other writers, found California congenial as an atmosphere in which to work but drew many of his themes from elsewhere. So did Edgar Rice Burroughs, originator of the banal Tarzan stories, Will Levington Comfort, Rupert Hughes, and James Hilton, who fall into the category of popularizers that kept up a voluminous and financially rewarding production. On a literary level of descending importance were Stuart Lake (*Wyatt Earp*, 1931), Paul Wellman (*The Iron Mistress*, 1951), and Ernest Haycox (*The Earthbreakers*, 1952). Their works were successful chiefly in that they reached large audiences through both movie and television adaptation.

A very different writer is Henry Miller, born in Manhattan in 1891. Most of his work is autobiographical; his best-known books are *Tropic of Cancer* (1934) and *Tropic of Capricorn* (1938), written during his expatriate period abroad. For many years Miller has lived on a secluded mountain top overlooking the Pacific Ocean at Big Sur, California, where he writes voluminously. His book *Big Sur and the Oranges of Hieronymus Bosch* (1956) describes his life in California. He takes his reader on a first hand tour of human depravity, and his central statement is that man has lost the art of living and that "until this colossal, senseless machine which we have made in America is smashed and scrapped there can be no hope."

A group reflecting Miller's influence, in many ways at least, grew up in the fifties. These were the spokesmen of the "Beat Generation." Prominent among them were Jack Kerouac and Allen Ginsberg, who made San Francisco their headquarters. Both expressed, with no perceptible inhibitions, the frustrations of many impatient young people who abhorred every aspect of postwar society and rejected its restrictions and obligations. Kerouac, who moved to California after defecting from Columbia University, originally coined the phrase "Beat Generation" to describe a close circle of disillusioned associates whom he portrayed in his writings. Ginsberg, having attended Columbia long enough to graduate, joined Kerouac in publishing some of his first writing in *Neurotica,* a journal that was built on "beat" compositions and that reflected a rebellion against "squares"— those mediocre conformists who lived a safe but dull and moral existence. Living in cold-water flats and studiously defying society's conventions, the "beatniks" clustered about the *cafe espresso* houses of San Francisco and the west side of Los Angeles. There, in a mood established as early as the 1920's by Kenneth Rexroth, they heard poetry readings and jazz or congregated at the "kookie" artistic colony of Sausalito on San Francisco Bay. Like Britain's "Angry Young Men" of the postwar decades, whom they resembled, these writers and artists achieved a considerable portion of the dramatic impact and public unpopularity they sought. They were considered by many to be little more than bearded bohemian eccentrics, and were on occasion called communists by conservative critics.

The "beatniks" themselves thought they were modern and avant garde, which perhaps they were in a way and for a little while. Probably the most representative of their works is Kerouac's *On the Road,* which is a kind of statement of the "beat" credo. Ginsberg's *Howl* (1956) also attracted particular attention. It was called on the one hand a tedious collection of raucous, wordy, and complex poems; on the other, critics found some astonishing effects and considerable perceptivity in this book. The most fair-minded appraisals seem to give Ginsberg and Kerouac credit for being competent, if sometimes confused, writers. For a time both men retained a loyal reading audience, composed in large part of young people. Although their writing can scarcely be called major, the "beats" have significantly drawn attention to modern man's increasing impotence in the face of mechanization, with its tendency to crush individualism and encourage conformity. Their poems contain many lines that are, furthermore, metrically superb, and their theme has the values of profound negation—considered intense and challenging by some, and adolescent and unrewarding by others. On occasion, the "beats" could become humorous; almost certainly they encouraged the social commentary of the comedian Mort Sahl, a former University of California student who has made a fortune in such nightclubs as San Francisco's Hungry i and Hollywood's Crescendo, as well as through such media as recordings and television. After World War II, thus, the spirit of protest took many forms, becoming much more complex than in the earlier messages of a Sinclair or a Steinbeck.

Periodical and Book Publishing

California's magazines have not progressed as significantly in recent times as might have been expected. With the exception of the short-lived *Pacific Spectator* (1947–1956), no periodical in California during the first half of the twentieth century even began to rival in impact the old *Overland Monthly*. Although *Westways*, *Frontier*, and the *Pacific Historical Review* print literary, political, and historical material for limited audiences, California remains today without a major literary or news magazine. Publications like *Westways* and *Sunset* cater primarily to homeowners and vacationers. Californians are forced to rely upon standard national magazines for other than regional interpretation of contemporary events.

In the mid-twentieth century, the crusading zeal and penetrating reporting which had characterized the early California press gave way to national editorial standardization. Hearst's fulminations against the Southern Pacific and General Otis' tirades against local labor bosses were replaced by nationally syndicated news and even editorial opinion, provided by eastern newsgathering and wire-service media. This is not to say that the local power of newspapers diminished. In numerous California communities only one newspaper exists. Because it has no competition, such a paper can frequently dominate local public opinion. The daily press is, indeed, often criticized for its lack of variety and high degree of monopolization. Even in California's large cities one or two papers tend to control news media. Yet, California's total number of newspapers is impressive. By 1960, there were 135 daily newspapers with a total circulation exceeding four million copies issued from within the state, as well as 600 others appearing biweekly or less often.

California has not yet produced a truly major book-publishing firm. There are, however, numerous fine printers, among them the Grabhorn Press and the John Henry Nash and Lawton Kennedy Presses at San Francisco, and the Ward Ritchie, Saul Marks, and Grant Dahlstrom operations at Los Angeles. Book dealers also publish occasionally. While both typographers and dealers have established a tradition for distinctive, deluxe printing, supported by the Book Club of California, and the Zamorano, Roxburghe, Rounce and Coffin Clubs, they generally produce books in limited editions, mostly with regional appeal. The University of California Press, the Stanford University Press, Westernlore, the Arthur H. Clark Company, Ritchie, and Fearon have instituted commercial operations resembling those of the publishing firms of the Eastern seaboard. Meanwhile, other commercial presses have sprung up at or near San Francisco in the postwar period, notably Wadsworth, W. H. Freeman, Howard Chandler, Hesperian, and Angel Island. Despite the lack of large-scale book manufacturing in California, a hopeful literary market has emerged.

Music and Drama

In the early twentieth century, the most important musical institutions in California were the Tivoli Opera House and the San Francisco Symphony. The Tivoli closed in 1913, but the San Francisco Opera Company filled the gap ten years later. Under a succession of talented impresarios, among them Gaetano Merola and Fortune Gallo, this organization has become world-famous. After 1932 it was given a home, the War Memorial Opera House, the first such municipal structure in the United States. The San Francisco Symphony, since its founding in 1911, has benefited from the leadership of an outstanding series of conductors. Among them have been Alfred Hertz and Pierre Monteux, who markedly improved both its reputation and quality and took the orchestra on national tours. In southern California, the Los Angeles Philharmonic Orchestra was founded in 1919, largely through the philanthropic efforts of William Andrews Clark, Jr. It too has attracted outstanding conductors, including Otto Klemperer, Alfred Wallenstein, and Eduard van Beinum. In addition, since 1921, the series of open-air concerts at the Hollywood Bowl have given local musicians and conductors an outlet for their talents. Local composers, however, have not been similarly favored, despite rich resources of talent. Similar civic performances, particularly of chamber music, have now been instituted by many communities throughout the state.

In the interwar period the early California resident song writers Charles Wakefield Cadman and Carrie Jacobs Bond were replaced by others. Ferdinand Rudolph (Ferde) Grofé, an arranger, and composer of the *Grand Canyon Suite*, began his career as an "extra" piano player at the Old Hippodrome Theater on San Francisco's Barbary Coast. On the eve of World War II a number of foreign composers sought refuge in California, among them Arnold Schönberg and Igor Stravinsky. For a time the French composer Darius Milhaud taught music at Mills College. These well-known musicians were apparently stimulated by the freedom of their new environment to pursue their experimental creative work.

California's strong thespian tradition has been discussed at some length. Although in the twentieth century it developed more slowly than previously, eclipsed somewhat by the films, many plays, pageants, and festivals have reflected the state's continuing interest in the dramatic arts. Among these have been the annual production of *Ramona* in the small community of Hemet, performances at Pasadena's Community Playhouse, productions of the Padua Hills Mexican Players, various experimental theater-in-the-round groups, and, since World War II, the activities of the Huntington Hartford Theater in Hollywood, and new repertory companies at San Francisco, Stanford, and Los Angeles. For many years a regular dramatic season was offered at theaters like the Biltmore in Los Angeles and a burgeoning "little theater" in its suburbs, particularly at U.C.L.A. in Westwood.

The Films and Television

Hollywood, which became the world's film capital, has drawn to California perhaps its greatest publicity in modern times, both good and bad. The development of the first motion-picture techniques in the United States was not specifically confined to Hollywood or California, although important cinematic experiments were conducted as early as 1872 at Sacramento. That year Eadweard Muybridge, a photographer, was commissioned by former Governor Leland Stanford to take some unique action shots of Stanford's favorite race horse, named Occident. Stanford, who owned a large stable, had bet a friend $25,000 that horses, while trotting, took all four hooves off the ground at one time during their stride. In order to prove this, Muybridge, with the aid of the engineering staff at Stanford's Southern Pacific Railway, lined up twenty-four cameras along a race track at Palo Alto. Numerous fine threads and wires were then stretched across the track. As the horse broke each thread, a camera shutter was released, with the result that a series of photographic prints were taken at stated intervals. The illusion was created that the horse was in motion when projection of the individual exposures onto a screen in rapid succession produced what was in essence a moving picture. When Stanford later went to Europe, he showed these pictures to photo expert Jean Meissonier. Muybridge's achievement thus attracted worldwide attention to the possibility of designing a motion-picture camera. He showed his photographs on the subject in a book entitled *The Attitudes of Animals in Motion* (1881). Credit for invention of the motion-picture camera, however, is usually but erroneously given to Thomas Alva Edison and his assistants. Their primitive Kinetoscope machine, using a strip film, was first demonstrated at the Chicago World's Fair in 1893.

For some years after the development of movie cameras, their use in the production of films was largely confined to New York and New Jersey. About 1907, however, producers, actors, cameramen, and scenario writers began to swarm toward Hollywood, for two main reasons. First, California's all-year climate and the variety of its scenery made it an ideal location for motion-picture production. Second, the state was far from Eastern debt collectors eager to hound financially desperate movie producers, and from the interference of New York State's motion-picture patent law, with its subpoenas and injunctions against producers who had infringed upon the basic patents held by Edison and other developers of cinema equipment. The fugitive producers with their bootleg cameras naturally had little capital with which to build a new industry. In southern California, however, since labor costs were lower than elsewhere, they found that they could operate on a shoestring budget if they pooled their resources. They rented second-hand equipment, painted their own sets, improvised lighting techniques—did everything possible to save money. In 1913 when Samuel Goldwyn, Jesse Lasky, and Cecil B. De Mille came West to produce *The Squaw Man* in a barn at the corner of Selma and Vine Streets, they had only a few thousand dollars and an unknown actress, Clara Kimball Young. This picture, and those that followed, quickly enriched the producers as orders poured in from hundreds of former vaudeville houses and nickelodeons now transformed into movie parlors.

In addition to these independent producers from New York, a number of pioneer film organizations began to grow up in California. One of the first of these was the Selig Polyscope Company, which in 1907–1908 filmed *The Count of Monte Cristo* near Los Angeles. Selig built a studio the next year at Edendale, another Los Angeles suburb. In 1909 the Bison Studios of New York arrived in Hollywood, followed by the Pathé organization and Biograph. The Vitagraph, Kalem, and Edison film companies appeared shortly thereafter. By 1914, when most of the Eastern companies had sent work forces to California, seventy-three firms were producing pictures in California. In those early years of the industry, a film company could literally grind out a "western" every other day.

Among the towns around Los Angeles (including Universal City, Inceville, and Edendale) whose names began to take on a special connotation through association with the film industry, the most spectacular changes took place in Hollywood. A sleepy little village founded by Kansas prohibitionists before the turn of the century, Hollywood had a town ordinance as late as 1903 which forbade the driving of more than two thousand sheep down Hollywood Boulevard at any one time. When the first motion-picture studios were established there, Hollywood could claim only a few thousand inhabitants; almost overnight it was to be transformed into the center of the film world.

During the early years of the Hollywood film industry, it passed through a megaphone and custard-pie-comedy phase that drew to it both hacks and persons of talent. That era gave rise to the stereotype of the autocratic director, typically clad in riding breeches and wearing his cap backward, who continually shouted orders at the droves of extras he employed to fill the background of his pictures. Among the most imaginative men who came West to "shoot pictures" was David Wark Griffith, producer of such enduring films as *The Birth of a Nation*. Due to its high cost of production ($100,000), this was the first American picture to command a two-dollar admission fee. It opened at Clune's Auditorium in Los Angeles on February 8, 1915, and ultimately grossed $20,000,000. This was also the first film to be honored with a showing at the White House, where President Wilson is said to have remarked: "It is like writing history with lightning."

In a few years Griffith and other entrepreneurs hurried the new medium of movie making from faltering adolescence into technical maturity. With the development of a "star system," the production of films became fantastically expensive. Outside the marquees of lavish, klieg-lighted premières, traffic stopped while fans ogled their favorite stars, most of them newcomers to fame and fortune. Charlie Chaplin, who became famous all over the world—probably the best-known film actor of all time—was an English comedian whose background was pantomime. With Mary Pickford, soon known as "America's Sweetheart," Chaplin worked for Mack Sennett's Keystone Company. In two years Chaplin's salary skyrocketed from $150 to $10,000 a week. Both of these stars were soon to command salaries in excess of $1,000,000 a year. Theda Bara, Dustin Farnum, Harold Lloyd, Lillian Gish,

Rudolph Valentino, and Greta Garbo were other performers whom adult fans idolized and wanted to see regularly. Similarly, the cowboy stars William S. Hart, Tom Mix, and Ed ("Hoot") Gibson became the heroes of countless small boys. A few of this group of actors had actually punched cattle on the range and were fine horsemen, as was the rustic comedian Will Rogers. In a category of her own, each week Pearl White left silent-film audiences breathlessly awaiting the next installment of *The Perils of Pauline*, which was first produced in 1914.

World War I led to the temporary collapse of movie making in Italy, Germany, and England. As a result, Hollywood producers gained virtual control of the world movie market. Mergers and consolidations, brought on by ruthless postwar competition and price-cutting, eventually reduced the number of studios to a handful. Single studios sometimes turned out fifty or sixty movies annually, with total production reaching a height of seven hundred pictures per year. In 1923, motion pictures already accounted for 20 per cent of the annual production of all manufactured products in California. More than 20,000 actors and actresses were by then working before cameras in 260 studios, their weekly payroll amounting to over a million dollars. That year *Harper's* magazine published an article on "Hollywood as a State of Mind." The mythology of Hollywood's scandalous folk tales continues to fascinate viewers and readers, for the myths of the motion picture industry seem to have a connection with "The American Dream," with materialistic and naive ambitions, successes, failures, and flaws. Someone has said that to explain Hollywood is to explain America.

The Hollywood of the 1920's is almost beyond recall today. In these lush years the flow of cash through the box offices staggered even the most avaricious of filmdom's pioneers. A baronial self-confidence led the movie moguls to festoon their studios with boastful pennants that read: "More Stars than There Are in Heaven" and "Hollywood, the Greatest Show on Earth." This was the era of matinee idols duly equipped with white silk shirts, bevies of aspiring starlets, sixteen-cylinder racing cars, and thirty-room white stucco palaces. Movie queens such as Pola Negri and Gloria Swanson spent thousands for perfume alone, helping to make Hollywood one of the most talked-of towns in the world. Gossip concerning the industry and its stars, in fact, was unquenchable. As early as 1923 the New York *World* wrote: "Hollywood has no art galleries, no institutions of learning aside from primary schools and kindergartens—nothing that makes the slightest pretense to culture, civic or otherwise. . . . But Beauty, ye gods, the place is choked, blocked, heaped to the gunwales with female beauty. One has to elbow beauties out of the way to make a passage down Hollywood Boulevard."

The stars' private lives drew criticism. In 1921, the career of popular comic Roscoe ("Fatty") Arbuckle was shattered by a scandal concerning the death of a young would-be actress in the course of a wild party in a hotel in San Francisco. Not only were Arbuckle's comedies thereafter banned from the screen in many communities, but a civic outcry for new moral standards was voiced. Sentiment for censorship grew so strong that in 1922 the major producers banded together to form the Motion Picture Producers and Distributors Association. Will H. Hays, former Postmaster General of the United States, was brought to Hollywood at a salary of $100,000 to impose discipline upon the industry. The Hays Office, which he established and headed for many years, was intended to restrain the industry from filming objectionable material; however, it did not prove wholly effective as an arbiter of morals and taste. Also, censorship seemed to dilute further the content of motion pictures. The Hays Office encouraged the "moral ending," a phenomenon which did much to transform honestly controversial pictures into vehicles for pious platitudes.

Among the technological innovations that contributed to Hollywood's almost miraculous success, one of the most dramatic was the addition of a sound track to the movie film strip. The Warner Brothers' production of *The Jazz Singer* was the first motion picture with sound. This "talkie," starring the song-and-dance man Al Jolson, revolutionized the industry when it appeared in 1927. Old stars with squeaky, high-pitched voices vanished and were replaced by others—the Clark Gables, Spencer Tracys, Claudette Colberts, and Joan Crawfords. Sound pictures, by attracting larger crowds than ever, soon led to the building of bigger and better theaters. It would have been hoped that this advance would also have resulted in movies of higher quality.

Instead, numerous brassy promoters encouraged what seemed to be a national craving for cheap entertainment combining the attractions of melodrama, vaudeville, and the circus. For twenty-five cents, in a carpeted atmosphere of popcorn and Coca Cola, America's moviegoers—who numbered at least 50,000,000 each week by the late 1920's—supported an industry built on stars, opportunistic agents, stunt men, writers, artists, electricians, scene painters, and thousands of hangers-on. Original and creative ideas often were squelched in the interest of money making. Only half-smiling could Hollywood's most famous lion roar "*Ars gratia artis"*—"Art for art's sake"—the caption that accompanied his every appearance. Actually, commercial considerations almost always triumphed over artistic ones. In those profitable years director-producer Cecil B. De Mille indulged his audiences with pretentious and lavish "historical" productions such the *The King of Kings* (1927) and *Cleopatra* (1934), whose purpose was spectacle, not significance. Such pictures were eminently vulnerable to the charge of tasteless vulgarity. De Mille himself once said: "Your poor person wants to see wealth, colorful, interesting, exotic." His films, with hundreds of paint-bedaubed extras, chariot races, and papier-mâché replicas of the monuments of antiquity, set an unfortunate pattern. Hollywood came to worship the "colossal" and "stupendous" as elephantine epics became the norm and as showmanship triumphed over art.

The commercialism of the movie producers can perhaps be partially attributed to their early insecurity and anxiety. Most of them had not been born into comfortable circumstances. William Fox was originally a cloth sponger on New York's East Side. Marcus Loew moved from dealing in furs to operating a penny arcade, as did Adolph Zukor. Lewis J. Selznick started out with a small jewelry business. Samuel Goldwyn was a glove salesman. Carl Laemmle, a German immigrant, managed a Wisconsin clothing store. Louis B. Mayer, who became one of the richest and most powerful of these pioneer "cellulords," began as a rag collector. Unprepared as they were for making artistic judgments, such men simply developed a technique for tailoring films with precision to the public taste.

Boy-meets-girl plots, big-laugh comedies, mawkish family dramas, and song-and-dance extravaganzas furnished an escape to viewers, especially during the depression years. Hollywood set the fashion for impressionable adolescents in dress, home furnishings, and married life; it clearly promoted the standardization of "culture." Many films were subject to the charge of glorifying crime, violence, corruption, and sex. In the 1920's civic groups claimed that even film titles had become too sensational, promising unwholesome attractions for the young and innocent. Representative of such titles were *Ladies Must Dress, Parlor, Bedroom, and Bath, The Love Flower, Old Wives for New, Paid to Love, The Price She Paid,* and *Theodora Goes Wild.* Parents resented the suggestive environment of darkened theaters and came to feel that the movies undermined morals, while churches accused the movie makers of deliberately marketing films that were spiritually debasing. Lurid advertisements of new pictures confirmed such suspicions. One newspaper ad of the 1930's spoke of a movie featuring "beautiful jazz babies, champagne baths, midnight revels, petting parties in the purple dawn, all ending in one terrific smashing climax that makes you gasp."

One striking feature of Hollywood is the literary and musical talent it attracted. The studios consistently paid large sums of money for movie scripts. Writers drawn to Hollywood included Peter B. Kyne, Rupert Hughes, F. Scott Fitzgerald, Nathanael West, William Faulkner, and Clifford Odets. In the early days musicians included Charles Wakefield Cadman, Carrie Jacobs Bond, and George and Ira Gershwin. Later, David Rose, Vincent Newman, Dmitri Tiomkin, and Miklos Rozsa joined the fold of studio song writers.

On rare occasions between the wars Hollywood produced excellent films like *All Quiet on the Western Front* (1930), *The Informer* (1935), and *Citizen Kane* (1940). In the late thirties the industry sometimes turned to various foreign stars and themes, in part to counter competition from such successful producers as England's Sir Alexander Korda. Among the new names were British actors Ronald Colman, Leslie Howard, and Robert Donat, as well as the Irish actress Greer Garson. The movies they made, such as *Mrs. Miniver* and *Goodbye, Mr. Chips*, earned for Hollywood a new measure of respect. Movies of substance, however, were more the exception than the rule.

After World War II, the trade journal *Variety* regularly carried reports indicating that the movies were headed for a financial nosedive. One of the last big moneymakers of the pre-television age was *The Best Years of Our Lives* (1946), a film starring Fredric March and directed by William Wyler. This sensitive production won most of the Academy Awards that year. At the same time Hollywood continued to flood the country with B-grade pictures, which it turned out in perhaps larger numbers than ever after 1945. A few postwar titles are illustrative: *Vice Raid*, *Drag Strip Girl*, and *High School Confidential*. Films of this type could hardly save the industry from the difficulties that lay ahead. Theater attendance was sagging, while the costs of making movies rose steadily as stars demanded larger shares of the profits. Increasingly high taxes absorbed another large part of Hollywood's revenues. As if to intensify a faltering industry's malaise, after 1948 government antitrust suits forced the major "Big Five" studios to divest themselves of their lucrative theater chains.

Gloom settled over Hollywood as it was beset by yet another difficulty—considerably increased competition from other contenders for America's leisure time. Prominent among these were paperback books, phonograph records, and such developing recreations as bowling, water skiing, and boating. Foreign films also made serious inroads on the American industry's markets, both in this country and abroad. By the late 1940's many producers and directors found it financially and artistically advantageous to film pictures out of the country, particularly at studios in Rome, Paris, and London. No longer did Hollywood produce 90 per cent of all films made in America and 65 per cent of the world's films.

Hollywood was hardest hit, however, by television, which offered free home entertainment. It too was a film medium, although its techniques and format generally differed from those in vogue at Hollywood. In time, television had great influence upon the movies. In imitation of television techniques, a wave of more realistic pictures was produced by "independents." Although these "independents" also produced many films of standard types, in general, they were a new breed of producer-directors. Few old-time directors, writers, or producers successfully shifted to TV production. The new generation of producers that arose were known for their previous achievements in acting and writing. A few had directed plays on the New York stage. In the 1950's director Elia Kazan and actor Marlon Brando were among those who contributed a directness of approach and a vividness of theme and plot to the films. These were qualities that the older Hollywood moguls had usually shunned as unprofitable. Films like *On the Waterfront* and *Baby Doll* attracted an audience that previously had found nothing to admire in the movies. Among the new forms which Hollywood developed in its struggle to compete were the independent production of films, sixteen millimeter home movies, educational films, color films, drive-in threaters, wide-angle screens, Cinerama, and three-dimensional productions. The survival of Hollywood came increasingly to depend upon the production of short films for use on television, as the town became a West Coast center of television filming and of transmission by the national networks.

The role of the cinema has been pervasive in our century. During World War II especially, this universal art form greatly increased contacts between nations. The movies have given many foreigners their first and sometimes their main impression of the United States. This is frequently regrettable. For better or for worse, the films have reached into the lives of millions, not only as entertainment but also as a means of instruction. Movies have been used to train workers and to impart learning. Plays and books have been revived and popularized through the films. Film versions of *Anna Karenina*, *Wuthering Heights*, and *War and*

Peace made these works familiar, loosely speaking, to many who would never have read them. Finally the cinema is characterized by such unique developments as Walt Disney's fantasies and cartoons, newsreels, and documentaries.

Fine Arts and Architecture

In the early twentieth century, other artists had come to California to take the place of Nahl, Keith, Audubon, and Bierstadt. Fresh styles of painting and drawing developed, often strange and difficult for traditionalist-minded viewers to comprehend. Oils and water color work reflected an especially imaginative use of color and design. Much of this new work was symbolical or evocative rather than explicit. But not all the new artists were experimental. Many traditional "sagebrush and eucalyptus" paintings continued to be produced.

In the 1930's the work of many artists reflected a consciousness of the disturbed economic and social conditions of the day that was parallel to the concern of writers such as John Steinbeck. Among the prominent new painters of the 1930's were Phil Dike, Barse Miller, and Rex Brandt.

First among California's sculptors was Gutzon Borglum, who began his career by studying art at San Francisco in the late 1880's. After a period of residence at Sierra Madre he was commissioned to carve the features of four American presidents in the granite cliffs of Mt. Rushmore, South Dakota; through this work he achieved national fame. Another California sculptor, and a book illustrator as well, Joe Mora, also became well-known outside the state, as did print-maker and painter Edward Borein. Mora settled at Pebble Beach and Borein opened a studio at Santa Barbara.

Outstanding among California's pioneer photographers were Carleton E. Watkins, Eadweard Muybridge, and Arnold Genthe. Watkins, a chum of Collis P. Huntington during boyhood days in New York, worked during the 1850's at San Francisco and, in 1861, was one of the first to photograph the Yosemite Valley. His pictures helped to influence public opinion in favor of legislation to establish the Yosemite as a national park. Due in part to the benefactions of his friend Huntington, Watkins became a well-known photographer who traveled all over the West. Regrettably, almost all of his photographic plates and his fine collection of pioneer daguerrotypes were destroyed in the San Francisco fire of 1906. Unable to recover from the shock of losing the results of his life's work, Watkins was committed to the state insane asylum at Napa in 1910 and died there, a very old man, six years later. The clarity and fidelity of his stereo views and other photographs, many of which are still in existence, won international prizes. Mount Watkins, a massive granite peak atop the Yosemite chasm, is named after him.

Muybridge was English-born; his original name was Edward Muggeridge. He was a well-known still photographer before he undertook the experiments for Leland Stanford which contributed to the development of the motion picture camera. In 1867, Muybridge photographed the Yosemite. His memorable views of the valley and other photographs of Alaska were exhibited across America and in Europe. In 1873, Muybridge took a series of unique photographs of the Modoc Indian War. Until 1881, he spent most of his time in California, frequently in Stanford's employ. On glass plates Muybridge recorded the movements of horses, dogs, cattle, rabbits, and men. That inclination of his work which made him one of the pioneers of motion pictures is apparent in a volume of photographic studies of San Francisco (1877), which was followed by *The Horse in Motion* (1878) and *Animal Locomotion* (1887). His work marked a great advance in the art of photography.

A third distinguished California photographer was the German-born Genthe. At San Francisco, after 1898, Genthe set up a remarkable studio. Holder of a Ph.D. degree, he was among the earliest photographers to develop a deliberate conception of his work as a distinctive art form. Genthe radically altered photographic techniques by the use of backlighting, and was highly experimental in his application of focus. He achieved great popularity at San Francisco. Women especially enjoyed sitting for their portraits by the handsome young Genthe. He also took some of the best pictures of the 1906 San Francisco fire and earthquake. For days he wandered along the city's streets, recording the devastation. Genthe's photos vividly caught the sense of shock on the faces of men, women, and children of the stricken city. He lived in San Francisco until 1911, and then moved to New York. His years in California had made a permanent mark upon Genthe, one of the great American photographers. In addition to his superb photographs of the state, Genthe left behind some indelible impressions of San Francisco in two books, *Old Chinatown* (1913) and *As I Remember* (1936), his autobiography.

The California photographers best known today are Edward Weston and Ansel Adams. Adams' black and white photos are sharp, vivid, and penetrating. Much of his work is devoted to the landscape of the Yosemite Valley. His is a latter-day complement to the superb oil paintings done in the Sierra before the first World War by Chris Jorgensen. The majestic spirit of California's land, water, and air governs the artistic impulse of Adams and Weston, and countless professional and amateur painters, water colorists, and etchers follow in this tradition.

Weston achieved an international reputation with his black and white photography, published in various books, among them Nancy Newhall's *The Photographs of Edward Weston* (1946). In 1941 he was asked to illustrate the first photographic edition of Walt Whitman's *Leaves of Grass*, an undertaking that led him, according to Miss Newhall, "to create a counterpoint to Whitman's vision." He traveled throughout America photographing its rivers, swamps, barns, flowers, trees and a people "strongly rooted in a quieter earth." Often he turned to subjects of social significance. Carmel was his home and his lens explored without rest the landscape of the Monterey peninsula. Weston died in 1957, having spent fifty years capturing subtleties of light and shadow. "Without ceremony," according to his friend and Carmel neighbor, the poet Robinson Jeffers, Weston "taught photography to be itself, not a facile substitute for painting, or an anxious imitator."

As early as the 1920's art colonies at Carmel, Santa Barbara, and Laguna Beach reflected the deepening interest in sculpture, painting, mosaic-work, and architectural design. Art institutes, among them Otis, Chouinard, the Los Angeles Art-Center school, and museums grew in their stature. The Huntington Art Gallery in San Marino obtained many more paintings of the English Renaissance while the Crocker Art Gallery at Sacramento and the De Young Museum in San Francisco's Golden Gate Park enlarged their collections. The Southwest Museum at Los Angeles likewise improved its holdings of aboriginal Indian materials.

In the colleges and universities a sense of freedom, as opposed to academicism, pervaded the teaching and execution of art. Experimentation in the plastic arts occurred at the Otis Art Institute, the Chouinard School, and at the California College of Arts and Crafts. Sculptor Merrill Gage lent distinction to the University of Southern California. Although California's modern sculpture has been described as bleak, in the 1950's Millard Sheets built a reputation as an artist and innovator who applied modern design to public and business edifices. Sheets had great influence upon architectural art. At the Los Angeles County Art Institute, of which Sheets was the first director, the approach was frankly experimental. At Immaculate Heart College a significant parallel specialty was the teaching of avant-garde mosaic art. San Francisco's art museum became a center for contemporary art.

In the post-World War II era numerous California artists, like the novelists, moved away from art that reflected the social compassion and consciousness of the 1930's. This had been of necessity representational in approach. Now non-objective, or abstract, forms predominated. The earthy, personal, and highly individualistic work of the Italian-born painter Rico Lebrun is representative of this movement. Lebrun is best known for "The Crucifixion" (1950), an immense tryptich. Some artists, of course, continued to paint in the traditional, representational style and at times intolerant critics wielded enough influence to secure the removal of "offending" works of painting and sculpture from museum exhibitions. Statues commissioned for public buildings were especially subject to criticism. Yet the public came increasingly to accept advances in artistic technique and execution. At the same time the work of modern foreign artists, such as Van Gogh, Toulouse-Lautrec, and Modigliani, found vastly increased appreciation. Museum attendance mounted markedly in the postwar decades.

One of the most bizarre artistic phenomena in modern California is the work of an Italian immigrant, Simon Rodia, builder of the Watts Towers. Located near Los Angeles, these novel creations, 99, 97, and 55 feet high, were fashioned out of bits of glass, tile, and artifacts garnered from nearby junk heaps. Without scaffolding, Rodia built the first of the towers in 1921. Five years later, when Los Angeles annexed the town of Watts, Rodia became involved in a long conflict with the city's Department of Building and Safety, because he had no building permit and because the towers were considered unsafe. While demolition and condemnation hearings dragged on for years, Rodia, who said he wanted to build something big, went on with his thirty-three years of erecting and defending a "gigantic fantasy of concrete, steel, and rubble." Called by art appreciators a "paramount achievement of twentieth century folk art in the United States," Rodia's towers were ultimately, and ironically, declared a local monument to be protected by a Los Angeles Cultural Heritage Board. When tested for safety, these filigree and mosaic-covered structures proved so strong that they could not easily be pulled down, even by steel cables attached to tractors. In 1954, at the age of eighty-one, Rodia tired of his project and left Los Angeles permanently for the northern town of Martinez. Public bickering over whether the towers were structurally sound left him embittered. He felt rejected by the society for which he had, as a monument of love, built the towers. Rodia never returned to Los Angeles. Why had he built the towers so strong? he was once asked. He replied, "If a man no have feet, he no stand."

Architecture was marked by an improved taste in housing standards and an increase in public affluence. In the 1890's the adobe, or Mexican ranch-style, house inspired a "mission revival" architecture, which featured the hollow plaster walls, phony arches, and imitation tile construction of a pretentious "Spanish style." From 1910 to 1930 this shared popularity with the wooden California bungalow of architects Charles Sumner Greene and Henry Mather Greene.

"Modern" architects, among them Frank Lloyd Wright, Rudolph M. Schindler, and Richard Neutra, built some of their first experimental structures in California, where architecture had already become a fascinating hodgepodge of affronts to one's sensibility. It is not unusual to find adjacent examples of Queen Anne style, Hawaiian or Oriental vestiges, Tudor or Jacobean mansions, French chateau affectations, Georgian or Mount Vernon colonial, Cape Cod fishermen's cottages, Egyptian and Mayan inspired houses, or Hopi Indian dwellings replete with ladders.

After 1900, at San Francisco, it was the age of the architects Willis Polk, Bernard Maybeck, and John Galen Howard. Polk was the designer of the famed Ferry building and one of the planners of the city's Civic Center. He also constructed the Hallidie Building, usually called the world's first glass skyscraper. Maybeck and Howard became, successively, the master planners of the University of California at Berkeley, aided by the benefactions of Phoebe Apperson Hearst. Maybeck also collaborated with Polk in designing the architecture for the Panama Pacific International Exposition of 1915.

At San Diego, after 1893, Irving Gill (trained, like Wright, under Chicago's Louis H. Sullivan) built some of that city's most original residences. Utilizing concrete, which he coated with plaster, Gill reduced the use of ornamentation in his buildings. Although the best known San Diego architect, he was not chosen as a designer for that city's Panama Pacific Exposition of 1915. Rather, the honor went to a devotee of Spanish colonial architecture, Bertram Goodhue, whose buildings ushered in a Hispanic revival that profoundly affected the California white stucco and red tile faddism of the period after 1910. Except for his leaner, more angular, Los Angeles Public Library, Goodhue's designs repeatedly utilized the Churriguresque motif that had pervaded Spanish and Mexican architecture in the eighteenth century.

Among California's modern architects, the Vienna-born Neutra became easily the most prominent. Associated previously with Wright, he moved to Los Angeles in 1926 to organize his own consulting and architectural firm. Neutra achieved renown because of his radical building and house designs. He also prepared new city plans for various communities. By the mid-1930's the Spanish-style house, once almost universally popular in California, had begun to give way to bolder, more functional experiments. Neutra's and Wright's most modernistic houses were designed for Californians who desired to replace Italian mannerist homes or extravagantly rococo Victorian residences. Both architects stressed the importance of the practical in residential construction, especially for "outdoor living." Their modernistic split-level houses offered greatly increased living space, wide windows, and enclosed recreation areas. Admirably suited to the California climate and environment, this architecture dominated many residential neighborhoods and contributed to the evolution of the widely-popular ranch-style residence.

Educational Advances

California has of course been obliged to keep pace with drastically expanding educational needs. Just as the nineteenth century saw the founding of major private collegiate institutions, the twentieth century witnessed the growth of numerous state-financed public campuses. In 1919 the State Normal School at Los Angeles became, by legislative act, the University of California, Southern Branch. Ten years later this rapidly-growing public institution—now entitled the University of California at Los Angeles, or U.C.L.A.—moved onto a beautiful new campus, at Westwood, near Beverly Hills. With its original campus at Berkeley, the state university, under the presidencies of Robert Gordon Sproul (1930–1958) and Clark Kerr (1958–1967), improved its faculty and broadened both its curriculum and the total range of its interests. It also expanded its multi-campus system; by the 1960's the University of California had campuses at Davis, Santa Barbara, Riverside, La Jolla, Santa Cruz, and at Irvine. Since the turn of the century the state university's professional and graduate schools have grown, with medicine, pharmacy, dentistry, education, business, law, journalism, and music among the disciplines encompassed.

California's state college system, a newer development than its university complex, grew out of a group of loosely related normal schools and teachers' colleges. After the 1940's eighteen state college campuses were located at Arcata, Chico, Dominguez Hills, Fullerton, Fresno, Hayward, Long Beach, Los Angeles, Northridge, Oakland, Orange, Rohnert Park, Sacramento, San Bernardino, San Diego, San Francisco, San Jose, and Turlock. With an enrollment of some 200,000 full- or part-time students in 1969, California's state colleges handled more students than its university system. That year University of California enrollment, full and part time, on all campuses was, however, in excess of 90,000. Teacher preparation and certification was once the major role of the state colleges, but their scope has widened in recent years to include the liberal arts and sciences. Another part of the state college system is its polytechnic colleges at San Luis Obispo, San Dimas, and Pomona. Also participating in public education are some ninety junior colleges.

By 1969 California had almost eighty four-year colleges and universities, both private and public. California's educational offerings include a large-scale "extension" system of training be-

UNIVERSITY OF CALIFORNIA, BERKELEY. CENTRAL CAMPUS DOMINATED BY ITS "CAMPANILE." (University of California photograph by Dennis Galloway.)

yond the high school. Utilitarian emphasis upon the applied arts is an important aspect of California's adult education program. The faculties of California's colleges and universities include more than their share of Nobel and Pulitzer prizewinners as well as Fulbright and Guggenheim Foundation fellows. After World War II the Ford Foundation founded at Palo Alto a Center for Advanced Study in the Behavioral Sciences, which aims to serve behavioral studies as the Institute for Advanced Studies at Princeton, N.J., serves the physical sciences.

In the pure sciences California has shown special prominence during the past half century. The California Institute of Technology at Pasadena, founded in 1890 as the Polytechnic or Throop College of Technology, was in the 1920's transformed into a virtually new institution by astronomer George Ellery Hale and pioneer atomic physicist Robert A. Millikan and a group of distinguished scientific associates. After Millikan was awarded the Nobel Prize in 1923 he drew around him a coterie of dedicated philanthropists and teachers who lent real distinction to "Caltech." In close cooperation with the Carnegie Institution of Washington, D.C., which operated the nearby Mount Wilson Solar Observatory, Millikan's group created one of the nation's two major national scientific research and technical institutes. The other is the Massachusetts Institute of Technology. Caltech and its scientists have demonstrated brilliance particularly in physics, biology, and genetics. In the late 1950's Caltech's Jet Propulsion Laboratory designed and supervised the manufacture of the United States' first artificial earth satellites. The institution also became deeply engaged in missile development and, on June 2, 1966, achieved the first of many later soft-landings on the surface of the moon. Jet Propulsion Laboratory remains a center of research for America's space program in conjunction with the National Aeronautic and Space Administration.

Another research center is the Lawrence Radiation Laboratory of the University of California at Livermore. Cyclotrons exist at both the Berkeley and Los Angeles campuses of the University. Its total scientific facilities, including medical schools, observatories, and institutes, have expanded rapidly. Another university campus specializing in science, the Scripps Institute of Oceanography at La Jolla, regularly charts the ocean's currents and maps its depths; it also operates oceanographic research vessels throughout the Pacific area. Also at La Jolla is the Salk Institute for Biological Studies, founded in the name of Jonas Salk, the research physician who has been given major credit for development of the first poliomyelitis vaccine.

In the field of astronomy the Lick Observatory at Mount Hamilton—technically also a campus of the University of California—was one of the first major observatories established in the United States. It has been in operation since 1874. An even better-known installation is the privately-operated Mount Wilson Observatory, whose 100-inch reflecting telescope has been in use since 1917. Its lens is exceeded in size only by the world's largest observatory—also located in California, at Mount Palomar in San Diego County. The Mount Palomar facility houses a 200-inch telescope, in operation since 1948. It was installed through the financial aid of the Rockefeller Foundation. The astronomers at Mount Palomar work closely with California Institute of Technology staff members and with astronomers at the Mount Wilson Observatory.

A Modern Culture

Associated with California's educational and scientific institutions are many centers of twentieth century cultural activity. California possesses two major historical societies, at San Francisco and Los Angeles, both of which produce quarterlies for their members. Several excellent research libraries publish significant books and professional journals. In the humanities and social sciences the Henry E. Huntington Library and Art Gallery at San Marino, the Bancroft Library of the University of California, Berkeley, and the Hoover Library of War, Revolution, and Peace at Stanford are internationally known. The Bancroft Library is a research center of Western American history and culture. The Huntington Library has become a center for humanistic studies in English and American literature and history. Its treasures include a copy of the *Gutenberg Bible* (1455), and the art collection has a sizable group of great paintings by English artists, among them Thomas Gainsborough's "Blue Boy."

Two huge amusement parks, Marineland and Disneyland, serve educational and recreational purposes; the latter is also a reservation of fantasy and illusion. California's prominence as a sports center has also attracted worldwide attention to the state. In the field of golf Billy Casper came from San Diego and Ken Venturi from San Francisco. Both became international champions. Richard "Pancho" Gonzalez, Jack Kramer, Ted Schroeder, and Dennis Ralston are only a few of California's tennis champions. Although sports do take the attention of thousands of fans away from government, culture, and education, the presence of professional teams in a city can also be unifying. Similar to talk about the weather, a spectator sport like baseball is a conversational common denominator. Pride in a team's achievement, indeed, often becomes a matter of fanatical devotion. In 1957 Los Angeles became the home of the former Brooklyn Dodgers National League Baseball Club and of another club, the Angels, a few years later. Similarly, San Francisco attracted the New York Giants to the West Coast. In 1960, Squaw Valley became the site of the winter Olympic Games.

Californians make heavy use of such diverse attractions as San Francisco's Golden Gate Park and Fleischacker Zoo, William Randolph Hearst's San Simeon estate—a treasure trove of art rarities—and the more than 200 free public library systems in the state which have sprung from the community libraries established by Andrew Carnegie. Local tax-supported libraries also maintain mobile book service in rural and remote areas of the state.

In recent years the noncommercial radio stations, KPFA in Berkeley, founded in 1949, and KPFK in Los Angeles, have employed unorthodox broadcasting practices to beam cultural programs to selected subscription audiences. Included on their schedules are unabridged performances of plays by dramatists from Aeschylus to Jean Paul Sartre, premier presentations of musical works by contemporary composers, poetry readings, and controversial discussions of present-day issues. Channel 28, a nonprofit education television station, performs a similar function for the TV media. The Commonwealth Club in San Francisco and Town Hall in Los Angeles have for years also sponsored vigorous discussions of public issues.

The cultural awareness of southern California gained impetus after the mid-1950's, and within a decade Los Angeles took important strides in the development of art and music. In 1964 the city completed a music pavilion, first structure of a $35 million cultural center. Three years later the Mark Taper Forum and Ahmanson Theater were added to it. Creation of resident repertory, ballet, and opera companies, as well as the emergence of nineteen symphony orchestras in Los Angeles County by 1967, underscored the rising interest in "culture." The Los Angeles County Art Museum was also completed in 1965 at a cost of almost $12 million. As the largest art museum west of the Mississippi River, and the biggest built in the United States in a quarter century, its Wilshire Boulevard complex was thereby formally launched into competition with America's other major art collections.

The 1960's offered further evidence that the Los Angeles renaissance had begun to shift at least part of California's leadership from north to south: a new arts council began to coordinate music center activities; funds were raised for a California Institute of Arts, in essence a proposed university of the fine arts; a museum of the communications industry opened in Hollywood; and Los Angeles became the nation's second biggest book-buying and art collecting market, the latter led by a new generation of "business collectors" like Norton Simon. The best art is shown in public museums or in the homes of the wealthy, some of whom regard its collection as status symbol or investment. A resurgence, incidentally, of more original and independent film-making in Hollywood accompanied the new mood of "art appreciation."

The cultural awakening of southern California seemed almost antithetical to the pattern established by the flood of midwestern migrants in the early 1900's. W. C. Fields once labeled Los Angeles "Double-Dubuque" while Sinclair Lewis called it "the retreat of all failures." The earlier farm-born conservative materialism had, indeed, probably contributed to cultural stagnation. Various forces seemed to change the pragmatic shallowness of the immediate past, the first of which was a shift in the incoming population toward persons with professional skills. Second was the continued prosperity of southern California's new industries, and, third, the emergence of a community cultural leadership with a demonstrated talent for fund-raising. Its members included Mrs. Norman Chandler, Edward W. Carter, and Howard Ahmanson, all of whom persuaded fraternal and service clubs as well as businesses and labor unions to contribute to cultural enterprises. The wide base of interest in the arts was shown by the fact that more than fifty per cent of private contributions to major cultural endeavors came from individuals. Despite the influx of funds for cultural purposes, local historical societies and theater workshops remained in dire financial straits.

Although the culture of Los Angeles still seemed largely unstructured and lingeringly garish, in the late 1960's the vitality of its artistic scene could no longer be denied. This, despite the fact that magazines, newspapers, and books like Alison Lurie's *The Nowhere City* (1966) and Christopher Rand's *Los Angeles: The Ultimate City* (1967), continued to satirize the area as a superficial "land of pop and honey." Yet the city which had played host to Stravinsky and Brecht found itself in the midst of its biggest era of cultural excitement.

A special aspect of California's culture is the effect of the influx of thousands of scientists and engineers, drawn first by the burgeoning aircraft industry and more recently by the electronics and missiles establishments of California. These newcomers have an intellectual orientation. The Rand (Research and Development) Corporation at Santa Monica, a semipublic, nonprofit agency created by the United States Air Force for the purpose of carrying on long-range strategic studies by "brainstorming" techniques, has brought together philosophers, political scientists, physicists, and mathematicians. They have created a new "think tank," or "R & D" intellectual "industry." Similar in purpose to the Rand Corporation but more technical in scope is the work of the Space Technology Laboratories of the Thompson, Ramo, Wooldridge organization at Canoga Park; they are the scientific and systems overseers of the United States Air Force's Ballistic Missile Division at nearby Los Angeles. Hughes Aircraft and International Telephone and Telegraph are among the companies with still other specialized research facilities in California. The Standard Oil Company of California has established at Richmond and La Habra a California Research Corporation whose exclusive activity is research, both primary and applied. Such centers attract personnel with interests that tend toward the intellectual. At San Diego the Hopkins Laboratory for Pure and Applied Science, sponsored by the General Dynamics Corporation, and the United States Navy Electronics Laboratory, have, through stressing "pure research," brought highly educated new citizens to that community.

These new Californians and their families tend to be independent-minded and intellectually curious. They are keenly interested in the activities of art museums, music centers, and other cultural institutions.

SELECTED READINGS

Descriptions of California's most recent cultural growth are numerous and varied. An attempt at synthesis, albeit dated and incomplete, was Aubrey Burns, "Regional Culture in California," *Southwest Review*, XVII (July, 1932), 373–394. Regarding journalism, see the sources on Hearst cited at the end of Chapter 32. Also informative is the autobiography of another ambitious California newspaperman, Thomas M. Storke's *California Editor* (Los Angeles, 1958). Among helpful works on literary figures, Harry T. Moore, *The Novels of John Steinbeck* (Chicago, 1939), is a study of California's best-known modern novelist.

There is no similar work on William Saroyan. His books, including *My Name Is Aram* (New York, 1940) and *The Human Comedy* (New York, 1943), are, however, partly autobiographical. Edmund Wilson, *The Boys in the Back Room: Notes on California Novelists* (San Francisco, 1941), deals almost allegorically with James M. Cain, John O'Hara, William Saroyan, Hans Otto Storm, and John Steinbeck. It is a delightful, incisive piece of literary criticism. Shorter and more academic is Frederick Bracher, "California's Literary Regionalism," *American Quarterly*, VII (Fall, 1955), 275–284. On Jeffers see Lawrence Clark Powell, *Robinson Jeffers: The Man and His Work* (Pasadena, 1940); Frederick J. Carpenter, *Robinson Jeffers* (New York, 1962); Radcliffe Squires, *The Loyalties of Robinson Jeffers* (Ann Arbor, Mich., 1956); and Melba Berry Bennett, *The Stone Mason of Tor House* (Los Angeles, 1966).

Art and architecture have been less thoroughly treated than literature. A blending of art and literature is to be found in a book by Carl Oscar Borg and Millard Sheets, *Cross, Sword, and Gold Pan . . .* (Los Angeles, 1936), which explains paintings of the settlement of the West. In the absence of a general history of California art, one must content himself with scanning exhibition literature, the occasional publications of such art institutes as Otis and Chouinard, and popular journals like *Sunset Magazine*. Frank J. Taylor provides an introduction to the history of architecture in his *Land of Homes* (Los Angeles, 1929). Treating the theme philosophically is Richard Neutra's *Mystery and Realities of the Site* (Scarsdale, 1951). Colonial architecture is studied in Kurt Baer's *Architecture of the California Missions* (Berkeley, 1958). An examination of style and tradition in the nineteenth century is Harold Kirker, *California's Architectural Frontier* (San Marino, 1960). This can be supplemented by Geoffrey E. Bangs, *Portals West: A Folio of Late Nineteenth Century Architecture in California* (San Francisco, 1960). Recent architecture is described in Esther McCoy's two books *Five California Architects* (New York, 1960) and *Richard Neutra* (New York, 1960), the latter an appreciation with photos. See also Frank Harris, ed., *A Guide to Contemporary Architecture in Southern California* (Los Angeles, 1951): Joseph A. Baird, Jr., *Time's Wondrous Changes, San Francisco's Architecture, 1776–1915* (San Francisco, 1962); and David Gebhard and Robert Winter, *A Guide to Architecture in Southern California* (Los Angeles, 1965). Consult also Gebhard's "The Spanish Colonial Revival in Southern California, 1895–1930," *Journal of the Society of Architectural History* (May, 1967). Regarding the art of printing, a good introduction is James D. Hart's *Fine Printing in California* (Berkeley, 1960). Ward Ritchie, "Fine Printing in Southern California," in *A Bookman's View of Los Angeles* (Los Angeles, 1961) is also useful.

Examples of notable photography, and some commentary upon it, are to be found in Joyce R. Muench, ed., *West Coast Portrait* (New York, 1946), and Edward Weston, *My Camera on Point Lobos* (Boston,

1950), as well as Charis Wilson Weston and Edward Weston, *California and the West* (New York, 1940). Ansel Adams has reproduced a number of his best photographs in book format. Recent examples (both in collaboration with Nancy Newhall) include *This Is the American Earth*, published by the Sierra Club (San Francisco, 1959), and *Yosemite Valley* (San Francisco, 1959). Early photography in the latter area is discussed in Mary V. Jessup Hood and Robert Bartlett Haas, "Eadweard Muybridge's Yosemite Valley Photographs, 1867–1872," California Historical Society *Quarterly*, XLII (March, 1963), 5–26. Rico Lebrun, *Drawings* (Berkeley, 1961), describes what has shaped a contemporary painter's viewpoint. Books by other California painters are virtually nonexistent.

A portrait of one of Hollywood's most renowned producer-directors is Richard Batman, "D. W. Griffith: The Lean Years," California Historical Society *Quarterly*, XLIV (September, 1965), 195–204. A penetrating study of the movies, now somewhat dated, is Leo C. Rosten, *Hollywood: The Movie Colony, the Movie Makers* (New York, 1941). Gordon Hendricks, *The Edison Motion Picture Myth* (Berkeley, 1961), shows that Edison had little to do with motion-picture invention. Histories of the industry include also Benjamin B. Hampton, *A History of the Movies* (New York, 1931), and Maurice Bardeche and Robert Brasillach, *A History of Motion Pictures* (New York, 1938). See also Terry Ramsaye, *A Million and One Nights* (New York, 1926). The problem of censorship is analyzed in Raymond Moley, *The Hays Office* (New York, 1945). Another significant analysis is Lewis Jacobs, *The Rise of the American Film* (New York, 1939). Skillful in its satire of movie making is Harry Leon Wilson's novel, *Merton of the Movies* (Garden City, 1922). Hollywood during the depression years is the subject of Nathanael West's novel *The Day of the Locust* (New York, 1939). Better-known fiction works are Budd Schulberg, *What Makes Sammy Run* (New York, 1941), a novel about the drive for power in Hollywood, and F. Scott Fitzgerald, *The Last Tycoon* (New York, 1941). A semi-allegorical treatment of the area around Hollywood, similar in theme, is Libbie Block, *The Hills of Beverly* (New York, 1957).

A searching modern look at one of the most powerful movie moguls is Bosley Crowther, *Hollywood Rajah: The Life and Times of Louis B. Mayer* (New York, 1960). See also A. R. Fulton, *Motion Pictures: The Development of an Art from Silent Films to the Age of Television* (Norman, Okla., 1960), and Edward Wagenknecht, *The Movies in the Age of Innocence* (Norman, Okla., 1962). Fred J. Balshofer and Arthur C. Miller, *One Reel A Week* (Berkeley, 1967), discusses the pre-World War I era of film making, while George N. Fenin and William K. Everson, *The Western, From Silents to Cinerama* (New York, 1962), gives a more composite view of the cinema. Kenneth MacGowan, *Behind the Screen: The History and Techniques of the Motion Picture* (New York, 1965), is a detailed illustrated account minus the "beautiful people" approach. A kind of "requiem for a dream town," written with sensitivity, is Beth Day's *This Was Hollywood* (New York, 1960). Two books that look at Hollywood almost sociologically, with attention to its folklore, taboos, and peculiarities, are Hortense Powdermaker, *Hollywood: The Dream Factory* (London, 1951), and Mervyn Le Roy, *It Takes More Than Talent* (New York, 1953). A penetrating and observant description of Los Angeles and Hollywood during the interwar period is Edmund Wilson, "The City of Our Lady, the Queen of the Angels," in *The American Earthquake* (New York, 1958).

The popular interpreters of life in California have included Joseph Henry Jackson, Carey McWilliams, Oscar Lewis, and Idwal Jones. In the columns of the press, as well as in their books, these writers have helped describe California's culture, past and present. Jackson was literary editor of the San Francisco *Chronicle* from the 1930's through the 1950's. He also edited such anthologies as *The Western Gate* (New York, 1952) and *Continent's End* (New York, 1944). Among Lewis's works are *Bay Window Bohemia* (Garden City, 1956), *Bonanza Inn* (New York, 1945), and *Here Lived the Californians* (New York, 1957). McWilliams, in his previously mentioned *Southern California Country* and *California: The Great Exception*, gives the reader some of the best analyses of the occultism and faddism discussed in this chapter. A life of Mrs. McPherson is Nancy Barr Mavity, *Sister Aimee* (Garden City, 1931); a later treatment of the same subject is Lately Thomas, *The Vanishing Evangelist* (New York, 1959). For a loyal adulation of a controversial facet of southern California's commercialized "cemetery culture" see Adela Rogers St. Johns, *First Step Up Toward Heaven* (Englewood Cliffs, 1959), which may be contrasted with Evelyn Waugh's satire *The Loved One* (Boston, 1948), and Aldous Huxley's earlier but equally acid novel, *After Many a Summer Dies the Swan* (New York, 1939). There are also studies available of utopian colonies, including Robert V. Hine, *California's Utopian Colonies* (San Marino, 1953), and Emmett A. Greenwalt, *The Point Loma Community in California, 1897–1942* (Berkeley, 1955).

A worthwhile collection of literary pieces is that edited by Robert Pearsall and Ursula Spier Erickson, *The Californians: Writings of Their Past and Present* (San Francisco, 1960). Another anthology is Robert Kirsch and William Murphy, *West of the West* (New York, 1967). A helpful bibliographical essay is Lawrence Clark Powell's *Land of Fiction* (Los Angeles, 1952). A recent lampooning of southern California is Cynthia Lindsay, *The Natives Are Restless* (New York, 1960). Another examination of this part of the state is Jessamyn West's *South of the Angels* (New York, 1960). Understanding of the "beatniks" is best gained by reading their writings. These are made partly available in Gene Feldman and Max Gartenberg, eds., *The Beat Generation and the Angry Young Men* (New York, 1958). Equally useful is Thomas Parkinson, ed., *A Casebook on the Beat* (New York, 1961), and Lawrence Lipton's *The Holy Barbarians* (New York, 1959).

California's recent educational developments are summarized and studied in James C. Stone and R. Ross Hempstead, *California Education Today* (New York, 1968).

34

Wartime Problems

During the years preceding United States entrance into World War II, Californians had become increasingly disturbed over the threat posed by the European dictators and the Japanese military clique. The unexpected attack upon Pearl Harbor in Hawaii by carrier-launched Japanese dive bombers on December 7, 1941, created a new mood. Japan went on to win all its objectives in Southeast Asia. Californians soon heard of the fall of New Britain in January, 1942, and, later, of the surrender of Sumatra, Java, Bali, Timor, Borneo, and the Philippines. A strange anxiety ran through California, to be alleviated only by America's Pacific victories.

The war years brought new economic dislocations and social tensions. Manpower problems, high taxation, rationing, transportation difficulties, and the urgent need of housing for defense workers were the order of the day. Military training camps, ship-yards, and aircraft factories had to be constructed quickly. Nothing must impede the job of getting planes, tanks, and guns to the fighting front. California's burgeoning war industries drew workers from all parts of the United States. The state dismantled its border "bum blockade" against "Okies" and "Arkies," thereby encouraging workers by the thousands to flock west-ward for employment in its new war plants. Local chambers of commerce focused attention upon getting whole industries to move to California, or at least to establish branch plants in the West.

Japanese Relocation

Long before Pearl Harbor, security had become a paramount consideration. During 1940, the state legislature passed the Dilworth Anti-Spy Bill, the Slater Anti-Sabotage Act, and the Tenney Anti-Subversive legislation. Before the war, as the United States and Japan became increasingly antagonistic, feeling against the Japanese had been mounting in California. The wartime atmosphere of suspicion and excitement was harmful to race relationships. By 1940 there were 120,000 Japanese in California. The Japanese immigrants' position had become economically stronger over the years, a factor that paradoxically made them more vulnerable to the old and ugly racist bugaboo that Orientals were unassimilable. As fishermen, cannery workers, and agriculturalists they still awakened the hostility of Caucasian competitors. Japanese truck farmers, in particular, more firmly entrenched than ever in the state's agricultural system, aroused widespread envy in California's agricultural areas.

Immediately after the Pearl Harbor attack, the Hawaiian Islands came under martial law. Rule of those islands was turned over to the commanding general of the United States Army in the Pacific and remained in his hands until 1944. Apprehension naturally spread to the mainland, especially during 1942 after a lone Japanese submarine surfaced at Goleta, near Santa Barbara, and fired a shell which splintered the end of a wooden jetty. Frightened residents put their houses up for sale and made plans to flee. On February 25, 1942, the California press erroneously reported that Japanese planes had bombed Los Angeles and its environs the night before, heavily damaging defense installations. Anti-aircraft fire had indeed been shot into the sky against imaginery aircraft, and the jittery ill-informed populace was ready for the worst.

At this point racial attitudes now came to be commingled with the argument of the military authorities that the proximity of California's Japanese to airfields, Army installations, and Navy bases was dangerous. The fact that many of the Japanese were second generation Nisei and that there was no evidence whatsoever that any of the Japanese were disloyal did not influence the military's considerations, and the military won the day. This was disastrous for the Japanese. Many had to sell their homes, businesses, and land at a fraction of their value. The Japanese-Americans suffered a property loss estimated at $365 million. Radios, arms, and other suspicious-looking personal effects were confiscated from them. German and Italian aliens were also interned, but in most cases quickly released.

By order of General John L. DeWitt, commanding the Western Defense Command from 1941 to 1943, a total of 112,000 West Coast Japanese, two thirds of whom were American citizens, were subject to relocation. Thousands were taken from their homes and businesses and herded into the interior. Among them were Issei (persons born in Japan), Nisei (American-born and educated), and Kibei (American-born but partly educated in Japan). This move was largely at the insistence of Earl Warren, state attorney general before he became governor in 1943. Warren was doubtless influenced by such nativist groups as the State Grange, the American Legion, the Native Sons and Daughters of the Golden West, and the State Federation of Labor. Together these sponsored the California Joint Immigration Committee, through which they voiced their views. Some Japanese were given the choice of "relocation" along the eastern seaboard. Others were sent to security camps at Heart Mountain, Wyoming, and Topaz, Utah. Some of the Japanese who were interned were from Washington, Oregon, and Arizona, but most came from California. At Tule Lake, Manzanar, and other California internment centers the evacuees lived behind barbed wire under military guard. They were charged with no crime. They were merely considered potential enemies by the Department of the Army, and no defender, in the government or outside it, arose to invoke the protection of the Constitution on their behalf. Some Californians, of course, were saddened by the necessity of complying with such wartime orders.

Although no openly identifiable cases of sabotage had occurred in Hawaii, rumors kept cropping up concerning collusion between the Hawaiian Japanese population and Japanese military forces. Only in 1944 were the first internees allowed to leave the relocation centers for coastal areas. By 1946 their incarceration had ended.

Only about 65,000 of the Japanese who had been forced to leave the West Coast ever returned. Some settled in the Middle West and in the East. Historians who have studied this forced evacuation in the calmer atmosphere of the postwar years have generally concluded that it was a fundamental and grievous violation of the constitutional rights of these individuals. The United States Supreme Court never fully conceded that the government was culpable, refusing to indemnify disappointed Japanese who appealed to the court. In the view of many critics, this episode shows how a democratic society is capable of grave error. Only long after World War II did California's Japanese gain sympathy for their grievances and then mainly on moral rather than legal grounds.

Yet a remarkable change occurred in the public attitude toward the Japanese. Whereas Californians had once believed that wartime Japan was little more than a nation of savages, a new respect flowered after Japan's defeat. Occupation troops acquired a taste for Oriental life, some even marrying Japanese brides. Americans, mesmerized by German technology, applied the same appreciation toward the makers of Japanese transistor radios and autos. The Nisei too had acquitted themselves magnificently during the war as members of the highly decorated 442d Regimental Combat Team, as professional men, or, in the case of Pat Suzuki, a graduate of San Jose State College, as the star of the 1956 Broadway musical, *Flower Drum Song*.

A Wartime Footing

By the year 1942 the political atmosphere of New Deal reform had largely been dissipated. After an election held under the shadow of wartime emergency, the administration of Culbert Olson was replaced on January 4, 1943, by that of Earl Warren, California's most renowned modern governor. Warren, state attorney general from 1939 to 1943, had a warm and attractive personality and great intelligence. He was, furthermore, a skilled political leader. A progressive-minded Republican, Warren stayed clear of feuds within his own party. His vigorous campaign against Olson showed Warren to be the most talented Republican strategist in many decades of the political history of the state.

Governor Warren's views were relatively nonpartisan, and he seldom mentioned either of the two leading political parties if he could avoid it. Like old Hiram Johnson, whose picture was the only one that hung in Warren's office, he called himself a Progressive. Also like Johnson, Warren attracted moderate voters of all parties. Always informal in manner, he improved steadily as an effective public speaker and personality. Warren projected a relaxed and reassuring image in difficult times, which was part of the magic of his success. Because of the war, a virtual moratorium on politics and labor difficulties characterized the Warren era. The waterfront strikes that had rocked the coast were a thing of the past. Most industrial disputes were handled now by voluntary arbitration; on occasion the governor himself was the arbitrator, for his judgment and good faith were trusted by all sides. Warren spent three terms at Sacramento, being easily reelected in 1946 and 1950.

About 85 per cent of the population growth from 1900 to 1940 was caused by immigration. The influx during World War II was far in excess of that during World War I. Not only did thousands of defense workers pour into the state; soldiers, sailors, and air-men came by the hundreds of thousands for military training or to be shipped overseas. Military posts became virtual cities, with their own supply, transportation, sanitation, and postal facilities. In south-central California, Camp Roberts housed upwards of 50,000 men. Another big army depot was Fort Ord, located between Monterey and Salinas. Camp Pendleton, near Oceanside, became a massive West Coast base for the marines, who played a large role in the Pacific campaigns during World War II. San Diego, Long Beach, and Mare Island, already major naval bases, increased their facilities many fold. And there were newly-ex-panded air training centers at March Field, the El Toro Marine Air Depot, and the Alameda Naval Air Station. San Francisco and Los Angeles became huge troop embarkation centers.

Industrial Expansion and Housing Shortages

Even before the attack on Pearl Harbor, California had begun to shift from peacetime to "defense" production. On the Rich-mond, Oakland, and San Pedro waterfronts the Todd and Beth-lehem shipyards in 1941 hammered out ships for the allied powers. Huge appropriations from the United States Maritime Commission also reopened shipbuilding installations at Sausa-lito and Vallejo that had been idle since World War I. A virtual industrial revival took place in the San Francisco Bay area. The shipyards of the Henry J. Kaiser enterprises began to build hun-dreds of cruisers, destroyers, cargo carriers, and auxiliary ves-sels. The labor force at Kaiser's Richmond Yard alone came to number more than 100,000. Kaiser controlled Calship at Los An-geles and also constructed, with the help of a Reconstruction Finance Corporation loan, the largest steel mill in the West in a vineyard at Fontana.

Numerous firms that produced steel products, chemicals, tex-tiles, and machine tools had been virtually on a wartime footing before 1941. Others quickly converted, after Pearl Harbor, to the production of tanks, jeeps, and munitions. Heavy industry was thereby introduced to California on a massive scale. As young civilian workers poured into the state, its towns expanded overnight. Typical was Vallejo, which jumped from a population of 20,000 in 1941 to 100,000 in 1943. New housing projects built with government money mushroomed, as did the need for streets and highways, sewer lines, water mains, health services, schools, and transportation facilities. Thousands of workers temporarily dwelt in trailer parks or in substandard housing and commuted to work, traveling as much as three or four hours per day. Train and bus facilities were heavily burdened. Crowding and strain were the order of the day.

The Aircraft Industry

No segment of the California economy grew more rapidly than the aircraft industry. Airplanes had been produced in the state since the years before World War I, and thus when World War II came an aircraft center was already in being there. The nation was fortunate in this fact.

In 1910 the first public aviation meet in America was held on the Dominguez Ranch near Los Angeles. This event drew almost 200,000 spectators, who saw Glen Curtis make the first successful West Coast flight, a thrilling spectacle that lasted for two whole minutes. Barnstorming pilots, "air circus" stunt flyers, and independently wealthy enthusiasts created a market for airplanes. At first these craft were literally held together with baling wire. Eventually, however, a measure of standardization led to improved construction. Southern California's airplane designers and builders began shortly after World War I to construct a variety of aircraft.

Among these builders was Donald Douglas, later an important figure in the aviation industry. He learned his trade with Glenn L. Martin, already renowned as an airplane engineer, At Los Angeles, Martin had established his own company in 1912 but later, in 1929, moved to Baltimore. Southern California's aircraft designers really broke into the national news in 1927. That year Charles A. Lindbergh, "The Lone Eagle," with private backing, commissioned San Diego's Ryan Aeronautical Corporation to build his "Spirit of Saint Louis," in which "Lindy" flew the Atlantic. All this historic activity was in the background of California's readiness as an aircraft center on the eve of World War II.

One of the giants of the American aircraft industry, the Lockheed Aircraft Company, was founded by Malcolm and Allan Loughead, who sold the company in 1932 to other owners, among them banker Robert E. Gross, through a federal receiver for only $40,000. Gross, the dominant figure in the development of the company, represented a reversal of the standard formula for success in the aircraft industry. Unlike aviation's earlier barnstorming heroes, Gross entered the field at the age of thirty-five as a cautious businessman, heading a corporation that was all but moribund. Lindbergh, Wiley Post, and Amelia Earhart began to set flying records in the company's planes. In 1933, Gross helped develop the twin-engined Electra, which earned Lockheed an international reputation.

In 1935 the output of California's aircraft industry had reached $20 million annually. By 1941, placement of orders for warplanes by foreign governments and by our own government had made California's aircraft companies vital to the rearmament program of the free nations of the world. The Douglas and Lockheed plants were the cornerstones of American airpower. Douglas-trained workers who had never previously operated an acetylene welding torch or a rivet gun put together Havoc Nightfighters for the British, Liberators, Flying Fortresses (B-17's), and various transports and dive bombers. At Burbank, Lockheed produced Hudson bombers for Britain, the P-38 fighter, the Ventura, and the 128-passenger Constitution. Lockheed employed a work force of 90,000 persons during the height of the war and was responsible for approximately six per cent of all United States plane production. During the war years this company built 20,000 planes.

Other plants, notably Consolidated Vultee (founded by Gerard Vultee), which later became part of the General Dynamics Corporation, Douglas, North American, Northrop, and the Hughes aircraft companies, expanded spectacularly during World War II.

California's role in World War II was of vital significance for the nation as well as for herself. The state's aviation industry alone made a remarkable contribution to the war effort. Conversely, the effect upon California of her participation in the conflict was great and lasting. The millions of dollars in government funds poured into her new steel mills, shipyards, and aircraft factories brought about a massive growth of her economy and population. After the war the aircraft companies diversified their activities and produced radar equipment, missiles, and jet aircraft. This stimulation assisted California in her effort to equal the industrial position of the older Midwestern and Eastern states. This growth inevitably changed the character of the state and effected an ever more drastic transformation from her Arcadian past.

Founding of the United Nations

In April, 1945, as the war in Europe was drawing to a close, representatives of 46 nations met at San Francisco to transform a wartime alliance against the Axis powers into a permanent structure for world peace. Despite almost constant disagreement between American and Russian delegates, all but disrupting the conference, the UN Charter was signed at San Francisco on June 26 by the delegates of all nations participating. On October 24, 1945, the new organization came into being. Thus San Francisco is forever associated with the UN Charter, whose purpose, as stated in its opening words, is "to save succeeding generations from the scourge of war." Among the reporters covering this event was a young, recently demobilized veteran named John F. Kennedy.

SELECTED READINGS

Discrimination against the Mexicans and Japanese has become a subject of popular interest. In her novel *Tumbleweeds* (New York, 1934), Marta Roberts portrays the demoralization of a Mexican couple dependent upon relief in California during the depression decades. Similarly, Cornelia Jessey uses her novel *Teach the Angry Spirit* (New York, 1949) to lament the hardships of life in the Mexican district of Los Angeles during World War II. Carey McWilliams presents a sympathetic view of another foreign group in *Prejudice: Japanese-Americans, Symbol of Racial Intolerance* (Boston, 1944). The army version of Japanese relocation, published by the United States War Department, is *Japanese Evacuation from the West Coast* (Washington, D.C., 1943). See also Stetson Conn, "The Decision to Evacuate the Japanese from the Pacific Coast, 1942," in Kent Roberts Greenfield, *Command Decisions* (New York, 1959), and Conn's *Guarding the United States and Its Outposts* (Washington, D.C., 1964), which carefully details the army's plans to evacuate aliens from the West Coast. An evacuee, Miné Okubo, has given her impressions of internment in *Citizen 13660* (New York, 1946). More critical is Morton Grodzins, *Americans Betrayed:*

Politics and the Japanese Evacuation (Chicago, 1949), and the previously cited book by ten Broek, Barnhart, and Matson, *Prejudice, War, and the Constitution*. Studies that are sociological in tone, such as Thomas and Nishimoto, *The Spoilage*, and Thomas, *The Salvage*, have appeared in the postwar period. Another of these is Leonard Bloom and Ruth Riemar, *Removal and Return . . .* (Berkeley, 1949). See also a useful recent article by Edward N. Barnhart, "The Individual Exclusion of Japanese Americans in World War II," *Pacific Historical Review*, XXIX (May, 1960), 111–130, and the already-mentioned volume by Daniels.

The economy of California during World War II is the subject of a study by the National Resources Planning Board, entitled *Pacific Southwest Region, Industrial Development* (Washington, D.C., 1942).

The literature concerning aviation is scattered and diverse. A history of sorts is Kenneth M. Johnson, *Aerial California: An Account of Early Flight in Northern and Southern California, 1849 to World War I* (Los Angeles, 1961). The story of Charles A. Lindbergh's epochal flight, with details about the building of the "Spirit of Saint Louis" in California, is told in his book *We* (New York, 1927). Various aviation journals began to be published at an early date, among them *Western Flying, Skyline* (North American), *Aircraftsman* (Lockheed), *Airview* (Douglas), *Consolidator* (Consolidated Aircraft). Other journals published by California aircraft firms include the *Lockheed Log*, the *Northrop News*, and the *Ryan Reporter*.

A general history of aviation, with attention to California, is Hugh Knowlton, *Air Transportation in the United States: Its Growth as a Business* (Chicago, 1941); another is Elsbeth Freudenthal, *The Aviation Business* (New York, 1940). The worldwide wartime implications of the aircraft industry are set forth in H. H. Arnold, *Global Mission* (New York, 1949). Postwar prospects are the subject of Bernard A. McDonald, *Air Transportation in the Immediate Post-War Period* (Buffalo, 1944). A company history is Western Air Lines, *Wings Over the West: The Story of America's Oldest Airline* (n.p., 1951).

35

California after World War II

California faced a variety of crucial problems at the end of the war. Only a handful of war contracts for production of aircraft and ships were extended beyond September 2, 1945, the date of Japan's surrender. As California began the process of reconversion from a war-stimulated economy to a peacetime one, the possibility of widespread business mortality among small war-born plants particularly worried civic leaders. Domination of postwar manufacturing by companies that had grown big during the war was another threat. A third source of anxiety concerned future employment of the great numbers of people which the war had drawn to the state. In the year of peak wartime employment, 1943, California's factories employed 1,165,000 persons, as compared with only 381,000 in 1939. It was feared that the bulk of the wartime labor force would leave California. In actuality, however, the state's population rose by another million persons from July, 1945, to July, 1947. These new residents were mostly wage and salary workers, rather than professional people. A startlingly high number of California veterans returned to the state. More than 300,000 service personnel from other parts of the country also elected to receive their discharges and to gather their belongings and to persuade their families to join them among the orange groves. The United States Veterans Administration estimated that more than half of California's resident World War II veterans came from other states.

Despite pessimistic expectations, a gratifying number of the G.I.'s who poured back into California found satisfactory work. Furthermore, most of the 274,300 persons who worked in the state's shipyards in 1943, as well as the majority of her 237,400 aircraft workers, succeeded in obtaining postwar employment. The migration into the state seemed to generate new employment to take the place of discontinued war industry. Emergency relief to discharged veterans under the benefits of the G.I. Bill of Rights helped take up the slack in unemployment. To help solve employment readjustments, Governor Warren and the legislature had wisely arranged to set aside certain revenues collected during the war as a "rainy day fund." In 1944 alone there had been a rise of 11 per cent in tax revenues and other state income; out of the surplus for that year, $34 million was put into this postwar employment reserve. A California State Reconstruction and Reemployment Commission was especially entrusted with supervision of a program of economic reconversion. In 1947 about 3,600,000 workers were employed in California. In most cases the state provided a higher standard of living for its workers than ever before. By 1958, the per capita income of California's millions of laborers reached $2,559, a figure 24 per cent above the national average.

Diversification and New Industry

The war not only gave new impetus to existing manufacturing industries; it also helped diversify industrial development. This adjustment was long overdue in California, where economic organization was clustered around too few major industries, among them orange growing, the movies, and oil. The war, furthermore, made the state increasingly prominent in the economy of the nation. It allowed California to draw a larger share of the nation's per capita income and population than ever before. California in the postwar years grew faster than almost any other part of the nation, and its very growth led to further heavy migration into the state.

Firms that had once served restricted local markets developed national distribution channels after the war. Rising transcontinental freight costs made it economical for some firms to establish permanent branches in California. The development of a specialized labor pool on the West Coast also encouraged Eastern manufacturers to move their plants. In addition to the well-established aircraft industry, significant expansion occurred in the manufacture of refrigeration equipment, technical instruments, heating and cooking apparatus, plumbing supplies, chemicals, hardware, and cosmetics for national markets.

Certain California products gained prominence in the postwar era. Among these were well-designed wearing apparel (especially sportswear), jewelry, and casual footwear for women. Los Angeles continued as an automobile assembly depot second only to Detroit. As a tube and tire center the city came to service much of the West. Before the war, smelting and refining of ferrous metals within the state had occurred on a virtually insignificant scale. After 1943, however, Kaiser's Fontana mill in southern California began to process quantities of iron ore from Eagle Mountain and tungsten from the Rand Mountains; by 1952, statewide steel production reached more than 3 million tons annually.

After the war secondary cities, among them Oakland, Stockton, Fresno, and San Diego, received a major share of the industries attracted to California. Included in this pattern by which California's manufacturing centers became more diversified were the new Western plants of such companies as Johns-Mansville, Continental Can, International Harvester, Procter and Gamble, Lever Brothers, Carnation, Alcoa, United States Steel, Bethlehem, and Goodyear. Also newly established in the state were the meat-packing operations of Swift, Armour, and Cudahy, and the food-processing plants of Heinz and Kraft. These were merely a few of the firms which operated extensively in California.

Boom

In the postwar years, California needed more of everything. Most of its new residents sought better houses, and more clothing, food, and services. Wartime facilities had often been flimsy and temporary. Concentrations of apartment houses, homes, schools, and facilities of all sorts had to be built. Business construction boomed. In 1947 alone Los Angeles built 215 new factories; 392 others were constructed that year in the San Francisco Bay area. Economists came to believe that such industrial expansion in California would continue only so long as population growth was maintained.

There seemed, however, to be no end to the migration into the state as the once tranquil paradise became crowded with people and automobiles. Statistics are revealing: In 1940 California had a population of 6,907,387; it ranked fifth among the states. Eight years later, by 1948, with a population of 10,031,000, the state passed Illinois and was contesting with Pennsylvania the right to call itself the nation's second largest state. By 1950, when the population reached 10,586,223 (up 53 per cent from 1940), Californians could decisively speak of their state as the second largest one. California had a birth rate two and a half times its death rate. Despite the noxious fumes of smog, which made city throats rasp and eyes smart, its rate of growth was uncomfortably spectacular. The state's highways became so jammed that it recorded the highest accident rate in the nation, and its schoolrooms grew so crowded that some schools were forced to offer classes in several shifts daily. California nevertheless steadily attracted new millions.

The shortage of housing after 1945 was grave, and the Korean War aggravated conditions further. For years, some families doubled up and even tripled up. Public housing projects, however, were often resisted by community groups who favored privately financed construction. From 1945 onward California experienced one of the great construction booms of all time. In small towns and big cities alike, acres of raw, green lumber framework, and innumerable stacks of bricks and sacks of cement went into thousands of new dwellings. Large-scale tract development occurred at the new postwar cities of Westchester, Lakewood, and West Covina in southern California and at Burlingame and Lafayette in the North. Formerly unincorporated communities, such as Saratoga, Campbell, Monte Sereno, Los Altos, and Milpitas in Santa Clara County, as well as Pacifica and Woodside in San Mateo County, voted to reincorporate as new communities of 25,000 to 50,000 persons.

Transportation

Closely tied to these projects was the development of new highways, including the building of the East Shore and Bayshore freeways. This road construction represented the execution of plans laid before the war. Massive freeway expansion now occurred throughout the state. In 1947, a ten-year highway construction program, to cost $3 million, was voted by the state legislature. By 1955, excluding city streets and federal highways, California had 136,570 miles of roads, of which about half were surfaced. In the early 1950's some 400 highway common carriers and autobus lines were engaged in the transportation of passengers and freight. By then the state was already spending more than $1 million per working day on new freeways and highways designed to relieve traffic congestion. This sum was bound to increase. The federal government also contributed heavily to highway projects. In 1956–1957 the state budget included $237 million for highways. The total auto registration in 1967 soared to 10 million, while highways reached 171,000 miles.

California's highway engineers planned a 12,500-mile statewide freeway system, to be built during the 1960's and 1970's. The estimated cost of this twenty-year project was over $10,000,000,000. A freeway system would link all cities in the state with a population of 5,000 or more persons, and would further serve to tie these cities into the federal highway program. Into the 1960's, Californians continued to spend more than a million dollars per day on highway construction. Automotive industries and services have become a key element in the state, while organizations like the Automobile Club of Southern California have grown politically powerful. By 1967, California had more drivers and cars (nearly a one-to-one ratio of registered drivers to registered vehicles)—about 10 million of each—and consumed more gasoline than any other state in the union. The Los Angeles area was the largest and fastest-growing gas and petroleum fuel market in the world, with 100 companies in competition.

CALIFORNIA FREEWAY INTRICACIES. (By courtesy of the Standard Oil Company of California.)

Meanwhile, traffic congestion grew particularly critical. Los Angeles County alone had 4.5 million vehicles in 1967. Local authorities foresaw 8 million cars, buses, and trucks clogging its streets by that Orwellian year, 1984. Although the legislature in 1964 had approved a Southern California Rapid Transit District (RTD) to plan intra-city transportation, obstacles were numerous. Irate citizens blamed politicians, the lobbying of used and new auto dealers, and the threat of high taxes for unconscionable delays in developing an alternative to transportation by the internal combustion engine.

Freeways continued to be controversial. Their opponents argued that urban land prices and "community values" should take precedence over freeway-user benefits. Supporters of an expanded highway network pointed out that California's metropolitan areas would remain automobile-oriented and that regional mobility was paramount. Whatever the arguments against automobile transportation, by 1966 the state was receiving $350 million per year in federal highway grants. But mass rapid transit by means other than automobiles was still mostly in the planning stage, except at San Francisco, where construction of the Bay Area Rapid Transit District proceeded after public opposition halted freeway construction in 1964.

Californians had made virtually no other provisions for surface movement of their mass society than by automobile. Ernest Marples, British Minister of Transport during the 1960's, called Los Angeles a "concrete desert" whose environment had been brutalized by the automobile. To him, reliance upon the auto as a single-approach solution to mass rapid transit had made that city the world's most horrible example of the consequences of non-experimentation.

San Francisco's freeway revolt resulted in failure to complete the Embarcadero Freeway as the city also struggled to keep the state's Panhandle Freeway out of Golden Gate Park. Freeway revolts also occurred in communities that were conscious of their uniqueness. At Laguna Beach and Pasadena, citizens sought to change an infamous federal and state "cost-benefit" formula by standing up to the state highway commission. Highway planners balanced the immediate cost of a freeway against savings to drivers in travel-time and money. The formula did not measure the social losses to a community when a freeway was rammed through it, bisecting residential areas with too little attention to aesthetic values, slashing through parks, destroying historical sites, cutting through redwood stands, and blighting the landscape. A similar shortsighted philosophy governed proposed dam construction, flood control projects, and other major public works. By stressing efficiency public agencies seemed to rationalize landscape destruction. Occasionally freeways were kept out of beauty spots, as at Laguna Beach, at Prairie Creek in Jedediah Smith Redwoods Park, and at Upper Crystal Springs Lake along the Junipero Serra Freeway—but only after prolonged public clamor.

At San Francisco critics averred that the narcissism and self-celebration of its satisfied citizens formed a barrier to reform in general. Reluctance to change occurred in still other communities. Carmel's residents resisted the installation of sidewalks, even though this meant the loss of mail privileges within village limits. Thus not every Californian, especially the conservationists, agreed that change necessarily meant progress.

Large numbers of harassed taxpayers, despite their disgust with smog and traffic jams, tolerated repeated roadblocks in developing a transportation system viably suited to the future rather than to the past. After 1967, as a conservative mood fastened itself upon California, retrenchment in state and local spending accompanied the same sort of indecision once experienced in water development.

Indeed, one of the black marks against California's record for progressivism has been its refusal to adopt mass rapid transit facilities beyond the automobile, the train, and the airplane. Repeated surveys resulted in unending debate by an affluent but shortsighted citizenry over whether Los Angeles even needed a rapid transit system. The Automobile Club of Southern California continued to oppose rapid transit beyond buses and autos. Major oil companies and auto dealers, too, vigorously discouraged the concept of rapid transit. These critics charged that public transportation systems could not survive upon densities of four to six families per acre, without some form of subsidy. Bond issues have repeatedly been sidelined and construction plans delayed.

At San Francisco, where the courageous revolt against freeways occurred, progress on mass transit has been better. In 1962, while Angelenos merely talked of constructing a 62-mile core line through the center of their city, the supposedly tradition-bound San Franciscans adopted a $725 million Bay Area Rapid Transit System. That year San Francisco, Alameda, and Contra Costa county voters approved construction of an electrified rail system to connect all the cities of the east bay. Tunnels under the bay would link them with subway stations on the peninsula.

At Los Angeles, RTD envisoned a $1.57 billion system. Each

year's delay in construction may cost RTD as much as $100 million, largely because of inflation. Meanwhile, RTD operated only smog-producing buses, which replaced its trolley system. Local rapid transit advocates continued to seek state offshore oil revenues and a percentage of motor vehicle taxes with which to begin construction. At Los Angeles voter approval of bond issues would be required before rapid transit progress materialized. No longer could California's major railroad lines be relied upon to furnish public transportation. One by one each had long since implored the state public utilities commission to suspend their antiquated, unprofitable passenger operations. So long as Angelenos agreed to put up with traffic jams, the delay in seeking alternate solutions to transportation problems would continue.

Civic Reconstruction

Los Angeles and San Francisco both undertook reconstruction of their central civic areas during the 1950's and 1960's. At Los Angeles this amounted to nothing less than face-lifting large areas of the downtown section of the city. Around a central mall that covered 228 acres, new buildings, twenty to forty stories high, were constructed to house federal, state, county and city government offices. This became the largest aggregate of government buildings outside the national capital. Another project was redevelopment, with federal aid, of a blighted slum area called Bunker Hill into a residential and commercial site at an estimated cost of $150 million; it followed years of controversy between the city fathers and residents ousted by the project, mostly elderly and dependent on a small income.

During the decade 1940–1950 the nation's population increased 14.5 per cent while the growth of the Los Angeles area was over three times as great, or 49.8 per cent. The 1960 census showed that Los Angeles had become the second largest city in the nation, with a population that year of 2,479,015. It was thus the only major city in the nation which had not lost residents to its suburbs in the decade preceding. Los Angeles County, with a population count of 6,038,771 persons was, in 1960, the most populous county in the United States. It had become a vast suburbia that multiplied almost yearly. During the late fifties the Los Angeles area grew by as much as 240,000 persons a year.

As the shift from single-family homes to apartments continued, the city skyline changed markedly. Construction became vertical rather than horizontal. Rising land costs made it uneconomical to build single-family dwellings in numerous area⌐ the 1950's a new style of architecture began to convert dɔᴡ. town Los Angeles and the nearby Wilshire district into an area of multi-storied apartments and office buildings, built of "high rise" light-weight metal and much window glass. In 1956, repeal of the 140-foot height limit on buildings was followed by construction of the first modern skyscrapers. An estimated one-third of the nation's architects, incidentally, supposedly live in California.

At San Francisco in the 1950's the process of building skyward was accelerated. On the bay shore of the lower peninsula the city built Candlestick Park, new home of the former New York Giants baseball club. Plans were also made in the fifties to construct tunnels under San Francisco Bay to handle the increasing flow of traffic in and out of the traffic-clogged city. In 1955 the James Lick Freeway, bisecting the city with a system of viaducts and overpasses, first opened to traffic. San Francisco's population grew almost imperceptibly in the postwar years. The decade 1940–1950 registered a larger growth for the city than did the following one. San Francisco's population in 1950 was 825,000, and in the next decade the city followed the national pattern of urban population loss. The city's hinterland population had, however, grown spectacularly. As compared to Los Angeles, which possessed room for expansion, San Francisco, confined to a peninsula, was forced to utilize its land space carefully.

Continued Defense Spending:
The Korean and Vietnam Wars

Continuing heavy defense expenditures by the federal government underwrote a large share of California's postwar construction. Defense activities that had been canceled after World War II were renewed as a result of the Korean War. After 1950, the manufacture of military aircraft became a more permanent business. A new round of government orders opened up branch plants of the major aircraft companies that had been closed since World War II. California increasingly possessed what amounted to a "nongovernmental civil service," that is, a large group of aircraft, missile component, and instrument workers who had come to rely upon government contracts for their jobs. This made for employment vulnerability whenever defense expenditures were cut. The continuing "cold war" with the Soviet

Union, however, indicated a relatively steady need for military production. Military personnel, whether in uniform or in civilian attire, played a large part in keeping California's economy buoyant.

But prosperity continued even after the end of the Korean War. Civilian employment in manufacturing has almost doubled since 1950. Southern California accounts for approximately three-quarters of this employment. In the five years from 1955 to 1960 the state continued to increase its percentage of the nation's total personal income (from 9.8 to 10.8 per cent) at a time when the other large states, including New York, Pennsylvania, Ohio, and Illinois, showed slight decreases.

The establishment in 1954 of the Air Force's Space Technology Laboratory at Inglewood and Canoga Park, and the founding of the I.B.M. Research Laboratory at San Jose and of Astronautics Inc. in San Diego, further immersed California in missile, rocket, and outer-space research and technology. A significant event of the late 1950's was the activation of the nation's first privately-financed nuclear power plant at Vallecitos. At the same time, the new Pacific Missile Range, extending several hundred miles along the California coast and far into the Pacific Ocean, became the scene of mounting military activity. A major launching site was located in this area, at the Vandenberg Air Force Base, just north of Lompoc. In a few years Vandenberg Air Force Base changed Lompoc from a rural town of only 6,500, concerned with mining diatomaceous soil and flower raising, to a city of 30,000 persons. Vandenberg became a rocketry center that also transformed nearby Santa Maria.

That segment of the state's industry which came to depend upon defense contracts received correspondingly greater federal supervision. Acquisition of too many such government contracts implied a loss of local independence; acquisition of too few of them, a decline in prosperity. The new term "Federal City" came to be applied to the Los Angeles area, where a close relationship between its economy and the central government flourished in the 1960's. Critics averred that industry in that municipality was more responsive to instructions and news from Washington than to word from Sacramento. California business and municipal leaders became involved in numerous classified negotiations with the national capital. Many of them insisted that California's paramount position in defense production not be sacrificed and that lucrative government contracts not be lost to East Coast competition. As a major center of science and technology the state's position was second to none. Here was the largest complex of military production in the entire nation. The Los Angeles region became better known for its missiles than for its once fabled movie premières. Several hundred companies, which employed more than 100,000 persons, settled within a mile of its international airport.

Each time the pattern of expenditures for weapons is altered in the direction of more arms for conventional warfare, this does not reassure California planners. Manufacturers in the Midwest and East have experience in producing vehicles, ordnance, and "soft goods," and in some cases boast a competitive advantage over the West Coast. The decision in the 1960's to award the contract for the TFX all-service fighter to a Texas corporation and the cloudy future of manned bombers, and of tactical and support aircraft, darkened the outlook for California's aircraft industry. Manufacture of commercial jet transports has not proved the boon to employment and profits that many expected. Also disquieting to Californians was the clamor raised in Congress over concentration of defense and space spending in relatively few states. Since California has taken a long lead over other states as a defense contractor of complex weapons systems, it has become a target for critics of concentration.

In 1962 California garnered $5.9 billion worth, or 23.9 per cent, of United States government military contracts. Some 54 per cent of California's military business was in missiles and 14 per cent in aircraft. From 1958 to 1962 about 40 per cent of the $6.1 billion in prime contracts for military experimental, developmental, test, and research work went to California. The presence of a "university-industrial" complex was an essential catalyst in building a sophisticated engineering and manufacturing force. By 1968 more than one-third of California's industrial production was in the defense and space fields.

California's former "defense" industry was changing and inventive. In the early 1960's North American's El Segundo plant developed the prototypes of the B-70 bomber, the most powerful yet designed. This same company produced the X-15 experimental supersonic rocket plane as well as the guidance and control systems of the Boeing Company's Minuteman missile. North American's Rocketdyne Division powered the ascent of 36 out of 40 American space probes, to mid-1961. Rocketdyne also developed the H-1 Saturn engine. The company delivered Hound Dog air-to-surface missiles to the Air Force and contributed to the design of the Tiros weather satellites. North American's Autonetics Division came to coordinate its efforts closely with those of the National Aeronautic and Space Administration, of

Caltech's Jet Propulsion Laboratory, and of the Space Technology Laboratories, operated for the Air Force by Thompson, Ramo, Wooldridge, Inc. North American became the prime contractor of the Apollo moonship.

The Lockheed corporation of Burbank and Sunnyvale, like North American, remained active both in missile and aircraft production. Its F-104 Starfighters were used in Canada, West Germany, Italy, Japan, the Netherlands, and Belgium. Lockheed, in addition to producing the Polaris for the United States Navy, was the prime contractor for the Midas system of detecting ICBM (Intercontinental Ballistic Missile) firings. Lockheed played a part as well in the development of the Agena and Polaris missiles and in the Samos "spy-in-the-sky" satellite.

At Santa Monica the Douglas enterprises manufactured the Thor-Able booster rocket, with the aid of the Aerojet General Corporation of Azusa and North American's Rocketdyne Division. Douglas also worked on the Nike-Zeus and Skybolt ballistic missiles. Douglas technicians were regularly stationed at launching sites at Cape Canaveral, Florida, at Vandenberg Air Force Base, and in Britain. The Douglas company also continued to manufacture its DC-8 jet airliner. At San Diego, Convair (later General Dynamics), builder of the F-106 Delta Dart and the 880 jet-airliner, also grew into a missile-designing organization. Its prize product was the Atlas ICBM, a missile with a range of almost 10,000 miles.

As time passed, key positions once available in the aircraft industry no longer existed. In fact, it had become in large measure a missiles industry.

Prior to the Vietnam War, California experienced occasional fears of an economic slump. Explosive growth had been replaced by moderate expansion in selected segments of the economy. Construction and manufacturing declined, unemployment rose, and most of the growth in jobs that did occur was in service-producing industries. To achieve full employment California needed an estimated 50,000 new jobs annually. A growing percentage of the labor force was occupied by eighteen- and nineteen-year-old postwar babies entering a hyper-technological labor market. Yet, after 1965, no state exceeded California in total personal income. That year California surpassed New York in such income (this figure increased 39.5 per cent to almost $60 billion between 1960 and 1965). Despite California's claim to a per capita income of 20 per cent above the national average, a feeling of uneasiness persisted among business leaders. Consumer prices continued to rise and government expenditures grew enormously throughout the early 1960's. Any cutback in defense-space contracts would leave the economy vulnerable. A kind of secondary civil service force had unconsciously been created by government spending.

The Vietnam War, especially after 1965, helped to make the aerospace industry a permanent feature of California's economic life. In southern California that year, four out of every ten manufacturing workers were employed in the defense-space field. It had evolved from equipment manufacturing into a research format that provided long-range military planning plus hardware for both the defense industry and outer space explorations. By the mid-1960's about 50 per cent of the contract dollars awarded by the National Aeronautics and Space Administration went to California firms. Some 60 per cent of the sales of such firms were attributable to their research and development projects.

More than 200 electronics firms have set up plants in the peninsular suburbs south of San Francisco alone, including most of the blue chips among "black box" makers: IBM, ITT, Ampex, Western Electric, Raytheon, Remington Rand, Sylvania, Sperry-Rand, Zenith, Motorola, Philco, and General Electric.

Economic Growth

The burgeoning needs of California's youthful population stimulated sales of housing, furniture, and appliances. By the late 1960's, more and more invested wealth, corporate and real estate, came to be centered in the West, as the state moved beyond economic regional domination into a pattern of national leadership.

With less than 10 per cent of the United States population, California had 11 per cent of the total national income, or about $69.1 billion in 1967. That year only four other states, led by New York, topped California in per capita income. Only New York State paid higher per capita state and local taxes (California, $395.27; New York, $409.94).

Internationally, too, California was economically important. If it were a separate nation, California would be the sixth largest economic force in the world. In 1967 the state's "gross product" amounted to $88.1 billion, a figure exceeded only by the United States, Russia, West Germany, France, and Japan. That year California's "gross product" was 8 per cent greater than Great Britain's gross national product. California's "GNP" is triple that of Communist China's, and the state's annual budget also ranks well above those of most foreign countries, exceeded only by the budgets of major nations.

California's foreign import and export figures have climbed sharply in recent years, making it the leading export state in the nation. Principal exports include aircraft and aircraft parts, armaments, raw cotton, refined petroleum products, industrial machinery, chemicals, iron ore concentrates, and agricultural products. Leading imports are motor vehicles, telecommunication apparatus, crude petroleum, iron and steel plates, newsprint, frozen meats, and such manufactured articles as musical instruments, toys, and jewelry.

Postwar Politics

When President Eisenhower called Governor Earl Warren to Washington in 1953 to become Chief Justice of the United States, an appointment that he was to hold for many years, California's "Warren era" of politics came to a close. In the 1948 national election Warren had been the running mate of that lusterless Republican presidential candidate New York Governor Thomas E. Dewey. Despite that unsuccessful campaign, Warren's nonpartisan appeal won the Republicans the governorship again in 1950. Governor Warren, as has been seen, was attractive to city workers, middle-class professionals, independent liberals, and conservative farmers alike. By avoiding extremes of either right or left he gained the support of both management and labor. Warren, although he was the head of the Republican Party in the state, appointed Democrats to public office and built his administration upon the talents and loyalties of both Republicans and Democrats. Thus the Warren administration secured the enactment of many of the welfare measures which California urgently needed in order to cope with its heavy influx of population. Warren pressed successfully for reform of the state workmen's compensation system, prison conditions, and old age pension standards. Only on the enactment of health insurance was Warren blocked, and then only through the efforts of the powerful California Medical Association lobby. He liked to refer to welfare measures as progressive and middle-of-the-road, rather than as liberal.

However, when Warren moved to Washington in 1953, he left a relatively weak Republican party organization behind in California. The state central committee was unwieldy and could not exert control as Warren had done. Sectional rivalries were revived, and these grew so serious that statewide political cooperation became almost impossible. At this point three ambitious Republican stalwarts assumed prominence in the politics of the state.

Lieutenant Governor Goodwin J. Knight, a party regular who had expressed scant support of Warren's liberal policies, succeeded him in the governorship. Knight in time became a moderate bidder for the labor vote who supported such social measures as increases in unemployment insurance, workmen's compensation benefits, aid to the aged, and construction of new health and mental hygiene facilities. Knight remained in office for five years, until 1958.

The second Republican leader to step into the California political limelight was Senator William F. Knowland. In 1945 Warren had appointed the thirty-seven-year-old Knowland to the United States Senate to fill the post left by the death of Hiram Johnson. Knowland was reelected to office in 1952 and kept the senatorship until he decided to run for governor in 1958. Knowland was vastly more conservative than Knight. During much of the 1950's Knowland was Senate Republican floor leader for the Eisenhower administration. However, after the death of Senator Robert A. Taft, he frequently opposed the administration in both domestic and international affairs, and his militant support of the Chinese nationalist regime gained him the half serious title of "the senator from Formosa."

The third politician to inherit part of Warren's power was Richard Milhous Nixon. His background was more varied than Knowland's or Knight's, and in both state and national politics he rose to greater power. Nixon was born at Yorba Linda, and graduated from Whittier College.

In 1946 those party leaders who had traditionally opposed Warren selected Nixon, then a young Navy veteran, to run in a controversial campaign to win the seat of liberal Congressman Jerry Voorhis, the incumbent Democrat in Nixon's home district. From the beginning, Nixon had the support of the conservative wing of the Republican Party in the state. Nixon won, and in 1950 he ran for the Senate against Helen Gahagan Douglas, wife of film star Melvyn Douglas. The Democrats accused Nixon of unfair tactics in both of these campaigns. Many felt that Nixon had repeatedly seemed to suggest that those opposing him were lacking in patriotism and in anti-communist conviction. This sentiment, just or not, was to mar Nixon's reputation for years to come. Nevertheless, Nixon developed a staunch corps of adherents, and became a national figure, known especially for his stand on matters of internal security.

No issue of the postwar years aroused greater tension within California than did the fear of communist infiltration conflicting with the constitutional obligation to preserve civil liberties. This was the McCarthy period of wholesale, unproven accusations of treason against persons in public office. Nixon's career was furthered considerably by the passage of the restrictive Mundt-Nixon Immigration Act and by his role in the startling trial and conviction of former State Department aide Alger Hiss for perjury, in connection with accusations of espionage. State Senator Jack B. Tenney headed a committee that claimed to have detected numerous active communists both in California's government and educational circles. A current remedy for uprooting subversives in public life was to require teachers and government employees to sign a "loyalty oath." The resulting atmosphere inevitably encouraged public timorousness and conformity.

For several years, beginning in 1949, a test-oath controversy raged on the campuses of the University of California. Numerous professors who refused to sign a non-communist oath imposed upon them by the regents of the university were dismissed. Ultimately the state supreme court ruled this oath invalid, on the ground that the power to require it belonged to the legislature, not to the university regents. In 1950, the legislature's Levering Act required an even more elaborate oath of all state employees. In the meantime the University of California had lost some of its most talented and independent-minded faculty members to other colleges and universities. In 1958, another California loyalty oath was struck down by the United States Supreme Court. This law, passed by the California legislature, would have required a non-communist oath from religious groups and from all veterans who sought tax exemptions. In recent years, however, the "loyalty" issue has attracted less interest, but the confrontation between university faculty and regents remained largely unresolved. From time to time this tension threatened to erupt into public debate.

A different type of factionalism continued to plague the unity of California's Republican Party. Its three stalwarts were never quite able to harmonize their differences. From 1952 until 1960 Vice President Nixon, as second ranking member of the Eisenhower administration, occupied the most prestigious position of any California Republican. He still had to cope, however, with the combined political power of Knowland and Knight. Operating within the state, they kept closer touch with California politics than Nixon.

Nixon, Knowland, and Knight all benefited from an almost solidly Republican press. Throughout the state's history its Republican newspapers had played a vigorous part in election campaigns, acting as a virtual arm of the party. Joseph Knowland, father of Senator Knowland, owned the Oakland *Tribune,* which consistently threw its support to Knowland's son in every political campaign. Similarly the Los Angeles *Times* gave strong support to at least one and sometimes all of the three Republican leaders. The Hearst chain of newspapers had usually been conservative Republican in outlook since the early New Deal period. The San Francisco *Chronicle,* although the most liberal major newspaper in California, ordinarily supported the Republicans at election times. The Sacramento, Modesto and Fresno *Bees* were generally independent newspapers. Thus, Los Angeles, San Francisco, San Diego, Oakland, and Fresno—the largest cities in the state—remained without actively Democratic papers. At Santa Barbara, publisher Thomas Storke's peppery *News-Press* generally took up the cudgels for the Democrats. The "big three" of California's more than 700 newspapers are the San Francisco *Chronicle,* Oakland *Tribune,* and Los Angeles *Times.*

The three Republican leaders also benefited from the fortuitous political device of cross-filing. From 1913 until 1959, when the privilege was abolished, any candidate could file for the nomination of more than one party. Through 1952, his party affiliation was not even printed on the party primary ballots. In California, where Democratic registration has traditionally been heavier than Republican, cross-filing worked in favor of the Republican candidate. The majority of the successful candidates for public office captured both nominations. Campaigning as a non-partisan, any candidate who won the nomination of both parties (for example, Governor Warren in 1946) could capitalize upon the large proportion of voters who were essentially independent. This tended to produce dull elections in which candidates avoided controversial issues. Too often each side sought to show conservative voters that its candidate was not too liberal while demonstrating to liberals that he was not too conservative either. Warren, Nixon, Knight, and later Governor Edmund G. ("Pat") Brown, to a degree, followed this pattern of campaigning.

Candidates also relied heavily upon professional public-relations firms to publicize their campaigns. California is especially known for the activity of such organizations, whose purpose is to use mass media to develop public sentiment in favor of a particular candidate or ballot proposal. Among public-relations firms specializing in electioneering the best known is Campaigns Incorporated.

Run since the 1930's by Whitaker and Baxter, it advertised itself as the first political campaign management organization in the United States. Offshoots of this firm included Baus and Ross as well as the Keene Associates—retained in 1952 and 1956 by presidential candidate Adlai Stevenson's forces in California. During the 1964 California primaries, New York Governor Nelson A. Rockefeller hired Spencer-Roberts and Associates of Los Angeles to manage his campaign. Baus and Ross also handled the 1964 California presidential primary of Barry Goldwater and the 1966 gubernatorial campaign of "Californians for Brown," a moderate Republican group. That year actor Ronald Reagan virtually turned his gubernatorial campaign over to public-relations experts (Spencer-Roberts-Haffner) with excellent results. Such firms have devised many of the campaign posters, slogans, and clichés of California's recent political history.

While the election activities of public-relations firms have been subject to question, there existed in postwar California a much less excusable variety of political lobbying. During the forties and early fifties Artie Samish, the "Mr. Big" of California politics, was influential at the state capital. Samish ran what some writers called "The Third House" of the California legislature. He became the spokesman for various truck and bus lines, liquor and beer interests, race tracks, and for many confidential clients who paid fat representation fees. In public, Samish treated the entire legislature with contempt, romping arrogantly through its halls as though he had prerogatives superior to those of its members. In private, his activities were equally effective and considerably less scrupulous.

Samish was finally exposed in a series of articles in the magazine *Collier's* during 1949, after which a special session of the legislature convened to examine lobbying practices. Unfortunately, basic reforms of lobbying were still not adopted, but the legislature that year authorized the registration and examination of all lobbyists. In 1953, Samish and his staff were convicted of evading federal income taxes. But the jailing of "Mr. Big" did not end high-pressure lobbying in California.

Not, however, to be likened to Samish are nearly four hundred organizations represented at the capitol during each legislative session. These pressure groups include organized business, labor, agriculture and the professions. They have replaced individual corporations like the Southern Pacific as new accumulations of political power in California. Their very number makes it unlikely that any one organization can effectively dominate state politics.

Recapture of California by the Democrats, 1958–1966

In 1958 the longstanding Republican political hegemony in California came to an abrupt end. That year an imprudent political squabble occurred among the Republicans. Senator Knowland sought the governorship, and, in effect, forced Governor Knight, who wanted to run for re-election, out of the gubernatorial race. After Knowland entered the contest for the governorship, powerful party pressure was exerted upon Knight to withdraw from the race and to seek Knowland's seat in the Senate. Many Republican voters were disillusioned by the way in which Knight was pushed aside by the Knowland faction of the party. Republican unity was temporarily shattered. The two Republican candidates found themselves actually supporting different sides of so vital an issue as the controversial "right to work," or anti-union shop, proposal. Knowland favored the measure and Knight opposed it. Democratic state Attorney General Brown was given an unexpected advantage in his battle for the governorship with Knowland. In fact, the Knight-Knowland quarrel forfeited the election of both men.

Like Warren before him, Brown had been state attorney general. He too had conducted nonpartisan political campaigns and avoided overly close association with his own Democratic Party. He was then a vigorous candidate, a native son, and a Catholic. During the gubernatorial race Brown slashed away at Knowland's ultraconservatism. While Knowland bull-headedly stuck to the outdated open-shop issue, Brown spoke of liberal reform and attracted thousands of new voters. He garnered not only the support of his own party but that of many independents tired of Republican rule, and was swept by a landslide into the governorship.

For the first time since 1888 the state legislature was firmly Democratic. Although there had been a Democratic majority of registered voters since 1934, sometimes numbering more than a million, California had elected Republican governors for more than fifty years, except for the Olson regime, elected in 1938. A number of ingredients combined with the Republican maladroitness to give the Democrats their 1958 victory. Many new Democratic voters had moved into the state. An infectious enthusiasm among young Democrats helped overcome strong Republican Party financial support of its candidates. A new California Democratic Council also generated peak interest within that party and reinvigorated it by a grass roots door-to-door campaign. In addition, the Hearst press and the San Francisco *Chronicle* in 1958 withheld their support of Senator Knowland for the governorship.

Governor Brown's election brought to California's Democratic Party responsibilities such as it had not known in recent times. Brown was immediately faced with controversial statewide problems, including traffic and smog control, water development, and a full-scale debate over capital punishment. The latter had become particularly heated because of the case of Caryl Chessman, the "red light bandit." Chessman's execution had been delayed eight times in twelve years. During this period he argued much of his own defense, claimed mistrials, wrote best-selling books about the injustice of capital punishment, and presented Governor Brown with a first-class legal dilemma. His protracted imprisonment caused worldwide criticism to be focused on the inconsistencies of American legal process and in particular on the state's death penalty. On May 2, 1960 Chessman finally died in San Quentin's gas chamber, after Brown refused him a last stay of execution. Brown personally opposed capital punishment but, in the absence of a state law terminating the practice, the governor saw no alternative but to send Chessman to his death. Smarting from criticism over his handling of this case, Brown called an extraordinary session of the legislature to debate the death penalty. The legislature, however, refused to revise the state's laws on this matter. Chessman's case cost Brown considerable popularity.

A period of fiscal reckoning coincided with the advent to power of Governor Brown. Failure to enact necessary new taxes, and temporizing with state finances by falling back on the state's "rainy day" fund, could not go on forever. To meet the state's $2.5 billion budget and to avert a treasury deficit, the legislature in 1959 increased personal income, inheritance, bank, corporation, and beer taxes. Added to new taxes on horse racing and cigarettes, these measures provide $222.7 million in additional revenue, or 18.5 per cent more than was anticipated from tax sources existing prior to the increases. Under the governor's goading, the legislature enacted the biggest spending and taxing program in the history of the state, raising taxes enough to trim a threatened $201 million annual deficit to $5 million.

In 1960, Vice President Nixon became the nominee of the Republican Party for the presidency. Governor Brown figured prominently in that election. At the Democratic National Convention held in Los Angeles' new Sports Arena, he helped to win the presidential nomination for Massachusetts Senator John F. Kennedy; not all the California delegates followed Brown's leadership and the galleries were packed with vociferous Stevenson supporters. Kennedy went on to fight for the state's political allegiance, campaigning forcefully in California, as did Nixon. Both candidates counted heavily upon California's thirty-two electoral votes. Although Nixon, as a native son, won the state by a narrow margin, his victory proved insufficient to prevent Kennedy's election.

Nixon was, however, encouraged sufficiently by the closeness of the voting to rally Republican forces for the California gubernatorial campaign of 1962. In the primary campaign he successfully discouraged two Republican rivals—former Governor Knight and the ultraconservative Assemblyman Joseph Shell. After winning the primary, Nixon went on to run against incumbent Governor Brown.

At stake in the Nixon–Brown race was Nixon's political future; a failure to win his native state would impair the 49-year-old Republican's chances of remaining a national figure. The campaign was bitter. Nixon accused Brown of being less than hard on Communists and of bungling the administration of the state, and pledged the death penalty for "big-time dope peddlers." He promised to drop "chiselers" from the state welfare rolls, held out the hope of lower taxes and reduced state expenditures, and promised greater efficiency at Sacramento. Brown, however, proudly defended his record on such matters as education, water development, and welfare. Both sides brought lawsuits to stop the circulation of pamphlets described as "smears." All indications were that the election would be close, and experts declined to predict the winner. Nixon lost by a margin six times wider than that by which he had carried the state against Kennedy in 1960. After the election Nixon assailed press coverage of his campaign, although he had received the editorial support of many more of California's large newspapers than had Brown. Thus California voters removed from the scene the third and most prominent of the three Republicans who had followed Warren into state and national leadership.

The 1964 election saw California's Republican Party badly split. A hot contest was waged between its conservatives who supported Arizona's Senator Barry Goldwater and moderates who favored the leader of the liberal or moderate Republicans, Senator Thomas Kuchel, Republican Whip in the United States Senate. He had been appointed to fill the Senate vacancy created by the election of Richard Nixon to the Eisenhower vice presidency. The onetime leader of the conservatives, former Senator Knowland, headed a huge volunteer organization in 1964 which rang doorbells and argued both against "Big Government" and the Republican "Eastern Establishment." After Goldwater had won the California primary, his bandwagon picked up momentum and he went on to the July, 1964, Republican National Convention in San Francisco to capture an overwhelming first-ballot nomination.

The 1964 election also resulted in a split among the Democrats. This break was, however, less involved with philosophies and more with personalities. During the primary, State Controller Alan Cranston campaigned against President Kennedy's former press secretary Pierre Salinger, seeking the Democratic nomination for the Senate post held by ailing incumbent Senator Clair Engle. Cranston gained the endorsement of Governor Brown and of the California Council of Democratic Clubs (CDC), but Salinger had the backing of Assembly Speaker Jesse Unruh and of Mrs. Jacqueline Kennedy. When Senator Engle died before the election, Governor Brown appointed Salinger to fill the unexpired term. 1n 1964, however, Salinger lost his Senate seat to George Murphy, a movie figure with virtually no governmental experience. Although Californians voted unanimously for President Lyndon Johnson—Kennedy's Vice President before the assassination—California's Democrats were to be unrepresented in the United States Senate during the Eighty-Eighth Congress.

A major factor that symbolized the dissension within California's Democratic Party was the role of the CDC, which had been formed after 1952 by a dedicated group of young Stevenson backers shocked by the defeat of their idol. Associated with the party, but not officially part of it, CDC felt free to gather in annual conventions and to endorse its own candidates. It built up a powerful statewide organization during the middle 1950's, then began to disintegrate, but not before clashing with old-line party officials, including Governor Brown himself. Brown had been criticized for his timid leadership of the party and for allowing factionalism to develop. This fratricidal in-fighting resembled the blood-letting that had wrecked California's Republican Party in 1958. The state's independent maverick Democrats included Samuel William Yorty, who had been elected mayor of Los Angeles in 1961 and who had bolted the party in 1960 to back Nixon against Kennedy. Assembly Speaker Jesse Unruh, like Yorty, had ambitions for higher office and became a kind of lone wolf who guarded his powerful role in Sacramento. Alan Cranston, state controller, for a time president of the CDC, posed a real threat to Unruh. Eventually these and other Democratic malcontents, unchecked by Governor Brown, found themselves with a fractured party on their hands—a party that stood against the growing conservative public mood that expressed itself in such crucial matters as anti-open-housing proposals (Proposition 14), part of the so-called "white backlash" against Negro agitation. The CDC leadership also split with Governor Brown over the Vietnam War as he insisted upon backing President Johnson's pro-war position.

Republican Resurgence, 1967—

California has been a political mystery since the mid-1930's. Although Democrats have a substantial edge in registration over Republicans (in 1968 the margin was about three to two), the Democrats, due to weak party organization, local conservatism, and poor financial support, have been relatively unsuccessful in electing candidates. While the Democrats controlled California politics from 1958 to 1966, the state has been in Republican hands during most of its history. Indeed, from 1950 to 1967 the eleven western states were governed by Republican administrations 69.4 per cent of the time.

The new wave of California's conservatism, which actually began to appear in 1964, had a variety of causes. Some analysts maintained that California's old midwestern farm population, once drawn to the state by the promise of the good life, had become terrified at the thought of political change. Other observers believed that the special strength of conservatism in southern California was caused by a significant self-made merchant mentality. This "new wealth" did not want its economic status threatened by change. The extreme-rightist presidential hopeful, Goldwater, benefited from such defensive feelings, especially in Los Angeles and Orange Counties, during the state primary victory over New York Governor Nelson Rockefeller in 1964. That year staunch conservatives had retained control of the California Republican Assembly, as well as of California's Young Republican organization. The right wing also directed the United Republicans of California, even after Goldwater's million-vote defeat by President Johnson in the general election. Actually, Goldwater carried only one of the eleven western states in 1964, his native Arizona. Yet conservative strength in California that November was reflected in the passage of Proposition 14, a measure designed to blunt the Rumford Fair Housing Act and to deny equal residential rights for Negroes.

California's gubernatorial election of 1966 was held in an atmosphere of mounting concern over an increased crime rate, high property taxes, and civil disturbances—including riots in the Negro sections of large cities and student rebellions at the state university in Berkeley. Racial tension and fiscal irresponsibility lurked incipiently in the background as Governor Brown sought a third term and actor Ronald Reagan assumed the role of non-professional politician. Although possessing an unusual record, Brown projected the image of a tired and ineffective campaigner. Reagan, instead, seemed youngish, confident, proud of his political inexperience, and he made excellent use of money provided by conservative businessmen to finance numerous television appearances. Reagan, like former Hollywood personality Senator George Murphy, and former child star Shirley Temple Black, who also sought office, had obvious "stage presence." A veteran of more than fifty motion pictures, in which he had frequently played the role of the "nice guy who doesn't get the girl," Reagan projected an easy, relaxed manner of self-possession before television cameras. Although considered the political heir of Goldwater, he managed to convince the electorate that he was a moderate genuinely aroused by the dangers of massive government social welfare programs. While the governor, the assembly speaker, and the CDC warred within the Democratic camp, Reagan quieted the old disputes inside California's Republican Party.

Republican moderates in 1966 were, however, angered that Senator Thomas Kuchel did not intervene within his own state party to construct a center-conservative consensus in opposition to the party's strong "reactionary" wing. Ultra-conservatives maintained control of the party apparatus. Despite the continuing Democratic advantage in registration, Reagan, originally identified with ultra-conservative causes, demonstrated a broad appeal that crossed party lines. He swept into office, defeating Brown by nearly one million votes, a surprisingly large margin, and his party captured all top state elective offices except that of attorney general. The Democrats, however, maintained narrow majorities in the newly apportioned legislature. In 1967 the Republican Party not only controlled the state administration but also both United States senatorships.

Confusion continued to be a major motif of California politics. The same electorate which in 1964 had given President Johnson a three to two victory over Goldwater, and which had refused to send Richard Nixon to Sacramento in 1962, had voted four to three for Reagan over Brown in 1966. Despite pre-election polls to the contrary, an anti-obscenity statute, the so-called CLEAN Amendment, was soundly defeated. In 1966 the voters also passed a constitutional revision package, which allowed annual legislative sessions of unlimited length and permitted the legislature to set its own salaries.

Reagan began his term of office by charging that the Democrats had left behind a severe economic crisis in state financing. Voters had forgotten how Governor Brown had made much the same charges against the Republicans in 1958. Now Reagan proposed budget slashes of 10 per cent in all departments, thereby causing a storm of demonstrations by students and teachers, as well as mental health and welfare advocates. Reagan's campaign promises had included systematic tax reform, especially for the elderly and for business, and voters waited patiently for the tax relief their new governor promised. In order not to raise taxes the new administration hoped to make government more frugal. When the governor proposed a sales tax on food, Democrats reacted furiously. Some voters were, however, pleased that he opposed witholding state income taxes from pay checks.

Reagan's critics found his program to be essentially a negative, reactionary one, and mumbled that he represented that predictable failure of leadership for which society occasionally yearns. Despite a movement, in 1968, to recall the governor, there was no use denying the general popularity of Reagan's entrenchment moves. What seemed like anti-intellectualism to academics was applauded by the public at large. The new governor's welfare and education cuts, especially in his first budget, were deeply resented by representatives of those professions. As a start Reagan proposed to slice $40 million from the $491 million requested by the state college and university systems for 1967–1968. Educators remonstrated that the overall effect of such cuts was to injure "quality education" in a state where its standards were high. Next, Reagan hoped to do away with the unique student freedom from tuition fees in California's university and state college system. He proposed charging $400 yearly tuition per student, in addition to fees already collected. Opponents argued that the governor's retrenchment maneuvers would deprive the poor of a college education. He contended that most college students came from middle-income families, and the public should not be taxed to subsidize them. Reagan settled, temporarily, for no increase in existing charges, but subsequently both the state university regents and state college trustees moved toward higher charges. Eventually the governor also restored part of his original cuts, although later budget requests for education continued to be severely curtailed. Among the state's education officials, Reagan enjoyed the backing of the strongly conservative superintendent of public instruction, Max Rafferty. As members of the university board of regents, both men favored the ouster in 1967 of university President Clark Kerr. Following disagreements over budgetary and other matters, President Kerr's advocates looked upon his firing as a kind of "sacrificial cleansing" toward erasing discord on the university's Berkeley campus. Later, Chancellors Franklin Murphy of UCLA and John Galbraith of San Diego also resigned, as did President John Summerskill of San Francisco State College.

Late in 1967 California's new governor proposed to trim 3,700 jobs from state public assistance agencies and to close eight mental health clinics in urban areas. A veritable uproar greeted the curtailment of mental health facilities; this remained the most sensitive of Reagan's economy issues. Whenever protests mounted, Reagan showed a tendency to hold back temporarily from announced courses of action. Critics like State Assembly Speaker Jesse Unruh, therefore, called Reagan's administration one that governed by crisis. Ultimately, Reagan did effect significant fiscal cuts, but, in the case of the state's mental health program, he relented.

One of the biggest Reagan economy targets was in funds for medical care of the elderly, the indigent, and other welfare recipients. He proposed slashes of up to $210 million in such programs and also called for changes in eligibility requirements and the lessening of various public services. As he had stated during his campaign, Reagan hoped to squeeze fraud and abuse out of California's welfare system. He feared the possibility of perpetuating poverty "by substituting a permanent dole for a paycheck," a longstanding preoccupation of California's far right.

So economy-minded was the Reagan administration that a new governor's mansion went unbuilt, although he called the old one such a firetrap that he refused to live in it. Toll collectors on bridges were forced to surrender revolvers, which were then sold. Travel by state employees was seriously curtailed as were the use of teletype and telephone services and the purchase of major equipment and supplies. The governor's office suspended publication of road maps, brochures, pamphlets, and a park and recreation magazine. It was announced that some $50,000 was saved in typewriter ribbons and $2 million in the state's phone bill during the first few months of Reagan's governorship. The governor also sold a state-owned airplane. Mostly, his economies were effected by item vetoes in appropriation bills.

Reagan ran up against the momentum of state growth as well as ingrained and costly governmental programs. He had relatively little success getting his economies through the state legislature, which stood fast on welfare and medical cuts in particular. Reagan continued to backtrack on occasion. Early in 1968 he first announced a deficit of $210 million in the "Medi-Cal" program, only to admit later that the alleged deficit had been paid and that a closer audit of "Medi-Cal's" finances had turned up a surplus of $30 million.

The new administration was stymied on matters other than economic. The Democrats in 1967 controlled the state assembly by 42 to 38 votes and the senate by 21 to 19. Reagan's conservative backers in the legislature laid great stress on public order. In 1967 he proposed six bills to deal with crime control, only one of which was enacted—a law that tripled the minimum penalty for rape, robbery, or burglary in cases where victims were injured. A stronger gun-control law passed the legislature in part because of a national mood toward such controls; also because a "Black Panther" group, armed with unloaded weapons, scared the legislature witless by bursting into that body while the law was being debated. True to his promises, the governor tried but failed to gain repeal of the controversial open-housing law. It will be recalled that voters, too, favored repeal in 1964 but that the state supreme court held the referendum invalid. Later, the legislature voted down the repeal measure. During his first year Governor Reagan also failed to gain passage of tighter obscenity laws, or the establishment of county welfare fraud units, or the institution of a merit system for judges, and reorganization of the state government along his own lines.

For several years Reagan remained popular. He was increas-

THE GOVERNOR'S MANSION, SACRAMENTO. (California State Library.)

ingly mentioned as a serious contender for the Republican presidential nomination in 1968, despite the opposition of more liberal Eastern leaders within his party. Reagan allowed his name to be placed in nomination at the Miami Beach Republican convention that year. As compared to Nixon, who received the presidential nomination, he made a relatively weak showing; this despite elaborate pre-convention preparations by powerful backers. Originally Reagan's insistence on state party unity supposedly led to his agreement to run as a favorite-son candidate that year.

Ultra-right-wing critics charged that Reagan achieved unity among California's Republicans by opportunistic coddling of all wings of the party. Outright critics, instead, saw an administration filled with businessmen who served on "task forces" and commissions without pay while urging the loosening of state controls over business. (In 1968 some 250 businessmen completed a survey for Reagan on efficiency and cost control, recommending sweeping economies designed to save $658 million over a period of years.)

When farm labor grew short during the 1967 harvest, the governor, echoing his view that farmers, businessmen, and government should work together, sent convicts into the field to help harvest crops. He also ordered use of employable welfare recipients where labor shortages existed. Labor, naturally, called such moves a subsidy to growers. Such controversies were symptomatic of California's most unusual gubernatorial administration of recent times.

By the 1960's a new voting pattern emerged in California. Two political extremes—the far right and the far left—became widely developed in the state. Hyper-conservative, retired elderly folk, yearning for the simplicity of earlier days, disliked "big government" and looked distrustfully at some of the young and restless "human tumble-weeds" who, without money and responsibility, flooded into the state. The John Birch Society had no more fertile seedbed than California, although, conversely, it has been attacked vigorously by important segments of the state's press and public. At the same time, California, occasionally a stronghold of liberal thought with a progressive tradition, increasingly shifted toward a "nonpartisanship" that moved slowly toward the right of center. For example, in 1962 state voters re-elected a Democratic governor by a margin of 300,000, yet sent a Republican to the United States Senate by a margin of over 700,000 votes. California politicians still like to stand in the middle, accusing their opponents of extremism, to the right or left.

A neutral stance, however, became increasingly difficult to maintain. In 1968 a strengthened brand of "far out" politics was reflected in the appearance of two new political parties on the California ballot. These were the first minor parties to qualify since the Prohibition Party had last appeared in the election of 1962. Representing the "states' rights" candidacy of former Alabama Governor George Wallace was the American Independence Party; the second fringe political group was the Peace and Freedom Party, a loose alliance of elements of the "new left." This group stood strongly against the Vietnam War and for civil rights. Both parties polarized California politics somewhat, but the ultra-rightists appeared to be much the stronger of the two.

Out of all this confusion it is difficult for political parties to construct an orderly or reliable voting pattern. Both major parties, of course, ponder the increasing national importance of the state, its changing voting complexion, and the thousands of new voters who come of age each year. Both Democrats and Republicans need to understand the complicated California voter in order to achieve future political victories. His growing affluence and hopes for the future are at the heart of such understanding.

SELECTED READINGS

Sources for studying the latest phases of California's economic and political development consist mainly of newspaper and journal articles. Relatively few up-to-date books on these matters exist. Among the interesting general articles about modern California, the following are quite useful: Carey McWilliams, "Look What's Happened to California," *Harper's*, October, 1949, pp. 21–29; the same author's "Population and Politics," *Nation*, July 8, 1950, pp. 35–37; and an earlier résumé by Governor Earl Warren and Frank J. Taylor, "California's Biggest Headache," *Saturday Evening Post*, August 14, 1948, pp. 20–21, 72, 74. Consult also Max Stern, "California's Next Hundred Years," *Atlantic Monthly*, September, 1949, pp. 53–57. Governor Warren's career is appraised in John D. Weaver, *Warren: The Man, the Court, the Era* (Boston, 1967), and in Leo Katcher, *Earl Warren: A Political Biography* (New York, 1967). Nixon's *Six Crises* (New York, 1962) sums up his career personally; see also Earl Mazo, *Richard Nixon: A Political and Personal Portrait* (New York, 1959) and William Costello, *The Facts About Nixon . . .* (New York, 1960). These should be supplemented by Horace Jeremiah (Jerry) Voorhis, *Confessions of a Congressman* (New York, 1947).

The series of articles by Lester Velie that exposed Samish's operations were entitled "The Secret Boss of California," *Collier's*, August 13, 1949, pp. 11–13, 71–73, and August 20, 1949, pp. 12–13, 60, 62–63. An article that throws light on election procedures is Francis M. Carney, "Auxiliary Party Organization in California," *Western Political Quarterly*, XI (June, 1958), 391–392. Similarly analytical is Currin V. Shields, "A Note on Party Organization: The Democrats in California," *Western Political Quarterly*, VII (December, 1954), 683 ff. The results of a crucial election are the subject of Mary Ellen Leary, "The Two-Party System Comes to California," *The Reporter*, February 7, 1957, p. 35. Gladwin Hill, "Dixieland Campaign in the Golden State," New York *Times* Magazine, September 28, 1958, pp. 69–70, discusses some aspects of the 1958 election. The use of professional public-relations advisers in elections is treated in Robert J. Pitchell, "The Influence of Professional Campaign Management Firms in Partisan Elections in California," *Western Political Science Quarterly*, XI (June, 1958), 286 ff. See also Eugene C. Lee and William Buchanan, "The 1960 Election in California," *Western Political Quarterly*, XVI (March, 1961), 309–326.

The publications of the Haynes Foundation in Los Angeles and of the Giannini Foundation at the University of California at Berkeley are also useful. For southern California, no better reports exist than those published by the Southern California Research Council, located on the campuses of Occidental and Pomona Colleges. The titles of these are: *The Effect of a Reduction of Defense Expenditures Upon the Los Angeles Economy* (1953); *The Los Angeles Economy: Its Strengths and Weaknesses* (1954); *The Next Fifteen Years—The Los Angeles Metropolitan Area, 1955–1970* (1955); *Guides to Prosperity for the Los Angeles Economy* (1956); *Manpower Outlook for the Los Angeles Area in the 1960's* (1957); *The Costs of Metropolitan Growth, 1958–1970* (1958); *The Southern California Metropolis—1980* (1959); *An Approach to an Orderly and Efficient Transportation System for the Southern California Metropolis* (1960). *Developing the Inland Empire* (1961); *Jobs For the Future: Southern California* (1962); *The Impact of Foreign Trade on Southern California* (1963); *Migration and the Southern California Economy* (1964); and *Crisis in School Finance* (1966) are illustrative. See also William L. Thomas, Jr., *Man, Time, and Space in Southern California* (Washington, D.C., 1961), and Winston W. Crouch and Beatrice Dinerman, *Southern California Metropolis: A Study in Development of Government for a Metropolitan Area* (Berkeley, 1964). The process by which city and county units have either merged or sought to maintain their identity from "metropolitanization" is examined in Richard Bigger *et al., Metropolitan Coast: San Diego and Orange Counties* (Berkeley, 1958). Two studies of urbanization in the San Fernando Valley are Richard E. Preston, *The Changing Landscape of the San Fernando Valley Between 1930 and 1964* (Northridge, 1966), a pamphlet, and Robert Durrenberger,

Leonard Pitt, and Richard E. Preston, *The San Fernando Valley: A Bibliography* (Northridge, 1967).

Regarding the problem of urbanization in northern California, there is a superbly conceived and generously designed book, Mel Scott's *The San Francisco Bay Area: A Metropolis in Perspective* (Berkeley, 1965). Edward Eichler and Marshall Kaplan, *The Community Builders* (Berkeley, 1967), focuses upon the development of new towns, especially in California.

A useful population study is Kathleen C. Doyle, *Californians: Who, Whence, Whither* (Los Angeles, 1956). Equally valuable in charting economic trends is "Economic Survey of California," *California Blue Book* (Sacramento, 1958), published by the State Chamber of Commerce. See also A. E. Karinen and D. W. Lantis, "Population of California: 1950–1961," *Annals* of the Association of American Geographers, LI (December, 1961), and *California Statistical Abstract* (Sacramento, 1958). The State Department of Finance publishes an annual publication entitled *California's Population*. *Western City* is the monthly periodical of the League of California Cities.

Books that deal with modern California government and politics include Leo J. Ryan, *Understanding California Government and Politics* (Palo Alto, 1966); Winston W. Crouch, Dean E. McHenry, John C. Bollens, and Stanley Scott, *California Government and Politics* (3d ed., Englewood Cliffs, N.J., 1964); Robert A. Walker and Floyd A. Cave, *How California Is Governed* (New York, 1953); Dean R. Cresap, *Party Politics in the Golden State* (Los Angeles, 1954); Bernard L. Hyink, Seyom Brown, and Ernest W. Thacker, *Politics and Government in California* (6th ed., New York, 1969); and Henry A. Turner and John A. Vieg, *The Government and Politics of California* (2d ed., New York, 1964). A helpful anthology is David Farrelly and Ivan Hinderaker, eds., *The Politics of California: A Book of Readings* (New York, 1951). See also Winston W. Crouch, *The Initiative and Referendum in California* (Los Angeles, 1950), and Joseph A. Beek, *The California Legislature* (Sacramento, 1957). Most of these books contain a minimum of historical interpretation, focusing attention on the structure of government. Somewhat more historical is Joseph P. Harris, *California Politics* (3d ed., Stanford, 1961). A book for young people is Anne B. Fisher's *The Story of California's Constitution and Laws* (Palo Alto, 1953).

California's bitter loyalty-oath controversy is the subject of David P. Gardner, *The California Oath Controversy* (Berkeley, 1967).

Political developments from the 1950's onward are discussed in B. Crick, "California Democratic Clubs: A Revolt in the Suburbs," *The Reporter*, May 31, 1956, pp. 35–39. Totten J. Anderson has written on "The 1956 Election in California" in *Western Politics and the 1956 Elections*, ed. by Frank H. Jonas (Salt Lake City, 1957). A short but useful article regarding the complexities of rightist sentiment is

Bruce Bliven, "How Did Southern California Get That Way?" *The Reporter*, January 18, 1962, pp. 39–40.

The relationship between politics and labor is explored in Steven Warshaw, "California: The Union Shop and the Amendment Game," *The Reporter*, October 30, 1958, pp. 14–16.

An attempt to forecast economic developments after the end of the war was made in a publication entitled *Postwar California* (*Monthly Digest of Information Published in Cooperation with the California State Reconstruction and Reemployment Commission*, Berkeley, 1945–   ). General postwar economic activity is the subject of Frank L. Kidner, *California Business Cycles* (Berkeley, 1946). See also James L. Clayton, "Defense Spending: Key to California's Growth," *Western Political Quarterly*, XV (June, 1962), 280–293. The increase in federal spending is examined in Sterling L. Brubaker, "The Impact of Federal Government Activities on California's Economic Growth, 1930–1956," Ph.D. dissertation, University of California, Berkeley (1959). Two industries affected by wartime expansion are analyzed in Ewald T. Grether, *The Steel and Steel-using Industries of California* (Berkeley, 1946), and George H. Hildebrand, *The Pacific Coast Maritime Shipping Industry, 1930–1948* (2 vols., Berkeley, 1952). Leonard J. Arrington and George Jensen, "Comparison of Income Changes in the Western States, 1929–1960," *Western Economic Journal*, I (Summer, 1963), 205–217, is useful in charting California's steady rise in personal income.

36

The Recent Past

As hundreds of thousands of new residents arrive annually in California, many problems become extremely urgent. These include overcrowded schools, hospitals, mental health facilities and sanitariums, a highway system that is dangerously outmoded, the need for reapportionment, taxation, water shortages, juvenile delinquency, and smog. Unending debate as to how best to handle these difficulties rages both in the press and in legislative halls. A glance at some of the physical problems that beset California should be helpful to an understanding of the human challenges discussed in the last chapter.

Smog

After World War II Los Angeles and San Francisco, especially the former, were increasingly plagued by one of the most troublesome problems than can afflict a modern city—air pollution in the form of "smog" (a combination of the words "smoke" and "fog"). The persistent, choking bluish haze grew more uncomfortable each year. It dirtied buildings, reduced visibility, irritated eyes, annoyed tourists, and created a public furor. Air pollution became an issue with statewide overtones. Politicians were elected to public office who promised to do something about the emission of fumes from oil refineries, local industries, and automobiles. In 1947, Los

LOS ANGELES SPRAWL, 1954. (By courtesy of William A. Garne

628

629

Angeles was forced to organize a County Air Pollution Control District, which spent millions of dollars trying to banish the fumes. Progress was slow, however. The city banned backyard incinerators only in 1957. Until a state law allowed the APCD, acting through the Los Angeles County Board of Supervisors, to override local jurisdiction, its air pollution ordinances could not be applied to the sixty-three municipalities that surrounded Los Angeles. The control of industries that produced sulphurous petrochemicals became part of the APCD program, as did laboratory investigation to determine the factors responsible for smog.

Geography emerged as the main culprit. Los Angeles is unfortunately located in a saucer-like basin which suffers from the lowest wind velocity of any major city of the United States. This condition creates disturbing "air inversions" sometimes lasting for days. If the air could escape the surrounding rim of mountains, where the atmosphere normally grows cooler with altitude, the condition would not be so troublesome. But a warm band of air overhead often makes this impossible. Indeed, constant bright sunshine on hot, sunny days causes photochemical regrouping of exhaust gas molecules. Then smog ozones form and the sulphurous plumes billowing out of industrial smokestacks refuse to go away. Hydrocarbons from auto exhausts and vapor leaks from gas tanks contribute to the smog.

In the San Francisco Bay area residents also became alarmed over smog. Although it was generally less of a problem in the north, San Francisco in 1955 organized a second Air Pollution Control District. This consisted of nine counties in the bay area. The next year this agency succeeded in banning open rubbish fires in six northern counties. Municipal dumps, which deposited layers of filthy air over the bay on windless days were forced to cover-and-fill city refuse. But in the San Francisco area, as in Los Angeles earlier, full smog control was never achieved. An "alert system" inaugurated at Los Angeles after 1956 was, however, helpful. When the concentration of pollution reached a prescribed level, local industries were notified by the city's APCD to reduce the burning of fuel. Beginning in 1959 business firms were forced to burn only natural gas from May through October.

Regulation of automotive exhausts at the state level has given suffering Californians their greatest hope of attacking the problem of smog control. While the legislature patiently awaited development, throughout the fifties, of an effective afterburner, it debated public imposition of such devices after they were made available by the auto industry. Automobiles emitted an estimated 96 per cent of Los Angeles toxic air pollution. State and local pressure was put upon the Detroit automakers to step up development of anti-smog devices. Eventually the automobile industry did change designs somewhat in order to reduce "blow-by," or gases escaping from crankcases. A state Motor Vehicle Control Act created a statewide pollution control board within the Department of Public Health, to supervise the testing of smog control devices and to supervise coordination of controls with future local and national standards. In 1959, to dramatize the need for auto exhaust controls, and to prod the automakers into action, one Los Angeles mayor gave up his black limousine for a small economy car. In 1960 Governor Brown signed into law an act that formalized adoption of afterburners on motor vehicles as soon as they became available. This legislation supplemented the "alert" system adopted at Los Angeles in 1956, whereby a public warning is sounded when the ozone-pollution count reaches a level which is considered dangerous to human health. With almost 10 million cars in the state by 1969, further smog control was absolutely unavoidable. Both the state and federal governments became increasingly interested in smog research.

Yet the smog persists. Each year during the 1960's the "smog season" seemed to lengthen. Californians experienced almost year-round smog conditions, even during the winter months. The damaging effects of air pollution upon human beings are still not entirely known. There is evidence that damage to the respiratory organs occurs after prolonged exposure. According to some, smog may even cause cancer, especially in the case of aged and infirm persons. Plant pathologists state that smog has been harmful to agriculture. The destructive effects of smog on foliage and flowers are well-known. Recently growers of leafy field crops, including lettuce and spinach, have complained that smog losses in the Los Angeles basin have run as high as $8 million per year. The reduction of fruit and vegetable yields is also demonstrable. When toxic leaf damage by hydrocarbons occurs, the leaves of avocado and orange trees dry up and turn gray and splotchy, severely reducing their crops. Meanwhile studies of the toxicity of ozones and other airborne chemical substances go forward, in order to ascertain their effects on plants, animals, and humans.

Reapportionment, Taxation, and the Constitution

Another continuing problem is the political imbalance between the northern and southern parts of California. Since the days of Mexican rule, relations between north and south have often been disturbed. As we have seen, there were occasions when the state was almost separated into two parts. In the earliest years of statehood, when the southland was distinctly rural, spokesmen at the state capital for the ranchos and sleepy pueblos of the south found themselves pitted against powerful representation from "the City," or San Francisco. For years virtually all important state appropriations were spent in northern California, where the bulk of the population resided. The state's earliest schools, hospitals, colleges, and other institutions were in the north.

The first constitution of California, written at Colton Hall in 1849, provided for a bicameral legislature, both houses of which were based on population. The constitution of 1879 had a similar provision. By the 1920's, the people of California had grown dissatisfied with it. The shift of population to the urban areas and to the south made the northern and rural areas fearful that their legitimate interests would be ignored by a legislature with both houses elected on a population basis.

It was proposed that the upper house of the legislature be patterned after the United States Senate, based on geographical area, no county having more than one senator and no more than three counties within one senatorial district. In 1926, this plan was adopted by the voters as a part of the California constitution, and in 1927, the legislature apportioned itself in accordance with the new constitutional provision. Opponents of the "federal plan," however, put the issue before the electorate again in the form of a referendum. Once more the people defeated the referendum. In 1948, in 1960, and again in 1962, ballot propositions in the form of constitutional amendments to modify California's "little federal plan" were rejected by the electorate.

Southern California's urban growth, however, reversed the state's population pattern. Today, southern Californians refer to the small, mountainous, thinly-populated northern regions of the state as "cow counties," a term once used to describe Los Angeles. Now more than 90 per cent of the state's population is urban. Until 1966, Los Angeles complained of poor representation at Sacramento. Although the population center of the state, it felt controlled and hampered by a northern rural minority in the legislature, a minority that drained it heavily of tax money. One who did not understand the history of the state might expect its second largest city, San Francisco, to lament non-urban rule over the state senate. After the 1920's, however, San Francisco was alarmed by the growth of Los Angeles at a rate that surpassed its own increase in population. Partly to retain its political power and to protect northern political and fiscal prerogatives, San Francisco frequently sided in the legislature with the rural, central-northern counties. The city's representatives also voted with farm lobbyists to block reapportionment of the legislature.

Critics maintained that, for all practical purposes, Los Angeles County had become disfranchised in the upper house of the legislature, and that an overwhelming proportion of the people of California were thus deprived of representation. Southern California's strength in the lower house of the legislature was relatively proportional, but the senate occupied a crucial position in determining legislation.

In 1960, although Los Angeles County had a population of over 6 million persons, the county then comprised but one senatorial district, which sent one senator to the state capital. Alpine, Mono, and Inyo counties, with a combined population of about 15,000 persons, also made up one senatorial district. Thus, in the northern mountain counties of California, one voter had more representation in the state senate than did 400 Los Angeles voters. The northern counties possessed the bulk of California's population during the Gold Rush era, when county lines were drawn. On the basis of their population at that time they achieved their voting strength. Non-urban northern areas frequently vetoed measures dealing with increased freeway construction, water development, flood control, taxation, smog prevention, and education. The relatively proportional representation in the state assembly did not offset the imbalance in the senate.

Most of this sectional discontent came to an end in 1964, when the United States Supreme Court ordered that both houses of all state legislatures be apportioned on a "one man, one vote" basis. That tribunal later upheld a lower court ruling which required the California state senate and assembly to be so districted. In October, 1965, a special session of the legislature completed the first senate reapportionment since 1926, and also slightly modified assembly districts. Eight southern counties (Los Angeles, Orange, Ventura, Santa Barbara, San Bernardino, Riverside, Imperial, and San Diego) were awarded 22 of the 40 seats and 46 of the 80 assembly seats. Los Angeles County alone increased its senate representation from 1 to 14, plus 1 seat shared with Orange County, while the central and northern region saw its allotment of senators shrink from 31 to 18. Thus, the long political struggle between northern and southern California took a definite turn in favor of the south. Opponents of reapportionment continued to maintain that the state's rural areas were more important than their population indicated, and hence deserving of disproportionate representation, and that the senate was the only agency in state politics

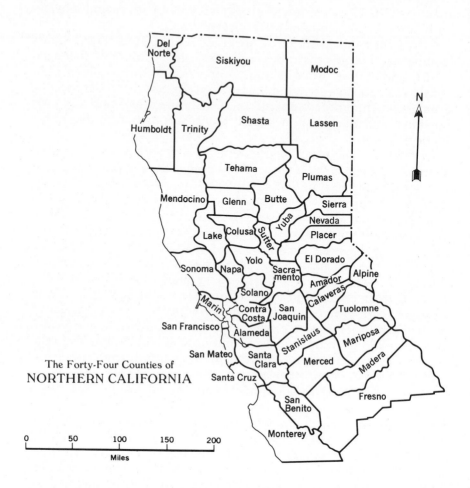

The Forty-Four Counties of
NORTHERN CALIFORNIA

which protected rural interests. The concentration of power in
the south was underscored in the election of 1966, when five of
California's top eight elected officers were southerners—including
the governor, lieutenant governor, controller, treasurer, and superintendent of public instruction.

Through the years, the dominant political party, usually the
Republicans, controlled the state through gerrymandering of assembly and congressional districts. When redistricting occurs, the
majority party seeks to concentrate the opposition's power in as
few districts as possible, spreading its own voting power as widely

The Fourteen Counties of
SOUTHERN CALIFORNIA

N

0   50   100   150   200

Miles

as possible by juggling the state's political units. In 1951 the Republicans vigorously gerrymandered state districts; in 1961 the
Democrats retaliated in kind. Control of the legislature is essential
to the success of such see-saw maneuvers. The restructuring of
political subdivisions in the state legislature is producing significant shifts in taxation, appropriations, and fiscal policies.

At the national level, in the redistribution of congressional seats
and electoral votes, resulting from the 1960 census, California
added 8 seats to its 30 in the House of Representatives, giving it
a total of 40 electoral votes (the formula is one vote for each

CONGRESSIONAL DISTRICTS, 1969-1971

Special "One Man, One Vote"
Reapportionment

1. Del Norte, Humboldt, Marin, Mendocino, Napa, Sonoma
2. Alpine, Amador, Butte, Calaveras, El Dorado, Inyo, Lassen, Madera, Mariposa, Modoc, Mono, Nevada, Placer, Plumas, Shasta, Sierra, Siskiyou, Tehama, Trinity, Tuolomne
3. Sacramento
4. Colusa, Glenn, Lake, Sacramento, Solano, Sutter
5. San Francisco
6. Marin
7-8. Alameda
9. Alameda, Santa Clara
10. San Benito, Santa Clara
11. San Mateo
12. Kings, Monterey, Santa Cruz, San Luis Obispo
13. Los Angeles, Santa Barbara, Ventura
14. Contra Costa
15. Merced, San Joaquin, Stanislaus
16. Fresno, Merced
17, 19-32. Kern, Los Angeles, Orange
33. San Bernardino
34. Orange
35. Orange, San Diego
36. San Diego
37. San Diego
38. Imperial, Riverside

0   50   100   150   200

Miles

636

state's seat in the House of Representatives plus two for its senators). As a result of this redistribution, the number of New York's electoral votes dropped from 45 to 43, and Pennsylvania lost three votes. But considerable inequality and unfairness of representation continues at the state level. The states of North Dakota, South Dakota, Montana, Wyoming, Colorado, New Mexico, Arizona, Utah, Nevada, Idaho, Oregon, Washington, Alaska, and Hawaii have a total of 28 votes in the United States Senate. California, with more than twice the total population of these 14 states, has only two votes in the senate. The federal constitution, furthermore, stipulates that this basic, and quite undemocratic, inequality can never be changed—even by constitutional amendment.

Revision of the state constitution is another matter of concern to reform-minded citizens. The last major revision of California's constitution was in 1879, and since then it has been amended over 300 times and has grown to 75,000 words, ten times the length of the United States constitution. It is exceeded in bulk only by the constitution of India and that of Louisiana. The state constitution, which resembles a telephone book in bulk, contains many provisions that should be in the statutory law of the state, and not in the basic document of the constitution. For example, the constitution provides that the legislature "shall have no power to prohibit wrestling and 12-round boxing contests in the State of California." The constitution requires that the trustees of the Huntington Library shall make an annual report to the secretary of state, and any person who fights a duel with deadly weapons, in or out of California, or sends or accepts a challenge to fight a duel, or acts as second, shall be prohibited from holding public office or voting in California.

After 1963 the state legislature's constitutional revision commission, following many hearings, proposed partial revisions of the constitution. Acceptance of revisions however, has, proved to be a complicated matter not likely to achieve rapid effect.

A New State Water Plan

We have seen that California's water supplies are located far from her population centers. Too often water is abundant only in the winter, when it is not needed—especially in the form of flash floods.

By the late 1940's it became evident that even Hoover Dam and the Boulder Canyon Project could not permanently provide water for southern California. In agricultural Kern County alone, underground wells were being overdrafted by an estimated 260 billion gallons per year. Overdraft of underground resources in coastal locations often causes the intrusion of sea water into fresh water deposits. In the Los Angeles basin of southern California, and to the north, in Suisun Bay and along the Sacramento-San Joaquin Delta, such intrusions have caused serious pollution and deterioration of existing supplies.

As we have noted, federal measures to control the flow of the Sacramento and San Joaquin Rivers and to generate hydroelectric power were authorized in the 1930's under the overall title of the Central Valley Project. Its chief units included Shasta Dam (completed in 1945), near the northern end of the Sacramento Valley, and the smaller Friant Dam (completed in 1942), near the headwaters of the San Joaquin, drained by the Friant-Kern Canal. Another canal, the Delta-Mendota, was finally placed in operation in 1951. Folsom Dam, 20 miles above Sacramento, on the American River, went into operation in 1955. Farther south the Tri-Dam Project was started the same year, as were Donnells, Beardsley, and Tulloch dams on the Stanislaus River. In 1955, also, construction of the federally-financed Trinity River Project, yet another unit of the Central Valley Project, was begun. Other portions of the San Joaquin Valley Project were expanded, in particular the harnessing of the King's River.

By 1960, after more than a quarter-century of effort, and the expenditure of $1 billion on its water development, California's Central Valley had been transformed into a virtual agricultural-urban empire. The Central Valley Project had, indeed, placed Fresno, Kern, and Tulare counties among the nation's ten most productive farm counties. State and local authorities, in cooperation with the Department of the Interior and Bureau of Reclamation, envisaged another $3 billion of federal outlays for water development in the area over the next fifty years.

But none of these developments provided a permanent solution to the water needs of urban centers outside the San Joaquin Valley. The major sources of water remained geographically maldistributed. Along California's northwest coast—where 41 per cent of the state's water resources originated—the Sacramento, the San Joaquin, and the Eel, Mad, and Klamath rivers continued to empty most of their water into the ocean.

A new non-federal approach to the conservation of California's wasted water resources had to be found. As early as 1948 advocates of a further water-development plan began to speak up for it in the state legislature. This was the Feather River Project. The

Feather, the most important tributary of the Sacramento River, has a seasonal runoff about one-fifth that of the entire Sacramento drainage basin. To achieve the purposes of the Feather River Project—to harness the energy and to conserve and distribute the waters of the Feather—a large reservoir capacity is needed, consisting of a series of costly dams and more than 800 miles of canals, tunnels, lakes, siphons, and penstocks. The cost of creating this capacity will be in excess of $2,600,000,000. But this project was only a small part of an $11 billion statewide master water plan which would be under construction until the year 2020 A.D. During 1957, site clearance began on "the world's largest dam," the 730-foot-high Oroville Dam, located on the Feather River above Sacramento. This was the first step toward completion of man's largest single construction project in California, a great downhill "natural stairway" of untapped hydroelectric power and water. This project was a comprehensive, far-reaching endeavor whose heart was the Feather River Project —which still has not been fully built.

However, in the 1950's a damaging debate over whether state or federal construction funds should be used—added to political sectionalism between northern and southern California—slowed down development of the Feather River Project. Even after construction had begun on the Oroville Dam, California's legislature remained locked in discord over the questions of whether to complete it and whether to build the dam projected to accompany it, San Luis Dam, 310 feet high, in Merced County southeast of San Francisco. California desperately needed agreement on a master water plan. An adamant stand by southern legislators against appropriating money for water which could be recaptured by northern "counties of origin" contributed to a ten-year stalemate that lasted through the 1950's. The wetter north required flood-control as urgently as the rapidly industrializing and populous but parched south needed additional water. Protection of the towns of Yuba City, Butte, and Marysville from floods had to be weighed with the need for life-giving water to southern California.

A persistent objection to the Feather River Project was the prospect of "unjust enrichment" of large landowners. Critics counseled application of a 160-acre limitation on the use of cheap water provided by the general taxpayer. They feared the further increase of "corporation farmers" whose thousands of productive acres would be nourished by water paid for by others, and pointed out that cheap subsidized water development in the San Joaquin Valley would produce more agricultural surpluses, already stockpiled with tax dollars by the federal government. A leading

FLOOD CONTROL ACTIVITY COMBINED WITH CONSERVATION. (Department of Water Resources.)

stumbling block to adoption of the Feather River Project was its great cost. Largely, however, the issue was one of the north's interests as opposed to the south's. For a time the water problem seriously disrupted state politics.

Not until after the election of Governor Brown in 1958 was the legislative deadlock broken. In a comprehensive water message to the legislature, Brown expressed regret that in a state so magnificently endowed by nature,

it has become the fashion in recent years to dwell on our water problems as being awesome and impossibly complicated. . . The result has been delay and frustration. This stalemate must come to an end. If we take courage and put our fears behind us, we can replace narrow sectional differences with confident, pioneering leadership.

In 1960 California voters endorsed Brown's first-step compromise water bond program and the long-delayed Feather River Project began to be built in earnest. When completed, the project will play a significant role in the transfer of water from northern California to points as far south as San Diego County. There nevertheless remained much concern over the cost of the plan.

Before this project could be passed upon by the legislature, and then by the voters, coordinated control over and utilization of the state's water resources had to be agreed upon. Protection of northern rights in the "counties of origin" is implicit in California's master water plan. Individual parts of the project will, however, be enacted upon a piecemeal basis. Envisioned was the construction of no less than the world's biggest water-transport system, the economic benefits of which greatly outweigh its public costs.

With its completion date set at 1972, the Feather River Aqueduct will run from Oroville, north of Sacramento, southward to the San Bernardino Mountains east of Los Angeles. Alongside the subsidiary functions of flood control, hydroelectric power generation, and recreation, the project's basic purpose is to conserve runoff water and to transfer it to areas of shortage for municipal and industrial use and for irrigation. This last purpose is crucial, since 95 per cent of California's crops are grown on irrigated land.

The new water network is, as previously noted, being built as the framework for a broader system to be constructed in the future; it will ultimately consist of 16 dams, 18 pumping stations, 9 power plants, and miles of aqueducts, canals, and pipelines. "The California Aqueduct's" main north-south artery, which will be 444 miles in length, includes the Delta Project, with its network of canals and pumping stations in the low-lying Sacramento-San Joaquin Valley. By 1990, the yield of the entire facility will be 4¼ million acre-feet, of which nearly one-half has been allotted to the Los Angeles Metropolitan Water District. The cost of transporting and storing the water will be paid by its sale to contracting regional authorities throughout the state.

About 2 million acre-feet of water will be allocated for use in the six heavily urbanized counties served by the new system. In southern California the Metropolitan Water District was among the first agencies to sign contracts with the state for Feather River water and is paying nearly 70 per cent of the state project's costs.

The transporting of this water into southern California posed a big construction problem, as the Tehachapi Mountains form a barrier between that area and the San Joaquin Valley. Water must be lifted over the Tehachapis and then sent via tunnels bored through the mountain ridges. To receive Feather River water, after it arrives at the state's terminal reservoir at Castaic, the Metropolitan Water District will construct a 300-mile system of feeder lines. A Tehachapi pumping plant will distribute this water from Los Angeles to San Diego.

The Feather River Project is being built in a region of steep-walled canyons and forested mountains, comprising some of the most breath-taking scenery in the West. The project also provides for fish and game protection as well as flood control and conservation. Sportsmen estimate that there are 1,000 miles of trout streams in the Feather River country, and bass, steelhead, and shad available in the river itself. In the woods are innumerable deer, bear, and mountain lion.

Observers have repeatedly pointed to another possible way of solving the water problem—large-scale desalination of sea water

AQUEDUCT CONSTRUCTION IN THE CENTRAL VALLEY. (Department of Water Resources.)

by mechanical means—although such a process would be tremendously costly. The popular conception of the economic feasibility of converting ocean water into fresh water has little foundation in fact. However, during the early sixties, the state had carefully explored all aspects of desalination. A desalination laboratory erected at Point Loma, near San Diego, with federal funds, began active experimentation along coastal waters. In 1967 President Johnson announced that the federal government would help to build the largest desalination plant in the country near San Diego. California cannot afford to ignore any possible means of developing its total water resources.

California suffered an obvious setback in 1960 when a water master, specially appointed by the United States Supreme Court to arbitrate the re-allocation of the water of the Colorado River, long claimed by both Arizona and California, recommended to the Supreme Court that certain rights be awarded to Arizona. If confirmed, this decision would severely curtail California's future share of Colorado River water. Diversion of that water eastward, toward the Rocky Mountain watershed, was now a legal possibility. Such a prospect was alarming to Californians in view of the fact that the state's water needs were expected to double in the years from 1960 to 1980.

Continued Agricultural Productivity

Aggressive water development has made possible the steady expansion of California, for most of its farms depend, wholly or in part, upon artificially supplied water. California has become an industrial state without ceasing to be an agricultural one. Aided by a vigorous farm lobby, by the Agricultural Extension Service, and by the Soil Conservation Service of the United States Department of Agriculture, farm acreage continues to expand, though the actual number of farms decreases annually. By the 1960's less than 30 per cent of California's land area was under cultivation. Yet the state has consistently led the nation in gross income from agricultural products. California is first nationally in the production of almost 40 crops, and no state even comes near its production of fruits and vegetables. Forty per cent of all the fruit consumed in the United States is grown in the state—including 85 per cent of the grapes and nearly every olive, lemon, apricot, date, almond, artichoke, fig, garlic clove, nectarine, persimmon, or pomegranate.

California's cash farm income by 1959 topped $3 billion, the largest yearly agricultural production registered by any American state. Farm income that year averaged more than $8,000 per farm, triple the national average. This increase resulted from both accelerated production and higher prices. California's farmers in 1959 accounted for 9 per cent of national net farm income. Yet the state has less than 2.5 per cent of the nation's farms and just over 3 per cent of its farm land.

In 1960 the agricultural production of four neighboring counties in the south San Joaquin Valley (Fresno, Kern, Tulare, and Kings) topped all but seven states outside California. That year Fresno County headed the nation's 3,134 counties in agricultural production for the past twelve years. Tulare remained in second place while Kern County was third.

The chief reason that California remains the leading agricultural state in the nation is that it continues to produce virtually every crop, indeed more than 275, that can be grown commercially in the temperate zone. Livestock, which is not a crop, accounted for about 15 per cent of its 1959 agricultural income. That year California also produced 6,063 million board feet of lumber, the highest in its history. California's main export is unmanufactured cotton, most of which goes to India and Japan, and she is also a major national producer of hay, rice, barley, hops, potatoes, tomatoes, dried beans, sugar beets, peaches, and pears. More than 90 per cent of all the apricots, dates, lemons, plums, dried prunes, figs, walnuts, lettuce, tomatoes, and broccoli in the United States are grown within California. Though faced with heavy competition from Florida, the state still contributes much of the nation's citrus production to domestic markets.

California agriculture has increased steadily in technological complexity as small, family-run farms have given way to large specialized and commercialized enterprises. The small farm is increasingly incapable of grossing an income sufficient to allow it to expand operations and compete successfully. Consequently, it is tending to be replaced by large mechanized "agri-businesses." These corporations include the Kern County Land Company, whose holdings in the Central Valley are gargantuan. The Irvine Ranch Company operates a vast acreage in Orange County and has become the major landowner in Imperial County as well. In the San Joaquin Valley, the DiGiorgio and Sawyer fruit and vegetable farms produce millions of dollars of income annually. The Maggio Company in the Imperial Valley is the largest single producer of commercially grown carrots in the United States. The Brock Ranches near El Centro, and the Antle Ranches, growers of Salinas lettuce and carrots in the Imperial Valley and Arizona,

MT. SHASTA, A TOWERING VOLCANIC PEAK OF THE CASCADE RANGE, REFLECTED IN A MILL POND. (Union Pacific Railroad.)

are among the leading producers of vegetables in the nation.

By adopting advanced techniques of industry, these large corporations not only increased the size of the average farm but markedly consolidated agricultural operations within the state. This new farming-business competence took advantage of crop and area diversity, technology, and corporate managerial skills. Large growers extended their operations into shipping, processing, and marketing, creating a vertical integration that controlled agriculture from planting through sale of the final product. Today's cattlemen breed, feed, finish, ship, and sell their own livestock; a few even grow the alfalfa and sorghum used in cattle fattening. By 1967 some 2 million cattle were fattened annually in California, as compared with only 50,000 in 1930. Yet, the state that year supported 4 million cattle on less space than it did almost fifty years ago when there were only 2 million cattle in California. Large rancher-farmers rely upon two-way radios to keep contact with employees; they operate motor pools, and they buy costly harvesters, tractors, and automatic potato pickers. This mechanization is a far cry from the nineteenth century's horse-drawn plows, haystacks, and milk wagons. Large capital investments are necessary to carry on the new agriculture.

Agriculture has, of course, yielded large areas of farm land to real estate subdivisions, industrial plants, and space-consuming highways. Real estate promoters today even "process the desert" to prepare new housing tracts. The decline of Los Angeles from its position as the first agricultural county in the nation has been caused by its shift toward industrialization. The annexation of the agricultural San Fernando Valley in 1915 brought 170 square miles of farm land into the Los Angeles city limits. But this agricultural zone has now become virtually urbanized. Despite the "cementing-in" of cattle feeding pens, lettuce and truck garden sites, orange groves, and orchards, the daily consumption demands of Los Angeles insure a continuing agricultural economy. Efficiency of operations has also helped Los Angeles to keep its rating as the nation's largest dairy county.

Heavy migration into Los Angeles and Orange counties has made the sight of orange orchards (once the symbol of southern California) a memory of the past. There was a time when the very name Orange County held a special enchantment no longer recapturable. As late as 1930, orange growing was clearly the first agricultural crop in the state, with dairies second and livestock third. But orange groves occupy too much land. With farm terrain soaring to $20,000 per acre during the 1950's, California's productive agricultural acreage fell 10 per cent in one decade. As ten newcomers step across the state line in search of sunshine and a better life, California loses an average of one more acre of farm land. Yet, California remains the nation's first farm income-producing state. True, crops have changed. The state's first agricultural activity today is the raising of livestock; dairying is the second largest; cotton has become the third largest crop; and grapes the fourth. Orange growing has tumbled to sixth place.

Today, grapes are grown on 475,000 acres of vineyards. California's 241 bonded wineries and wine cellars are valued at approximately $700 million and employ a peak labor force of 111,000 persons. Wine storage capacity exceeds 335 million gallons. Grapes, more than half of which are crushed for wine and brandy, rank as the state's most valuable fruit harvest and are third among all cultivated crops. About eighty per cent of the wine consumed in the United States originates in California. While Californians consume twice as much wine as the national average (.9 of a gallon per capita annually in the nation), more than three-fourths of California wine is shipped out of the state.

In recent years pessimists have seen California agriculture as fading; optimists, conversely, characterize it as dynamic in productivity as well as diversified and still in a period of growth. Some 15 million acres are regularly farmed or are potential farmland. Unfortunately, 90 per cent of the prime 5 million acres adjoins growing urban areas; much of this acreage continues to disappear at an estimated rate of 140,000 acres per year. Undeveloped lands are of lower soil quality, in a less desirable climatic zone, and require more water per acre and more "ingredient inputs" to produce crops.

These factors reduce the ability of California farmers to compete with other states producing the same crops. Advocates of large farms attack a 160-acre limitation on lands that qualify for water from federally-sponsored projects. They argue that no one can make a living unless he grows at least 160 acres of crops. Owners of large farms call enforcement of this law unrealistic and a serious challenge to agriculture. As a result, some farmers have moved to Mexico, where they find that cheap labor and land are plentiful.

California farmers, however, still lead the nation in farm sales (in 1966 $1 billion per year higher than second-ranking Iowa). They generate 8 per cent of national farm receipts. Severe competition for land and water has, however, made it necessary to squeeze higher yields from the soil. From 1955 to 1965 alone, Orange County's farm acreage dropped from 143,092 acres to 64,247 acres. County crop acreage in Los Angeles dropped from

320,493 acres in 1950 to 145,987 acres in 1960, and will drop an estimated 88,500 acres in 1970 and 60,000 acres by 1980. California's farm employment, which averaged 369,000 in 1958, had also dropped to 305,000 persons by 1966. Only the efficient handling, processing, and marketing of farm products has enabled the state to retain national farm leadership.

During 1966 California's gross agricultural income exceeded the $4 billion mark for the first time in the state's history. For the nineteenth consecutive year California retained its position as the nation's first agricultural state. That year Fresno remained the leading agricultural county in the nation, while second place went to Kern County and fourth place to Tulare County. Six of the nation's top ten agricultural counties were located in California. Agricultural production that year stood 28 per cent above the amount recorded for 1960.

One should not lose sight of California's ancillary food-producing industry. Aside from widespread fruit and vegetable canning operations, the state remains a significant center of commercial poultry raising, viniculture, dairying, and fish canning. Fish and shellfish landed at California ports annually exceed a billion pounds, the largest catch of any state in the Union. Meeting heavy foreign competition, fish canneries are located at San Francisco, Monterey, San Pedro, and San Diego.

Commercial fishing, described earlier, has remained an important part of California's food-producing industries. The state ranks as the leading commercial fishing state in the nation, slightly ahead of second-place Alaska. While the total value of its catch has generally risen, the number of pounds of fish actually landed has trended downward for the past thirty years. California's 1964 catch of 493 million pounds was less than a third that of the peak year 1936. Directly responsible for this sharp decline has been the virtual disappearance of the sardine as a major commercial part of the fishing industry. Annual landings of sardines, which had been above one billion pounds prior to 1940, dropped to only 7 million pounds in 1963. Conservationists have charged that this diminution was in large part caused by the massive misuse of sardines as fish fertilizer.

Tuna is now by far the most important species of fish caught in California waters. Four varieties—yellowfin, skipjack, albacore, and bluefin—account for more than 85 per cent of the total fish catch. Other leading commercial species include jack and Pacific mackerel, abalone, spiny lobsters, sea trout, red snapper, and white seabass.

Wetbacks and Migrants

One of the unsolved problems that continues to face California concerns its migratory labor. Although increasingly mechanized, modern agriculture still requires large numbers of hand laborers. They hoe and thin sugar beets, cut spinach, feed livestock, and prune grape vineyards. During both winter and summer, fruit, vegetable, and cotton pickers range throughout the state looking for work. Uncertain market conditions and the maladjustment between labor demands and the supply of workers keep wages depressed. Migrant laborers, traditionally non-unionized, are also dependent upon the harvest itself. A bad freeze or drought period drastically reduces their income. They live in substandard housing, are rarely fed adequately, and their children seldom complete even a grade-school education. In California and throughout the United States their way of life has been described by the late Edward R. Murrow as a "harvest of shame." Leslie S. Clark has attempted to capture poetically the plight of the migrants:

> These are the drifting, rootless ones,
>   Like tumbleweeds
> They blow on bitter winds of fate;
>   No pathway leads
> Toward home and small loved garden plot
>   Their fathers hoed . . .
> For them—a stranger's shack and crop;
>   For them—the road!

In California the migrants have come into severe economic competition with Mexican farm workers. Racial implications of this migration have already been discussed. The debased condition of cherry pickers and almond harvesters has not improved markedly, in part due to the competition of laborers from Mexico. By the thousands these *braceros* were imported into California precisely because they formed a cheap and willing labor pool. The low wages they received north of the border seemed opulent by Mexican standards. After the war as many as 750,000 of these workers entered the United States as supplementary farm laborers, many under Public Law 28. Illegal "wetbacks" were also shepherded across the Rio Grande into Texas and other parts of the rural Southwest. Man-snatching *coyotes*, or middle-men, made a business of secreting laborers and even stealing and marketing whole labor crews to employers. The Mexican government frequently protested the illegal profiteering that resulted from the exploitation of Mexican labor in California and elsewhere.

Carey McWilliams points out:

After 1900 the increasing urbanization of population, the disappearance of the backyard garden, the development of new canning processes, and the introduction of refrigerator cars, brought about an enormous increase in the production of fruits and vegetables on large-scale commercial farms in the irrigated portions of the Southwest. . . . This fabulous increase in production—which set the Southwest on its feet financially—could never have taken place so rapidly without the use of Mexican labor. . . . Unorganized Mexican labor in inexhaustible quantities made this production possible.

Unprotected by the lack of interstate agreements to control or improve the conditions of migrants, foreign or domestic, laborers wandered from farm to farm, following the harvests as birds follow the sun. Until 1964, when the *bracero* in-migration was sharply curtailed, Mexican officials were assured that foreign contract laborers—those who remained legally in the United States for several years—would receive the same wages as American workers, but these wages were depressed and working conditions poor. Women and children slept nightly in abandoned barns, frame shacks, adobe huts, empty corrals, on straw in warehouses —any place where rent was not demanded. Even today the hovels in which they live have dirt floors, or tin roofs with no ceilings. Cheese cloth or flour sacks are hung over window openings to keep insects out, but flies, attracted by primitive toilet facilities, find their way into sleeping areas. Poorer "houses" are patched together from scraps of lumber, flattened oil cans, old signboards, or tar paper. They have no indoor pipes or cooking facilities. Migrants often cook outside over open fires in warm weather and inside out of wash tubs when it rains. These laborers are the modern equivalent of the poorest nineteenth century squatter— wretchedly clad, housed, and fed, and unwanted. Among them are illiterate and shiftless persons who would be almost unemployable in a more regulated job. Only a relatively small number of California harvest workers have been very successful, economically.

In part because of their lack of skills, the unionization of farm labor has traditionally failed. Since the days when the I.W.W. tried unsuccessfully to organize the Central Valley, and later, in the 1930's, when the AFL and CIO also failed, the drive to organize

California's army of migrants has found the growers' resistance virtually impregnable. Growers, organized into a Council of California Growers, insist that their unstable and unpredictable "industry" does not lend itself to traditional unionization. They claim that once a crop is ready for harvest, a strike becomes an impossibility, as they cannot shut down picking operations to negotiate. Nevertheless they faced renewed threats during 1960 from the Agricultural Workers Organizing Committee, which sought a minimum wage of $1.25 per hour. That year this union claimed success in obtaining wage increases of 12 to 17 cents for each box of peaches picked and from 15 to 17 cents per box for tomatoes. In 1961 the Teamster's Union signed a union-shop contract at Salinas with various large ranches. But these were sporadic gains, without general significance. California's long-term failure to improve the condition of its migrant labor suggests that federal control may be forthcoming. Recent unionization attempts will be examined later.

Tidelands Oil and Federal Tension

California has been one of the leading states in the Union in the production of all minerals. Petroleum fuels have contributed the largest proportion of the value of mineral production. To keep up with growing natural gas requirements, large quantities of that fuel are imported from Texas and New Mexico. In 1958 construction began on a 1,300-mile pipeline which would bring natural gas from Alberta, Canada. California, once second only to Texas as an oil-producing state, has in recent years found its production curve leveling off at about 300 million barrels of oil a year, or a little over 800,000 barrels a day, while its own consumption goes on climbing. In oil, California is now third in the nation, as the offshore fields of Louisiana, one of the last great untapped reserves of America, come into production. California is, however, still the colossus of oil production on the Pacific Coast.

Unique among the three greatest oil-producing states, California itself now consumes all the oil it produces and more. The state's production demands have risen to 900,000 barrels a day and are still climbing. There seems to be no leveling off in sight for California's curve of rising demand for oil products. To outsiders it seemed fantastic that a state which still produced a sizable share of the world's oil should be on an import basis.

Despite depletion of such large oil-producing zones as Signal

Hill and Santa Fe Springs, new sources of oil continued to be discovered throughout California. During the war, when the need for oil was vastly increased, exploration was stepped up and prospecting techniques markedly improved. Careful supervision of drilling, to conserve dwindling underground reserves, became more common. Both the state and federal governments were drawn into the management of the petroleum industry. As California became an oil-importing state after the war, governmental and private attention was given to its valuable offshore oil resources. This, in turn, gave rise to the tidelands controversy, a battle for jurisdiction over vast deposits under the sea, extending outward many miles from the shoreline. Various southern states claimed that historic state limits of jurisdiction extended for ten miles out to sea. Under international law, three miles was the accepted jurisdiction of a nation on the high seas. A further complication involved the fact that California in the 1940's leased tideland drilling rights to private companies and reaped large royalties from these leases. In 1945 the federal government brought suit against the state to stop this practice. In 1947, furthermore, Supreme Court decisions established the "paramount rights" of the federal government.

However, this controversy became a political one, subject to all the passions of sectional and local feeling. In the presidential election campaign of 1952, Dwight D. Eisenhower championed turning back the undersea oil reserves to the states. In one of his last acts in office, however, President Truman declared such tidelands a naval reserve. A major conflict developed within the next Congress, the Eighty-third, over this issue. In May, 1953, the federal government, under the Holland Bill, was instructed to turn over its tidelands oil reserves to various states within "historic boundary limits" of three miles. Non-tidelands states immediately questioned the constitutionality of allowing seaboard states to reap the benefits of such offshore reserves. The seaboard states, however, continued to maintain rights beyond the federally-recognized three-mile limit. Because the offshore jurisdiction of neither state nor federal government was firmly established, California extended its claims as far as 30 miles out to sea. The federal Submerged Lands Act of 1953 gave coastal states the tidelands out to three miles from shore but made it possible for states to claim more if they could prove that their historical boundaries lay further out. In 1961 the United States Supreme Court awarded Texas and Florida ownership of submerged tidelands out to the ten and a half mile limit. Alabama, Mississippi, and Louisiana, however, were granted only those lands out to three and a half

THE RICHMOND REFINERY OF THE STANDARD OIL COMPANY OF CALIFORNIA. (By courtesy of the Standard Oil Company of California.)

miles offshore. The status of California's tidelands remained nebulous until 1965, when the Supreme Court denied almost all of California's claims to submerged tidelands oil, valued at more than $1 billion. Only Monterey Bay, less than 100,000 acres of the 6 million acres claimed by the state, was awarded to California. The high court's decision appeared to end the twenty-year dispute, unless the national Congress passes a law granting California underwater rights to San Pedro, Santa Monica, and San Luis Obispo bays. The chance for enactment of such legislation is faint.

The federal and state tidelands controversy also came to involve local municipalities. At Long Beach, city officials after World War II leased offshore reserves to independent oil operators in defiance of both state and federal claims. Only after a lengthy dispute throughout the 1950's was a three-way agreement reached between the federal government, the state, and various California coastal municipalities. The state became the principal beneficiary of its offshore reserves. In return for this concession, the state government had to agree to spend a sizable part of its oil and gas revenues for the improvement of beaches and parks. The result was a major beautification of fomerly polluted beach sites and of cramped picnic and camping areas. Residents and tourists today flock to recreational facilities made possible from offshore oil funds. Tidelands oil revenues have also been earmarked for water development and other worthy state projects.

It can be said that such funds are used for the benefit of the state's people. Care, however, has to be exercised that its shoreline and coastal waters do not become too heavily forested with offshore drilling rigs on platforms that rival thirty-story buildings in height. Scrupulous attention is given by the State Lands Commission to limit drilling by operators who have leased thousands of acres of beach land, from north of the Ventura County line beyond Carpinteria and Santa Barbara to Gaviota.

Forming part of past federal-state tension over tidelands oil were other disputes which evoked sharp public reactions, one of which was the Fallbrook Affair. Fallbrook, a relatively small inland town in southern California, is almost wholly dependent upon a tiny river, the Santa Margarita, for its water supply. This is one of those elusive western streams that ebb and flow according to the dryness of each season. After 1942, when the Marine base at nearby Camp Pendleton also began to utilize the waters of the Santa Margarita, at the expense of Fallbrook, a controversy was fought out in both press and radio. The Navy Department maintained it had purchased rights to the Santa Margarita watershed when it acquired the rancho on which its Marine base was built. Public opinion, however, took a dim view of the federal government bullying a tiny community. Fallbrook also received the weighty support of the Los Angeles *Times*. By 1951 the federal government, in effect, was forced to back down; California had won a victory for states' rights.

Educational Expansion

Postwar California also faced grave problems of educational expansion. As thousands of "war babies" reached school age the state had to provide adequate schools and teachers for them. Unfortunately the great bulge in the school-age population came at a time of vastly increased demand for other facilities—roads, dams, prisons, hospitals, and parks. The facilities of local school districts were taxed to the utmost. Bond issue after bond issue had to be passed to provide funds needed to construct hundreds of new schools, to employ thousands of teachers, and to alleviate hardship in impoverished school districts. From 1947 to 1960 the state spent more than $1,200,000,000 on new school construction, but much more was needed. Each year the need for educational funds mounted. Public enrollment reached 4,238,000 by 1967 and was expected to reach 5 million by 1970. Education became the largest item in the state budget each year, amounting to about 40 per cent of California's total expenditures. Annual appropriations for education were apportioned over 1,600 school districts.

Closely related to educational finance has been the recruitment of teachers. An annual shortage of teachers continues to exist in California. The demand for elementary school teachers is expected to exceed the supply at least until 1970. Although teachers' salaries have steadily increased and are among the highest in the nation, only with difficulty does the state meet the challenge posed by its advancing school population. Thousands of elementary and high school youngsters still attend half-day sessions, and many teachers continue to teach on emergency credentials. Education at the collegiate level also underwent mounting strain in recent years. Costs of buildings and land spiraled at a time when California needed large-scale expansion of its state colleges and university campuses. To chart the future of higher education in California, Governor Brown initiated a state master-plan survey in 1959. Chaired by President Arthur G. Coons, then of Occidental College, a survey team made vigorous new recommendations, including establishment of a Coordinating Council for Higher Education, with representation from the private and state colleges and universities as well as California's junior colleges. The 1960 legislature put into motion vast building expenditures for the state colleges and its university. California's new master plan for higher education divorced the state colleges from the California Department of Education and placed them under a separate board of control similar to the regents of the University of California, whose own multi-campus structure was expanded. In effect, this represented a fair-trade agreement between the state colleges and the state university; each undertook to accept a stated share of students, legislative funds, and overall educational responsibilities.

With an expected enrollment of 500,000 full-time college and university students by 1970, California had to plan boldly for the future. New building costs alone for public school structures in the decade of the 1960's were to be in excess of $2 billion.

Another $2 million per year, roughly half of which comes from the state, must be spent on public education from kindergarten through the junior college years. To keep pace California must build at least one new school per day. In one way or another, by

1970, almost 6 million Californians will be enrolled in schools. A great expansion of teacher recruitment must accompany this physical expansion. Educational demands have imposed a heavy burden on Californians. Despite the fact that the state boasts 10,000 P.T.A. organizations, taxpayer resistance to rising costs has mounted in recent years. An obsolete tax structure places much of the state education budget on local property taxation. After 1959 the rate of passage of local school bond issues declined precipitously; the state constitution requires a two-thirds vote for their enactment. The lowest acceptance of educational tax measures was recorded in the 1966 elections.

Regrettably, the 1960's were educationally acrimonious years. In 1962 Max Rafferty, a colorful but controversial ultra-conservative, was elected state superintendent of public instruction. Governor Brown, who had the right to appoint members of the State Board of Education, chose Thomas W. Braden as its chairman. Braden, a liberal newspaperman, bitterly contested Rafferty's ideas. After the Reagan administration assumed office in 1966, the new governor gave Rafferty a strongly conservative board and chairman with which to work.

Population Explosion

The Gold Rush migration was numerically insignificant compared to California's recent growth in population. In the 1950's the state's population continued to swell by about half a million every year. During the ten years from 1950 to 1960, California's population increased by 48.5 per cent, or 5,130,981 persons. Demographic predictions of population growth are proving to be startlingly accurate. The California State Department of Finance's 1961 calculations estimated that the state's population will reach 22 million by 1970.

The majority of today's Californians, originally migrants into the state from elsewhere, represent a selection rather than a cross-section of persons from all parts of the United States and throughout the world. In the decade 1950–1960, 70 per cent of these immigrants settled in southern California. Enthusiasts have fallen into the habit of extending southern California's "zone of influence" considerably above Tehachapi Pass, the traditional demarcation line. Real estate and chamber of commerce promoters claim California's "fourteen southern counties": San Luis Obispo, Kings, Tulare, Inyo, Mono, Kern, Santa Barbara, Ventura, Los Angeles, San Bernardino, Orange, Riverside, San Diego, and Imperial.

From about 1940 to 1960 California experienced a flight of population to the suburbs, with a consequent denuding of the economic drawing power of its largest cities. In 1930 Los Angeles' downtown stores commanded 88 per cent of that metropolitan area's retail sales, but by 1959, their share of total sales had sunk to 19.6 per cent. Like Los Angeles, San Francisco also experienced considerable loss of population to its suburbs.

Today's California has fourteen "core cities," or Standard Metropolitan Statistical Areas of more than 250,000 each. Between 1950 and 1960, the largest of these, the Los Angeles-Long Beach area, increased in population by 27.1 per cent, while areas outside the two core cities increased by 82.6 per cent. Another core area is Kern County (1960 population, 291,984). There, Bakersfield increased by 63.4 per cent between 1950 and 1960, versus 27.9 per cent for Kern County. The San Francisco-Oakland metropolitan area, with a population of 2,783,359 in 1960, gained by 24.2 per cent in population from 1950 to 1960, but its central cities lost 4.5 per cent.

By 1960, 86.4 per cent of California's population was urban. Population density in the state was then 100.4 persons per square mile, almost twice the average for the United States (50.5). Orange, Santa Barbara, and San Diego Counties each gained more people between 1950 and 1960 than any of 33 states. San Bernardino County gained more than any of 23 states. Between 1950 and 1960, the population of Orange County expanded 225.6 per cent, and various northern counties registered gains ranging from 51.5 to 120 per cent. Fresno County had a 1960 population of 365,945 while the San Jose-Santa Clara County area that year numbered 642,315.

Sacramento had a 1960 county population of 502,778. Between 1950 and 1960 the area surrounding Sacramento increased by 122.9 per cent, versus 39.3 per cent for the city alone. The San Bernardino-Riverside-Ontario region had a 1960 population of 809,782. In San Diego the 1960 county population was 1,033,011. Dynamic growth occurred outside the city between 1950 and 1960 as its suburbs increased by 106.7 per cent, versus 71.4 per cent for San Diego proper.

By 1980 one out of every six Americans may be living in California. Almost certainly they will be unevenly distributed. In 1960, about 90 per cent of the population was clustered around nine metropolitan areas, encompassing less than 5 per cent of California's land.

In the Los Angeles 5-County Area (Los Angeles, Orange, San Bernardino, Riverside, and Ventura), the population is expected to climb from 9.4 million in 1965 to 11.9 million in 1975, and 15 million in 1985, or a 60 per cent gain over the 20-year period. This compares with an expected increase of almost exactly the same percentage in the nine-county San Francisco Bay area, comprising Alameda, Contra Costa, Marin, Napa, San Francisco, San Mateo, Santa Clara, Solano, and Sonoma—the population of which is projected to rise from 4.3 million in 1965 to 6.9 million in 1985.

Growth will continue to pose grave problems. The labor market must expand unceasingly to absorb millions of new workers. In an era of labor-saving technological mechanization this promises to be a challenging task. No new mammoth growth industry, unless it be space-technology, seems likely to stimulate the state's economy as did the defense industries during the 1950's. Possibly space-technology may hold the key to California's expansion. In 1962 Californians had a share in the production of such scientific marvels as the instrumentation which put America's astronauts into orbit.

Because the older segment of California's population has also grown, fear is occasionally voiced that a serious economic recession would gravely burden the state's relief rolls. Thousands of "senior citizens" over the age of 60 have flocked to southern California. The term "senior citizen," a euphemism of questionable felicitousness, possibly invented to mask society's indifference, could be applied to more than 10 per cent of California's population. Thus far, the economy has proved expansive enough to allow successful economic integration of aged persons into the California labor market. But, as long as per capita income remains the highest in the nation ($2,871 as against $2,351 nationally), workers in search of jobs will be strongly attracted to California.

Perhaps inevitably the newcomers to California have been primarily workers; a large proportion of the new residents are in the young-adult age bracket. The newcomers also tend to be well-educated. California has also drawn part of its new society from less privileged areas of the country. Overall, these new Californians are in no way less able or less trained workers than the bulk of the population resident in the state before World War II. Governor Warren once said of California's unending flow of new residents that the state was profiting from a "population bargain."

Californians have also been considerably concerned with the rising cost of state government. In the past three decades, the state government has become a veritable behemoth. Since 1930 the number of state employees jumped about 600 per cent—from 17,-000 to 115,000 in 1960, far in excess of the rate of population growth.

Today California can be reached readily from every quarter of the globe. The state is now serviced by major railroads and air-lines; a total of 462 air fields provide flights to cities of the United States, Mexico, Central and South America, Hawaii, and the Far East. At least 4 million tourists visit California each year, among them, in 1959, then Soviet Premier Nikita Khrushchev. California has become increasingly the point of departure for the popular polar route to Europe.

Urbanization and Its Consequences

As we have seen, smog, which has damaged the state's attrac-tiveness, poses only one representative problem. A host of other difficulties have arisen out of California's shift from an agri-cultural to an industrial way of life. Inordinate delay in develop-ing new water resources, for example, could well deter expansion. Additional industry and investment capital must be attracted to the state. Sorely needed educational facilities must continue to be created. Coordination of mass transportation is crucial. Traffic congestion has grown acute and requires quick solution. Even the newest roadways are overcrowded and dangerous. The freeways of today become obsolete almost before they are built. Traffic jams now require helicopter surveillance-scouting and air-to-ground radio reports. There exist grave shortages of hospitals, jails, fire stations, police facilities, sewage plants, and community rehabilitation centers.

Dynamite and the bulldozer have ruined irreplaceable scenic sites, and the landscape has been gouged by deep scars. Talk of rejuvenation projects and pedestrian malls is dwarfed by con-tinued deterioration of the environment. In 1963 James K. Carr, a Californian, and President Kennedy's Under Secretary of the In-terior, took a pessimistic view of this change:

Smog too often hangs like a pall over all our cities, causing discom-fort, damage, and even death. In a single generation we have almost ruined the superb, Mediterranean climate of southern California. Some shore lines foam with detergents, fish and wildlife are threatened, and scenic beauty is destroyed. Cities slobber over into the countryside, cluttered with billboards, spawning sleazy developments that have brought new, ugly words to our California lexicon—slurbs and slurburbia.

The shores of Lake Tahoe, the jewel of the Sierra, already bear the permanent scars of uncontrolled, unplanned commercialism un-checked; this kind of slurbanization can despoil forever our cherished, scenic recreation areas. The redwoods, noble sentries of this "unique bright land," are increasingly victims of the chain saw, being logged in many places with no other control than the laws of the market place, as though these trees were just another species of timber. In some instances, the logged-over hillsides bleed silt into the streams where fish no longer swim. . . . We will have to establish Orange Grove State Park in southern California to show future generations a real orange grove.

The National Park Service has estimated that there were once more than 2 million acres of redwoods between Monterey Bay and southern Oregon, but now only 15 per cent of that virgin forest remains. During the 1960's these tallest of trees continued to be cut down at the incredible rate of a billion board feet per year. Were it not for an organization known as the Save the Redwoods League most of the virgin forests would have vanished. West coast architects, accustomed to designing redwood-type buildings, require increased quanties of this wood. Even the 50,000 acres of redwood within the state's parklands (a bare 3 per cent of the remaining virgin forest) is in danger. After 1964 there were demands that the state cut an expressway through the very heart of its coastal redwood forests. California's forests are being destroyed by logging and other causes twice as fast as they are being replenished by natural growth.

Furthermore, only some 10 per cent of the state is still farmland; Californians are paving this over at the rate of 90,000 acres a year—an area three times the size of San Francisco. The Bay region's 4 million people, indeed, are spilling over even into the once tranquil and green wine-growing Napa and Livermore Valleys. As elsewhere, a freeway will soon replace the meandering two-lane road that runs the length of the Napa Valley, which will probably touch off a development boom along its route. Bold action will be required to preserve even agricultural areas from commercial encroachment. Conservationists have, therefore, suggested establishment of national agricultural reserves, just as seashore and historical areas have been created to protect man's avarice.

Not all urbanization has led to spoliation. One of the genuinely spectacular land developments of recent times has been the opening up of the formerly restricted Irvine Ranch properties in Orange County. In 1864 the San Francisco merchant James Irvine with three partners purchased Rancho San Joaquin. By 1889 he had expanded the Irvine Ranch to 105,000 acres, weaving two other ranches into a single parcel of land. His holdings, six times the size of Manhattan, extended 22 miles inland from the coast. Later his son incorporated the holdings to form the Irvine Com-

ALAMEDA INTERCHANGE WITH BAY BRIDGE IN BACKGROUND. (Division of Highways.)

pany, whose real estate value soared to $1 billion. Before 1960 the company leased nearby fertile land on which to run sheep and cattle and to raise barley, potatoes, wheat, and, later, citrus. In 1960 a master plan was drawn up for development of Irvine's agricultural lands also for residential, industrial, recreational, and cultural uses. A new campus of the University of California was built on land donated by the company to the state. By the year 1990 the college expects to have an enrollment of 27,500 students. On a hill where Spanish conquistadores once viewed the Pacific Ocean stands a massive new "Fashion Island." Irvine's master plan includes 622 acres for four major department stores with 50 smaller establishments to serve shoppers in southern California. The Irvine development is graced by the nearby resort cities of Newport, Balboa, and Laguna Beach.

Reorganization of older sites for modern purposes has also

occurred at San Francisco. In 1967 that city restored its Palace of Fine Arts, the last remaining proud remnant of its 1915 Panama Pacific International Exhibition. Along the Marina Shoreline visitors see a 160-foot-high domed rotunda on the east and a semicircular 48-foot-high gallery on the west, the tour de force of the architect Bernard Maybeck. The Victorian Ghirardelli chocolate factory has also been restored as one of the most charming places in the country to wine, dine, and shop. Conversion of an adjacent antique cannery near Fisherman's Wharf and of the city's intriguing cable car barn (whose machinery has been repainted in gay colors) combines preservation of historic sites with today's functional needs.

Conservationists remain concerned not only with preserving urban and rural values; they wish to save nature itself. Repeated demands have been made that San Francisco Bay be filled in to accommodate more population. In 1965 the state legislature created a Bay Conservation and Development Commission, a step partly designed to stop the Berkeley city council from doubling that city's area by expanding into the bay. This has become a major regional political issue, as have other proposals concerning the use of land, water, and air.

Steadily criticized, for example, were the Atomic Energy Commission tapline at Woodside, despoliation of scenic coastlands and redwoods, and the unsystematic use of arable lands. The harmful commercialism of neon signs, haphazard garbage disposal, and the lack of parks in urban areas also offended thinking persons. Threats to such green belts as San Francisco's Golden Gate Park and Los Angeles' Elysian Park were increasingly condemned. After 1965, a new voice in all this criticism, the magazine *Cry California*, was launched by a non-profit conservationist group called "California Tomorrows."

There is a correlation between California's deteriorating environment and a diminishing public pride. Avaricious developers have located cheaply constructed tract homes in areas isolated from productive centers of employment. Such houses quickly fall into a state of disrepair; deserted by working folk, they sometimes lapse into the hands of the unemployed or of migrants. Such poor planning by selfish vested interests has led to an environmental deterioration which spawns riots and other antisocial behavior. Ulcerated nests of poverty, ugly slum conditions, and a shrinking countryside press in upon and weaken local government while splashy billboards, set against a backdrop of junkyards and ramshackle houses, undermine community morale.

An "artificial landscape" consumes much of the countryside.

Even the amusement parks so popular in today's California are a synthetic alternative to the greenery obliterated by her largest municipalities. Lewis Mumford has attempted to make us aware of the senseless cannibalism of the modern "gridiron cities." As more freeways are developed, to transport workers in an increasingly hive-like environment, traffic congestion mounts. Not only do California's freeways erase the countryside; they also take valuable land off the public tax rolls. Freeways consume up to 28 acres of land per mile of construction. An interchange uses up to 80 acres. By the late 1960's the San Francisco Bay area alone lost an estimated 21 square miles of countryside every year, while southern California surrendered 70 square miles annually to concrete ribbons and "urban sprawl." When taxes go up, due primarily to shortsighted zoning, farmers are forced to sell valuable agricultural land. The chance for future beautification of the countryside is thus lost.

At Los Angeles, this type of squandering is at its worst. Mumford estimates that two-thirds of the central part of that city is occupied by streets, freeways, parking facilities, and garages. Without these provisions for the movement of large numbers of persons, however, an even more chaotic urban center would probably exist. The failure to develop a mass transportation system into the center of Los Angeles has speeded dispersal of that city to its suburbs. It is doubtful that "L.A.'s" westward extension toward its Wilshire district would have expanded nearly so rapidly had downtown rapid transit become a reality. Paradoxically, the late 1960's witnessed a counter-trend back into the centers of both San Francisco and Los Angeles. The decline of city core areas there and elsewhere has ended, and real estate values have been moving upward. Los Angeles' central city boom began with construction of a new Music Center, the 42-story Union Bank Building, and the 55-story Richfield-Bank of America complex (planned as a West Coast version of New York's Rockefeller Center). Urban residents, however, continue to move to outlying areas and to orient their lives around such suburban shopping centers as Newport, rather than revived urban cores.

A new type of planning is needed if Californians are not to live in hopeless congestion and if they are to safeguard their woodlands, lakes, seashore, and desert areas. The state's skyline has become markedly different in configuration. As the tide of life rushes up through its valleys, overwhelming the countryside, thousands of new ranch-style houses are hammered together. As a result, California's physical appearance is changing radically. Urbanization, industrialization, and the freeways are the chief causes.

SAN FRANCISCO. (Courtesy of William A. Garne

Peacefulness has departed, perhaps forever, from many areas. The whine of rubber tires on concrete and the drone or explosive clatter of overhead aircraft seem to be ever-present. Repeatedly, engineering-minded planners have placed the maintenance of California's scenic beauty relatively low on their order of priorities. The obligation to create and to improve the livability of its communities is, however, at least as important as moving traffic or building new high tension power lines. Hopefully, new state parks at Angel Island, Point Reyes, and in the Channel Islands off Santa Barbara will be developed. If these sanctuaries become a reality, future generations may be able to see something of what this land was like before the coming of the white man, also renewing both mind and spirit in an age of increasing complexity.

The tendency of California's cities to grow without planning continues to result in the sacrifice of aesthetic values, for metropolitan planning is still in its infancy, especially in the West. Eastern cities were among the earliest to embrace the tools and resources necessary to combat urban blight. California's Community Redevelopment Law encourages local communities to redevelop their neighborhoods with the help of federal loans and grants, but squabbling among local officials often prevents action. Instead of finding better ways to house lower-income residents, energy has been dissipated in bitter debates over whether there should be more public housing in its present form or none at all. Urban renewal has lost political appeal with voters because of its imperfections rather than because of its need. Conservatives charge that it is impossible to write regulations in Washington which apply to each state, county, or city; California, especially, seems too diverse and its problems are sometimes unique. Federal controls which Ronald Reagan has called "financial strait jackets" infuriate conservative critics of public housing. Large Negro ghettos, as in the Watts area, have, meanwhile become pockets of poverty and reservoirs of unemployed labor. By 1980, some 90 per cent of the population will be living in urban areas, where housing problems become more acute.

One day a solid city will stretch northward from San Diego to Los Angeles, then to Santa Barbara and perhaps even to San Luis Obispo. Its east-west line will probably run from the Sierra Madre Mountains to the ocean. In northern California a second decentralized, sprawling urban complex may become a continuous metropolis around the fingers of San Francisco Bay—with offshoots into the valleys northward, southward, and inland from the bay. The planning of these super-cities of the future must go forward rapidly.

Urbanization is erasing the functionally impractical and artificial boundaries created by past generations. Smaller cities have, in numerous instances, become economically, socially, and politically obsolete. As new governmental entities evolve out of the re-districting of these communities, Californians seek to maintain local autonomy. Just as freeways may have to give way to lightweight monorail lines, so must local government evolve more subtle new forms to meet the challenge of the urban sprawl. In an age of rapid transition, society requires cooperation between the older city and county units of government and such essential new agencies as metropolitan water districts, metropolitan transit authorities, and air pollution control districts. As the megalopolis inundates man's land and his activities, government becomes remote from the governed, and irrelevant to their needs.

When California celebrated its new status as the most populous state, many recalled an earlier comment of Chief Justice Warren, a former great governor, who said:

I would not celebrate with fireworks, or by dancing in the street. I would make it a day of contemplation as to how we might better provide for the happiness of these millions. . . .

SELECTED READINGS

Basic materials concerning California's most pressing social problems are available for the most part in government reports rather than in book form. There is as yet no significant or comprehensive study of smog as a modern problem of industrial society, though the publications of the Los Angeles County Air Pollution Control District, mostly in mimeograph form, may be of some use to the student. Pertinent data on water development are to be found in various publications of the State Water Resources Board, notably *Water Resources of California* (Bulletin No. 1, Sacramento, 1951), and *The California Water Plan* (Bulletin No. 3, Sacramento, 1957). See also Mary Montgomery and Marion Clawson, *History of Legislation and Policy Formation of the Central Valley Project* (Berkeley, 1946). A detailed study of the relationship of politics to water development is Vincent Ostrom, *Water and Politics: A Study of Water Policies and Administration in the Development of Los Angeles* (Los Angeles, 1953). The Commonwealth Club of San Francisco also treats the question in its *Transactions* for March, 1950, pp. 183 ff., under the title "Who Should Develop California's Water Resources for Water and Power?" A worthwhile article that argues for the necessity of the Feather River Project is Sydney Kossen, "California's $2 Billion Thirst," *Harper's*, March, 1961, pp. 94–102.

Paul S. Taylor has written an imposing series of research monographs on the role of Mexicans in the United States. His *Mexican Labor in the United States* (Berkeley, 1928–1934), a multi-volume study, is basic to the subject. Volume I is entitled *Imperial Valley*. With Dorothy Lange Taylor, he also published *An American Exodus: A Record of Human Erosion* (New York, 1939). Carey McWilliams treats this same subject in his previously mentioned *Factories in the Fields*, as well as in *North from Mexico* (Philadelphia, 1949). In a similar vein is Ruth D. Tuck, *Not with the Fist* (New York, 1946). Useful also is Harry Schwartz, *Seasonal Farm Labor in the United States* (New York, 1945). Leonard Pitt's *The Decline of the Californios: A Social History of the Spanish-Speaking Californians* (Berkeley, 1966), treats the Mexican-American story from 1846 to 1890. A modern discussion of the problem in relation to a vital California crop is N. Fogelberg and A. W. McKay, *The Citrus Industry and the California Fruit Growers Exchange System* (Washington, 1940). See also California State Chamber of Commerce, *Migrants: A National Problem and Its Impact upon California* (San Francisco, 1940), and N. Ray Gilmore and Gladys W. Gilmore, "The Bracero in California," *Pacific Historical Review*, XXXII (August, 1963), 265–282.

The best overall discussion of the offshore oil controversy is Ernest R. Bartley, *The Tidelands Oil Controversy* (Austin, 1953). This is an expansion of the same author's "The Tidelands Oil Controversy," *Western Political Quarterly*, II (March, 1949), 135–153. Another useful article is Robert B. Krueger, "State Tidelands Leasing in California," *U.C.L.A. Law Review*, V (May, 1958), 427–489. The United States Supreme Court decision which ruled that California should temporarily refrain from leasing its offshore oil lands was *United States v. California*, 332 U.S. 19 (1947).

The Fallbrook controversy was the subject of Ed Ainsworth and Cameron Shipp's "Government's Big Grab," *Saturday Evening Post*, January 5, 1952, pp. 26 ff., and, by the same authors in the same journal, "Fallbrook Case Explodes in the Bureaucrats' Faces," October 11, 1952, pp. 10 ff.

Reapportionment problems are treated in Thomas S. Barclay, "The Reapportionment Struggle in California in 1948," *Western Political Quarterly*, IV (June, 1951), 315–316, and in Ivan Hinderaker and Laughlin E. Waters, "A Case Study in Reapportionment—California 1951," *Law and Contemporary Problems*, XVII (Spring, 1952), 440–449. Critical of the selection of state senators by counties is Dean E. McHenry, "Should State Senators Represent People or Space?" *Frontier*, I (March, 1950), 4–6. Similarly informative is J. C. Peppin, "Municipal Home Rule in California," *California Law Review*, XXX (March, 1942), 272–332.

The Southern California Research Council's reports on the past and future growth of that area are listed in the "Selected Readings" for Chapter 35. Consult also a study by the Stanford Research Institute entitled *The California Economy, 1947–1980* (December, 1960).

Urbanization and its problems are creating a literature more national than regional. Gordon Mitchell, *Sick Cities* (New York, 1963), however, includes a devastatingly factual probe of Los Angeles as a prototype. Implied criticisms of that city include Christopher Rand, *Los Angeles, the Ultimate City* (New York, 1967), and Alison Lurie, *The Nowhere City* (New York, 1966). More objective but less imaginative is Robert M. Fogelson, *The Fragmented Metropolis, Los Angeles, 1850–1930* (Cambridge, Mass., 1967). Consult also John L. Chapman, *Incredible Los Angeles* (New York, 1967). Raymond F. Dasmann, *The Destruction of California* (New York, 1965), reflects the shock of a trained biologist and zoologist concerning what has been happening to California. Even more critical is William Bronson's *How to Kill A Golden State* (New York, 1968). Another look at the sullied landscape which man is creating appears in Richard Lillard, *Eden in Jeopardy, Man's Prodigal Meddling With His Environment: The Southern California Experience* (New York, 1966).

Surprisingly, no popular book has yet been written regarding the smog problem. Government reports do exist, however, beginning with *Air Pollution and the Public Health* (Sacramento, 1957). The Air Pollution Foundation has also published *The Air Pollution Problem: An Appraisal* (San Marino, 1960).

37

The Present

Few events in America's history can match California's emergence as a major force in our national existence. Yet pursuit of "the good life" in California veils both its past achievements and future challenges. The unstructured routine of Californians also obscures specific answers to baffling economic, political, and social questions. Some of California's most pressing problems have developed only in the last three decades. A sense of history, therefore, may not seem especially useful to their solution. The widely differing beliefs of Californians reflect not only the confusions that exist but also the state's variety of residents. The clash between contending social outlooks has not completely watered down a common pride; yet today's Californians are divided about their goals and how to achieve them.

Glowing or Clouded Future

One can celebrate California's recent material growth with good reason. Not so certainly does the historian of today find her people assured of their future. Population pressure alone has caused some decline in the state's sense of an unlimited horizon. The confusions of this age have seemed to disorient the heritage of the forefathers. For several generations material success did inspire a yeasty confidence. A relatively free educational and social system produced idealism; but this has not assured the development of a critical temper in America, of which California is a reflection. A resourceful and practical people once had faith in the ability of the common man to do almost anything by himself; however, this created an antipathy to planning. A tendency to let things drift, nationally and locally, has been more characteristic than has preparation for long-range results. Inexperience with planning may, in fact, be a major disability of national and state progress, California's included. Not until the time of Hiram Johnson, during the almost accidental presidency of Theodore Roosevelt, did "experts in government" begin to appear. City planners were virtually unheard of before 1910. Later, haphazard emergency "planning" during the New Deal years made that word suspect in the vocabulary of older persons. Yet there must be skillful, non-political planning in the lives of nations and states, just as there is in that of individuals. In an age of mass complexity, the absence of order can lead to chaos. There is evidence that California has been caught up in the tendency toward overpowering environmental disorder.

Ours is an age of surplus population, where smog is only one of many waste products. Thoughtful people are alarmed by the loss of purpose and the uneasy defeatism that seem to have punctured California's glowing record. To the right or left of center, old and young alike seem increasingly discontented. The historian can only be impressed and humbled, for them, by the magnitude of the tasks that lie ahead as he seeks to examine the roots of alienation in their midst. If not met, some of California's most pressing social problems—the scummy air and garbage-strewn shorelines, stubborn race relations, traffic congestion, critical fiscal demands (particularly for education and crime control), and violation of the landscape—will become a limiting factor upon the state's future.

Continued Agricultural Unrest

Matters of labor and race lie at the very heart of California's turmoil. In 1968 its working population numbered almost 8 million. While the percentage of agricultural workers has steadily declined, some of the most serious problems of labor remain rooted in the rural sector of California's economy. As we have seen, the state's "wetback" and migrant problem, spanning the period from 1930 into the postwar era, has generated continuing discontent.

California attracts one out of every seven Americans who move

from one state to another. Some of these persons are restless. Reflective of the continuing rootlessness of field laborers was a massive strike—after September, 1965—of some 4,500 grape harvesters near Delano, a Central Valley community. The protracted
strike reminded Californians of the disorganization among the
state's 500,000 seasonal farm laborers. Their problems had
plagued the state since before Steinbeck wrote *Grapes of Wrath*.
The strikers, many of whom belonged to minority groups, sought
$1.40 per hour from growers. In addition, these field workers
wanted union recognition, better housing and working conditions,
unemployment insurance, and the right to bargain collectively. At
first farm owners refused to discuss these demands, and some
even dusted the strikers with insecticides. Laborers imported by
the growers met aggressive picket lines shouting "Viva la Huel-
ga!" while firing marbles with sling shots. Then labor organizers
imposed a statewide sympathetic boycott upon Delano grapes and
beverages. Several chain stores agreed not to stock these items.
Leaflets explaining the boycott flooded into stores which had not
agreed to ban such merchandise. The strike was backed by the
Congress of Racial Equality (CORE) and various student groups,
with support from local clergymen. To dramatize their cause, the
grape-strikers marched 300 miles to Sacramento to confer with
Governor Brown. Three years later, grape-strikers again marched
on the capital to present their demands to Governor Reagan.

In subsequent negotiations with large farm operators, the striking field hands were represented by two new labor groups, the
National Farm Workers Association and the AFL-CIO United
Farm Workers Organizing Committee. Personally leading the farm
workers was Cesar Chavez, a magnetic idealist who had spent his
youth in the labor camps of Imperial Valley. On one occasion
when members of his union were accused of advocating violence
he went on a hunger strike. Ultimately most of his demands were
met and, by 1968, the minimum rate for fruit pickers had reached
$1.70 per hour. But trouble in the fields was not over.

The Mexican-Americans

No racial group, except perhaps the Negroes, has aroused more
recent public attention than California's 1,600,000 Mexican-Americans. They formed, like the Negroes, not a large percentage of the
population. Indeed, by 1960 only 8.5 per cent of all Californians
were foreign-born, the biggest numbers from Mexico, Canada,
Italy, Britain, and Germany, in that order. California's Mexican-

Americans, however, outnumber its Negroes by a two to one ratio. Their birthrate is some 50 per cent higher than the general population. Also, the Mexican-American community's average age is ten years younger than the total population. Increasingly, however, both major political parties realized the latent importance of the once inarticulate Mexican-American segment of the state's population. In 1963 California's Mexican-Americans were shocked by the assassination of President Kennedy. A fellow Catholic, he had been nominated for the presidency at Los Angeles, hub of the Mexican-American population, and had campaigned with special vigor among the "Viva Kennedy" clubs organized during the 1960 presidential campaign.

Early in 1964 Kennedy's successor, President Lyndon B. Johnson, scheduled a series of unprecedented conferences in Los Angeles with Mexico's President Lopez Mateos. These covered the whole range of United States relations with Mexico and were also attended by Secretary of State Dean Rusk. In addition to discussing the sharing of Colorado River water and the *bracero* problem, the two chiefs of state dealt with the social reforms championed by Kennedy's Alliance for Progress program throughout the Americas. Astute observers of local politics did not, however, miss the importance of the setting in which the Democratic Party had chosen to hold these talks, or the emerging political role of the Mexican-Americans. Los Angeles contains the largest Mexican population of any city outside Mexico City.

Widespread dissatisfaction continues in California's Mexican-American community. Less than five years after President Kennedy's death their grief was to be repeated. In June, 1968, his brother, Senator Robert F. Kennedy of New York, was assassinated at Los Angeles following a stunning presidential primary victory in which the Mexican-Americans had strongly participated.

While the discrimination directed against them may not seem so overt as that which the Negro encounters, the status of that minority remains deprived. Seventy-six per cent of California's 1968 adult population of Mexican background was employed in unskilled occupations. Statistically they were then two full years behind the Negro in scholastic achievement, and four years behind non-minority citizens of the state. The Californian of Mexican descent continued to live on a smaller per capita income than any other group in its population, including Negroes. Some California *Latino* leaders referred to the plight of their people as that of *desgraciados*, people "born without grace." For a populace so rich in tradition and so proud of its ancestral heritage, such a status is little short of humiliating.

Stereotyped attitudes toward the Mexican-Americans have grown in California since the Treaty of Guadalupe Hidalgo deceptively guaranteed a defeated people equal rights with other residents. Their years of employment as stoop laborers in the fields, presumed to be satisfied with menial jobs, cast some Mexican-Americans in the role of inferior members of the social order. Their children at times endured segregated seating in schools and special handling at the hands of white Anglo-Saxon Protestant (or WASP) authorities. Some Mexican-American children dropped out of school by the time they reached the eighth grade, the legal limit within which a child must attend classes. Such a child, who joined his father in the fields, also symbolically joined the ranks of thousands who were sidetracked from a college education.

While better educated Mexican-Americans escaped discrimination by rapid assimilation, others were apathetic about solving the problems of less advantaged compatriots. Some converts to the "Anglo" social order were content to move into the pleasant grass-green, middle-class neighborhoods of Oakland, Whittier, or Glendale. Politically naive, such folk were of little help to those devoted Mexican-American leaders anxious to improve the plight of their people. Among those who furnished leadership was Los Angeles City Councilman Edward Roybal who, in 1962, went on to become a congressman. Roybal had organized the Mexican-American Political Association, the most vocal of several such groups. Another leader was Dr. Julian Nava, a professor who served vigorously on the Los Angeles school board after 1967. Restiveness among California's Mexican-Americans, however, remained far from allayed by the slight political success they have had.

In March, 1968, various demonstrations and boycotts by hundreds of Mexican-American students and some of their teachers occurred in seven Los Angeles high schools. Several high schools whose population is predominantly Negro also closed down during this period of uprising. The city's school board was forced to promise implementation of various reforms after denying that it would not do so "on a shotgun basis." Among these was the appointment of at least one Negro school principal to replace a white principal as well as provision for improved school cafeterias, alleviation of restrictions on hair-styles and clothing, more bilingual instruction, smaller classes, and a modernized industrial training program for minority-group students who would not go on to college.

Accused of sparking the school walkouts were members of a new Mexican-American group called "the Brown Berets," whose goals stood in contrast to "the Green Berets" of the United States

Army in Vietnam. Their leaders sought to unite what they called "La Raza" (the race) in the *barrios* of California. Wearing clothing that resembled the revolutionary garb of Fidel Castro and his Cuban followers, these critics carried signs which read "Viva la Revolucion!" Despite their ominous appearance, fairly wide community support served to intimidate both the press and educational officials into a wider admission of the need for reform. As with the Negroes, the unrest of this significant minority posed many touchy and unresolved questions about their future.

The Negroes and Watts

Negroes remained clustered mostly in California's southland. The oldest Negro newspaper in the state, *The California Eagle*, has been published at Los Angeles since 1879. Negro communities grew slowly until the 1880's, after which larger numbers of Negroes piled into nascent ghettoes, including custodians, waiters, cooks, porters off railroad trains, domestics in the homes of the rich, handymen, and gardeners. The economic stimulus of World War I attracted still more Negroes westward. After the war these benefited from the national restrictive immigration laws of 1921 and 1924, which opened up jobs normally filled by foreigners.

Negroes from the southern states increasingly flocked to California. World War II added to the in-migration of Negroes. By 1944 the Japanese district of Los Angeles ("Little Tokyo") felt the inroads of 80,000 new Negro residents. Better established Negroes moved into Pasadena and into San Francisco from Oakland. "Lily white" cities, like Glendale or San Marino, had, however, virtually no Negro residents. The colored population founded an all-Negro community at Val Verde Park in the Tehachapi foothills and an important all-Negro insurance corporation, as well as a few Negro resorts. From the 1950's through the 1960's, about a thousand Negroes per month came into Los Angeles County alone. In that decade California's Negro populace grew by 91 per cent while its overall population increased by only 48 per cent. During the same decade more Negroes (over 350,000) moved to California than to any other state. Yet they remained a definite minority in total percentage of the population.

Negroes not only moved gradually into white neighborhoods; they also took jobs formerly held by Caucasians. In the professions, in sports, and in the political world they slowly challenged white supremacy, collectively and individually. Dr. Ralph Bunche, a graduate of UCLA, went from a State Department career to become Under Secretary at the United Nations; Jackie Robinson began his baseball prominence at Pasadena Junior College; Leslie Shaw became postmaster of Los Angeles in 1965; Thomas Bradley was only one Negro who came to be seated as a city councilman.

While entertainers like Nat "King" Cole or Sammy Davis, Jr., became well-known, relatively few Negroes made the progress to which they felt entitled. Crowded into dilapidated lower-class neighborhoods, they chafed at prejudice, segregation, and social deprivation. In southeast Los Angeles the sprawling all-Negro ghetto of Watts became an especially unwholesome sore spot. Although some of its streets were lined with palm trees, crowded slums were bound, eventually, to produce violence, directed against symbolic white oppressors.

California's Negroes detested what they considered rank legal and extra-legal discrimination. True, the Rumford Fair Housing Act, passed by the legislature in 1963, had broadened existing prohibitions against discrimination to include the sale or rental of private dwellings containing more than four units. Yet large segments of the population pressed for its repeal. Along with the 1959 Unruh Civil Rights Act (which had outlawed housing discrimination by business establishments), the Rumford Act formed the heart of the state's laws against discrimination in housing. In 1964 the voters adopted the controversial Proposition 14, which nullified the state's open housing provisions. This setback for Negroes occurred almost on the eve of the Watts riots. Not until 1966 did the state supreme court strike down Proposition 14. The Supreme Court of the United States confirmed that decision only in 1967. Meanwhile, continuing attempts to dismantle the state's fair housing laws were deeply resented by California's Negro community.

The "Negro Revolution" that swept across America in the 1960's was to reap tragic repercussions in the riots that broke out during August, 1965, at Watts. These violent uprisings epitomized the malaise of disenchanted Negroes and deeply upset Californians. Hundreds of crazed rioters, shouting the anti-white epithets "Burn Baby Burn" and "Get Whitey," looted stores, set buildings afire, and shot at firemen and police. Governor Brown ordered National Guard troops into Los Angeles to help local policemen restore order and to establish a curfew. The riots, which lasted for several days, caused the deaths of 35 persons (mostly Negroes), injury to 600 others, and $40 million in damage. Some 4,000 persons were arrested, mostly in a one square mile burned-over area. Rioters charged arresting police with brutality in Watts and later at Oakland and San Francisco, where "aftershocks" were felt for many months. The police asserted that criminal elements had taken control of the riots.

The seemingly motiveless violence of some Watts rioters undermined the authority of responsible Negro leaders. The riots also deepened the gulf between uninterested middle-class Negroes and their fellows at the bottom of the social heap. As acts of rage, black outbursts underscored a savage sense of hopelessness which grew out of economic misery, a diffuse Negro family structure, envy of the white man's luxuries, and resentment against "Establishment" forces of law and order. The anti-white rowdyism of the ignorant, however, made these upheavals only partly racial. The search for material goods led marauders to sack furniture stores filled with television sets, freezers, and high-fidelity phonographs —as if to defy the traditional white monopoly of "success." The orgy of looting at Watts had seemingly escalated into a racial outburst.

Various key terms or phrases repeated in California after the Watts riots symptomatically depicted the problems of "inner-city" streets there and elsewhere: "discrimination, anarchy, mob violence, looting, illegitimacy, drug addicts, venereal disease, employment inequality, police brutality, attacks on policemen and school teachers, white and non-white attitudes toward transportation to schools."

The Watts disturbances rate among the first serious racial conflicts in the postwar United States. The riots did little, however, to alter fear and hatred of disenchanted poor Negroes toward whites. There were, nevertheless, various moves toward reform, one of which was to focus attention on the building of a cultural center at Watts as well as a hospital. Educated Negroes from ghetto areas were listened to with greater attention than before; yet there was a continuing failure to delve into the quality of the African past and the meaning of race. The Mexican-Americans also keenly felt the lack of genuine white Anglo-Saxon Protestant accommodation to their way of life. The McCone Commission, a state investigatory body, chaired by the former head of the Central Intelligence Agency, was appointed by Governor Brown, and it interviewed dozens of Watts residents. A dialogue between the police and Negroes, in order to reduce community tension, accompanied demands for better local transportation and recreation facilities. Businessmen also tried to widen employment opportunities, in order to mollify the distrust and sense of despair of rootless male Negroes.

Some observers look upon California as the prototype of future societies. Its recent history partly confirms this belief. We now know that the stupor of fear and hatred so evident in the Watts riots was later to be repeated in Detroit, New Haven, Chicago, Newark, and elsewhere. During 1968, aftershocks of the Watts riots occurred. In the midst of that year's summer Watts festival, several persons were killed in armed encounters with the law. As in other instances of clashes between blacks and whites, police brutality was charged.

California's racial history had once actually seemed like a model one, when compared with that of some other states. Revamping run-down neighborhoods and pouring money into welfare programs, the state had never sponsored a poll tax. Although its cities long had separate Mexican-American and Chinese sectors, impacted Negro sections did not emerge until after World War II. Schools were officially integrated long ago.

Yet in 1964, as we have seen, state fair-housing provisions were callously repealed. Negroes blamed the real estate lobby for legalized segregation in housing. But bigotry seemed widespread among California's voters. Even after the Watts riots, many attempts were made in the legislature to repeal the Rumford Act, although, as a result, California stood to lose millions of dollars in federal redevelopment funds for non-segregated neighborhoods. In summary, despite the gains Negroes had made, they still lacked legal and social equality as well as earning power. While conditions for the California Negro improved marginally after the Watts riots, a rising level of expectation accompanied dissatisfaction over slowness in achieving parity with whites. "Black Power" advocates constantly reiterated the themes of discrimination and inequality. A growing population of idle young Negroes continues to expect realization of the promises of civil rights legislators, and of the sponsors of such national anti-poverty measures and educational programs as "Head Start" and "Upward Bound."

Racial Tally

In 1960 only 8 per cent of California's people were non-white. The rapidly expanding Negro population then constituted a clear majority of the non-whites, but still only 7.4 per cent of total state population. In 1960 California's residents comprised 14,455,230 Caucasians (including the Mexican Americans), 883,861 Negroes, 157,317 Japanese, 95,600 Chinese, 65,459 Filipinos, and 39,014 American Indians.

During 1962, President Kennedy issued a directive permitting refugees from Hong Kong and Taiwan to join family members in the United States. Many of these came to San Francisco's Chinatown, traditional center of America's West Coast Orientals. The next year President Johnson signed into law a bill amending the Immigration and Nationality Act. The new law provided for abolition of the national origins quota system by 1968. This would result in a future increase of Oriental immigration.

Student Unrest

Not all of California's problems were concerned with labor or race. Reflective of the national impatience of students, the mid-1960's stood in genuine contrast to the placidity of "the silent generation" during the 1950's. After 1963, especially, repeated student demonstrations occurred on California's campuses, particularly at the University of California at Berkeley. There were also numerous protest rallies at San Francisco State College and other collegiate centers. A "Free Speech Movement" at Berkeley kept the university in the headlines as "agitator-students" like Mario Savio and Bettina Aptheker insisted upon a greater voice in university administration. The right of political assembly was particularly dear to activists. Student drama, journalism, and music came to reflect their discontent. Wide-eyed young fans of the folksingers Bob Dylan and Joan Baez wanted action as well as words.

Following massive sit-ins during the fall of 1964, the Free Speech Movement grew politically unpopular. The blatant use of obscenity by some of its leaders was particularly unwise. In response to public demands, local police were called onto the Berkeley campus when order could not be maintained. More than 700 youths, not all of them students, were dragged out of Sproul Hall, the administrative center, and jailed. Almost 600 of these (including Savio) were pronounced guilty of illegal trespassing and resisting arrest. Repeatedly Ronald Reagan spoke of the need to clean up the Berkeley environment and its left-wing extremism.

Contributing to continued student malaise were stalemates encountered in both the civil rights struggle and in prosecution of the Vietnam War. The San Francisco Bay area became a national center of agitation both for Negro rights and against the war. Students threatened to burn draft cards, defied law and order, and remonstrated against "the Establishment." At Berkeley, especially, they resented the presence on campus of representatives from napalm-producing firms as well as armed service recruiters. As the Vietnam War dragged on, student and other rioters blocked the nearby Oakland Induction Center, turning in draft cards and, on occasion, even repudiating educational deferments.

Undergraduates and graduates alike wished to expand radically the role they played in collegiate government on the campuses of the state university. The wisdom of conservative, business-oriented regents, appointed for 16-year terms by past governors, was increasingly questioned. Students were impatient also with the depersonalization of academic life and they argued for decentralization of the state university. Pursuant to a regent-authorized investigation of 1965 (which culminated in the Byrne Report), the university eventually did take steps to decentralize its campuses; it also strengthened the authority of individual chancellors. Small undergraduate colleges similar to those at Oxford represented a student ideal, partly realized by the founding of a new university campus at Santa Cruz. At Berkeley and at other campuses, faculty study groups sought to find added ways to reduce mechanization and to disarm hostility and student disloyalty by sharing authority with them. The 1967 Muscatine Report of a faculty committee recommended various means by which teaching could be reinvigorated and the university decentralized.

After the Reagan administration came to office, public distrust of the state university reached new heights, as did student criticism not only of their authorities but particularly of the governor himself. A 96-page student-faculty (Berkeley) commission report of 1967 read: "The inroads on civil liberties and academic freedom made in the past year are warnings that for the first time in many years we are faced with a consistently unfriendly state administration whose theories of educational financing are a logical accompaniment to its suspicions of this campus." The resignations of University of California President Clark Kerr (1967) and President John Summerskill (1968) of San Francisco State College highlighted the tension between the academic world and various state authorities. Summerskill complained not only of educational budgets "inadequate to maintain operations at their present level"; he also predicted that the state college system would "break down if the trustees and politicians are going to hire and fire professors." He thereby referred to a nasty incident on the state college campus at Fullerton which involved censorship of a controversial dramatic production entitled *The Beard*. In 1968 this was to be followed by criticism of various sculpture and art shows on other state college campuses, which were labeled pornographic by critics in nearby municipalities.

There was no denying, especially after 1967, that California's academic community was in disfavor with a large segment of the state's voters. The public remained upset that college campuses had become centers of opposition to the Vietnam War as well as centers of criticism of American society. Taxpayers, confused by the mystique of revolt, believed that the state's colleges and universities should teach students only those skills with which they could make a living, and nothing else. Such critics did not feel that state-operated campuses should become the seats of independent inquiry, public criticism, or distasteful dramatic and artistic productions. At Berkeley, a city in which the university dominates the community in a monolithic way, the tension between town and gown continued unabated. Civic power remained in the hands of older residents who showed scant understanding of the radically different younger generation. The "generation gap" was partly related to a difference in goals between new and earlier residents.

The Hippies

In the 1960's the California environment came to reflect the alienation from society of a wide variety of young persons. The disgust of a new type of rebel called Hippies grew to be so great that they created a species of "underground culture." Instead of expressing open aggression against parents, the Hippies took a cool look at modern life, decided it was beyond hope, and "dropped out." Cloistered in the ghettoes of San Francisco, Oakland, or Venice West, they grew more and more resentful of the war in Vietnam, which took millions of dollars for armaments, while racial bigotry, poverty, and ignorance seemed to be troweled over. Disgust over automation, the suppression of individuality, and with what they considered the shallow materialism and phony morals of adults, led to further estrangement.

In California the Hippie generation sought distinctive salvation in a new life-style that involved the imaginative use of colors—sometimes called psychedelic. To transcend the monotony of ordinary existence some Hippies used drugs and were strongly preoccupied with the search for "inward values." In various pockets of communal living the Hippies emphasized love and the sharing of food and property. Hippiedom—the Haight-Ashbury district of San Francisco—became a national focal point, and on weekends Haight Street was jammed with curious sightseers, sometimes bringing traffic to a halt.

Magazines and newspapers, as well as radio and television stations, featured descriptions of young rebels. Parents could not understand how their children, who had enjoyed superior advantages, could leave their middle-class homes and, in the language of disillusioned youth, "turn on, tune in, and drop out." Increasingly youth was not impressed by materialism. For example, the fact that California reputedly has half the swimming pools in the United States was the sort of statistic not celebrated by the young. They were more apt to be impressed by the failures of conservationists in a struggle to create even a small national redwoods park on the California coast. Cancellation in 1967 by "civic groups" of a Renaissance Fair in the San Fernando Valley and of the Monterey Jazz Festival the next year represented the sort of intolerance against which youth chafed. California's Galanos-designed dresses, the cotillion balls of the society page, and the coming out of debutantes were far from the interests of experimenters with marijuana and Zen.

Hippies let their hair grow, dressed as they pleased, and often wore no shoes. Parents, however, frequently saw only outward appearances and seldom listened to their ideas, or so their children believed. Young rebels expressed these ideas in what came to be known as the "underground press." The Los Angeles *Free Press* was sold at curbside along the Sunset Strip. In the Bay Area the Berkeley *Barb* and San Francisco *Oracle* also assumed a semi-subversive anti-Establishment stance. The *Barb* defined underground people as "that part of the population which lives at odds with the Establishment," and stated that the paper would "push any movement that will push the Establishment in a socially humanistic direction."

Following the lurid publicity, and the ogling tourists who frequented the Haight-Ashbury district, came commercialization. Furthermore, the Hippie movement did not seem to diminish inherent avarice, aggressiveness, and other shortcomings in its adherents. Their ghetto resembled everyone else's; it too was ridden by malnutrition, poverty, illegitimacy, murder, suicide, and drug addiction. Distrust gradually arose among those who came to feel that their way of life had proved no better than society's. Drugs like LSD may have given new depth and meaning to a few users; to others, bad trips or looking inward did not sustain personal growth but sometimes represented a temporary fling or permanent tragedy. For the drug user, however, re-entry into the dull routine of one's society proved difficult, for drugs deadened the drive to work and produce. Sociologists and psychologists felt that the Hippies raised valid questions about society's ethics; yet these malcontents did not provide solutions. Critics of the Hippies believed that they had refused to face real issues and that this constituted a form of hypocrisy.

Hippies began to leave San Francisco and to start communes in rural areas of California when their utopian ideals seemed to falter. Meditation, taught by advocates of various eastern religions, attracted some of them. Looking inward to find peace without drugs was another approach, but the use of drugs remained widespread. Some lawyers advocated loosening state and federal penalties, particularly concerning the use of marijuana. Others hoped against hope that the Hippies would, in time, go back into the mainstream of California society and try to improve it. That society had apparently created as many anxieties for them as it had provided challenges.

California's Formless Style

The Hippies served to dramatize California's continuing lack of cohesion. Tension between its urban and rural elements, between the wealthy and the poor as well as the old and the young, unbalances the state's society. Yet variety and experiment remain part of the scene, as does the desire to hold fast to the known. Just as the Sierra Club guards the freshness of California's back country, San Franciscans take parochial pride in such historic symbols of the past as their cable cars, restaurants, and hotels. Los Angeles, instead, focuses upon the modern, material or artistic.

To outsiders California's people seem both provincial and cosmopolitan. Despite their economic successes, adjustment to the present appears awkward and ill-defined. The populace has reacted with mixed emotions to its technologically-oriented culture, at times valuing means over ends. There was a frontier brashness and individualism in the disparate masses that first came to California, characterized by the slogan "nothing succeeds like excess." As bizarre cults gave way to psychiatrists and group therapy, observers wondered if sophistication was taking place or not.

Some of California's oldest residents have found adjustment to non-frontier complexities difficult. Ultra-conservatives flocked to the John Birch Society, headquartered in San Marino, for deliverance from that confusing environment symbolized by the Beatniks and Hippies. The elderly felt especially alienated. Even to agree concerning the creative use of leisure was difficult. Priorities and appropriate political leadership offered still a greater forum for dispute. The unity to knit together diverse outlooks will not necessarily come via informality or by self-congratulation and overstatement or in a frantic search for freedom from anxiety.

Someone has said California attracts, but Californians repulse.

A westering force does garner young migrants as well as the aged. And the state offers unusual opportunities to educated and skilled persons. Yet California can be a disappointment for those who have little to contribute to its society. To such folk the state may seem impersonal and industrial rather than rural and friendly. California may lead the rootless, cut off from old ties and tradition, simply not to care about its future. It makes others insecure.

We have seen that resistance to planning has become as typical of modern Californians as almost any characteristic. This, despite the complexity of today's society which requires increased co-ordination and integration. Indeed, achievement of a balance between conflicting sectors of California life seems as imperative as individualism itself. Unlimited individualism (crime, for example) can be cripplingly disruptive in a mass culture. Yet the maximizing of a people's resources need not mean the sacrifice of individual freedom. The alternative—social disintegration—can result from the refusal to make those adaptive changes which altered conditions require. The ideals of the frontier can be preserved but readjusted to new frontiers—including the art of living in one of the world's most complex societies.

Hopeful Horizon?

Like the rest of the nation, Californians belong to a consumer-oriented society—one that is constantly reassured by the advertising media that its greatest strength and virtue derive from the production, distribution, and consumption of more and more goods. Consequent confusion over human values is not surprising. Nevertheless, in an age of commuting autoists, traffic roar, and contorted megalopolises, Californians may yet be able to salvage their expansive style of shuttle-living. This is not only a matter of revitalizing ugly city cores and polluted suburbs—tomorrow's slums. California needs to match its material advance with cultural and social cohesion. Along with the look-alike supermarket chains, industrial parks, pedestrian malls, rejuvenated housing projects, pool-flanked houses, and sports cars, social and cultural depth is yet to be achieved. Otherwise freedom from formality will be California's most deep-rooted tradition; that is, the lack of tradition itself. It is a long road from the leafy environment of suburbia's glistening outdoor barbecues to the building of a heritage of noble dimensions.

Californians are no longer frontiersmen. The extravagances of the past have been tempered by wealth and the responsibility that comes from power. As we have seen, a society geared to commerce can yearn for culture. Without conforming to a rigid pattern of conduct, Californians have built a new center of political and economic life. This fluid, vital society, with its freer style of work, has attracted international attention. Critics may call Californians sports-mad, or loungers in a lotus-land, but they also see California as a window into the future. Californians remain favored by climate, history, and enthusiasm. That their state will continue to expand—in population, economy, and power—is a prediction easily made. That this expansion will beget cultural depth and significance cannot be forecast so readily. We can only be certain that California's potentialities are vast.

The big, the new, and the innovative do not assure quality. In fact, these attributes can actually retard California from maturing into that scarce fusion of culture, willpower to excel, and desire for change that characterized fifth-century Greece, Republican Rome, or the Renaissance cities. Motion sometimes defies stability.

California has been likened to Italy in variety; Los Angeles to Rome in amorphousness; and San Francisco to Florence in style and atmosphere. Beauty, grace, humor, and wit develop slowly in any civilization. To move from frontier conditions into urban grandeur provides a great challenge for any culture. One day a new faith in their future may help Californians to build more than plastic cities pockmarked by ugliness, crowding, and the blight of impersonality. At that point materialist boosterism will have given way to the confidence of solid achievement. Beauty lost will have become beauty rewon.

Finally, out of respect for California's future history, we do well to heed the immortal lines of William Shakespeare:

> There is a tide in the affairs of men,
> Which, taken at the flood, leads on to fortune;
> Omitted, all the voyage of their life
> Is bound in shallows and in miseries.
> On such a full sea are we now afloat,
> And we must take the current when it serves,
> Or lose our ventures.

SELECTED READINGS

In addition to the sources cited in Chapter 36, various recent studies of the Mexican-Americans concern their role in agriculture. These include John Gregory Dunne, *Delano—The Anatomy of the Great California Grapeworkers Strike* (New York, 1967); John C. Elac, "The Employment of Mexican Workers in U.S. Agriculture, 1900–1960," Ph.D. dissertation, UCLA (1961); James F. Rooney, "The Effects of Imported Mexican Farm Labor in a California County," *American Journal of Economics and Sociology*, XX (October, 1961), 513–521; W. Willard Wirtz (U.S. Secretary of Labor), *The Year of Transition: Seasonal Farm Labor* (Washington, 1966); Ernesto Galarza, *Merchants of Labor: The Mexican Bracero Story* (San Jose, 1964); Otey M. Scruggs, "The Evolution of the Mexican Farm Labor Agreement of 1942," *Agricultural History*, XXXIV (July, 1960), 140–149; and Truman E. Moore, *The Slaves We Rent* (New York, 1965). More general are Manuel P. Servín, "The Pre-World War II Mexican-American: An Interpretation," *California Historical Society Quarterly* (December, 1966), 325–328; Fernando Penalosa, "The Changing Mexican-American in Southern California," *Sociology and Social Research*, LI (July, 1967), 405–417; Michael Mathes, "The Two Californias During World War II," *California Historical Society Quarterly*, XLIV (December, 1965), 323–332; and John R. Martinez, "Mexican Immigration to the United States, 1910–1930," Ph.D. dissertation, University of California, Berkeley (1957).

The Division of Fair Employment Practices, California Department of Industrial Relations, has published a series of valuable pamphlets, including *Californians of Spanish Surname* (1964); *Negroes and Mexican Americans in Southeast Los Angeles* (1966); *Negro Californians* (1963); and *Californians of Japanese, Chinese, and Filipino Ancestry* (1965). See also Helen Rowan, "A Minority Nobody Knows," *Atlantic*, Vol. 219 (June, 1967), pp. 47–52.

Relatively recent appraisals of the Negro include F. Ray Marshall, *The Negro and Organized Labor* (New York, 1965); Edward E. France, "Some Aspects of the Migration of the Negro to the San Francisco Bay Area Since 1940," Ph.D. dissertation, University of California, Berkeley (1962); and Luigi Laurenti, *Property Values and Race* (New York, 1961). Journalistic literature on the Watts riots is already substantial. A basic document is the McCone Commission report, entitled *Violence in the City—An End or a Beginning* (Los Angeles, 1965), which can be supplemented by Jerry Cohen and William Murphy, *Burn Baby Burn: The Los Angeles Race Riot, August, 1965* (New York, 1966), which reproduces photos taken during the riots. Other accounts are Spencer Crump, *Black Riot in Los Angeles: The Story of the Watts Tragedy* (Los Angeles, 1966), and Robert Conot, *Rivers of Blood, Years of Darkness* (New York, 1967), which includes case histories, interviews, and sociological material concerning the Watts riots. One of the best photographic records of the riots is "La Revolte de Los Angeles," *Paris Match*, August 28, 1965.

Clark Kerr, *The Uses of a University* (New York, 1963), relates higher education to the needs of a technological society. More immediately focused upon California is Arthur G. Coons, *Crises in California Education* (Los Angeles, 1968). The Muscatine Report has been published as *Education at Berkeley* (Berkeley, 1967). Seymour M. Lipset and Sheldon S. Wolin, eds., *The Berkeley Student Revolt: Facts and Interpretations* (New York, 1965), will inevitably be followed by similar books, as will the first "life" of Ronald Reagan (with Richard Hubler), *Where's the Rest of Me?* (New York, 1965). A survey of recent California politics is Eugene C. Lee, ed., *The California Governmental Process: Problems and Issues* (Boston, 1966). Publicist Thomas M. Storke's battle against the John Birch Society is described in his *I Write for Freedom* (Fresno, 1963), with a preface by Adlai Stevenson. Charles M. Price ed., *Consensus and Cleavage: Issues in California Politics* (San Francisco, 1968), is a compilation of selected articles about persistent political problems. Similar in tone, but reaching further back, are the readings edited by Leonard Pitt, entitled *California Controversies: Major Issues in the History of the State* (New York, 1967).

The past decade has seen the publication of numerous articles in national journals concerning California's politics, economics, society, racial problems, style of life, and future. Mostly, they offer a stereotyped view that stresses the modern, the adventuresome, and the bizarre. Here are a few of the most prominent issues of such magazines: "The Call of California," *Life*, October 19, 1962; "California: 62 Pages of Words and Pictures," *Look*, September 25, 1962; "California Without Cliches," *Holiday*, October, 1965; "California," *Look*, June 28, 1966; "California, The Nation Within a Nation," *Saturday Review*, September 23, 1967.

Two retrospective as well as forecastive issues of the magazine *Los Angeles* were published in January, 1966, and January, 1967. R. A. Smith, "Los Angeles, Prototype of Supercity," *Fortune*, LXXI (March, 1965), 99–103, is self-descriptive as is Mellier Scott, *Partnership in the Arts: Public and Private Support of Cultural Activities in the San Francisco Bay Area* (Berkeley, 1963). Arthur Bloomfield, *The San Francisco Opera, 1923–1961* (San Francisco, 1961), also concerns the growth of culture in the Bay area. A glance at the tensions exerted upon a middle-class southern California suburb is Richard M. Elman, *Ill-at-Ease in Compton* (New York, 1968).

Finally, several books, written in a popular vein, seek to fathom the most recent intricacies of state politics. Among these are Gladwin Hill, *Dancing Bear: The Inside Look at California Politics* (New York, 1968), Bill Boyarsky, *The Rise of Ronald Reagan* (New York, 1968), Joseph Lewis, *What Makes Reagan Run?: A Political Profile* (New York, 1968), and Carey McWilliams, ed., *The California Revolution* (New York, 1968). The last is an uneven collection of seventeen essays on modern California.

Appendix

The Governors of California

SPANISH REGIME, 1767–1821

Dates of service in the case of each governor are from
assumption to surrender of office

GASPAR DE PORTOLÁ
November 30, 1767, to July 9, 1770

From May 21, 1769, Portolá's position was that of *Comandante-militar*
for Alta California. Fom July 9, 1770, to May 25, 1774, the position of
Comandante was filled by Pedro Fages; and from May 25, 1774, to
February, 1777, by Fernando Rivera y Moncada.

MATÍAS DE ARMONA
June 12, 1769, to November 9, 1770

FELIPE DE BARRI
March ?, 1770, to March 4, 1775

Governor of *Las Californias*, residing at Loreto.

FELIPE DE NEVE
March 4, 1775, to July 12, 1782

In February, 1777, Neve arrived from Loreto and took up his residence at Monterey in Alta California. Rivera y Moncada went south to assume the lieutenant-governorship at Loreto. The acting lieutenant-governor, pending Rivera's arrival, was Joaquín Cañete.

PEDRO FAGES
July 12, 1782, to April 16, 1791

On July 18, 1781, Rivera y Moncada was killed on the Colorado River, and Joaquín Cañete served as lieutenant-governor until late in November, 1783, when he was succeeded by José Joaquín de Arrillaga.

JOSÉ ANTONIO ROMÉU
April 16, 1791, to April 9, 1792

JOSÉ JOAQUÍN DE ARRILLAGA
April 9, 1792, to May 14, 1794

During this period, Arrillaga was lieutenant-governor and Comandante of Lower California, and governor of *Las Californias ad interim*.

DIEGO DE BORICA
May 14, 1794, to March 8, 1800

JOSÉ JOAQUÍN DE ARRILLAGA
March 8, 1800, to July 24, 1814

Until March 11, 1802, when he died, Pedro de Alberni was *Comandante-militar* for Alta California. The decree making Alta California a separate province bore the date August 29, 1804, and it reached Arrillaga November 16.

JOSÉ DARÍO ARGÜELLO
July 24, 1814, to August 30, 1815

Governor *ad interim*.

PABLO VICENTE DE SOLÁ
August 30, 1815, to November 10, 1822

Held over from Spanish regime to November, 1822.

MEXICAN REGIME, 1821–1847

Luís Antonio Argüello
November 10, 1822, to November ?, 1825

Until April 2, 1823, Argüello's authority was derived from the Spanish Regency. After that date until November 17 it was derived from Iturbide as Agustín I. After November 17 it was derived from the *Congreso Constituyente* (National Congress). In March, 1823, Iturbide named Naval Captain Bonifacio de Tosta governor of Alta California. In 1824 José Miñón was appointed governor of Alta California, but he declined the office.

José María de Echeandía
November ?, 1825, to January 31, 1831

Antonia García was first appointed as Echeandía's successor, but the appointment was revoked.

Manuel Victoria
January 31, 1831, to December 6, 1831

José María de Echeandía
December 6, 1831, to January 14, 1833

De facto *jefe político* and *jefe militar* in the district south of, but not including, Santa Bárbara.

Pío Pico
January 27 to February 16, 1832

Jefe político by appointment of the *Diputación* for only twenty days.

Agustín Vicente Zamorano
February 1, 1832, to January 14, 1833

De facto *jefe militar* only in the district north of and including Santa Bárbara.

José Figueroa
January 14, 1833, to September 29, 1835

Early in 1833 Figueroa asked to be relieved of office. On July 16, 1833, José María Híjar was appointed *jefe político*, but the appointment was revoked by Mexico's President Santa Anna on July 25. On July 18, 1834, Figueroa withdrew his request to be relieved.

JOSÉ CASTRO
September 29, 1835, to January 2, 1836

From October 8, 1835, to January 1, 1836, the position of *jefe militar* was held by Nicolás Gutiérrez.

NICOLÁS GUTIÉRREZ
January 2 to May 3, 1836

MARIANO CHICO
May 3 to August 1, 1836

NICOLÁS GUTIÉRREZ
August 1 to November 5, 1836

JOSÉ CASTRO
November 5 to December 7, 1836

Castro was *jefe militar* until November 29, when he was succeeded by Mariano Guadalupe Vallejo. He then became Acting Governor.

JUAN BAUTISTA ALVARADO
December 7, 1836, to December 31, 1842

Until August 7, 1839, Alvarado was governor *ad interim*. On June 6, 1837, Carlos Carrillo was appointed governor, and on December 6, he assumed office at Los Angeles, but he was arrested and deposed by Alvarado on May 20, 1838.

MANUEL MICHELTORENA
December 31, 1842, to February 22, 1845

PÍO PICO
February 22, 1845, to August 10, 1846

By the departmental junta Pío Pico was declared governor *ad interim* on February 15, 1845. José Castro served as *jefe militar* for the same period.

JOSÉ MARÍA FLORES
October 31, 1846, to January 11, 1847

ANDRÉS PICO
January 11 to January 13, 1847

AMERICAN GOVERNORS UNDER MILITARY RULE

COMMODORE JOHN D. SLOAT, July 7, 1846.

COMMODORE ROBERT F. STOCKTON, July 29, 1846.

CAPTAIN JOHN C. FRÉMONT, January 19, 1847.

GENERAL STEPHEN W. KEARNY, March 1, 1847.

COLONEL RICHARD B. MASON, May 31, 1847.

GENERAL PERSIFOR F. SMITH, February 28, 1849.

GENERAL BENNETT RILEY, April 12, 1849.

GOVERNORS OF THE STATE OF CALIFORNIA

NAME	PARTY	DATE OF INAUGURATION
Peter H. Burnett	Ind. Dem.	Dec. 20, 1849
John McDougal	Ind. Dem.	Jan. 9, 1851
John Bigler	Dem.	Jan. 8, 1852
John Neely Johnson	Amer.	Jan. 9, 1856
John B. Weller	Dem.	Jan. 8, 1858
Milton S. Latham	Lecomp. Dem.	Jan. 9, 1860
John G. Downey	Lecomp. Dem.	Jan. 14, 1860
Leland Stanford	Rep.	Jan. 10, 1862
Frederick F. Low	Union	Dec. 10, 1863
Henry H. Haight	Dem.	Dec. 5, 1867
Newton Booth	Rep.	Dec. 8, 1871
Romualdo Pacheco	Rep.	Feb. 27, 1875
William Irwin	Dem.	Dec. 9, 1875
George C. Perkins	Rep.	Jan. 8, 1880
George Stoneman	Dem.	Jan. 10, 1883
Washington Bartlett	Dem.	Jan. 8, 1887
Robert W. Waterman	Rep.	Sept. 13, 1887
Henry H. Markham	Rep.	Jan. 8, 1891
James H. Budd	Dem.	Jan. 11, 1895
Henry T. Gage	Rep.	Jan. 4, 1899
George C. Pardee	Rep.	Jan. 7, 1903
James N. Gillett	Rep.	Jan. 9, 1907
Hiram W. Johnson	Prog. Rep.	Jan. 3, 1911
William D. Stephens	Rep.	Mar. 15, 1917
Friend W. Richardson	Rep.	Jan. 8, 1923
Clement C. Young	Rep.	Jan. 4, 1927
James Rolph, Jr.	Rep.	Jan. 6, 1931
Frank F. Merriam	Rep.	Jan. 7, 1935
Culbert L. Olson	Dem.	Jan. 2, 1939
Earl F. Warren	Rep.	Jan. 4, 1943
Goodwin F. Knight	Rep.	Oct. 5, 1953
Edmund G. Brown	Dem.	Jan. 5, 1959
Ronald Reagan	Rep.	Jan. 5, 1967

The Twenty-One Missions

With dates of their founding and their founders

1. SAN DIEGO DE ALCALÁ, July 16, 1769. Junípero Serra.
2. SAN CARLOS BORROMÉO, June 3, 1770. Junípero Serra.
3. SAN ANTONIO DE PADUA, July 14, 1771. Junípero Serra.
4. SAN GABRIEL ARCÁNGEL, September 8, 1771. Junípero Serra.
5. SAN LUÍS OBISPO DE TOLOSA, September 1, 1772. Junípero Serra.
6. SAN FRANCISCO DE ASIS, October 9 (or 8), 1776. Francisco Palóu.
7. SAN JUAN CAPISTRANO, November 1, 1776. Fermín Francisco de Lasuén.
8. SANTA CLARA, January 12, 1777. Tomás de la Peña.
9. SAN BUENAVENTURA, March 31, 1782. Junípero Serra.
10. SANTA BARBARA, December 4, 1786. Fermín Francisco de Lasuén.
11. PURISÍMA CONCEPCIÓN, December 8, 1787. Fermín Francisco de Lasuén.
12. SANTA CRUZ, September 25 (or August 28), 1791. Fermín Francisco de Lasuén.
13. NUESTRA SEÑORA DE LA SOLEDAD, October 9, 1791. Fermín Francisco de Lasuén.
14. SAN JOSÉ DE GUADALUPE, June 11, 1797. Fermín Francisco de Lasuén.
15. SAN JUAN BAUTISTA, June 24, 1797. Fermín Francisco de Lasuén.
16. SAN MIGUEL ARCÁNGEL, July 25, 1797. Fermín Francisco de Lasuén.
17. SAN FERNANDO REY DE ESPAÑA, September 8, 1797. Fermín Francisco de Lasuén.
18. SAN LUÍS REY DE FRANCIA, June 13, 1798. Fermín Francisco de Lasuén.
19. SANTA INÉS, September 17, 1804. Estevan Tapis.
20. SAN RAFAEL ARCÁNGEL, December 14, 1817. Vicente Francisco Sarría.
21. SAN FRANCISCO SOLANO (Sonoma), July 4, 1823. José Altimira.

PRESIDENTS OF THE MISSIONS

Fray Junípero Serra	1769–1784
Fray Francisco Palóu	1784–1785
Fray Fermín Francisco de Lasuén	1785–1803
Fray Estevan Tapis	1803–1812
Fray José Señan	1812–1815
Fray Mariano Payeras	1815–1819
Fray José Señan	1819–1823

PRESIDENTS OF THE MISSION (*cont.*)

Fray Vicente Francisco Sarría	1823–1825
Fray Narciso Durán	1825–1827
Fray José Bernardo Sánchez	1827–1831
Fray Narciso Durán	1831–1838
Fray José Joaquín Jimeno	1838–1844
Fray Narciso Durán	1844–1846

Presidios, Municipalities, and Mission Pueblos

With dates of their founding

PRESIDIOS AND MILITARY TOWNS

PRESIDIO OF SAN DIEGO, July 16, 1769.

PRESIDIO OF MONTEREY, June 3, 1770.

PRESIDIO OF SAN FRANCISCO, September 17, 1776.

PRESIDIO OF SANTA BARBARA, April 21, 1782.

CIVIC MUNICIPALITIES

SAN JOSÉ, November 29, 1777.

LOS ANGELES, September 4, 1781.

BRANCIFORTE (now extinct), 1797.

MISSION PUEBLOS

SAN LUÍS OBISPO, September 1, 1772.

SAN JUAN CAPISTRANO, November 1, 1776.

SAN JUAN BAUTISTA, June 24, 1797.

SONOMA, July 4, 1823.

Counties of California

NAME OF COUNTY	COUNTY SEAT	YEAR OF CREATION
1. Butte	Oroville	1850
2. Calaveras	San Andreas	1850
3. Colusa	Colusa	1850
4. Contra Costa	Martinez	1850
5. El Dorado	Placerville	1850
6. Los Angeles	Los Angeles	1850
7. Marin	San Rafael	1850

COUNTIES OF CALIFORNIA (*cont.*)

NAME OF COUNTY	COUNTY SEAT	YEAR OF CREATION
8. Mariposa	Mariposa	1850
9. Mendocino	Ukiah	1850
10. Monterey	Salinas	1850
11. Napa	Napa	1850
12. Sacramento	Sacramento	1850
13. San Diego	San Diego	1850
14. San Francisco	San Francisco	1850
15. San Joaquin	Stockton	1850
16. San Luis Obispo	San Luis Obispo	1850
17. Santa Barbara	Santa Barbara	1850
18. Santa Clara	San Jose	1850
19. Santa Cruz	Santa Cruz	1850
20. Shasta	Redding	1850
21. Solano	Fairfield	1850
22. Sonoma	Santa Rosa	1850
23. Sutter	Yuba City	1850
24. Trinity	Weaverville	1850
25. Tuolumne	Sonora	1850
26. Yolo	Woodland	1850
27. Yuba	Marysville	1850
28. Nevada	Nevada City	1851
29. Placer	Auburn	1851
30. Siskiyou	Yreka	1852
31. Sierra	Downieville	1852
32. Tulare	Visalia	1852
33. Alameda	Oakland	1853
34. San Bernardino	San Bernardino	1853
35. Humboldt	Eureka	1853
36. Plumas	Quincy	1854
37. Stanislaus	Modesto	1854
38. Amador	Jackson	1854
39. Merced	Merced	1855
40. Tehama	Red Bluff	1856
41. Fresno	Fresno	1856
42. San Mateo	Redwood City	1856
43. Del Norte	Crescent City	1857
44. Mono	Bridgeport	1861
45. Lake	Lakeport	1861
46. Alpine	Markleeville	1864
47. Lassen	Susanville	1864
48. Inyo	Independence	1866
49. Kern	Bakersfield	1866
50. Ventura	San Buenaventura	1872
51. San Benito	Hollister	1874

COUNTIES OF CALIFORNIA (*cont.*)

NAME OF COUNTY	COUNTY SEAT	YEAR OF CREATION
52. Modoc	Alturas	1874
53. Orange	Santa Ana	1889
54. Glenn	Willows	1891
55. Madera	Madera	1893
56. Riverside	Riverside	1893
57. Kings	Hanford	1893
58. Imperial	El Centro	1907

Index of Authors Cited

Index

St. Vrain, Ceran, 177
Salinas, 6, 130, 364
  agriculture in valley of, 364, 651
  during conquest era, 197, 204
Salinas River, 66, 182
Salinger, Pierre, 616
Salk Institute for Biological Studies,
  578
Salt Lake City, 287
Salton Sea, 371
Salvatierra, Juan María de, 60
Samish, Artie, 612
San Agustín, vessel, 55
San Antonio, mission, 130
San Antonio, vessel, 64–65, 68–69
San Bernardino, 325, 346, 577
San Bernardino County, 109, 633, 657
San Bernardino Mountains, 495, 641
San Bernardino Valley, 176, 364
San Bernardo, Rancho, 206
San Blas, Mexico, 68, 86, 95, 140, 157,
  164
San Buenaventura (later Ventura),
  45, 162
San Buenaventura, vessel, 55
San Carlos, vessel, 52, 64, 65, 81
San Carlos Borroméo, mission, 69,
  75–76
San Clemente, 482–83
San Diego, 73, 90, 91, 94, 102, 138, 147,
  153, 172, 202, 204, 206, 338, 373–74,
  481, 495, 550, 579, 591, 643, 657
  air industry at, 481, 591, 606
  architecture at, 575
  Bay formation at, 14
  Davis as town founder of, 373–74
  defenses of, 101
  expeditions to, 44, 63, 65–66, 68
  fish canneries at, 648
  labor at, 542
  new "science industries" of, 582,
  606
  origin of name of, 56
  Panama-California Exposition at,
  481
  population growth of, 481, 657
  Portolá at, 68–69
  as presidio pueblo, 78
  provincial custom house
    controversy at, 162
  returns to Mexican rule, 165

San Diego (*cont.*)
  settlement of, 66, 79, 373–74, 481
  state college at, 577
  water titles at, 125
  weather at, 8
  wine industry near, 366
San Diego County, 125, 316, 633, 641,
  656
San Diego de Alcalá, mission, 68, 365
San Diego *Herald*, 446
San Diego *Union*, 446
San Dimas, 577
San Feliciano Canyon, 1842 gold
  discovery at, 212
San Felipe Rancho, 114–15
San Fernando, 480
San Fernando Rey de España,
  mission, 89, 222
San Fernando Valley, 154, 207, 365,
  646
  agriculture in, 6, 366
  aqueduct in, 503
San Francisco, 91, 104, 106, 108, 202,
  208, 220, 232, 237, 255, 256, 260,
  269, 273, 274, 278, 286, 289, 290,
  293, 298, 309, 310, 319, 334, 344,
  345, 415, 416, 424, 433, 445, 453,
  481, 495, 498, 579, 580, 639, 685
  artists and theater activities in
    after Gold Rush, 274–78
  Chinese at, 383–89, 415
  climate of, 8
  cosmopolitanism of, 453–54
  cultural life of after Gold Rush,
    264–78
  culture of in 1870's, 429, 449–51
  defenses of, 101
  earthquake and fire of 1906, 449,
    465–66, 479
  fire of 1851, 308
  fish canneries at, 648
  founding of the United Nations at,
    593
  foreigners in, 395–96
  freeway revolt at, 600
  during Gold Rush, 215–18
  as Hippie center, 681–83
  labor agitation at, 415–16, 524–26,
    543, 544
  Legislative Assembly of, 238–39
  likened to Florence, Italy, 685